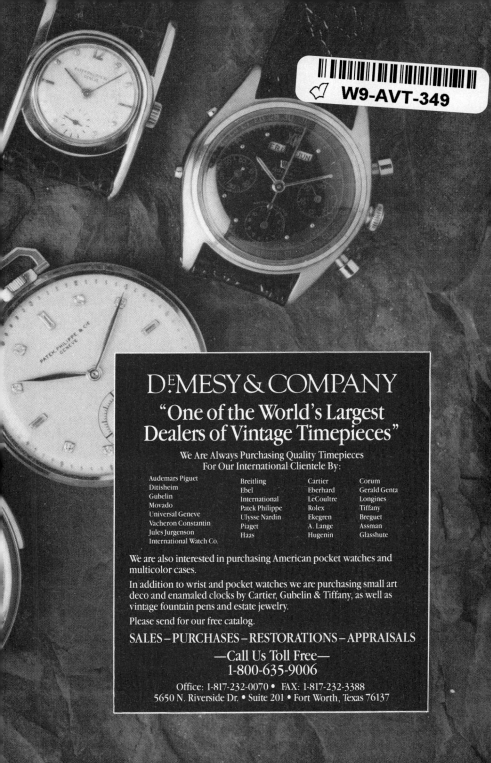

Copyright 1992 by Cooksey Shugart

All rights reserved under International and Pan-American Copyright Conventions.

Published by:
COOKSEY SHUGART PUBLICATIONS
P. O. BOX 3147
CLEVELAND, TN. 37320-3147

Distributed by:
COLLECTOR BOOKS
P. O. BOX 3009,
5801 KENTUCKY DAM ROAD
PADUCAH, KY. 42001

Manufactured in the United States of America

ISBN 0–89145–507–8
TWELFTH EDITION: JAN. 1992

10 9 8 7 6 5 4 3 2

COMPLETE
PRICE GUIDE TO
WATCHES

BY
COOKSEY SHUGART & RICHARD E. GILBERT

EDITED BY MARTHA SHUGART

SPECIAL ADVISOR TOM ENGLE

WITH HELPFUL ASSISTANCE BY:
NORMAN HOWARD,   PAUL A. DUGGAN
HENRY B. FRIED & DAVID SEARLES

TABLE OF CONTENTS

Vintage and special interest Swatch watches for the discriminating collector.

Also handling all vintage Patek, Philippe, Vacheron Constantin, Rolex, and Audemers Piquet wrist and pocket watches.

Coming Soon – Full color Swatch catalogue. Send name and address or call **(212) 354-694**

Ye Olde Timekeepers, Inc.

52 West 47th Street, Suite 201, New York, NY 10036
(212) 354-6944 • (516) 596-1615 Evenings and Weekends • FAX (516) 593-3354
Linda and Dennis Nichinson, *Horologists, N.A.W.C.C. 048702, A.W.I.*

ACKNOWLEDGMENTS

I am especially appreciative of Bob Overstreet, author of The Overstreet Comic Book Price Guide, for his encouragement.

To my wife Martha, for her complete understanding and assistance in compiling this book.

To TOM ENGLE whose help is invaluable a very special thanks.

A very special thanks to Henry B. Fried.

To the NAWCC Museum, Hamilton Watch Co., and Bowman Technical School, for allowing us to photograph their watches.

To Christie's, Jonathan Snellenburg, Osvaldo Patrizzi and Joseph Auction for photographs of watches.

And to the following people whose help was invaluable and will be long remembered: Frank Irick, John Cubbins, Harold Harris, Paul Gibson, Robert L. Ravel, M.D., William C. Heilman Jr., M.D., Thomas McEntyre, Paul Morgan, Bill Selover, Oscar Laube, Ed Kieft, Charles Wallace, Bob Walters, Jack Warren, Howard Schroeder, Edward M. McGinnis, James Gardner, Paul Zuercher, Irving E. Roth, Don Bass, Stephen Polednak, Dick Stacy, Ernest J. Lewis, Herbert McDonald, David Steger, Fred Favour, Ralph Warner, Estus Harris, Charles Cleves, Tom McIntyre, Ralph Ferone, Arnold C. Varey, Jeffrey Ollswang, Tom Rohr, Leon Beard, Glenn Smith, Kenneth Vergin, Thomas Rumpf, Frank Diggs, Tom Thacker, Bob Lavoie, Norman Howard, Constantin Tanasecu, Rod Minter, Ernest Luffman, John Amneus, Lawrence D. Harnden, Mike Kirkpatrick, Clint B. Geller, Art W. Rontree, Denford Jones Photographics; and a special thanks to Peter Kushnir, Dr. J. Mauss, Robert D. Gruen, Jeff Hess, Col. R. A. Mulholland, Dick Ziebell, Jack Warren, Ron Starnes, Dick Flaute, Ralph Vinge, Edward Fletcher, Richard Walker, Alex Wolanguk, Carl Goetz, Miles Sandler, Dave Mycko, and Martin Cullen, Benji Rook, Phillip Welsh, Paul Craft.

* * *

Send only corrections, additions, deletions and comments to **COOKSEY SHUGART, P. O. BOX 3147, CLEVELAND, TN. 37320-3147.**

When corresponding, please send a self-addressed, stamped envelope.

Special Consultants:

David Searles

Paul A. Duggan

Norman Howard

Dan Crawley

Geoff White

Dennis Nichinson

Jeff Cohen

POCKET WATCHES ONLY

Avoid the Middleman
Sell Direct to an Authority!

WE BUY
POCKET WATCHES!

TOP PRICES QUOTED

If It Has Anything to Do with
Pocket Watches, We Buy It.
• MOVEMENTS • CASES • DIALS
• MATERIALS • ADVERTISING • TOOLS

**OUR 30 YEARS EXPERIENCE MEANS
KNOWLEDGE, DEPENDABILITY, & FINANCIAL RESPONSIBILITY.**

WE BUY EVERYTHING,
FROM INDIVIDUAL PIECES, TO ENTIRE
ACCUMULATIONS, ESTATES AND COLLECTIONS!
WE WILL <u>BUY</u> YOUR <u>ENTIRE</u> <u>COLLECTION</u>,
NOT JUST THE BEST ITEMS.

CALL TODAY!

OFFICE: (310) 826-7778
ANY TIME: (310) 476-2332
FAX #: (310) 207-3976
NAWCC 15075 / HOURS BY APPOINTMENT

JON HANSON

Box 5499, Beverly Hills, California 90210

INTRODUCTION

This book is dedicated to all watch collectors who we hope will find it an enjoyable and valuable reference to carry on buying trips or to trace the lost history of that priceless family heirloom.

The origin of this book began when I was given a pocket watch that had been in our family for many years. After receiving the prized heirloom I wanted to know its complete history, and thus the search began. Because of the lack of a comprehensive reference on American pocket watches the venture took me through volume after volume. Over the course of ten years many hours were accumulated in running down the history of this one watch. The research sparked my interest in the pocket watch field and pointed to the need for a book such as this one. We hope it will provide the information that you are looking for.

— The Authors

Watches are unique collectibles and since the beginning of civilization man has held a fascination for time. When man scooped up a handful of sand and created the hourglass, portable timepieces have been in demand for the wealthy and poor alike. Man has sought constantly to improve his time-measuring instruments and has made them with the finest metals and jewels. The pocket watch, in particular, became an ornamentation and a source of pride, and this accounts for its value among families for generation after generation.

The watch has become precious and sentimental to so many because it is one of the true personal companions of the individual night and day. Mahatma Gandhi, the father of India and one of the rare people in history who was able to renounce worldly possessions, was obsessed with the proper use of his time. Each minute, he held, was to be used in the service of his fellowman. His own days were ordered by one of his few personal possessions, a sixteen-year-old, eight-shilling Ingersoll pocket watch that was always tied to his waist with a piece of string.

Another factor that has made watches unique collectibles is the intricate artisanship with which they are put together. Many of the watches of yesteryear, which were assembled with extreme accuracy and fine workmanship, continue to be reliable timepieces today. They stand out as unique because that type of watch is no longer manufactured. In today's world of mass production, the watch with indiviual craftmanship containing precious jewels and metals can rarely be found — and, if found, it is rarely affordable.

The well-made watch is a tribute to man's skills, artisanship and craftsmanship at their finest level. That is why the watch holds a special place in the collectible field.

In America, there are about 80,000 avid watch collectors. About 5 million people own two or more watches, and an untold number possess at least one of these precious heirlooms.

The Complete Price Guide to Watches does not attempt to estabtablish or fix values or selling prices in the watch trade market.

It does, however, reflect the trends of buying and selling in the collector market. Prices listed in this volume are based on data collected and analyzed from dealers and shops all over the country.

These prices should serve the collector as a guide only. The price you pay for any watch will be determined by the value it has to you. The intrinsic value of any particular watch can be measured only by you, the collector, and a fair price can be derived only after mutual agreement between both the buyer and the seller.

It is our hope that this volume can help make your watch collecting venture both pleasurable and profitable.

Information contained herein may not necessarily apply to every situation. Data is still being found, which may alter statements made in this book. These changes, however, will be reflected in future editions.

Hopefully, everyone interested in horology will research the watch and add to his library on the subject.

COLLECTAMANIA
Hobby — Business — Pastime — Entertainment

Just name it. More than likely someone will want to buy or sell it: books, coins, stamps, bottles, beer cans, gold, glassware, baseball cards, guns, clocks, watches, comics, art, cars, and the list goes on and on.

Most Americans seem to be caught up in collectamania . More and more Americans are spending hour after hour searching through antique shops, auctions, flea markets and yard sales for those rare treasures of delight that have been lying tucked away for generations just waiting to be found.

This sudden boom in the field of collecting may have been influenced by fears of inflation or disenchantment with other types of investments. But more people are coming into the field because they gain some degree of nostalgic satisfaction from these new tangible ties with yesteryear. Collecting provides great fun and excitement. The tales of collecting and the resultant "fabulous finds" could fill volumes and inspire even the non-collector to embark upon a treasure hunt.

Collecting for the primary purpose of investment may prove to have many pitfalls for the amateur. The lack of sufficient knowledge is the main cause of disappointment. The inability to spot fakes or flawed merchandise can turn excitement into disappointment. And, in many fields, high-class forgers are at work, doing good and faithful reproductions in large quantities that can sometimes fool even the experts the first time they see them.

Collecting for fun and profit can be just that if you observe a fair amount of caution. Always remember, amidst your enthusiasm, that an object may not be what it would first appear. Below are a few guidelines that may be helpful to you:

1. **Make up your mind** as to what you want to collect and concentrate in this area. Your field of collecting should be one that you have a genuine liking for, and it helps if you can use the objects. It may help also to narrow your field even further, for instance, in collecting watches, to choose only one company or one type of pocket watch.

2. **Gain all the knowledge you can** about the objects you collect. The more knowledge you have the more successful you will be in finding valuable, quality pieces. Amassing the knowledge required to be a good collector is easier if you have narrowed your scope of interest. Otherwise, it may take years to become an "expert." Don't try to learn everything there is to know about a variety of fields. This will end in frustration and disappointment. Specialize.

3. **Buy the best you can afford**, assuming the prices are fair. The advanced collector may want only mint articles; but the novice collector may be willing to accept something far less than mint condition due to caution and economics. Collectible items in better condition continue to rise in value at a steady rate.

4. **Deal with reputable dealers** whom you can trust. Talk with the dealer; get to know the seller; get a business card; know where you can contact the dealer if you have problems, or if you want the dealer to help you find something else you may be looking for.

HOROLOGICAL PUZZLE

The Sum Is
Always 13

HOW TO USE THIS BOOK

The Complete Price Guide to Watches is a simple reference, with clear and carefully selected information. The first part of the book is devoted to history, general information, and a how-to section. The second part of the guide consists mainly of a listing of watch manufacturers, identification guides, and prices. This is a unique book because it is designed to be taken along as a handy pocket reference for identifying and pricing watches. With the aid of this book, the collector should be able to make on-the-spot judgments as to identification, age, quality, and value. This complete guide and a pocket magnifying glass will be all you need to take on your buying trips.

*   *   *

Watch collecting is fast growing as a hobby and business. Many people collect for the enjoyment and profit. The popularity of watches continues to rise because watches are a part of history. The American railroad brought about the greatest watch of that time the railroad pocket watch. Since that time America has produced some of the best quality pocket watches that money could buy. The gold-filled cases made in America have never been surpassed in quality or price in the foreign market. With the quality of movement and cases being made with guaranteed high standards as well as beauty, the American pocket watch became very desirable. Because they are no longer being made in the U. S. A., pocket watches continue to rise in value.

The watch is collected for its beauty, quality in movement and case, and the value of metal content. Solid gold and platinum are the top of the line; silver is also very desirable. (Consider that some watches in the early 1900's sold between $700 and $1,000. This is equal to or greater than the price of a good car of the same period.)

As with limited edition prints, a watch of supreme excellence is also limited and will increase in value. There is universal appeal and excitement in owning a piece of history, and your heirloom is just that. At one time pocket watches were a status symbol. Everyone competed for beauty and quality in the movement and case. Solid gold cases were adorned with elaborate engravings, diamonds, and other precious jewels. The movements were beautiful and of high quality. Manufacturers went to great lengths to provide movements that were both accurate and lovely. Fancy damaskeening on the back plates of nickel with gold lettering, 26 jewels in gold settings, and a solid gold train (gears) were features of some of the more elaborate timepieces. The jewels were red rubies, or diamond-end stones, or sapphires for the pallet stones. There were gold timing screws, and more. The faces were made by the best artisans of the day hand-painted, jewel-studded, with fancy hands and double-sunk dials made of enamel and precious metals.

HOW TO DETERMINE MANUFACTURER

When identifying a watch, look on the face or dial for the name of the company and then refer to the alphabetical list of watch companies in this book. If the face or dial does not reveal the company name you will have to seek information from the movement's back plate. The company name or the town where it was manufactured will likely be inscribed there. The name engraved on the back plate is referred to as the "signature." After locating the place of manufacture, see what companies manufactured in that town. This may require reading the histories of several companies to find the exact one. Use the process of elimination to narrow the list. Note: Some of the hard-to-identify watches are extremely collectible and valuable. Therefore, it is important to learn to identify them.

HOW TO DETERMINE AGE

After establishing the name of the manufacturer, you may be interested in the age of the watch. This information can be obtained by using the serial number inscribed on the back movement plate and referring to the production table. It is often difficult to establish the exact age, but this method will put you within a two or three-year period of the date of the manufacture.

The case that houses the movement is not necessarily a good clue to the origin of the movement. It was a common practice for manufacturers to ship the movements to the jewelers and watchmakers uncased. The customer then married the movement and case. That explains why an expensive movement can be found in a cheaper case or vice versa.

If the "manufacturer's" name and location are no help, the inscription could possibly be that of a jeweler and his location. Then it becomes obvious there is no quick and easy way to identify some American made watches. However, the following steps may be helpful. Some watches can be identified by comparing the models of each company until the correct model is found. Start by sizing the watch and then comparing the varied plate shapes and styles. The cock or bridge for the balance may also be a clue. The general arrangement of the movement as to jeweling, whether it is an open face or hunting case, and style of regulators may help to find the correct identification of the manufacturer of the movement.

Numbers on a watch case should not be considered as clues to the age of the movement because cases were both American and foreign made, and many of the good watches were re-cased through the years.

APPRAISING WATCHES

Watch collecting is still young when compared to fields of the standard collectibles: coins and stamps. The watch collecting field is growing but information is still scarce, fragmented, and sometimes unreliable. To be knowledgeable in any field, one must spend the time required to study it.

The value of any collectible is determined first by demand. Without demand there is no market. In the watch trade, the law of supply and demand is also true. The supply of the American watches has stopped and the demand among collectors continues to rise. There are many factors that make a watch desired or in demand. Only time and study will tell a collector just which pieces are most collectible. After the collector or investor finds out what is desirable, then a value must be placed on it before it is sold. If it is priced too high, the watch will not sell; but, on the other hand, if it is priced too low, it will be hard to replace at the selling price. The dealer must arrive at a fair market price that will move the watch.

There are no two watches alike. This makes the appraising more difficult and often-times arbitrary. But there are certain guidelines one can follow to arrive at a fair market price. When watches were manufactured, most companies sold the movements to a jeweler, and the buyer had a choice of dials and cases. Some high-grade movements were placed in a low-grade case and vice versa. Some had hand-painted multi-colored dials; some were plain. The list of contrasts goes on. Conditions of watches will vary greatly, and this is a big factor in the value. The best movement in the best original case will bring the top price for any type of watch.

Prices are constantly changing in the watch field. Gold and silver markets affect the price of the cases. Scarcity and age also affect the value. These prices will fluctuate regularly.

APPRAISING GUIDELINES

Demand, supply, condition, and value must be the prime factors in appraising an old watch.

Demand is the most important element. Demand can be determined by the number of buyers for the particular item. A simple but true axiom is that value is determined by the price someone is willing to pay.

In order to obtain a better knowledge in appraising and judging watches, the following guidelines are most useful. Consider all these factors before placing a value on the watch. (There is no rank or priority to the considerations listed.)

1. Demand: Is it high or low?
2. Availability: How rare or scarce is the watch?
   How many of the total production remain?
3. Condition of both the case and movement (very important) .
4. Low serial numbers: The first one made would be more
   valuable than later models.
5. Historical value.
6. Age.
7. Is it an early handmade watch?
8. Type of case: beauty and eye appeal; value of metal content.
9. Is it in its original case? (very important).
10. Complications: Repeaters, for example.

11. Type of escapement.
12. Size, number of jewels, type of plates (3/4, full and bridge), type of balance, type of winding (key-wind, lever-set, etc.), number of adjustments, gold jeweled settings, damaskeening, gold train.
13. What grade of condition is it? Pristine, Mint, Extra Fine, Average, Fair, or Scrap?
14. Identification ability.
15. Future potential as an investment.
16. Quality (high or low grade), or low cost production watches (dollar watch).
17. How much will this watch scrap for?

GRADING WATCHES

Pricing in this book is based on the following grading system:

PRISTINE MINT (G-10): Absolutely factory new; sealed in factory box with wax paper still intact.

MINT PLUS (G-9): Still in factory box; has had paper removed for inspection only; has never been used.

MINT (G-8): Same as factory new but with very little use; no faint scratches; is original in every way crystal, hands, dial, case, movement; used briefly and stored away; may be in box.

NEAR MINT (G-7): Completely original in every way; faint marks may be seen with a loop only; expertly repaired; movement may have been cleaned and oiled.

EXTRA FINE (G-6): May or may not be in factory box; looks as though watch was used very little; crystal may have been replaced; original case, hands, dial, and movement. If watch has been repaired, all original replacement parts have been used. Faint case scratches are evident but hard to detect with the eye. No dents and no hairline on dial are detectable.

FINE (G-5): May have new hands and new crystal, but original case, dial and movement; faint hairline in dial; no large scratches on case; slight stain on movement; movement must be sharp with only minor scratches.

AVERAGE (G-4): Original case, dial and movement; movement may have had a part replaced, but part was near to original; slight brass showing through on gold-filled case; no rust or chips in dial; may have hairlines in dial that are hard to see. All marks are hard to detect, but may be seen without a loop.

FAIR (G-3): Hairlines in dial and small chips; brass can be seen through worn spots on gold-filled case; rust marks in movement; a small dent in case; wear in case, dial, and movement; well used; may not have original dial or case.

POOR (G-2): Watch may not run; needs new dial; case well worn, with many dents; hands may be gone; replacement crystal may be needed.

SCRAP (G-1): Not running; bad dial; rusty movement; brass showing badly; may not have case; some parts not original; no crystal or hands. Good for parts.

Below is an example of how the price is affected by the different grades of the same watch:

Hamilton 992B

G-10	$295
G-9	$260
G-8	$235
G-7	$215
G-6	$200
G-5	$180
G-4	$175
G-3	$75
G-2	$45
G-1	$35

The value of a watch can only be assessed after the watch has been carefully inspected and graded. It may be difficult to evaluate a watch honestly and objectively, especially in the rare or scarce models.

If the watch has any defects, such as a small scratch on it, it can not be Pristine. It is important to realize that older watches in grades of Extra Fine or above are extremely rare and may never be found.

COLLECTING ON A LIMITED BUDGET

Most collectors are always looking for that sleeper, which is out there waiting to be found. One story goes that the collector went into a pawn shop and asked the owner if he had any gold pocket watches for sale. The pawn broker replied, "No, but I have a 23J silver cased pocket watch at a good price." Even though the pocket watch was in a cheaper case, the collector decided to further explore the movement. When he opened the back to look at the movement, there he saw engraved on the plates 24J Bunn Special and knew immediately he wanted to buy the pocket watch. The movement was running, and looked to be in first grade shape. The collector asked the price. The broker said he has been trying to get rid of the pocket watch, but had no luck and if he wanted it, he would sell it for $35. The collector took the pocket watch and replaced the bent-up silver case for a gold-filled J. Boss case, and sold it a month later for $400. He had a total of $100 invested when he sold it, netting a cool $300 profit.

Most collectors want a pocket watch that is in mint or near-mint condition and original in every way. But consider the railroad pocket watches such as the Bunn Special in a cheaper case. The railroad man was compelled to buy a watch with a quality movement, even though he may have only been able to afford a cheap case. The railroad man had to have a pocket watch that met certain standards set by the railroad company. A watch should always be judged on quality and performance and not just on its appearance. The American railroad pocket watch was unsurpassed in reliability. It was durable and accurate for its time, and that accounts for its continuing value today.

If you are a limited-budget collector, you would be well advised not to go beyond your means. But watch collecting can still be an interesting, adventurous, and profitable hobby. If you are to be successful in quadrupling your purchases that you believe to be sleepers, you must first be a hard worker, have perserverence and let shrewdness and skill of knowledge take the place of money. A good starting place is to get a working knowledge of how a pocket watch works. Learn the basic skills such as cleaning, mainspring and staff replacement. One does not have to be a watchmaker, but should learn the names of parts and what they do. If a watch that you are considering buying does not work, you should know how and what it takes to get it in good running order or pass it by. Stay away from pocket watches that do not wind and set. Also avoid "odd" movements that you hope to be able to find a case for.

Old watches with broken or missing parts are expensive and all but impossible to have repaired. Some parts must be made by hand. The odd and low-cost production watches are fun to get but hard to repair. Start out on the more common basic-jeweled lever pocket watches. The older the watch, the harder it is to get parts. Buy an inexpensive pocket watch movement that runs and play with it. Get the one that is newer and for which parts can be bought; and get a book on watch repairing.

You will need to know the history and demand of a watch. Know what collectors are looking for in your area. If you cannot find a buyer, then, of course, someone else's stock has become yours.

SELLING AT CHRISTIE'S

Christie, Manson & Woods International, Inc. is an auction house of superior reputation, known thoughout the world for its sales of the finest works of art and collectibles. Frequently in the news for record breaking sales in the art market, Christie's is respected in the watch world for its professional presentation and sale of the best in pocket and wrist watches.

Under the expert direction of Christie's Vice-President Jonathan Snellenburg, the New York gallery's watch sales have enjoyed great success. The catalogues are reliable, estimates sensible and attractive to bidders, and the merchandise selected for sale is both original and excellent.

Those interested in selling fine watches at auction may contact Mr. Snellenburg who will then evaluate the watches and their suitability for auction, as well as discuss timetables, sales strategy, photos and commission rates. Typical commission rates on goods over $7,500 are 10% and 6% to the trade. Insurance is also available, as well as certain repair services. Should an agreeable arrangement be made, a contract is drawn up and the goods are prepared for cataloguing and marketing. Clients examine the goods at a preview and may leave order bids or attend the sale by phone or in person. The seller, if successful, then receives payment within the contracted period, usually 35 days.

One of the keys to successful sales lies in establishing reasonable estimates and reserves (minimum selling price acceptable to seller), so as to attract competition and obtain the best price. Overestimation alienates prospective buyers, while underestimation may jeopardize the seller. The art is to find the right balance, this is where Mr. Snellenburg's experience pays off.

THAT GREAT AMERICAN
RAILROAD POCKET WATCH

It was the late nineteenth century in America. The automobile had not yet been discovered. The personal Kodak camera was still not on the market. Women wore long dresses, and the rub board was still the most common way to wash clothes. Few homes had electricity, and certainly the radio had not yet invaded their lives. Benjamin Harrison was president. To be sure, those days of yesteryear were not quite as nostalgically simple as most reminiscing would have them be. They were slower, yes, because it took longer to get things done and longer to get from one place to another. The U.S. mail was the chief form of communication linking this country together, as America was inching toward the Twentieth Century.

The tremendous impact of the railroad on the country during this era should not be underestimated. Most of the progress since the 1830s had chugged along on the back of the black giant locomotives that belched steam and fire, up and down the countryside. In fact, the trains brought much life and hope to the people all across the country, delivering their goods and food, bringing people from one city to another, carrying the U.S. mail, and bringing the democratic process to the people by enabling candidates for the U.S. Presidency to meet and talk with people in every state.

Truly the train station held memories for most everyone and had a link with every family.

In 1891, the country had just eased into the period that historians would later term the "Gay Nineties." It was on April 19 of that year that events occurred near Cleveland, Ohio, that clearly pointed out that the nation's chief form of transportation was running on timepieces that were not reliable. The time had come for strict standards for pocket watches used by the railroaders.

From the ashes of this smoldering Ohio disaster rose the phoenix in the form of the great American railroad pocket watch, a watch unrivaled in quality and reliability.

That April morning the fast mail train, known as No. 4, was going East. On the same track an accommodation train was going West. It was near Elyria, about 25 miles from Cleveland, Ohio, that the engineer and conductor of the accommodation train were given written orders to let the fast mail train pass them at Kipton, a small station west of Oberlin.

As the accommodation train was leaving the station at Elyria, the telegraph operator ran to the platform and verbally cautioned the engineer and conductor, "Be careful, No. 4 is on time." The conductor replied, "Go to thunder. I know my business."

The train left Elyria on time according to the engineer's watch. What was not known was that the engineer's watch had stopped for four minutes and then started up again. Had the conductor looked at his own watch, the impending disaster could have been avoided.

The two trains met their destiny at Kipton; the accommodation train was under full brakes, but the fast mail was full speed ahead. Both engineers were killed as well as nine other people. The railroad companies (Lake Shore Railroad and Michigan Southern Railway) sustained great losses in property as did the U.S. Post Office.

Following this disaster, a commission was appointed to come up with standards for timepieces that would be accepted and adopted by all railroads. The commission learned that, up to the time of the Kipton crash, conductors on freight trains were depending on cheap alarm clocks. The railroading industry had grown, fast new trains were now in service, and the same lines were used by several different railways. Very often, in only a short space of time, two trains would cover the same track. The industry now had to demand precision in its timekeeping.

By 1893 the General Railroad Timepiece Standards were adopted, and any watch being used in rail service by railroaders responsible for schedules was required to meet the following specifications:

Be open faced, size 18 or 16, have a minimum of 17 jewels, adjusted to at least five positions, keep time accurately to within a gain or loss of only 30 seconds a week, adjusted to temperatures of 34 to 100 degrees Fahrenheit, have a double roller, steel escape wheel, lever set, micrometric regulator, winding stem at 12 o'clock, grade on back plate, use plain Arabic numbers printed bold and black on a white dial, and have bold black hands.

Some also wanted a Breguet hairspring, adjusted to isochronism and 30 degrees Fahrenheit with a minimum of 19 jewels.

The railroad man was compelled to buy a timepiece more accurate than many scientific instruments of precision used in laboratories. The American pocket watch industry was compelled to produce just such an instrument which it did. The railroad watch was a phenomenal timekeeper and durable in long life and service. It had the most minute adjustments, no small feat because watchmaking was rendered far more difficult than clockmaking, due to the fact that a clock is always in one position and powered by a constant force-it's weights,while watches must be accurate in several positions with a variable power source.

The 1893 railroad pocket watch standards were adopted by almost every railroad line. While each company had its individual standards, most all of them included the basic recommendations of the commission.

The key figure in developing the railroad watch standards was Webb C. Ball of Cleveland, Ohio, the general time inspector for over 125,000 miles of railroad in the U.S., Mexico, and Canada. Ball was authorized by railroad officials to establish the timepiece inspection system. After Ball presented his guidelines, most American manufacturers set out to meet those standards and a list of the different manufacturers producing watches of the grade that would pass inspection, was soon available.

According to the regulations, if a watch fell behind or gained 30 seconds in 7 to 14 days, it must be sent in for adjustment or repair. Small cards were given to the engineers and conductors the railroad timekeepers and a complete record of the watch's performance was written in ink. All repairs and adjustments were conducted by experienced and approved watchmakers; inspections were conducted by authorized inspectors.

Because this system was adopted universally and adhered to, and because American watch manufacturers produced a superior railroad watch, the traveling public was assured of increased safety and indeed the number of railroad accidents occurring as a result of faulty timepieces was minimized.

Prior to the 1891 collision, some railroad companies had already initiated standards and were issuing lists of those watches approved for railroad use. Included were the Waltham 18s, 1883 model, Crescent Street Grade, and the B.W. Raymond, 18s, both in open and hunter cases with lever set or pendant set.

By the mid 1890s hunter cases were being turned down as well as pendant set. Watches meeting approval then included Waltham, 18s, 1892 model; Elgin, 7th model; and Hamilton, 17j, open face, lever set.

Hamilton Grade 992, 17 size, 21 jewels, nickel 3/4 plate movement, lever set only, gold jewel settings, gold center wheel, steel escape wheel, micrometric regulator, compensating balance. Adjusted to temperature, isochronism and 5 positions.

By 1900 the double roller sapphire pallets and steel escape wheels with a minimum of five positions were required.

The early Ball Watch Co. movements, made by Howard, used initials of railroad labor organizations such as "B. of L.E. Standard" and "B. of L.F. Standard." Ball also used the trademark "999" and "Official Railroad Standard." Some watches may turn up that are marked as "loaners." These were issued by the railroad inspectors when a watch had to be kept for repairs.

By 1920 the 18 size watch had lost popularity with the railroad men and by 1950 most railroad companies were turning them down all together.

In 1936 duty on Swiss watches were lowered by 50 percent, and by 1950 the Swiss imports had reached a level of five million a year.

In 1969 the last American railroad pocket watch was sold by Hamilton Watch Co.

RAILROAD GRADE WATCH ADJUSTMENTS

The railroad watch, as well as other fine timepieces, had to compensate for several factors in order to be reliable and accurate at all times. These compensations, called adjustments, were for heat and cold, isochronism, and five to six different positions. These adjustments were perfected only after experimentation and a great deal of careful hand labor on each individual movement.

All railroad grade watches were adjusted to a closer rate to compensate for heat and cold. The compensation balance has screws in the rim of the balance wheel which can be regulated by the watchmaker. The movement was tested in an ice box and in an oven, and if it did not keep the same time in both temperature extremes, as well as under average conditions, the screws in the balance wheel was shifted or adjusted until accuracy was achieved.

The isochronism adjustment maintained accuracy of the watch both when the mainspring was fully wound up and when it was nearly run down. This was achieved by selecting a hairspring of exact proportions to cause the balance wheel to give the same length of arc of rotation regardless of the amount of the mainspring that had been spent.

Railroad watches were adjusted to be accurate whether they were laying on their face or back, or being carried on their edges with pendants up or down, or with the three up or the nine up. These adjustments were accomplished by having the jewels, in which the balance pivots rest, of proper thickness in proportion to the diameter of the pivot and, at the same time, equal to the surface on the end of the pivot which rests on the cap jewel. To

* * * * * * * *

NOTE: Railroad grade watches had a compensation balance made of brass and steel. Brass was used on the outside rim and steel on the inside. Brass is twice as sensitive to temperature changes and twice as thick as the steel balance (one-piece is welded to the steel balance wheel) and after finishing, the rim is cut at one end near the arm of the balance and at the same spot 180 across. In higher temperature, the dominant brass would "grow" longer but welded to the steel rim, it would curve inward, thus, in effect, placing the mass of the balance closer to the center of the balance wheel. This would cause the balance to go faster. However, the steel hairspring in rising temperature would also grow longer but more important would also lose some of its resilience. This would cause the watch to lose time. The balance, remember under the same condition, in effect became smaller and this action by the balance compensated for the loss of the hairspring's elasticity and lengthening. In cold temperatures, the opposite effect took place. This is why the balance is called a "compensation" balance. (It compensates for the temperature errors in the hairspring.)

be fully adjusted for positions, the balance wheel and the pallet and escape wheel must be perfectly poised. Perfect poise is achieved when the pivots can be supported on two knife-edged surfaces, perfectly smooth and polished and when the wheel is placed in any edge, it will remain exactly as it is placed. If it is not perfectly poised, the heaviest part of the wheel will always turn to the point immediately under the lines of support.

The micrometric regulator or the patent regulator is a device used on all railroad grade and higher grade watches for the purpose of assisting in the finer manipulation of the regulator. It is arranged so that the regulator can be moved the shortest possible distance without fear of moving it too far. There is always a fine graduated index attached which makes it possible to determine just how much the regulator has been moved.

E. Howard Watch Co. Railroad Chronometer, Series 11, 16 size, 21 jewels, expressly designed for the railroad trade.

The hairspring used on the so-called ordinary and medium-grade watches is known as the flat hairspring. The Breguet hairspring was an improvement over the flat hairspring and was used on railroad and high-grade watches. The inside coil of any hairspring is attached to a collet on the balance staff and the end of the outside coil of the hairspring is attached to a stud which is held firmly by a screw in the balance wheel bridge. Two small regulator pins are fastened to the regulator. These pins clasp the outer side of the hairspring a short distance from the hairspring stud. If the regulator index is moved toward the "S," the regulator pins will move, allowing the hairspring to lengthen and the balance wheel to make a longer arc of rotation. This causes the watch to run slower because it requires a longer time for the wheel to perform the longer arc.

When the regulator is moved toward the "F" these regulator pins are moved from the stud which shortens the hairspring and makes shorter arcs of the balance wheel, thus causing the movement to run faster. Sometimes, after a heavy jolt, the coil next to the outside one will catch between these regulator pins and this will shorten the length of the hairspring just one round, causing a gaining rate of one hour per day. When this occurs, the hairspring can be easily released and will resume its former rate.

The Breguet hairspring, which is used on railroad grade movements, prevented the hairspring from catching on the regulator pins and protected against any lateral or side motion of the balance wheel ensuring equal expansion of the outside coil.

Railroad grade watches also used the patent or safety pinion which was developed to protect the train of gears from damage in the event of breakage of the mainspring. These pinions unscrewed in event of mainspring breakage, allowing the force to be harmlessly spent by the spinning barrel.

Some earlier railroad grade watches had non-magnetic movements. This was achieved by the use of non-magnetic metals for the balance wheel, hairspring, roller table and pallet. Two of the metals used were iridium and paladium, both very expensive.

Rockford Grades 805-Hunting & 905-Open Face, 18 size, 21 extra fine ruby jewels in gold settings, beautifully damaskeened nickel plates, gold lettering, adjusted to temperature, isochronism and 5 positions, Breguet hair spring, double roller escapement, steel escape wheel, sapphire pallets, micrometric regulator, compensating balance in recess.

RAILROAD WATCH DIALS

Railroad watch dials are distinguished by their simplicity. A true railroad watch dial contained no fancy lettering or beautiful backgrounds. The watches were designed to be functional and in order to achieve that, the dials contained bold black Arabic numbers against a white background. This facilitated ease of reading the time under even the most adverse conditions.

True railroad watches had the winding stem at the 12 o'clock position. The so-called "side winder," that winds at the 3 o'clock position, was not approved for railroad use. (The side winder is a watch movement designed for a hunter case but one that has been placed in an open-faced case.)

One railroad watch dial design was patented by a Mr. Ferguson. On this dial, the five minute numbers were much larger than the hour numbers which were on the inside. This dial never became very popular.

About 1910 the Montgomery dials began to appear. The distinguishing feature of the Montgomery dial is that each minute is numbered around the hour chapter. The five-minute divisions were in red, and the true Montgomery dial has the number "6" inside the minute register. These dials were favored by the railroad men.

The so-called Canadian dial had a 24-hour division inside the hour chapter.

The double-time hands are also found on some railroad grade watches. One hour hand was in black and the other was in red, one hour apart, to compensate for passing from one time zone to another.

Ball Watch Co. Motto: "Carry a Ball and Time Them All." This case is an example of Ball's patented Stirrup Bow. With the simple easy to read dial, this watch was a favorite among railroad men.

RAILROAD WATCH CASES

Open face cases were the only ones approved for railroad use. Railroad men sought a case that was tough and durable; one that would provide a dust-free environment for the movement.

The swing-out case offered the best protection against dust, but the screw-on back and bezel were the most popular open-face cases.

The lever-set was a must for railroad-approved watches and some of the case manufacturers patented their own styles of cases, most with a heavy bow. One example is the Stirrup Bow by the Ball Watch Co. Hamilton used a bar above the crown to prevent the stem from being pulled out. Glass was most commonly used for the crystal because it was not as likely to scratch.

RAILROAD GRADE OR
RAILROAD APPROVED WATCHES

Note: Not all watches listed here are railroad approved, even though all are railroad grade. See Ball Watch Co. for railroad standards.

BALL
All official R.R. standard with 19, 21, & 23J, hci5p, 18 &16S, open face.

COLUMBUS WATCH CO.
Columbus King, 21, 23, 25J; Railway King, 17-25J; Time King, 21-25J, 18S; Ruby Model, 16S.

ELGIN
1. "Pennsylvania Railroad Co." on dial, 18S, 15J & 17J, key wind and set, first model "B. W. Raymond."
2. "No. 349," 18S, seventh model, 17-21J.
3. Veritas, B. W. Raymond, or Father Time, 18S, 21-23J.
4. Grades 162, 270, 280, or 342 marked on back plate, 16S, 17-21J.
5. Veritas, Father Time, or Paillard Non-Magnetic, 16S, 19-23J.
6. 571, 21J or 572, 16S, 19J.
7. All wind indicator models.

HAMILTON
1. Grade 946, 23J, 18S.
2. Grades 940, 942, 21J, 18S.
3. Grade 944, 19J, 18S.
4. Grades 924, 926, 934, 936, 938, 948, 17J, 18S.
5. Grades 950, 950B, 950E, 23J, 16S.
6. Grades 992, 992B, 992E, 954, 960, 970, 994, 990, 21J, 16S.
7. Grade 996, 19J, 16S.
8. Grades 972, 968, 964, 17J, 16S.

HAMPDEN
1. Sp. Railway, 17J, 21J, 23J; New Railway, 23J & 17J; No. Am. RR22J., Wm. McKinley, 21J; John Hancock, 21J & 23J; John C. Duber, 21J, 18S
2. 105, 21J; 104, 23J; John C. Duber, 21J; Wm. McKinley, 17, 21, & 23J; New Railway, 21J; Railway, 19J; Special Railway, 23J, 16S.

E. HOWARD & CO.
1. All Howard models marked "Adjusted" or deer symbol.
2. Split plate models, 18S or N size; 16S or L size.

HOWARD WATCH CO.
All 16S with 19, 21, & 23J.

ILLINOIS
1. Bunn 15J marked "Adjusted," & Stuart, 15J marked "Adjusted," 18S.
2. Benjamin Franklin, 17-26J; Bunn 17, 19, 21, 24J; Bunn Special, 21-26J; Chesapeake & Ohio Sp., 24J; Interstate Chronometer, 23J;Lafayette, 24J; A. Lincoln, 21J; Paillard W. Co., 17-24J; Trainsmen, 23J; Pennsylvania Special 17-26J; The Railroader & Railroad King, 18S.
3. Benjamin Franklin, 17-25J; Bunn, 17-19J; Bunn Special, 21-23J; Diamond Ruby Sapphire, 21 & 23J; Interstate Chronometer, 23J; Lafayette, 23J; A. Lincoln, 21J; Paillard Non-Magnetic W. Co., 17 & 21J; Pennsylvania Special, 17, 21, & 23J; Santa Fe Special, 21J; Sangamo, 21-26J; Sangamo Special, 19-23J; Grades 161, 161A, 163, 163A, 187, and 189, 17J, 16S.

PEORIA WATCH CO.
15 & 17J with a patented regulator, 18S.

ROCKFORD
1. All 21 or more jewels, 16-18S, and wind indicators.
2. Grades 900, 905, 910, 912, 918, 945, 200, 205, 18S.
3. Winnebago, 17-21J, 505, 515, 525, 535, 545, 555, 16S.

SETH THOMAS
Maiden Lane, 21-28J; Henry Molineux, 20J; 260 Model, 18S.

SOUTH BEND
1. Studebaker 329, Grade Nos. 323, and 327, 17-21J, 18S.
2. Studebaker 229, Grade Nos. 223, 227, 293, 295, 299, 17-21J, 16S.
3. Polaris.

UNITED STATES WATCH CO., MARION
United States, 19J, gold train.

U. S. WATCH CO., WALTHAM
The President, 17J, 18S.

WALTHAM

1. 1857 KW with Pennsylvania R.R. on dial, Appleton Tracy & Co. on movement.
2. Crescent Street, 17-23J; 1883 & 1892 Models; Appleton Tracy & Co., 1892 Model; Railroader, 1892 Model; Pennsylvania Railroad; Special RR, Special RR King, Vanguard, 17 -23J, 1892 Model; Grade 845, 18S.
3. American Watch Co., 17-21J, 1872 Models; American Watch Co., 17-23J, Bridge Models; Crescent Street, 17-21J, 1899 & 1908 Models; Premier Maximus; Railroader; Riverside Maximus, 21-23J; Vanguard, 19-23J; 645, 16S.
4. All wind indicators.

American Waltham Watch Co. Vanguard , 16 size, 19-23 jewels, winding indicator which alerts user to how far up or down the mainspring is wound. This watch was made to promote new sales in the railway industry.

Hamilton Watch Co. A Favorite raiload style case by Hamilton. Note the Montgomery style dial as well as the bar above the crown.

CANADIAN PACIFIC SERVICE
RAILROAD APPROVED WATCHES 1899
WALTHAM

Vanguard, 18-16S, 19-21-23 jewels
Crescent St., 18S, 19J; 18-16S, 21J
Appleton-Tracy 17J; also No. 845, 21J
Riverside 16S, 19J; Riverside Maximus, 16S, 23J; and 16S, No. 645, 21J
C. P. R. 18-16S, 17J; also C. T. S. 18-16S, 17J

ELGIN
  Veritas, 18-16S, 21-23J
  B. W. R. 18-16S, 17-19-21J
  Father Time 18-16S, 21J
  Grade 349, 18S, 21J
HAMILTON
  18S, 946, 23J; 940-942, 21J; 944, 19J; 936-938, 17J
  16S, 950, 23J; 960-990-992, 21J; 952, 19J; 972, 17J
SOUTH BEND
  18S, 327-329, 21J; 323, 17J
  16S, 227-229, 21J; 223, 17J
BALL
  All Balls 18S, 16S, 17-19-21-23J
ILLINOIS
  Bunn Special, 18-16S, 21-23J; also Bunn 18-16S, 17-19J
  A. Lincoln, 18-16S, 21J
  Sangamo Special, 16S, 19-21-23J
SETH THOMAS
  Maiden Lane, 18S, 25J; No. 260, 21J; No. 382, 17J
E. HOWARD WATCH CO.
  16S Series, 0-23J, 5-19J, 2-17J, 10-21J; also No. 1, 21J
ROCKFORD
  18S, Grade 918-905, 21J; Winnebago, 17J; also Grade 900, 24J
  16S, Grades 545, 525, 515, 505, 21J; 655 W.I., 21J; and Grade 405, 17J
LONGINES
  18S, Express Monarch, 17-19-21-23J
  16S, Express Monarch, 17-19-21-23J
BRANDT-OMEGA
  18S, D.D.R., 23J; C.C.C.R., 23J; C.D.R., 19J; C.C.R., 19J

AMERICAN RAILROAD APPROVED WATCHES—1930

The following requirements for railroad approved watches are outlined by Mr. R. D. Montgomery, General Watch Inspector of the Santa Fe Railway System:

"The regulation watch designated as of 1930 to be standard is described as follows:"

"16 size, American, lever-setting, 19 jewels or more, open face, winding at '12,' double-roller escapement, steel escape wheel, adjusted to 5 positions, temperature and isochronism, which will rate within a variation not exceeding 6 seconds in 72 hour tests, pendant up, dial up and dial down, and be regulated to run within a variation not exceeding 30 seconds per week."

"The following listed makes and grades meet the requirements and comprise a complete list of watches acceptable. Watches bearing the name of jewelers or other names not standard trade marks or trade numbers will not be accepted:"

American Waltham Watch Co.
(16 Size)
- 23J Premier Maximus
- 23J Riverside Maximus
- 23J Vanguard
  6 position
  winding indicator
- 23J Vanguard
  6 position
- 21J Crescent Street
- 21J No. 645
- 19J Vanguard
- 19J Riverside

Ball Watch Co.
(16 Size)
- 23J Official R.R. Standard
- 21J Official R.R. Standard
- 19J Official R.R. Standard

Elgin Watch Co.
(16 Size)
- 23J Veritas
- 21J Veritas
- 21J B. W. Raymond
- 21J Father Time
- 21J No. 270

Hamilton Watch Co.
(16 Size)
- 23J No. 950
- 21J No. 990
- 21J No. 992
- 19J No. 952
- 19J No. 996

Hampden Watch Co.
(16 Size)
- 23J Special Railway
- 21J New Railway
- 19J Railway

Howard Watch Co.
(16 Size)
- All 23J
- All 21J
- All 19J

Illinois Watch Co.
(16 Size)
- 23J Sangamo Special
- 23J Sangamo
- 23J Bunn Special
- 21J Bunn Special
- 21J Sangamo
- 21J A. Lincoln
- 19J Bunn

South Bend Watch Co.
(16 Size)
- 21J No. 227
- 21J No. 229
- 21J No. 295
- 19J No. 293

APPROVED POCKET WATCHES IN CP RAIL SERVICE AS OF FEBRUARY 1, 1957

Waltham (16 Size)
- 23J Vanguard No. 29, 634, 001 and up

Elgin (16 Size)
- 21J B.W.R.
- 21J No. 571

Hamilton (16 Size)
- 23J No. 950B
- 21J No. 992B

Ball (16 Size)
- 21J (Hamilton) No. 992C
- 21J No. 435C

Zenith (16 Size)
- 21J Extra RR 56

APPROVED WRIST WATCHES IN CP RAIL SERVICE

Cyma
- 17J RR 2852 M
- 25J RR 2872 A

Girard Perregaux
- 17J CP 307H.F.

Longines
- 17J RR 280

Universal
- 19J RR 1205

Zenith
- 18J RR 120 T

APPROVED WRIST WATCHES IN
CP RAIL SERVICE
BATTERY POWERED

Bulova Accutron	Rodania	Wittnauer
17J 214	13J RR 2780 Calendar	13J RR 12 WT Calendar
17J 218 Calendar		

APPROVED WRIST WATCHES SEMI-MECHANICAL
QUARTZ ANALOG BATTERY POWERED
IN CP RAIL SERVICE AS OF 1978

Cyma	Rodania	Wyler
7J Calendar RR 9361 Q	6J Calendar 9952.111RR	7J Calendar RR 9361 Q
6J Calendar RR 960 Q	7J Calendar RR 9361 Q	
		Wittnauer
Bulova	Rotary	7J Calendar RR 2 Q 115 C
7J Calendar RR 9362 Q	7J Calendar RR 9366 Q	
6J Calendar RR 960.111Q		

ADJUSTMENTS

There are nine basic adjustments for watch movements. They are:

heat ... 1	positions ... 6
cold ... 1	TOTAL ... 9
isochronism ... 1	

THE SIX POSITION ADJUSTMENTS ARE:

Stem UP

Stem Down

This position adjustment not required on railroad watches.

Stem Left   Stem Right

Dial Up   Dial Down

A watch with eight adjustments (the most common) will be listed in this book as: "Adj.5P" (heat, cold, isochronism, 5 positions).

The total number of pocket watches made for the railroad industry was small in comparison to the total pocket watches produced. Generally, watches defined as "Railroad Watches" fall into five categories:

1. **Railroad Approved-** Grades and Models approved by the railway companies.
2. **Railroad Grade-**Those advertised as being able to pass railroad inspection.
3. **Pre-Commission Watches-**Those used by the railroads before 1893.
4. **Company Watches-**Those with a railroad logo or company name on the dial.
5. **Train Watches-**Those with a locomotive painted on the dial or inscribed on the case.

*   *   *   *   *

1. Not all railroad employees were required to purchase or use approved watches, just the employees that were responsible for schedules. But many employees did buy the approved watches because they were the standard in reliability.

2. These were used primarily by those railroaders who were not required to submit their watches for inspection.

3. There were many watches made for railroad use prior to 1893. Some of the key wind ones, especially, are good quality and highly collectible.

4. Some manufacturers inscribed terms such as railroader, special railroad, dispatcher, etc. on the back plates of the movements.

COLONIAL WATCHMAKERS

Early American watchmakers came from Europe; little is known about them, and few of their watches exist today. Their hand-fabricated watches were made largely from imported parts. It was common practice for a watchmaker to use rough castings made by several craftsmen. These were referred to as "movements in the gray." The watchmaker finished these parts and assembled them to make a complete watch. He would then engrave his name on the finished timepiece.

Some of the early American watchmakers designed the cases or other parts, but most imported what they needed. The early colonial watchmakers showed little originality as designers and we can only guess how many watches were really made in America.

These early hand-made watches are almost non-existent; therefore, only the name of the watchmaker will be listed. This compilation comes from old ads in newspapers and journals and other sources. It is not considered to be complete.

Because of the rarity and condition of these early watches, prices may vary widely from $400 to $2,000.

Example of watch paper placed inside a pair-cased watch by a watch maker. This was a form of advertisement placed in the watch after repair was made.

Ephraim Clark, 18 size, non-jeweled, made between 1780-1790; a good example of a colonial watch. These early watches usually included chain driven fusees, verge type escapements, hand pierced balance cock, key wind & set; note the circular shaped regulator on the far left side of the illustrated example.

Nath. Hawxhurst, N.Y., 18 size, non-jeweled, ca. 1770-1780, chain driven fusee, verge type escapement, notice hand-pierced cock.

J.F. Bartlett, Clinton, Mass. Example of watch paper placed inside a pair-cased watch by the watch maker, ca. 1850.

EARLY AMERICAN WATCHMAKERS
(With Location and Approximate Date)

Adams, Nathan (Boston, MA, 1800)
Adams, William (Boston, MA, 1810)
Aldrich, Jacob (Wilmington, DE, 1802)
Allebach, Jacob (Phila., PA, 1825-1840)
Atherton, Nathan (Phila., PA, 1825)
Atkinson, James (Boston, MA, 1745)
Backhouse, John (Lancaster, PA, 1725)
Bagnall, Benjamin (Phila., PA, 1750)
Bailey, John (Boston, MA, 1810)
Bailey, William (Phila., PA, 1820)
Baker, Benjamin (Phila., PA, 1825)
Banks, Joseph (Phila., PA, 1790)
Barnhill, Robert (Phila., PA, 1775)
Barrow, Samuel (Phila., PA, 1771)
Barry, Standish (Baltimore, MD, 1785)
Basset, John F. (Phila., PA, 1798)
Belknap, William (Boston, MA, 1815)
Bell, William (Phila., PA, 1805)
Benedict, S. W. (New York, NY, 1835)
Bigger & Clarke (Baltimore, MD, 1783)
Billion, C. (Phila., PA, 1775-1800)
Bingham & Bricerly (Phila., PA, 1778-1799)
Birnie, Laurence (Phila., PA, 1774)
Blundy, Charles (Charleston, SC, 1750)
Blunt & Nichols (New York, NY, 1850)
Bond, William (Boston, MA, 1800-1810)
Bonnaud (Phila., PA, 1799)
Bower, Michael (Phila., PA, 1790-1800)
Bowman, Joseph (Lancaster, PA, 1821-1844)
Boyd & Richards (Phila., PA, 1808)
Boyter, Daniel (Lancaster, PA, 1805)
Brands & Matthey (Phila., PA, 1799)
Brandt, Aime (Phila., PA, 1820)
Brant, Brown & Lewis (Phila., PA, 1795)
Brazier, Amable (Phila., PA, 1795)
Brearley, James (Phila., PA, 1790-1800)
Brewer, William (Phila., PA, 1785-1791)
Brewster &Ingraham(Bristol,CT,1827-1839)
Brown, Garven (Boston, MA, 1767)
Brown, John (Lancaster, PA, 1840)
Brownell, A. P. (New Bedford, MA)
Burkelow, Samuel (Phila., PA, 1791-1799)
Bush, George (Easton, PA, 1790-1800)
Campbell, Charles (Phila., PA, 1796)
Campbell, William (Carlisle, PA, 1765)
Capper, Michael (Phila., PA, 1799)
Carey, James (Brunswick, ME, 1830)
Carrell, John (Phila., PA, 1791-1793)
Carter, Jacob (Phila., PA, 1805)
Carter, Thomas (Phila., PA, 1823)

Carver, Jacob (Phila., PA, 1790)
Carvill, James (New York, NY, 1803)
Chandlee, John(Wilmington,DE,1795-1810)
Chaudron (Phila., PA, 1799)
Chauncey & Joseph Ives (Bristol, CT, 1825)
Cheney, Martin (Windsor, VT, 1800)
Chick, M. M. (Concord, NH, 1845)
Clark,Benjamin(Wilmington,DE,1737-1750)
Clark, Ephraim (Phila., PA, 1780-1800)
Clark, John (New York, NY, 1770-1790)
Clark, John (Phila., PA, 1799)
Clark, Thomas (Boston, MA, 1764)
Claudon, John-George (Charleston SC,1773)
Cook, William (Boston, MA, 1810)
Crow, George (Wilmington, DE, 1740-1770)
Crow, John (Wilmington, DE, 1770-1798)
Crow, Thomas (Wilmington, DE, 1770-1798)
Currier & Trott (Boston, MA, 1800)
Curtis, Solomon (Phila., PA, 1793-1795)
Dakin, James (Boston, MA, 1795)
Davis, Samuel (Boston, MA, 1820)
Delaplaine, James K.(New York, 1786-1800)
DeVacht, Joseph & Frances (Gallipolis, OH, 1792)
Dix, Joseph (Phila., PA, 1770)
Downes, Anson (Bristol, CT, 1830)
Downes, Arthur (Charleston, SC, 1765)
Downes, Ephriam (Bristol, CT, 1830)
Droz, Hannah (Phila., PA, 1840)
Droz, Humbert (Phila., PA, 1793-1799)
Duffield, Edward W. (Whiteland, PA, 1775)
Dunheim, Andrew (New York, NY, 1775)
Dupuy, John (Phila., PA, 1770)
Dupuy, Odran (Phila., PA, 1735)
Dutch, Stephen, Jr. (Boston, MA, 1800-1810)
Eberman, George (Lancaster, PA, 1800)
Eberman, John (Lancaster, PA, 1780-1820)
Ellicott, Joseph (Buckingham, PA, 1763)
Elsworth, David (Baltimore, MD, 1780-1800)
Embree, Effingham (New York, NY, 1785)
Evans, David (Baltimore, MD, 1770-1773)
Fales, James (New Bedford, MA, 1810-1820)
Ferris, Tiba (Wilmington, DE, 1812-1850)
Fessler, John (Phila., PA, 1785-1820)
Feton, J. (Phila., PA, 1825-1840)
Filder, John (Lancaster, PA, 1810-1825)
Fister, Amon (Phila., PA, 1794)
Fix, Joseph (Reading, PA, 1820-1840)
Fowell, J & N (Boston, MA, 1800-1810)
Frances, Basil & Alexander Vuille
   Baltimore, MD, 1766)

Galbraith, Patrick (Phila., PA, 1795)
Gibbons, Thomas (Phila., PA, 1750)
Goodfellow, William (Phila., PA, 1793-1795)
Goodfellow & Son, William (Phila., PA, 1796-1799)
Gooding, Henry (Boston, MA, 1810-1820)
Green, John (Phila., PA, 1794)
Groppengeiser, J. L. (Phila., PA, 1840)
Grotz, Issac (Easton, PA, 1810-1835)
Hall, Jonas (Boston, MA, 1848-1858)
Harland, Theodore (Norwich, CT,1750-1790)
Harland, Thomas (Norwich, CT, 1802)
Harrison, James (Shrewbury, MA, 1805)
Hawxhurst, Nath. (New York, NY, 1784)
Heilig, Jacob (Phila., PA, 1770-1824)
Heilig, John (Germantown, PA, 1824-1830)
Hepton, Frederick (Phila., PA, 1785)
Heron, Isaac (New York, NY, 1770-1780)
Hodgson, William (Phila., PA, 1785)
Hoff, John (Lancaster, PA, 1800)
Hoffner, Henry (Phila., PA, 1791)
Howard, Thomas (Phila., PA, 1789-1791)
Howe, Jubal (Shrewbury, MA, 1800)
Huguenail, Charles (Phila., PA, 1799)
Hunt, Hiram (Robbinston, ME, 1800)
Hutchins, Abel (Concord, MA, 1785-1818)
Hutchins, Levi (Concord, MA, 1785-1815)
Hyde, John E. (New York, NY, 1805)
Hyde & Goodrich (New Orleans, LA, 1850)
Ingersoll, Daniel B. (Boston, MA, 1800-1810)
Ingold, Pierre Frederick (NY, NY,1845-1850)
Ives, Chauncy & Joseph (Bristol, CT, 1825)
Jacob, Charles & Claude (Annapolis,MD, 1775)
Jackson, Joseph H. (Phila., PA, 1802-1810)
Jessop, Jonathan (Park Town, PA, 1790)
Jeunit, Joseph (Meadville, PA, 1763)
Johnson, David (Boston, MA, 1690)
Johnson, John (Charleston, SC, 1763)
Jones, George (Wilmington, DE, 1815-1835)
Jones, Low & Ball (Boston, MA, 1830)
Keith, William (Shrewbury, MA, 1810)
Kennedy, Patrick (Phila., PA, 1795-1799)
Kincaid, Thomas (Christiana Bridge, DE, 1775)
Kirkwood, John (Charleston, SC, 1761)
Launy, David F. (Boston & New York, 1800)
Leavenworth, Mark (Waterbury, CT, 1820)
Leavenworth, Wm. (Waterbury, CT, 1810)
Leslie & Co., Baltimore, MD, 1795)
Leslie & Price (Phila., PA, 1793-1799)
Leslie, Robert (Baltimore, MD, 1788-1791)
Levely, George (Phila., PA, 1774)
Levi, Michael & Issac (Baltimore, MD, 1785)
Limeburner, John (Phila., PA, 1790)
Lind, John (Phila., PA, 1791-1799)
Lowens, David (Phila., PA, 1785)
Ludwig, John (Phila., PA, 1791)
Lufkins & Johnson (Boston, MA, 1800-1810)
Lukins, Isaac (Phila., PA, 1825)

MacDowell, Robert (Phila., PA, 1798)
MacFarlane, John (Boston, MA, 1800-1810)
Mahve, Matthew (Phila., PA, 1761)
Manross, Elisha (Bristol, CT, 1827)
Martin, Patrick (Phila., PA, 1830)
Maunroe & Whitney (Concord, MA, 1805-1825)
Maus, Frederick (Phila., PA, 1785- 1793)
Maynard, George(New York,NY, 1702-1730)
McCabe, John (Baltimore, MD, 1774)
McDowell, James (Phila., PA, 1795)
McGraw, Donald (Annapolis, MD, 1767)
Mends, James (Phila., PA, 1795)
Merriman, Titus (Bristol, CT, 1830)
Merry, Charles F. (Phila., PA, 1799)
Meters, John (Fredricktown, MD,1795-1825)
Miller, Abraham (Easton, PA, 1810-1830)
Mitchell & Atkins (Bristol, CT, 1830)
Mitchell, Henry (New York, NY, 1787-1800)
Mohler, Jacob (Baltimore, MD, 1773)
Moir, J & W (Waterbury, CT, 1790)
Montandon, Julien (Shrewbury, CT, 1812)
Moollinger, Henry (Phila., PA, 1794)
Morgan, Thomas (Phila. & Balti., 1774-1793)
Moris, William (Grafton, MA, 1765-1775)
Mulford, J. H. (Albany, NY, 1845)
Mulliken, Nathaniel (Boston, MA, 1765)
Munroe & Whitney (Concord, MA, 1820)
Narney, Joseph (Charleston, SC, 1753)
Neiser, Augustine (Phila., PA, 1739-1780)
Nicholls, George (New York, NY, 1728-1750)
Nicollette, Mary (Phila., PA, 1793-1799)
O'Hara, Charles (Phila., PA, 1799)
Oliver, Griffith (Phila., PA, 1785-1793)
Ormsby, James (Baltimore, MD, 1771)
Palmer, John (Phila., PA, 1795)
Palmer, John Peter (Phila., PA, 1795)
Park, Seth (Parktown, PA, 1790)
Parke, Solomon (Phila., PA, 1791-1795)
Parke, Solomon & Co. (Phila., PA, 1799)
Parker, James (Cambridge, OH, 1790)
Parker, Thomas (Phila., PA, 1783)
Parry, John J. (Phila., PA, 1795-1800)
Patton, Abraham (Phila., PA, 1799)
Patton, David (Phila., PA, 1800)
Payne, Lawrence (New York, NY,1732- 1755)
Pearman, W. (Richmond, VA, 1834)
Perkins, Thomas (Phila., PA. 1785-1800)
Perry, Marvin (New York, NY, 1770-1780)
Perry, Thomas (New York, NY, 1750-1775)
Phillips, Joseph (New York, NY, 1713-1735)
Pierret, Mathew (Phila., PA, 1795)
Pope, Joseph (Boston, MA, 1790)
Price, Philip (Phila., PA, 1825)
Proctor, Cardan (New York, NY, 1747-1775)
Proctor, William (New York,NY, 1737-1760)
Proud, R. (Newport, RI, 1775)
Purse, Thomas (Baltimore, MD, 1805)
Quimby, Phineas & William (Belfast, ME, 1825)

Reily, John (Phila., PA, 1785-1795)
Rich, John (Bristol, CT, 1800)
Richardson, Francis (Phila., PA, 1736)
Ritchie, George (Phila., PA, 1785-1790)
Roberts, John (Phila., PA, 1799)
Roberts, S & E (Trenton, NJ, 1830)
Rode, William (Phila., PA, 1785)
Rodger, James (New York, NY, 1822-1878)
Rodgers, Samuel (Plymouth,MA, 1790-1804)
Russell, George (Phila., PA, 1840)
Saxton & Lukens (Phila., PA, 1828)
Schriner, Martin (Lancaster, PA, 1790-1830)
Schriner, M & P (Lancaster, PA, 1830-1840)
Seddinger, Margaret (Phila., PA, 1846)
Severberg, Christian (NY, NY, 1755-1775)
Sherman, Robert (Wilmington, DE,
    1760-1770)
Sibley, O. E. (New York, NY, 1820)
Smith, J. L. (Middletown, CT, 1830)
Smith & Goodrich (Bristol, CT, 1827-1840)
Soloman, Henry (Boston, MA, 1820)
Souza, Sammuel (Phila., PA, 1820)
Sprogell, John (Phila., PA, 1791)
Spurck, Peter (Phila., PA, 1795-1799)
Stanton, Job (New York, NY, 1810)
Stein, Abraham (Phila., PA, 1799)
Stever & Bryant (Wigville, CT, 1830)
Stillas, John (Phila., PA, 1785-1793)

Stinnett, John (Phila., PA, 1769)
Stokel, John (New York, NY, 1820-1840)
Store, Marmaduke (Phila., PA, 1742)
Strech, Thomas (Phila., PA, 1782)
Syderman, Philip (Phila., PA, 1785)
Taf, John James (Phila., PA, 1794)
Taylor, Samuel (Phila, PA, 1799)
Tonchure, Francis (Baltimore, MD, 1805)
Townsend, Charles (Phila., PA, 1799)
Townsend, David (Boston, MA, 1800)
Trott, Andrew (Boston, MA, 1800-1810)
Turrell, Samuel (Boston, MA, 1790)
Voight, Henry (Phila., PA, 1775-1793)
Voight, Sebastian (Phila., PA, 1775-1799)
Voight, Thomas (Henry's son) (Phila., PA,
    1811-1835)
Vuille, Alexander (Baltimore, MD, 1766)
Warner, George T. (New York, NY, 1795)
Weller, Francis (Phila., PA, 1780)
Wells, George & Co. (Boston, MA, 1825)
Wells, J.S. (Boston, MA, 1800)
Wetherell, Nathan (Phila., PA, 1830-1840)
Wheaton, Caleb (Providence, RI, 1800)
White, Sebastian (Phila., PA, 1795)
Whittaker, William (NY, NY, 1731-1755)
Wood, John (Phila., PA, 1770-1793)
Wright, John (New York, NY, 1712-1735)
Zahm, G.M. (Lancaster, PA, 1865)

Baldwin Jones, Boston, 18 size, early American key wind watch with date calendar, verge chain driven fusee, ca. 1800.

H. Mitchell, New York, 18 size, verge chain driven fusee; note regulator below hand-pierced cock, ca. 1790.

10 20 30 40 50 60 70 80 90 100 110

MILLIMETERS

AMERICAN MOVEMENT SIZES
LANCASHIRE GAUGE

Size	Inches	Inches	mm	Lignes	Size	Inches	Inches	mm	Lignes
18/0	18/30	.600	15.24	6 3/4	2	1 7/30	1.233	31.32	13 7/8
17/0	19/30	.633	16.08	7 1/8	3	1 8/30	1.266	32.16	14 1/4
16/0	20/30	.666	16.92	7 1/2	4	1 9/30	1.300	33.02	14 7/8
15/0	21/30	.700	17.78	7 7/8	5	1 10/30	1.333	33.86	15 1/8
14/0	22/30	.733	18.62	8 1/4	6	1 11/30	1.366	34.70	15 3/8
13/0	23/30	.766	19.46	8 5/8	7	1 12/30	1.400	35.56	15 3/4
12/0	24/30	.800	20.32	9 1/8	8	1 13/30	1.433	36.40	16 1/8
11/0	25/30	.833	21.16	9 3/8	9	1 14/30	1.466	37.24	16 1/2
10/0	26/30	.866	22.00	9 3/4	10	1 15/30	1.500	38.10	16 7/8
9/0	27/30	.900	22.86	10 1/8	11	1 16/30	1.533	38.94	17 1/4
8/0	28/30	.933	23.70	10 1/2	12	1 17/30	1.566	39.78	17 5/8
7/0	29/30	.966	24.54	10 7/8	13	1 18/30	1.600	40.64	18 1/8
6/0	1	1.000	25.40	11 1/4	14	1 19/30	1.633	41.48	18 3/8
5/0	1 1/30	1.033	26.24	11 5/8	15	1 20/30	1.666	42.32	18 3/4
4/0	1 2/30	1.066	27.08	12 1/8	16	1 21/30	1.700	43.18	19 1/8
3/0	1 3/30	1.100	27.94	12 3/8	17	1 22/30	1.733	44.02	19 1/2
2/0	1 4/30	1.133	28.78	12 3/4	18	1 23/30	1.766	44.86	19 7/8
0	1 5/30	1.166	29.62	13 1/8	19	1 24/30	1.800	45.72	20 1/4
1	1 6/30	1.200	30.48	13 1/2	20	1 25/30	1.833	46.56	20 3/4

SWISS MOVEMENT SIZES
Lignes With Their Equivalents in Millimeters and Decimal Parts of an Inch

Lignes	Inches Decimals	Millimeters
7	.622	15.79
8	.710	18.05
9	.799	20.30
10	.888	22.56
11	.977	24.81
12	1.066	27.07
13	1.154	29.32
14	1.243	31.58
15	1.332	33.84
16	1.421	36.09
17	1.510	38.35
18	1.599	40.60
19	1.687	42.86
20	1.776	45.11
21	1.865	47.37
22	1.954	49.63

GAUGES FOR MEASURING YOUR WATCH SIZE

The size of a watch is determined by measuring the outside diameter of the dial side of the lower pillar plate. The gauges below may be placed across the face of your watch to calculate its approximate size.

AMER. MOVEMENT SIZES

SWISS MOVEMENT SIZES
LIGNES

SOLID GOLD MARKS

GOLD-FILLED CASES

The first patent for gold-filled cases was given to J. Boss on **May 3, 1859.**
Gold-filled cases are far more common than solid gold cases. Only about 5 percent of the cases were solid gold. In making the gold-filled case, the following process was used: two bars of gold, 12" long, 2" wide, and 1/2 " thick were placed on either side of a bar of base metal. The bar of base metal was 3/4" thick and the same length and width as the gold bars. These three bars were soldered together under pressure at high temperature. The bars were sent through rolling mills under tremendous pressure; this rolling was repeated until the desired thickness was reached. The new sandwich-type gold was now in a sheet. Discs were punched out of the sheet and pressed in a die to form a dish-shaped cover. Finally the lip, or ridge, was added. The bezel, snap, and dust caps were added in the finishing room. Gold-filled cases are usually 10k or 14k gold. The cases were marked ten-year, fifteen-year, twenty-year, twenty-five-year, or thirty-year. The number of years indicated the duration of guarantee that the gold on the case would not wear through to the base metal. The higher the number of years indicates that more gold was used and that a higher original price was paid.

In 1924 the government prohibited any further use of the guarantee terms of 5, 10, 15, 20, 25, or 30 years. After that, manufacturers marked their cases 10k or 14k Gold-Filled and 10k Rolled Gold Plate. Anytime you see the terms "5, 10, 15, 20, 25 and 30-year" this immediately identifies the case as being gold-filled. The word "guaranteed" on the case also denotes gold-filled.

Rolled Gold

Rolled gold involved rolling gold into a micro thinness and, under extreme pressure, bonding it to each sheet of base metal. Rolled gold carried a five-year guarantee. The thickness of the gold sheet varied and had a direct bearing on value, as did the richness of the engraving.

Gold Gilding

Brass plates, wheels and cases are often gilded with gold. To do this, the parts are hung by a copper wire in a vessel or porous cell of a galvanic battery filled with a solution of ferro-cyanide of potassium, carbonate of soda, chloride of gold, and distilled water. An electric current deposits the gold evenly over the surface in about a six-minute period. One ounce of gold is enough for heavy gilding of six hundred watches. After gilding, the plates are polished with a soft buff using powdered rouge mixed with water and alcohol. The older method is fire-gilt which uses a gold and mercury solution. The metal is subjected to a high temperature so the mercury will evaporate and leave the gold plating. This is a very dangerous method, however, due to the harmful mercury vapor.

GOLD-FILLED MARKS

The following gold-filled and rolled gold plate marks are not complete, but if you have any doubt that the case is solid gold, pay only the gold-filled price.

GOLD FILLED MARKS

C.W.C.CO

TRADE ⭐ 🌙 MARK

PIONEER

☆ 10 K ROLLED GOLD PLATE

BEE HIVE

(14K. Filled.)

(Jas. Boss
10K. Filled.
20 Years.)

CROWN 14K. FILLED
(25 Years.)

(Keystone Extra,
Substitute for
All-Gold Case.)

CROWN 10K. FILLED
(20 Years.)

(Rolled Gold.)

(Jas. Boss
14K. Filled.
25 Years.)

EMPRESS
(Gold Filled, 10 Years.)

FORTUNE
(Gold Filled, 20 Years.)

(10 Years.)

PREMIER
(Gold Filled, 25 Years.)

(14K. Filled.)

xv.

v.

**THE BELL
14K.**
(25 Years.)

xx.

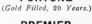

CASHIER
(Gold Filled, 25 Years.)

(10K. Gold Filled.)

(5 Years.)

(15 Years.)

(20 Years.)

(25 Years.)

THE COMET
(10 Years.)

SILVER CASE MARKS

A.W.W.CO.

WALTHAM.

STERLING.

A.W.W.CO.
COIN.

STERLING

(Coin Silver with Albata Cap)
(Discontinued.)

(Discontinued.)

(Discontinued.)

(Coin Silver with Silver Cap)
(Discontinued.)

(Coin Silver, with Silver Caps,
Gold Joints and Crowns.)

**STERLING
925/1000
FINE**

(Sterling Silver.)

Sterling Silver

SILVER CASE MARKS

(Sterling Silver.)

STERLING
SILVER
UNITED STATES
ASSAY
925./1000
FINE.

ILLINOIS
W.C.CO,
ELGIN
STERLING

HUNTING CASES

A hunting case is identifed by a cover over the face of the watch. The case is opened by pressing the stem or the crown of the watch.The hunter style watch was used for protection of the watch and carried by men of status and used as a dress watch.

HOW TO HANDLE A HUNTING CASE WATCH

Hold the watch in your right hand with the bow or swing ring between the index finger and thumb. Press on the pendant-crown with the right thumb to release the cover exposing the face.

When closing, don't snap the cover. Press the crown to move the catch in, close the cover, then release the crown. This will prevent wear to the soft gold on the rim and catch.

Above: Example of a hunting case

Right: Example of a swing-out case

SWING-OUT MOVEMENT

On some pocket watches the movement swings out from the front. On these type watches the movement can be swung out by unscrewing the crystal and pulling the stem out to **release** the movement. See example above.

Demi-Hunting case

Example of a 14 carat gold boxed hinged case, selling for $94 in 1890.

Below: Example of a reversible case to either hunting or open face.

Left: Example of a screw bezel and screw back case.

Note: The screw on bezel was invented by E. C. Fitch in 1886.

38

MOVEMENT IDENTIFICATION

1. Grade Number. **2.** Nickel Motor Barrel Bridge. **3.** Center Wheel (2nd Wheel). **4.** Winding Wheel with Jewel Setting. **5.** First Barrel Wheel. **6.** Winding Click. **7.** Case Screw. **8.** Pendant Crown. **9.** Pendant Bow or Swing Ring. **10.** Crown Wheel with Screw. **11** Damaskeening-horizontal pattern. **12.** Number of Jewels. **13.** Center Wheel Jewel with Setting. **14.** Adjusted to Heat, Cold, Isochronism & 5 Positions. **15.** Patented Regulator with Index & Spring. **16.** Balance End Stones (Diamonds, Rubys, & Sapphires were used). **17.** Balance Screws. **18.** Compensating Balance Wheel. **19.** Hairspring. **20.** Escapement Bridge. **21.** Escapement Wheel Jewel with Setting (Diamonds, Rubys, & Sapphires were used). **22.** Escapement Wheel. **23.** Fourth Wheel Jewel with Setting. **24.** Third Wheel. **25.** Fourth Wheel. **26.** Fourth Wheel Bridge. **27.** Third Wheel Jewel with Setting. **28.** Center & Third Wheel Bridge. **29.** Bridge Screw. **30.** Manufacturers Name & Location. **31.** Jewel Setting Screw.

NOMENCLATURE
OF
WATCH PARTS

Ratchet Wheel

Crown or Main Wheel

Click Spring

Setting Cam

Bevel Pinion

Crown or Main
Screw Washer

Winding Arbor

Winding and
Setting Clutch

Setting Spring

Setting
Lever

Click

Setting
Spring Cam

Winding Sleeve

Clutch Lever

NOMENCLATURE
OF
WATCH PARTS

Barrel

Center Wheel

Third Wheel

Minute Wheel

Hour Wheel

Fourth Wheel

Escape Wheel

Center Arbor Washer

Third Pinion

Fourth Pinion

Center Staff

Center Pinion

Escape Pinion

Cannon Pinion

Balance Staff

Pallet Fork and Arbor

Regulator

Combination Roller

Barrel Arbor

Overcoil Hairspring

Balance Wheel

CASE PRICES

Case prices are for complete cases with bezel, crystal, stem, crown and bow. Hunting case style watches must have workable lift spring.

SILVEROID CASES

Size and Style	Avg	Ex-Fn	Mint
18S, OF, SW	$10	$15	$25
18S, OF, KW	20	25	35
18S, HC, SW	20	25	40
18S, HC, KW	25	40	50
16S, OF	10	15	20
16S, HC	20	25	35
12S, OF	5	8	10
12S, HC	10	15	20
6S, OF	5	8	10
6S, HC	10	15	20

COIN-SILVER CASES

Size and Style	Avg	Ex-Fn	Mint
18S, OF, SW	$20	$30	$40
18S, OF, KW	30	50	70
18S, HC, SW	35	45	60
18S, HC, KW	50	70	100
16S, OF	20	25	35
16S, HC	40	45	55
12S, OF	5	10	15
12S, HC	15	30	50
6S, OF	10	15	20
6S, HC	20	30	50

GOLD-FILLED CASES

Size and Style	Avg	Ex-Fn	Mint
18S, OF, Plain	$55	$65	$75
18S, OF, Fancy	65	75	100
18S, HC, Plain	75	85	150
18S, HC, BOX & Fancy	100	150	200
18S, HC, MULTI-COLOR BOX & Fancy	300	375	500
16S, OF, Plain	50	60	70
16S, OF, Fancy	55	65	85
16S, HC, Plain	65	75	120
16S, HC, BOX & Fancy	200	250	300
16S, HC, MULTI-COLOR BOX & Fancy	250	300	400
12S, OF, Plain	15	20	30
12S, OF, Fancy	20	25	35
12S, HC, Plain	25	35	50
12S, HC, Fancy	30	40	55
6S, OF, Plain	10	20	30
6S, OF, Fancy	15	25	35
6S, HC, Plain	25	30	45
6S, HC, BOX	55	75	125
6S, HC, MULTI-color BOX	125	150	200

☞ **Note:** Plain enamel single sunk dial brings $15 to $30.

14K SOLID GOLD CASES

Size and Style	Avg	Ex-Fn	Mint
18S, OF, Plain	$300	$350	$425
18S, OF, Fancy	350	375	450
18S, HC, Plain	375	425	475
18S, HC, Fancy	400	450	575
18S, HC, BOX & Fancy	475	600	800
16S, OF, Plain	250	275	350
16S, OF, Fancy	300	325	375
16S, HC, Plain	350	375	400
16S, HC, Fancy	375	400	450
16S, HC, BOX & Fancy	425	550	750
12S, OF, Plain	150	160	175
12S, OF, Fancy	200	235	285
12S, HC, Plain	225	255	300
12S, HC, Fancy	265	285	325
6S, OF,	125	155	185
6S, HC, Plain	155	185	225
6S, HC, BOX	200	225	300

18K SOLID GOLD CASES

Size and Style	Avg	Ex-Fn	Mint
18S, OF, Plain	$500	$550	$625
18S, OF, Fancy	550	600	725
18S, HC, Plain	650	700	800
18S, HC, Fancy	750	800	1,000
18S, HC, BOX & Fancy	900	1,000	1,200
16S, OF, Plain	400	450	500
16S, OF, Fancy	450	500	625
16S, HC, Plain	500	600	725
16S, HC, Fancy	550	650	825
16S, HC, BOX & Fancy	650	725	900
12S, OF, Plain	250	275	335
12S, OF, Fancy	275	300	335
12S, HC, Plain	350	375	425
12S, HC, Fancy	400	450	500
6S, OF,	155	185	225
6S, HC, Plain	200	250	300
6S, HC, BOX	300	350	425

14K MULTI–COLOR SOLID GOLD CASES

Size and Style	Avg	Ex-Fn	Mint
18S, OF, Plain	$650	$700	$800
18S, OF, BOX	700	750	850
18S, HC, Plain	850	900	950
18S, HC, BOX	1,000	1,300	1,800
18S, HC, BOX & Fancy	1,200	1,600	2,500
16S, OF, Plain	500	650	700
16S, OF, BOX	650	700	750
16S, HC, Plain	700	800	900
16S, HC, BOX	800	900	1,100
16S, HC, BOX & Fancy	900	1,200	1,500
6S, OF,	300	350	400
6S, HC, Plain	400	450	500
6S, HC, BOX & Fancy	450	500	575

INSPECTING OPEN-FACED WATCHES

For watches with a screw-on front and back, as in railroad models, hold the watch in the left hand and, with the right hand, turn the bezel counter clockwise. While removing the bezel, hold onto the stem and swing ring in order not to drop the watch. Lay the bezel down, check the dial for cracks and crazing nicks, chips, etc. Look for lever and check to see that it will allow hands to be set. After close examination, replace the bezel and turn the watch over. Again, while holding the stem between the left thumb and index finger, remove the back cover. If it is a screw-on back cover, turn it counter clockwise. If it is a snap on cover, look for the lip on the back and use a pocket knife to pry the back off.

DAMASKEENING

Damaskeening (pronounced dam-a-skeening) is the process of applying ornate designs on metal by inlaying gold or by etching. Damaskeening on watch plates became popular in the late 1870s. This kind of beauty and quality in the movement was a direct result of the competition in the watch industry. Illinois, Waltham, Rockford, and Seth Thomas competed fiercely for beauty. Some damaskeening was in two colors of metal such as copper and nickel. The process derives its name from Damascus, a city in Syria, most famous for its metal work. A kind of steel was made there with designs of wavy or varigated lines etched or inlaid on their swords.

Left: Example of open face case

Below: Example of Damaskeening

DISPLAY CASE WATCHES

Display case watches were used by salesmen and in jewelry stores to show the customer the movement. Both front and back had a glass crystal. These are not rare, but they are nice to have in a collection to show off a nice watch movement.

WATCH CASE PRODUCTION

Before the Civil War, watchmaking was being done on a very small scale, and most of the companies in business were making their own movements as well as their own cases. After the War, tradesmen set up shops specializing exclusively in cases, while other artisans were making the movements. The case factories, because of mass production, could supply watch manufacturers with cases more economically than the manufacturers could produce their own.

A patent was granted to James Boss on May 3, 1859, and the first gold-filled watch cases were made from sandwich-type sheets of metal. Boss was not the first to use gold-filled, but he did invent a new process that proved to be very successful, resulting in a durable metal that Boss sold with a 20-year money-back guarantee.

Gold
Base Metal
Gold

The illustration at left is a sandwiched type gold-filled case.

GOLD CASE
WEIGHTS BY SIZE

Size & Style of Case	Ex. Heavy	Heavy	Medium	Light	Ex. Light
18 size Hunting Case	60 to 65	50 to 55	45 to 50	40 to 45	35
16 size Hunting Case	55 to 60	45 to 50	40 to 45	35 to 40	32
18 size Open Face Case		40 to 45	38	35	
16 size Open Face Case		40	36	30	
12 size Open Face Case (Thin)					14
6 size Hunting Case	24	22	20	18	
0 size Hunting Case					14 to 16

Pennyweights (DWT)

An 18 size movement with a full plate weighs 50 DWT; a 16 size movement with a ¾ plate weighs 35 DWT. These weights do not include the case.

CARE OF WATCHES

To some people a watch is just a device that keeps time. They do not know the history of its development nor how it operates. They have no appreciation for improvements made over the years. That the watch is a true miracle of mechanical genius and skill, is seldom more than a fleeting thought. The average person will know it must be wound to run, that it has a mainspring and possibly a hairspring. Some even realize there are wheels and gears and, by some strange method, these work in harmony to keep time. If for some reason the watch should stop, the owner will merely take it to a watch repair shop and await the verdict on damage and cost.

To be a good collector one must have some knowledge of the components of a watch and how they work and the history of the development of the watch. To buy a watch on blind faith is indeed risky, but many collectors do it every day because they have limited knowledge.

How does a watch measure time and perform so well? Within the case one can find the fulcrum, lever, gear, bearing, axle, wheel, screw, and the spring which overcomes nature's law of gravity. All these parts harmonize to provide an accurate reading minute by minute. A good collector will be able to identify all of them.

After acquiring a watch, you will want to take good care of it. A watch should be cleaned inside and out. Dirt will wear it out much faster, and gummy oil will restrict it and keep it from running all together. After the watch has been cleaned it should be stored in a dry place. Rust is the No. 1 enemy. A watch is a delicate instrument but, if it is given proper care, it will provide many years of quality service. A pocket watch should be wound at regular intervals about once every 24 hours, early each morning so the mainspring has its full power to withstand the abuse of daily use. Do not carry a watch in the same pocket with articles that will scratch or tarnish the case. A fully wound watch can withstand a jar easier than a watch that has been allowed to run down. Always wind a watch and leave it running when you ship it. If you are one who enjoys carrying a watch be sure to have it cleaned at least once every two years.

EXAMINATION AND INSPECTION OF A WATCH
BEFORE PURCHASING

The examination and inspection of a watch before purchasing is of paramount importance. This is by no means a simple task for there are many steps involved in a complete inspection.

The first thing you should do is to listen to a watch and see how it sounds. Many times the trained ear can pick up problems in the escapement and balance. The discriminating buyer will know that sounds cannot be relied on entirely because each watch sounds different, but the sound test is worthwhile and is comparable to the doctor putting the stethescope to a patient's heart as his first source of data.

Check the bow to see if it is securely fastened to the case and look at the case to see if correction is necessary at the joints. The case should close firmly at both the back and front. (Should the case close too firmly, rub the rim with beeswax which will ease the condition and prolong the life of the rim.)

Take note of the dents, scratches, wear and other evidences of mis-use. Does the watch have a generally good appearance? Check the bezel for proper fit and the crystal to see if it is free of chips.

Remove the bezel and check the dial for chips and hairline cracks. Look for stains and discoloration; and check to see if the dial is loose. It is important to note that a simple dial with only a single sunk dial is by nature a stronger unit due to the fact that a double sunk dial is constructed of three separate pieces.

If it is a stem-winder, try winding and setting. Problems in this area can be hard to correct. Parts are hard to locate and may possibly have to be handmade. If it is a lever set, pull the lever out to see if it sets properly into gear. Also check to see that the hands have proper clearance.

Now that the external parts have been inspected, open the case to view the movement. Check to see that the screws hold the movement in place securely. Note any repair marks and any missing screws. Make a visual check for rust and discoloration, dust, dirt and general appearance. If the movement needs cleaning and oiling, this should be deducted from the price of the watch, as well as any repair that will have to be made.

Note the quality of the movement. Does it have raised gold jewel settings or a gold train (center wheel or all gears)? Are the jewels set in or pressed in? Does it have gold screws in the balance wheel? Sapphire pallets? Diamond end stones? Jeweled motor barrel? How many adjustments does it have? Does it have overall beauty and eye appeal?

Examine the balance for truth. First look directly down upon the balance to detect error truth in the roundness. Then look at it from the side to detect error in the flat swing or rotation. It should be smooth in appearance.

Examine the hairspring in the same manner to detect errors in truth. When a spring is true in the round, there will be no appearance of jumping when it is viewed from the upper side. The coils will appear to uniformly dilate and contract in perfect rhythm when the balance is in motion. Check the exposed portion of the train wheels for burred, bent, or broken teeth. Inspect pinions and pivots for wear. If a watch has complicated features such as a repeater, push the slides, plungers, and buttons to see that they are in good working order.

After the movement and case have been examined to your satisfaction and all the errors and faults are found, talk to the owner as to the history and his personal thoughts about the watch. Is the movement in the original case? Is the dial the original one? Just what has been replaced?

Has the watch been cleaned? Does it need any repairs? If so, can the seller recommend anyone to repair the watch?

Finally, see if the seller makes any type of guarantee, and get an address and phone number. It may be valuable if problems arise, or if you want to buy another watch in the future.

WATCH MOVEMENT PARTS

Mechanical watches are small engines powered by a spring, which keeps the balance in motion. The uniformity of this motion relies on the balance; the durability rests on the quality of material and construction of the complete movement.

HOW A WATCH WORKS

There are five basic components of a watch:

1. The mainspring, and its winding mechanism, which provides power.
2. The train which consists of gears, wheels and pinions that turn the hands.
3. The escapement consisting of the escape wheel and balance that regulates or controls.
4. The dial and hands that tell the time.
5. The housing consisting of the case and plates that protect.

The motion of the balance serves the watch the same as a pendulum serves a clock. The balance wheel and roller oscillate in each direction moving the fork and lever by means of a ruby pin. As the lever moves back and forth it allows the escape wheel to unlock at even intervals (about 1/5 sec.) and causes the train of gears to move in one direction under the power of the mainspring. Thus, the mainspring is allowed to be let down or unwind one pulse at a time.

Power unit for modern watch showing the various parts.

Early style watch with a stackfreed (tear shaped cam).
Note the balance is dumbell shaped.

THE MAINSPRING

Watches were developed from the early portable clocks. The coiled spring or mainspring provided the drive power. The first coiled springs were applied to clocks about 1450. For the small portable watch, coiled springs were first used about 1470. The power from a mainspring is not consistent and this irregular power was disastrous to the first watches.

The Germans' answer to irregular power was a device called a stackfreed. Another apparatus employed was the fusee. The fusee proved to be the best choice. At first catgut was used between the spring barrel and fusee. By around 1660 the catgut was replaced by a chain. Today, the fusee is still used in naval chronometers. One drawback to the fusee is the amount of space it takes up in the watch. Generally, the simplest devices are best.

The mainspring is made of a piece of hardened and tempered steel about 20 inches long and coiled in a closed barrel between the upper and lower plates of the movement. It is matched in degree of strength, width, and thickness most suitable for the watch's need or design. It is subject to differing conditions of temperature and tensions (the wound-up position having the greatest tension). The lack of uniformity in the mainspring affects the timekeeping qualities of a watch.

The power assembly in a watch consists of the mainspring, mainspring barrel, arbor, and cap. The mainspring furnishes the power to run the watch. It is coiled around the arbor and is contained in the mainspring barrel, which is cylindrical and has a gear on it which serves as the first wheel of the train. The arbor is a cylindrical shaft with a hook for the mainspring in the center of the body. The cap is a flat disk which snaps into a recess in the barrel. A hook on the inside of the mainspring barrel is for attaching the mainspring to the barrel.

Jeweled Motor Barrel Unit: 1. Barrel top jewel screw. 2. Barrel top jewel and setting. 3. Ratchet wheel. 4. Barrel bridge. 5. Barrel hub. 6. Barrel head. 7. Mainspring (in barrel). 8. Barrel. 9. Barrel arbor (riveted to barrel). 10. Barrel lower jewel and setting. 11. Pillar plate.

The mainspring is made of a long thin strip of steel, hardened to give the desired resiliency. Mainsprings vary in size but are similar in design; they have a hook on the outer end to attach to the mainspring barrel, and a hole in the inner end to fasten to the mainspring barrel arbor.

By turning the crown clockwise, the barrel arbor is rotated and the mainspring is wound around it. The mainspring barrel arbor is held stationary after winding by means of the ratchet wheel and click. As the mainspring uncoils, it causes the mainspring barrel to revolve. The barrel is meshed with the pinion on the center wheel, and as it revolves it sets the train wheels in motion. Pocket and wrist watches, in most cases, will run up to 40 hours on one winding.

Curb pins adjusted to vary the length of hairspring

Fig. 1

Fig. 2

Fig. 1. Bottom view of Hairspring & cock

Fig. 2. A side and top view of hairspring

THE HAIRSPRING

The hairspring is the brain of the watch and is kept in motion by the mainspring. The hairspring is the most delicate tension spring made. It is a piece of flat wire about 12 inches long, 1/100th of an inch wide, 0.05mm or 0.0019685 inches thick, and weighs only about 1/9,000th of a pound. Thousands of these hairsprings can be made from one pound of steel. The hairspring controls the action of the balance wheel. The hairspring steel is drawn through the diamond surfaces to a third the size of a human hair. There are two kinds of hairsprings in the watches of later times, the flat one and the Breguet. The Breguet (named for its French inventor) is an overcoil given to the spring. There are two methods for overcoil, the oldest is the way the spring is bent by hand; and with the other method the overcoil is bent or completed in a form at one end and at the same time is hardened and tempered in the form. The hairspring contracts and expands 432,000 times a day.

REGULATORS
Identification

Overcoil concentric to travel of regulator pins
Regulator pins
Curve of Hairspring overcoil
Hairspring stud
Hairspring stud screw
Regulator
Balance Cock

E. Howard & Co.

South Bend

Waltham

Breguet

Swiss

Ball Hamilton 18s

Ball Elgin 18s

Ball Hamilton 16s

Ball Illinois 16s

Ball Waltham 16s

Hampden

Marion

E. Howard & Co.

J.P. Stevens

F R S

Agassiz

Waltham

Petek Philippe

swiss- 2 piece

Fasoldt

Hampden

U.S. Waltham

U.S. Waltham

Waltham

REGULATORS
Identification

Keystone

Waltham

Keystone

Fredonia & Peoria

J. Jurgensen

Illinois

Otay

U.S. Waltham

Elgin

Elgin COCK

Rockford

Columbus

Improved Swiss

Thomas Tompion
1638-1700

ROBT HOOKE
FIRST MAINSPRING
1675

Hamilton

English & American 1800-1850

Undersprung

Nathaniel Barrow 1750

Grossman Glasshutte

A modern style **Regulator**. Note triangular shaped hairspring stud which is located on the balance bridge between the screw and curb pin.

THE TRAIN

The time train consists of the mainspring barrel, center wheel and pinion, third wheel and pinion, fourth wheel and pinion, and escape wheel which is part of the escapement. The function of the time train is to reduce the power of the mainspring and extend its time to 36 hours or more. The mainspring supplies energy in small units to the escapement, and the escapement delays the power from being spent too quickly.

The long center wheel arbor projects through the pillar plate and above the dial to receive the cannon pinion and hour wheel. The cannon pinion receives the minute hand and the hour wheel the hour hand. As the mainspring drives the barrel, the center wheel is rotated once each hour.

Actual alignment of **Train Unit**

The second or center wheel of the watch turns once every hour. It is the second largest wheel in the watch, and the arbor or post of the center wheel carries the minute hand. The center wheel pinion is in mesh with the mainspring barrel (pinions follow and the wheel supplies the power). The center wheel is in mesh with the third wheel pinion (the third wheel makes eight turns to each turn of the center wheel). The third wheel is in mesh with the fourth wheel pinion, and the fourth wheel pinion is in mesh with the escape wheel pinion. The fourth wheel post carries the second hand and is in a 1:60 ratio to the center wheel (the center wheel turns once every hour and the fourth wheel turns 60 turns every hour). The escape wheel has 15 teeth (shaped like a flat foot) and works with two pallets on the lever. The two pallet jewels lock and unlock the escape wheel at intervals (1/5 sec.) allowing the train of gears to move in one direction under the influence of the mainspring. The lever (quick train) vibrates 18,000 times to one turn of the center wheel (every hour). The hour hand works from a motion train. The mainspring barrel generally makes about five turns every 36 hours.

SOLID GOLD TRAIN

Some watches have a gold train instead of brass wheels. These watches are more desirable. To identify gold wheels within the train, look at a Hamilton 992; the center wheel is made of gold and the other wheels are made of brass. Why a gold train? Gold is soft, but it has a smooth surface and it molds easily. Therefore, the wheels have less friction. These wheels do not move fast, and a smooth action is more important than a hard metal. Gold does not tarnish or rust and is non-magnetic. The arbors and pinions in these watches will be steel. Many watches have some gold in them, and the collector should learn to distinguish it.

Above: Top view of early "s" shaped cock. Note dumbbell balance and cock is pinned to the plate.

Left: Early verge style escapement with dumbbell balance. 1. Lower pallet. 2. Upper pallet. 3. Verge. 4. Dumbbell balance.

TYPES OF ESCAPEMENTS

The verge escapement is the earliest form of escapement. It was first used in clocks as far back as the early 1300s. The verge escapement consists of a crown escape wheel, a verge which has two flags called pallets, and a balance. Early German watches had a balance shaped like a dumbbell, called a "foliot." Later most other watches used a balance shaped like a wheel. The crude weights of the foliot could be adjusted closer to or farther from the center of the balance for better timekeeping. Another design from that period was the circular balance. The circular balance was used by Christian Huygens in 1675 when he introduced the hairspring. This remarkable invention was used from that time onward.

The verge escapement was used by Luther Goddard in America as well as most of the Colonial watchmakers.

Balance Wheel
Pallet
Verge
Pallet
Contrate Wheel
Crown or Escape Wheel

*A later style **Verge Escapement** with a more common balance wheel.*

About 1725 the cylinder escapement was invented by George Graham, an Englishman. His cylinder escapement was a great improvement over the verge. Even so, the cylinder escapement was not popular until Abraham Louis Breguet adopted the idea in the late 1700s.

☞ **Note:** *We have never seen a Colonial watch that used a cylinder escapement in a movement. If you have one or know where one is, please contact the author.*

Cylinder Escapement

Duplex Escapement

Balance Wheel
Impulse Pin
Short Impulse Tooth
Long Tooth
Escape Wheel

Illustrating and American form of the
Duplex Escapement as first employed
by the Waterbury Watch Co.

Impulse Pin
Long Tooth
Escape Wheel
Short Impulse Tooth

The duplex escapement is accredited generally to Pierre LeRoy, a Frenchman, around 1750, but was never popular in France. This type of escapement was favored in England up to the mid 1850s. The New England Watch Co. of Waterbury, Conn., used the duplex from 1898 until 1910. The Waterbury Watch Company used it from 1880 to 1898.

The roller and lever action escapement was invented by Thomas Mudge in 1750.

Rack and lever escapement. 1. Balance wheel pinion. 2. Rack. 3. Lever. 4. Ratchet escape wheel.

English style right angle lever which was used in earlier American made watches.

The rack lever escapement was invented by Hautefeuille in 1722. The famous Breguet used the detached lever escapement early in the 1800s. By 1830 the English watchmakers had established the superiority of the lever escapement. In France and Switzerland the teeth of the lever escapement wheel were boot-shaped to provide a wider impulse plane. In England, pointed or ratchet teeth were preferred, and the right-angle lever was preferred over the straight line lever, also referred to as the Swiss lever. Pitkins and Custer both used the lever escapements. The right-angle lever was used in the Warren & Samuel Curtis as well as early Elgin, Newark, Tremont, New York, early Hampden, early Illinois, and Cornell watches. The American factories settled on a Swiss style escapement (straight line lever and club tooth escape wheel) by the 1870s.

Purpose of Escape Wheel

If a movement consisted only of the mainspring and a train of wheels, and the mainspring were wound up, the train would run at full speed resulting in the power being spent in a few moments. For this reason, the escapement has been arranged to check it. The duty of the escapement is to allow each tooth of the escape wheel to pass at a regulated interval. The escapement is of no service alone and, therefore, must have some other arrangement to measure and regulate these intervals. This is accomplished by the balance assembly.

The escape wheel is in most cases made of steel and is staked on a pinion and arbor. It is the last wheel of the train and connects the train with the escapement. It is constructed so that the pallet jewels move in and out between its teeth, allowing but one tooth to escape at a time, turnstile fashion. The teeth are club-foot-shaped because of the addition of impulse face to the end of the teeth.

The pallet jewels are set at an angle to make their inside corners reach over three teeth and two spaces of the escape wheel. The outside corners of the jewels will reach over two teeth and three spaces of the escape wheel with a small amount of clearance. At the opposite end of the pallet, directly under the center of the fork slot, is a steel or brass pin called the guard pin. The fork is the connecting link to the balance assembly.

BALANCE AND HAIRSPRING

The rotation of the balance wheel is controlled by the hairspring. The inner end of the hairspring is pinned to the collet, and the collet is held friction-tight on the staff above the balance wheel. The outer end of the hairspring is pinned to a stud which is held stationary on the balance cock by the stud screw. The roller jewel is cemented in the large roller assembly, which is mounted on the staff directly under the balance wheel. Under the first roller is a smaller one which acts as a safety roller. This is necessary because of the crescent cut out in the roller table which allows the guard pin of the escapement assembly to pass through.

The balance wheel rotates clockwise and counterclockwise on its axis by means of the impulse it receives from the escapement. The motion of the balance wheel is constant due to the coiling and uncoiling of the hairspring. The impulse, transmitted to the roller jewel by the swinging of the pallet fork

Modern or Swiss Lever Escapement

A. Lever
B. Entrance pallet
C. Exit pallet
D. Fork
E. Banking pins
F. Fork slot
G. Horns
H. Impulse roller jewel
K. Safety finger
L. Notch of small plate M
M. Safety roller
N. Roller table
P. Impulse plane of the teeth of the wheel
R. Escape wheel

to the left, causes the balance to rotate in a counterclockwise direction. The position of the fork allows the roller jewel to move out of the slot of the fork freely and in the same direction. The fork continues on until it reaches the banking pin. Meanwhile the balance continues in the same direction until the tension of the hairspring overcomes the momentum of the balance wheel. When this occurs the balance returns to its original position, which causes the roller jewel to again enter the slot of the fork.

Pallet and Escape Tooth Action. The momentum that has been built up during the return of the balance, causes the roller pin to impart an impulse on the inside of the fork slot. This impulse is great enough to push the fork away from its position against the banking pin. As the fork is pushed away, it causes the pallet stone to slide on the toe of the escape wheel tooth. When the pallet stone has slid down to its edge, it frees the escape wheel tooth, thereby unlocking the escape wheel. The escape wheel, being impelled by the force of the mainspring, starts to rotate. As the escape wheel turns, the tooth glides along the impulse face of the pallet jewel, forcing it to move out of the way. The moving pallet carries the fork with it and imparts the impulse to the roller jewel. The right pallet stone intercepts a tooth of the escape wheel to lock it, as the fork moves toward the banking pin. Having a short "run" left to the banking pin, the pressure of the escape wheel tooth against the locking face of the pallet jewel draws the stone deeper into the escape wheel and, therefore, causes the fork to complete its run and holds it against the banking pin. Meanwhile the balance continues in a clockwise direction until the tension of the hairspring overcomes the momentum of the balance and returns it to its original position.

Rate of Escape Tooth Release. Through the motion of the escapement, the mainspring keeps the balance vibrating, and the balance regulates the train. The escape wheel has 15 teeth and is allowed to revolve 10 turns per minute. Thus, 150 teeth glide over each pallet stone in 1 minute. The gliding of the escape wheel teeth over the impulse faces of the pallet stones will cause the balance to vibrate 300 vibrations or beats per minute. These vibrations will continue until the force of the mainspring is spent.

SCREWS

Screws used in watches are very small and precise. These screws measure 254 threads to the inch and 47,000 of them can be put into a thimble. The screws were hardened and tempered and polished to a cold hard brilliance. By looking at these screws through a magnifying glass one can see the uniformity.

Equidistant form of escapement   Circular form of escapement

EQUIDISTANT ESCAPEMENT

The term Equidistant Escapement is a form of lever escapement. The locking of each pallet takes place at the same distance from the pallet arbor. A similar form of escapement is the circular pallet with the circular form of escapement. The impulses are given at equal distance from the center line. The Swiss preferred the equidistant while the Americans preferred the circular. There is little difference in performance between these two types of escapement.

THE PLATES

The movement of a watch has two plates and the works are sandwiched in between. The plates are called the top plate and the pillar plate. The top plate fully covers the movement. The 3/4 plate watch and the balance cock are flush and about 1/4 of a full plate is cut out to allow for the balance, thus the 3/4 plate. The bridge style watch has two or three fingers to hold the wheels in place and together are called a bridge. The term bridge (horologically) is one that is anchored at both ends. A cock is a wheel support that is attached at one end only. English balance cock for verge watches and lever watches have but one screw. French and Dutch verge watches have their balance bridges secured at both ends. The metal is generally brass, but on better grade watches, nickel is used. The full plate is held apart by four pillars. In older watches the pillars were very fancy, and the plates were pinned, not screwed, together. The plates can be gilded or engraved when using brass. Some of the nickel plates have damaskeening. There are a few watches with plates made of gold. The plates are also used to hold the jewels, settings, etc. Over 30 holes are drilled in each plate for pillars, pivots, and screws.

TRAIN
BRIDGE

ESCAPE BRIDGE

WATCH — TRAIN SIDE

PILLAR PLATE

PALLET
BRIDGE

BALANCE COCK

BARREL BRIDGE

The plates and bridges which hold all the parts in proper relation to each other.

The pinion is the smaller of the two wheels that exist on the shaft or arbor. They are small steel gears and usually have six teeth called leaves. Steel is used wherever there is great strain, but where there is much friction, steel and brass are used together; one gear of brass, and a pinion of steel. After the leaves have been cut, the pinions are hardened, tempered, and polished.

Invented in 1525

FUSEE

SPRING
BARREL

THE FUSEE

A mainspring gives less and less power as it lets down. To equalize the power a fusee was first used. Fusee leverage increases as the main spring lets down. A fusee is smaller at the top for a full mainspring. When the chain is at the bottom, the mainspring is almost spent, and the fusee has more leverage. Leonardo da Vinci is said to have invented the fusee.

When the mainspring is fully wound, it also pulls the hardest. At that time the chain is at the small end of the fusee. As the spring grows weaker, the chain descends to the larger part of the fusee. In shifting the tension, it equalizes the power.

On the American watch, the fusee was abandoned for the most part in 1850 and an adjustment is used on the hairspring and balance wheel to equalize the power through the 24 hours. When a watch is first wound the mainspring has no more power than it does when it is nearly run down. With or without the fusee, the number of parts in a watch are about the same: close to 300.

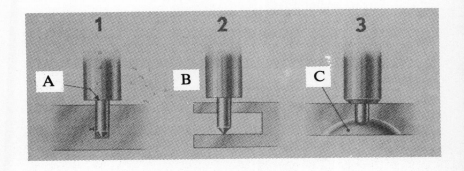

1. Illustration of pivot before 1700. 2. Pivot used in early 1700s. 3. Pivot used in late 1700s to present

JEWELS AND PIVOTS

Before 1700, holes were drilled only part way into the plates and the pivot rested directly on the bottom of the hole, as in Illustration No. 1. The shoulder of the pivot was above the plate, however, reducing part of the function, as in Illustration No. 1A.

In the early 1700s, a French watchmaker, Sully, improved the pivot friction as seen in Illustration No. 2B. Illustration No. 3 shows a later improvement. Perfected by Julien Le Roy.

N.F. de Duiller of Geneva, in conjunction with Peter and Jacob Debaufre, French immigrants living in London, developed a method of piercing jewels. This method was patented in 1704; however, it was not until around 1800 that holed jewels started to appear in watch movements and then only in high grade watches.

In the mid-1800s experiments were already being made for artificial rubies. In 1891 Fremy solved the problem and by the early 1900s the reconstructed ruby was popular.

SHOCK ABSORBERS

When a watch is dropped or subjected to a hard shock, the balance and pivots usually suffer the most.

A shock-resisting device was invented by Breguet in 1789; he called it a parachute. This device was a spring steel arm supporting the endstone. The parachute gives a cushioning effect to the balance staff.

The American pocket watch industry tried to find a device to protect pocket watch pivots, but it was the Swiss who perfected the devices for wristwatches around 1930.

Above: Incabloc
Left: Parachute
Below: Illustrates shock absorbing system. Note end stone and spring in raised position giving a cushioning effect to the balance staff.

JEWEL COUNT

Jewels are used as bearings to reduce metal-to-metal contacts which produce friction and wear. They improve the performance and accuracy of the watch, and materially prolong its usefulness. The materials used for making watch jewels are diamonds, sapphires, rubies, and garnets. The diamond is the hardest but is seldom used except for cap jewels. The sapphire is the next in hardness and is the most commonly used because of its fine texture. Garnets are softer than sapphires and rubies.

Two views showing upper and lower jewel locations in the plates and bridges.

Types of Jewels. Watch jewels are of four distinct types, each type having a particular function.

(1) **HOLE JEWELS.** Hole jewels are used to form the bearing surface for wheel arbors and balance staff pivots.

(2) **CAP JEWELS**. Cap jewels (also called end stones) are flat jewels. They are positioned at the ends of wheel staffs, outside the hole jewels, and limit the end thrust of the staff.

(3) **ROLLER JEWELS.** The roller jewel (pin) is positioned on the roller table to receive the impulse for the balance from the fork.

(4) **PALLET JEWELS.** The pallet jewels (stones) are the angular shaped jewels positioned in the pallet to engage the teeth of the escape wheel.

Number and Location of Jewels. Most watches have either 7, 9, 11, 15, 17, 19, 21, or 23 jewels. The location of the jewels varies somewhat in different makes and grades, but the general practice is as follows:

7-JEWEL WATCHES. Seven-jewel watches have: one hole jewel at each end of the balance staff; one cap jewel at each end of the balance staff; one roller jewel; and two pallet jewels.

9-JEWEL WATCHES. These have the seven jewels mentioned in 7-jewel watches, with the addition of a hole jewel at each end of the escape wheel.

11-JEWEL WATCHES. In these, seven are used in the escapement as in 7-jewel watches. In addition, the four top pivots (the third wheel, the fourth wheel, the escape wheel, and the pallet) are jeweled.

15-JEWEL WATCHES. These watches have the nine jewels found in 9-jewel watches, with the addition of the following: one hole jewel at each end of the pallet staff; one hole jewel at each end of the fourth wheel staff; and one hole jewel at each end of the third-wheel staff.

17-JEWEL WATCHES. The 15 jewels in 15-jewel watches are used with the addition of one hole jewel located at each end of the center wheel staff.

19-JEWEL WATCHES. In these watches, the jewels are distributed as in the 17-jewel watch, with the addition of one for each pivot of the barrel or mainspring.

21-JEWEL WATCHES. The jewels in these are distributed as in the 17-jeweled grade, with the addition of two cap jewels each for the pallet and escape wheel.

Location of jewels in balance

23-JEWEL WATCHES. The jewels are distributed as in the 21-jewel watch, with the addition of one for each pivot of the barrel or mainspring.

24J., 25J., and 26 JEWEL WATCHES. In all of these watches, the additional jewels were distributed as cap jewels. These were not very functional but were offered as prestige movements for the person who wanted more.

In many cases, these jewel arrangements varied according to manufacturer. All jeweled watches will not fit these descriptions.

WINDING AND SETTING

The simplest but not the most practical method for winding up the mainspring of a pocket watch was to wind the barrel staff by means of a key, but then it is necessary to open up the watch case. And the key method of winding proved unpopular, as oftentimes the key became lost.

WINDING & SETTING PARTS

1. Ratchet Wheel	6. Stem and Crown	10. Clutch Lever	14. Hour Wheel
2. Crown Wheel	7. Winding Pinion	11. Clutch Lever Spring	15. Minute Wheel
3. Crown Wheel Center	8. Clutch Wheel	12. Setting Wheel	16. Dial Washer
4. Click	9. Setting Lever	13. Yoke	17. Cannon Pinion
5. Click Spring			

WINDING MECHANISM. a-Winding and setting clutch. p-Winding pinion. b-Barrel. r-Ratchet wheel. c-Crown or main wheel. t- Winding arbor.

The modern principle of the winding of the mainspring and handsetting by pulling on the crown, dates back to 1842. We owe this combination to Adrian Philippe, associate of Patek, of Geneva.

The winding and setting mechanism consists of the stem, crown, winding pinion, clutch wheel, setting wheel, setting lever, clutch lever, clutch spring, crown wheel, and ratchet wheel. When the stem is pushed in, the clutch lever throws the clutch wheel to winding position. Then, when the stem is turned clockwise, it causes the winding pinion to turn the crown and ratchet wheels. The ratchet wheel is fitted on the square of the mainspring arbor and is held in place with a screw. When the stem and crown are turned, the ratchet wheel turns and revolves the arbor which winds the mainspring, thereby giving motive power to the train. Pulling the stem and crown outward pushes the setting lever against the clutch lever, engaging the clutch wheel with the setting wheel. The setting wheel is in constant mesh with the minute wheel; therefore, turning the stem and crown permits setting the hands to any desired time.

SETTING MECHANISM. Clutch a. meshes with m. and the minute works wheel b. The minute works wheel meshes with the cannon pinion h. The hour cannon d. bears the hour hand H. C. center wheel M. Minute hand.

The dial train consists of the cannon pinion, minute, and hour wheels. The cannon pinion is a hollow steel pinion which is mounted on the center wheel arbor. A stud which is secured in the pillar plate holds the minute wheel in mesh with the cannon pinion. A small pinion is attached to the minute wheel which is meshed with the hour wheel.

The center arbor revolves once per hour. A hand affixed to the cannon pinion on the center arbor would travel around the dial once per hour. This hand is used to denote minutes. The hour wheel has a pipe that allows the hour wheel to telescope over the cannon pinion. The hour wheel meshes with the minute wheel pinion. This completes the train of the cannon pinion, minute wheel, and hour wheel. The ratio between the cannon pinion and the hour wheel is 12 to 1; therefore, the hand affixed to the hour wheel is to denote the hours. With this arrangement, time is recorded and read.

A—PINION
B—CLUTCH WHEEL
C—SETTING WHEEL
D—MINUTE WHEEL
E—CANNON PINION
F—HOUR WHEEL
G—CLUTCH LEVER
H—SETTING SPRING
J—SETTING SPRING CAM

Automatic Winding. The self-winding watch uses the movements of the body in order to wind up the mainspring slowly and nearly continuously. The first pocket self-winding watches were executed by a watchmaker from Le Locle, Abraham-Louis Perrelet, around 1770. They were improved soon

Early self wind pocket watch by Breguet.

ETERNA-MATIC AUTOMATIC WINDING MECHANISM. 1–Oscillating weight. 2–Oscillating gear. 3–Upper wheel of auxiliary pawl-wheel. 4–Lower wheel of auxiliary pawl-wheel. 5–Pawl-wheel with pinion. 6–Lower wheel of pawl-wheel with pinion. 7–Transmission-wheel with pinion. 8–Crown-wheel yoke. 9–Winding pinion. 10–Crown-wheel. 11–Ratchet-wheel. 12–Barrel. 13–Driving runner for ratchet-wheel. 14–Winding stem. 15–Winding button.

after by Abraham-Louis Breguet. In the case of the pocket watch, the movements causing the winding of the watch were essentially the result of walking. This system of winding was never widely adopted. The watch was a fancy model and not a really useful one. Herman von der Heydt was the only maker in America to work with the self-winding pocket watch. However, inventors always kept the idea of the self-winding watch in mind.

In 1923, the British firm Harwood took up once again the solution of the problem of automatic winding, for wrist watches. This was the spark which rapidly resulted in research to improve and simplify this type of mechanism. A company was formed in London to manufacture Harwood's watch, and before long over 500 jewelers in the United Kingdom were selling his automatic watch. A second company was formed in France, and a third in the United States. The business flourished about two and one-half years. Then, in 1931, these companies were liquidated.

Illustration of Self Winding mechanism used by Harwood.   This 1931 wrist watch made by Perpetual Self-Winding Watch Co. of America originally sold for $29.75.

THE BALANCE ARC OF VIBRATION

If the watch is to function with any degree of satisfaction, the proper arc of motion of a balance must be no less than 225 degrees in a single vibration direction. Wind up the watch, stop the balance; upon releasing the balance, carefully observe the extent of the swing or vibration. After 30 seconds it should have reached its maximum. If it takes longer, the full power of the mainspring is not being communicated strongly enough. With the watch fully wound, the balance should vibrate between 225 degrees and 315 degrees in a single vibration direction.

HIGH ARC   LOW ARC

COTTAGE INDUSTRY WATCHMAKING
IN COLONIAL AMERICA

The cottage industry (pre-1700s to 1800s) consisted of organized, skilled craftsmen having separate divisions for the purpose of producing watches. The movements were handmade using manpowered tools. The parts generally were not given a final finish. The cottage industries were in most countries including France, England, Switzerland, Germany, and others, but not in America. Each skilled parts maker specialized in a specific part of the watch. There were fusee makers, wheel makers, plate and cock makers, spring makers, case makers and enamelers, to name a few. In the cottage industry each maker became an expert in his field. Expenses and overhead were less because fewer tools and less labor were required. Because all components were produced separately, a larger volume of watches resulted.

The enterprising colonial watchmaker in America would order all the parts and assemble them to complete a finished movement. This finisher, or watchmaker, would detail the parts, such as filing them to fit, polishing and gilding the parts, fitting the movement to a case, installing a dial, and adjusting the movement to perform. The finisher would then engrave his name and town of manufacture to the movement or dial. The finisher determined the timekeeping quality of the completed watch, thus gaining a good reputation for some watchmakers.

Most watchmakers used this system during this period; even, to some extent, Abraham L. Breguet. A colonial watchmaker or finisher could produce about 50 watches a year. There were few colonial watchmakers because only the wealthy could afford such a prized possession as a watch. Most colonial watchmakers struggled financially, and supplemented their businesses with repair work on European-made watches. Since most of them understood the verge escapement, and imported this type of part from England to produce watches, many colonial watches have the verge escapement. Few colonial watches survive today.

Side-view of 17th Century single-hand movement with fusee and catgut line to barrel. This three-wheel movement normally ran from 15 to 16 hours between windings. Also note the balance has no hairspring.

EBAUCHES

The stamping out of plates and bridges began with Frederic Japy of Beaucort, France, around 1770. At first, ebauches consisted of two plates with barrel and train bridges, the cock and fusee, pillars, and the clicks and assembly screws. The ebauches were stamped-out or rough movements. Japy invented machinery a common laborer could operate, including a circular saw to cut brass sheets into strips, a machine for cutting teeth in a wheel, a machine for making pillars, a press for the balance, and more. These machines were semi-automatic and hard to keep in alignment or register. But, with the aid of these new machines the principal parts of the movement could be produced in a short period of time with some precision. However, the parts of watches at this time were not interchangeable. These movements in the rough or "grey" were purchased by finishers. The finisher was responsible for fitting and polishing all parts and seeing to the freedom and depth of these wheels and working parts. He had to drill the holes to fit the dial and hands. The plates, cock and wheel, after being fitted and polished, were gilded. After the parts were gilded, the movement would be reassembled, regulated for good timekeeping, and placed in a case. The finisher had to be a master watchmaker.

In England, during the 1800s, Lancashire became the center of the movement trade. One of the better known English ebauche makers was Joseph Preston & Sons of Prescot. The movements were stamped J. P. Some Swiss ebauches would imitate or stylize the movement for the country in which they were to be sold, making it even harder to identify the origin.

As the watch industry progressed, the transformation of the ebauche to a more completed movement occurred. Automation eventually made possible the watch with interchangeable parts, standard sizing, and precision movements that did not need retouching. This automation began about 1850 (in America) with such talented mechanics as Pierre Fredric Ingold, the Pitkins Brothers, A. L. Dennison, G. A. Leschot with Vacheron and Constantin, Patek, Phillipe, and Frederic Japy of Beaucount. The pioneers in the 1850s who set the standards for modern watchmaking included the American Pitkin Brothers, Dennison, Howard, and Jacob Custer. By 1880 most other countries had begun to follow the lead of America in the manufacture of the complete pocket watch with interchangeable parts.

Five typical Ebauches. Three with bar movements, one with a three -quarter plate, one with a half plate. Four with lever escapements, one with a cylinder escapement. The age ranges from 1860 to 1890.

Ebauches S.A.

Ebauches S.A. with its main office in Neuchatel, Switzerland, at one time the following 17 affiliated firms were part of Ebauche S.A.

 A. Schild S.A., Grenchen

 Fabrique d'Ebauches de Fleurier S.A., Fleurier

 Fabrique d'Horlogerie de Fontainemelon, fontainemelon

 Fabrique d' Ebauches de Peseux S.A., Peseux

 Eta S.A., Fabrique d'Ebauches, Grenchen

 Fabriques d'Ebauches Reunies Arogno S.A., Arogno

 Fabrique d'Horlogerie de Fontainemelon, Succursale du Landeron, Le Landeron

 Fabriques d'Ebauches de bettlach, Bettlach

 A. Michel S.A., Grenchen

 Fabrique d'Ebauches de Chezard S.A., Chezard

 Felsa S.A., Grenchen

 Derby S.A., La Chaux-de-Fonds

 Fabriques d'Ebauches Bernoises S.A., Etablissement Aurore, Villeret

 Nouvelle Fabrique S.A., Tavannes

Fabrique d'Ebauches Venus S.A., Moutier

Valjoux S.A., Les Bioux

Fabrique d'Ebauches Unitas S.A., Tramelan

Examples of four ebauches: **Upper left:** Example of a Chinese duplex. **Lower left:** An ebauche circa 1900-1930. **Upper right:** A three-finger bridge movement, circa 1890-1910. **Lower right:** Bridge movement, circa 1885-1900.

WORM GEAR ESCAPEMENT

This oddity was advertised as "The Watch With a Worm in It." Robert J. Clay of Jersey City was given a patent on October 16, 1886. Mr. Clay said, "The principal object of my invention is to provide a watch movement which is very simple and has but few parts." The worm gear or continuous screw was by no means simple. Mr. Clay and William Hanson of Brooklyn revamped the original worm gear and obtained another patent on January 18, 1887.

The first watch containing a worm gear escapement reached the market in 1887. However, the New York Standard Watch Co. soon converted to a more conventional lever escapement. About 12,000 watches with the worm gear were made, but few survived.

Enlarged worm gear escapement. Note endless screw was referred to by the New York Watch Co. as "a watch with a worm in it."

Movement with top plate removed.

DIAL MAKING

Watch dials were basically hand produced. The base is copper and the coating is generally enamel. In the process the copper plate is covered with a fine white enamel, spread with a knife to a thickness of 3/100ths of an inch. It is then allowed to dry at which time it is placed on a plate and inserted into a red hot furnace. The dial is turned frequently with a pair of long tongs. The copper would melt if it were not coated with the enamel. After the dial has been in the furnace for one minute it is removed and the resulting enamel is soft. The dial is now baked onto the copper plate or "set." The surface is rough after cooling, and it is sanded smooth with sandstone and emery, then baked again. The dial is now ready for the painter, who draws six lines across the dial using a lead pencil. Then, with a pencil of black enamel, he traces the numbers, finishing the ends to make them symmetrical. Then the minute marks are made. Lastly, the name of the watch company is painted onto the dial. The dial is glazed and fired again, then polished. The dial artist used a magnifying glass and a fine camelhair brush to paint the dials and produced about one dozen per hour.

Top and side view of Single and Double sunk dial. Single sunk is one level below the hour ring. Double sunk is two levels below the hour ring.

FIRST DIALS

Henri Foucy was the first man to make enamel dials in America. He came to New York from Geneva, Switzerland, in 1856 and was employed by the American Watch Factory.

CRAZING

The word "craze" means a minute crack in the glaze of the enamel. This is not a crack in the dial because the dial has a backing of copper. Crazing does little damage to the structure of the enamel, even though it may go all the way through to the copper.

ENAMEL

Enamel may be transparent or colored. Enamel acts as a protective surface on the metals. It is resistant to acid, corrosion, and weather. Enamel is made of feldspar, quartz, silica, borax, lead, and mineral oxides. These materials are ground into a fine powder and then fired at a temperature of about 1500 degrees Fahrenheit. The heat melts the enamel powder and unites it with the surface of the metal.

PIN LEVER ESCAPEMENT (DOLLAR WATCHES)

The pin lever escapement is sometimes erroneously referred to as "Roskopf escapement" and watches with pin lever escapements are sometimes referred to as "Roskopf watches."

The original Roskopf watch, which was publicly exhibited at the Paris Exposition in 1867, was a rugged "poor man's watch." The chief Roskopf patent, decreases the number of wheels by creating a large barrel whose diameter encroached upon the center of the watch. The loose cannon pinion and hour wheel were driven by a friction-clutch minute wheel mounted to the barrel cover and enmeshing with the loose cannon pinion and hour wheel. The cannon pinion rode loosely on a steel pin threaded to the center of the main plate. The true term, "Roskopf" applies to the barrel with its clutch fitted minute wheel driving the dial train and the Roskopf watch was made in LA Chaux-de-Fonds, Switzerland.

☞ NOTE: Some fakes use the name "**Rosskopf.**"

LOW COST PRODUCTION WATCHES
(DOLLAR WATCHES)

Jason R. Hopkins hoped to produce a watch that would sell for no more than 50 cents as early as the 1870s. He had a plan for which he received a patent (No. 161513) on July 20, 1875. It was a noble idea even though it was never fully realized. In 1876, Mr. Hopkins met a Mr. Fowle who bought an interest in the Hopkins watch. The movement was developed by the Auburndale Watch Co., and the Auburndale Rotary Watch was marketed in 1877. It cost $10, and 1,000 were made. The 20 size had two jewels and was open-face, pendant wind, lever set, and detent escapement. The 18 size had no jewels and was open-face.

In December, 1878, D. A. A. Buck introduced a new watch, at a record low price of $3.50, under the name of Benedict and Burnham Manufacturing Co. It was a rotary watch, open-face, with a skeleton dial which was covered with paper and celluloid. The movement turned around in the case, once every hour, and carried the minute hand with it. There were 58 parts and all of them were interchangeable. They had no jewels but did have a duplex style escapement. The teeth on the brass escape wheel were alternately long and short, and the short teeth were bent down to give the impulse. The main spring was about nine feet long and laid on a plate on the bed of the case. The click was also fastened to the case. The extremely long mainspring took 140 half turns of the stem to be fully wound. It came to be known as the "long wind" Waterbury and was the source of many jokes, "Here, wind my Waterbury for awhile; when you get tired, I'll finish winding it."

In 1892 R. H. Ingersoll ordered 1,000 watches produced at a cost of 85 cents each. He offered the watch for sale in his mail-order catalog for $1 each and advertised it as, "The Watch that Made the Dollar Famous."

Above: Example of a Waterbury longwind showing the nine foot long spring.

Left: Face illustration of a Waterbury Longwind. The movement can be seen through open skeleton area around edge or face.

Right: Example of a two wheel train rather than the standard four wheel train.

Left: Example of the escape wheel for the duplex escapement.

These watches were thick, sturdy and noisy and were wound from the back like a clock. The wages in 1892 were about 8 cents per hour, so it took some 13 hours of work to buy a Dollar Watch.

The E. N. Welch Manufacturing Co. was the next low cost production watch manufacturer. Then came the New York City Watch Co., who in 1895, produced a watch with a unique pendant crank to wind the movement. In 1899 came the Western Clock Mfg. Co., which later became the Westclox Corporation.

Also, among the low cost production watches were the "comic character" watches. They have become prime collectibles in recent years.

About 70 percent of the watches sold in the U. S. were Dollar type. These watches were characterized by the pin lever, non-jeweled (for the most part), and with a face of paper or other inexpensive material. These watches were difficult to repair and the repairs cost more than the price of a new one. Thus they were thrown away, and today it is hard to find one in good condition.

DOLLAR WATCH CHARACTERISTICS:

1. Sold at a price that almost everyone could afford.
2. Used pin lever or duplex escapement.
3. Stamped or pressed out parts; also used fewer parts overall.
4. Were non-jeweled (except for a few) but rugged and practical.
5. Dial made of paper or other inexpensive material.
6. Case and movement were sold as one unit.

Personalized watch movement by ROCKFORD. Engraved on movement. "W.G. Gane, Special Railway, 17j, Adj, serial No. 344551." To identify, see the Identification of Movement section of all watch companies, noting plate design & screw locations to determine that it is a ROCK-FORD Model No. 8.

Personalized watch movement by HAMILTON. Engraved on movement, "Mayer, Chattanooga, Tenn., Adjusted, 21 jewels, serial No. 254507." To identify, see the Identification of Movement section of all watch companies, noting plate design & screw locations to determine that it is an 18 size, open face HAMILTON model. Then by using the serial number, the grade can be determined.

Model 8, 18 size, Rockford, full plate, hunting, lever set. This illustration from the identification section matches the model above.

Grade 936, 18 size, Hamilton, open face. This matches the model above.

PERSONALIZED WATCHES

It was common practice for some watch manufacturers to personalize watches for jobbers, jewelry firms, and individuals. This was done either by engraving the movement or painting on the dial. Probably the Ball Watch Co. did more of this than any other jobber.

Each manufacturer used its own serial number system even though there may have been a variety of names on the movements and/or dials. Knowledge of this will aid the collector in identifying watches as well as determining age.

"Remington Watch Co."-marked on movement and case, made by N.Y. Standard Watch Co., 16 size, 11 jewels.

"E.F. Randolph"-marked on movement, made by Illinois Watch Co., 23j, hunting, model No. 4.

16 size, No. 390, made by New York Standard Watch Co. Watch. Same model as above.

Model 4, 16 size, made by Illinois Watch Co. Same model as above.

In order to establish the true manufacturer of the movement, one must study the construction, taking note of the shape of the balance, shape of the plates, location of jewels, etc. Compare each company in this volume until the manufacturer is located. The best place to start is at the Hamilton and Illinois sections because these two companies made most of the personalized watches.

After the correct manufacturer has been determined, the serial number can be used to determine the age. Taking the age, grade, size, and manufacturer into consideration, the approximate value can be determined by comparing similar watches from the parent company. If a jeweler's name and location are on the watch, this particular watch will command a higher price in that area.

SWISS IMPORTED FAKES

Before 1871 a flood of pocket watches were made which had names strikingly similar to many well-known American watches. These were made in foreign countries as well as in America and looked and sounded like high quality watches. But they were fakes, inferior in quality.

These key-wind imitations of American pocket watches are a fascinating and inexpensive watch type that would make a good collection. The watches closely resembled the ones they were intended to emulate. Names such as "Hampton Watch Company" might fool the casual buyer into thinking he had purchased a watch from Hampden. "Rockville Watch Co." could easily be mistaken for the American Rockford Watch Co. Initials were also used such as H. W. Co., R. W. Co., and W. W. Co., making it even harder to determine the true identity.

In 1871 Congress passed a law requiring all watches to be marked with the country of origin. The Swiss tried to get around this by printing "Swiss" so small on the movement that it was almost impossible to see. Also the word "Swiss" was printed on the top of the scroll or on a highly engraved area of the movement, making it difficult to spot.

By 1885 these Swiss imitations were of better quality and resembled even more closely what was popular in America. But the Swiss fakes did not succeed, and by 1900 they were no longer being sold here.

Example of a Swiss imported fake. Note misspelled signature "P.S. Barrett." The authentic American Waltham watch is spelled "P.S. Bartlett."

Example of a Swiss imported fake. Note similarity to E. Howard & Co. watches. Some were made by the (International Watch CO.)

HOW TO IDENTIFY A SWISS FAKE

1. At first they were keywind and keyset; then they became stem wind, full plate, about 18 size, large jewels on the plate side, and used Roman numerals.

2. Most had American-sounding names so close to the original that it looks merely like a misspelling.

3. The material was often crudely finished with very light gilding.

4. The dial used two feet; American watches used three.

5. The balance wheel was made to look like a compensated balance, but it did not have the cut in the balance wheel.

6. The large flat capped jewels were blue in color.

These characteristics are not present with all imported fakes. Some or none of these factors may be present. The later the date, the more closely the fake resembled the American watch.

Example of a NEW HAVEN WATCH CO. imported Swiss fake. Marked on movement New Haven Watch Co. New Haven Conn. 778883.

MARKET REPORT
1991

The antique timpiece and collectible wrist watch market under went significant changes and intriguing new trends appeared in the past year.

Due in part to an economic slow-down and the limited availability of merchandise, every area of the watch market was affected and subsequently pushed in new directions.

Common and Better American pocket watches (i.e. railroad watches, keywind, gold cased watches) have long held steady in price and dealers even experienced a "slow market" in the past few years. This year affirmed that the availability of *fine condition* pocket watches and "finds" of **large quantities** have definitely become a thing of the past. The result implies higher prices, **high demand** and a **strong market** in these areas during the next *few years*.

Scarce and high grade U.S. models were also hard to find in 1990 – 1991, and although the demand was high for rare U.S. pieces (early high grade American Walthams, rare Howards and high jewelled watches), major collections did not **surface**. This demand was offset by a slow-down in the secondary scarce U.S. market (i.e. Marions, Fredonias, and other low production models). This area is long overdue for a renewal of interest.

The wrist watch market was volatile and extremely mixed. Contrary to previous "boom years", this area tried to clarify its values and directions during the past year. Demand seems to fluctuate between several areas of collecting (early U.S. watches, chronographs, unsual, complicated, etc.). There are still **great buys** in this relatively new market, especially in the medium to lower-priced arena. The higher-end market also experienced *ups and downs,* but the result will most likely be a more stable and predictable market in the long run.

The foreign watch market (early timepieces, complicated repeaters, fine enamels and unsual watches) has shown slow and steady *increases in demand* by U.S. collectors. This has been an undervalued and misunderstood market in the U.S. market for many years. This area of the watch field promises to be **a solid investment**, and possibly the next **strong market** during the upcoming years.

AMERICAN LISTINGS
Pricing at Retail Level
(Complete Watches Only)

Watches listed in this book are priced at the retail level and as complete watches, having an original 14k gold-filled case with an original white enamel single sunk dial. The entire original movement is in good working order with no repairs needed, unless otherwise noted. Watches listed as 14k and 18k are solid gold cases. Coin or silveroid-type and stainless steel cases will be listed as such. Keywind and keyset watches are listed as having original coin silver cases. Dollar-type watches or low cost production watches are listed as having a base metal type case and a composition dial. Wrist watches are priced as having original gold-filled case with the movement being all original and in good working order, and the wrist watch band being made of leather except where bracelet is described.

Many of the watch manufacturers were commissioned to put jewelers' or jobbers' names on their movements in place of their own. Due to this practice, the true manufacturers of these movements are difficult to identify. These watch models are listed under the original manufacturer and can be identified by comparison with the model sections under each manufacturer. See "Personalized Watches" for more detailed information.

The prices shown were averaged from dealers' lists just prior to publication and are an indication of the retail level or what collectors will pay. Prices are provided in three categories: average condition, extra fine, and mint condition, and are shown in whole dollar amounts only. The values listed are a guide for the retail level and are provided for your information only. Dealers will not necessarily pay full retail price. Prices listed are for watches with original cases and dials.

☞ Note: Descriptions and serial number ranges listed for early watches cannot be considered 100 percent accurate due to the manner in which records were kept by these companies.

WARNING: It has been reported to us that 24 Jeweled watches are being faked, especially in Illinois and Rockford watches. One method known is the altering of the number 21 on the movement to a 24. Before buying a 24 Jewel watch, compare the movement with a known 24 Jewel.

INFORMATION NEEDED — We are interested in any facts and information you might have that should possibly be considered for future editions. Documented facts are needed, so please send photo or sources of information. Send to: Cooksey Shugart, P. O. BOX 3147, Cleveland, Tennessee 37320-3147. (When corresponding, please include a self-addressed, stamped envelope.)

ABBREVIATIONS USED IN
THE COMPLETE PRICE GUIDE TO WATCHES

★★★★ — Extremely rare; less than 20 known to exist.
★★★ — Rare; less than 100 known to exist.
★★ — Scarce; less than 500 known to exist.
★ — Uncommon; less than 2,500 known to exist.
ADJ — Adjusted (to temperature, heat and cold, also isochronism)
BASE — Base metal used in cases; e.g., silveroid
BC — Box case
BRG — Bridge plate design movement
C&B — Case and Band
COIN — Coin silver
DB — Double back
DES — Diamond end stones
DMK — Damaskeened
DS — Double sunk dial
DR — Double roller
DWT — Penny weight: 1/20 Troy ounce
ETP — Estimated total production
ESCAP. — Escapement
EX — Extra nice; far above average
FULL — Full plate design movement
    3/4—3/4 plate design movement
    F brg — One finger bridge design and a 3/4 plate (see Illinois 16s M#5)
    2F brg — Two finger bridge design
    3F brg — Three finger bridge design
GF — Gold filled
GJS — Gold jewel settings
G# — Grade number
GT — Gold train (gold gears)
GCW — Gold center wheel
GRO — Good running order
HC — Hunter case
HL — Hairline crack
(illo.) — Illustration of watches
J — jewel (as 21J)
K — Karat (as 14k solid gold — not gold filled)
KS — Key set
KW — Key wind
KW/SW — (Key wind/stem wind) transition

LS — Lever set
MCBC — Multi-color box case
MCC — Multi-color case
MCD — Multi-color dial
MD — Montgomery type dial
M# — Model number
Mvt. — OnlyDial and movement; no case
NI — Nickel plates or frames
OF — Open face
P — Position (5 positions adj)
PS — Pendant set
RGP — Rolled gold plate
RR — Railroad
RRA — Railroad approved
RRG — Railroad grade
S — Size
SBB — Screw back and bezel
SRC — Swing ring case
SS — Stainless steel
SW — Stem wind
S# — Serial number
TEMP — Temperature
TP — Total production
2T — Two-tone
WGF — White gold filled
WI — Wind indicator (also as up and down indicator)
WW — Wrist watch
YGF — Yellow gold filled

Abbott Stem Wind Attachment. Left: Normal view of an Illinois watch movement with 'hidden' Abbott Stem Wind Attachment (pat. Jan., 18th, 1881). Right: Same watch with dial removed exposing the Abbott Stem Wind Attachment. Serial number 52045. Add $100 to $250 to value of watch with this attachment.

ABBOTT'S STEM WIND
HENRY ABBOTT

Henry Abbott first patented his stem wind attachment on June 30, 1876. The complete Abbott's stem wind mechanism is arranged in such a way as to convert key wind to stem wind. He also made a repeater-type slide mechanism for winding. On January 18, 1881, he received a patent for an improved stem wind attachment. On the new model the watch could be wound with the crown. Abbott sold over 50,000 of these stem-wind attachments, and many of them were placed on Waltham, Elgin, and Illinois watches.

ABBOTT WATCH CO.
(MADE BY HOWARD WATCH CO.)
1908 - 1912

Abbott Sure Time Watches were made by the E. Howard WatchCo.(Keystone), and are similar to Howard Watch Co. 1905 model. These watches sold for $8.75 and had 17 jewels. Some of the open face watches are actually hunting case models without the second bits register.

Description	Avg	Ex-Fn	Mint
Abbott Sure Time, 16S, 17J, OF, GF Case	$150	$225	$300
Abbott Sure Time, 16S, 17J, HC, GF Case	200	275	350
Abbott Sure Time, 16S, 17J, OF or HC, Coin	170	235	325
Abbott Sure Time, 16S, 17J, Silveroid	100	170	250
Abbott Sure Time, 16S, 17J, 18K, HC	550	600	700
Abbott Sure Time, 16S, 17J, 14K, HC	450	500	600

Example of Abbott Watch Co., 16 size, 17 jewels, gold jeweled settings, hunting case. Note similarity to the Howard Watch Co. model 1905. Serial number 993932.

Example of Abbott Watch Co., 16 size, 17 jewels, gold jeweled settings, open face. Note similarity to the Howard Watch Co. series 9.

ADAMS AND PERRY WATCH MANUFACTURING CO.
Lancaster, Pennsylvania
1874 - 1877

This company, like so many others, did not have sufficient capital to stay in business for long. The first year was spent in setting up and becoming incorporated. The building was completed in mid-1875, and watches were being produced by September. The first watches were limited to three grades, and the escapement and balance were bought from other sources. By December 1875, the company was short of money and,by the spring of 1876, they had standardized their movements to 18 size. The first movement went on sale April 7, 1876. The next year the company remained idle. In August 1877 the company was sold to the Lancaster Watch Company, after making only about 800 to 1,000 watches. In 1892 Hamilton acquired the assets.

Description		Avg	Ex-Fn	Mint
20S, 20J, GJS, PS, KW, 18K original	★★★	$2,200	$2,700	$3,300
18S, 20J, GJS, PS	★★★	1,000	1,500	2,200
18S, 17J, GJS, PS	★★	700	1,200	1,600
18S, 17J, GJS, PS, Coin, Original	★★	900	1,500	2,000

Example of Adams & Perry Watch Co.movement. This basic model consists of 19 jewels, gold jeweled settings, key wind and pendant set, serial number 1681.

J. H. ALLISON movement 16 jewels,gold train and escape wheel with a spring detent, key wind and key set, serial no.19.

J. H. ALLISON
Detroit, Michigan
1853 - 1890

The first watch J. H. Allison made was in 1853; it was a chronometer with full plate and a fusee with chain drive. The balance had time screws and sliding weights. In 1864, he made a 3/4 plate chronometer with gold wheels. He also damaskeened the nickel movement. He produced only about 25 watches, of which 20 were chronometers. By 1883 he was making

3/4 plate movements with a stem wind of his own design. Allison made most of his own parts and designed his own tools. He also altered some key wind watches to stem wind. Allison died in 1890.

Description	Avg	Ex-Fn	Mint
Full Plate & 3\4 Plate, GT, NI, DMK .... ★★★★	$6,500	$8,500	$10,000
Detent Chronometer Escapement, 16J, KW/KS, GT ...... ★★★★	10,000	12,000	14,000

AMERICAN REPEATING WATCH CO.

Elizabeth, New Jersey

1885 - 1892

Around 1675, a repeating mechanism was attached to a clock for the first time. The first repeating watch was made about 1687 by Thomas Tompion or Daniel Quare. Five-minute, quarter-hour and half-hour repeaters were popular by 1730. The minute repeater became common about 1830.

Fred Terstegen applied for a patent on August 21, 1882, for a repeating attachment that would work with any American key-wind or stem-wind watch. He was granted three patents: No. 311,270 on January 27, 1885; No. 3,421,844 on February 18, 1890; and No. 3,436,162 in September 1890. Waltham was the only watch company to fabricate repeating watches in America. It is not known how many repeaters were made, but it is estimated to be from 1,300 to 3,000.

Add $1,200 to $2,400 to value of a watch with this attachment.

American Repeating Attachment. Illustration at left shows Terstegen's patented repeating attachment only. Illustration at right shows attachment as normally found on movement. The two outside circles on left illustration are wire gongs. The hammer can be seen at upper right.

THE AMERICAN WALTHAM WATCH CO.
1851 - 1957

To trace the roots of the Waltham family one must start with the year 1850 in Roxbury, Massachusetts, No. 34 Water Street. That fall David Davis, a Mr. Dennison, and Mr. Howard together formed a watch company. Howard and Dennison had a dream of producing watches with interchangeable parts that were less expensive and did not result in less quality.

Howard served an apprenticeship to Aaron Willard Jr. in about 1829. Several years later, in 1842, Howard formed a clock and balance scale manufacturing company with Davis. Howard and Dennison combined their ideas and, with financing provided by Samuel Curtis, the first of their watches was made in 1850. But they had problems. They were trying out ideas such as using jewels, making dials, and producing steel with mirror finishes. This required all new machinery and resulted in a great financial burden. They discovered, too, that although all watches were produced on the same machines and of the same style, each watch was individual with its own set of errors to be corrected. This they had not anticipated. It took months to adjust the watches to the point they were any better than any other timepieces on the market.

But Howard had perfected and patented many automatic watchmaking machines that produced precision watch parts. In 1851 the factory building was completed and the name American Horologe Company was chosen. It was not until late 1852 that the first watches were completed bearing the signature "The Warren Mfg. Co.," after a famed Revolutionary War hero. The first 17 watches were not placed on the market but went to officials of the company. Watches numbered 18 through 110 were marked "WarrenBoston;" the next 800 were marked "Samuel Curtis;" a few were marked "Fellows & Schell" and sold for $40.

The name was changed to the Boston Watch Company in September 1853, and a factory was built in Waltham, Massachusetts, in October 1854. The movements that were produced here carried serial numbers 1,001 to 5,000 and were marked "Dennison, Howard & Davis," "C. T. Parker," and "P. S. Bartlett." Boston Watch Company failed in 1857 and was sold at a sheriff's auction to Royal E. Robbins. In May 1857, it was reorganized as the Appleton, Tracy & Co., and the watches produced carried serial numbers 5,001 to 14,000, model 1857. The first movements were marked Appleton, Tracy & Co. The C. T. Parker was introduced as model 1857 and sold for $12.00 399 of these models were made. Also 598 chronodrometers were produced and in January 1858 the P. S. Bartlett watch was made.

Example of a Warren model, 18 size, 15 jewels, serial number 44. Note: This movement was made for an English case and will not fit a standard 18 size American case.

Example of a Samuel Curtis model, 18 size, 15 jewels, serial number 112. This movement was also made for an English case.

In January 1859 the Waltham Improvement Co. and the Appleton, Tracy & Co. merged to form the American Watch Company. In 1860, as Lincoln was elected president and the country was in Civil War, the American Watch Co. was faced with serious problems. The next year, business came to a standstill. There seemed to be little hope of finding a market for watches, and bankruptcy again seemed close at hand. At this point it was decided to cut expenditures to the lowest possible figure and keep the factory in operation.

American horology owes much to members of the Waltham Watch group such as Bacon, Church, Dennison, Fogg, Howard Marsh, Webster, and Woerd, who contributed much to its development and success. In early 1861, the name "J. Watson" appeared on model 1857 (first run: Nos. 23,601 to 24,300 total production 1,200).

The next model 1857 was the "R. E. Robbins" of which 2,800 were made.

The William Ellery, marked "Wm. Ellery," (model 1857) was then introduced with the first serial number of 46,201. It was key wind and key set and had 7 to 15 jewels.

A size 10 woman's watch was marketed with first serial numbers of 44,201. It was key wind and key set, 3/4 plate, 13 to 15 jewels. Some were marked "P S Bartlett" and a 15 jewel was marked "Appleton, Tracy & Co." A special model, 10 size, serial numbers of 45,801 to 46,200, is extremely rare. The first stem wind, beginning with serial number 410,698, was produced in 1868. By 1880 all watches were quick train. The last key wind was serial No. 22,577,000, about 1919, 18 size, 1883 model, 7J, sterling, produced for export.

WALTHAM ESTIMATED SERIAL NUMBERS AND PRODUCTION DATES

Date	Serial No.	Date	Serial No.	Date	Serial No.
1852	50	1888	3,800,000	1924	24,550,000
1853	400	1889	4,200,000	1925	24,800,000
1854	1,000	1890	4,700,000	1926	25,200,000
1855	2,500	1891	5,200,000	1927	26,100,000
1856	4,000	1892	5,800,000	1928	26,400,000
1857	6,000	1893	6,300,000	1929	26,900,000
1858	10,000	1894	6,700,000	1930	27,100,000
1859	15,000	1895	7,100,000	1931	27,300,000
1860	20,000	1896	7,450,000	1932	27,550,000
1861	30,000	1897	8,100,000	1933	27,750,000
1862	45,000	1898	8,400,000	1934	28,100,000
1863	65,000	1899	9,000,000	1935	28,600,000
1864	110,000	1900	9,500,000	1936	29,100,000
1865	180,000	1901	10,200,000	1937	29,400,000
1866	260,000	1902	11,100,000	1938	29,750,000
1867	330,000	1903	12,100,000	1939	30,050,000
1868	410,000	1904	13,500,000	1940	30,250,000
1869	460,000	1905	14,300,000	1941	30,750,000
1870	500,000	1906	14,700,000	1942	31,050,000
1871	540,000	1907	15,500,000	1943	31,400,000
1872	590,000	1908	16,400,000	1944	31,700,000
1873	680,000	1909	17,600,000	1945	32,100,000
1874	730,000	1910	17,900,000	1946	32,350,000
1875	810,000	1911	18,100,000	1947	32,750,000
1876	910,000	1912	18,200,000	1948	33,100,000
1877	1,000,000	1913	18,900,000	1949	33,500,000
1878	1,150,000	1914	19,500,000	1950	33,560,000
1879	1,350,000	1915	20,000,000	1951	33,600,000
1880	1,500,000	1916	20,500,000	1952	33,700,000
1881	1,670,000	1917	20,900,000	1953	33,800,000
1882	1,835,000	1918	21,800,000	1954	34,100,000
1883	2,000,000	1919	22,500,000	1955	34,450,000
1884	2,350,000	1920	23,400,000	1956	34,700,000
1885	2,650,000	1921	23,900,000	1957	35,000,000
1886	3,000,000	1922	24,100,000		
1887	3,400,000	1923	24,300,000		

The above list is provided for determining the approximate age of your watch. Match serial number with date.

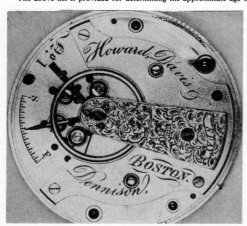

HOWARD, DAVIS & DENNISON:
20 size, 15 jewels, 8 day, two mainsprings,
gilt movement. The first 17 were made for
the officials of the companny, Ca.1852.

20 SIZE
MODEL 1862,-20-KW
T. P. 3,500

Grade or Name–Description	Avg	Ex -Fn	Mint
American Watch Co., 19J, KW, 18K, HC, all original ....★★	$3,700	$4,500	$6,000
American Watch Co., 15 & 17J, KW, KS,3/4, vibrating hair-spring stud, silver case ....★★	1,400	2,000	2,500
American Watch Co., 15 & 17J, KW, KS, 3/4, vibrating hairspring stud, 18K HC, all original .... ★★	3,500	4,000	5,500
American Watch Co., 15 & 17J,3/4, KW, ADJ .... ★	500	700	900
American Watch Co., 19J,3/4, KW, ADJ ....★★	2,200	2,600	3,200
American Watch Co., 19J,3/4, KW, ADJ, with Maltese cross stopwork, all original silver case ....★★	2,800	3,200	4,000
American W. Co., 15J,3/4, KW .... ★	400	600	800
American W. Co., 7-11J,3/4, KW .... ★	300	400	550
American W. Co., 19J,3/4W, Stratons Pat. Barrel ....★★	2,000	2,500	3,500
American W. Co., Nashua S# under dial, (below 51,000)..★★★	4,000	5,000	6,000
American W. Co., Woerd's Pat., Cam Reg...........................★★★	2,200	2,500	3,300
Am'n W. Co., 15J, KW,3/4, coin case .... ★	300	375	450
Am'n W. Co., 15J, KW,3/4, Mvt. only...	150	200	275
Appleton, Tracy & Co., 15J,3/4, KW, with Maltese cross stopwork, all original .... ★	500	700	900
Appleton, Tracy & Co., 15 & 17J,3/4,KW gol balance .... ★	450	550	700
Appleton, Tracy & Co., 15 & 17J,3/4, KW	250	400	550
Appleton, Tracy & Co., 15 & 17J,3/4, KW, vibrating hair spring stud, silver case...★★	1,000	1,200	1,600
Appleton, Tracy & Co., 15 & 17J,3/4, KW, vibrating hair spring stud, 18K HC ....★★★	2,800	3,200	3,600
Appleton Tracy & Co., 15J, KW,3\4, Mvt. only	125	150	225
Appleton Tracy & Co., 15J, KW, Vibrating hairspring stud Straton barrel, Foggs Pat. ....★★	800	1,000	1,200

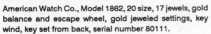

American Watch Co., Model 1862, 20 size, 17 jewels, gold balance and escape wheel, gold jeweled settings, key wind, key set from back, serial number 80111.

Appleton Tracy & Co., Model 20KW, 20 size, 15 jewels, serial number 125004. Note vibrating hairspring stud.

Appleton Tracy & Co., Model 18KW, 18 size, 15 jewels, serial number 32006. Reversible center pinion, patented Nov. 30th, 1858.

Model 1857, 18 size, 16 jewels, "Chronodrometer" on dial, "Appleton Tracy & Co." or "P.S. Bartlett on back plate, key wind & set.

18 SIZE
MODELS 1857, 18KW =1859, 1870, 1877, 1879, 1883, 1892

Grade or Name – Description	Avg	Ex-Fn	Mint
American Watch Co., 17J,3/4, KW, M#18KW .... ★★★	$1,400	$1,700	$2,200
American Watch Co., 19J, M#1859, 3/4 .... ★★★★	2,800	3,400	4,200
American Watch Co., 19J, M#1888, HC, silver...................... ★★	800	1,000	1,400
American Watch Co., 17J, M#1883..	75	100	150
American Watch Co., 21J, M#1883, ADJ, GJS .... ★★★	400	500	700
American Watch Co., 15J, M#1859,3/4, Pat. Nov. 30, 1858, reverse pinion, original silver case................................★★★	3,000	3,500	4,000
American Watch Co., 17J, M#1859,3/4, KW, Fitts Pat. Reversing Pinion, Originial 18K case	4,000	5,000	6,000
American Watch Co., 15J, M#1870, KW	200	250	350
Am. Watch Co., 15J, M#1857, KW, KS...	75	100	150
Am. Watch Co., 17J, M#1857, KW, KS .... ★	200	250	350
Am. Watch Co., 14K, HC, heavy box hinged, multi-color (4 colors)	2,200	2,400	3,200
Am. Watch Co., 11J, thin model, KW, 3/4,s plate .... ★	175	275	500
Am. Watch Co., 15 & 17J, M#1870, KW, ADJ	150	200	300
Am. Watch Co., 11J, M#1883, SW or KW	55	75	125
Am. Watch Co., 17J, M#1892, LS	75	100	150
Am. Watch Co., 17J, M#1892, PS..	75	100	150
Am. Watch Co., 21J, M#1892, LS	150	175	225
Am. Watch Co., 21J, M#1892, PS..	150	175	225
Am. Watch Co., 7J, M#1877	55	75	100
Am. Watch Co., 7J, M#1883, KW	75	100	150
Am. Watch Co., 11J, M#1877	55	75	100
Am. Watch Co., 11J, M#1883, KW	75	100	150
Am. Watch Co., 15J, M#1857, SW .... ★	200	300	450
Appleton, Tracy & Co., 15J, M#1857, SW	100	125	175
Appleton, Tracy & Co., 7-11J, KW, M#1857	125	150	200

Grade or Name–Description	Avg	Ex-Fn	Mint
Appleton, Tracy & Co., 15J, M#18KW, 3/4, reverse pinion, Pat. Nov. 30, 1858, orig. silver case ....★★★	$1,200	$1,600	$1,800
Appleton, Tracy & Co., KW, 3/4 ....★	275	350	450
Appleton, Tracy & Co., 11J, thin model, KW,3/4 ....★	250	350	250
Appleton, Tracy & Co., 15J,3/4, KW, with vibrating hairspring stud, Foggs Pat., coin case ....★★★	1,400	1,600	2,000
Appleton, Tracy & Co., 15J,3/4, KW, with vibrating hairspring stud, orig. 18K case ....★★★	2,000	2,400	2,800
Appleton,Tracy & Co., Sporting,(Chronodrometer),M#1857, 16J, KW,KS, orig. case, with stop feature ....★★	1,500	2,000	2,500
Appleton, Tracy & Co., 15J, KW, Fitts Pat., pinion................★★	400	500	600
Appleton, Tracy & Co., 15J, 3/4, KW...★	150	200	285
Appleton, Tracy & Co., 15J, M#1857, KW, 18K	600	700	1,000
Appleton, Tracy & Co., 15J, M#1857, KW	100	125	175
Appleton, Tracy & Co., 11J, M#s 1877, 1879, SW	55	75	100
Appleton, Tracy & Co., 17J, M#1892, SW, Premiere	75	100	150
Appleton, Tracy & Co., 15J, M#1892, SW, OF	60	85	100
Appleton, Tracy & Co., 17J, M#1892, SW, OF	70	95	125
Appleton, Tracy & Co., 19J, M#1892, SW, OF	85	115	150
Appleton, Tracy & Co., 21J, M#1892, SW, OF	90	125	175
Appleton, Tracy & Co., 15J, M#1883, SW, OF	55	65	95
Appleton, Tracy & Co., 15J, M#1877, KW	60	75	110
Appleton, Tracy & Co., 15J, M#1879, SW, OF	55	65	95
Appleton, Tracy & Co., 17J, M#1883, OF	60	80	100
Appleton, Tracy & Co., 17J, M#1892, SW, HC	75	100	150
Appleton, Tracy & Co., 19J, M#1892, SW, HC	100	125	175
Appleton, Tracy & Co., 21J, M#1892, SW, HC	100	125	175
Appleton, Tracy & Co., 15J, M#1883, SW, HC	75	100	150
Appleton, Tracy & Co., 15J, M#1879, SW, HC	75	100	150
Appleton, Tracy & Co., 17J, M#1883, SW, 2 tone mvt. Lehigh Valley Railroad ....★	500	650	800
Appleton, Tracy & Co., 17J, M#1883, SW, HC	75	100	150

Appleton, Tracy & Co.18 size, 15 jewels, with vibrating hairspring stud, key wind & set from back, serial number 140030.

P..S. Bartlett, Model 18KW, 18 size, 11 jewels, key wind & set from back, serial number 41597.

Grade or Name – Description	Avg	Ex-Fn	Mint
A. W. W. Co., 7J, M#1883, SW, OF	$55	$65	$75
A. W. W. Co., 11J, M#1883, SW, OF	55	65	75
A. W. W. Co., 7J, M#1883, KW, OF	55	75	125
A. W. W. Co., 11J, M#1879, OF	35	45	75
A. W. W. Co., 15J, M#1879, OF	55	65	90
A. W. W. Co., 11J, M#1883, OF	55	65	75
A. W. W. Co., 15J, M#1883, OF	55	65	85
A. W. W. Co., 17J, M#1883, OF	60	70	90
A. W. W. Co., 17J, M#1892, LS, OF	80	90	135
A. W. W. Co., 17J, M#1892, PS, OF	70	80	125
A. W. W. Co., 17J, M#1892, HC	75	100	150
A. W. W. Co., 19J, M#1892	90	115	160
A. W. W. Co., 21J, M#1892	100	125	175
A. W. W. Co., 17J, "for R.R. Service" on dial	200	250	350
A. W. W. Co., 15J, OF	55	60	90
A. W. W. Co., 15J, 14K multi-color boxcase HC	1,500	2,000	2,500
A. W. W. Co., 11J, LS, HC	75	100	150
A. W. W. Co., 15J, HC	75	100	150

P.S. Bartlett, 18 size, 15 jewels, Model 1857, Engraved on back "4 PR. Jewels." Serial number 13446.

Canadian Railway Time Service, Model 1892, 18 size, 17 jewels, serial number 22,017,534.

Grade or Name – Description	Avg	Ex-Fn	Mint
P. S. Bartlett, 7J, M#1857, KW, 1st Run	$300	$350	$450
P. S. Bartlett, 11J, M#1857, KW, 1st Run	300	350	450
P. S. Bartlett, 11J, M#1857, KW, 2nd-3rd Run	75	100	125
P. S. Bartlett, 15J, M#1857, KW, 2nd-3rd Run	100	125	150
P. S. Bartlett, 11J, LS, HC, 14K	550	650	850
P. S. Bartlett, 15J, M#1857, KW, below S#5000	300	350	450
P. S. Bartlett, 11J, M#1879, KW	55	75	125
P. S. Bartlett, 11J, M#1857, KW, Eagle inside case lid	125	150	175
P. S. Bartlett, 15J, M#1879, KW	75	100	150

Grade or Name – Description	Avg	Ex-Fn	Mint
P. S. Bartlett, 15J, M#1879, SW	$55	$65	$80
P. S. Bartlett, 11-15J, M#1870, SW	75	85	100
P. S. Bartlett, 11-15J, M#1877, KW	100	125	175
P. S. Bartlett, 11J, M#1883, SW	50	70	100
P. S. Bartlett, 15J, M#1883, KW	75	100	150
P. S. Bartlett, 17J, M#1883, SW	55	70	100
P. S. Bartlett, 15J, M#1883, SW	55	70	100
P. S. Bartlett, 11J, M#1859, 3/4, thin model, KS from back	275	350	450
P. S. Bartlett, 11J, M#1859, 3/4, Pat. Nov. 30, 1858	400	500	675
P. S. Bartlett, 15J, pinned plates, KW ★	400	500	600
P. S. Bartlett, 15J, M#1892, SW	65	75	100
P. S. Bartlett, 17J, M#1892, SW, OF, LS	75	85	110
P. S. Bartlett, 17J, M#1892, SW, HC	125	150	175
P. S. Bartlett, 17J, M#1892, SW, OF, PS	75	80	110
P. S. Bartlett, 17J, M#1892, SW, 2-Tone	85	95	120
P. S. Bartlett, 19J, M#1892, SW	95	105	130
P. S. Bartlett, 21J, M#1892, SW	95	105	140
P. S. Bartlett, 21J, M#1892, SW, 2-Tone	100	115	150
Broadway, 7J, M#1857, KW, HC	75	100	150
Broadway, 11J, M#1857, KW, HC	75	100	150
Broadway, 11J, M#1877, KW, SW, NI, HC	75	100	150
Broadway, 7J, M#1883, KW, HC	75	100	150
Broadway, 11J, M#1883, KW, HC	75	100	150
Broadway, 11J, M#1883, SW, HC	75	100	150
Canadian Railway Time Service, 17J, M#1892, Adj.5P	200	250	300
Central Park, 15J, M#1857, KW	150	175	225
Champion, 15J, M#1877, OF	50	75	100
Crescent Park, 15J M#1857	150	175	225
Crescent Street, 15J, M#1870, KW	150	200	225
Crescent Street, 15J, M#1870, pin or nail set	160	250	250
Crescent Street, 17J, M#1870, KW ★	200	225	300

Appleton, Tracy & Co. 18 size, 15 jewels, Model # 1877, stem wind, quick train, huting case, serial # 1,389,078.

Crescent Street, Model 1870, 18 size, 15 J., Key wind & set from back, serial number 552,526.

Grade or Name–Description	Avg	Ex-Fn	Mint
Crescent Street, 15J, M#1870, SW	$125	$150	$200
Crescent Street, 15J, M#1883, SW, non-magnetic, OF	100	150	200
Crescent Street, 15J, M#1883, SW, non-magnetic, HC	100	125	175
Crescent Street, 15J, M#1883, SW, 2-Tone	100	125	175
Crescent Street, 17J, M#1883, SW, OF	75	100	150
Crescent Street, 17J, M#1883, SW, HC	100	125	175
Crescent Street, 19J, M#1883 .... ★	200	275	325
Crescent Street, 17J, M#1892, SW, GJS	100	125	175
Crescent Street, 17J, M#1892, SW, OF	75	100	135
Crescent Street, 17J, M#1892, SW, HC	100	125	175
Crescent Street, 19J, M#1892, SW, Adj.5P, GJS	100	125	175
Crescent Street, 21J, M#1892, SW, Adj.5P, GJS	100	125	175
Crescent Street, 21J, M#1892, Wind Indicator	800	1,000	1,300
Crescent Street, 19J, M#1899, SW, OF	75	100	150
Crescent Street, 19J, M#1899, SW, HC	100	125	175
Crescent Street, 21J, M#1899, GJS, OF	100	125	175
Crescent Street, 21J, M#1899, GJS, HC	150	175	225
Samuel Curtis, 11-15J, M#1857, KW, S# less than200, original 17S silver case .... ★★	2,500	3,000	4,000
Samuel Curtis, 11-15J, M#1857, KW, S# less than 400, original 17S silver case .... ★★	2,300	2,800	3,800
Samuel Curtis, 11-15J, M#1857, KW, S# less than 600, original 17S silver case .... ★★	2,000	2,500	3,500
Samuel Curtis, 11-15J, M#1857, KW, S# less than 1,000, original 17S silver case .... ★	1,700	2,200	3,200
(Samuel Curtis not in original silver case, deduct $800 to $1,000 from value)			
Dennison, Howard, Davis, 7J, M#1857, KW, orig. case	600	800	1,000
Dennison, Howard, Davis, 11J, M#1857, KW, orig. case	750	950	1,200
Dennison, Howard, Davis, 15J, M#1857, KW, orig. case	900	1,100	1,300
Dennison, Howard, Davis, 15J, M#1857, KW, S# less than 2,000, original case	950	1,150	1,400

Dennison, Howard, Davis, Model 1857, 18 size, 15 jewels, under sprung, key wind, serial number 1205.

Howard & Rice, Model 1857, 18 size, 15 jewels, under sprung, serial number 6003.

Grade or Name –Description	Avg	Ex-Fn	Mint
Denver & Rio Grande, 21J, M#1892, GJS, Adj.3P	950	1,200	1,500
Dominion Railway, 15J, M#1883, OF, SW, train on dial	700	900	1,200
Wm. Ellery, 7-11J, M#1857, Boston, Mass.	75	100	125
Wm. Ellery, 7-11J, M#1857, KW	65	90	110
Wm. Ellery, 7-11J, M#KW, 3/4	150	175	250
Wm. Ellery, 15J, KW, 3/4	320	380	450
Wm. Ellery, 7-11J, M#18KW, KW-KS from back, 18K HC	1,000	1,200	1,500
Wm. Ellery, 7J, M#1857, KW, KS from back	175	200	275
Wm. Ellery, 15J, M#1857, KW	75	100	150
Wm. Ellery, 15J, M#1857, SW .... ★	200	300	450
Wm. Ellery, 7-11J, M#1877, M#1879, KW	75	100	150
Wm. Ellery, 11-15J, M#1877, SW	55	75	100
Wm. Ellery, 7-11J, M#1883	55	75	100
Excelsior, M#1877, KW	80	95	140
Export, 7-11J, M#1877	55	75	120
Export, 7-11J, M#1883, KW	75	100	150
Favorite, 15J, M#1877	75	100	150
Fellows & Schell, 15J, KW, KS .... ★★★	$1,500	$1,700	$2,000
Franklin, 7J, M#1877, SW	125	150	200
Home Watch Co., 7-11J, M#1857, KW	75	100	125
Home Watch Co., 7J, M#1877, KW	75	100	125
Home Watch Co., 7-11J, M#1879, SW	75	100	125
Howard, Davis & Dennison, S#1-17.............. ★★★★	30,000	40,000	50,000
Howard & Rice, 15J, M#1857, KW, KS (serial numbers range from 6000 to 6500) .... ★★	1,200	1,400	1,700
E. Howard & Co., Boston (on dial & mvt.), English style escape wheel, upright pallets, 15J, M#1857, KW, KS, S#s about 6,400 to 6,500 .... ★★★	2,500	2,800	3,500
Martyn Square, 7-11J, M#1857, KW, SW (exported)	120	150	200
Mermod, Jaccard & KingParagon Timekeeper, 23J, M#1892, Vanguard, LS, GJS, HC........................	200	250	300

Pennsylvania Special, Model 1892, 18 size, 21 jewels, serial number 14,000,015.

Railroad, Model 1892, 18 size, 19 jewels, Adj5P, open face, note engine & coal car engraved on movement, serial number 10,099,625.

Grade or Name –Description	Avg	Ex-Fn	Mint
Non-Magnetic, 15J, SW, LS, NI	$100	$125	$175
Non-Magnetic, 17J, M#1892, SW, LS	150	175	250
Paragon, 15J, M#1883, HC	100	125	175
C. T. Parker, 7J, M#1857, KW, 14K, HC ★★	1,200	1,400	1,800
Pennsylvania R.R. on dial, Appleton, Tracy & Co. on Mvt., KW, KS, M# 1859 ★★	2,500	3,000	3,500
Pennsylvania Special, 21J, M#1892, HC ★★★	1,400	1,700	2,000
Pennsylvania Special, 21J, M#1892, OF ★★★	1,200	1,500	1,800
Pennsylvania Special, 21J, M#1892, HC GOLD DAMASKEENED ★★★★★	10,000	12,000	15,000
Pennsylvania Special, 23J, M#1892, OF ★★★	2,000	2,200	2,600
Pioneer, 7J, M#1883	55	75	100
Premier, 17J, M#1892, LS, OF	125	150	175
Railroad, 17J, M#1892, LS	200	250	350
Railroad, 21J, M#1892, LS	250	300	400
Railroader, 17J, M#1892, LS,Adj,GJS, OF ★★	500	600	800
Railroad King, 15J, M#1883, LS	200	250	350
Railroad King, 15J, M#1883, 2-Tone	250	300	400
Railroad King, 17J, Special, M#1883, LS	250	300	400
(Railroad Watches with R.R. names on dial and movement as follows:)			
Canadian Pacific R.R., 17J, M#1883	225	275	325
Canadian Pacific R.R., 17J, M#1892	350	450	550
Canadian Pacific R.R., 21J, M#1892	400	500	600
Santa Fe Route, 17J, M#1883	350	450	550
Santa Fe Route, 17J, M#1892 ★	500	600	750
Riverside, 7J, M#1857	100	125	175
Riverside, 17J, M#1892 ★	300	350	450
Roadmaster, 17J, M#1892, LS ★	300	350	450
R. E. Robbins, 11J, M#1857, KW ★	600	700	800
R. E. Robbins, 15J, M#1877, KW	200	250	350
R. E. Robbins, 13J, M#1883	100	125	175

Sidereal, model #1892, 17j, 24 hour dial used by astronomers.

Vanguard, Model 1892, 18 size, 23 jewels, diamond end stone, gold jewel settings, exposed winding gears, serial number 10,533,465.

Grade or Name – Description	Avg	Ex-Fn	Mint
Sol, 7J, M#1883, OF	$55	$75	$100
Sol, 17J, OF, PS	75	100	125
Special Railroad, 17J, M#1883, LS, OF	300	350	450
Special R. R. King, 15J, M#1883	300	350	450
Special R. R. King, 17J, M#1883, HC	355	375	485
454, 21J, GT, 3/4,	200	250	325
Sterling, 7J, M#1857, KW, Silver	100	125	150
Sterling, 7-11J, M#1877, M#1879	55	75	100
Sterling, 7-11J, M#1883, KW	55	75	100
Sterling, 11-15J, M#1883, SW	55	75	100
Tourist, 11J, M#1877	55	75	100
Tourist, 7J, M#1877	55	75	100
Tracy, Baker & Co., 15J, 18K original A.W.W. Co. case ★★★★	4,900	5,500	6,300
Vanguard, 17J, M#1892, GJS, HC ★★★	400	500	650
Vanguard, 17J, M#1892, LS, Adj.5P, DR, GJS, OF ★★	300	400	550
Vanguard, 17J, M#1892, Wind Indicator, Adj.5P, DR, GJS	800	1,000	1,200
Vanguard, 19J, M#1892, LS, Adj.5P, Diamond end stones	125	150	200
Vanguard, 19J, M#1892, LS, Adj.5P, DR, GJS, OF	125	150	200
Vanguard, 19J, M#1892, Wind Indicator, LS, Adj.5P, DR, GJS	1,000	1,200	1,400
Vanguard, 19J, M#1892, Adj.5P, GJS, HC ★	250	350	450
Vanguard, 21J, M#1892, Adj.5P, PS	125	150	175
Vanguard, 21J, M#1892, HC, GJS, Adj.5P	200	250	300
Vanguard, 21J, M#1892, LS, Adj.5P, DR, GJS, OF	125	150	175
Vanguard, 21J, M#1892, LS, Adj.5P, Diamond end stone	150	175	200
Vanguard, 21J, M#1892, WI, LS, Adj.5P, DR, GJS ★	1,000	1,200	1,400
Vanguard, 23J, M#1892, LS, Adj.5P, DR, GJS, OF	175	250	350
Vanguard, 23J, M#1892, LS, Adj.5P, DR, GJS, HC	250	325	425
Vanguard, 23J, M#1892, LS, Adj.5P, DR, GJS, Diamond end stone	200	275	375

American Waltham Watch Co., Model 1883, 18 size, 15 jewels, serial number 3,093,425

845,Model 1892,18 size, 21 jewels, railroad grade, Adj..5P, serial number 15,097,475

Grade or Name – Description	Avg	Ex-Fn	Mint
Vanguard, 23J, M#1892, PS, Adj.5P, DR, GJS, OF	$175	$250	$350
Vanguard, 23J, M#1892, Wind Indicator, LS, Adj.5P, DR,GJS.. ★	1,100	1,300	1,600
Vermont, 15J, gilded full plate, Of..	125	165	225
Warren, 15J, M#1857, KW, KS, S#18-29, original 17S silver case..★★★	18,000	23,000	28,000
Warren, 15J, M#1857, KW, KS, S#30-60, original 17S silver case..★★★	12,000	16,000	20,000
Warren, 15J, M#1857, KW, KS, S#61-90, original 17S silver case..★★★	10,000	14,000	18,000
Warren, 15J, M#1857, KW, KS, S#91-110, original 17S silver case..★★★	9,000	12,000	15,000
(Warren not in original silver case, deduct $1,000 to $2,500)			
George Washington, M#1857, KW	275	350	450
J. Watson, 7J, M#1857, KW, KS, "Boston" ....★	500	700	1,000
J. Watson, 7-11J, M#1857, KW, KS, "London"......................... ★	500	700	1,000
45, 19J, GJS, 2-Tone, HC ....★★	500	600	800
845, 21J, M#1892, OF..	125	150	175
845, 21J, M#1892, HC..	200	250	300
820, 825, M#1883..	55	75	100
836, 17J, DR, Adj.4P, LS, OF	75	100	125
M#1892, 19J, Sidereal, OF ....★★★	1,200	1,500	2,000
M#1892, 17J, Astronomical Sidereal ....★★★	1,000	1,300	1,800

☞ Note: Some grades are not included. Their values can be determined by comparing with similar models and grades listed.

American Watch Co., Model 16KW or Model 1868,16 size, 11-15 jewels, key wind and set from back, serial number 330,635.

American Watch Co., Model 1888, 16 size, 19 jewels, gold jeweled settings, gold train, hunting case. Waltham's highest grade; serial number 5,000,297.

☞ Note: Watches listed in this book are priced at the retail level, as complete watches having an original 14k gold-filled case, an original white enamel single sunk dial, and with the entire original movement in good working order with no repairs needed.

16 SIZE
MODELS 16KW = 1860, 1868, 1872, 1888, 1899, 1908, BRIDGE MODEL

Grade or Name – Description	Avg	Ex-Fn	Mint
Am. Watch Co., 11J, M#16KW, KW & KS from back, original silver case ......★★	$400	$450	$575
Am. Watch Co., 15J, M#16KW, KW & KS from back ....★★	400	450	575
Am. Watch Co., 11J, M#1868, 3/4, KW	175	200	250
Am. Watch Co., 15-17J, M#1868, 3/4, KW	200	225	275
Am. Watch Co., 15J, M#1872, 3/4, SW..	100	125	175
Am. Watch Co., 16-17J, M#1872, 3/4, SW	150	175	225
Am. Watch Co., 19J, M#1872, 3/4, SW.............................★★★	600	800	1,000
Am. Watch Co., 7-11J, M#1888, 3/4, SW	50	75	100
Am. Watch Co., 15J, M#1888, 3/4, SW..	50	75	100
Am. Watch Co., 17J, M#1899	75	100	125
Am. Watch Co., 7-11J, M#1899	50	75	100
Am. Watch Co., 13J, M#1899	50	75	100
Am. Watch Co. 15-16J, M#1899, HC..	100	125	175
Am. Watch Co., 15J, M#1899, SW, HC..	100	125	175

American Watch Co., Model 1888, 16 size, 21 jewels, gold train, note tadpole regulator.

American Watch Co., Bridge Model, 16size, 23 jewels gold train, Adj.5P.

Grade or Name –Description	Avg	Ex-Fn	Mint
Am. Watch Co., 15J, M#1899, SW, OF	$50	$75	$100
American Watch Co., 19J Maltese cross stopwork, gilt mvt. all original 1860 Model, 18K ....★★	1,500	1,800	2,200
American Watch Co., 17-19J, 3/4, KW & KS from back, vibrating hairspring stud, 1860 Model, 18K ....★★★	1,200	1,500	1,900
American Watch Co., 19J, 3/4 , KW & KS from back, nickel mvt. 1860 Model, original case, 18K.....................................★★★	2,500	3,000	3,500
American Watch Co., 15J, M#1868, 3/4, KW, Silver ....★★★	300	350	475
American Watch Co., 17J, M#1868, 3/4, KW, ADJ, Silver ..★★	400	450	550
American Watch Co., 18J, M#1868, SW, nickel mvt....................	450	500	600
American Watch Co., 19J, M#1868, SW, nickel mvt. Silver case ....★★★	1,500	1,800	2,400

Grade or Name — Description	Avg	Ex-Fn	Mint
American Watch Co., 17J, M#1872,3/4,SW,HC,14K .... ★	$900	$1,100	$1,250
American Watch Co., 19J, M#1872, 3/4, SW ....★★★	600	700	900
American Watch Co., 19J, M#1872, 3/4, GJS, Woerd's			
Pat. sawtooth balance, all original ....★★★	2,000	2,500	3,200
American Watch Co., 21J, M#1872, 3/4, SW.......................★★	1,200	1,350	1,550
American Watch Co., 21J, M#1872, 3/4, SW, 18k ....★★★	1,500	1,800	2,200
American Watch Co., 19J, M#1888, 14K ....★★	700	900	1,050
American Watch Co., 19J, M#1888 ....★	300	400	550
American Watch Co., 21J, M#1888, NI, 3/4 ....★★	400	500	650
American Watch Co., 23J, M# 1899, Adj.5P, GT, GJS	600	700	800
American Watch Co., 23J, BRG, Adj.5P, GT, GJS, 14K			
original case..★★★	1,300	1,800	2,200
American Watch Co., 23J, BRG, Adj.5P, GT, GJS, 18K			
original case..★★★	1,500	1,900	2,400
American Watch Co., 23J, BRG, Adj.5P, GT, GJS .... ★	900	1,200	1,600
American Watch Co., 21J, BRG, Adj.5P, GT, GJS .... ★	500	550	650
American Watch Co., 19J, BRG, Adj.5P, GT, GJS .... ★	400	450	550
American Watch Co., 17J, BRG, Adj.5P, GT, GJS .... ★	300	350	450
Appleton, Tracy & Co., 15J, M#1860, 3/4, KW & KS from			
back, all original silver case	500	600	700
Appleton, Tracy & Co., 15J, M#1868, 3/4, KW	300	350	450
Appleton, Tracy & Co., 15J, 3/4, KW, with vibrating			
hairspring stud, all original, silver case ....★★	700	800	1,200
Appleton, Tracy & Co., 15J, 3/4, KW, with vibrating			
hairspring stud, 18K, original case................................★★	1,200	1,500	2,200
A. W. Co., 7J, M#1872, SW, HC...	100	125	175
A. W. Co., 11J, M#1872, SW, HC...	100	125	175
A. W. Co., 17J, M#1872, SW, DMK, GJS, DES, HC	200	300	450
A. W. Co., 7J, M#1899, SW DMK..	50	55	65
A. W. Co., 9J, SW, NI	50	55	75
A. W. Co., 11J, M#1899, SW	50	55	75
A. W. W. Co., 7J, SW, M#1888	50	55	65
A. W. W. Co., 11J, M#1888	50	55	75

P.S. Bartlett, Model 1908, 16 size, 17 jewels, serial number 10,014,478.

Crescent Street, Model 1899, 16 size, 21 jewels, Adj5p, serial number 16,179,418.

Grade or Name–Descripion	Avg	Ex-Fn	Mint
A. W. W. Co., 13J, M#1888, OF	$50	$55	$75
A. W. W. Co., 15J, M#1899, OF	50	55	75
A. W. W. Co., 15J, M#1888, SW, HC	65	75	95
A. W. W. Co., 16J, M#1888, SW, OF	55	65	100
A. W. W. Co., 16J, M#1899, SW, DMK, HC	65	80	125
A. W. W. Co., 17J, M#1899, SW, OF	75	85	100
P. S. Bartlett, 17J, M#1899, OF	55	65	80
P. S. Bartlett, 17J, M#1899, HC	100	125	175
P. S. Bartlett, 17J, M#1908, OF	55	75	100
Bond St., 7J, M#1888	50	55	65
Bond St., 11J, M#1888	55	75	100
Bond St. 15J, M#1888	55	75	100
Bond St., 7J, M#1899	50	55	65
Canadian Railway Time Service, M#1908 ★	275	350	450
Crescent St., 19J, M#1899, Adj.5P, LS, OF	75	100	150
Crescent St., 19J, M#1899, Adj.5P, PS, OF	75	100	150
Crescent St., 19J, M#1899, Adj.5P, LS, HC	125	150	200
Crescent St., 19J, M#1899, Adj.5P, PS, HC	125	150	200
Crescent St., 21J, M#1899, Adj.5P, PS, OF	125	150	175
Crescent St., 21J, M#1899, Adj.5P, LS, OF	125	150	175
Crescent St., 21J, M#1899, Adj.5P, PS, HC	125	150	200
Crescent St., 19J, M#1908, Adj.5P, LS, OF	100	125	150
Crescent St., 19J, M#1908, Adj.5P, PS, OF	100	125	150
Crescent St., 21J, M#1908, Adj.5P, LS, OF	125	150	175
Crescent St., 21J, M#1908, Adj.5P, PS, OF	125	150	175
Crescent St., 21J, M#1908, Adj.6P, LS, OF	125	150	175
Crescent St., 21J, M#1908, Adj.5P, PS, HC	150	175	200
Crescent St., 21J, M#1908, Adj.5P, LS, Wind Indicator	350	400	450
Crescent St., 21J, M#1912, Adj.5P, LS, Wind Indicator	350	400	450
Chronometro Superior, 21J, M#1899, LS, OF	150	200	250
Chronometro Victoria, 21J, M#1899, HC	175	225	275
Chronometro Victoria, 15J, M#1899, PS, OF	75	100	125
Diamond Express, 17J, M#1888, PS, OF, Diamond End Stones ★	400	500	550
EIGHT DAY, 15J, double mainspring barrels, (not 22 size aircraft clock) 3/4 plate, nickel, SW, PS, OF, 16 size (43mm) ★★★			
Electric Railway, 17J, OF, LS, Adj.3P	100	125	150
Equity, 7-11J, PS, OF, 16 1/2 Size	50	55	65
Equity, 7-11J, PS, HC, 16 1/2 Size	60	65	75
Equity, 15-17J, PS, OF, 16 1/2 Size	55	65	75
Equity, 15-17J, PS, HC, 16 1/2 Size	65	75	90
Hillside, 7J, M#1868, ADJ	100	125	175
Hillside, 7J, M#1868, sweep sec. ★★	450	600	850
Marquis, 15J, M#1899, LS	65	75	100
Marquis, 15J, M#1908, LS	65	75	100
Non-Magnetic, 15J, NI, HC	135	155	185
Park Road, 16-17J, M#1872, PS	100	150	200

☞ Note: Some grades are not included. Their values can be determined by comparing with similar models or grades listed.

Premier Maximus, "Premier" on movement. "Maximus" on dial, 16 size, 23 jewels (two diamond end stones), open face, pendant set, serial number 17,000,014.

American Waltham Watch Co., 5 minute repeater, 16 size, 16 jewels, 3/4 plate, grade 1888, adj, 2 gongs, ca. 1900.

Grade or Name — Description	Avg	Ex-Fn	Mint
Park Road, 11-15J, M#1872, PS	$90	$110	$135
Premier, 9J, M#1908, PS, OF	50	55	70
Premier, 11J, M#1908	50	60	75
Premier, 15J, M#1908, LS, OF	70	85	100
Premier, 17J, M#1908, PS, OF	75	90	105
Premier, 17J, M#1908, PS, OF, Silveroid	50	60	70
Premier, 21J, M#1908, Silveroid	100	125	150
Premier, 21J, M#1908, LS, OF	125	150	175
Premier Maximus, 23J, M#1908, GT, gold case, LS,GJS, Adj.6P, WI, DR, 18K Maximus case,box & papers ★★	8,000	9,000	10,000
Premier Maximus, 23J, M#1908, GT, gold case, LS, GJS,Adj.6P, WI, DR, 18K Maximus case, no box ★★	6,000	7,000	8,000
Premier Maximus, 23J, M#1908, GT, gold case, LS,GJS,Adj.6P, WI, DR, 18K Maximus case, sterling box and papers, extra crystal & mainspring ★★	9,000	10,000	11,000
Premier Maximus, 23J, M#1908, GT, YGF recased ★★	2,000	2,500	3,000
Railroader, 17J, M#1888, LS, NI ★★	300	350	535
Railroad King, 17J, 2-Tone ★	195	240	375
Railroad Watches with R. R. names on dial and movement, such as Canadian Pacific RR, Santa Fe Route, etc., M#s 1888, 1899, 1908 ★	255	450	750
Repeater, 16J, M#1872, original coin case, 5 min ★★	2,000	2,500	3,000
Repeater, 16J, M#1888, 5 Min., 14K ★★	3,000	3,500	4,000
Repeater, 16J, M#1872, 5 min., 18K ★★★	3,500	4,000	5,500
Repeater, 16J, M#1872, 5 min., chronograph with register, 18K ★★★★	4,000	5,000	6,500
Repeater, 1 min. moon phase, M#1872, Perpetual Cal., 18K case, all original ★★★★	30,000	35,000	45,000

(Prices are with gold filled cases except where noted.)

Grade or Name – Description	Avg	Ex-Fn	Mint
Riverside, 15J, M#1872, PS, NI, OF	$75	$100	$125
Riverside, 15J, M#1872, PS, gilted, OF	75	100	125
Riverside, 16-17J, M#1888, NI, OF, 14K	400	475	600
Riverside, 16-17J, M#1888, NI, OF	75	100	125
Riverside, 17J, M#1888, gilded, OF	75	100	125
Riverside, 15J, M#1888, gilded, OF	75	100	125
Riverside, 17J, M#1888, checker goldtone DMK, raised gold jewel settings, OF	150	175	225
Riverside, 17J, M#1899, LS, DR, OF	75	100	125
Riverside, 17J, M#1899, LS, DR, HC	100	125	150
Riverside, 19J, M#1899, LS, DR, OF	100	125	150
Riverside, 19J, M#1899, PS, DR, OF	100	125	150
Riverside, 21J, M#1899, LS, DR, OF	125	150	175
Riverside, 19-21J, M#1908, Adj.5P, LS, DR	100	125	150
Riverside, 19J, M#1908, Adj.5P, PS, DR, OF	100	125	150
Riverside Maximus, 21J, M#1888, LS, ADJ, GJS, GT, DR, HC, GF ★★	600	700	850
Riverside Maximus, 21J, M#1888, LS, ADJ, GJS, GT, DR, HC, 14K ★★	1,000	1,100	1,250
Riverside Maximus, 21J, M#1899, PS, Adj.5P, GJS, GT, DR	300	400	550
Riverside Maximus, 21J, M#1899, LS, Adj.5P, GJS, GT, DR	350	450	600
Riverside Maximus, 23J, M#1899, LS, Adj.5P, GJS, GT, DR	400	500	650
Riverside Maximus, 23J, M#1908, LS, Adj.5P, GJS, GT, DR	400	500	650
Riverside Maximus, 23J, M#1908, LS, Adj.5P, GJS, GT, DR	400	500	650
Riverside Maximus, 23J, M#1908, PS, Adj.5P, GJS, GT, DR, HC, GF ★	600	700	850
Riverside Maximus, 23J, M#1908, PS, Adj.5P, GJS, GT, DR, 14K, HC ★	1,050	1,200	1,350
Riverside Maximus, 21J, M#1888, LS, GT, Diamond end stones, OF ★★	500	600	750

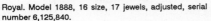

Royal. Model 1888, 16 size, 17 jewels, adjusted, serial number 6,125,840.

Vanguard, Model 1908, 16 size, 23 jewels, diamond end stone, gold jewel settings, exposed winding gears, serial number 11,012,533.

Stone Mountain, 16 size, 17 jewels, crystal plates, Model 1872, gold train, gold jeweled settings, Adj5p, serial number 20.

Vanguard, 16 size, 23 jewels, Adj6p, note pressed-in jewels rather than gold jewel settings. c. 1945.

Grade or Name – Description	Avg	Ex-Fn	Mint
Riverside Maximus, 21J, M#1899,LS,GT,Diamond end stone, OF .... ★	$375	$475	$625
Riverside Maximus, 21J, M#1899, LS, GT, Diamond end stone, HC .... ★	500	600	750
Riverside Maximus, 23J, M#1908, LS, Adj.5P, Wind Indicator ....★★	2,500	3,000	3,500
Roadmaster, 17J, M#1899, LS, OF GJS .... ★	200	250	350
Royal, 15J, M#1872, PS, OF	70	95	120
Royal, 17J, M#1888, PS, OF	75	100	125
Royal, 17J, M#1888, PS, HC	100	125	150
Royal, 17J, M#1899, Adj.3P, OF	65	85	110
Royal, 17J, M#1899, LS, Adj.5P	75	100	125
Royal, 17J, M#1899, PS, Adj.5P	70	95	120
Royal Special, 17J, M#1888	100	125	175
Sol, 7J, M#1888	50	75	100
Sol, 7J, M#1908	50	75	100
Stone Mountain, Crystal plates, 17J, M#1872, GT,GJS, no crackes in CRYSTAL PLATES ....★★★★	7,000	9,000	15,000
Traveler, 7J, M#1888, 1899, 1908	40	50	60
Vanguard, 19J, M#1899, PS, LS, Adj.5P, GJS, DR, OF	100	125	170
Vanguard, 19J, M#1899, PS, LS, Adj.5P, GJS, DR, HC	150	175	225
Vanguard, 21J, M#1899, Adj.5P	125	150	175
Vanguard, 23J, M#1899, Adj.5P, HC	250	275	350
Vanguard, 23J, M#1899, Adj.6P, OF	175	200	250
Vanguard, 23J, M#1899, LS, Adj.5P, GJS, DR, OF	150	175	200
Vanguard, 23J, M#1899, PS, Adj.5P, GJS, DR, OF	150	175	200
Vanguard, 23J, M#1899, PS, Wind Indicator, Adj.5P, GJS, DR	350	400	450
Vanguard, 19J, M#1908, LS & PS, Adj.5P, GJS, DR	100	125	175

Grade or Name – Description	Avg	Ex-Fn	Mint
Vanguard, 21J, M#1908, Adj.5P, GJS, DR, Diamond end stone	$125	$150	$175
Vanguard, 21J, M#1908, Adj.5P, GJS, DR, PS, LS, OF	125	150	175
Vanguard, 21J, M#1908, Adj.5P, GJS, DR, PS, LS, HC	150	200	225
Vanguard, 23J, M#1908, LS, Adj.5P, GJS, DR, OF	150	175	200
Vanguard, 23J, M#1908, LS, Adj.5P, GJS, DR, HC	250	275	300
Vanguard, 23J, M#1908, PS, Adj.5P, GJS, DR	150	175	200
Vanguard, 23J, M#1908, Adj.5P, Wind Indicator, GJS, DR	350	400	450
Vanguard, 23J, M#1908, Adj.5P, GJS , Diamond end stone	150	175	200
Vanguard, 23J, M#1908, Adj.5P, GJS, HC	275	300	400
Vanguard, 23J, OF, LS or PS, 14K	500	550	675
Vanguard, 23J, M#1908, Adj.6P, Wind Indicator, GJS, DR	360	400	450
Vanguard, 23J, M#1908, Adj.6P, Wind Indicator, Lossier, GJS, DR	350	400	450
Vanguard, 23J, M#1912, Press Jewels	100	125	150
Vanguard, 23J, M#1912, PS, military (case), Wind Indicator ...	400	435	475
Vanguard, 24J, (marked 9J. & 24J.) Adj.6P, center sec.,wind indicator, military W.W.11			
George Washington, 11J, M#1857 .... ★	225	300	375
Weems, 23j, Navigation watch, Wind Indicator .... ★★★	650	800	950
M#665, 19J, GJS, BRG, HC .... ★★	600	700	800
M#1888, G #s 650, 640	60	70	85
M#1899, G #s 610, 615, 618, 620, 625, 628, 630	60	70	85
M#1908, G #s 610, 611, 613, 614, 618, 620, 621, 623, 625, 628, 630, 635, 636, 637, 640, 641, 642	60	70	85
M#645, 21J, GCW, OF, LS	125	150	175
M#645, 19J, OF, LS	80	105	130
M#16-A, 22J, Adj.3P, 24 hr. dial	125	150	175
M#16-A, 17J, Adj.5P	65	75	80
M#1621, 21J, Adj.5P	125	150	175
M#1623, 23J, Adj.5P	150	200	225

Weems Navigation watch, 21j, Weems pat. seconds dial, pusher for seconds scale setting, ca. 1942.

Grade 645, Model 1899, 16 size, 21 jewels, Adj5p, gold center wheel.

14 SIZE
MODELS 14KW, 1874, FULL PLATE
1884, 1895, 1897, COLONIAL-A

Grade or Name – Description	Avg	Ex-Fn	Mint
Adams Street, 7J, M#14KW, KW, Coin	$100	$125	$175
Adams Street, 11J, M#14KW, KW, Coin	100	125	175
Adams Street, 15J, M#14KW, KW	100	125	175
A. W. Co., 7J, M#14KW, , KW	50	75	100
A. W. W. Co., 7J, M#1874, SW, LS, HC	75	100	125
A. W. W. Co., 15-16J, M#1874, SW	50	65	85
A. W. W. Co., 7-11J, M#s FP, 1884, & 1895	40	50	65
A. W. W. Co., 13J, M#1884	40	50	65
A.W.Co., 19J, GJS, GCW	65	75	95
Am. Watch Co., 7-11J, KW, ...	35	45	60
Am. Watch Co., 13J, M#1874, SW	65	75	95
Am. Watch Co., 15J, M#1874, ...	70	80	100
Am. Watch Co., 16J, M#1874, SW	70	80	100
Am. Watch Co., 7-11J, M#FP, KW	50	65	85
Am. Watch Co., 16J, M#1884, SW	55	75	95
Am. Watch Co., 15J, M#1897, SW	40	60	90
Bond St., 7J, M#1895, SW	40	55	75
Bond St., 9J, M#1884, KW	75	100	125
Bond St., 7J, M#1884, SW, PS	50	60	90
Beacon, 15J, M#1897, SW	50	60	90
Chronograph, 13J, M#1884, 14K, OF, Am. W. Co. case	600	800	1,000
Chronograph, 13J, M#1884, 14K, HC, Am. W. Co. case	700	900	1,100
Chronograph, 13J, M#1884, 18K, HC, Am. W. Co. case .... ★	1,000	1,200	1,400
Chronograph, 13J, M#1884, 14K OF with register, Am. W. Co. case	750	950	1,150

Chronograph, Model 1874, split-second, 14 size. Note two split second hands on dial.

Bond St., 14 size, 7 jewels, stem wind, open face, note pin set, serial number 2,437,666. c. 1884.

Grade or Name — Description	Avg	Ex-Fn	Mint
Chronograph, 13J, M#1884, 14K HC with register, Am. W. Co. case	$850	$950	$1,350
Chronograph, 13J, M#1884, 18K HC with register, Am. W. Co. case	1,200	1,400	1,600
Chronograph, 13J, M#1884	175	225	300
Chronograph, 15J, M#1884	185	250	335
Chronograph, 17J, M#1884	195	270	365
Chronograph, 17J, M#1874, split second, Am. W. Co. case .. ★	350	425	550
Chronograph, 15J, M#1874, split sec., 14K, HC ★★	1,200	1,400	1,600
Chronograph, 15J, M#1874, split second, min. register, 14K Am. W. Co. HC ★★	1,400	1,800	2,000
(Above in 18K case, add $250 to $400 to value)			
Chronograph, 16J, double dial, M#1874, 18K, Am. W. Co. case	2,000	2,500	3,500
Chronometro Victoria, 15J, M#1897, ★★	65	75	95
Church St., 7J, M#1884,	40	60	75
Crescent Garden, 7-11J, M#14KW, KW	60	75	100
Crescent Garden, 7J, M#FP, KW	60	75	90
Wm. Ellery, 7J, M#1874, SW	35	45	75
Gentleman, 7J, M#1884, SW	35	45	75
Hillside, 7-15J, M#1874, SW	35	45	75
Hillside, 7-11J, M#FP, SW	35	45	75
Hillside, 7-13J, M#1884, KW	35	45	75
Hillside, 11J, M#1884, KW	35	45	75
Hillside, 15J, M#1884, SW	65	75	100
Hillside, 16J, M#1874, (calendar date only on outside chapter) SW, GJS, OF,(calendar sets from with lever) ★★★	400	500	700
Maximus, 21J, Colonial A	145	185	275
Maximus, 21J, Colonial A, 14K	300	400	575
Night Clock, 7J, M#1884, KW	50	70	95
Repeater (5 min.), 16J, M#1884, SW, LS, 14K ★	3,500	4,000	5,000
Repeater (5 min.), 16J, M#1884, SW, LS, 18K ★	3,800	4,800	6,300

Chronograph, Model 1874-double dial, 14 size, 15 jewels, hunting. case.

Chronogrpah, Model 1874-Split Second, 14 size, 15 jewels, open face, gold escape wheel, gold train, serial number 303,094.

Five Minute Repeater, Model 1884, 14 size, 13-15 jewels, hunting case, slide actuated, serial number 2,809,551.

Grade or Name — Description	Avg	Ex-Fn	Mint
Repeater (5 min.), 16J, M#1884, split second chrono graph, 18K case	$5,000	$6,000	$7,500
Repeater (5 min.), 16J, M#1884, SW, LS, chronograph with register, 14K Am. W. Co. case	3,500	4,000	5,000
Repeater (5 min.), 16J, M#1884, SW, LS, chronograph with register, 18K Am. W. Co. case	4,000	5,000	6,500
Repeater (5 min.), 16J, M#1884, SW, LS, original Coin,	2,000	2,500	3,000
Repeater (5 Min.), 18K, HC ★★	3,000	4,000	5,500
Repeater (1 Min.), perpetual calendar, moon ph., 18K ★★★	30,000	37,000	50,000
Riverside, 11-15J, M#s 1874, HC ★	150	175	250
Riverside, 15J, M#1884, OF	55	60	80
Riverside, 19-21J, Colonial A, OF ★★	150	175	250
Royal, 11-13J, M#s 1874, 1884	40	55	65
Seaside, 7-11J, M#1884, SW	40	55	65
Special, 7J, M#1895, HC	75	100	125
Sterling, 7J, M#1884	40	55	65
Waltham, Mass., 7J, Full Plate, KW	75	100	125

12 SIZE
MODELS KW, 1894, BRIDGE, COLONIAL SERIES

Grade or Name — Description	Avg	Ex-Fn	Mint
A. W. W. Co., 7J, M#1894, 14K, OF	$200	$225	$275
A. W. W. Co., 11J, M#1894, Colonial	40	50	60
A. W. W. Co., 15J, M#1894, Colonial	40	50	60
A. W. W. Co., 15J, M#1894, Colonial, 14K, HC	250	275	350
A. W. W. Co., 17J, M#1894, Colonial	40	50	60
A. W. W. Co., 17J, M#1894, Colonial, 14K OF	200	225	275
P. S. Bartlett, 19J, M#1894, 14K, HC	275	300	375
P. S. Bartlett, 19J, M#1894	50	60	70
Bond St., 7J, M#1894	40	50	60

Actual size illustration of a cushion style shaped watch depicting thinness with emphasis on style and beauty. This watch was popular in the 1930s.

Grade or Name – Description	Avg	Ex-Fn	Mint
Bridge Model, 19J, GJS, Adj.5P, GT	$100	$150	$200
Bridge Model, 19J, GJS, Adj.5P, GT, 18K, HC	500	550	575
Bridge Model, 21J, GJS, Adj.5P, GT, OF	100	150	200
Bridge Model, 21J, GJS, Adj.5P, GT, HC, 14K .... ★★	600	700	850
Bridge Model, 23J, GJS, Adj.5P, GT	200	250	300
Duke, 7-15J, M#1894	40	50	70
Digital Hour & Second Window, 17J	75	100	125
Elite, 17J, OF	40	50	70
Ensign, 7J, OF	25	35	45
Martyn Square, 7-11J, M#KW	100	125	175
Maximus, 21J, GJS, GT	175	200	250
Premier, 17-19J, M#1894	65	80	100
Premier, 21J, M#1894	65	80	100
Riverside, 17-19J, M#1894, Colonial	60	70	80
Riverside, 19-21J, M#1894, Colonial	70	80	90

A.W.W.Co., Model 1894, 12 size, 7-11 jewels, open face, serial number 7,565,004.

Riverside, Colonial series, 12 size, 19 jewels, open face or hunting, Adj5p, double roller.

Grade or Name – Description	Avg	Ex-Fn	Mint
Riverside, 19-21J, M#1894, Colonial, 14K, HC	$225	$275	$375
Riverside Maximus, 21J, M#1894, Colonial, GT, GJS, 14K	400	475	575
Riverside Maximus, 21J, M#1894, Colonial, GT, GJS................	175	225	325
Riverside Maximus, 23J, M#1894, Colonial, GT, GJS............ ★	225	275	375
Riverside Maximus, 23J, M#1894, Colonial, GT, GJS, 14K	425	475	575
Royal, 17J, OF, PS	45	55	65
Royal, 19J, OF, PS	55	65	75
Secometer, 17J, (revolving seconds dial only) of........................	45	55	65

10 SIZE
MODEL KW, 1861, 1874

☞ NOTE: These watches (excluding Colonial) are usually found with solid gold cases, and are therefore priced accordingly. Without cases, these watches have very little value due to the fact that the cases are difficult to find. Many of the cases came in octagon, decagon, hexagon, cushion and triad shapes.

Grade or Name – Description	Avg	Ex-Fn	Mint
Am. W. Co., 7-15J, M#1874, KW, 14K	$200	$250	$350
American Watch Co., 11-15J, M#1874, 14K, HC	275	325	425
Appleton, Tracy & Co., 15J, M#1861 or 1874, 14K	200	250	350
Appleton, Tracy & Co., 15J, M#1861, 18K multi-color box case ....★★	650	750	900
P. S. Bartlett, 11J, M#1861, KW, 14K	275	300	375
P. S. Bartlett, 13J, M#KW, gold balance, 1st S# 45,801, last 46,200, 14K, Pat. Nov. 3, 1858 ....★★	300	375	525
P. S. Bartlett, 13J, M#KW, gold balance, 1st S#45,801, last 46,200, 18K	600	750	850
P. S. Bartlett, 13J, M#1861, KW, 14K	200	250	300
Colonial A , 21J,OF...	45	50	60
Crescent Garden, 7J, M#1861, KW, 14K	200	250	300
Wm. Ellery, 7,11,15J, M#1861, KW, 14K	200	250	300
Home W. Co., 7J, M#1874, KW, 14K	200	250	300
Martyn Square, 7-11J, M#1861, 14K	200	250	350
Maximus "A", 21J, 14K ....★★	400	475	600

Appleton Tracy & Co., Model 10KW, 10 size, 11-15 jewels, key wind and set from back, serial number 370,411.

Am. W. Co., Model 1873, 8 size, 15 jewels, serial number 691,001.

Grade or Name – Description	Avg	Ex-Fn	Mint
Maximus "A", 23J, 14K ....★★	$425	$500	$600
Riverside, 19J–21, Adj.5P, GF	65	75	100
Riverside Maximus, 19-21J, Adj.5P, GJS, GF	125	200	275
Riverside Maximus, 19-21J, Adj.5P, GJS, 18K	450	525	625
Riverside Maximus, 23J, Adj.5P, GJS, GF	200	250	375
Royal, 15J, Adj.5P, GF	55	65	80

8 SIZE
MODEL 1873

NOTE: Collectors usually want solid gold cases in small watches.

Grade or Name – Description	Avg	Ex-Fn	Mint
Am. W. Co., 15J, M#1873, 14K, Multi-Color Box Hinged case	$500	$700	$900
Am. W. Co., 15J, M#1873	65	75	85
P. S. Bartlett, 15-16J, M#1873	40	50	60
Wm. Ellery, 7-11J, M#1873	40	50	60
Wm. Ellery, 7J, 14K, HC	200	275	350
Riverside, 7-11J, M#1873, 18K, HC	325	400	600
Riverside, 7-11J, M#1873	65	75	85
Royal, 7-13J, M#1873	40	50	60
Victoria, 11-15J, tu-tone movement, 18k HC...............★	325	400	600

VICTORIA, 8 size 1873 model, 11-15 jewels, tu-tone high grade movement, HC, S# 871256

6 size Ladies movement this basic model came in the following grades: J = 7 jewels, gilt; Y = 7 jewels, nickel; N = 15 jewels, gilded or nickel; X = 15 jewels, nickel, gold jewel settings; K = 16 jewels nickel, raised gold settings; RIVERSIDE = 17 jewels, nickel, raised gold settings.

6 SIZE
MODEL 1873, 1889

Grade or Name – Description	Avg	Ex-Fn	Mint
A,B,C,D,E,F,G,H,J,K	$65	$70	$85
A,B,C,D,E,F,G,H,J,K, 14K, HC	200	275	325
A. W. W. Co., 19J, 18K, HC	325	400	475
A. W. W. Co., 19J, 14K, Multi-Color gold case	450	600	800
A. W. W. Co., 7J, M#1873	40	45	55

Grade or Name – Description	Avg	Ex-Fn	Mint
A. W. W. Co., 15J, multi-color GF HC	$175	$200	$275
A. W. W. Co., 15J, 2 tone mvt., HC	75	100	150
A. W. W. Co., 11J, HC, LS	75	100	150
Am. W. Co., 7J, M#1889	40	45	55
American W. Co., 7J, KW & KS from back, 10K, HC	175	225	275
Wm. Ellery, 7J, M#1873	40	50	70
Lady Waltham, 16J, M#1873, Demi, HC, 14K	275	300	350
Lady Waltham, 16J, M#1873, 18K	300	325	375
Riverside Maximus, 21J, GT, DR	225	250	300
Riverside, 15-17J, PS	50	75	100
Seaside, 7J, M#1873	40	45	55

American Watch Co., Model 1889, 6 size 7 jewels, serial number 4,700,246 Stone

Stone Movement or Crystal Plate movement, size 4, 16 jewels, gold train, open face, serial number 28.

4 SIZE

Grade or Name – Description	Avg	Ex-Fn	Mint
Stone Movement or crystal movement, 4 size, crystal, 16 ruby jewels in gold settings, gold train, exposed pallets, compensation balance adjusted to temperature, isochronism, position, Breguet hairspring, and crystal top plate, 14K ★★★★	$4,000	$5,000	$6,000

☞ NOTE: Watches listed in this book are priced at the retail level, as complete watches having an original 14k goldfilled case, an original white enamel single sunk dial, and with the entire original movement in good working order with no repairs needed, unless otherwise noted.

0 SIZE
MODELS 1882, 1891, 1900, 1907

Grade or Name – Description	Avg	Ex-Fn	Mint
A.W.Co., 7-15J, multi-color 14K HC	$350	$475	$600
A. W. Co., 7J, 14K, HC	175	275	350
A. W. Co., 7J, SW, 14K, GF, OF	50	60	70
A. W. Co., 7!15 J, SW, HC	75	100	150
American Watch Co., 15J, SW, OF & HC	75	100	150

Lady Waltham, Model 1900, 0 size, 16 jewels, open face or hunting, adjusted, stem wind, pendant set.

A.W. Co., Model 1891, 0 size, 7 jewels, stem wind, originally sold for $13.00.

Grade or Name – Description	Avg	Ex-Fn	Mint
American Watch Co., 15J, SW, 14K, HC	$175	$275	$350
P. S. Bartlett, 11J, M#1891, OF, 14K	125	150	175
P. S. Bartlett, 16J, 14K, HC	175	275	350
Lady Waltham, 15J, SW, 14K, HC	175	275	350
Lady Waltham, 15-16, SW, HC	100	125	175
Maximus, 19J, SW, HC	100	125	175
Riverside, 15,16,17J, SW, HC	100	125	175
Riverside, 15,16,17J, SW, HC, 14K	175	275	350
Riverside Maximus, 21J, GT, multi-color gold HC, 14K ★★	500	675	850
Riverside Maximus, 21J, GT	125	150	175
Riverside Maximus, 19J,, SW, HC	150	175	250
Riverside Maximus, 19J, HC, 14K ★	275	350	475
Royal, 16J, SW, HC	75	100	125
Seaside, 15J, SW, HC, 14K	175	275	350
Seaside, 11J, SW, OF, multi-color dial, no chips	125	175	200
Seaside, 11J, SW, HC	75	100	125
Seaside, 7J, HC	65	75	100
Seaside, 7J, HC, 14K	175	275	350
Special, 11J, M#1891, OF, 14K	125	175	200

Riverside, Jewel Series, 6/0 size, 17 ruby jewels, raised gold settings, gold center wheel.

Ruby, Jewel Series, 6/0 size, 15 jewels, adjusted to temperature, open face or hunting.

JEWEL SERIES 6/0

Grade or Name – Description	Avg	Ex -Fn	Mint
Diamond, 15J, HC, 14K	$200	$250	$300
Patrician, 15J, pin set, GJS, OF, 18k ★			
Riverside J Size, 17J, HC, 14K	200	250	300
Ruby J Size, 15J, OF, 14K	150	200	250
Sapphire, 15J, OF, 14K	150	200	250

AMERICAN WALTHAM WATCH CO.
IDENTIFICATION OF MOVEMENTS
BY MODEL NUMBER

How to Identify Your Watch: Compare the movement of your watch with the illustrations in this section. Upon matching the movement exactly, the model number and size can be determined. When comparing, note the location of the balance, jewels, screws, gears and type of back plate (Full, ¾, Bridge) which will be clues to identifying the movement you have. Having determined the size and model number, you can now find your watch in the main price listing by name or number (which is engraved on the movement).

20 size, 1862 or KW 20 model. Note vibrating hairspring stud. 1st serial number 50,001

18 size, key wind model 1st serial number 28,821

Model 1857, KW, KS. 1st serial number 1,001

Model 1870, KW, KS from back 1st serial number 500,001

Model 1877, 18 size

Model 1879, 18 size

Model 1883, hunting
1st serial number 2,354,001

Model 1883, open face

Model 1892, open face

Model 1892, hunting.
1st serial number 6,026,001

16½ size, Equity open face

**Model 1868 or Model 16KW,
16 size**

Model 1872, 16 size

**Stone Mountain crystal plates,
16 size**

Model 1888, 16 size, hunting

Bridge Model, 16 size

**Model 1899 or Model 1908,
16 size, open face**

**Model 1899 or Model 1908,
16 size, hunting**

**Model 1899 or Model 1908,
16 size, open face**

Model 16-A, 16 size

**Model 1622, Deck Watch
16 size, sweep second**

Model 1874 & 1884, 14 size

Model 1874, 14 size, hunting

Model 1884, 14 size, open face

5 Minute Repeater, 14 size

5 Minute Repeater, 14 size

Model 1874, 14 size

Model 1884, 14 size

**Model 1895, 14 size,
open face**

Model 1897, 14 size

Colonial A Model, 14 size

Colonial Series, 14 size

Model 1924, The Colonial

Model 1894, 12 size

Model 1894, 12 size

Model 10KW, 10 size

Colonial A, 10 size

Model 1873, 8 size

Model 1873, 8&6 size

Model 1889, 6 size

Model 1890, 6 size

Model 1890, 6 size

Stone Mtn, 4 size

Model 1882, 1 size

Model 1891, 0 size

Model 1900, 0 size   Model 1907, 0 size   Jewel Series

Model 1900, 0/3 size, open face   Model 1907, 0/3 size, hunting   Model 1898 & 1912, 0/6 size, hunting

Model 1898 & 1912, 0/6 size, open face   10½ ligne   10 ligne

☞ Note: Watches listed in this book are priced at the retail level, as complete watches having an original 14k gold-filled case, an original white enamel single sunk dial, and with the entire original movement in good working order with no repairs needed.

☞ Note: Some grades or styles are not included. Their values can be determined by comparing with similar age, models, styles and grades listed.

ANSONIA CLOCK CO.

Brooklyn, New York
1904 - 1929

The Ansonia Watch Co. was owned by the Ansonia Clock Company in Ansonia, Connecticut. Ansonia started making clocks in about 1850 and began manufacturing watches in 1904. They produced about 10,000,000 dollar- type watches. The company was sold to a Russian investor in 1930. "Patented April 17, 1888," is on the back plate of some Ansonia watches.

Ansonia Watch Company. Example of a basic movement, 16 size, stem wind.

Ansonia Watch Co., Sequi-Centennial model.

Grade or Name–Description	Avg	Ex-Fn	Mint
Ansonia White Dial	$40	$50	$70
Ansonia Radium Dial	45	55	75
Ansonia in NI case, Black Dial	40	45	60
Ascot	40	55	75
Bonnie Laddie Shoes	60	95	115
Dispatch	30	40	60
Faultless	40	45	55
Guide	40	55	70
Lenox	35	40	50
Mentor	35	45	55
Picadilly	45	60	75
Rural	35	47	70
Sesqui-Centennial	250	275	350
Superior	45	60	75
Tutor	45	60	75

APPLETON WATCH CO.

(REMINGTON WATCH CO.)

Appleton, Wisconsin

1901 - 1903

In 1901, O. E. Bell bought the machinery of the defunct Cheshire Watch Company and moved it to Appleton, Wisconsin, where he had organized the Remington Watch Company. The first watches were shipped from the factory in February 1902; production ceased in mid-1903 and the contents were sold off before the end of that year. Most movements made by this firm were modified Cheshire movements and were marked "Appleton Watch Company." Advertisements for the firm in 1903 stated that they made 16 and 18 size movements with 11, 15, or 17 jewels. Serial numbers range from 90,000 to 104,950. During the two years they were in business, the company produced about 2,000 to 3,000 watches.

Appleton Watch Co., 18 size, 7 jewels, "The Appleton Watch Co." on dial. Engraved on movement "Appleton Watch Co., Appleton, Wis." Note that the stem is attached to movement. Serial number 93,106.

Description		Avg	Ex-Fn	Mint
18S, 7J, OF, NI, 3/4, DMK, SW, PS, stem attached ....★★★		$450	$500	$600
18S, 7J, OF, NI, 3/4, DMK, SW, PS, Coin, OF ....★★★		400	500	600
18S, 15J, NI, LS, SW, 3/4, M#2 ....★★★★		500	600	700
16S, 7-11J, 3/4, stem attached .... ★★★		450	550	750

☞ Note:Original APPLETON cases add $100. to $200 more. This case is difficult to find.

AUBURNDALE WATCH CO.

Auburndale, Massachusetts

1876 - 1883

This company was the first to attempt an inexpensive watch. Jason R. Hopkins was issued two patents in 1875 covering the "rotary design." The rotary design eliminated the need of adjusting to various positions, resulting in a less expensive watch. The company was formed about 1876, and the first watches were known as the "Auburndale Rotary." In 1876, equipment was purchased from the Marion Watch Co., and the first rotary designed watches were placed on the market for $10 in 1877. Auburndale produced about 3,230 watches before closing in 1883.

Auburndale Timer, 18 size, 7 jewels, stem wind, 10 minute, second jump timer.

Auburndale Rotary, 20 size, 2 jewels, lever set, stem-wind, detent escapement.

Grade or Name – Description	Avg	Ex-Fn	Mint
Auburndale Rotary, 20S, 2J, LS, SW, NI case, detent ....★★★	$1,500	$1,900	$2,500
Auburndale Rotary, 18S, 2J, SW, LS, NI case, lever ....★★	1,000	1,300	2,000
Bentley, 18S, 7J, LS, NI case, SW, 3/4 ....★★	600	800	1,100
Lincoln, 18S, 7J, LS, NI case, KW, 3/4 ....★★	600	800	1,100
Auburndale Timer, 18S, 7J, SW, NI case, 10 min. timer, 1/4 sec. jump, Chronograph	200	250	375
Auburndale Timer, 18S, 7J, KW, NI case, 10 min. timer, 1/4 sec. jump with split seconds, Chronograph...............★★	500	700	900
Auburndale Timer,18S, marked "207", gold balance, OF............	225	300	400

Bentley, 18 size, 7 jewels, 3/4 plate, stem wind, serial number 2.

Auburndale Rotary, 18 size, 2 jewels, stem wind, lever set, serial number 448.

AURORA WATCH CO.

Aurora, Illinois

1883 - 1892

Aurora Watch Co. was organized in mid-1883 with the goal of getting one jeweler in every town to handle Aurora watches. The first movements were 18S, full plate, and were first sold in the fall of 1884. There were several watches marked No. 1. The total production was about 215,000; over 100,000 were 18 Size, and some were 6 size ladies' watches. For the most part Aurora produced medium to low grade; and at one time made about 150 movements per day. The Hamilton Watch Co. purchased the company on June 19, 1890.

AURORA WATCH CO.
Estimated Serial Nos. and Production Dates

1884 - 10,001	1887 - 160,000	1889 - 215,000
1885 - 60,000	1888 - 200,000	1891 - 230,901
1886 - 110,000		

Aurora Watch Co., 18 size, 15 jewels, serial number 142,060. Made for railroad service. New model.

Aurora Watch Co., 18 size, 15 jewels, Adj, engraved on movement "Made expressly R.J.A.," serial number 73,529.

Description	Avg	Ex-Fn	Mint
18S, 7J, KW, KS, Gilded, OF	$125	$150	$175
18S, 7J, KW, KS, Gilded, HC	135	165	195
18S, 7J, 5th pinion, Gilded, LS, SW, OF	135	165	195
18S, 7J, LS, SW, Gilded, new model, HC	200	250	325
18S, 11J, KW, KS, Gilded, HC	135	165	195
18S, 11J, KW, KS, Gilded, OF	135	165	195
18S, 11J, 5th pinion, LS, SW, Gilded, new model, OF	150	185	225
18S, 11J, 5th pinion, LS, SW, NI, GJS, OF	140	170	200
18S, 11J, 5th pinion, LS, SW, NI, GJS, new model, OF	160	190	230
18S, 11J, LS, SW, Gilded, HC, made expressly for the guild	150	185	225
18S, 11J, 5th pinion, LS, SW, NI, OF, made expressly for the guild	170	190	240
18S, 15J, KW, KS, NI, GJS, DMK, OF or HC ★	225	275	350
18S, 15J, 5th pinion, LS, SW, Gilded, OF	200	250	325
18S, 15J, 5th pinion, LS, SW, NI, GJS, DMK, ADT, OF	225	275	350
18S, 15J, 5th pinion, LS, SW, NI, GJS, DMK, ADJ, new model, OF	300	350	400
18S, 15J, LS, SW, NI, GJS, DMK, ADJ, new model, HC	300	350	400
18S, 15J, LS, SW, NI, GJS, ADJ, 2 Tone DMK, checkerboard or snowflake HC	325	375	425
18S, 15J, LS, SW, NI, GJS, ADJ, 2 Tone DMK, checkerboard or snowflake, 5th pinion, OF ★	400	550	750

Size and Description	Avg	Ex-Fn	Mint
18S, 15J, LS, SW, NI, GJS, DMK, ADJ, Railroad Time Service or Caufield Watch, new model, HC .... ★	$400	$550	$675
18S, marked 15 Ruby Jewels but has 17J, 5th pinion, LS, SW, NI, GJS, 2 Tone, ADJ, OF ....★★	600	700	900
18S, marked 15 Ruby Jewels, only 15J, LS, SW, NI, GJS, 2 Tone DMK, ADJ, HC......................	400	500	600
18S, marked 15 Ruby Jewels, only 15J, LS, SW, NI, GJS, ADJ, 2 Tone DMK, OF .... ★	450	525	600
18S, 15J, Chronometer, LS, SW, NI, DMK, ADJ, ...ew model HC......................★★	400	500	600
18S, 15J, Chronometer, LS, SW, NI, GJS, DMK, ADJ, HC ... ★	375	450	525
18S, 15J, LS, Gilded, "Eclipse, Chicago", new model, HC.........	275	300	385
18S, 15J, LS, SW, NI, DMK, HC, made expressly for the guild..	250	300	375
18S, 15J, 5th pinion, LS, SW, Gilded, OF, made expressly for the guild...........................	300	350	400
18S, 15J, LS, SW, Gilded, HC, made expressly for the "RJA" (Retails Jeweler's Assoc.)...........................	300	350	400
6S, 11-15J, LS, SW, Gilded, 3/4, HC.............................	125	150	200
6S, 11-15J, LS, SW, NI, GJS, DMK, 3/4, HC	150	175	225
6S, 11-15J, LS, SW, 3/4 plate, 14K, HC.............................	250	300	400

BALL WATCH CO.

Cleveland, Ohio
1879 - 1969

The Ball Watch Company did not manufacture watches but did help formulate the specifications of watches used for railroad service. Webb C. Ball of Cleveland, Ohio, was the general time inspector for over 125,000 miles of railroad in the U. S., Mexico, and Canada. In 1891 there was a collision between the Lake Shore and Michigan Southern Railways at Kipton, Ohio. The collision was reported to have occurred because an engineer's watch had stopped, for about four minutes, then started running again. The railroad officials commissioned Ball to establish the timepiece inspection system. Ball knew that the key to safe operations of the railroad was the manufacturing of sturdy, precision timepieces. He also knew they must be able to withstand hard use and still be accurate. Before this time, each railroad company had its own rules and standards. After Ball presented his guidelines, most American manufacturers set out to meet these standards and soon a list was made of the manufacturers that produced watches of the grade that would pass inspection. Each railroad employee had a card that he carried showing the record of how his watch performed on inspection. Ball was also instrumental in the formation of the Horological Institute of America.

A 1902 advertisement for Ball Watch Company read, "We do not sell movements or cases separately."

200,000 railroad watches, plus 150,000 non-railroad grade watches, were made and sold by the Ball Watch Co., totaling approximately 350,000.

ESTIMATED SERIAL NUMBERS AND PRODUCTION DATES
FOR RAILROAD GRADE WATCHES

Hamilton		Waltham		Elgin
Date	**Serial No.**	**Date**	**Serial No.**	**Date**
1895	13,000	1900	060,700	1904 - 1906
1897	20,500	1905	202,000	S# range:
1900	42,000	1910	216,200	11,853,000 - 12,282,000
1902	170,000	1915	250,000	
1905	462,000	1920	260,000	**E. Howard & Co.**
1910	600,000	1925	270,000	
1915	603,000			**Date**
1920	610,000	**Illinois W. Co.**		1893 - 1895
1925	620,000			S# range:
1930	637,000	**Date**	**Serial No.**	226,000 - 308,000
1935	641,000	1929	800,000	
1938	647,000	1930	801,000	**Hampden**
1939	650,000	1931	803,000	
1940	651,000	1932	804,000	**Date**
1941	652,000			1890 - 1892
1942	654,000			S# range:
				626,750 - 657,960 -
				759,720

BALL — AURORA
18 SIZE

Description		Avg	Ex-Fn	Mint
17J, OF, marked Ball .... ★★		$1,500	$1,750	$2,000

Ball-Elgin, Grade 333, 18 size, 17 jewels, rare hunting
case model, serial number 11,958,002.

Ball-Elgin, Grade 333, 18 size, 17 jewels, open
face model, serial number 11,856,801.

BALL — ELGIN
18 SIZE G. F. CASES

Description		Avg	Ex-Fn	Mint
16J, G#327, OF, LS .... ★		$275	$350	$475
17J, G#328, OF, LS .... ★		300	375	500

Description	Avg	Ex-Fn	Mint
17J, G#328, Coin, OF, LS .... ★	$250	$325	$450
17J, G#329, NI, Adj.5P, LS, HC .... ★	1,200	1,500	1,800
21J, G#330, LS, official RR std., HC .... ★★★★	2,000	2,500	3,000
16J, G#331, NI, OF, Adj.5P, PS, Commercial Std. .... ★★	375	400	550
17J, G#331, NI, OF, Adj.5P, PS........................	165	255	325
17J, G#332, OF, PS........................ ★	300	350	400
17J, G#333, NI, OF, Adj.5P, LS	175	200	275
17J, G#333, NI, HC, Adj.5P, LS .... ★★★	1,300	1,600	1,900
21J, G#333, NI, OF, Adj.5P, LS.....................	200	250	325
21J, G#334, NI, OF, Adj.5P, LS.....................	325	375	425

☞ Note: 18 Size Ball watches in hunting cases are scarce.

BALL — HAMILTON
18 SIZE G. F. CASES

Description	Avg	Ex-Fn	Mint
17J, M#936, Superior Grade, early run .... ★★★	$1,500	$2,000	$3,000
17J, M#938, NI, OF, DR, ...	575	625	750
17J, M#999, Commercial Standard	300	400	500
17J, Off. Ball marked jewelers name on dial & mvt., OF .... ★	350	450	575
17J, M#999, NI, OF, Adj.5P, LS, Coin	150	200	275
17J, M#999, NI, OF, Adj.5P, LS.....................	150	200	275
17J, M#999, "A" model adj. .... ★	300	375	495
17J, M#999, NI, OF, Adj.5P, marked "Loaner" on case	200	275	375
19J, M#999, NI, OF, Adj.5P, LS.....................	175	225	300
21J, M#999, NI, OF, Adj.5P, LS.....................	225	275	375
23J, M#999, NI, OF, Adj.5P, LS ,14K case .... ★★★	6,000	7,500	10,000
23J, M#999, NI, HC, Adj.5P, LS,14K case .... ★★★★	7,000	9,000	12,000
Ball & Co., 17J, SR, Coin	450	600	800
Brotherhood of Locomotive Engineers, 17J, OF.........	400	500	675
Brotherhood of Locomotive Engineers, 19J, OF.........	500	600	775

BALL-HAMILTON, Grade 999, 18 size, 17 jewels, serial number 458,623

BALL-HAMILTON, Grade 999, 18 size, 17 jewels, marked "Railroad Watch Co." serial number 20,793.

Ball Watch Co., Brotherhood of RR trainmen, 18 size, 17 jewels; movement made by Hamilton, serial number 13,020.

Ball Watch Co. (Hamilton). Grade 999, 18 size, 21 J., sun ray damaskeening, serial number 548,157, c.1906.

Description	Avg	Ex-Fn	Mint
Brotherhood of Locomotive Engineers, 21J, OF	$600	$700	$875
Brotherhood of Locomotive Firemen, 17J, OF	400	500	675
Brotherhood of Locomotive Firemen, 19J, OF	500	600	775
Brotherhood of Locomotive Firemen, 21J, OF	600	700	875
Brotherhood of Railroad Trainsmen, 17J, OF	400	500	675
Brotherhood of Railroad Trainsmen, 19J, OF	500	600	775
Brotherhood of Railroad Trainsmen, 21J, OF	600	700	875
Order of Railroad Conductors, 17J, OF	400	500	650
Order of Railroad Conductors, 19J, OF	500	600	750
Order of Railroad Conductors, 21J, OF	600	700	850
Order of Railroad Telegraphers, 17J, OF	400	500	650
Order of Railroad Telegraphers, 19J, OF	500	600	750
Order of Railroad Telegraphers, 21J, OF"	600	700	850
Ball Standard RR. W. Co., 16J, OF, LS, marked dial ★★	900	1,200	1,750
Ball Standard RR. W. Co., 17J, OF, LS, marked dial ★★	1,000	1,300	1,850

BALL– DeLONG ESCAPEMENT
16 SIZE

Description	Avg	Ex-Fn	Mint
21J, 14K OF Case ★★★	$2,000	$2,500	$3,000

Ball-Hamilton, Model 998 Elinvar, 16 size, 23 jewels, with center bridge.

BALL W. CO.(HAMILTON),16size, 21jewels, offical RR standard, ADJ.5p, serial no.611429

BALL — HAMILTON
16 SIZE G. F. CASES

Description	Avg	Ex-Fn	Mint
16J, M#976, 977, NI, OF, LS	$125	$150	$200
17J, M#974, NI, OF, LS	125	150	200
17J, Official RR Standard, OF	150	175	225
19J, Official RR Standard, OF	300	350	425
19J, M#999, NI, OF, LS	150	175	225
21J, M#999, NI, OF, LS	175	200	250
21J, M#999B (marked), NI, OF, LS, Adj.6P	300	350	400
21J, M#999, Coin case	150	175	225
21J, M#999 Loaner, marked case	175	200	250
23J, M#999B, NI, OF, LS, Adj.6P	500	600	700
23J, M#998 Elinvar, Adj.5P	475	575	650
23J, M#999, NI, OF, LS	450	550	650
1J, M#992-B, NI, OF, LS, Webb C. Ball ★★★	600	750	1,000
Brotherhood of Locomotive Engineers, OF	325	375	500
Brotherhood of Locomotive Firemen, OF	325	375	500
Brotherhood of Railroad Trainmen, OF	325	375	500
Order of Railroad Conductors, OF	325	375	500

BALL — HAMPDEN
18 SIZE

Description	Avg	Ex-Fn	Mint
17J, LS, SW, OF, marked "Superior Grade" ★★★	$1,250	$1,400	$1,850
17J, LS, SW, OF, not marked "Superior Grade" ★★	1,000	1,200	1,600
15J, LS, SW, OF	200	250	300
15J, LS, SW, HC ★★★	400	500	650

Ball-Hampden, 18 size, 17 jewels, serial number 759,728.

Ball-Hampden, marked "Superior Grade," 18 size, 17 jewels, serial number 626,754.

BALL — E. HOWARD & CO.
18 SIZE

Description	Avg	Ex-Fn	Mint
17J, 3/4, HC, PS, GJS, 18K, VII, orig. gold HC ....★★★	$4,000	$5,000	$6,500
17J, 3/4, OF, PS, GJS, 14K, VIII, orig. gold OF case ....★★	2,500	3,000	5,000
17J, 3/4, OF, PS, GJS, 14K, VIII, Brotherhood of Locomotive Engineers........★★★	3,000	4,000	6,000

BALL & CO. (E. HOWARD & CO.), Series VIII, 18 size, 17 jewels. Order of Railway Conductors, serial number 307,488. c.1900.

BALL-E. HOWARD WATCH CO., 16 size, 21 jewels (Keystone). This watch believed to be one-of-a-kind prototype, serial number 982,201.

BALL — E. HOWARD WATCH CO.

16 SIZE

Description	Avg	Ex-Fn	Mint
17J, OF, GJS..	$2,000	$2,500	$3,500
21J, OF, GJS... ★★★	2,500	3,000	4,000

Ball Watch Co., Illinois Model, 16 size, 23 jewels. To identify, note back plates that circle around balance wheel, serial number B801,758.

BALL regulator identification, note: styles and location of hairspring stud.

BALL — ILLINOIS

16 SIZE

Description	Avg	Ex-Fn	Mint
23J, 3/4, LS, OF, GJS .... ★★	$800	$1000	$1,200
23J, 3/4, LS, OF, GJS, marked 60 hr. .... ★★	1,200	1,400	1,600

Top Left: Ball-Hamilton, 16 size, 23 jewels. Bottom left: Ball-Illinois, 16 size, 23 jewels. Above: Ball Waltham, 16 size, 23 jewels. These three movements are similar in appearance. To identify, note where the hair spring stud attaches to the balance bridge, which is slightly different on each movement.

BALL — SETH THOMAS
18 SIZE

Description	Avg	Ex-Fn	Mint
17J, M#3, LS, OF,3/4, GJS......★★★★	$2,200	$2,800	$3,500

BALL — WALTHAM
18 SIZE

Description	Avg	Ex-Fn	Mint
1892, 15J, OF, LS, SW, marked Webb C. Ball, Cleveland .....★★	$1,300	$1,500	$2,000

BALL — WALTHAM
16 SIZE

Description	Avg	Ex-Fn	Mint
15J, HC, GCW......★★	$325	$400	$550
15J, Commercial Std.,3/4, OF......	75	100	155
16J, Commercial std., OF......	75	100	155
16J, Commercial std., HC......	95	125	185
17J, Commercial std., OF	75	100	150
17J, Commercial std., HC......	95	125	185
17J, OF, LS, 3/4, Adj.5P, Multi-color case, GF	250	300	400
17J, OF, LS, 3/4, Adj.5P	150	200	275
17J,Official RR std., HC......★★	800	1,000	1,300
19J,Official RR std., LS, GCW,GJS, OF......	175	225	275
21J,Official RR std., LS, GCW,GJS, OF......	175	225	275

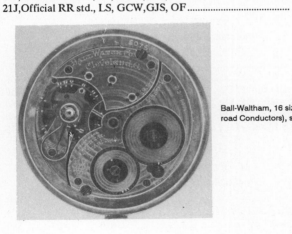

Ball-Waltham, 16 size, 19 jewels, ORC (Order of Railroad Conductors), serial number B204,475.

Description	Avg	Ex-Fn	Mint
19J, BLF&E......	$450	$500	$650
21J, Brotherhood, marked ORC, BOFLE	500	600	750
19J, Hunting case......★★	900	1,100	1,400
19J, OF, LS, 14K......	575	650	750
19J, OF, LS, stirrup style case	150	200	225

Description	Avg	Ex-Fn	Mint
19J, OF, LS, Coin	$100	$125	$175
19J, OF, LS, 3/4, Adj.5P	150	200	275
19J, OF, LS, 3/4, Adj.5P, Wind Indicator ★★	2,500	3,000	4,000
21J, OF, LS, 3/4, Adj.5P	225	250	300
21J, LS, OF, Adj.5P, marked Loaner	250	275	350
23J, LS, OF, Adj.5P, NI, GJS ★	550	650	850

Ball Watch Co. by Waltham, 12 size, 19 jewels, open face, digital seconds

12 SIZE
(Not Railroad Grade)

Description	Avg	Ex-Fn	Mint
19J, Illinois, OF, PS	$135	$175	$250
19J, Illinois, HC, PS	200	300	450
15J, Waltham, Commerical Standard, OF, PS,	150	200	250
16J, Waltham, Commerical Standard, OF, PS,	160	210	260
17J, Waltham, Commerical Standard, OF, PS,	150	160	180
19J, Waltham, OF, PS, rotating digital sec	150	200	275

0 SIZE
(Not Railroad Grade)

Description	Avg	Ex-Fn	Mint
17-19J, Waltham, OF, PS	$225	$275	$375
19J, HC, PS, "Queen" in Ball case	350	400	550

FOR CANADA R.R. SERVICE

Description	Avg	Ex-Fn	Mint
16S, 3/4, LS, OF, GJS	$500	$600	$750

RAILROAD INSPECTOR'S OR JEWELRY CO. NAME
ON DIAL AND MOVEMENT

Description	Avg	Ex-Fn	Mint
18S, 17J, Adj.5P, OF	$700	$850	$1,000

Ball-Audemars Piguet & Co., 14 size, 31 jewels, minute repeater, open face, serial number 4,220.

Ball-Vacheron & Constantin, 43mm, 18 jewels, hunting; note wolf-teeth winding.

BALL — SWISS
16 SIZE

Description	Avg	Ex-Fn	Mint
17J, "Garland"	$100	$125	$175
21J, Time Ball Special, OF	50	60	75
21J, M#435-B, OF, LS, Adj.6P, Ball case, stirrup bow	175	225	275
21J, M#435-C, OF, LS, Adj.6P, Ball case, stirrup bow	175	225	275
21J, M#477-B, Adj.6P (BXC-Record Watch Co.)	150	175	225
40mm Audemar Piguet, min. repeater, jeweled thru hammers, 18K, OF, triple signed Webb C. Ball	6,000	7,500	9,500
43mm Vacheron & Constantin, 18J, HC, 18K	800	900	1,100

BANNATYNE WATCH CO.
1905 - 1911

Mr. Bannatyne had previously worked for Ansonia, in charge of watch production. Bannatyne made non-jeweled watches that sold for about $1.50. Ingraham bought this company in 1912.

ESTIMATED SERIAL NUMBERS AND PRODUCTION DATES

Date	Serial No.	Date	Serial No.	Date	Serial No.
1906	40,000	1908	140,000	1910	250,000

Description	Avg	Ex-Fn	Mint
18S, OF, SW, NI case ★	$500	$600	$800

Bannatyne Watch Co. (left), Ingraham Watch Co. (right). Note similarity of movements. Both patented Aug. 27th, 1907 & Sept. 3rd, 1907.

BENEDICT & BURNHAM MFG. CO.
Waterbury, Connecticut
1878 - 1880

This name will be found on the dial of the first 1,000 "long wind" Waterbury watches made in 1878. These watches had skeleton type movements with open dials that made the works visible. They contained 58 parts and were very attractive. The company was reorganized in March 1880 as the Waterbury Watch Co. and in 1886 became the New England Watch Co.

Description		Avg	Ex-Fn	Mint
18S, long wind, NI case .... ★★★		$700	$900	$1,100

Benedict & Burnham Mfg. Co. dial & movement, 18 size, long wind, skeletonized dial.

BOWMAN WATCH CO.

Lancaster, Pennsylvania
1877 - 1882

In March 1879, Ezra F. Bowman, a native of Lancaster, Pa., opened a retail jewelry and watch business. He employed William H. Todd to supervise his watch manufacturing. Todd had previously been employed by the Elgin and Lancaster Watch companies. Bowman made a 17S, 3/4 plate, fully-jeweled movement. The escape wheel was a star tooth design, fully capped, similar to those made by Charles Frodsham, an English watch maker. They were stem wind with dials made by another company. Enough parts were made and bought for 300 watches, but only about 50 watches were completed and sold. Those performed very well. The company was sold to J. P. Stevens of Atlanta, Ga.

Description	Avg	Ex-Fn	Mint
18S, 17J, Hamilton 928, OF, marked E. F. Bowman	$300	$400	$550
17S, 19-21J, 3/4, GJS, NI, LS, SW ....★★★	8,000	11,000	16,000
16S, 21J, Hamilton 960, OF, marked E. F. Bowman....................	300	400	550

Bowman Watch Co., 16-18 size, 17 jewels, 3/4 plate, gold jewel settings, lever set, stem wind. Note free sprung balance. Serial number 17, c.1880.

ROBERT BROWN & SON
1833 - 1856
J. R. BROWN & SHARPE
1856
Providence, Rhode Island

Description	Avg	Ex-Fn	Mint
18S, KW, KS, FULL..★★★	$2,200	$2,700	$3,800

California Watch Co., 18 size, 15 jewels, full plate.

California Watch Co., 18 size, 7 jewels, full plate, serial number 29,029.

CALIFORNIA WATCH CO.

Berkeley, California
1876 - 1877

The Cornell Watch Co. was reorganized in early 1876 as the California Watch Co. The new company bought machinery to make watch cases of gold and silver. In a short time the company was in bad financial trouble and even paid its employees with watches. The business closed in the summer of 1876. Albert Troller bought the unfinished watches that were left. In about four months, he found a buyer in San Francisco. The factory was then closed and sold to the Independent Watch Co. Only about 5,000 watches were made by the California Watch Company. Serial numbers range from 25,115 to 30,174. Inscribed on the movements is "Berkeley."

Description		Avg	Ex-Fn	Mint
18S, 15J, FULL, KW, KS, "Berkeley" ....★★		$1,300	$1,600	$2,000
18S, 11J, FULL, KW, KS.. ★		1,000	1,200	1,600

CHESHIRE WATCH CO.

Cheshire, Connecticut
1883 - 1890

In October 1883, the Cheshire Watch Company was formed by George J. Capewell with D. A. A. Buck (designer of the long-wind Waterbury) as superintendent. Their first movement was 18S, 3/4 gilt plate, stem wind, stem set, with the pendant attached to the movement. It fit into a nickel case which was also made at the Cheshire factory. The first watches were completed in April 1885. A new 18S nickel movement with a second hand was made to fit standard size American cases, and was introduced in 1887. By that date production was at about 200 watches per day. Serial numbers range from 201 to 89,650. All Cheshire watches were sold through L. W. Sweet, general selling agent, in New York City. The factory closed in 1890, going into receivership. The receiver had 3,000 movements finished in 1892. In 1901 O. E. Bell bought the machinery and had it shipped to Appleton, Wisconsin, where he had formed the Remington Watch Company. The watches produced by Remington are marked "Appleton Watch Co." on the movements.

Cheshire Watch Co., 18-20 size, 4 jewels, model number 1. Note stem attached and will not fit standard size case, serial number 201.

Description	Avg	Ex-Fn	Mint
20S, 4-7J, FULL, OF, SW, NI case, stem attached, 1st model, closed top plate .... ★★★	$450	$550	$700
18S, 4-7J, 3/4, SW, OF, NI case, stem attached, 2nd model ..... ★	300	350	450
18S, 7J, OF, fits standard case .... ★	250	300	375
18S, 11J, OF, SW, standard case, 3rd model .... ★	275	325	400
18S, 15J, OF, NI, ADJ, standard case, 3rd model .... ★	300	350	450
18S, 21J, OF, SW, Coin, standard case, 3rd model .... ★★	400	450	550
6S, 3/4, OF, SW, NI case .... ★	200	275	350

Cheshire Watch Co., 18 size, 4-7 jewels. This model number 2 was manufactured with the stem attached and requires a special case.

Cheshire Watch Co., 18 size, 4-7 jewels. This model fits standard 18 size cases. Model number 3.

 NOTE : 1st & 2nd model Cheshire movements will not fit standard 18 size cases.

Chicago Watch Co., 18 size, 15 jewels, open face nickel movement, serial number 209,145.

CHICAGO WATCH CO.

Chicago, Illinois
1895 - 1903

The Chicago Watch Company's watches were 18S, 7J, open-faced, had silveroid type cases, and were produced at low cost. They are believed to have been made by another manufacturer and sold by Chicago Watch Co.

Description	Avg	Ex-Fn	Mint
18S, 7J, OF	$100	$150	$200
18S, 7-11J, HC or OF, Swiss fake	40	50	65
18S, 11J, KW	325	375	450
18S, 15J, OF, SW	175	200	300
Columbus, 18S, 15J, SW, NI, HC ★★	200	225	325
Illinois, 18S, 11J, SW, NI ★★	200	225	325
Waltham, 18S, 15J ★★	200	225	325
12S, 15J, OF	100	150	200
12S, 15J, YGF, HC	200	225	325

COLUMBIA WATCH CO.

Waltham, Massachusetts
1896 - 1899

The Columbia Watch Company was organized in 1896 by Edward A. Locke, formerly General Manager of the Waterbury Watch Company. The firm began manufacturing an 0-size, 4-jewel gilt movement with duplex escapement in 1897. These movements were marked "Columbia Watch Co./Waltham, Mass." The firm also made movements marked "Hollers Watch Co./Brooklyn, NY," as well as nickeled movements marked "Cambridge Watch Co./New York."

Locke turned the business over to his son-in-law, Renton Whidden, in 1898, and the firm changed to an 0-size, 7- jewel nickel movement with lever escapement called the Suffolk. The firm name was not changed until early 1901.

Description	Avg	Ex-Fn	Mint
0S, 4J, SW, OF, HC, Duplex, gilded	$50	$60	$75
0S, 7J, SW, OF, lever escapement	60	75	85

Columbia Watch Co., 0 size, 4 jewels, stem wind, open face and hunting, duplex escapement, the escape wheel teeth were milled to give better quality than the Waterbury movements.

COLUMBUS WATCH CO.

Columbus, Ohio
1882 - 1903

The Columbus Watch Co. grew from the Columbus Watch Mfg. Co. which was started in 1876 by D. Gruen and W. J. Savage. The company finished Swiss -imported movements in 8, 16, and 18 sizes to fit American-made cases. They continued to import movements until Nov. 18, 1882, at which time a factory was built. By Aug. 18, 1883, the first movements had been produced. There are several features that separate the Columbus from other American watches. The train is different because the barrel has 72 teeth, the center wheel 72, center pinion 11, third wheel 11 leaves. No cases were made by the company, and the mainsprings and hairsprings, as well as the jewels, were imported. The company started making its own dials in 1884. They were producing watches at the rate of 150 a day in 1888. Serial numbers range from 20,000 to 383,000 for standard grade movements. In 1894 a block of numbers from 500,000 to 505,800 was assigned to some higher grade movements. Also in that year some movements bore the name 'New Columbus Watch Co." In 1903 the Columbus Watch Co. was sold to the South Bend Watch Co.

18 SIZE

Grade or Name — Description	Avg	Ex-Fn	Mint
Champion, 15J, NI, FULL, HC	$125	$150	$185
Champion, 15J, gilt, FULL, HC	125	150	185
Champion, 15J, gilt, FULL, Coin, OF	100	125	175
Champion, 16J, NI, ADJ, FULL, DMK, OF	85	110	140
Columbus W. Co., 15J, OF, LS	85	110	140
Columbus W. Co., 16J, OF, LS	95	120	150
Columbus W. Co., 17J, OF, LS	100	125	175
Columbus W. Co., 17J, OF, LS, 2-Tone	135	160	200
Columbus W. Co., 16J, KW, KS, HC ★★★	400	550	775

Columbus Watch Co., 18 size, 15 jewels, key wind and set, "Ohio Watch Co." on dial, "Col. Watch Co." on movement.

Columbus Watch Co., Railway King, 18 size, 23 jewels, with a "choo choo" dial.

Grade or Name — Description	Avg	Ex-Fn	Mint
Columbus W. Co., 11-15J, KW, KS, HC	$200	$300	$450
Columbus W. Co., 15J, KW, KS, 18K, HC	700	800	950
Columbus W. Co., 15J, HC, LS, KW/SW Trans.	125	150	200
Columbus W. Co., 15J, Multi-color 14K box hinge HC	1,600	1,800	2,500
Columbus W. Co., 15J, Coin	75	100	125
Columbus W. Co., 15J, "New Columbus W. Co." on mvt.	75	100	125
Columbus W. Co., 11J, Coin	75	100	125
Columbus W. Co., 11J, HC, LS	125	150	200
Columbus W. Co., 13J, HC, LS	125	150	200
Columbus W. Co., 17J, HC, LS, Trans.	125	150	200
Columbus King, 17J, HC	250	275	350
Columbus Watch Co., 17J, NI, 14K Multi-color box hinge HC	1,600	1,800	2,200
Columbus King, 21J, HC	275	300	375
Columbus King, 23J, HC	700	1,000	1,350
Columbus King, 25J, HC ★★	2,000	2,500	3,500
Jay Gould, 15J, OF	200	275	375
Jackson Park, 15J, NI, ADJ, OF	200	275	375
North Star, 11J, NI, FULL, HC	75	100	125
North Star, 11J, gilt, FULL, HC	75	100	125
North Star, 15J, gilt, FULL, Coin, HC	85	110	140
North Star, 15J, NI, FULL, HC	85	110	140
Ohio Watch Co., 13J, OF, KW, KS ★★	300	375	475
Ohio Watch Co., 11-13J, OF, transition KW/KS to SW/LS ★	200	275	375

Grade or Name — Description	Avg	Ex-Fn	Mint
Railroad Monarch, 17J, ADJ, OF	$200	$275	$375
Railway King, 16J, ADJ, GJS, 2-Tone, Choo Choo dial, HC	250	325	425
Railway King, 17J, ADJ, GJS, Choo Choo dial, HC	250	325	425
Railway King, 17J, 2-Tone, HC	175	225	300
Railway King, 19J, GJS, Adj.5P, HC ★★	500	600	700
Railway King, 19J, GJS, Adj.5P, OF ★★	500	600	700
Railway King, 21J, GT, Adj.6P, DMK, GJS, HC	250	300	400
Railway King, 21J, GT, Adj.6P, DMK, GJS, 2-Tone, HC	300	375	475
Railway King, 23J, Adj.6P, DMK, GJS, HC ★	800	1,100	1,450
Railway King, 25J, GT, Adj.6P, DMK, GJS, OF ★★	2,000	2,500	3,500
Railway King, 25J, GT, Adj.6P, DMK, GJS, HC ★★★	2,500	3,000	4,000
Railway King Special	200	275	375
R. W. K. Special, 17J, OF, LS, 2-Tone	225	275	375
R. W. K. Special, 19J, HC, LS, 2-Tone	250	325	425
Railway Regulator, 17J, OF	200	250	350
Railway Time Service, 17J, OF, NI	175	225	300
Time King, 17J, 2-Tone, OF	150	175	200
Time King, 21J, GT, Adj.6P, DMK, GJS, 2-Tone, HC	275	325	400
Time King, 23J, GT, Adj.6P, DMK, GJS, HC	800	1,100	1,450
Time King, 25J, GT, Adj.6P, DMK, GJS ★★	2,000	2,500	3,500
G#18, 16J, HC, Adj.6P, GJS, DMK, NI	150	175	200
G#20-21, 7-11J, HC	100	125	175
G#28, 16J, HC, FULL, ADJ, GJS, DMK	125	150	175
G#34, 15J, HC, FULL, NI	125	150	175
G#32, 15J, HC, FULL, gilded	125	150	175
G#90, 7J, gilt, OF, FULL	75	100	125
G#90, 7J, gilt, OF, Coin	75	100	125
G#93, 15J, gilt, OF, FULL	85	110	140
G#94, 15J, NI, OF, FULL	85	110	140

Columbus King, 18 size, 25 jewels, hunting case, stem wind, serial number 503,094.

Railway King, 18 size, 23 jewels, adjusted, stem wind, open face, serial number 503,315.

Grade or Name — Description	Avg	Ex-Fn	Mint
G#95, 15J, NI, OF, FULL, ADJ, GJS	$75	$100	$125
G#98, 16J, NI, OF, FULL, ADJ, GJS, DMK	85	110	140
G#99, 16J, NI, OF, FULL, Adj.6P, GJS, DMK	100	125	150
G#105, 19J, GJS, 2-Tone, HC......................................★	1,000	1,200	1,500
Swiss-made 18S, 7J, HC, SW, LS,3/4 Plate..........................	75	100	125
Swiss-made 18S, 11J, HC, SW, LS, 3/4 Plate........................	75	100	125
Swiss-made 18S, 15J, HC, SW, LS, 3/4 Plate........................	85	110	140
Swiss-made 18S, 16J, HC, SW, LS, 3/4 Plate........................	85	110	140

Columbus Watch Co., 16 size, 17 jewels, gold train, serial number 228,188.

Columbus Watch Co., Ruby Model, 16 size, 21 jewels, three quarter plate, gold jewel settings, gold train, Adj.6p.

16 SIZE

Grade or Name — Description	Avg	Ex-Fn	Mint
New Columbus Watch Co., 11J, 3/4, OF..............................	$50	$75	$100
New Columbus Watch Co., 15J, 3/4, OF..............................	50	75	100
New Columbus Watch Co., 16J, 3/4, OF..............................	50	75	100
New Columbus Watch Co., 17J, 14K, Multi-color HC	1,000	1,200	1,500
New Columbus Watch Co., 17J, 2-Tone	75	100	125
Ruby Model, 21J, 3/4, NI, GJS, GT, OF, 2-tone ....★★	525	600	725
Ruby Model, 21J, 3/4, NI, GJS, Adj.6P, GT, HC ....★	425	500	625
G#41, 11J, gilt, 3/4, HC..	75	100	125
G#43, 11J, NI, 3/4, HC...	75	100	125
G#44, 15J, NI, GJS, ADJ, 3/4, HC..................................	85	110	140
G#45, 19J, GJS, 2-Tone, HC ....★★	800	1,000	1,300
G#46, 15J, NI, GJS, ADJ, 3/4, HC..................................	75	100	125
G#47, 16J, NI, ADJ, GJS, 3/4, HC.................................	85	110	140
G#81, 11J, OF, gilt, 3/4	50	75	100
G#83, 11J, OF, NI, 3/4	50	75	100
G#84, 15J, OF, NI, GJS, ADJ, 3/4	50	75	100
G#86, 15J, OF, NI, GJS, ADJ, 3/4	75	100	125
G#87, 16J, OF, Adj.3P, GJS, 3/4, NI, DMK	85	110	140
G#88, 16J, OF, Adj.6p, 14K, GJS, 3/4, DMK, NI	475	500	600

Grade or Name — Description	Avg	Ex-Fn	Mint
Swiss-made 16S, 15J, SW, LS, OF..	$50	$75	$100
Swiss-made 16S, 15J, SW, LS, HC..	75	100	125
Swiss-made 16S, 16J, SW, LS, OF..	50	75	100
Swiss-made 16S, 16J, SW, LS, HC..	85	110	140

Columbus Watch Co., 6 size, 15 jewels, 3/4 plate, stem wind, serial number 377,489.

New Columbus Watch Co. Example of a basic model for 6 size. 3/4 plate, 7-16 jewels, gilded and nickel.

6 SIZE

Grade or Name — Description	Avg	Ex-Fn	Mint
G#102-G#50, 7J, gilded, HC	$75	$100	$125
G#101-G#51, 11J, gilded, HC	75	100	125
G#53, 11J, NI, HC	75	100	125
G#55, 15J, GJS, NI, 18K, HC..	375	425	575
G#55, 15J, GJS, NI, HC...	75	100	125
G#104-G#57, 16J, GJS, DMK, NI, HC	75	100	125
Swiss made 6S, 11-15J, SW, LS, HC..	50	75	100

4 SIZE

Grade or Name — Description	Avg	Ex-Fn	Mint
Columbus Watch Co., 15J, HC, gilt mvt.	$100	$150	$200
Columbus Watch Co., 15J, HC, nickel mvt.	110	160	220

COLUMBUS
ESTIMATED SERIAL NUMBERS AND PRODUCTION DATES

Date	Serial No.	Date	Serial No.	Special Block of Serial Nos.	
1883	23,000	1893	207,000		
1884	30,000	1894	229,000		
1885	40,000	1895	251,000	Date	Serial No.
1886	53,000	1896	273,000	1894	500,001
1887	75,000	1897	295,000	1896	501,500
1888	97,000	1898	317,000	1898	503,000
1889	119,000	1899	339,000	1900	504,500
1890	141,000	1900	361,000	1902	505,800
1891	163,000	1901	383,000		
1892	185,000				

CORNELL WATCH CO.

Chicago, Illinois
1870 - 1874
San Francisco, California
1875 - 1876

The Cornell Watch Co. bought the Newark Watch Co. and greatly improved the movements being produced. In the fall of 1874, the company moved to San Francisco, Calif., with about 60 of its employees. The movements made in California were virtually the same as those made in Chicago. The company wanted to employ Chinese who would work cheaper, but the skilled employees refused to go along and went on strike. The company stayed alive until 1875 and was sold to the California Watch Co. in January 1876. But death came a few months later.

The Chronology of the Development of Cornell Watch Co.:
Newark Watch Co. 1864-1870; S#s 6901-12,000
Cornell Watch Co., Chicago, Ill. 1870-1874; S#s 12,001 to 25,000;
Cornell Watch Co., San Francisco, Calif. 1874-Jan. 1876; S# s 25,001 to 35,000;
California Watch Co., Jan. 1876-mid 1876.

Cornell Watch Co., J.C. Adams, 18 size, 11 jewels, key wind & set, made in Chicago, Ill, serial number 13,647.

Cornell Watch Co., 18 size, 15 jewels, key wind & set, marked "John Evans," serial number 16,868.

18 SIZE

Grade or Name — Description		Avg	Ex-Fn	Mint
J. C. Adams, 11J, KW	★	$400	$500	$650
C. T. Bowen, FULL, KW	★	350	450	600
C. M. Cady, 15J, SW	★	400	500	650
Cornell, 7J, San Francisco on mvt., KW	★	900	1,100	1,400
Cornell, 11J, KW	★	300	400	550
Cornell, 11J, San Francisco on mvt., KW	★	900	1,100	1,400
Cornell, 15J, KW	★	350	450	600
Cornell W. Co., 15J, San Francisco on mvt., KW	★	1,100	1,300	1,600

Grade or Name — Description	Avg	Ex-Fn	Mint
Cornell W. Co., 15J, San Francisco on mvt., SW ★★	$1,200	$1,400	$1,800
Paul Cornell, 19J, GJS, HCI5P, SW ★★★	1,500	1,800	2,500
John Evans, 15J, KW ★	350	450	600
Excelsior, 15J, FULL, KW, KS	300	400	550
H. N. Hibbard, 11J, KW, ADJ ★	400	500	650
C.L. Kidder, 7J, KWKS, OF ★	300	350	400
George F. Root, 15J, KW ★★	550	700	900
George Waite, 7J, (Hyde Park), KW ★★	400	550	650
E. J. Williams, 7J, KW ★	350	450	600
Ladies Stemwind ★	150	200	300
Eugene Smith, 17J ★	350	450	600

JACOB D. CUSTER

Norristown, Pennsylvania
1840 - 1845

At the age of 19, Jacob Custer repaired his father's watch. He was then asked to repair all the watches within his community. Custer was basically self-taught and had very little formal education and little training in clocks and watches. He made all the parts except the hairspring and fusee chains. The watches were about 14 size, and only 12 to 15 watches were made. The 14S fusee watches had lever escapement, 3/4 plate and were sold in his own gold cases. He made a few chronometers, one with a helical spring.

J.D. Custer, 14-16 size, engraved on movement "J.D. Custer, Norristown, Pa. Patented Feb. 4, 1843.

Description	Avg	Ex-Fn	Mint
14S, OF, engraved on mvt. "J. D. Custer, Patented Feb. 4, 1843, #2,939" ★★★★★	$8,500	$12,000	$18,000

DUDLEY WATCH CO.
Lancaster, Pennsylvania
1920 - 1925

William Wallace Dudley became interested in watches and horology at the age of 13 and became an apprentice making ship chronometers in Canada. When he moved to America, he worked for the South Bend and Illinois Watch companies and the Trenton Watch Co. before going to Hamilton Watch Co. in Lancaster. He left Hamilton at age 69 to start his own watch company. In 1922 his first watches were produced; they were 14S, 19J, and were labeled Models 1894 and 1897. Watch parts, dials and hands were Swiss made. The winding mechanism was made at the Dudley factory. The cases came from Wadsworth Keystone and the Star Watch Case Co. Dudley also made a 12S, 19J watch. By 1924, the company was heavily in debt, and on February 20, 1925, a petition for bankruptcy was filed. The Masonic Watch was his most unusual.

Dudley Watches				Total Production
Dudley Watch Co.	1920-1925	Model No. 1	S# 500-1,900	1,400
P. W. Baker Co.	1925-1935	Model No. 2	S# 2,001-4,800	1,600
XL Watch Co., N.Y.	1935-1976	Model No. 3	S# 4,801-6,500	1,000
			Total	4,000

Model No. 1, 14S, 19J, OF, can be distinguished by the "Holy Bible" engraved on the winding arbor plate.

Model No. 2, 12S, 19J, used the 910 and 912 Hamilton wheels and escapement, has a flat silver-colored Bible.

Model No. 3, 12S, can be distinguished by the silver Bible which was riveted in place and was more three-dimensional.

Dudley Watch Co., Model 1,
14 size, 19 jewels, open face,
flip back, serial number 1232.

12 SIZE - 14 SIZE
"MASONS" MODEL

Grade or Name — Description	Avg	Ex-Fn	Mint
14S, Dudley, 19J, 14K, flip open back, Serial #1 (made 5 experimental models with Serial #1) ....★★★	$5,000	$7,000	$10,000
14S, M#1, 19J, OF, 14K, flip open back ....★	3,000	3,200	3,600
12S, M#1, 19J, OF, 14K, flip open back, w/box & papers ......★	3,500	3,800	4,000
12S, M#2, 19J, OF, flip open back, GF ....★	1,600	1,800	2,300
12S, M#2, 19J, OF, 14K, flip open back case ....★	2,000	2,200	2,600
12S, M#2, 19J, OF, 14K display case ....★	1,850	2,200	2,400
12S, M#3, 19J, OF, display case, GF ....★	1,600	1,800	2,275
12S, M#3, 19J, OF, 14K flip open case ....★	2,000	2,200	2,600

Dudley Watch Co., Model 2, 12 size, 19 jewels, open face, serial number 2,420.

Dudley Watch Co., Model 3, 12 size, 19 jewels, open face.

ELGIN WATCH CO.
(NATIONAL WATCH CO.)
Elgin, Illinois
1864 - 1964

This was the largest watch company in terms of production; in fact, Elgin produced half of the total number of pocket watches (dollar-type not included). Some of the organizers came from Waltham Watch Co., including P. S. Bartlett, D. G. Currier, Otis Hoyt, Charles H. Mason and others. The idea of beginning a large watch company for the mid-West was discussed by J. C. Adams, Bartlett and Blake. After a trip to Waltham, Adams went back to Chicago and approached Benjamin W. Raymond, a former mayor of Chicago, to put up the necessary capital to get the company started. Adams and Raymond succeeded in getting others to pledge their financial support also. The National Watch Co. (Elgin) was formed in August 1864. The factory site was in Elgin, Illinois, where the city had donated 35 acres of land. The factory was completed in 1866, movement was a B. W. Raymond, 18S, full plate design. The first watches were put on the market in 1867, selling for about $115, and all were quick train. The first stem wind model was an H. L. Culver with serial No. 155,001, lever set and quick train. In 1874 the name was changed to the Elgin National Watch Co. and they produced watches into the 1950s.

The first wrist watch made by Elgin was sold in 1910. This watch, Serial No. 101, sold for $12,000 in 1988.

Elgin Movements

	1st. App.	1st S#		1st. App.	1st. S#
18S B. W. Raymond	April 1867	101	10S Lady Elgin	Jan. 1869	40,001
18S H. L. Culver	July 1867	1,001	10S Frances Rubie	Aug. 1870	50,001
18S J. T. Ryerson	Oct. 1867	5,001	10S Gail Borden	Sept. 1871	185,001
18S H. H. Taylor	Nov. 1867	25,001	10S Dexter Street	Dec. 1871	201,001
18S G. M. Wheeler	Nov. 1867	6,001	First Stem Wind	June 1873	
18S Matt Laflin	Jan. 1868	9,001	1st Nickel Movement	Aug.15, 1879	
18S Father Time	No date	2,300,001	Convertible	Fall 1878	
18S Veritas	No date	8,400,001			

Some Serial Nos. have the first two numbers replaced by a letter; i.e., 39,482,000 would be X482,000.

X—39	V—46
C,E,T&Y—42	H—47
L—43	N—48
U—44	F—49
J—45	S—50

ELGIN ESTIMATED SERIAL NUMBERS
AND PRODUCTION DATES

Date	Serial #	Date	Serial #	Date	Serial #
1867	10,000	1897	7,100,000	1926	29,100,000
1868	35,000	1898	7,550,000	1927	30,050,000
1869	65,000	1899	8,200,000	1928	31,500,000
1870	95,000	1900	9,000,000	1929	32,000,000
1871	120,000	1901	9,250,000	1930	32,500,000
1872	155,000	1902	9,700,000	1931	33,000,000
1873	170,000	1903	10,100,000	1932	33,800,000
1874	210,000	1904	10,900,000	1933	35,100,000
1875	320,000	1905	11,900,000	1934	35,000,000
1876	390,000	1906	12,600,000	1935	35,750,000
1877	475,000	1907	12,900,000	1936	36,200,000
1878	500,000	1908	13,550,000	1937	37,100,000
1879	580,000	1909	14,000,000	1938	37,900,000
1880	750,000	1910	14,900,000	1939	38,200,000
1881	900,000	1911	15,900,000	1940	39,100,000
1882	1,000,000	1912	16,500,000	1941	40,200,000
1883	1,300,000	1913	17,200,000	1942	41,100,000
1884	1,500,000	1914	17,900,000	1943	42,200,000
1885	1,700,000	1915	18,400,000	1944	42,600,000
1886	2,000,000	1916	19,500,000	1945	43,200,000
1887	2,400,000	1917	20,100,000	1946	43,800,000
1888	2,900,000	1918	21,000,000	1947	44,200,000
1889	3,400,000	1919	22,000,000	1948	45,100,000
1890	3,900,000	1920	23,000,000	1949	46,000,000
1891	4,500,000	1921	24,050,000	1950	47,000,000
1892	4,800,000	1922	25,100,000	1951	48,000,000
1893	4,900,000	1923	26,050,000	1952	49,000,000
1894	5,550,000	1924	27,000,000	1953	50,000,000
1895	5,900,000	1925	28,050,000	1956	55,000,000
1896	6,550,000				

Some collectors seek out low serial numbers and will usually pay a premium for them. The lower the number, the more desirable the watch. The table shown below lists the first serial number of each size watch made by Elgin.

Size	1st Serial Nos.	Size	1st Serial Nos.
18	101	10	40,001
17	356,001	6	570,001
16	600,001	0	2,889,001
14	351,001		

Elgin Watch Co., Lord Elgin, Grade 351, 16 size, 23 jewels, gold train, raised gold jewel settings, serial number 12,718,340 (1st run).

Father Time, 18 size, 21 jewels, model #8 with wind indicator, free sprung model, serial number 22,888,020

18 SIZE

Grade or Name — Description	Avg	Ex-Fn	Mint
Advance, 11J, gilded, KW, HC, FULL	$75	$100	$125
Atlas Watch Co., 7J, HC, LS, FULL	75	100	125
California Watch, 15J, gilded, HC, KW, KS, FULL	125	150	200
Chief, 7J, gilded, KW, FULL, HC	75	100	125
Convertible, 7J, G#98	75	100	125
H. L. Culver, 15J, gilded, KW, KS, FULL, HC, ADJ, low S#	200	250	325
H. L. Culver, 15J, gilded, KW, KS, FULL, HC, ADJ	125	150	200
H. L. Culver, 15J, KW, KS, 14K, HC	525	550	600
H. L. Culver, 15J, gilded, KW, KS, FULL, HC	100	125	175
H. L. Culver, 15J, gilded, SW, FULL, HC	75	100	125
H. L. Culver, 15J, gilded, KW, FULL, LS, HC	75	100	125
Elgin W. Co., 7J, OF, SW	55	75	100
Elgin W. Co., 7J, KW, gilded, HC	75	100	125
Elgin W. Co., 11J, KW, LS	55	75	100
Elgin W. Co., 11J, LS, SW, HC, 9K-10K	325	375	475
Elgin W. Co., 11J, LS, SW, HC, Silveroid	40	50	65
Elgin W. Co., 11J, LS, , SW, OF	55	70	100
Elgin W. Co., 13J, SW, PS/LS, Silveroid	40	50	65
Elgin W. Co., 13J, SW, PS/LS	55	75	100

California Watch, 18 size, 15 jewels, gilded, key wind & set, serial number 200,700.

Convertible, 18 size, 21 jewels, converts to either hunting or open face.

Grade or Name — Description	Avg	Ex-Fn	Mint
Elgin W. Co., 15J, KW, LS, HC	$75	$100	$150
Elgin W. Co., 15J, SW, LS, OF	55	75	100
Elgin W. Co., 15-17J, SW, LS, box–hinge YGFilled, HC	125	150	200
Elgin W. Co., 15-17J, SW, LS, box–hinge 14k gold,HC	1,000	1,200	1,600
Elgin W. Co., 15J-17, SW, LS, "Multi-color" box YGFilled,HC	300	385	550
Elgin W. Co., 15-17J, SW, 14K case, OF	300	350	425
Elgin W. Co., 15-17J, SW, 14K case, HC	375	425	475
Elgin W. Co., 15-17J, SW, 18K case, HC	650	700	800
Elgin W. Co., 15-17J, SW, Multi-color, 14K, HC	1,500	1,800	2,200
Elgin W. Co., 15-17J, SW, LS, "COIN"Silver 6 OZ	100	125	175
Elgin W. Co., 15-17J, SW, LS, "COIN"Silver"	55	75	100
Elgin W. Co., 15J, SW, LS, HC	75	100	125
Elgin W. Co., 15J, KW, hidden key	125	150	175
Elgin W. Co., 17J, SW, LS, Silveroid	55	60	75
Elgin W. Co., 17J, SW, LS or PS, OF	55	75	100
Elgin W. Co., 21J, SW, LS or PS, OF	100	125	175
Elgin W. Co., 21J, SW, LS, box case, GF	175	200	275
Elgin W. Co., 21J, LS, HC, 14K	575	600	675
Elgin W. Co., 21J, SW, LS, Silveroid	75	90	125
Elgin W. Co., 21J, SW, LS, HC	125	150	175

Elgin W. Co., Grade 297, 18 size, 15 jewels.

Charles Fargo, 18 size, 7 jewels, gilded, key wind & set, hunting case.

Pennsylvania Railroad Co. on dial. B.W. Raymond on movement. One of the first railroad watches commissioned by Penn. RR Co., 18 size, 15 jewels, key wind and set, serial number 123,245, c. 1874.

Grade or Name — Description	Avg	Ex-Fn	Mint
Elgin W. Co., 21J, Wind Indicator	$600	$800	$1,000
Elgin W. Co., 21J, Wind Indicator, free sprung	600	800	1,000
Charles Fargo, 7J, gilded, KW, HC	150	175	200
J. V. Farwell, 11J, gilded, KW, HC ★	250	300	375
Father Time, 17J, NI, KW, FULL, HC, DMK ★	250	350	450
Father Time, 17J, NI, FULL, OF, DMK	100	125	175
Father Time, 17J, SW, OF, Silveroid	55	60	80
Father Time, 17J, SW, HC	125	150	200
Father Time, 20J, NI, SW, FULL, HC, DMK ★	250	300	375
Father Time, 21J, NI, SW, FULL, OF, GJS, DMK	150	175	200
Father Time, 21J, NI, SW, 3/4, GJS, DMK, HC	125	150	200
Father Time, 21J, NI, SW, 3/4, OF, GJS, DMK	125	150	200
Father Time, 21J, GJT, HCI5P, Diamond end stone	125	150	200
Father Time, 21J, NI, SW, 3/4, OF, GJS, Wind Indicator	800	1,000	1,300
Father Time, 21J, SW, 3/4, GJS, wind indicator, HC	1,000	1,200	1,500
Father Time, G#367, 21J, NI, SW, 3/4, OF, GJS, military wind indicator, free sprung, 602 sterling case	1,200	1,400	1,700
W. H. Ferry, 15J, gilded, KW, HC	125	150	175
W. H. Ferry, 11J, gilded, KW, HC	125	150	175
Mat Laflin, 7J, gilded, KW, HC	125	150	175
National W. Co., 7J, KW, KS	75	100	125
National W. Co., 11J, KW, KS	75	100	125
National W. Co., 15J, KW, KS	85	110	135
M. D. Ogden, 15J, KW, HC	125	150	175
M. D. Ogden, 11J, gilded, KW, HC	125	150	175
Overland, 17J, NI, KW, HC, DMK	150	175	200
Overland, 17J, NI, SW, HC, DMK	100	125	175
Pennsylvania Railroad Co. on dial, B. W. Raymond on mvt., 15J, KW, KS (1st RR watches) ★★★	900	1,200	1,500
Railway Timer, 15J, FULL, HC ★	300	400	500

B.W. Raymond, 18 size, 23 jewels, wind indicator. Note small winding indicator gear next to crown wheel.

H.H. Taylor, 18 size, 15 jewels, key wind & set, serial number 288,797.

Grade or Name — Description	Avg	Ex-Fn	Mint
B. W. Raymond, 15-17J, KW, low S# under 1000	$400	$500	$700
B. W. Raymond, 15J, gilded, KW, FULL, HC	125	150	175
B. W. Raymond, 17J, gilded, KW, FULL, HC	125	150	175
B. W. Raymond, 15J, SW, HC	75	100	125
B. W. Raymond, 17J, NI, FULL, OF	55	75	100
B. W. Raymond, 17J, Silveroid	40	60	80
B. W. Raymond, 17J, NI, FULL, HC	100	125	175
B. W. Raymond, 15J, box case, 14K	700	800	1,200
B. W. Raymond, 17J, gilded, NI, SW, FULL, ADJ	75	100	125
B. W. Raymond, 19J, NI, 3/4, SW, OF, GJS, DMK, GT	75	100	150
B. W. Raymond, 19J, 3/4, SW, OF, GJS, Wind Indicator, DMK	500	600	850
B. W. Raymond, 19J, 3/4, GJS, GT, Diamond end stone	75	100	125
B. W. Raymond, 21J, 3/4, GJS, GT, Diamond end stone, OF	125	150	175
B. W. Raymond, 21J, SW, Silveroid	100	125	150
B. W. Raymond, 21J, SW, GJS, GT, DES, HC	175	200	250
B. W. Raymond, 21J, NI, 3/4, SW, GJS, DMK, GT	125	150	175
B. W. Raymond, 21J, NI, 3/4, SW, GJS, Wind Indicator, DMK.	650	750	950
J. T. Ryerson, 7J, gilded, FULL, KW, HC	75	100	125
Solar W. Co., 15J, Multi-color dial	75	100	150
Standard, 17J, OF, LS	100	125	150
Sundial, 7J, SW, PS	55	60	75
H. H. Taylor, 15J, gilded, FULL, KW, HC	100	125	175
H. H. Taylor, 15J, NI, FULL, KW, HC, DMK	100	125	175
H. H. Taylor, 15J, NI, FULL, SW, HC, DMK, quick train	100	125	175
H. H. Taylor, 15J, SW, Silveroid	40	50	65
H. H. Taylor, 15J, SW, slow train	60	70	85
Veritas, 21J, SW, PS, HC	175	225	300
Veritas, 21J, SW, LS, GJS, GT, HC	175	225	300

Veritas, 18 size, 23 jewels, solid gold train, gold jewel settings, diamond end stone, serial number 9,542,678.

G.M. Wheeler, Grade 369, 18 size, 17 jewels, open face, gold jewel settings, serial number 14,788,315

Grade or Name — Description	Avg	Ex-Fn	Mint
Veritas, 21J, 3/4, NI, GJS, OF, DMK, GT	$125	$150	$175
Veritas, 21J, 3/4, GJS, GT, Diamond end stones	125	150	175
Veritas, 21J, 3/4, GJS, GT, Diamond end stones, HC	175	225	300
Veritas, 21J, 3/4, NI, GJS, OF, Wind Indicator, DMK	1,000	1,100	1,300
Veritas, 21J, 3/4, NI, GJS, HC, Wind Indicator, DMK	1,000	1,200	1,400
Veritas, 23J, 3/4, NI, GJS, OF, DMK, GT	175	225	300
Veritas, 23J, 3/4, NI, GJS, OF, DMK, GT, Diamond end stone	200	225	300
Veritas, 23J, 3/4, Wind Indicator, GJS, OF, DMK, GT, 14K	1,400	1,600	2,000
Veritas, 23J, G#214, 3/4, NI, GJS, OF, Wind Indicator, DMK	800	1,000	1,300
Veritas, 23J, G#214, SW, OF	125	150	200
Veritas, 23J, 3/4, SW, NI, GJS, GT, LS, HC ★★★★	250	270	350
Veritas, 23J, SW, OF, 14K	550	575	650
G. M. Wheeler, 11J, gilded, KW, HC	75	100	150
G. M. Wheeler, 13-15J, gilded, FULL, KW	75	100	150
G. M. Wheeler, 15J, NI, FULL, KW, DMK, HC	75	100	150
G. M. Wheeler, 15J, SW, NI, FULL, DMK, OF	55	75	100
G. M. Wheeler, 17J, KW, NI, FULL, DMK, OF	100	125	175
G. M. Wheeler, 17J, SW, NI, FULL, DMK, OF	55	75	125

MOVEMENTS WITH NO NAME

	Avg	Ex-Fn	Mint
No. 5 & No. 17, 7J, gilded, FULL, HC	$75	$100	$125
No. 23 & No. 18, 11J, gilded, FULL, HC	75	100	125
No. 69, 15J, M#1, KW, quick train, HC	75	100	125
No. 316, 15J, NI, FULL, HC, DMK	75	100	150
No. 317, 15J, NI, FULL, ADJ, OF, DMK	75	100	150

Grade or Name — Description	Avg	Ex-Fn	Mint
No. 316 & No. 317, 15J, Silveroid	$40	$50	$65
No. 326, 15J, OF	60	70	80
No. 327, 15J, HC	75	100	150
No. 335, 17J, HC	75	100	150
No. 336, 17J, NI, FULL, OF, DMK	55	75	150
No. 345, 19J, GJS, 2-Tone, HC ★	600	700	900
No. 348, 21J, NI, FULL, HC, GJS, DMK	100	125	175
No. 349, 21J, OF	100	125	150
No. 378, 19J, NI, FULL, HC, DMK	75	100	150
No. 379, 19J, OF	55	75	125

Elgin Watch Co., 17 size, 11 jewels, key wind & set, made for English market, serial number 418,220.

Elgin Watch Co., 17 size, 7 jewels, key wind & set, serial number 199,076. Made for Kennedy & Co.

17 SIZE

Grade or Name — Description	Avg	Ex-Fn	Mint
Avery, 7J, gilded, KW, FULL, HC	$75	$100	$150
Inter–Ocean, 7J, KW KS, HC	85	110	160
Leader, 7J, gilded, KW, FULL, HC	75	100	150
Leader, 7J, gilded, KW, FULL, HC, early movement	75	100	150
Sunshine, 15J, KW, KS from back	100	125	175
The Age, 7J, gilded, KW, FULL, HC	125	175	225
M#11, 14, 15, 51, 59, 7J, gilded, KW, FULL, HC	100	125	175
17 Size, KW, Silveroid	50	75	85

16 SIZE

Grade or Name — Description	Avg	Ex-Fn	Mint
Blind Man's Watch, 9-17J, HC	$75	$100	$150
Convertible Model, 11J, BRG, OF	50	75	125
Convertible Model, 13J, BRG, OF	50	75	125
Convertible Model, 15J, BRG, ADJ, 14K, HC	450	475	525
Convertible Model, 15J, ADJ, DMK, 3F BRG, HC	75	100	150
Convertible Model, 15J, 3/4, ADJ, DMK, GJS	75	100	150

Elgin Watch Co., 16 size, 21 jewels, converts to open face or hunting case, serial number 607,061.

Elgin W. Co., 16 size, 21 jewels, three-fingered bridge model, adjusted, gold jewel settings, gold train, serial number 6,469,814.

Grade or Name — Description	Avg	Ex-Fn	Mint
Convertible Model, 15J, Silveroid	$50	$60	$90
Convertible Model, 15J, 3F BRG, OF	50	75	125
Convertible Model, 21J, 3F BRG	900	1,100	1,450
Convertible Model, 21J, G#72, 3/4, ADJ, , GJS, 14K ....★★	1,000	1,200	1,500
Convertible Model, 21J, G#91, 3F BRG, 14K ....★★	1,400	1,800	2,000
Doctors Watch, 15J, 4th Model, NI, GT, sweep second hand, GF case	150	185	225
Doctors Watch, 15J, 4th Model, gilded, sweep second hand, coin silver case	150	185	225
Doctors Watch, 15J, 4th Model, sweep second hand, 14K	500	600	700
Elgin W. Co., 7J, OF	50	75	125
Elgin W. Co., 7J, HC..	75	100	150

Doctors Watch, 16 size, 15 jewels, fourth model, gold jewel settings, gold train, sweep second hand, serial number 926,458.

Grade or Name — Description	Avg	Ex-Fn	Mint
Elgin W. Co., 9J, OF	$50	$75	$125
Elgin W. Co., 11J, OF	50	75	125
Elgin W. Co., 11J, HC	75	100	150
Elgin W. Co., 13J, OF	50	125	125
Elgin W. Co., 13J, OF, Silveroid	40	50	70
Elgin W. Co., 13J, HC	75	100	150
Elgin W. Co., 15J, HC	75	100	150
Elgin W. Co., 15J, OF, Silveroid	40	50	70
Elgin W. Co., 15J, OF	50	75	125
Elgin W. Co., 15J, OF 14K OF case	285	325	400
Elgin W. Co., 15J, HC, 14K	400	450	550
Elgin W. Co., 17J, OF	50	75	125
Elgin W. Co., 17J, 14K, HC	400	450	550
Elgin W. Co., 17J, G#280, 9th model, ADJ5P	100	125	175
Elgin W. Co., 17J, HC	100	125	175
Elgin W. Co., 19J, OF, LS	75	100	150
Elgin W. Co., 21J, HC	150	175	225
Elgin W. Co., 21J, OF, Silveroid	75	100	125
Elgin W. Co., 21J, OF	100	125	175
Elgin W. Co., 17J, LS, multi-color HC, GF	250	300	400
Elgin W. Co., 17J, multi-color HC, 14K	1,000	1,200	1,600
3F Bridge Model, 15J, NI, DMK	50	75	125
3F Bridge Model, 17J, Adj.3P, NI, DMK, GJS	50	75	125
3F Bridge Model, 17J, Adj.5P, NI, DMK, GJS, GT	75	100	150
3F Bridge Model, 21J, Adj.5P, NI, DMK, GJS, GT	200	250	325
Father Time, 17J, 3/4, NI, OF, GJS, DR, DMK	100	125	175
Father Time, 21J, 3/4, NI, HC, GJS, DR, DMK	175	200	275
Father Time, 21J, 3/4, NI, OF, GJS, DR, Wind Indicator	400	450	500
Father Time, 21J, Silveroid	75	100	125
Father Time, 21J, NI, GJS, DR, OF	125	150	175
Lord Elgin, 21J, GJS, DR, Adj.5P, 3F BRG, 14K ★★	1,200	1,500	2,000

Father Time, 16 size, 21 jewels, gold train; Note up and down wind indicator.

Father Time, 16 size, 21 jewels, gold train; Note model 19 up and down wind indicator movement does show the differential wheel as does the 18 size, serial number 18,106,465.

Lord Elgin, 16 size, 23 jewels, gold train, raised gold jewel settings, serial number 12,718,340.

B.W. Raymond, 16 size, 19 jewels, gold jewel settings, serial number 17,822,991.

Grade or Name — Description	Avg	Ex-Fn	Mint
Lord Elgin, 23J, GJS, DR, Adj.5P, 3/4, 14K, OF ....★★	$1,000	$1,200	$1,400
B. W. Raymond, 17J, 3/4, GJS, 14K, OF..	475	525	650
B. W. Raymond, 17J, 3/4, GJS, SW, HC	200	275	350
B. W. Raymond, 17J, 3F BRG ....★★	400	500	650
B. W. Raymond, 17J, LS, NI, Wind Indicator .... ★	300	350	400
B. W. Raymond, 17J, GJS, SW, OF..	150	200	250
B. W. Raymond, 17J, 3/4, GJS, DR, Adj.5P, DMK......................	175	225	275
B. W. Raymond, 19J, 3/4, GJS, DR, Adj.5P, DMK, OF..............	75	100	150
B. W. Raymond, 19J, OF, 14K, 30 DWT......................................	400	450	500
B. W. Raymond, 19J, 3/4, GJS, DR, HCI5P, DMK, Wind			
Indicator	350	400	450
B. W. Raymond, 19J, M#8, G#240, OF, Adj.5P	75	100	150
B. W. Raymond, 19J, GJS, Adj.5P, HC.......................................	150	175	225
B. W. Raymond, 21J, 14K, OF..	425	475	525
B. W. Raymond, 21J, G#389, OF	125	150	175
B. W. Raymond, 21J, G#571, 3/4, Adj.5P, OF	125	150	175
B. W. Raymond, 21J, 3/4, GJS, DR, Adj.5P, HC.........................	175	225	275
B. W. Raymond, 21J, 3/4, GJS, DR, Adj.5P, DMK, OF..............	125	150	175
B. W. Raymond, 21J, 3/4, GJS, DR, Adj.5P, DMK, W I.............	350	400	450
B. W. Raymond, 22J, WWII Model, sweep second hand	125	150	175
B. W. Raymond, 23J, 3/4, GJS, DR, Adj.5P, DMK......................	250	300	375
B. W. Raymond, 23J, 3/4, GJS, DR, Adj.5P, DMK, W I.............	475	525	600
B. W. Raymond, 23J, 3/4, GJS, DR, Adj.5P, DMK, W I,			
military style	425	475	550
Repeater, Terstegen, 5 min., 21J, 2 gongs ....★★	2,500	3,000	4,500
Veritas, 21J, 3F brg, GJS.. ★	225	275	350
Veritas, 21J, GJS, DR, Adj.5P, DMK, 3/4, HC	250	300	375

Veritas, 16 size, 23 jewels, solid gold train, gold jeweled settings, Adj5p, serial number 16,678,681.

Grade 340, 16 size, 17 jewels, three-fingered bridge model, open face.

Grade or Name — Description	Avg	Ex-Fn	Mint
Veritas, 21J, GJS, DR, Adj.5P, DMK, 3/4, Wind Indicator	$550	$600	$700
Veritas, 21J, GJS, SW, Grade 360.................................... ★	375	400	475
Veritas, 21J, GJS, SW, Adj.5P, OF, Grade 270	125	150	200
Veritas, 23J, GJS, Adj.5P, 14K, OF..................................	575	675	800
Veritas, 23J, GJS, Adj.5P, HC.......................................	300	400	500
Veritas, 23J, GJS, DR, Adj.5P, DMK, 3/4, OF, Grade 376	350	400	500
Veritas, 23J, GJS, DR, Adj.5P, DMK, 3/4, Diamond end stone, Grade 350... ★	375	425	525
Veritas, 23J, GJS, DR, Adj.5P, DMK, 3/4, Wind Indicator	600	650	750
G. M. Wheeler, 17J, DR, Adj.3P, DMK, 3/4..........................	50	75	90
G. M. Wheeler, 17J, 3F BRG	50	75	90
G. M. Wheeler, 17J, HC, 14K...	450	475	525
WWII Model, 17J, OF	100	125	175
WWII Model, 21J, OF	125	150	200
M#13, 9J, HC...	75	85	100
M#48, 13J, HC..	75	100	150

(Add $50 to hunting case models listed as open face)

MODELS WITH NO NAMES

Grade or Name — Description	Avg	Ex-Fn	Mint
Grade #72, 21J, ADJ, 3/4, HC...................................... ★	$450	$600	$800
Grade #91, 21J, 3F BRG .... ★★	450	550	700
Grade #145, 19J, GJS, BRG, HC .... ★★	650	750	900
Grade #155, 17J, GT, GJS, HC.......................................	100	125	150
Grade #156, 21J, 3/4, NI, DR, DMK, GT, GJS, HC .... ★	250	275	325
Grade #156, 21J, 3/4, NI, DR, DMK, GT, GJS, HC, 14K ...... ★	475	500	625
Grade #162, 21J, SW, PS, NI, GJS, GT OF........................... ★	225	275	350
Grade #270, 21J, 3F BRG, GJS, marked mvt.	150	175	225
Grade #280, 17J, marked on mvt.....................................	125	150	200
Grade #290 & #291, 7J, OF, 3/4, NI, DMK	50	75	90

Grade or Name — Description	Avg	Ex-Fn	Mint
Grade #291, 7J, 3/4, HC, 14K	$400	$450	$550
Grade #312 & #313, 15J, 3/4, NI, DR, DMK, OF	50	75	90
Grade #372, 19J, M#15, LS, OF, Adj.5P	250	300	375
Grade #374, 21J, M#15, LS, OF, Adj.5P	275	325	400
Grade #381 & #382, 17J, 3/4, NI, DR, DMK, OF	65	85	125
Grade #391, 21J, M#15, LS, OF, Adj.5P	300	350	450
Grade #571, 21J, Adj.5P, OF	100	125	175
Grade #572, 19J, Adj.5P, OF	100	125	175
Grade #573, 17J, Adj.5P, OF	90	110	125

14 SIZE

Grade or Name — Description	Avg	Ex-Fn	Mint
Lord Elgin, 17J, SS, OF	$200	$225	$275
7J, M#1, gilded, KW, 14K, HC	300	350	400
7J, M#1, gilded, KW, YGF, HC	75	100	150
11J, M#1, gilded, KW, YGF, HC	75	100	150
11J, M#1, gilded, KW, YGF, OF	50	60	85
13J, M#1, gilded, KW, OF	50	60	85
15J, M#1, gilded, KW, OF	50	60	85
7J, M#2, SW, OF	50	60	85
15J, M#2, SW, OF	60	75	100
15J, M#2, SW, 14K, HC	275	325	375
15J, M#1, Grade # 46, 3/4, KW, HC	75	95	125

12 SIZE

Grade or Name — Description	Avg	Ex -Fn	Mint
Eight Day, 21J, 8-Day Wind Indicator, BRG ★★★★	$2,000	$2,500	$3,000

ELGIN, 14 size, model # 1, grade # 46, 3/4 plate design, key wind and key set, hunting case, serial # 474,414.

Elgin Eight Day, 12 size, 21 jewels, wind indicator, bridge movement, open face, serial number 12,345,678.

Example of a 12 size 17 jewel Elgin with a personalized logo on dial.

Lord Elgin, 12 size, 21 jewels, gold train, gold jewel settings, serial number 24,999,947.

Grade or Name — Description	Avg	Ex-Fn	Mint
Elgin W. Co. #30, 7J, gilded, KW, OF	$45	$55	$85
Elgin W. Co. #189, 19J, HC, NI	75	100	150
Elgin W. Co. #190-194, 23J, OF, GJS, Adj.5P, NI, DMK, GT	125	150	200
Elgin W. Co. #190-194, 23J, HC, GJS, Adj.5P, NI, DMK, GT	150	175	225
Elgin W. Co. #236 & #237, 21J, OF, GJS, Adj.5P, NI, DMK, GT	75	100	150
Elgin W. Co. #236 & #237, 21J, HC, GJS, Adj.5P, NI, DMK, GT	100	125	175
Elgin W. Co. #301 & #302, 7J, HC, NI	50	65	85
Elgin W. Co. #314 & #315, 15J, HC, NI	50	65	85
Elgin W. Co. #383 & #384, 17J, HC, NI	60	70	95
Elgin W. Co., 15J, 14K, Multi-color	500	600	750
Elgin W. Co., 15J, OF, GF	50	60	75
Elgin W. Co., 15J, HC, 14K	300	350	425
Elgin W. Co., 17J, OF, 14K	275	300	350
Elgin W. Co., 19J, HC, 14K	325	375	450
Elgin W. Co., 19J, 14K, OF	275	300	350
C. H. Hulburd, 19J, thin BRG model, 14K case ★	800	1,000	1,200
C. H. Hulburd, 19J, thin BRG model, 18K ★	1,000	1,200	1,400
Lord Elgin, 23J, HC, GJS, DR, Adj.5P, DMK, NI	175	200	275
Lord Elgin, 17J, HC	75	100	150
Lord Elgin, 19J, HC	75	100	150
Lord Elgin, 21J, 14K, OF	275	300	375
Lord Elgin, 21J, HC	75	100	150

☞ Note: Watches listed in this book are priced at the retail level, as complete watches having an original 14k gold-filled case, an original white enamel single sunk dial, and with the entire original movement in good working order with no repairs needed.

☞ Note: Some grades are not included. Their values can be determined by comparing with similar models and grades listed.

Lord Elgin, 12 size, 23 jewels, gold jewel settings, Adj.5p, originally sold for $110.00.

G.M. Wheeler, 12 size, 17 jewels, Adj3p, originally sold for $27.00.

Grade or Name — Description	Avg	Ex-Fn	Mint
Pierce Arrow, 17j, OF	$125	$150	$185
B. W. Raymond, 19J, HC, GJS, Adj.5P, DR, DMK, NI	75	100	125
G. M. Wheeler, 17J, DR, Adj.5P, DMK, NI, OF	45	60	75
G. M. Wheeler, 17J, DR, Adj.5P, DMK, NI, HC	65	90	110
194, 23J, DR, GJS, Adj.5P, DMK, NI, OF	185	200	230

Frances Rubie, Grade 23, 10 size, 15 jewels, key wind & set.

Gail Borden, Grade 22, 10 size, 11 jewels, key wind & set, serial number 947,696.

10 SIZE
(HC)

Grade or Name — Description	Avg	Ex-Fn	Mint
Dexter St., 7J, KW, HC, 14K	$200	$275	$325
Dexter St., 7J, KW, HC, 18K	250	325	375
Dexter St., 7J, gilded, KW, HC, gold filled	50	75	125
Frances Rubie, 15J, gilded, KW, HC, 14K ★	550	600	700
Frances Rubie, 15J, KW, HC, 18K ★★	600	650	750

☞ Note: Watches listed in this book are priced at the retail level, as complete watches having an original 14k gold-filled case, an original white enamel single sunk dial, and with the entire original movement in good working order with no repairs needed.

Grade or Name — Description	Avg	Ex-Fn	Mint
Gail Borden, 11J, gilded, KW, HC, 14K	$200	$275	$325
Gail Borden, 11J, KW, HC, gold filled	50	75	125
Gail Borden, 11J, KW, HC, 18K	250	325	375
Lady Elgin, 15J, gilded, KW, HC, 14K	200	275	325
Lady Elgin, 15J, KW, HC, 18K	250	325	375
G# 21 or 28, 7J, gilded, KW, HC, gold filled	50	75	125
Elgin, multi-color case, gold filled, HC	200	225	275
Elgin, 15J, Silveroid, HC	30	40	50
Elgin, 15J, YGF, HC	55	75	125

Elgin W. Co., Grade 121, 6 size, 15 jewels, hunting, serial number 4,500,445.

Elgin W. Co., Grade 67, 6 size, 11 jewels, serial number 1,149,615.

6 SIZE
(HC Only)

Grade or Name — Description	Avg	Ex-Fn	Mint
Atlas, 7J, HC	$50	$75	$125
Elgin W. Co. #168, 16J, HC	50	75	125
Elgin W. Co. #286, 7J, HC, DMK, NI	50	75	125
Elgin W. Co. #295, 15J, HC, DMK, NI	50	75	125
Elgin W. Co., 7J, HC, 14K	175	225	300
Elgin W. Co., 15J, SW, HC, Enamel case, 18K	800	1,000	1,300
Elgin W. Co., 15J, YGF, HC	50	75	125
Elgin W. Co., 15J, HC, 14K	175	225	300
Elgin W. Co., 15J, HC, 10K	150	175	225
Elgin W. Co., 15J, HC, 18K	250	325	375
Elgin W. Co., 15J, HC, GF multi-color case	200	225	275
Elgin W. Co., 11J, HC, 14K	175	225	300
Elgin W. Co., 15J, demi-HC	75	100	150
Elgin W. Co., 15J, 14K, Multi-color HC	450	500	650

Elgin W. Co., 6 size, 15 jewels

Elgin W. Co., Grade 201-HC, 205-OF, 0 size, 19 jewels, gold train.

Elgin W. Co., Grade 200-HC, 204-OF, 0 size, 17 jewels, gold jewel settings.

0 SIZE

Grade or Name — Description	Avg	Ex-Fn	Mint
Atlas W. Co., 7J, HC	$75	$100	$150
Elgin W. Co., 7J, NI, DR, DMK, OF	35	40	50
Elgin W. Co., 15J, NI, DR, DMK, OF	40	45	55
Elgin W. Co., 15J, NI, DR, DMK, HC	75	100	150
Elgin W. Co., 17J, NI, DR, DMK, ADJ, OF	55	60	80
Elgin W. Co., 19J, NI, DR, DMK, GJS, ADJ, OF	55	75	95
Elgin W. Co., 15J, OF, 14K	135	175	225
Elgin W. Co., 15J, HC, 14K	175	225	300
Elgin W. Co., 15J, HC, multi-color GF	175	200	250
Elgin W. Co., 15J, OF, multi-color dial	100	125	175
Elgin W. Co., 15J, HC, 10K	150	175	225
Elgin W. Co., 15J, 14K, Multi-color case	400	450	525
Elgin W. Co., 15J, 14K, Multi-color case + diamond	500	550	625
Frances Rubie, 19J, HC ★	200	225	300

Lady Elgin, 5/0 size, 17 jewels, gold jewel settings, originally sold for $42.50.

Lady Raymond, 5/0 size, 15 jewels, originally sold for $24.20.

3/0 and 5/0 SIZE
(HC ONLY)

Grade or Name — Description	Avg	Ex-Fn	Mint
Lady Elgin, 15J, PS, HC	$75	$100	$150
Lady Elgin, 15J, 14K, HC	200	225	275
Lady Raymond, 15J, PS, HC	75	100	150
Elgin W. Co., 7J, HC	75	100	150

ELGIN NATIONAL WATCH CO.
IDENTIFICATION OF MOVEMENTS
BY MODEL NUMBER

How to Identify Your Watch: Compare the movement of your watch with the illustrations in this section. Upon matching the movement exactly, the model number and size can be determined. While comparing, note the location of the balance, jewels, screws, gears and type of back plate (Full, ¾, Bridge) which will be clues in identifying the movement you have. Having determined the size and model number, you can now find your watch in the main price listing by name or number (which is engraved on the movement).

Model 1, 18 size, full plate, hunting, key wind & set, first serial number 101, Apr., 1867.

Model 2-4, 18 size, full plate, hunting, lever set, first serial number 155,001, June, 1873.

Model 5, 18 size, full plate, open face, pendant set, first serial number, 2,110,001, Grade 43, Dec., 1885.

Model 6, 18 size, three-quarter plate, hunting, open face, pendant set.

Model 7, 18 size, full plate, open face, lever set, first serial number 6,563,821, Grade 265, Apr., 1897.

Model 8, 18 size, three-quarter plate, open face, lever set, first serial number 8,400,001, Grade 214, Dec., 1900.

Model 8, 18 size, three-quarter plate, open face, lever set with winding indicator.

Model 9, 18 size, three-quarter plate, hunting, lever set, first serial number 9,625,001, Grade 274, May, 1904.

Model 9, 18 size, three-quarter plate, hunting, lever set with winding indicator.

Model 1, 17 size, full plate, hunting, key wind and set.

Model 2, 17 size, full plate, hunting, lever set.

Model 1, 16 size, three-quarter plate, hunting & open face, lever set.

Model 2, 16 size, three-quarter plate, bridge, hunting & open face, lever set.

Model 3, 16 size, three-quarter plate, hunting, lever set, first serial number 625,001, Grade 1, Feb., 1879.

Model 4, 16 size, three-quarter plate, sweep second, hunting & open face, lever set.

Model 5, 16 size, three-quarter plate, open face, pendant set.

Model 5, 16 size, three-quarter plate, open face, pendant set, first serial number 2,811,001, Grade 105, Oct., 1887.

Model 6, 16 size, three-quarter plate, hunting, pendant set, first serial number 6,458,001, Grade 151, Aug., 1895.

Model 6, 16 size, three-quarter plate, bridge, hunting, pendant set, first serial number 6,463,001, Grade 156, May, 1896.

Model 7, 16 size, three-quarter plate, open face, pendant set, first serial number 6,464,001. Grade 157, Sept., 1895.

Model 7, 16 size, three-quarter plate, bridge, open face, pendant set, first serial number 6,469,001, Grade 162, Apr., 1896.

Model 8, 16 size, three-quarter plate, bridge, hunting, lever set, serial number 12,283,001, Grade 341, Jan., 1907.

Model 9, 16 size, three-quarter plate, bridge, open face, lever set, first serial number 9,250,001, Grade 270, July, 1902.

Model 13, 16 size, three-quarter plate, open face, lever set, first serial number 12,717,001, Grade 350, June, 1908.

Model 14, 16 size, three-quarter plate, hunting, lever set.

Model 15, 16 size, three-quarter plate, open face, lever set.

Model 17, 16 size, three-quarter plate, hunting, lever set.

Model 19, 16 size, three-quarter plate, open face, lever set with winding indicator.

Model 20, 16 size, three-quarter plate, open face, Grades 571, 572, 573, 574, 575, 616.

Model 1, 14 size, three-quarter plate, hunting, key wind and set.

Model 2, 14 size, three-quarter plate, open face, pendant set.

Model 1, 12 size, three-quarter plate, hunting, key wind and set.

Model 2, 12 size, three-quarter plate, hunting, pendant set, first serial #7,410,001, Grade 188, Dec., 1897.

Model 2, 12 size, three-quarter plate, spread to 16 size, hunting, pendant set.

Model 3, 12 size, three-quarter plate, open face, pendant set, serial number 7,423,001, Grade 192, May 1898.

Model 3, 12 size, three-quarter plate, spread to 16 size, open face, pendant set.

Model 4, 12 size, three-quarter plate, open face, pendant set, serial number 16,311,001, Grade 392, July, 1912.

Model 1, 10 size, three-quarter plate, style 1, hunting, key wind and set.

Model 2, 10 size, three-quarter plate, hunting, key wind and set.

Model 3, 10 size, three-quarter plate, hunting.

Model 4, 10 size, three-quarter plate, hunting.

Model 5 & 6, 10 size, three-quarter plate.

Model 1, 6 size, three-quarter plate, hunting.

Model 1, 6 size, three-quarter plate, hunting.

Model 2, 6 size, three-quarter plate, hunting.

Model 1, 0 size, three-quarter plate, hunting.

Model 2, 0 size, three-quarter plate, hunting.

Model 2, 0 size, three-quarter plate, hunting.

Model 3, 0 size, three-quarter plate, open face.

Model 3, 0 size, three-quarter plate, open face.

Model 2, 3-0 size, three-quarter plate, hunting.

Charles Fasoldt, 18-20 size, 16 jewels, gold jewel settings, key wind & set, bar movement, serial number 90.

Charles Fasoldt, 18-20 size, 16 jewels, key wind & set, bar movement; note patented regulator, series II.

CHARLES FASOLDT WATCH CO.
Rome, New York   1849 - 1861
Albany, New York   1861 - 1878

Charles Fasoldt came to the United States in 1848. One of his first watches, Serial No. 27, was for General Armstrong and was an eight-day movement. At about that same time, he made several large regulators and a few pocket chronometers. He displayed some of his work at fairs in Utica and Syracuse and received four First-Class Premiums and two diplomas. In 1850, he patented a micrometric regulator (generally called the Howard Regulator because Howard bought the patent). He also patented a chronometer escapement in 1855-1865, a watch regulator in 1864, and a hairspring stud in 1877. He was also known for his tower clocks, for which he received many awards and medals. He made about 500 watches in Albany and about 50 watches in Rome.

Charles Fasoldt, 18-20 size, 16 jewels, stem wind, key set, bar movement, series III.

Charles Fasoldt, 18-20 size, 16 jewels, stem wind, key set, bar movement, series III.

Year	Model	Style	Serial # Range
1855 - 1864	Series I	KW, ½ plate	5- 40
1865 - 1868	Series II	KW, Bar	41-330
1868 - 1878	Series III	SW, Bar	331-540

Grade or Name — Description		Avg	Ex-Fn	Mint
18 — 20 SIZE, 22J, chronograph,dual mainsprings & dual train, GJS, KW or SW, 18K case	★★★★	$10,000	$12,000	$16,000
18 — 20 SIZE, 16J, GJS, KW, KS 18K	★★★	8,000	10,000	14,000
10 — 12 SIZE, 16J, GJS, KW & SW, KS, 14K		3,500	4,000	5,000
Otto H. Fasoldt, 18S, 15J, SW, Swiss made or American		175	200	250

FITCHBURG WATCH CO.
Fitchburg, Massachusetts
1875 - 1878

In 1875 S. Sawyer decided to manufacture watches. He hired personnel from the U. S. Watch Company to build the machinery, but by 1878 the company had failed. It is not known how many, if any, watches were made. The equipment was sold to Cornell and other watch companies.

E.H. Flint dial and movement, 18 size, 4-7 jewels, open face, key wind & set, "Lancaster Pa." on dial, "Patented Sept. 18th,1877" on movement.

E. H. FLINT
Cincinnati, Ohio
1877 - 1879

The Flint watch was patented September 18, 1877, and about 50 watches were made. The serial number is found under the dial.

Grade orName — Description		Avg	Ex-Fn	Mint
18 Size, 4–7J, KW, Full Plate, OF, Coin	★★★	$2,000	$2,500	$3,500
18 Size, 4–7J, KW, Full Plate, 18K, HC	★★★	4,000	4,500	5,500

Fredonia Watch Co., 18 size, 15 jewels, signature on movement "Cyrus N. Gibbs, Mas," key wind & set, serial number 4403.

Fredonia Watch Co., 18 size, 15 jewels, adjusted, serial number 8,368. NOTE: FREDONIA Regulator disc will have teeth all around the disc.

FREDONIA WATCH CO.
Fredonia, New York
1883 - 1885

This company sold the finished movements acquired from the Independent Watch Co. These movements had been made by other companies. The Fredonia Watch Company was sold to the Peoria Watch Co. in 1885, after having produced approximately 20,000 watches.

Chronology of the Development of Fredonia:

Independent Watch Co.	1880 –1883
Fredonia Watch Co.	1883 –1885
Peoria Watch Co.	1885 –1895

Fredonia Watch Co., with a reversible case; changes to either hunting or open face.

Grade or Name — Description	Avg	Ex-Fn	Mint
18S, 7J, SW, OF	$150	$200	$300
18S, 7J, SW, HC	175	225	325
18S, 9J, SW, OF	150	200	300
18S, 9J, SW, HC	175	225	325
18S, 11J, SW, OF	150	200	300
18S, 11J, KW, KS, HC, Coin	175	225	325
18S, 15J, SW, Multi-color, 14K, HC	1,600	1,800	2,200
18S, KW, Reversible case	300	350	450
18S, 15J, SW, LS, Gilt, OF	175	200	300
18S, 15J, straight line escapement, NI	300	350	450
18S, 15J, HC, low serial number	300	350	450
18S, 15J, personalized mvt.	200	250	350
18S, 15J, KW, HC, marked Lakeshore W. Co.	250	300	400

FREEPORT WATCH CO.

Freeport, Illinois
1874 - 1875

Probably less than 20 watches made by Freeport have survived. Their machinery was purchased from Mozart Co., and a Mr. Hoyt was engaged as superintendent. The building erected was destroyed by fire on Oct. 21, 1875. A safe taken from the ruins contained 300 completed movements which were said to be ruined.

Grade or Name — Description		Avg	Ex-Fn	Mint
18S, 19J, KW, SW, gold train, raised gold jewel settings				
18K case	★★★★	$6,000	$7,000	$8,000
18S, 15J, KW, KS, gold train, friction jewels				
18K case	★★★	$5,500	$6,000	$7,000

Freeport Watch Co., Example of a basic movement, 18 size, 15 jewels, key wind & set, pressed jewels, gold train, high grade movement, serial number 11.

SMITH D. FRENCH

Wabash, Indiana
1866 - 1878

On August 21, 1866, Mr. French was issued a patent for an improved escapement for watches. The escape wheel has triangular shaped pins and the lever has two hook-shaped pallets.

The pin wheel escapement was probably first used by Robert Robin, about 1795, for pocket watches. Antoine Tavan also used this style escape wheel around 1800. Mr. French's improved pin wheel and hook shaped lever (about 70 total production) can be seen through a cutout in the plates of his watches.

Illustration from the patent office, patent number 57,310, patented Aug. 21, 1866. Note pin wheel escapement with adjustable hook shaped lever.

Grade or Name — Description		Avg	Ex-Fn	Mint
18S, 15J, 3/4, KW, KS, gilt, pin wheel escapement, Silver case	★★★★	$4,000	$5,500	$6,000
18S, 15J, 3/4, KW, KS, gilt, pin wheel escapement, 18K case	★★★★★	5,000	6,500	8,000

S.D. French, about 18 size, 15 jewels, gilt 3/4 movement, key wind & set, with pin wheel escapement, engraved on movement "S.D. French, Walbash Ind., Aug. 21. 1866, No. 24."

L. Goddard, 55mm, 7 jewels, full plate movement with solid cock, chain driven fusee, flat steel balance, serial number 235, ca. 1809-1817.

LUTHER GODDARD

Shrewsbury, Massachusetts

1809 - 1825

The first significant attempt to produce watches in America was made by Luther Goddard. William H. Keith, who became president of Waltham Watch Co. (1861 -1866) and was once apprenticed to Goddard, said that the hands, dials, round and dovetail brass, steel wire, mainsprings and hairsprings, balance, verge, chains, and pinions were all imported. The plates, wheels, and brass parts were cast at the Goddard shop, however. He also made the cases for his movements which were of the usual style open faced double case-and somewhat in advance of the prevalent style of thick bull's eye watches of the day. About 600 watches were made which were of good quality and more expensive than the imported type. The first watch was produced about 1812 and was sold to the father of ex-governor Lincoln of Worcester, Massachusetts. In 1820 his watches sold for about $60.00.

About 1870 Goddard built a shop one story high with a hip roof about 18' square; it had a lean-to at the back for casting. The building was for making clocks, but a need for watches developed and Goddard made watches there. He earned the distinction of establishing the first watch factory in America.

His movements were marked as follows: L. GODDARD, L.GODDARD & CO., LUTHER GODDARD & SON, P. GODDARD, L. & P. GODDARD, D.P. GODDARD & CO., D. & P. GODDARD.

Frank A. Knowlton purchased the company and operated it until 1933.

Chronology of the Development of Luther Goddard:

Luther Goddard, L. Goddard, L. Goddard & Son 1809-1825

L. Goddard & Son 1817-1825

P.& D. Goddard 1825-1842

D. Goddard & Son 1842-1850

Luther D. Goddard 1850-1857

Goddard & Co. 1857-1860

D. Goddard & Co., Benjamen Goddard 1860-1872

D. Goddard, 18-20, 15 jewels, "Worcester, Mass." on movement, key wind & set, solid balance, under sprung, serial number 8.

L. Goddard & Co.,16-18 size, pair case, open face-thick bulls-eye type, and of high quality for the time.

☞ NOTE: Watches listed below are with original silver cases.

Grade or Name — Description	Avg	Ex-Fn	Mint
Benjamin Goddard	$1,000	$1,200	$1,500
Luther Goddard, S#1-35 with eagle on balance bridge ★★★	5,000	6,000	7,500
Luther Goddard without eagle on cock ★	2,500	3,000	3,500
Luther Goddard,L.Goddard, Luther Goddard & Son ★	2,000	3,200	4,200

L. Goddard & Son. Example of basic movement, about 18 size, open face, pair case; most of the parts are made in America but resemble the English style.

L. Goddard & Son, about 18 size, pair case, verge escapement, engraved on movement "L. Goddard & Son, Shrewsbury," serial number 460.

Grade or Name—Description	Avg	Ex-Fn	Mint
L. Goddard & Co., D. Goddard & Son .... ★	$1,200	$1,400	$1,700
Luther D. Goddard, Goddard & Co., D. Goddard & Co........ ★	1,000	1,200	1,500
P. Goddard, with eagle on cock.. ★	1,000	1,200	1,500
P & D Goddard, 7J.,(Worcester),fusee, KWKS, OF...................	800	900	1,200

JONAS G. HALL

Montpelier, Vermont

1850 - 1870

Millwood Park, Roxbury, Vermont

1870 - 1890

Jonas G. Hall was born in 1822 in Calais, Vermont. He opened a shop in Montpelier where he sold watches, jewelry, silverware, and fancy goods. While at this location, he produced more than 60 full plate, lever style watches. Hall later established a business in Roxbury where he manufactured watch staking tools and other watchmaking tools. At Roxbury, he made at least one watch which was a three-quarter plate model. He also produced a few chronometers, about 20-size with a fusee and detent escapement and a wind indicator on the dial.

Hall was employed by the American Waltham Watch Co. for a short time and helped design the first lady's model. He also worked for Tremont Watch Co., E. Howard & Co., and the United States Watch Co. of Marion, New Jersey.

Style or Name–Description	Avg	Ex-Fn	Mint
18S, 15J, Full plate, KW KS	$1,500	$2,000	$2,800
18S, 15J, 3/4 plate, gilded, KW KS	2,500	3,000	3,600
20S, 15J, Detent Chronometer, KW KS	4,000	5,000	7,500

J.G. Hall, 18 size, 15 jewels, full plate, key wind & set, engraved on movement "J.G. Hall, Montpelier, VT.," serial number 25, ca. 1857.

J.G. Hall, 18 size, 15 jewels, 3/4 plate, key wind and set, engraved on movement "J.G. Hall, Millwood Park, Roxbury, VT," no serial number, ca. 1880.

HAMILTON WATCH CO.

Lancaster, Pennsylvania
December 14, 1892 - Present

Hamilton's roots go back to the Adams & Perry Watch Manufacturing Co. On Sept. 26, 1874, E. F. Bowman made a model watch, and the first movement was produced on April 7, 1876. It was larger than an 18S, or about a 19S. The movement had a snap on dial and the patented stem-setting arrangement. They decided to start making the watches a standard size of 18, and no more than 1,000 of the large-size watches were made. Work had commenced on Sept. 1, 1877, at the Lancaster Watch Co. The watches were designed to sell at a cheaper price than normal. It had a one-piece top 3/4 plate and a pillar plate that was fully ruby-jeweled (4 1/2 pairs). It had a gilt or nickel movement and a new stem-wind device designed by Mosely & Todd. By mid-1878, the Lancaster Watch Co. had made 150 movements. Four grades of watches were produced: Keystone, Fulton, Franklin, and Melrose. In September 1879 the company had manufactured 334 movements. In 1880 some 1,250 movements had been made. In mid-1882, about 17,000 movements had been assembled. All totaled, about 20,000 movements were made.

Grade 936, 18 size, 17 jewels, serial number 1. c. 1893.   Grade 936, 18 size, 17 jewels, serial number 2, c. 1893.

The first Hamilton movement to be sold was No. 15 to W. C. Davis on January 31, 1893. The No. 1 movement was finished on April 25, 1896, and was never sold. The No. 2 was finished on April 25, 1893, and was shipped to Smythe & Ashe of Rochester, N. Y. Nos. 1 & 2 are at the N.A.W.C.C. museum.

Chronology of the Development of Hamilton:

Adams & Perry Watch Co.	Sept. 1874-May 1876
Lancaster, Pa., Watch Co.	Aug. 1877-Oct. 1887
Lancaster, Pa., Watch Co.	Nov. 1877-May 1879
Lancaster Watch Co.	May 1883-1886
Keystone Standard Watch Co.	1886-1890
Hamilton Watch Co.	Dec. 14, 1892-1969

In 1893 the first watch was produced with the Hamilton label. The watches became very popular with railroad men and by 1923 some 53 percent of Hamilton's production were railroad watches. The 940 model watch was discontinued in 1910. Most Hamilton movements were fitted

Grade 937, 18 size, 17 jewels, hunting case. Note serial   Hamilton Watch Co., 18 size, 7 jewels, serial number
number 1047. Hunting case models began with 1001.   2934.

with a 42-hour mainspring. The Elinvar hairspring was patented in 1931 and used in all movements thereafter. On October 15, 1940, Hamilton introduced the 992B which were fitted with the Elinvar hairspring. Elinvar and Invar are tradenames and are the same 36 percent nickel steel. Although the Hamilton Watch Co. is still in business today making modern type watches, they last produced Americanmade watches in 1969.

HAMILTON ESTIMATED SERIAL NUMBERS
AND PRODUCTION DATES

Date	Serial No.	Date	Serial No.	Date	Serial No.	Date	Serial No.
1893	1-2,000	1906	590,000	1919	1,700,000	1932	2,500,000
1894	5,000	1907	756,000	1920	1,790,000	1933	2,600,000
1895	10,000	1908	921,000	1921	1,860,000	1934	2,700,000
1896	14,000	1909	1,087,000	1922	1,900,000	1935	2,800,000
1897	20,000	1910	1,050,500	1923	1,950,000	1936	2,900,000
1898	30,000	1911	1,290,500	1924	2,000,000	1937	3,000,000
1899	40,000	1912	1,331,000	1925	2,100,000	1938	3,200,000
1900	50,000	1913	1,370,000	1926	2,200,000	1939	3,400,000
1901	90,000	1914	1,410,500	1927	2,250,000	1940	3,600,000
1902	150,000	1915	1,450,500	1928	2,300,000	1941	3,800,000
1903	260,000	1916	1,517,000	1929	2,350,000	1942	4,025,000
1904	340,000	1917	1,580,000	1930	2,400,000		
1905	425,000	1918	1,650,000	1931	2,450,000		

NOTE: The serial numbers and dates listed above are only close approximations. The actual date of your watch could vary 2 to 3 years from the listed date.

The Hamilton Masterpiece

The adjoining illustration shows the Masterpiece in a platinum case. The dial is sterling silver with raised gold numbers and solid gold hands. This watch sold for $685.00 in 1930. All 922 MP Models included the following: 23 jewels, were adjusted to heat, cold, isochronism, and five positions, with a motor barrel, solid gold train, steel escape wheel, double roller, sapphire pallets and a micrometric regulator.

HAMILTON SERIAL NUMBERS AND GRADES

To help determine the size and grade of your watch, the following serial number list is provided. Serial numbers 30,001 through 32,000, which are omitted from the list, were not listed by Hamilton. To identify your watch, simply look up its serial number which will identify the grade. After determining the grade, your watch can be easily located in the pricing section.

Serial	Grade	Serial	Grade	Serial	Grade	Serial	Grade
1-20	936	27001-28000	929	56801-900	974	73001-200	975
21-30	932	28001-29000	999	56901-57000	976	73201-300	973
31-60	936	29001-800	927	57001-300	977	73301-74000	977
61-400	932	29801-30000	935	57301-500	975	74001-400	974
401-1000	936	32001-300	926	57501-600	973	74401-600	972
1001-20	937	32301-700	930	57601-800	975	74601-75000	976
1021-30	933	32701-33000	934	57801-58000	977	75001-76799	HWW*
1031-60	937	33001-500	931	58001-100	972	76002-76800	HWW*
1061-1100	933	33501-800	927	58101-200	974	77001-100	969
1101-300	937	33801-34000	935	58201-300	972	77101-300	973
1301-600	933	34001-500	928	58301-400	966	77301-500	975
1601-2000	937	34501-700	930	58401-500	976	77501-600	971
2001-3000	7J	34701-800	926	58501-600	972	77601-700	973
3001-100	931	34801-35000	934	58601-800	974	77701-900	975
3101-500	935	35001-800	931	58801-59000	976	77901-78000	977
3501-600	931	35801-36000	935	59001-300	973	78001-500	970
3601-900	935	36001-37000	928	59301-500	967	78501-700	972
3901-4000	931	37001-38000	929	59501-700	975	78701-900	974
4001-300	930	38001-500	926	59701-60000	977	78901-79000	976
4301-5100	934	38501-600	930	60001-500	976	79001-100	973
5101-400	926	38601-900	934	60501-700	974	79101-300	975
5401-600	934	38901-39000	926	60701-61000	976	79301-700	977
5601-6000	930	39001-200	931	61001-200	975	79701-900	975
6001-700	936	39201-500	935	61201-500	977	79901-80000	973
6601-700	938	39501-700	927	61501-600	973	80001-200	972
6701-800	936	39701-900	935	61601-800	975	80201-400	974
6801-7000	932	39901-40000	931	61801-62000	977	80401-600	970
7001-10	17J	40001-200	930	62001-100	972	80601-700	972
7011-600	937	40201-500	934	62101-300	974	80701-900	974
7601-700	939	40501-41000	926	62301-500	976	80901-81000	976
7701-800	937	41001-500	929	62501-700	974	81001-300	961
7801-8000	933	41501-42000	927	62701-900	972	81301-500	965
8001-700	936	42001-43000	999	62901-63000	974	81501-82000	961
8701-800	938	43001-300	941	63001-500	977	82001-300	972
8801-9000	936	43301-500	943	63501-600	975	82301-500	974
9001-300	937	43501-700	937	63601-800	977	82501-600	970
9301-600	939	43701-900	941	63801-900	975	82601-700	972
9601-800	937	43901-44000	943	63901-64000	973	82701-800	974
9801-900	933	44001-02	21J	64001-100	976	82801-900	968
9901-10000	939	44003-400	938	64101-200	972	82901-83000	976
10001-200	938	44401-500	942	64201-300	974	83001-400	977
10201-400	936	44501-45000	936	64301-600	972	83401-500	971
10401-50	932	45001-46000	929	64601-700	976	83501-700	975
10451-500	936	46001-500	926	64701-900	974	83701-800	973
10501-700	938	46501-800	934	64901-65000	976	83801-900	975
10701-900	936	46801-47000	930	65001-200	973	83901-84000	969
10901-11000	938	47001-500	927	65201-300	977	84001-400	974
11001-12000	936	47501-700	935	65301-400	975	84401-500	970
12001-200	939	47701-48000	931	65401-500	973	84501-700	972
12201-13000	937	48001-05	942	65501-700	977	84701-800	968
13001-400	999	48006-300	940	65701-900	975	84801-85000	976
13401-14000	938	48301-500	942	65901-66000	977	85001-200	937
14001-15000	999	48501-900	940	66001-200	976	85201-900	941
15001-300	939	48901-49000	942	66201-300	974	85901-86000	943
15301-15401	21J	49001-400	927	66301-500	972	86001-87000	928
15302-700	937	49401-900	925	66501-600	976	87001-88000	929
15701-16000	939	49901-50	11J	66601-700	974	88001-500	926
16001-100	931	50071-500	962	66701-800	972	88501-89000	930
16101-200	930	50501-750	960	66801-67000	974	89001-500	941
16201-300	927	50751-50850	964	67001-100	977	89501-90000	937
16301-400	931	50851-51000	960	67101-300	975	90001-100	926
16401-600	927	51001-51300	16s	67301-600	973	90101-950	999
16601-17000	931	51301-400	963	67601-800	975	91001-92000	925
17001-500	929	51401-650	961	67801-68000	977	92001-200	940
17501-18000	931	51651-750	965	68001-800	960	92201-93000	936
18001-200	928	51751-52000	961	68801-69000	964	93001-94000	927
18201-300	926	52001-300	16s	69001-100	977	94001-003	934
18301-500	928	52301-500	976	69101-200	975	94004-95000	928
18501-19500	930	52501-700	974	69201-400	973	95001-96000	923
19501-700	926	52701-800	966	69401-600	975	96001-100	942
19701-20000	930	52801-53000	976	69601-70000	977	96101-700	940
20001-300	934	53001-53070	16s	70001-200	976	96701-97000	936
20301-500	926	53071-53500	977	70201-400	970	97001-900	929
20501-21000	999	53501-900	975	70401-600	968	97901-98000	927
21001-300	935	53901-54000	967	70601-900	972	98001-99000	924
21301-500	927	54001-200	972	70901-71000	974	99001-100000	925
21501-800	935	54201-300	974	71001-200	975	100001-101000	924
21801-22500	927	54301-500	976	71201-500	971	101001-102000	925
22501-800	931	54501-700	974	71501-700	975	102001-103000	922
22801-23000	935	54701-800	968	71701-90	973	103001-104000	927
23001-200	928	54801-55000	976	71791-800	969	104001-105000	940
23201-500	7J	55001-300	973	71801-900	977	105001-500	925
24001-500	926	55301-600	977	71901-72000	974	105501-106000	927
24501-25000	934	55601-700	969	72001-100	976	106001-107000	940
25001-100	11J	55701-800	977	72101-300	974	107001-400	941
25101-400	927	55801-56000	975	72301-600	974	107401-500	943
25401-800	931	56001-300	974	72601-700	968	107501-800	941
25801-26000	935	56301-500	976	72701-900	976	107801-108000	943
26001-500	930	56501-600	966	72901-73000	972	108001-200	928
26501-27000	928	56601-800	972				

108201-109000	926	186001-187000	942	275202-460	HWW*	322001-323000	974
109001-500	927	187001-188000	927	275462-500	HWW*	323001-700	975
109501-110000	925	188001-189000	924	276001-277000	940	323701-324000	973
110001-900	940	189001-190000	925	277001-278000	941	324001-325000	960
110901-111000	942	190001-191000	926	278001-279000	940	325001-100	965
111001-500	937	191001-192000	927	279001-280000	925	325101-326000	961
111501-112000	941	192001-193000	924	280001-281000	936	326001-327000	974
112001-200	928	193001-194000	925	281001-282000	927	327001-300	971
112201-113000	926	194001-195000	926	282001-283000	926	327301-500	973
113001-114000	925	195001-500	935	283001-284000	925	327501-328000	975
114001-003	940	195501-196000	927	284001-500	934	328001-300	992
114004-115000	936	196001-197000	926	284501-900	924	328301-500	990
115001-116000	927	197001-198000	937	284901-285000	999	328501-329000	992
116001-117000	940	198001-199000	936	285001-286000	925	329001-330000	975
117001-118000	925	199001-200000	925	286001-287000	940	330001-100	992
118001-119000	999	200001-201000	926	287001-288000	927	330101-500	990
119001-120000	925	201001-202000	925	288001-289000	940	330501-331000	992
120001-121000	924	202001-500	926	289001-290000	927	331001-200	973
121001-500	941	202501-203000	934	290001-800	936	331201-400	975
121501-122000	943	203001-204000	927	290801-291000	938	331401-500	969
122001-300	940	204001-100	934	291001-292000	925	331501-700	971
122301-400	942	204101-500	926	292001-500	940	331701-800	973
122401-123000	940	204501-205000	934	292501-293000	942	331801-332000	975
123001-124000	941	205001-206000	941	293001-294000	925	332001-200	992
124001-100	942	206001-207000	940	294001-295000	926	332201-800	972
124101-800	940	207001-208000	927	295001-296000	927	332801-333000	974
124801-125000	942	208001-900	999	296001-297000	940	333001-500	975
125001-126000	927	208901-209000	940	297001-298000	927	333501-700	971
126001-127000	924	209001-210000	925	298001-299000	940	333701-900	973
127001-128000	941	210001-211000	940	299001-300000	925	333901-334000	975
128001-129000	936	211001-212000	927	300001-300	972	334001-200	972
129001-130000	925	212001-213000	940	300301-500	970	334201-800	992
130001-500	924	213001-500	941	300501-900	974	334801-335000	990
130501-131000	926	213501-600	937	300901-301000	968	335001-600	975
131001-132000	925	213601-214000	925	301001-400	975	335601-800	971
132001-100	926	214001-215000	924	301401-500	971	335801-900	973
132101-200	934	215001-216000	927	301501-302000	973	335901-336000	975
132201-500	926	216001-217000	940	302001-100	990	336001-200	972
132501-133000	924	217001-218000	927	302101-200	992	336201-337000	974
133001-134000	937	218001-219000	940	302201-300	990	337001-338000	975
134001-135000	924	219001-220000	925	302301-900	992	338001-200	974
135001-136000	925	220001-221000	924	302901-303000	990	338201-900	992
136001-137000	926	221001-222000	927	303001-100	973	338901-339000	990
137001-100	11J	222001-223000	926	303101-300	975	339001-300	971
137101-138000	927	223001-02	927	303301-800	975	339301-500	973
138001-139000	940	223003-04	941	303801-304000	973	339501-340000	975
139001-140000	937	223005	937	304001-100	970	340001-200	974
140001-300	938	223006-224000	927	304101-400	972	340201-300	972
140301-141000	942	224001-225000	924	304401-305000	974	340301-600	970
141001-142000	941	225001-226000	927	305001-100	973	340601-341000	974
142001-143000	940	226001-227000	940	305101-200	971	341001-200	973
143001-100	927	227001-228000	925	305201-300	969	341201-342000	975
143101-144000	925	228001-229000	924	305301-900	975	342001-300	990
144001-145000	924	229001-230000	925	305901-306000	973	342301-343000	992
145001-146000	925	230001-500	926	306001-400	972	343001-344000	975
146001-400	934	230501-231000	924	306401-307000	974	344001-200	970
146401-147000	924	231001-565	937	307001-100	975	344201-400	972
147001-148000	927	231566-232000	927	307101-300	971	344401-345000	974
148001-149000	940	232001-233000	940	307301-400	975	345001-346000	975
149001-150000	925	233001-234000	941	307401-500	973	346001-300	992
150001-151000	924	234001-235000	940	307501-600	975	346301-347000	974
151001-400	927	235001-236000	941	307601-700	971	347001-180	993
151401-500	935	236001-237000	936	307701-900	975	347181-200	991
151501-152000	927	237001-238000	941	307901-308000	969	347201-300	975
152001-153000	936	238001-239000	926	308001-700	990	347301-400	973
153001-154000	941	239001-500	943	308701-309000	992	347401-700	993
154001-155000	936	239501-240000	941	309001-100	971	347701-900	991
155001-156000	927	240001-241000	940	309101-400	973	347901-348000	973
156001-157000	940	241001-242000	941	309401-310000	975	348001-200	975
157001-158000	925	242001-243000	940	310001-400	970	348201-800	974
158001-159000	940	243001-244000	927	310401-311000	974	348801-349000	972
159001-160000	941	244001-245000	936	311001-700	975	349001-350000	975
160001-161000	940	245001-246000	925	311701-312000	973	350001-300	990
161001-162000	941	246001-247000	940	312001-200	970	350301-400	974
162001-163000	926	247001-248000	927	312201-500	972	350401-600	990
163001-164000	943	248001-249000	940	312501-600	968	350601-351000	992
164001-165000	940	249001-250000	927	312601-313000	974	351001-352000	975
165001-166000	925	250001-251000	926	313001-100	973	352001-100	968
166001-167000	924	251001-252000	927	313101-400	971	352101-353000	974
167001-168000	927	252001-253000	924	313401-600	969	353001-354000	975
168001-169000	940	253001-254000	925	313601-314000	975	354001-400	992
169001-400	935	254001-255000	940	314001-600	974	354401-355000	974
169401-170000	927	255001-256000	925	314601-900	972	355001-800	973
170001-171000	999	256001-257000	926	314901-315000	970	355801-900	993
171001-172000	925	257001-258000	941	315001-100	971	355901-356000	993
172001-100	934	258001-259000	924	315101-400	973	356001-500	990
172101-173000	926	259001-260000	941	315401-316000	975	356501-357000	974
173001-174000	924	260001-261000	940	316001-200	992	357001-358000	975
174001-175000	924	261001-262000	927	316201-300	972	358001-359000	975
175002-176000	HWW*	262001-263000	926	316301-500	992	359001-360000	975
176001-699	HWW*	263001-264000	927	316501-317000	972	360001-550	960
176001-177000	940	264001-265000	940	317001-600	975	360801-361000	960
177001-178000	927	265001-266000	927	317601-700	969	361001-100	993
178001-179000	942	266001-267000	940	317701-318000	973	361101-300	991
179001-500	935	267001-268000	925	318001-100	972	361301-400	993
179501-180000	927	268001-269000	940	318101-900	974	361401-700	975
180001-181000	940	269001-270000	927	318901-319000	970	361701-20	973
181001-182000	941	270001-271000	940	319001-100	971	361721-362000	975
182001-300	926	271001-272000	925	319101-320000	975	362001-900	974
182301-400	934	272001-273000	926	320001-300	972	362901-363000	990
182401-183000	926	273001-274000	941	320301-400	968	363001-364000	975
183001-184000	941	274001-275000	924	320401-321000	974	364001-365000	974
184001-185000	940	275002-100	HWW*	321001-200	973	365001-100	975
185001-186000	925	275102-200	HWW*	321201-322000	975	365101-300	973

HAMILTON SERIAL NUMBERS AND GRADES

To help determine the size and grade of your watch, the following serial number list is provided. Serial numbers 30,001 through 32,000, which are omitted from the list, were not listed by Hamilton. To identify your watch, simply look up its serial number which will identify the grade. After determining the grade, your watch can be easily located in the pricing section.

Serial	Grade	Serial	Grade	Serial	Grade	Serial	Grade
1-20	936	27001-28000	929	56801-900	974	73001-200	975
21-30	932	28001-29000	999	56901-57000	976	73201-300	973
31-60	936	29001-800	927	57001-300	977	73301-74000	977
61-400	932	29801-30000	935	57301-500	975	74001-400	974
401-1000	936	32001-300	926	57501-600	973	74401-600	972
1001-20	937	32301-700	930	57601-800	975	74601-75000	976
1021-30	933	32701-33000	934	57801-58000	977	75001-76799	HWW*
1031-60	937	33001-500	931	58001-100	972	76002-76800	HWW*
1061-1100	933	33501-800	927	58101-200	974	77001-100	969
1101-300	937	33801-34000	935	58201-300	972	77101-300	973
1301-600	933	34001-500	928	58301-400	968	77301-500	975
1601-2000	937	34501-700	930	58401-500	976	77501-600	971
2001-3000	7J	34701-800	926	58501-600	972	77601-700	973
3001-100	931	34801-35000	934	58601-800	974	77701-900	975
3101-500	935	35001-800	931	58801-59000	976	77901-78000	977
3501-600	931	35801-36000	935	59001-300	973	78001-500	970
3601-900	935	36001-37000	928	59301-500	967	78501-700	972
3901-4000	931	37001-38000	929	59501-700	975	78701-900	974
4001-300	930	38001-500	926	59701-60000	977	78901-79000	976
4301-5100	934	38501-600	930	60001-500	976	79001-100	973
5101-400	926	38601-900	934	60501-700	974	79101-300	975
5401-600	934	38901-39000	926	60701-61000	976	79301-700	977
5601-6000	930	39001-200	931	61001-200	975	79701-900	975
6001-600	936	39201-500	935	61201-500	977	79901-80000	973
6601-700	938	39501-700	927	61501-600	973	80001-200	972
6701-800	936	39701-900	935	61601-800	975	80201-400	974
6801-7000	932	39901-40000	931	61801-62000	977	80401-600	970
7001-10	17J	40001-200	930	62001-100	972	80601-700	972
7011-600	937	40201-500	934	62101-300	974	80701-900	974
7601-700	939	40501-41000	926	62301-500	976	80901-81000	976
7701-800	937	41001-500	929	62501-700	974	81001-300	961
7801-8000	933	41501-42000	927	62701-900	972	81301-500	965
8001-700	936	42001-43000	999	62901-63000	974	81501-82000	961
8701-800	936	43001-300	941	63001-500	977	82001-300	972
8801-9000	938	43301-500	943	63501-600	975	82301-500	974
9001-300	937	43501-700	937	63601-800	977	82501-600	970
9301-600	939	43701-900	941	63801-900	975	82601-700	972
9601-800	937	43901-44000	943	63901-64000	973	82701-800	974
9801-900	933	44001-02	21J	64001-100	976	82801-900	968
9901-10000	939	44003-400	938	64101-200	972	82901-83000	976
10001-200	938	44401-500	942	64201-300	974	83001-400	977
10201-400	936	44501-45000	936	64301-600	972	83401-500	971
10401-50	932	45001-46000	929	64601-700	976	83501-700	975
10451-500	936	46001-500	926	64701-900	974	83701-800	973
10501-700	938	46501-800	934	64901-65000	976	83801-900	975
10701-900	936	46801-47000	930	65001-200	973	83901-84000	969
10901-11000	938	47001-500	927	65201-300	977	84001-400	974
11001-12000	936	47501-700	935	65301-400	975	84401-500	970
12001-200	939	47701-48000	931	65401-500	973	84501-700	972
12201-13000	937	48001-05	942	65501-700	977	84701-800	968
13001-400	999	48006-300	940	65701-900	975	84801-85000	976
13401-14000	938	48301-500	942	65901-66000	977	85001-200	937
14001-15000	999	48501-900	940	66001-200	976	85201-900	941
15001-300	939	48901-49000	942	66201-300	974	85901-86000	943
15301-15401	21J	49001-400	927	66301-500	972	86001-87000	928
15302-700	937	49401-900	925	66501-600	976	87001-88000	929
15701-16000	939	49901-50	11J	66601-700	974	88001-500	928
16001-100	931	50071-500	962	66701-800	972	88501-89000	930
16101-200	930	50501-750	960	66801-67000	974	89001-500	941
16201-300	927	50751-50850	964	67001-100	977	89501-90000	937
16301-400	931	50851-51000	960	67101-300	975	90001-100	926
16401-600	927	51001-51300	16s	67301-600	973	90101-950	999
16601-17000	931	51301-400	963	67601-800	975	91001-92000	925
17001-500	929	51401-650	961	67801-68000	977	92001-200	940
17501-18000	931	51651-750	965	68001-800	960	92201-93000	936
18001-200	928	51751-52000	961	68801-69000	964	93001-94000	927
18201-300	926	52001-300	16s	69001-100	977	94001-003	934
18301-500	928	52301-500	976	69101-200	975	94004-95000	928
18501-19500	930	52501-700	974	69201-400	973	95001-96000	923
19501-700	926	52701-800	966	69401-600	975	96001-100	942
19701-20000	930	52801-53000	976	69601-70000	977	96101-700	940
20001-300	934	53001-53070	16s	70001-200	976	96701-97000	936
20301-500	926	53071-53500	977	70201-400	970	97001-900	929
20501-21000	999	53501-900	975	70401-600	968	97901-98000	927
21001-300	935	53901-54000	967	70601-900	972	98001-99000	924
21301-500	927	54001-200	972	70901-71000	974	99001-100000	925
21501-800	935	54201-300	974	71001-200	975	100001-101000	924
21801-22500	927	54301-500	976	71201-500	971	101001-102000	925
22501-800	931	54501-700	974	71501-700	975	102001-103000	922
22801-23000	935	54701-800	968	71701-90	973	103001-104000	927
23001-200	928	54801-55000	976	71791-800	969	104001-105000	940
23201-500	7J	55001-300	973	71801-900	977	105001-500	925
24001-500	926	55301-600	977	71901-72000	975	105501-106000	927
24501-25000	934	55601-700	969	72001-100	974	106001-107000	940
25001-100	11J	55701-800	977	72101-300	976	107001-400	941
25101-400	927	55801-56000	975	72301-600	974	107401-500	943
25401-800	931	56001-300	974	72601-700	968	107501-800	941
25801-26000	935	56301-500	976	72701-900	976	107801-108000	943
26001-500	930	56501-600	966	72901-73000	972	108001-200	928
26501-27000	928	56601-800	972				

108201-109000	926
109001-500	927
109501-110000	925
110001-900	940
110901-111000	942
111001-500	937
111501-112000	941
112001-200	928
112201-113000	926
113001-114000	925
114001-003	940
114004-115000	936
115001-116000	927
116001-117000	940
117001-118000	925
118001-119000	999
119001-120000	925
120001-121000	924
121001-500	941
121501-122000	943
122001-300	940
122301-400	942
122401-123000	940
123001-124000	941
124001-100	942
124101-800	940
124801-125000	942
125001-126000	927
126001-127000	924
127001-128000	941
128001-129000	936
129001-130000	925
130001-500	924
130501-131000	926
131001-132000	925
132001-100	926
132101-200	934
132201-500	926
132501-133000	924
133001-134000	937
134001-135000	924
135001-136000	925
136001-137000	926
137001-100	11J
137101-138000	927
138001-139000	940
139001-140000	937
140001-300	938
140301-141000	942
141001-142000	941
142001-143000	940
143001-100	927
143101-144000	925
144001-145000	924
145001-146000	925
146001-400	934
146401-147000	924
147001-148000	927
148001-149000	940
149001-150000	925
150001-151000	924
151001-400	927
151401-500	935
151501-152000	927
152001-153000	936
153001-154000	941
154001-155000	936
155001-156000	927
156001-157000	940
157001-158000	925
158001-159000	940
159001-160000	941
160001-161000	940
161001-162000	941
162001-163000	926
163001-164000	943
164001-165000	940
165001-166000	925
166001-167000	924
167001-168000	927
168001-169000	940
169001-400	935
169401-170000	927
170001-171000	999
171001-172000	925
172001-100	934
172101-173000	926
173001-174000	925
174001-175000	924
175002-176000	HWW*
175001-699	HWW*
176001-177000	940
177001-178000	927
178001-179000	942
179001-500	935
179501-180000	927
180001-181000	940
181001-182000	941
182001-300	926
182301-400	934
182401-183000	926
183001-184000	941
184001-185000	940
185001-186000	925
186001-187000	942
187001-188000	927
188001-189000	924
189001-190000	925
190001-191000	926
191001-192000	924
192001-193000	924
193001-194000	925
194001-195000	926
195001-500	935
195501-196000	927
196001-197000	926
197001-198000	937
198001-199000	936
199001-200000	925
200001-201000	926
201001-202000	925
202001-500	926
202501-203000	934
203001-204000	927
204001-100	934
204101-500	926
204501-205000	934
205001-206000	941
206001-207000	940
207001-208000	927
208001-900	999
208901-209000	940
209001-210000	925
210001-211000	940
211001-212000	927
212001-213000	940
213001-500	941
213501-600	937
213601-214000	925
214001-215000	924
215001-216000	927
216001-217000	940
217001-218000	937
218001-219000	940
219001-220000	925
220001-221000	924
221001-222000	927
222001-223000	926
223001-02	927
223003-04	941
223005	937
223006-224000	927
224001-225000	924
225001-226000	927
226001-227000	940
227001-228000	925
228001-229000	924
229001-230000	925
230001-500	926
230501-231000	924
231001-565	937
231566-232000	927
232001-233000	940
233001-234000	941
234001-235000	940
235001-236000	941
236001-237000	936
237001-238000	941
238001-239000	926
239001-500	943
239501-240000	941
240001-241000	940
241001-242000	941
242001-243000	940
243001-244000	927
244001-245000	936
245001-246000	925
246001-247000	940
247001-248000	927
248001-249000	940
249001-250000	927
250001-251000	926
251001-252000	927
252001-253000	924
253001-254000	925
254001-255000	940
255001-256000	925
256001-257000	926
257001-258000	941
258001-259000	924
259001-260000	941
260001-261000	940
261001-262000	927
262001-263000	926
263001-264000	925
264001-265000	940
265001-266000	927
266001-267000	940
267001-268000	925
268001-269000	940
269001-270000	927
270001-271000	940
271001-272000	925
272001-273000	926
273001-274000	941
274001-275000	927
275002-100	HWW*
275102-200	HWW*
275202-460	HWW*
275462-500	HWW*
276001-277000	940
277001-278000	941
278001-279000	940
279001-280000	925
280001-281000	936
281001-282000	927
282001-283000	926
283001-284000	925
284001-500	934
284501-900	924
284901-285000	999
285001-286000	925
286001-287000	940
287001-288000	927
288001-289000	940
289001-290000	927
290001-800	936
290801-291000	938
291001-292000	925
292001-500	940
292501-293000	942
293001-294000	925
294001-295000	926
295001-296000	927
296001-297000	940
297001-298000	927
298001-299000	940
299001-300000	925
300001-300	927
300301-500	970
300501-900	974
300901-301000	968
301001-400	975
301401-500	971
301501-302000	973
302001-100	990
302101-200	992
302201-300	990
302301-900	992
302901-303000	990
303001-100	973
303101-300	971
303301-800	975
303801-304000	973
304001-100	970
304101-400	972
304401-305000	974
305001-100	973
305101-200	971
305201-300	969
305301-900	975
305501-306000	973
306001-400	972
306401-307000	974
307001-100	975
307101-300	971
307301-400	975
307401-500	973
307501-600	975
307601-700	971
307701-900	975
307901-308000	969
308001-700	990
308701-309000	992
309001-100	971
309101-400	973
309401-310000	975
310001-400	970
310401-311000	974
311001-700	975
311701-312000	973
312001-200	970
312201-500	972
312501-600	968
312601-313000	974
313001-100	973
313101-400	971
313401-600	969
313601-314000	975
314001-600	974
314601-900	972
314901-315000	970
315001-100	971
315101-400	973
315401-316000	975
316001-200	992
316201-300	972
316301-500	992
316501-317000	972
317001-600	975
317601-700	969
317701-318000	973
318001-100	972
318101-900	974
318901-319000	970
319001-100	971
319101-320000	975
320001-300	972
320301-400	968
320401-321000	974
321001-200	973
321201-322000	975
322001-323000	974
323001-700	975
323701-324000	973
324001-325000	960
325001-100	965
325101-326000	961
326001-327000	974
327001-300	971
327301-500	973
327501-328000	975
328001-300	992
328301-500	990
328501-329000	992
329001-330000	975
330001-100	992
330101-500	990
330501-331000	992
331001-200	973
331201-400	975
331401-500	969
331501-700	971
331701-800	973
331801-332000	975
332001-200	992
332201-800	972
332801-333000	974
333001-500	975
333501-700	971
333701-900	973
333901-334000	975
334001-200	972
334201-800	990
334801-335000	992
335001-600	975
335601-800	971
335801-900	973
335901-336000	975
336001-200	972
336201-337000	974
337001-338000	975
338001-200	974
338201-900	992
338901-339000	990
339001-300	971
339301-500	973
339501-340000	975
340001-200	974
340201-300	972
340301-600	970
340601-341000	974
341001-200	973
341201-342000	975
342001-300	990
342301-343000	992
343001-344000	975
344001-200	970
344201-400	972
344401-345000	974
345001-346000	975
346001-300	992
346301-347000	974
347001-180	993
347181-200	991
347201-300	975
347301-400	973
347401-700	993
347701-900	991
347901-348000	973
348001-200	970
348201-300	974
348801-349000	972
349001-350000	975
350001-300	990
350301-400	974
350401-600	990
350601-351000	992
351001-352000	975
352001-100	968
352101-353000	974
353001-354000	975
354001-400	992
354401-355000	974
355001-800	975
355801-900	973
355901-356000	993
356001-500	990
356501-357000	974
357001-358000	975
358001-359000	974
359001-360000	975
360001-550	960
360580-361000	960
361001-100	993
361101-300	991
361301-400	993
361401-700	975
361701-20	973
361721-362000	975
362001-900	990
362901-363000	990
363001-364000	975
364001-365000	974
365001-100	975
365101-300	973

Serial Numbers	Grade
365301-366000	975
366001-367000	974
367001-500	975
367501-368000	993
368001-369000	974
369001-370000	992
370001-100	990
370101-400	992
370401-500	974
370501-800	990
370801-371400	992
371401-500	972
371501-373500	974
373501-700	990
373701-374000	992
374001-200	974
374201-700	990
374701-375000	974
375001-100	993
375101-500	991
375501-376000	975
376001-200	972
376201-500	974
376501-377000	992
377001-200	973
377201-378000	975
377801-379000	974
379001-380080	992
380801-381000	990
381001-382000	992
382001-100	990
382101-383000	974
383001-300	992
383301-700	990
383701-384000	972
384001-700	974
384701-900	972
384901-385000	974
385001-600	972
385601-800	974
385801-386000	990
386001-800	974
386801-900	992
386901-387000	972
387001-100	990
387101-900	992
387901-388000	972
388001-400	990
388401-389000	992
389001-391000	974
391001-300	972
391301-392000	974
392001-800	992
392801-393000	990
393001-400	975
393401-600	973
393601-394000	993
394001-200	972
394201-395000	974
395001-100	993
395101-900	991
395901-396000	993
396001-397000	992
397001-200	990
397201-398000	992
398001-200	972
398201-399000	992
399001-600	993
399601-400000	975
400001-401000	924
401001-402000	940
402001-404000	924
404001-405000	926
405001-406000	924
406001-407000	940
407001-408000	926
408001-416000	940
416001-417000	926
417001-418000	940
418001-419000	926
419001-420000	941
420001-421000	940
421001-422000	926
422001-423000	924
423001-425000	926
425001-426000	924
426001-500	936
426501-427000	944
427001-428000	924
428001-429000	926
429001-430000	925
430001-431000	924
431001-432000	925
432001-433000	940
433001-434000	924
434001-500	940
434501-600	942
434601-435000	946
435001-436000	924
436001-438500	940
438501-800	946
438801-900	942
438901-440000	946
440001-441000	924
441001-442000	940
442001-400	946
442401-500	942
442501-443000	946
443001-444000	926
444001-445000	924
445001-446000	927
446001-447000	924
447001-448000	925
448001-449000	926
449001-450000	924
450001-451000	926
451001-452000	925
452001-453000	940
453001-454000	924
454001-456000	940
456001-457000	999
457001-458000	940
458001-459000	999
459001-110	946
459111-118	942
459119-200	946
459201-700	942
459701-460000	946
460001-461900	940
461901-462000	940
462001-463000	940
463001-500	940
463501-464000	940
464001-466000	926
466001-467000	924
467001-468000	926
468001-469000	940
469001-470000	924
470001-471000	926
471001-472000	946
472001-473000	924
473001-474000	940
474001-475000	924
475001-476000	940
476001-477000	924
477001-478000	940
478001-479000	926
479001-480000	944
480001-481000	926
481001-482000	927
482001-483000	924
483001-484000	926
484001-485000	940
485001-486000	925
486001-487000	999
487001-488000	924
488001-489000	999
489001-492000	924
492001-493000	940
493001-494000	946
494001-495000	944
495001-496000	940
496001-497000	925
497001-498000	999
498001-499000	936
499001-501000	940
501001-900	926
501901-502000	934
502001-503000	926
503001-504000	999
504001-507000	940
507001-508000	999
508001-509000	940
509001-510000	942
509901-510000	942
510001-511500	940
511501-700	942
511701-517000	940
517001-519000	924
519001-521000	925
521001-523000	944
523001-524000	946
524001-531000	940
531001-532000	926
532001-10	934
532011-533000	926
533001-535500	999
535501-536000	940
536001-537000	936
537001-538000	924
538001-543000	940
543001-544000	927
544001-200	934
544201-545000	926
545001-546000	925
546001-547000	924
547001-548000	926
548001-549000	999
549001-551000	946
551001-553000	944
553001-555000	940
555001-556000	936
556001-558000	924
558001-560000	925
560001-561000	999
561001-562000	926
562001-564000	924
564001-565000	926
565001-568000	940
568001-569000	936
569001-571000	924
571001-576000	940
576001-200	942
576201-578000	940
578001-580000	924
580001-582000	926
582001-584000	925
584001-585000	927
585001-587000	999
587001-592000	940
592001-593000	926
593001-594000	924
594001-601000	940
B600001-601000	999 Ball
601001-601800	926
B601001-601800	999 Ball
601801-602000	934
B601801-602000	999 Ball
602001-603000	926
B602001-603000	999 Ball
603001-604000	926
B603001-604000	999 Ball
604001-605000	926
B604001-605000	999 Ball
605001-606000	925
B605001-606000	999 Ball
606001-607000	925
B606001-607000	999 Ball
607001-608000	925
B607001-608000	999 Ball
608001-613000	924
B608001-613000	999 Ball
613001-614000	925
B613001-614000	999 Ball
614001-616500	924
B614001-616500	999 Ball
616501-617000	934
B616501-617000	999 Ball
617001-619000	926
B617001-619000	999 Ball
619001-620000	927
B619001-620000	999 Ball
620001-622700	940
B620001-622700	999 Ball
622701-623000	942
B622701-623000	999 Ball
623001-624000	941
B623001-624000	999 Ball
624001-625000	936
B624001-625000	999 Ball
625001-626000	925
B625001-626000	999 Ball
626001-627000	926
B626001-627000	999 Ball
627001-628000	924
B627001-628000	999 Ball
628001-630800	925
B628001-630800	999 Ball
631001-636000	940
B631001-636000	999 Ball
636001-637000	941
B636001-637000	999 Ball
637001-638000	936
B637001-638000	999 Ball
638001-639000	926
B638001-639000	999 Ball
639001-640000	925
B639001-640000	999 Ball
640001-642000	924
B640001-644400	999 Ball
644401-645000	940
B644501-645500	999 Ball
645501-646000	925
B645501-646000	999 Ball
646001-647000	926
B646001-647000	999 Ball
647001-648000	940
B647001-648000	999 Ball
648001-649000	940
B648001-649000	998 Ball
649001-650000	940
B649001-650000	998 Ball
650001-651000	940
B650001-651000	999 Ball
651001-652000	940
B651001-652000	998 Ball
652001-652700	924
B652001-652700	998 Ball
652701-652800	924
652801-652900	927
652901-653000	937
653001-655000	940
B653001-655000	999 Ball
655001-655200	924
B655001-655200	999 Ball
655201-656000	924
656001-657000	926
657001-659000	924
659001-660000	925
660001-661000	927
661001-662000	924
662001-664000	940
664001-666000	924
666001-667000	940
667001-668000	941
668001-669000	926
669001-670000	999
670001-100	937
670501-673000	925
673001-675000	926
675001-677000	940
677001-678000	924
678001-679200	927
679201-680000	926
680001-685000	924
685001-687000	940
687001-688000	925
688001-689000	946
689001-694000	940
694001-696000	924
696001-697000	941
697001-700000	924
700001-702000	974
702001-703800	992
703801-704000	990
704001-400	992
704401-705000	990
705001-700	972
705701-706000	974
706001-707000	990
707001-800	972
707801-708000	990
708001-709500	975
709501-710000	973
710001-800	993
710801-711000	991
711001-300	973
711301-712000	975
712001-600	993
712601-713000	991
713001-714900	975
714901-715000	991
715001-716000	993
716001-100	972
716101-717000	974
717001-200	991
717201-718000	975L
718001-721500	974
721501-722000	992
722001-724000	974
724001-725000	972
725001-726000	974
726001-727000	992
727001-728000	974
728001-729000	992
729001-730000	975
730001-731000	992
731001-732000	975
732001-734000	992
734001-735000	975
735001-736000	974
736001-738000	975
738001-739000	974
739001-740000	975
740001-100	974
740101-200	972
740201-900	974
740901-741000	975
741001-742000	992
742001-743000	974
743001-300	975
743301-400	993
743401-744000	975
744001-500	974
744501-745000	992
745001-747000	975
747001-700	974
747701-748000	972
748001-749500	992
749501-750000	974
750001-100	961
750101-200	961
750201-700	950
750701-751000	952
751001-752000	960
752001-500	952
752501-753000	950
753001-500	952
753501-754000	950
754001-100	960
754101-500	952
754501-755000	960
755001-400	992
755401-500	974
755501-700	972
755701-900	974
755901-756000	972
756001-757000	974
757001-300	975
757301-500	993
757501-758000	975
758001-100	972
758101-759000	992
759001-760000	975
760001-400	992
760401-600	972
760601-800	974
760801-761000	992

Serial	Grade
761001-400	975
761401-600	993
761601-762000	975
762001-200	992
762201-300	972
762301-763000	974
763001-300	993
763301-600	973
763601-764000	975
764001-300	992
764301-400	972
764401-765000	974
765001-300	992
765301-767000	974
767001-600	992
767601-800	972
767801-768000	974
768001-769000	975
769001-700	992
769701-770000	972
770001-100	974
770101-771200	992
771201-400	972
771401-772000	974
772001-773000	975
773001-800	992
773801-774000	972
774001-775000	975
775001-500	952
775501-776000	950
776001-300	973
776301-700	993
776701-777000	975
777001-300	972
777301-778300	974
778301-800	992
778801-900	972
778901-779300	974
779301-780100	992
780101-300	972
780301-781300	992
781301-400	972
781401-500	974
781501-782000	992
782001-783000	975
783001-600	992
783601-784000	974
784001-785000	992
785001-500	952
785501-786000	950
786001-787000	992
787001-400	974
787401-788000	972
788001-791300	992
791301-792600	974
792601-900	972
792901-793700	992
793701-900	990
793901-794000	992
794001-200	972
794201-795000	974
795001-796400	992
796401-800	972
796801-797200	974
797201-500	954
797501-798000	974
798001-500	990
798501-800	972
798801-799000	954
799001-200	972
799201-600	992
799601-800000	954
800001-802000	974
802001-200	954
802201-2	972
802203-300	954
802301-500	972
802501-803700	974
803701-804200	954
804201-806000	974
806001-807000	975
807001-500	993
807501-808500	993
808801-809000	993
809001-500	974
809501-600	972
809601-810000	974
810001-300	990
810301-812000	974
812001-700	992
812701-813000	974
813001-814000	974P
814001-800	974L
814801-815900	992
815901-816000	974L
816001-817000	974P
817001-819000	974L
819001-820000	974P
820001-821500	974L
821501-822000	990L
822001-700	992L
822701-823000	974L
823001-824000	974P
824001-826000	975P

Serial	Grade
826001-500	975L
826501-827000	993
827001-828000	975P
828001-829000	974L
829001-830000	974P
830001-500	990L
830501-831000	992L
831001-100	954P
831101-200	972P
831201-500	954P
831501-832000	974P
832001-400	974L
832401-833000	992L
833001-834000	990L
834001-600	974P
834601-800	974L
834801-835000	974P
835001-600	992L
835601-800	990L
835801-836000	974L
836001-500	974P
836501-900	954P
836901-837000	974P
837001-838000	975P
838001-839000	975L
839001-400	974L
839401-700	992L
839701-840000	990L
840001-400	952L
840401-900	950L
840901-841000	952L
841001-842000	975P
842001-843000	974L
843001-844000	974P
844001-200	993
844201-845000	993
845001-200	992
845201-400	972
845401-700	954
845701-846000	972
846001-500	952
846501-847000	950
847001-200	972
847201-849000	974
849001-850000	975
850001-300	992
850301-800	990
850801-851000	972
851001-400	993
851401-852000	975
852001-853000	992
853001-854000	974
854001-600	950
854601-900	952
854901-855100	960L
855101-856000	950L
856001-857840	975
857841-858000	975L
858001-500	974
858501-859000	972
859001-860000	974
860001-862300	992
862301-400	954
862401-500	972
862501-600	954
862601-800	972
862801-863000	974
863001-864000	992
864001-865000	975
865001-866000	992
866001-600	974
866601-700	954
866701-867000	972
867001-868000	975
868001-869000	992
869001-870000	975
870001-872000	992
872001-200	993
872201-874000	975
874001-800	974
874801-875000	975
875001-300	952
875301-876000	975
876001-600	993
876601-877000	975
877001-400	992
877401-700	975
877701-878000	993
878001-879400	975
879401-880000	992
880001-600	992
880601-882400	974
882401-883400	992
883401-884100	974
884101-885300	992
885301-886000	974
886001-887000	992
887001-300	974
887301-890300	992
890301-891000	974
891001-600	992
891601-892200	978
892201-896200	974
896201-897800	974
897801-898000	972

Serial	Grade
898001-899100	992
899101-500	978
899501-900000	974
900001-902000	940
902001-904000	926
904001-906000	924
906001-914000	940
914001-916000	926
916001-917000	927
917001-919000	925
919001-921000	940
921001-923000	924
923001-500	999
923501-924000	925
924001-926000	940
926001-100	927
927001-929000	926
929001-933000	924
933001-935000	925
935001-937000	926
937001-939000	940
939001-941000	924
941001-944000	940
944001-949000	926
949001-952000	925
952001-953000	924
953001-956000	926
956001-960000	940
960001-968000	926
968001-970000	940
970001-971700	924
971701-972000	948
972001-973000	924
973001-974000	936
974001-975400	926
975401-25 Spec.	926
975426-976000	924
976001-979000	940
979001-100	942
979101-981000	940
981001-982000	948
982001-984000	924
984001-986000	940
986001-987000	946
987001-988000	936
988001-992000	940
992001-996000	924
996001-999998	940
999999-1000000	947
1000001-1003000	972
1000301-1003000	992
1003001-1004000	974
1004001-900	992
1004901-1007100	974
1007101-1008300	992
1008301-1009500	974
1009501-1010700	992
1010701-1011200	972
1011201-1012700	974
1012701-1013000	992
1013001-1015000	978
1015001-300	974
1015301-1016000	992
1016001-300	975
1016301-600	973
1016601-1018000	993
1018001-1020000	992
1020001-1022600	950
1022601-1023000	952
1023001-700	992
1023701-1024500	974
1024501-600	974
1024601-1025000	972
1025001-1027000	975
1027001-400	993
1027401-1029600	975
1029601-1030000	973
1030001-1032000	992
1032001-1033000	974
1033001-200	972
1033201-800	954
1033801-1035300	974
1035301-600	972
1035601-1036000	974
1036001-300	972
1036301-800	954
1036801-1037000	992L
1037001-1038000	974
1038001-1039000	992
1039001-200	972
1039201-500	978
1039501-1040300	974
1040301-1041000	992
1041001-1042000	974
1042001-700	992
1042701-1043000	972
1043001-700	978
1043701-1044000	992
1044001-1045000	974
1045001-1046000	992
1046001-1047000	975
1047001-1048000	974L
1048001-1049000	992
1049001-500	990
1049501-1051000	992

Serial	Grade
1051001-200	975
1051201-1052000	993
1052001-500	972P
1052501-900	954
1052901-1053000	974
1053001-1054000	992
1054001-1056000	974
1056001-1057000	975
1057001-1061300	992
1061301-1062300	972
1062301-1066000	992
1066001-1068000	974
1068001-1069000	975
1069001-1070000	974
1070001-1071000	992L
1071001-1073000	975P
1073001-1075000	992
1075001-1076200	974L
1076201-700	972L
1076701-1077000	978L
1077001-1079000	974P
1079001-1080000	992L
1080001-100	952L
1080101-200	960L
1080201-400	994L
1080401-1081000	950L
1081001-1082000	978L
1082001-400	993L
1082401-1083000	973L
1083001-1084000	990L
1084001-1085000	992L
1085001-1086000	992L
1086001-1088000	974P
1088001-1091000	992L
1091001-200	978L
1091201-1092000	974L
1092001-1093000	992L
1093001-1095000	974P
1095001-1096000	992P
1096001-400	974L
1096401-1097000	974P
1097001-1098000	992L
1098001-400	975P
1098401-1099000	975L
1099001-600	993L
1099601-1100000	975P
1100001-1104000	992L
1104001-1105000	974P
1105001-1106000	992L
1106001-500	978L
1106501-1107000	972L
1107001-1109000	992L
1109001-1111000	972L
1111001-1112000	974L
1112001-1113000	974P
1113001-1116000	992L
1116001-900	974P
1116901-1117000	974L
1117001-1119000	992L
1119001-1120000	978L
1120001-1122000	992L
1122001-1123000	974P
1123001-500	972P
1123501-1125000	974P
1125001-1127000	992L
1127001-1128000	972L
1128001-1129000	974L
1129001-1130500	974P
1130501-1131000	956P
1131001-1132000	992L
1132001-1133000	990L
1133001-1134000	978L
1134001-1135000	972L
1135001-1137000	992L
1137001-1138000	956P
1138001-1139000	956P
1139001-1140000	978L
1140001-1141000	972L
1141001-1142000	956P
1142001-500	974P
1142501-1145000	974L
1145001-1146000	975P
1146001-500	956P
1146501-1149000	974P
1149001-1150000	974L
1150001-600	950L
1150601-1151800	952L
1151801-1152000	952P
1152001-900	950P
1152901-1153200	992L
1153201-300	
1153301-500	994P
1153501-800	994L
1153801-1154000	960L
1154001-500	950L
1154501-1155000	950P
1155001-200	994P
1155201-500	994L
1156001-1158000	996L
1158001-1160000	974P
1160001-1162000	992L
1162001-500	993L
1162501-1164000	992L
1164001-1166000	974P

Serial Range	Grade
1166001-1167000	974L
1167001-1168000	956P
1168001-1169000	975P
1169001-1170000	974P
1170001-1174000	956P
1174001-1176000	974P
1176001-1177000	992L
1177001-1178000	956P
1178001-1179000	974P
1179001-1181000	996L
1181001-1182000	992L
1182001-1183000	996L
1183001-1184400	974P
1184401-1185400	956P
1185401-1186000	974P
1186001-1187000	992L
1187001-1188000	996L
1188001-1189000	992L
1189001-1190000	974P
1190001-1192000	996L
1192001-1193000	975P
1193001-1194000	974P
1194001-1195000	956P
1195001-1196000	974P
1196001-1199000	992L
1199001-1201000	974P
1201001-1202000	975P
1202001-1203000	992L
1203001-1204000	974P
1204001-500	956P
1204501-1206000	974P
1206001-1207000	992L
1207001-1210000	974P
1210001-1212000	992L
1212001-1213000	974P
1213001-500	996L
1213501-1214000	992L
1214001-1214600	993L
1214601-1215000	975P
1215001-1216000	974L
1216001-1219000	992L
1219001-1220000	974P
1220001-1221000	992L
1221001-1223500	974P
1223501-1224000	956P
1224001-1227000	992L
1227001-1228000	972L
1228001-700	992L
1228701-1229000	990L
1229001-500	956P
1229501-1230000	974P
1230001-1231000	974L
1231001-1232000	992L
1232001-1233000	974P
1233001-1236000	992L
1236001-500	974P
1236501-1237000	956P
1237001-500	996L
1237501-1238000	992L
1238001-1239000	956P
1239001-1241000	992L
1241001-1242000	975P
1242001-400	974L
1242401-1243000	972L
1243001-500	996L
1243501-1244000	992L
1244001-1245000	974P
1245001-1246000	992L
1246001-300	974P
1246301-800	956P
1246801-1247000	974L
1247001-1248000	992L
1248001-1249700	974P
1249701-1250000	956P
1250001-1252000	983
1252001-1253000	985
1253001-1257000	983
1257001-900	985
1260001-970	Chro.*
1260971-1265000	
1265001-1266000	956P
1266001-1267000	974P
1267001-1268200	978L
1268201-1269000	978L
1269001-600	992L
1269601-1270000	992L
1270001-1271700	992L
1271701-1272000	974P
1272001-1274000	996L
1274001-500	993L
1274501-700	992L
1274701-1275000	992L
1275001-1276000	972L
1276001-1277000	974L
1277001-1278000	992L
1278001-1279000	975P
1279001-1280000	974P
1280001-1281000	992L
1281001-800	974P
1281801-1282000	956P
1282001-1284000	996L
1284001-1285000	992L
1285001-1286000	956P
1286001-1288000	978L
1288001-500	993L
1288501-1289100	992L
1289101-700	990L
1289701-1290000	992L
1290001-1291500	974P
1291501-1292000	992P
1292001-1297000	992L
1297001-1298000	974P
1298001-1299000	992L
1299001-1300000	975P
1300001-1301000	974P
1301001-1302000	974L
1302001-500	992L
1302501-1303000	990L
1303001-500	972L
1303501-1304000	972P
1304001-1305000	978L
1305001-1306000	956P
1306001-1307000	974P
1307001-1308500	992L
1308501-1309000	993L
1309001-1310000	974L
1310001-1311000	972L
1311001-1312000	992L
1312001-800	974P
1312801-1313000	956P
1313001-1317000	992L
1317001-1318000	956P
1318001-1321000	992L
1321001-300	990L
1321301-1322000	992L
1322001-700	974L
1322701-1323000	972L
1323001-1324000	992L
1324001-1325000	996L
1325001-1326500	975P
1326501-1327000	993L
1327001-300	956P
1327301-1329000	974P
1329001-1330000	992L
1330001-1331300	974L
1331301-800	972L
1331801-1332000	978L
1332001-1334000	992L
1334001-400	974P
1334401-1335000	956P
1335001-300	978L
1335301-1336000	972L
1336001-1337000	992L
1337001-1338200	996L
1338201-1339000	996L
1339001-1340000	956P
1340001-1341000	992L
1341001-300	972L
1341301-500	974L
1341501-1342000	978L
1342001-1343000	992L
1343001-400	956P
1343401-1344000	974P
1344001-1345000	992L
1345001-600	974L
1345601-1346000	972L
1346001-1348000	975P
1348001-1349000	974P
1349001-1350000	992L
1350001-600	972L
1350601-1351000	974L
1351001-1352000	993L
1351501-1352000	974L
1352001-1352300	974L
1352301-800	978L
1352801-1353000	974L
1353001-500	972P
1353501-1354200	956P
1354201-700	992P
1354701-1355000	974P
1355001-1356000	992L
1356001-1357000	974P
1357001-1359800	992L
1359801-1361000	996L
1361001-1362000	992L
1362001-600	974P
1362601-1363000	956P
1363001-1364000	992L
1364001-1365000	975P
1365001-800	956P
1365801-1367000	974P
1367001-1369400	992L
1369401-1370000	996L
1370001-1371000	974L
1371001-600	996L
1371601-1373000	975P
1373001-1374000	992L
1374001-1375000	950L
1375001-1376000	992L
1376001-1377000	992L
1377001-1378300	974P
1378301-1379000	956P
1379001-1380200	972L
1380201-1381000	978L
1381001-500	956P
1381501-1383000	974P
1383001-1384000	992L
1384001-1386100	974P
1386101-1387000	992L
1387001-1388000	992L
1388001-400	978L
1388401-1389000	978L
1389001-300	956P
1389301-1390000	956P
1390001-1391000	992L
1391001-500	956P
1391501-1392000	974P
1392001-1393000	992L
1393001-1394000	974P
1394001-1396000	992L
1396001-500	972L
1396501-1398000	974L
1398001-400	974P
1398401-1399000	956P
1399001-1400000	992L
1400001-1401000	936
1401001-1403000	924
1403001-1409000	940
1409001-500	946
1409501-1410000	940
1410001-1414000	924
1414001-300	941
1414501-1415000	925
1415001-1417000	924
1417001-1419000	940
1419001-1420000	924
1420001-1421000	940
1421001-1422000	924
1422001-1424000	940
1424001-1428000	924
1428001-1430000	940
1430001-200	924
1430201-400	948
1430401-1431000	924
1431001-1433000	940
1433001-1438000	924
1438001-500	926
1438501-1439500	924
1439501-1440000	926
1440001-1441000	940
1441001-1442000	924
1442001-500	926
1442501-1444000	924
1444001-1445000	940
1445001-1447000	924
1447001-1448200	940
1449001-1450500	924
1500001-600	974P
1500601-1501200	956P
1501201-1502000	974P
1502001-1503000	993L
1503001-1504000	996L
1504001-500	974L
1504501-1505200	972L
1505201-700	978L
1505701-1506000	974L
1506001-1507000	975P
1507001-1508000	992L
1508001-400	974P
1508401-1509000	956P
1509001-1510000	992L
1510001-1511000	974L
1511001-1512000	975P
1512001-1513200	992L
1513201-600	992P
1513601-1514000	992L
1514001-200	956P
1514201-1515000	974P
1515001-1516000	992L
1516001-1517000	974P
1517001-1520000	992L
1520001-1521200	974L
1521201-1522000	978L
1522001-600	974P
1522601-1525000	956P
1525001-1527000	996L
1527001-1528000	992L
1528001-1531000	974P
1531001-1533000	992L
1533001-600	974P
1533601-1534000	956P
1534001-100	975P
1535101-200	975P
1535201-600	975P
1535601-1536000	993L
1536001-1537000	972L
1537001-1538000	992L
1538001-800	956P
1538801-1539000	974P
1539001-1540000	992L
1540001-500	992P
1540501-1541000	992L
1541001-1542200	974P
1542201-800	956P
1542801-1543000	974P
1543001-1544000	996L
1544001-1545000	992L
1545001-400	978L
1545401-1546000	974L
1546001-1548000	992L
1548001-600	974L
1548601-1549000	972L
1549001-1550000	974P
1550001-500	972P
1550501-1552000	974P
1552001-1555000	992L
1555001-1557000	993P
1557001-800	972L
1557801-1558000	974L
1558001-500	956
1558501-1559700	956P
1559701-1560000	974P
1560001-1561000	975P
1561001-1563000	992L
1563001-1565000	978L
1565001-1567000	992L
1567001-1568000	974L
1568001-1569000	992L
1569001-1571000	972L
1571001-1572000	974P
1572001-1573000	975P
1573001-1575000	974P
1575001-400	950L
1575401-1576000	950P
1576001-1577000	950L
1577001-1578000	975P
1578001-1580000	992L
1580001-1581200	974L
1581201-1582000	956P
1582001-1583000	974P
1583001-1584000	992L
1584001-1585000	978L
1585001-1586000	992L
1586001-1587000	992L
1587001-500	992P
1587501-1589000	992L
1589001-500	956P
1589501-1590000	974P
1590001-1591000	974L
1591001-1592000	992L
1592001-1593000	974P
1593001-1595000	992L
1595001-200	974P
1595201-900	956P
1595901-1596000	974P
1596001-1611000	992L
1611001-1612100	974P
1612101-1613000	956P
1613001-600	996L
1614001-900	956P
1614901-1615000	974P
1615001-1625000	992L
1625001-200	950L
1625201-1626000	952L
1626001-1627000	974P
1627001-1633000	992L
1633001-1635000	950L
1635001-1636000	992L
1636001-1637000	956P
1637001-1638000	974P
1638001-1642800	992L
1642801-1643000	992P
1643001-1644000	992L
1644001-1646000	974L
1646001-1648000	972L
1648001-1649000	992L
1649001-1652000	974P
1652001-1653000	950L
1653001-1654000	956P
1654001-1657000	974P
1657001-1660000	992L
1660001-1661000	978L
1661001-1663000	974P
1663001-1664000	974L
1664001-1665000	950L
1665001-1666000	974P
1666001-1667000	956P
1667001-1669000	974P
1669001-1670000	978L
1670001-1671000	974P
1671001-300	992L
1671301-900	992P
1671901-1672000	992L
1672001-1676000	974P
1676001-1678000	992L
1678001-1679000	974P
1679001-1681000	974L
1681001-1682000	974P
1682001-1683000	956P
1683001-1685000	974P
1685001-1686000	992L
1686001-1688000	974P
1688001-500	978L
1689001-600	975P
1690001-1691000	956
1691001-1693000	992L
1693001-1696000	956P
1696001-1699000	992L
1699001-1703000	974P
1703001-1704000	992L
1704001-1705000	956P
1705001-1706000	974P
1706001-1707100	992L
1708001-1714000	992L
1714001-1715000	974P
1715001-1717000	992L
1717001-900	956
1718001-1750000	992L
1750001-1761000	900
1761001-1765000	914
1765001-1767000	920
1767001-1768000	914
1768001-1769000	900
1769001-1770000	920
1770001-1778200	914
1778201-1779000	910
1779001-1780000	920
1780001-1782000	910
1782001-500	920
1782501-1783000	900
1783001-1808000	910
1808001-1810000	914
1810001-1811000	910
1811001-1813000	900
1813001-1818000	910
1818001-1819000	914
1819001-1821000	910

Serial Numbers	Grade
1821001-1822000	914
1822001-1827000	910
1827001-600	914
1827601-1829100	910
1829101-500	914
1829501-1830000	910
1830001-1831000	900
1831001-1832000	920
1832001-700	910
1832701-1833300	914
1833301-1834500	910
1834501-1835400	914
1835401-1836900	910
1836901-1837400	914
1837401-1839000	910
1839001-500	914
1839501-1844700	910
1844701-1845700	914
1845701-1848300	910
1848301-1849500	914
1849501-1851900	910
1851901-1853100	914
1853101-1856800	910
1856801-1857900	914
1857901-1860300	910
1860301-1861000	914
1861001-1863000	900
1863001-700	920
1863701-1864300	900
1864301-1865000	920
1865001-500	914
1865501-1870300	910
1870301-1871500	914
1871501-1875100	910
1875101-600	914
1875601-1876500	910
1876501-1877500	914
1877501-1878700	910
1878701-1880000	914
1880001-300	920
1880301-1881500	900
1881501-700	920
1881701-900	900
1881901-1882900	920
1882901-1885000	900
1885001-1887400	910
1887401-1888600	914
1888601-1891000	910
1891001-1892200	914
1892201-1894600	910
1894601-1895800	914
1895801-1899000	910
1899001-300	900
1899301-1900000	920
1900001-400	910
1900401-1902100	914
1902101-1907000	910
1907001-1909000	914
1909001-1910000	910
1910001-500	920
1910501-1911000	900
1911001-1913000	920
1913001-1914000	900
1914001-1920000	910
1920001-1922000	920
1922001-1924000	910
1924001-1925000	900
1925001-1936000	910
1936001-1937000	920
1937001-900	900
1940001-1941000	914
1941001-1949000	910
1949001-1950000	914
1950001-1962000	910
1962001-1963000	914
1963001-1975000	910
1975001-1976000	914
1976001-1980000	910
1980001-1981000	914
1981001-1988500	910

Serial Numbers	Grade
1989001-400	914
2000001-2001700	988
2001701-2002400	986
2002401-800	988
2002801-2003100	986
2004001-2035000	986
2035001-2037200	981
2040001-2064000	986
2100001-2191300	986A
2200001-2248000	987
2248001-2300000	987F
2300001-2311000	992L
2311001-2312000	974L
2312001-2321700	992L
2321701-2323000	974L
2323001-2326000	992L
2326001-2327000	974P
2327001-2333000	992L
2333001-2336000	974P
2336001-2338000	992L
2338001-2339000	974P
2339001-2340000	974L
2340001-2341000	974P
2341001-2346000	992L
2346001-2347000	974P
2347001-2356000	992L
2356001-2358000	974P
2358001-2364000	992L
2364001-2365000	974P
2365001-2374000	992L
2374001-2375000	974P
2375001-2378000	992L
2378001-2380000	974L
2380001-2383000	992L
2383001-2384000	950L
2384001-2385000	992L
2385001-2396000	974P
2386001-2390000	992L
2390001-2391000	974P
2391001-2393000	992L
2393001-2395000	974P
2395001-2397000	992L
2397001-2399000	974L
2398001-2401000	992L
2401001-2402000	974P
2402001-2407000	992L
2407001-2409000	974P
2409001-2413000	992L
2413001-2414000	974P
2414001-2415000	974L
2415001-2418000	992L
2418001-2420000	974P
2420001-2422000	992L
2422001-2423000	974P
2423001-2432000	992L
2432001-2433000	974P
2433001-2434000	992L
2434001-2435000	974P
2435001-2437000	992L
2437001-2438000	974P
2438001-2442000	992L
2442001-2445000	974P
2445001-2451000	992L
2451001-2453000	974P
2453001-2455000	992L
2455001-2456000	974P
2456001-2457000	992L
2457001-2458000	950L
2458001-2459000	974L
2459001-2461000	992L
2461001-2462000	974L
2462001-2464000	992L
2464001-2466000	974P
2466001-2468000	992L
2468001-2469000	974P
2469001-2472000	992L
2472001-2473000	974P
2473001-2474000	992L
2474001-2475000	974P

Serial Numbers	Grade
2475001-2476000	992L
2476001-2477000	974P
2477001-2490000	992L
2490001-2492000	974L
2492001-2504000	992L
2504001-2505000	950L
2505001-300	950L
2506001-2526000	992L
2526001-2528000	974P
2528001-2533000	992L
2533001-2534000	974P
2534001-2535000	992L
2535001-2536000	974P
2536001-2537000	974P
2537001-2538000	974P
2538001-2539000	974L
2539001-2542000	974P
2542001-2543000	992L
2543001-2545000	974P
2545001-2547000	992L
2547001-2548400	974P
2548401-2548600	974L
2548601-2548700	974P
2548701-2550000	974L
2550001-2551000	992L
2551001-2552000	974L
2552001-2555000	992L
2555001-2555600	974L
2555701-2557000	974L
2558001-2560000	992L
2560001-2561000	974L
2561001-2563000	992L
2563001-2564000	974L
2564001-2566000	992L
2566001-2566600	974L
2567001-2581000	992L
2581001-2583900	992E
2583901-2584300	992L
2584301-2596000	992E
2596001-2597000	974L
2597001-2608000	992E
2608001-2608800	974L
2609001-2611000	992E
2611001-2611400	950L
2611401-2613000	950E
2613001-2618000	992E
2618001-2619000	950E
2619001-2631000	992E
2631001-2631600	950E
2631801-2632000	950E
2632001-2639000	992E
2639001-2641000	950E
2641001-2649000	992E
2649001-2650600	950E
2651001-2655300	992E
2900001-2911500	979
2911601-2931900	979F
3000001-3002300	922
3002301-3002500	922M.P.
3002501-3003800	922
3003801-3004000	922M.P.
3004001-3006100	922
3006101-3006300	922M.P.
3006301-3008000	922
3008001-3008600	922M.P.
3008601-3010000	922
3010001-3010500	922
3010501-3010700	922M.P.
3010701-3011900	922
3011901-3012500	922M.P.
3012501-3013100	922
3013101-3013700	922M.P.
3013701-3015700	922
3050001-3054800	902
3054801-3056000	922
3056001-3060800	902
3061001-3065100	904
3100001-3133800	916
3135001-3152700	918
3200001-3460900	912
4000001-4447201	987F
4447301-4523000	987E

Serial Numbers	Grade
A-001 to A-8450	980B
1B-001 to 1B-4000	999B
2B-001 to 2B-700	999B
2B-701 to 2B-800	950B
C-001 to C-169000	992B
E-001 to E-114000	989
E-114001 to E-140400	989E
F-101 to F-57600	995
F-57601 to F-59850	995A
F-59851 to F-62000	995
F-62001 to F-63000	995A
F-63001 to F-63800	995
F-63801 to F-286200	995A
G-001 to G-13600	980
G-13601 to G-14600	980 & 980A
G-14601 to G-44500	980
G-44501 to G-45000	980A
G-45001 to G-47400	980
G-47401 to G-48400	980A
G-48401 to G-58200	980
G-58201 to G-58700	980A
G-58701 to G-61600	980
G-61601 to G-62500	980A
G-62501 to G-67500	980
G-67501 to G-68600	980A
G-68601- to G-486000	980
H-001 to H-1000	921
H-1001 to H-1800	400 & 921
H-1801 to H-2000	921
H-2001 to H-2800	400 & 921
H-2801 to H-3500	400
H-3501 to H-30000	921
H-50001 to H-57500	401
J-001 to J-320000	982
M-001 to M-58000	982M
N-001 to N-223000	721
O-1 to 0408000	987A
R-001 to R-1400	923
S-001 to S-3400	950B
SS-001 to SS-71500	987S
T-001 to T-312000	911
V-001 to V-38000	911M
X-001 to X-125000	917

*Hamilton 36 size chronometer watch

*Haydn W. Wheeler model

NOTE: The above serial number and grade listing is an actual Hamilton factory list and is accurate in most cases. However, it has been brought to our attention that in rare cases the serial number and grade number do not match the list. One example is the Hayden W. Wheeler model.

(See Hamilton Watch Co. **Serial Numbers and Grades** section located at the end of the Hamilton Watch price section to identify the movement, size and grade of your watch.)

NOTE: Watches listed in this book are priced at the retail level, as complete watches having an original 14k gold-filled case, an original white enamel single sunk dial, and with the entire original movement in good working order with no repairs needed.

Grade 925, 18 size, 17 jewels, hunting case, serial number 101,495.

Grade 932, 18 size, 16 jewels, open face, serial number 6,888.

HAMILTON
18 SIZE

Grade or Name — Description		Avg	Ex-Fn	Mint
7J, OF, LS, FULL	★★	$800	$1,000	$1,200
11J, HC, LS, FULL	★★★	1,200	1,400	1,700
11J, OF, LS, FULL	★★★★	1,500	1,700	2,000
922, 15J, OF	★★	450	550	700
923, 15J, HC	★★	500	600	750
924, 17J, NI, OF, DMK		55	75	100
925, 17J, NI, HC, DMK		100	125	175
926, 17J, NI, OF, DMK, ADJ		55	75	100
927, 17J, NI, HC, DMK, ADJ		100	125	175
928, 15J, NI, OF		125	150	200
929, 15J, NI, HC, 14K		600	700	800
929, 15J, NI, HC		175	225	300
930, 16J, NI, OF		150	200	275
931, 16J, NI, HC		200	250	325
932 or 936, serial #s less than 50, OF	★★★	1,500	1,900	2,500
932, 16J, NI, OF	★★	400	450	525
932 *(S#s less than 400 up to $1,200)*				
933, 16J, NI, HC	★★	500	550	625
933 *((Serial #s started at 1021, S#s less than 1,300 up to $1,400)*				
934, 17J, NI, OF, DMK, DR, Adj.5P		100	125	175
934, 17J, NI, OF, Adj.5P, Coin		75	100	150
935, 17J, NI, HC, DMK, DR, Adj.5P	★	250	300	375
936, 17J, NI, OF, DMK, DR		75	100	150
936 *(S#s less than 400 up to $1,200)*				
937, 17J, NI, HC, DMK, DR		150	200	275
937 *(Serial #s started at 1001, S#s less than 1,300 up to $1,200)*				

Grade or Name — Description	Avg	Ex-Fn	Mint
938, 17J, NI, OF, DMK, DR .... ★★	$500	$600	$775
939, 17J, NI, HC, DMK, DR... ★★	600	700	875
940, 21J, NI, OF, Mermod Jaccards St. Louis Paragon Time Keeper & an hour glass on mvt.	275	325	400
940, 21J, NI, OF, DMK, DR, Adj.5P, GJS	125	175	250
940, 21J, NI, OF, 2-Tone..	150	200	275
940, 21J, NI, OF, Extra..	175	225	300
940, 21J, NI, OF, Coin...	100	150	175
940, 21J, NI, OF, Special..	175	225	300
941, 21J, NI, HC, GJS, Marked	125	175	250
941, 21J, NI, HC, GJS, Special..	275	350	450
941, 21J, NI, HC, DMK, DR, Adj.5P, GJS	200	275	375
942, 21J, NI, OF, DMK, DR, Adj.5P, GJS	175	250	300
943, 21J, NI, HC, DMK, DR, Adj.5P, GJS .... ★	225	300	350
943, Burlington Special, 21J .... ★	550	650	800
944, 19J, NI, OF, DMK, DR, Adj.5P, GJS	150	200	275
945, 19J, GJS, 2-Tone, HC.. ★★	1,000	1,200	1,500
946, Anderson (jobber name on movement), 14K.......................	800	1,000	1,300
946, 23J, Extra, OF, GJS..	500	550	625
946, 23J, "Loaner" on case..	425	475	575
946, 23J, NI, OF, DMK, DR, Adj.5P, GJS	400	450	525
946, 23J, NI, OF, DMK, Adj.5P, GJS, unmarked........................	350	400	425
947, 23J, NI, HC, DMK, DR, Adj.5P, GJS, 14K, HC, not marked "947" .... ★	3,500	4,000	5,000

☞ Note: Some 18 size movements are marked with grade numbers, some are not. Collectors prefer marked movement.

☞ Note: The first hunting case was a Model number 937 which begins with serial number 1001.

Grade 947 (marked), 18 size, 23 jewels, gold jewel settings, hunting case, Adj6p, serial number 163,219.

Burlington Special, 18 size, 21 jewels, Grade 943, open face, serial number 121,614.

☞ NOTE: Watches listed in this book are priced at the retail level, as complete watches having an original 14k goldfilled case, an original white enamel single sunk dial, and with the entire original movement in good working order with no repairs needed, unless otherwise noted.

Grade or Name — Description	Avg	Ex-Fn	Mint
947, 23J, NI, Adj.5P, GJS, 14K, HC, marked "947" ....★★★	$4,500	$5,500	$6,500
947, 23J, NI, GJS, Adj.5P, marked 947 Extra, 14K, HC ..★★★★	5,000	6,000	7,500
948, 17J, NI, OF, DMK, DR, Adj.5P, GJS .... ★	300	350	425
948, 17J, NI, DMK, DR, Adj.5P, GJS, OF, Coin .... ★	300	350	425
The Banner, 928, 15J, NI, OF...	125	150	200
The Banner, 940, 21J, NI, OF...	150	175	225
The Banner, 941, 21J, NI, HC...	200	225	275
The Banner, 17J, M#927, HC, ADJ...	125	150	200
Burlington Special, 17J, Adj.5P, OF.......................................	300	350	425
Burlington Special, 17J, Adj.5P, HC.......................................	350	400	475
Burlington Special, 21J, Adj.5P, OF.......................................	400	450	525
Burlington Special, 21J, Adj.5P, HC.......................................	450	500	575
Imperial Canada, GRADE 922, OF.. ★	600	700	850
Imperial Canada, GRADE 923, HC.. ★	700	850	975
Inspectors Standard, 21J, OF	300	350	475
The Union, 17J..	125	150	200
The Union Special, 17J...	125	150	200
The Union, 17J, G#925, HC..	200	225	275

Grade 950, 16 size, 23 jewels, pendant set, gold train, gold jewel settings, serial number 1,020,650.

Grade 961, 16 size, 21 jewels, gold train, gold jewel settings, serial number 81,848.

16 SIZE

Grade or Name — Description	Avg	Ex-Fn	Mint
950, 23J, LS, DR, GT, 14K..	$700	$800	$900
950, 23J, LS, DR, OF, BRG, GJS, Adj.5P, NI, GT	325	375	450
950, 23J, PS, DR, OF, GJS, BRG, Adj.5P, NI, GT	350	400	475
950B, 23J, LS, OF, Adj.5P, NI, DR, BRG	350	400	450
950E, 23J, LS, OF, Adj.5P, NI, DR, BRG	350	400	450
951, 23J, LS, Adj.5P, NI, GT, GJS, DR, HC ....★★★	3,500	4,000	5,000
951, 23J, PS, HC, Adj.5P, NI, GT, GJS, DR ....★★★	3,500	4,000	5,000
951, 23J, PS, HC, Adj.5P, NI, GT, GJS, DR, 14K ....★★★	4,000	4,500	5,500
952, 19J, LS or PS, OF, BRG, Adj.5P, NI, GJS, DR....................	175	200	275
952, 19J, LS or PS, Adj.5P, OF, 14K......................................	475	525	600
953, 19J, LS or PS, HC, GJS, GT................................★★	2,000	2,500	3,000

Grade or Name — Description	Avg	Ex-Fn	Mint
954, 17J, LS or PS, OF, 3/4, DR, Adj.5P	$75	$100	$150
956, 17J, PS, OF, 3/4, DR, Adj.5P	75	100	150
960, 21J, PS, OF, BRG, GJS, GT, DR, Adj.5P ★	300	325	400
960, 21J, LS, OF, BRG, GJS, GT, DR, Adj.5P ★	325	350	425
961, 21J, PS & LS, HC, BRG, GJS, GT, DR, Adj.5P ★	400	450	500
962, 17J, PS, OF, BRG ★★	500	600	700
963, 17J, PS, HC, BRG ★★	550	650	750
964, 17J, PS, OF, BRG ★★	650	700	800
965, 17J, PS, HC, BRG ★★	500	550	650
966, 17J, PS, OF, 3/4 ★★	600	650	750
967, 17J, PS, HC, 3/4 ★★	625	675	775
968, 17J, PS, OF, 3/4 ★	325	375	475
969, 17J, PS, HC, 3/4 ★	425	450	500
970, 21J, PS, OF, 3/4	150	175	225
971, 23J, Adj.5P, Swiss made	75	100	135
971, 21J, PS, HC, 3/4	175	200	250
972, 17J, PS & LS, OF, 3/4, NI, GJS, DR, Adj.5P, DMK	100	125	175
973, 17J, PS & LS, HC, 3/4, NI, DR, Adj.5P	150	175	225
974, 17J, LS, OF, 3/4, NI, Adj.3P	50	75	100
974, 17J, OF, PS, Adj.3P	50	75	100
974, 17J, OF, 2-tone	125	150	200
2974B, 17J, OF, Adj.3P	125	150	175
975, 17J, PS & LS, HC, 3/4, NI, Adj.3P	75	100	150
976, 16J, PS, OF, 3/4	150	175	225
977, 16J, PS, HC, 3/4	150	175	225
978, 17J, LS, OF, 3/4, NI, DMK	50	75	100
990, 21J, LS, OF, GJS, DR, Adj.5P, DMK, NI, 3/4, GT	150	175	225
991, 21J, LS, HC, 3/4, GJS, Adj.5P, DMK, NI, GT	175	200	250
992, 21J, OF, 3/4, LS, GJS, Adj.5P, DR, NI, DMK	125	150	200
992, 21J, OF, 3/4, PS & LS, GJS, Adj.5P, DR, NI, DMK, 2 -Tone	150	175	225
992, 21J, Extra, OF, 3/4, PS & LS, GJS, Adj.5P, DR, NI, DMK.	150	175	225

Grade 992B, 16 size, 21 jewels, Adj5p.

Grade 4992B, 16 size, 22 jewels, Adj6p.

Grade 996, 16 size, 19 jewels, open face, gold jewel settings, serial number 152,060.

Hayden W. Wheeler, 16 size, 17 jewels, adjusted to heat & cold, serial number 76,029.

Grade or Name — Description	Avg	Ex-Fn	Mint
992, 21J, 3/4, PS, GJS, Adj.5P, OF	$125	$150	$200
992, 21J, Elinvar, 3/4, GJS, Adj.5P	175	200	225
992, 21J, Special, OF, 3/4, PS & LS, GJS, Adj.5P, DR, NI, DMK, Adj. for RR Service' on dial	350	400	500
992B, 21J, 2-Tone	200	250	300
992B, 21J, LS, OF, 3/4	175	200	235
992B, 21J, OF, 3/4, silver case	175	200	235
3992B, 22J, Adj.6P, 12 hr. dial, silver case ★	200	250	300
4992B, 22J, LS, OF, 3/4, 24-hr. dial, Greenwich Civil Time	125	150	200
993, 21J, PS, HC, GJS, Adj.5P, DR, NI, DMK	200	225	275
993, 21J, LS, HC, GJS, Adj.5P, DMK, DR, NI	175	200	250
993, 21J, LS, HC, GJS, Adj.5P, DMK, DR, NI, 14K	550	600	700

ADMIRAL,16 size, 16 jewels, Damaskeened on nickel 3/4 plate, serial no. 57821.

Chronograph, Grade 23, 16 size, 19 jewels, start-stop-reset to 0.

Grade or Name — Description	Avg	Ex-Fn	Mint
993, 21J, LS, HC, GJS, Adj.5P, DMK, DR, NI,(GF multi color case)	$275	$325	$400
994, 21J, BRG, OF, GJS, GT, DR, Adj.5P, DMK, PS ★	750	900	1,100
994, 21J, BRG, OF, GJS, GT, DR, Adj.5P, DMK, LS ★	850	1,000	1,200
995, 19J, GJS, BRG, HC ★★	900	1,000	1,200
996, 19J, LS, OF, 3/4 GJS, DR, Adj.5P, DMK	125	150	200
Admiral, 16J., Grade 977, 3/4 plate, OF, ★★★	120	135	155
DeLong Escapement, 21J, 992-B	1,000	1,100	1,300
Electric Interurban, 17J, G#974, OF	100	125	175
Official Standard, 17J, OF	175	200	275
Union Special, 17J	100	125	200
Hayden W. Wheeler, 17J, OF ★	400	500	650
Hayden W. Wheeler, 17J, HC ★	400	500	600
Hayden W. Wheeler, 21J ★	500	600	700
Hayden W. Wheeler, 21J, 14K H.W.W. case ★	900	1,000	1,100
Swiss Mfg., 17J, Adj.2P, GF case	85	100	145
Admiral,16J,NI, ADJ., DMK, HC	120	135	155

CHRONOGRAPH
Grade 23

Grade or Name — Description	Avg	Ex-Fn	Mint
16S, 19J, start-stop-reset to 0	$175	$200	$300

12 SIZE
(Some cases were octagon, decagon, cushion, etc.)

Grade or Name — Description	Avg	Ex-Fn	Mint
900, 19J, BRG, DR, Adj.5P, GJS, OF, 14K	$275	$300	$375
900, 19J, BRG, DR, Adj.5P, GJS, OF	75	100	175
902, 19J, BRG, DR, Adj.5P, GJS	100	125	200

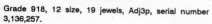

Grade 918, 12 size, 19 jewels, Adj3p, serial number 3,136,257.

Grade 920, 12 size, 23 jewels, gold train, gold jewel settings, serial number 1,863,381.

Grade or Name — Description	Avg	Ex-Fn	Mint
902, 19J, BRG, DR, Adj.5P, GJS, 14K	$300	$325	$375
904, 21J, BRG, DR, Adj.5P, GJS, GT	100	125	175
910, 17J, 3/4, DR, ADJ	40	50	70
912, 17J, Digital model, rotating seconds, OF	80	110	150
912, 17J, 3/4, DR, ADJ	40	50	70
914, 17J, 3/4, DR, Adj.3P, GJS	40	50	70
914, 17J, 3/4, DR, Adj.3P, GJS, 14K	225	250	300
916, 17J, 3/4, DR, Adj.3P	40	50	70
916, 17J, Adj.3P, silver case	30	40	60
918, 19J, Adj.3P, WGF	75	100	150
918, 19J, 3/4, DR, Adj.3P, GJS, OF	75	100	150
920, 23J, BRG, DR, Adj.5P, GJS, GT, OF	200	250	325
920, 23J, BRG, DR, Adj.5P, GJS, GT, 14K	400	450	525
922, 23J, BRG, DR, Adj.5P, GJS, GT, 14K	400	450	525
922, 23J, BRG, DR, Adj.5P, GJS, GT, OF	200	250	325
922 MP, (MASTERPIECE), 18K case, ★	800	900	1,100
922 MP, GF, Hamilton case	300	400	550
400, 21J, 3/4, ADJ ★	300	400	550

Grade 922MP, 12 size, 23 jewels, serial number 3,013,390, c. 1930.

Grade 912, 12 size, 17 jewels, with Secometer dial, originally sold for $88.70.

10 SIZE

Grade or Name — Description	Avg	Ex-Fn	Mint
917, 17J, 3/4, DR, Adj.3P	$40	$50	$70
917, 17J, 3/4, DR, Adj.3P, 14K	200	225	300
921, 21J, BRG, DR, Adj.5P	60	70	90
923, 23J, BRG, DR, Adj.5P	150	175	250
923, 23J, G.F.	275	300	375
923, 23J, 18K, and box	500	600	700
945, 23J, Adj.5P	125	150	225

0 SIZE

Grade or Name — Description	Avg	Ex-Fn	Mint
981, 17J, 3/4, Adj.3P, DR, 18K, HC	$275	$300	$350
983, 17J, Adj.3P, DR, GJS, 18K, HC	275	300	350
985, 19J, BRG, Adj.3P, DR, GJS, GT, 18K, HC	300	325	375
Lady Hamilton, 14K case, OF	200	225	300
Lady Hamilton, 23J, GJS, gold filled OF	125	150	200

Top: Pocket Chronometer, 36 size, 21 jewels, gold jewel settings, Adj5p, serial number 1,260,382.

Right: Chronometer in gimbals and box, 35 size, wind indicator.

CHRONOMETER

Grade or Name — Description	Avg	Ex-Fn	Mint
35S, M#22, 21J, Wind Indicator, Adj.6P, in gimbals and box, lever	$500	$600	$700
35S, M#22, 21J, Wind Indicator, Adj.6P, in a large base metal OF case	400	500	600
36S, M#36, 21J, Wind Indicator, in gimbals and box	1,200	1,400	1,600
36S, M#36, 21J, Wind Indicator, in Hamilton sterling pocket watch case with bow	1,500	1,700	2,000
85S, M#21, 14J, KW, KS, Fusee, Detent Escapement with helical hairspring, gimbals and box	1,300	1,500	1,800

HAMILTON WATCH COMPANY
IDENTIFICATION OF MOVEMENT
BY MODEL NUMBER

How to Identify Your Watch: Compare the movement with the illustrations in this section. While comparing, note the location of the balance, jewels, screws, gears, and back plate (Full, ¾, Bridge) which will be clues in identifying the movement you have. Having determined the size, the Grade can also be found by looking up the serial number of your watch in the Hamilton Serial Number and Grades list.

Grade 936, 18 size

Open face, 17 jewels, single roller before No. 426,001, double roller after No. 426,000.

Grade 925, 18 size

Hunting, 17 jewels, single roller

Grade 971, 16 size

Hunting, 21 jewels, ¾ plate movt.

Grade 992, 16 size

Open face, ¾ plate movt., 21 jewels, single roller before No. 377,001, double roller after No. 379,000.

Grade 992B, 16 size
Open face, ¾ plate movt., 21 jewels, double roller

Grade 950, 16 size
Open face, bridge movt., 23 jewels, double roller

Grade 950B, 16 size
Open face, bridge movt., 23 jewels, double roller

Grade 902, 12 size
Open face, bridge movt., 19 jewels, double roller

Grade 912, 12 size
Open face, ¾ plate movt., 17 jewels, double roller

Grade 918, 12 size
Open face, ¾ plate movt., 19 jewels, double roller

Grade 922, 12 size
Open face, bridge movt., 23 jewels, double roller

Grade 917, 10 size
Open face, ¾ plate movt., 17 jewels, double roller

Grade 921, 10 size
Open face, bridge movt., 21 jewels, double roller

Grade 923, 10 size
Open face, bridge movt., 23 jewels, double roller

Grade 983, 0 size
Hunting, bridge movt., 17 jewels,
double roller

Grade 979,6/0 size
Hunting, ¾ plate movt., 19
jewels, double roller

Grade 986, 6/0 size
Open face, ¾ plate movt., 17
jewels, double roller

HAMPDEN WATCH CO.
(DUEBER WATCH CO.)
Springfield, Massachusetts
Canton, Ohio
1876 - 1930

The New York Watch Co. preceded Hampden, and before that Don J. Mozart (1864) produced his three-wheel watch. Mozart was assisted by George Samuel Rice of New York and, as a result of their joint efforts, the New York Watch Co. was formed in 1866 in Providence, Rhode Island. It was moved in 1867 to Springfield, Massachusetts. Two grades of watches were decided on, and the company started with a 18S, 3/4 plate engraved "Springfield." They were sold for $60 to $75. The 18S, 3/4 plate were standard production, and the highest grade was a "George Walker" that sold for about $200 and a 16S, 3/4 plate "State Street" which had steel parts and exposed balance and escape wheels that were gold plated.

John C. Dueber started manufacturing watch cases in 1864 and bought a controlling interest in a company in 1886. At about this time a disagreement arose between Elgin, Waltham, and the Illinois Watch companies. Also, at this time, an anti-trust law was passed, and the watch case manufacturers formed a boycott against Dueber. Dueber was faced with a major decision, whether to stay in business, surrender to the watch case companies or buy a watch company. He decided to buy the Hampden Watch Co. of Springfield, Mass. By 1889 the operation had moved to Canton, Ohio. By the end of the year the company was turning out 600 watches a day. The first 16 size watch was produced in 1890. In 1894 Hampden introduced the first 23J movement made in America.

HAMPDEN ESTIMATED SERIAL NUMBER
AND PRODUCTION DATES

Date	Serial No.	Date	Serial No.	Date	Serial No.
1877	60,000	1893	775,000	1909	2,536,000
1878	91,000	1894	833,000	1910	2,664,000
1879	122,000	1895	888,500	1911	2,792,000
1880	153,000	1896	944,000	1912	2,920,000
1881	184,000	1897	1,000,000	1913	3,048,000
1882	215,000	1898	1,128,000	1914	3,176,000
1883	250,000	1899	1,256,000	1915	3,304,000
1884	300,000	1900	1,384,000	1916	3,432,000
1885	350,000	1901	1,512,000	1917	3,560,000
1886	400,000	1902	1,642,000	1918	3,680,000
1887	450,000	1903	1,768,000	1919	3,816,000
1888	500,000	1904	1,896,000	1920	3,944,000
1889	555,500	1905	2,024,000	1921	4,072,000
1890	611,000	1906	2,152,000	1922	4,200,000
1891	666,500	1907	2,280,000	1923	4,400,000
1892	722,000	1908	2,408,000	1924	4,600,000

Chronology of the Development of Hampden Watch Co.:
The Mozart Watch Co., Providence, R. I. –1864-1866
New York Watch Co., Providence, R. I. –1866-1867
New York Watch Co., Springfield, Mass. –1867-1875
New York Watch Mfg. Co., Springfield, Mass. –1875-1876
Hampden Watch Co., Springfield, Mass. –1877-1886
Hampden-Dueber Watch Co., Springfield, Mass.–1886-1888
Hampden Watch Co., Canton, Ohio –1888–1923
Dueber Watch Co., Canton, Ohio –1888–1923
Dueber-Hampden Watch Co., Canton, Ohio –1923–1931
Amtorg, U.S.S.R. –1930–Present

Issued 1890

Issued 1892

Issued 1895

Dueber Watch Co., 18 size, 15 jewels, nickel movement.   Dueber Grand, 18 size, 17 jewels, open face, originally
Model 3, hunting case.   sold for $20.00.

HAMPDEN
18 SIZE

Grade or Name — Description	Avg	Ex-Fn	Mint
Anchor, 17J, ADJ, GJS, DMK, OF	$75	$100	$150
"3" Ball, 17J, ADJ, NI, DMK, OF	100	125	175
Champion, 7-11J, ADJ, FULL, gilded, or, NI, OF	55	75	95
Champion, 7-11J, ADJ, FULL, gilded, or, NI, HC	100	125	150
Champion, 15-17J, ADJ, FULL, gilded, or, NI, OF	65	75	100
Champion, 15-17J, ADJ, FULL, gilded, or, NI, HC	125	135	165
Correct Time, 15J, HC	125	150	200
Dueber, 16J, gilded, DMK, OF	75	100	150
Dueber, 17J, gilded, DMK, OF	75	100	150
John C. Dueber, 15J, gilded, DMK, OF	75	100	150
John C. Dueber, 17J, gilded, ADJ, DMK, OF	70	100	150
John C. Dueber, Sp., 17J, gilded, ADJ, DMK, OF	75	100	150
John C. Dueber, 17J, HC	100	125	175
John C. Dueber, 21J, HC	150	165	225
Dueber Grand, 17J, OF	75	100	150
Dueber Grand, 17J, ADJ, HC	100	125	175
Dueber Grand, 21J, ADJ, DMK, NI, HC	150	175	225
Dueber W. Co., 11J, OF	75	100	125
Dueber W. Co., 15J, DMK, OF	75	100	135
Dueber W. Co., 15J, DMK, HC	100	125	175
Dueber W. Co., 16J, OF	75	100	150
Dueber W. Co., 16J, HC	100	125	175
Dueber W. Co., 17J, DMK, ADJ, OF	75	100	150
Dueber W. Co., 17J, Gilded	75	100	150
Dueber W. Co., 17J, DMK, ADJ, HC	100	125	175
Dueber W. Co., 19J, ADJ, GJS, HC ★	400	475	550
Dueber W. Co., 21J, Adj.5P, GJS, OF	125	150	175
Dueber W. Co., 21J, GJS, Adj.5P, HC	150	175	225

John C. Dueber Special, 18 size, 17 jewels, serial number 949,097.

Oriental, 18 size, 15 jewels, open face, serial number 117,825.

Grade or Name — Description	Avg	Ex-Fn	Mint
Homer Foot, gilded, KW, OF (Early)	$150	$175	$225
Gladiator, KW, OF	75	100	150
Gladiator, 11J, NI, DMK, OF	75	100	150
Gulf Stream Sp., 21J, R.R. grade, OF, LS	400	500	600
Hampden W. Co., 7J, KW, KS, OF	75	100	150
Hampden W. Co., 7J, SW, OF	55	75	100
Hampden W. Co., 11J, OF, KW	75	100	135
Hampden W. Co., 11J, HC, KW	100	125	150
Hampden W. Co., 11J, OF, SW	75	100	135
Hampden W. Co., 11J, HC, SW	100	125	175
Hampden W. Co., 15J, OF, KW	75	100	150
Hampden W. Co. 15J, HC, KW	100	125	175
Hampden W. Co., 15J, HC, SW	100	125	175
Hampden W. Co., 15J, SW, Gilded, OF	75	100	150
Hampden W. Co., 15J, SW, NI, OF	75	100	150
Hampden W. Co., 15J, Multi-color, 14K, HC	1,600	1,800	2,200
Hampden W. Co., 16J, OF	75	100	150
Hampden W. Co., 17J, SW, Gilded	75	100	150
Hampden W. Co., 17J, SW, NI, OF	75	100	150
Hampden W. Co., 17J, HC, SW	100	125	175
Hampden W. Co., 17J, LS, HC, 14K	500	550	625
Hampden W. Co., 17J, LS, HC, 10K	350	400	475
Hampden W. Co., 21J, OF, HC, SW	150	175	225
John Hancock, 7J, Adj., OF	55	75	100
John Hancock, 15J, Adj.3P, OF	70	90	135
John Hancock, 17J, GJS, Adj.3P, OF	75	100	150
John Hancock, 17J, GJS, Adj.3P, HC	125	150	200
John Hancock, 21J, GJS, Adj.3P, OF	125	150	200
John Hancock, 23J, GJS, Adj.5P, OF	200	250	325
Hayward, 15J, KW	100	125	200
Hayward, 11J, SW	75	100	125

Menlo Park, 18 size, 17 jewels, serial number 1,184,116.

New Railway, 18 size, 23 jewels, open face only, gold jewel settings, originally sold for $50.00, Model 2.

Grade or Name — Description	Avg	Ex-Fn	Mint
Lafayette, 11J, NI	$75	$85	$125
Lafayette, 15J, NI, KW	125	150	200
Lafayette, 15J, NI	100	125	175
Lakeside, 15J, NI, SW	100	125	175
M. J. & Co. Railroad Watch Co., 15J, HC	300	400	525
Menlo Park, 17J, NI, ADJ, OF	100	125	175
Mermod, Jaccard & Co., 15J, KW, HC	125	150	200
Metropolis, 15J, NI, SW, OF	75	100	150
Wm. McKinley, 17J, Adj.3P, OF	75	100	150
Wm. McKinley, 21J, GJS, Adj.5P	125	150	200
New Railway, 17J, GJS, Adj.5P, OF	75	100	150
New Railway, 19J, GJS, Adj.5P, OF	150	175	225
New Railway, 19J, GJS, Adj.5P, HC	150	175	225

Railway, 18 size, 17 jewels, key wind & set; early railroad watch.

Special Railway, 18 size, 23 jewels, Adj5p, serial number 3,357,284.

Grade or Name — Description	Avg	Ex-Fn	Mint
New Railway, 21J, GJS, Adj.5P, HC	$150	$175	$200
New Railway, 21J, GJS, Adj.5P, OF	125	150	175
New Railway, 23J, GJS, Adj.5P	175	225	300
New Railway, 23J, GJS, Adj.5P, 14K, OF	550	575	625
North Am. RR, 21J, GJS, Adj.5P, OF, LS	125	150	200
North Am. RR, 21J, GJS, Adj.3P, HC, PS	150	175	225
Pennsylvania Special, 17J, GJS, Adj.5P, DR, NI ★★	700	900	1,200
J. C. Perry, 15J, KW, gilded, HC	125	150	200
J. C. Perry, 15J, NI, SW, OF	70	80	95
J. C. Perry, 15J, gilded, SW, OF	75	100	150
Railway, 15J, gilded, OF	75	100	150
Railway, 17J, NI, OF	75	100	150
Railway, 15J, KW, marked on mvt., HC ★★	500	600	800
Railroad with R.R. names on dial and movement:			
Canadian Pacific RR, 17J, OF ★	500	600	800
Canadian Pacific RR, 21J, OF ★	550	700	900
Special Railway, 17J, GJS, Adj.5P, NI, DR, OF	75	100	150
Special Railway, 21J, GJS, Adj.5P, NI, DR, 2-Tone, OF	125	150	200
Special Railway, 23J, GJS, Adj.5P, NI, DR, 2-Tone, OF	200	275	375
Special Railway, 23J, Adj.5P, HC	225	300	400
Special Railway, 23J, 14K, HC	625	675	750
Springfield, 7-11J, KW, gilded, HC	100	125	175
Springfield, 7-11J, SW, NI, HC	100	125	175
Standard, 15J, gilded, HC	100	125	175
State Street, 15J, NI, LS, (Early KW)	150	175	225
Theo. Studley, 15J, KW, KS, HC	125	150	200
Tramway Special, 17J, NI	125	150	200
Woolworth, 11J, KW	100	125	175
Grade 45 HC & 65 OF, 11J	75	100	150
Grade 60, 15J, LS, OF	75	100	150
Grade 80 & 81, 17J, ADJ, OF	75	100	150
Grade 85, 19J, GJS, 2-Tone, HC ★★	500	600	750
Grade 95, 21J, GJS, OF	125	150	175
Grade 125, 21J, Adj.3P, OF	125	150	200

16 SIZE

Grade or Name — Description	Avg	Ex-Fn	Mint
Champion, 7J, NI, 3/4, gilded, coin, OF	$50	$75	$100
Champion, 7J, NI, 3/4, gilded, OF	50	75	100
Champion, 7J, NI, 3/4, gilded, HC	100	125	175
Chronometer, 21J, detent escapement, NI, Adj.3P, GJS	300	400	500
John C. Dueber, 17J, GJS, NI, Adj.5P, 3/4	75	100	150
John C. Dueber, 21J, GJS, NI, Adj.5P, 3/4	100	125	175
John C. Dueber, 21J, GJS, NI, Adj.5P, DR, BRG	125	150	200
Dueber Watch Co., 17J, ADJ, 3/4	75	100	150

Hampden W. Co., Bridge Model, 16 size, 23 jewels, 2-tone movement, serial number 1,899,430.

Hampden W. Co., 16 size, 17 jewels, gold jewel settings, serial number 3,075,235.

Grade or Name — Description	Av	Ex-Fn	Mint
Hampden W. Co., 7J, SW, OF	$50	$75	$125
Hampden W. Co., 7J, SW, HC	75	100	150
Hampden W. Co., 11J, SW, OF	50	75	125
Hampden W. Co., 11J, SW, HC	75	100	150
Hampden W. Co., 15J, SW, OF	50	75	125
Hampden W. Co., 15J, SW, HC	75	100	150
Hampden W. Co., 17J, SW, OF	50	75	125
Hampden W. Co., 17J, 14K, Multi-color, HC	1,200	1,400	1,600
Hampden W. Co., 17J, SW, HC	75	100	150
Hampden W. Co., 21J, SW, HC	150	175	225
Hampden W. Co., 21J, SW, OF	125	150	175
Hampden W. Co., 23J, Adj.5P, GJS, 3/4	200	225	300
Hampden W. Co., 23J, Series 2, HC "Freesprung", GJS, GT ★★★	375	450	550
Masonic Dial, 23J, GJS, 2-Tone porcelain dial	350	400	500

Hampden W. Co., Series I, 16 size, 15 jewels, stem wind, open face.

Railway, 16 size, 17 jewels, Adj5p, serial number 2,271,866.

Grade 104, 16 size, 23 jewels, gold jewel settings, gold train, Adj5p, serial number 2,801,184.

Grade 108, 16 size, 17 jewels, open face and hunting, serial number 1,042,051.

Grade or Name — Description	Avg	Ex-Fn	Mint
Wm. McKinley, 17J, GJS, Adj.5P, NI, DR, 3/4	$75	$100	$150
Wm. McKinley, 21J, GJS, Adj.5P, NI, DR, 3/4	125	150	175
Wm. McKinley, 21J, GJS, Adj.5P, NI, DR, 3/4, Coin	125	150	175
Wm. McKinley, 21J, GJS, Adj.5P, NI, DR, BRG	125	150	175
New Railway, 21J, GJS, Adj.5P	125	150	175
New Railway, 23J, GJS, Adj.5P, LS, HC	250	300	375
Ohioan, 21J, Adj.3P, GJS, 3/4	150	175	225
Railway, 19J, GJS, Adj.5P, BRG, DR	125	150	175
Special Railway, 23J, Adj.5P, NI, BRG, DR	225	275	350
Gen'l Stark, 15J, DMK, BRG	75	100	150
Gen'l Stark, 17J, DMK, BRG	75	100	150
95, 21J, marked "95", GJS, Adj.5P,	125	150	175
97 HC, 98 HC, & 108 OF, 17J, Adj.3P, NI, 3/4, DMK	75	100	150
99, 15J, 3/4, HC	100	125	175
103, 21J, GJS, Adj.5P, NI, BRG, DR	125	150	175
104, 23J, GJS, Adj.5P, NI, BRG, DR, DMK, HC	275	375	500
105, 21J, GJS, Adj.5P, NI, 3/4, DR, DMK	125	150	175
106, 107 OF, & 108, 17J, SW, NI	75	100	150
109, 15J, 3/4, OF	75	100	150
110, 11J, 3/4	60	70	85
115-120, 21J, SW, NI, OF	100	125	175
340, 17J, SW, NI	75	100	150
440, 15J, 2-tone	100	125	175
555, 21J, GT, GJS, Chronometer on dial & mvt.	200	250	325
600, 17J, SW, NI	75	100	150

12 SIZE

Grade or Name — Description	Avg	Ex-Fn	Mint
Champion, 7J, SW	$40	$50	$70
Dueber Grand, 17J, BRG, OF	50	60	80

Dueber Grand, 12 size, 17 jewels, gold jewel settings, hunting case, serial number 1,737,354.

Dueber Grand, 12 size, 17 jewels, gold jewel settings, open face, pin set, serial number 1,732,255.

Grade or Name — Description	Avg	Ex-Fn	Mint
Dueber Grand, 17J, BRG, HC	$55	$65	$85
Hampden W. Co., 7J, SW, OF	40	50	75
Hampden W. Co., 17J, 14K, Multi-color, HC	700	800	1,000
John Hancock, 21J, BRG	55	65	85
Gen'l Stark, 15J, BRG	40	50	75
Gen'l Stark, 15J, pin set	40	50	75
207-300 HC & 302 OF, 7J, 3/4 (add $25 for HC)	40	50	75
304 HC & 306 OF, 15J, 3/4 (add $25 for HC)	40	50	75
305-308 HC & 310 OF, 17J, 3/4	40	50	75
307, 17J	40	50	75
310, 17J, gold filled OF case	40	50	75
310, 17J, 14K OF case	150	175	200
312, 21J, 3/4, Adj.5P, DMK, HC	55	75	125
314, 21J, DR, Adj. 5P, DMK, OF	50	65	110
31 OF, 17J, SW, 14K	275	325	400

Paul Revere. Example of Hampden Watch Co.'s thin series showing face and movement, 12 size, 17-19 jewels, Adj5p.

12 SIZE (THIN MODEL)

Grade or Name — Description	Avg	Ex-Fn	Mint
Aviator, 17J, Adj.4P	$40	$50	$75
Aviator, 19J, Adj.4P	45	60	85
Beacon, 17J	40	50	75
Nathan Hale, 15J ★	40	50	75
Minuteman, 17J ★	50	60	85
Paul Revere, 17J, OF 14K	275	325	400
Paul Revere, 17J	50	60	85
Paul Revere, 19J	60	70	95

☞ Note: Some 12 Sizes came in cases of octagon, decagon, hexagon, triad, and cushion shapes, and these usually bring slightly higher prices.

6 SIZE

Grade or Name — Description	Avg	Ex-Fn	Mint
200, 7J (add $25 for HC)	$40	$50	$75
206, 11J (add $25 for HC)	40	50	75
213, 15J (add $25 for HC)	40	50	75
220, 17J (add $25 for HC)	40	50	75
Hampden W. Co., 15J, multi-color GF, HC	150	200	275
Hampden W. Co., 15J, Multi-color, 14K, HC	375	425	500

Molly Stark, 000 size, 7 jewels, hunting or open face, originally sold for $12.00.

000 SIZE

Grade or Name — Description	Avg	Ex-Fn	Mint
Diadem, 15J, 14K, OF Case	$100	$150	$200
Diadem, 15J, HC, 14K	200	250	325
Diadem, 15J, HC	100	125	175
Molly Stark, 7J, HC	100	125	175
Molly Stark, 7J, 14K, HC	200	250	325
Molly Stark, 7J, Pin Set, OF	50	75	125
Four Hundred, 11, 15, 16, & 17J, HC	100	125	175
14K Multi-color, HC	375	425	500

HAMPDEN WATCH CO.
IDENTIFICATION OF MOVEMENTS

How to Identify Your Watch: Compare the movement of your watch with the illustrations in this section. While comparing, note the location of the balance, jewels, screws, gears, and type of back plate (Full, 3/4, Bridge) which will be clues in identifying the movement you have.

Series I, 18 size
Hunting or open face, key wind & set

Series II, 18 size
Hunting, stem wind, pendant or lever set

Series III, 18 size
Hunting, stem wind, pendant or lever set

Series IV, 18 size
Open face, stem wind, lever set

Series 1, 16 size
Open face, stem wind, pendant or lever set

Series II, 16 size
Hunting, stem wind, pendant or lever set

Series III, 16 size
Open face, stem wind, pendant set

Series IV, 16 size
Hunting, stem wind, pendant or lever set

Series V, 16 size
Open face, stem wind, pendant or lever set

Series VI, 16 size
Hunting, stem wind, pendant set

Series VII, 16 size
Open face, stem wind, pendant set

Series III, 12 size
Open face, stem wind, pendant set

Series I, 12 size
Hunting, stem wind, lever set

Series II, 12 size
Open face, stem wind, lever set

Series IV, 12 size
Open face, stem wind, pendant

Series V, 12 size
Open face, stem wind, pendant set

Series I, 6 size
Open face, stem wind

Series I, 3/0 size
Hunting, stem wind

Series II, 3/0 size
Open face, stem wind, pendant

Series III, 3/0 size
Hunting, lever or pendant

Series IV, 3/0 size
Hunting, stem wind, pendant

HERMAN VON DER HEYDT
CHICAGO SELF–WINDING WATCH CO.
Chicago, Illinois
1883

Herman von der Heydt patented a self-winding watch on Feb. 19, 1884. A total of 35 watches were hand-made by von der Heydt. The watches were 18S, full plate, lever escapement and fully-jeweled. The wind mechanism was a gravity type made of heavy steel and shaped like a crescent. The body motion let the heavy crescent move which was connected to a ratchet on the winding arbor, resulting in self-winding. Five movements were nickel and sold for about $90; the gilded model sold for about $75.

Grade or Name — Description		Avg	Ex-Fn	Mint
18S, 19J, FULL, NI.. ★★★★		$12,000	$14,000	$16,000
18S, 19J, FULL, gilded .... ★★★★		10,000	12,000	14,000

Example of Herman Von Der Heydt, 18 size self winding watch. "Chicago S. W. Co." on dial.

Herman Von Der Heydt, 18 size, 19 jewels; America's only self winding pocket watch. Note crescent shaped winding weight.

E. HOWARD & CO.
Boston (Roxbury), Massachusetts
December 11, 1858 - 1903

After the failure of the Boston Watch Company (1853 -57), Edward Howard decided to personally attempt the successful production of watches using the interchangeable machine-made parts system. He and Charles Rice, his financial backer, were unable to buy out the defunct watch company in Waltham, however, they did remove (per a prior claim) the watches in progress, the tools and the machinery to Howard and Davis' Roxbury factory (first watch factory in America), in late 1857. During their first year, the machinery was retooled for the production of a revolutionary new watch of Howard's design. Also, the remaining Boston Watch Co. movements were completed (E. Howard & Co. dials, Howard & Rice on the movement). By the summer of 1858, Edward Howard had produced his first watch. On December 11, 1858 the firm of E. Howard & Co. was formed for the manufacture of high-grade watches. Howard's first model was entirely different from any watch previously made. It introduced the more accurate "quick beat" train to American watchmaking. The top plate was in two sections and had six pillars instead of the usual four pillars in a full plate. The balance was gold or steel at first, then later it was a compensation balance loaded with gold screws. Reed's patented barrel was used for the first time. The size, based on the Dennison system, was a little larger than the regular 18 size. In 1861, a 3/4 plate model was put on the market. Most movements were being stamped with "N" to designate Howard's 18 size. On February 4, 1868 Howard patented a new steel motor barrel which was to supersede the Reed's, but not before some 28,000 had been produced. Also, in 1868 Howard introduced the stemwinding movement and was probably the first company to market such a watch in the U. S. By 1869, Howard was producing their "L" or 16 size as well as their first nickel movements. In 1870, G. P. Reed's micrometer regulator was patented for use by E. Howard & Co. The Reed style "whiplash" regulator has been used in more pocket watches, worldwide, than any other type. In 1878, the manufacturing of keywind movements was discontinued. Mr. Howard retired in 1882, but the company continued to produce watch movements of the grade and style set by him until 1903. This company was the first to adjust to all six positions. Their dials were always a hard enamel and always bore the name "E. Howard & Co., Boston." In 1903, the company transferred all rights to use the name "Edward Howard," in conjunction with the production of watches, to the Keystone Watch Case Co. Most of their models were stamped "Howard" on the dial and "E. Howard Watch Co., Boston. U.S.A." on the movement. Edward Howard's company never produced its own watch cases, the great majority of which were solid gold or silver. Keystone, however, produced complete watches, many of which were gold filled.

CHRONOLOGICAL DEVELOPMENT OF E. HOWARD & CO.:
Howard, Davis & Dennison, Roxbury, Mass., 1850
American Horologue Company, Roxbury, Mass., 1851
Warren Manufacturing Company, Roxbury, Mass., 1851-53
Boston Watch Co., Roxbury, Mass. —1853-1854/Waltham, Mass., 1854-57
Howard & Rice, Roxbury, Mass., 1857-58 (E. Howard & Co. on dials)
E. Howard & Co., Roxbury, Mass. —1858-1903
Keystone Watch Case Co. (Howard line), Jersey City, N. J., 1903-30

LEFT: Balance cock unmarked = UNADJUSTED
CENTER: Balance cock marked heat &cold = adjusted to TEMPERATURE
RIGHT: Balance cock marked adjusted = FULLY ADJUSTED

E. HOWARD & CO.
APPROXIMATE DATES, SERIAL NOS., AND TOTAL PRODUCTION

Serial Number	Date	Series	Total Prod.
131-1,800	-1860	I (18S)	1,800
1,801-3,000	1860-1861	II (18S)	1,200
3,001-3,200	1861	K(14S)	100
3,201-3,400	1861	i(10S)	100
3,501-28,000	1861-1871	III (18S)	24,500
30,001-50,000	1868-1882	IV (18S)	20,000
50,001-71,000	1869-1899	V (16S)	21,000
100,001-105,500	1869-1899	VI (6S)	5,500
200,001-227,000	1880-1899	VII (18S)	27,000
*228,001-231,000	1895	VII (18S)	3,000
300,001-309,000	1884-1899	VIII (18S)	9,000
*309,001-310,000	1895	VIII (18S)	1,000
400,001-405,000	1890-1895	IX (18S)	5,000
500,001-501,500	1890-1899	X (12S)	1,500
*600,001-601,500	1896	XI (16S)	1,500
*700,001-701,500	1896	XII (16S)	1,500

* ¾ Split Plates with 17 Jewels

E. HOWARD & CO. WATCH SIZES

Letter	Inches	Approx. Size
N	1 13/16	18
L	1 11/16	16
K	1 10/16	14
J	1 9/16	12
I	1 8/16	10
H	1 7/16	8
G	1 6/16	6
F	1 5/16	4
E	1 4/16	2
D	1 3/16	0

Standard Escapement

Coles Escapement

Deer
Adjusted to
Hcl6P

Horse
Adjusted to
HCI-No
positions

Hound
Unadjusted

NOTE: E. Howard & Co. movements will not fit standard cases properly.

18 or N size, 15 jewels, right angle lever escapement, experimental model, serial number 3,122.

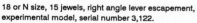

10 or I size, 15 jewels; note cut-out to view esape wheel, experimental model, serial number 3,472.

E. HOWARD & CO.
N SIZE (18)
(In Original Cases)

Series or Name — Description	Avg	Ex-Fn	Mint
E. Howard & Co. on dial and movement, 1857 Model, upright pallets, English style escape wheel, KW & KS, silver case ....★★	$1,600	$2,000	$2,500
I, II or III, Isochronism, 15J, gilded, KW, helical hairspring ....★★★	5,000	6,000	8,000

Series 1, 18 size, 15 jewels, note the compensating balance on this early movement, serial number 133.

Series II, 18 size, 15 jewels, key wind & set, serial number 2,477.

Grade or Name — Description	Avg	Ex-Fn	Mint
I, 15J, with serial # below 100	$5,000	$6,000	$7,500
I, 15J, with serial # below 200	2,000	3,000	4,500
I, 15J, with serial # below 300	1,000	2,000	3,000
I, 15J, gilded, KW, 18K, HC or OF, upright pallets ....★★	2,200	2,800	3,500
I, 15J, gilded, KW, 18K, HC or OF, horizontal pallets .... ★	1,800	2,000	2,500
I, 15J, gilded, KW, silver HC..................................... ★	1,000	1,200	1,400
I, 15J, (movement only)..................................... ★	500	600	700
II, 15J, gilded, KW, 18K, HC or OF................................ ★	1,600	1,800	2,000
II, 15J, gilded, KW, silver HC................................ ★	800	1,000	1,200
II, 15J, (movement only) .... ★	450	550	650
III, 15J, gilded, KW, 18K, HC....................................	1,300	1,500	1,800
III, 15J, gilded, KW, silver case	600	800	1,000
III, 15J, nickel, KW, silver case................................	700	900	1,100
III, 15J, gilded, KW, 18K, Mershon's Patent....................	1,500	1,800	2,000
III, 15J, gilded, KW, 18K, Coles Escapement ....★★	1,600	1,900	2,300
III, 15J, NI, Private label	800	1,000	1,200
III, 15J , (movement only).....................................	150	175	225
IV, 15J, gilded or nickel, KW, 18K, HC	1,200	1,400	1,700
IV, 15J, gilded or nickel, SW, 18K, HC	1,000	1,200	1,400

Series III, 18 size, 15 jewels, note center wheel rack regulator, serial number 22,693.

Series III, 18 size, 15 jewels, note high balance wheel over center wheel, serial number 7,000.

Series IV, 18 size, 15 jewels, key wind and set, serial number 37,893.

Series VII, 18 size, 15 jewels, nickel movement, note running deer on movement, "adjusted" on bridge, serial number 219,304.

Series or Name — Description		Avg	Ex-Fn	Mint
IV, personalized with jobber's name, silver	★★	$500	$600	$800
IV, 15J, gilded, Cole's Escapement	★★★	1,500	1,600	1,700
IV, 15J (movement only)		90	110	150
VII, 15J, gilded or nickel, SW, 14K, HC		1,000	1,200	1,500
VII, 17J, nickel, split plate, SW, 14K, HC	★	1,200	1,400	1,700
VII, 17J, nickel, split plate, SW, silver, HC	★	600	700	900
VII, 19J, nickel, split plate, SW, 14K HC	★★★	2,500	3,000	4,000
VII, 15J (movement only)		95	100	115
VII, Ball, 17J, nickel, SW, 14K, HC	★★★	3,500	4,000	6,000
VII, Ball, 17J, nickel, SW, GF, HC	★★★	2,200	2,800	3,500
VIII, 15J, gilded or nickel, SW, 14K, OF		900	1,000	1,400
VIII, 17J, nickel, split plate, SW, 14K, OF	★	1,200	1,400	1,700
VIII, 17J, nickel, split plate, SW, silver, OF	★	425	525	650
VIII, 15J (movement only)		85	90	100
VIII, Ball, 17J, nickel, SW, 14K, OF	★★	3,000	3,500	4,000
VIII, Ball, 17J, nickel, SW, GF, OF	★★	1,000	1,500	2,000

Series VII, 18 size, 17 jewels, 3/4 split plate, serial number 228,055.

Series VIII, 18 size, 15 jewels, serial number 308,455.

Series VIII, 18 size, 17 jewels, split plate model, gold jewel settings, serial number 309,904.

Series IX, 18 size, 15 jewels, hunting. This series is gilded only and hound grade exclusively, serial number 402,873.

Series or Name — Description	Avg	Ex-Fn	Mint
IX, 15J, gilded, SW, 14K, HC	$900	$1,100	$1,400
IX, 15J, gilded, SW, silver, HC	425	525	650
IX, 15J (movement only)	80	85	100

L SIZE (16)
(In Original Cases)

Series or Name — Description	Avg	Ex-Fn	Mint
V, 15J, gilded, KW, 18K, HC	$1,000	$1,200	$1,500
V, 15J, gilded, KW, 18K, Coles Escapement ★	1,300	1,500	1,800
V, 15J, gilded or nickel, SW, 14K, HC	800	1,000	1,300
V, 15J, gilded, SW, 14K, Coles Escapement ★	1,100	1,300	1,600
Prescott, 15J., gilded, SW, (Series V movement only) ★	1,000	1,500	2,000

Series V, 16 or L size, Prescott Model, 15 jewels, hunting, serial number 50,434.

Series XI, 16 size, 17 jewels, split plate model, nickel movement, gold jewel settings, serial number 600,021.

Series XII, L-16 size, 21 jewels, split plate model, nickel movement, gold lettering, gold jewel settings, serial number 700,899.

Series K, 14 or K size, 15 jewels, key wind & set, serial number 3,005.

Series or Name — Description	Avg	Ex-Fn	Mint
V, 15J (movement only)	$90	$100	$125
XI, 17J, nickel, split plate, SW, 14K, HC .... ★	1,100	1,300	1,600
XI, 17J, nickel, split plate, SW, silver, HC .... ★	400	500	650
XI, 17J (movement only)..	200	300	450
XII, 17J, nickel, split plate, SW, 14K, OF .... ★	1,000	1,200	1,500
XII, 17J, nickel, split plate, SW, silver, OF .... ★	375	475	625
XII, 17J (movement only)	100	150	175
XII, 21J, nickel, split plate, SW, 14K OF ....★★★	2,500	3,000	4,000

K SIZE (14)
(In Original Cases)

Series or Name — Description	Avg	Ex-Fn	Mint
K, 15J, gilded, KW, 18K, HC .... ★★★★	$4,000	$5,000	$6,500

J SIZE (12)
(In Original Cases)

Series or Name – Description	Avg	Ex-Fn	Mint
X, 15J, nickel, hound, SW, 14K, OF .... ★	$700	$900	$1,200
X, 15J, nickel, horse, SW, 14K, OF........................... ★	800	1,000	1,300
X, 15J, nickel, deer, SW, 14K, OF............................ ★	900	1,100	1,400
X, 15J, hound (movement only)................................ ★	200	250	300

Series X, 12 or J size, 15 jewels, note deer on movement, serial number 501,361.

I size (10 size), 15 jewels, gilded, key wind, serial number 3,404.

I SIZE (10)
(In Original Cases)

Series or Name — Description	Avg	Ex-Fn	Mint
I, 15J, gilded, KW, 18K HC .... ★★★	$2,800	$3,400	$4,200

G SIZE (6)
(In Original Cases)

Series or Name — Description	Avg	Ex-Fn	Mint
VI, 15J, gilded, KW, 18K, HC .... ★★	$1,400	$1,800	$2,400
VI, 15J, gilded or nickel, SW, 18K, HC	1,000	1,200	1,500
VI, 15J, gilded or nickel, SW, 14K, HC	700	850	1,000
VI, 15J (movement only)	175	200	300

Series VI, 6 or G size, 15 jewels, stem wind.

Series VI, 6 or G size, 15 jewels, stem wind, serial number 104,520.

E. HOWARD WATCH CO.
Waltham, Massachusetts
1902 - 1930

The Howard name was purchased by the Keystone Watch Case Co. in 1902. The watches are marked "E. Howard Watch Co. Boston, U. S. A." There were no patent rights transferred, just the Howard name. The "Edward Howard" chronometer was the highest grade, 16 size, and was introduced in 1912 for $350.

Keystone Howard gained control of U. S. Watch Co. of Waltham and N. Y. Standard Watch Co.

ESTIMATED SERIAL NUMBERS
AND PRODUCTION DATES

Date	Serial No.
1902	850,000
1903	900,000
1909	980,000
1912	1,100,000
1915	1,285,000
1917	1,340,000
1921	1,400,000
1930	1,500,000

The arrows denote number of jewels and adjustments in each grade.

Cross—23 jewel, 5 positions

Star—21 jewel, 5 positions

Triangle—19 jewel, 5 positions

Circle—17 jewel, 3 positions

SERIES 1905, 16 size, 17 jewels. This model can be identified by the slant parallel damaskeening. This represents the middle grade.

SERIES 9, 16 size, 17 jewels. This model can be identified by the checkerboard damaskeening. This represents the top grade.

SERIES 3, 16 size, 17 jewels. This model can be identified by the circular damaskeening. This represents the lowest grade of the three.

E. Howard Watch Co., Series 0, 16 size, 23 jewels, in original E. Howard Watch Co. swing-out movement Keystone Extra gold filled OpenFace case.

E. HOWARD WATCH CO. Series 0 (not marked), 16S, 23J., Hunting Case,

☞ NOTE: unmarked Series 0, 1, 2, 5 & 10 look the same as the 2 above illustrations, 0 = 23J, 1&10 = 21J, 2 = 17J, 5 = 19J.

E. HOWARD WATCH CO.
(KEYSTONE)
16 SIZE

Series or Name — Description	Avg	Ex-Fn	Mint
No. 0, 23J, BRG, Adj.5P, DR, OF	$425	$500	$600
Series 0, 23J, BRG, Adj.5P, DR, Ruby banking pins	425	500	600
Series 0, 23J, BRG, Adj.5P, DR, jeweled barrel	450	525	625
Series 0, 23J, BRG, Adj.5P, DR, OF, 14K	700	900	1,200
Series 0, 23J, BRG, Adj.5P, DR, HC, 14K	1,000	1,200	1,500
No. 1, 21J, BRG, Adj.5P, DR ★	275	300	375
Series 1, 21J, BRG, Adj.5P, DR	275	300	375
Series 2, 17J, BRG, Adj.5P, DR, HC	175	200	250

☞ Note: Add $75-$100 for original box and papers. Add $50 for hunting case models listed as open face.

Series II, Railroad Chronometer, 16 size, 21 jewels, Adj5p, serial number 1,217,534.

Edward Howard Model, 16 size, 23 blue sapphire jewels, frosted gold bridge, wolfteeth wind, serial number 77. c.1914.

E. Howard Watch Co., 16 size, 23 jewels, by Waltham, raised gold jewel settings, Adj5p, hunting case, bridge style movement.

E. Howard Watch Co., 16 size 19 jewels, by Waltham, gold jewel settings, Adj3p, hunting case, 3/4 plate movement.

Series or Name — Description	Avg	Ex-Fn	Mint
Series 2, 17J, BRG, Adj.5P, DR, OF	$125	$150	$175
Series 3, 17J, 3/4, Adj.3P, circular DMK	100	125	150
Series 3, 17J, OF, Adj.3P, 14K, circular DMK	500	525	550
No. 5, 19J, GJS, BRG, HC ★	400	425	450
Series 5, 19J, BRG, Adj.5P, DR, 14K	550	575	600
Series 5, 19J, BRG, Adj.5P, DR, 1907 Model	200	225	275
1905, 17J, 3/4, Adj.5P, DR, RGJS, slant parallel DMK, OF	125	150	175
1905, 17J, 3/4, Adj.5P, DR, RGJS, slant parallel DMK, HC	175	200	250
Series 9, 17J, 3/4, Adj.5P, DR, LS, checkerboard DMK	175	200	250
Series 9, 17J, 3/4, Adj.5P, DR, 14K, checkerboard DMK (railroad grade)	475	500	550
Series 10, 21J, BRG, Adj.5P, DR Marked Non–Magnetic ★	250	325	475
Series 10, 21J, BRG, Adj.5P, DR	250	300	375
No. 10, 21J, BRG, Adj.5P, DR	250	300	375
Series 11, 21J, R.R. Chrono., Adj.5P, DR	300	350	425
Edward Howard," 23 blue sapphire J, Adj.6P, GJS, GT, DR Serial numbers below 300, without box ★★	8,000	9,000	10,000
Edward Howard," 23 blue sapphire J, Adj.6P, GJS, GT, DR Serial numbers below 300, with original box and papers, with a 18K Edward Howard case ★★★	9,000	10,000	11,000
23J, E. Howard W. Co. on movement (mfg. by Waltham), 14K, Brg model ★★	1,200	1,400	1,700
23J, E. Howard W. Co. on movement (mfg. by Waltham), OF, gold filled	500	600	700
23J, E. Howard W. Co. on movement (mfg. by Waltham), HC, gold filled	600	700	800
21J, Waltham Model, 3/4, OF	275	300	350
19J, Waltham Model, 3/4, OF	275	300	350

Series or Name — Description	Avg	Ex-Fn	Mint
17J, Waltham Model, 3/4, OF..	$225	$250	$300
Climax,7J.,(made for export), gilded, OF.....................................	60	70	90
Unmarked, 23J, BRG, Adj.5P, DR, OF....................................	425	450	500

☞ Note: Add $100 for original wood box and papers on 16 size watches.

12 SIZE

Series or Name — Description	Avg	Ex-Fn	Mint
Series 6, 19J, BRG, DR, Adj.5P, 1908 Model, 14K, HC	$300	$350	$425
Series 6, 19J, BRG, DR, Adj.5P, 14K, OF....................................	200	250	325
Series 6, 19J, BRG, DR, Adj.5P, OF.....................................	70	90	125
Series 7, 17J, BRG, DR, Adj.3P, 14K, OF....................................	200	250	325
Series 7, 17J, BRG, DR, Adj.3P, OF.....................................	70	90	125
Series 8, 21J, BRG, DR, Adj.5P, OF......................................	85	100	150
Series 8, 23J, BRG, DR, Adj.5P, 14K, OF....................................	350	400	475
Series 8, 23J, BRG, DR, Adj.5P, OF......................................	100	150	200
Series 8, 23J, BRG, DR, Adj.5P, 14K, HC....................................	450	550	650

☞ NOTE: Add $25 for gold filled hunting case.

Series 8, 12 size, 21 jewels, open face, stop works, extra thin.

E. Howard Watch Co., 10 size, 17 jewels, Adj3p, serial number 61,230. (Serial numbers started at about 1,001 on this model.)

10 SIZE

☞ NOTE: Serial numbers start at about 1,001 on this model.

Series or Name — Description	Avg	Ex-Fn	Mint
Thin Model, 21J, ADJ, 14K case, OF..	$250	$275	$325
Thin Model, 19J, ADJ, 14K case, OF..	225	250	300
Thin Model, 17J, ADJ, 14K case, OF...	200	225	275

ILLINOIS WATCH CO.
Springfield, Illinois
1869 - 1927

The Illinois Watch Company was organized mainly through the efforts of J. C. Adams. The first directors were J. T. Stuart, W. B. Miller, John Williams, John W. Bunn, George Black and George Passfield. In 1879 the company changed all its watches to a quick train movement by changing the number of teeth in the fourth wheel. The first mainspring made by the company was used in 1882. The next year soft enamel dials were used.

The Illinois Watch Co. used more names on its movements than any other watch manufacturer. To identify all of them requires extensive knowledge by the collector plus a good working knowledge of watch mechanics. Engraved on some early movements, for example, are "S. W. Co." or "I. W. Co., Springfield, Ill." To the novice these ab breviations might be hard to understand, thus making Illinois watches difficult to identify. But one saving clue is that the location "Springfield, Illinois" appears on most of these watches. It is important to learn how to identify these type watches because some of them are extremely collectible. Examples of some of the more valuable of these are: the Benjamin Franklin (size 18 or 16, 25 or 26 jewels), Paillard's Non-Magnetic, Pennsylvania Special, C & O, and B & O railroad models.

The earliest movements made by the Illinois Watch Co. are listed below. They made the first watch in early 1872, but the company really didn't get off the ground until 1875. Going by the serial number, the first watch made was the Stuart. Next was the Mason, followed by the Bunn, the Miller, and finally the Currier. The first stem-wind was made in 1875.

The Illinois Watch Company was sold to Hamilton Watch Co. in 1927. The Illinois factory continued to produce Illinois watches under the new management until 1932. After 1933 Hamilton produced watches bearing the Illinois name in their own factory until 1939.

ILLINOIS WATCH CO., Bates Model, 18 size, 7 jewels, key wind & set, serial number 43,876, c.1874.

BUNN, 18 size, 16 jewels, hunting case, serial number 1,185,809.

CHRONOLOGY OF THE DEVELOPMENT OF ILLINOIS WATCH CO.:
Illinois Springfield Watch Co. 1869-1879
Springfield Illinois Watch Co. 1879-1885
Illinois Watch Co. 1885-1927
Illinois Watch Co. was sold to Hamilton Watch Co. in 1927.

ILLINOIS ESTIMATED SERIAL NUMBERS AND PRODUCTION DATES

Date	Serial No.	Date	Serial No.	Date	Serial No.
1872	5,000	1893	1,120,000	1914	2,600,000
1873	20,000	1894	1,160,000	1915	2,700,000
1874	50,000	1895	1,220,000	1916	2,800,000
1875	75,000	1896	1,250,000	1917	3,000,000
1876	100,000	1897	1,290,000	1918	3,200,000
1877	145,000	1898	1,330,000	1919	3,400,000
1878	210,000	1899	1,370,000	1920	3,600,000
1879	250,000	1900	1,410,000	1921	3,750,000
1880	300,000	1901	1,450,000	1922	3,900,000
1881	350,000	1902	1,500,000	1923	4,000,000
1882	400,000	1903	1,650,000	1924	4,500,000
1883	450,000	1904	1,700,000	1925	4,700,000
1884	500,000	1905	1,800,000	1926	4,800,000
1885	550,000	1906	1,840,000	1927	5,000,000
1886	600,000	1907	1,900,000	(Sold to Hamilton)	
1887	700,000	1908	2,100,000	1928	5,200,000
1888	800,000	1909	2,150,000	1929	5,350,000
1889	900,000	1910	2,200,000	1930	5,400,000
1890	1,000,000	1911	2,300,000	1931	5,500,000
1891	1,040,000	1912	2,400,000	1932	5,600,000
1892	1,080,000	1913	2,500,000		

(See Illinois Identification of Movements section located at the end of the Illinois price section to identify the movement, size and model number of your watch.)

ILLINOIS
18 SIZE

Grade or Name — Description	Avg	Ex-Fn	Mint
Alleghany, 11J, KW, gilded, OF	$55	$75	$125
Alleghany, 11J, M#1, NI, KWM#	100	125	175
Alleghany, 11J, M#2, NI, Transition	100	125	175
America, 7J, M#3, Silveroid	50	65	95
America, 7J, M#1-2, KW, FULL	100	125	175
America Special, 7J, M#1-2, KW, FULL	150	175	225
Army & Navy, 19J, GJS, Adj.5P, FULL	225	250	300
Army & Navy, 21J, GJS, Adj.5P, FULL	275	300	350
Baltimore & Ohio R.R. Special, 17J, GJS, ADJ	500	700	900
Baltimore & Ohio R.R. Special, 21J, GJS, NI, ADJ	800	1,000	1,200
Baltimore & Ohio R.R. Standard, 24J, GJS, ADJ	1,300	1,600	1,800
Bates, 7J, M#1-2, KW, FULL	125	150	185
Benjamin Franklin U.S.A., 17J, ADJ, NI	500	600	750

☞ NOTE: (Prices are with gold filled cases except where noted.)

Illinois Watch Co., 18 size, railroad watch with a Ferguson dial.

Army and Navy, 18 size, 19 jewels, engraved on movement "Washington Watch Co.," serial number 1,606,612.

Grade or Name — Description	Avg	Ex-Fn	Mint
Benjamin Franklin U.S.A., 21J, GJS, Adj.6P, NI .... ★	$900	$1,000	$1,150
Benjamin Franklin U.S.A., 21J, GJS, Adj.5P, NI .... ★	800	900	1,050
Benjamin Franklin U.S.A., 24J, GJS, Adj.6P, FULL, NI, DMK.. ★	2,000	2,500	3,000
Benjamin Franklin U.S.A., 25J, GJS, Adj.6P, FULL, NI, DMK.. ★★★★	6,000	6,500	7,500
Benjamin Franklin U.S.A., 26J, GJS, Adj.6P, FULL, DR, NI, DMK... ★★★	5,000	5,500	7,000
Bunn, 15J, M#1, KW, KS, FULL, OF..	500	600	775
Bunn, 15J, M#1, KW, KS, ADJ, FULL...........................	550	650	825
Bunn, 15J, KW/SW transition	425	500	650
Bunn, 15J, M#1, KW, Coin	500	600	775
Bunn, 15J, KW, M#1, HC....................................	550	650	825
Bunn, 16J, KW, OF	500	600	775
Bunn, 16J, KW, HC......................................	550	650	825
Bunn, 17J, SW, M#1, HC... ★	650	750	925
Bunn, 17J, M#2, SW, NI, FULL, HC	150	200	275
Bunn, 17J, SW, NI, Coin...............................	125	150	200
Bunn, 17J, SW, M#3, 5th pinion, gilded, OF	350	400	475
Bunn, 17J, M#4, SW, NI, FULL, OF................................	125	150	200
Bunn, 17J, M#5, SW, NI, FULL, HC	150	200	275
Bunn, 17J, M#6, SW, NI, FULL, OF...................................	125	150	200
Bunn, 19J, SW, NI, FULL, OF, DR, LS, GJS, Adj.5P, J. barrel	250	300	325
Bunn, 19J, SW, OF, Adj.6P, DR, J. barrel	300	350	425
Bunn, 19J, SW, GJS, FULL, HC, DR, Adj.5P, J. barrel......... ★	350	400	500
Bunn Special, 21J, SW, Coin...................................	150	175	225
Bunn Special, 21J, GJS, ADJ, HC....................................	300	350	400

Bunn Special, 18 size, 24 jewels, adjusted, serial number 1,413,435

Bunn Special, 18 size, 26 Ruby jewels, "J. Home & Co." on dial,adjusted to six positions, gold jewel settings, serial number 2,019,415.

Grade or Name — Description	Avg	Ex-Fn	Mint
Bunn Special, 21J, GJS, ADJ, DR, OF	$150	$175	$225
Bunn Special, 21J, GJS, DR, Adj.5P, OF	155	180	230
Bunn Special, 21J, GJS, DR, Adj.6P, OF	160	185	235
Bunn Special, 21J, GJS, Adj.5P, HC, 14K	700	750	825
Bunn Special, 21J, GJS, ADJ, 2-Tone	175	200	250
Bunn Special, 21J, GJS, Adj.5P, DR	175	200	250
Bunn Special, 21J," EXTRA", GJS ★	375	500	575
Bunn Special, 23J, GJS, ADJ, DR, OF	350	375	425
Bunn Special, 23J, GJS, Adj.6P, DR, OF	375	400	450
Bunn Special, 23J, GJS, Adj.6P, DR, 2-Tone, OF	375	400	450
Bunn Special, 23J, GJS, ADJ, DR, HC ★★	1,800	2,200	2,500
Bunn Special, 24J, GJS, Adj.5P, DR, HC	600	700	850
Bunn Special, 24J, GJS, Adj.5P, DR, 14K, HC	1,300	1,400	1,600
Bunn Special, 24J, GJS, Adj.5P, DR, OF	500	575	650
Bunn Special, 24J, GJS, Adj.6P, DR, OF	525	625	750
Bunn Special, 24J, GJS, Adj.5P, single roller	475	525	600
Bunn Special, 25J, GJS, Adj.6P, DR ★★★	5,000	5,500	6,500
Bunn Special, 26J, GJS, Adj.6P, DR ★★	4,500	5,000	6,000
Central Truck Railroad, 15J, KW, KS ★	350	400	475
Chesapeake & Ohio, 17J, ADJ, OF ★	400	500	600
Chesapeake & Ohio Special, 21J, GJS, 2-Tone ★	900	1,100	1,400
Chesapeake & Ohio Special, 24J, NI, ADJ, GJS ★	1,600	1,800	2,100
Chronometer, 15J, M#2, HC	150	175	225
Columbia, 11J, M#3, 5th Pinion	100	125	175
Columbia, 11J, M#1 & 2, FULL, KW	100	125	175
Columbia, 11J, M#1 & 2, Silveroid	75	100	150
Columbia Special, 11J, M#1-2-3, FULL, KW	100	125	175
Columbia Special, 11J, M#1-2-3, FULL, KW, transition	75	100	125
Comet, 11J, M#3, OF, LS, SW	75	100	125

Diurnal, 18 size, 7 jewels, key wind & set, only one run, total production 2,000, serial number 86,757.

Emperor, 18 size, 21 jewels, Adj3p, serial number 2,396,628.

Grade or Name — Description	Avg	Ex-Fn	Mint
Commodore, 17J, HC	$150	$175	$225
Currier, 11J, KW, FULL, OF	100	125	175
Currier, 11J, KW, FULL, Coin	100	125	175
Currier, 11J, KW, HC	125	175	225
Currier, 11J, KW/SW, HC	100	150	200
Currier, 11J, transition, OF	75	100	125
Currier, 11J, M#3, OF	75	100	125
Currier, 13–15J, M#3, OF	75	100	125
Dauntless, 11J	75	100	125
Dean, 15J, M#1, KW, FULL, HC ★	250	350	450
Diurnal, 7J, KW, KS, HC, Coin ★	200	250	325
Dominion Railway, with train on dial ★	800	900	1,200
Eastlake, 11J, SW, KW, Transition	100	125	175
Emperor, 11J, M#6, LS, SW, ADJ	150	175	225
Enterprise, M#2, ADJ	100	125	175
Eureka, 11J	100	125	175
Forest City, 7–11J, SW, LS, HC	125	150	200
Forest City, 17J, KW/SW, gilted, FULL	150	175	225
General Grant or General Lee, 11J, M#1, KW	225	250	300
Hoyt, 9-11J, M#1-2, KW, FULL	75	100	150
Illinois Watch Co., 11J, M#1-2, KW, FULL	75	100	125
Illinois Watch Co., 11J, M#3	55	75	100
Illinois Watch Co., 13J, M#1-2, KW, FULL	100	125	175
Illinois Watch Co., 15J, M#1-2, KW, FULL	100	125	175
Illinois Watch Co., 15J, G#106, KW, ADJ, FULL, NI	125	150	200
Illinois Watch Co., 15J, SW, ADJ, DMK, NI	75	100	125
Illinois Watch Co., 15J, transition	60	75	100
Illinois Watch Co., 15J, SW, Silveroid	50	60	75
Illinois Watch Co., 15J, SW, 9K, HC	300	400	550
Illinois Watch Co., 17J, SW, Silveroid	50	60	75
Illinois Watch Co., 17J, M#3, 5th Pinion	200	225	275
Illinois Watch Co., 17J, SW, 2 tone mvt,	65	95	145

Ill. W. Co., 18 size, 17 jewels, adjusted, 2-tone movement, serial number 1,404,442.

Miller, 18 size, 17 jewels, 5th pinion model which changes hunting case to open face.

Grade or Name — Description	Avg	Ex-Fn	Mint
Illinois Watch Co., 17J, SW, ADJ	$75	$100	$125
Illinois Watch Co., 17J, transition	75	100	125
Illinois Watch Co., 19J, OF	150	175	225
Illinois Watch Co., 21J, OF	150	175	225
Illinois Watch Co., 21J, HC	175	200	250
Interior, 7J, KW, FULL	100	125	175
Interior, 7J, M#3	75	100	150
Interstate Chronometer, 17J, HC	400	500	650
Interstate Chronometer, 17J, OF	300	400	550
Interstate Chronometer, 23J, Adj.5P, GJS, NI, OF	850	950	1,150
Interstate Chronometer, 23J, Adj.5P, GJS, NI, HC	950	1,050	1,250
Iowa W. Co., 7J, M#1-2, KW, FULL	175	200	250
Iowa W. Co., 11J, M#1-2, KW	175	200	250
King of the Road, 16 &17J, NI, OF & HC, LS, FULL, ADJ . ★	400	500	625
Lafayette, 24J, GJS, Adj.6P, NI, SW, OF	950	1,050	1,250
Lakeshore, 17J, OF, LS, NI, FULL, SW	100	125	175
Landis W. Co., 7-11J	75	100	150
Liberty Bell, 17J, NI, SW, FULL	100	125	175
Liberty Bell, 17J, Silveroid	75	100	150
A. Lincoln, 21J, Silveroid	125	150	175
A. Lincoln, 21J, Adj.5P, NI, DR, GJS, HC	250	300	375
A. Lincoln, 21J, Adj.5P, NI, FULL, DR, OF, GJS	150	175	225
Maiden Lane, 17J, 5th Pinion	350	400	475
Manhattan, 11J, NI, FULL, KW, LS, HC or OF	125	140	185
Manhattan, 15–17J, NI, FULL, KW, LS,HC or OF	130	155	200
Mason, 7J, KW, KS, HC, FULL	125	150	200
Miller, 15J, Silveroid	75	100	125
Miller, 15J, M#1, HC, KW, FULL	150	175	225
Miller, 15J, M#1, HC, KW, FULL, ADJ	175	200	250
Miller, 15J, KW, FULL, OF	125	150	200

Paillard Non-Magnetic W. Co., 18 size, 24 jewels, gold jewel settings, serial number 1,397,812.

Pennsylvania Special, 18 size, 26 jewels, Adj6p, 2-tone movement, serial number 1,742,913.

Grade or Name — Description	Avg	Ex-Fn	Mint
Miller, 17J, 5th Pinion, ADJ	$275	$300	$375
Monarch W. Co., 17J, NI, ADJ, SW, FULL	125	150	200
Montgomery Ward, 17J, OF, GJS	125	150	200
Montgomery Ward, 21J	150	175	225
Montgomery Ward Timer, 21J, ★	150	200	250
Montgomery Ward, 24J, OF	950	1,050	1,250
Montgomery Ward, 24J, HC ★	1,200	1,400	1,700
Muscatine W. Co., 15J, LS, NI, HC	150	175	225
The National, 11J, SW, LS, OF	75	100	135
Non-Magnetic W. Co., 21J, OF ★	225	275	350
A.Norton, 7J, KW, KS,	75	95	125
Paillard Non-Magnetic W. Co., 15J, NI, OF	75	100	150
Paillard Non-Magnetic W. Co., 17J, GJS, NI, Adj.5P, OF	100	125	155
Paillard Non-Magnetic W. Co., 21J, GJS, NI, Adj.5P, OF	200	250	325
Paillard Non-Magnetic W. Co., 23J, GJS, NI, Adj.5P, OF	850	900	1,150
Paillard Non-Magnetic W. Co., 24J, GJS, NI, Adj.5P, OF	950	1,050	1,250
Pennsylvania Special, 17J, GJS, Adj.3P ★	600	750	900
Pennsylvania Special, 21J, DR, Adj.5P ★	1,200	1,400	1,800
Pennsylvania Special, 24J, DR, GJS, ADJ ★	1,800	2,000	2,400
Pennsylvania Special, 25J, DR, GJS, ADJ, NI ★★★★	5,000	5,500	6,500
Pennsylvania Special, 26J, DR, GJS, ADJ, NI ★★	4,500	5,000	6,000
Pierce Arrow, 17J, "automaker logo" ★	350	425	575
Plymouth W. Co., 15-17J, SW, FULL	65	95	125
Potomac, 17J, OF, FULL, ADJ, NI	125	150	200
The President, 15J, FULL, NI, OF	125	150	200
The President, 17J, DMK, FULL, 14K gold case	600	700	850
Railroad Construction, 17J, OF	200	250	325
Railroad Dispatcher Extra, 17J, OF	200	250	325
Railroad King, 15J, FULL, NI, ADJ	225	250	275
Railroad King, 16J, FULL, NI, ADJ ★	300	350	425
Railroad King, 17J, FULL, NI, ADJ ★	300	350	425
The Railroader, 15J, OF, FULL, ADJ, NI	250	300	375
Railway Engineer, 15J	250	300	375

The President, 18 size, 17 jewels, chalmer patented regulator, serial number 1,240,909.

Railroad King, 18 size, 17 jewels, Fifth Pinion Model, adjusted. Note Chalmer patented regulator, serial number 1,160,836.

Grade or Name — Description	Avg	Ex-Fn	Mint
Railway Regulator, 15J, KW, KS, gilt	$400	$500	$675
Remington W.Co. 17J, OF ★	175	200	300
S. W. Co., 15J, M#1, KW, HC	125	150	200
R.W. Sears W.Co.Chicago,"Defiance" model, HC	650	750	900
Sears & Roebuck Special, 17J, GJS, NI, DMK, ADJ	125	150	200
Senate, 17J, NI, DMK, FULL	125	150	200
Southern R.R. Special, 21J, LS, ADJ, OF ★	800	1,000	1,250
Southern R.R. Special, 21J, M#5, LS, ADJ, HC ★	1,200	1,400	1,650
Star Light, 17J, 5th pinion, Chalmers Reg. OF	175	225	300
J. P. Stevens, 17J, SW. FULL, NI	600	700	850
Stuart, 15J, M#1, KW, KS	500	600	750
Stuart, 15J, M#1, KW, KS, transition ★	300	350	450
Stuart, 15J, M#1, KW, KS, marked ADJ ★★	500	650	825
Stuart, ADJ, KW, Abbotts Conversion, 18K, HC ★★	1,500	1,700	2,000
Stuart, 15J, M#1, KW, KS, Coin ★★	500	600	775
Stuart, 15J, M#1, KW, KS, HC, the 1st run and the serial # under" l0" ★★★★	5,000	6,500	8,500

Sears & Roebuck Special, 18 size, 17 jewels, serial number 1,481,879.

Washington W. Co., Lafayette model, 18 size, 24 Ruby jewels, gold jewel settings, adjusted, serial # 3,392,897.

Vault Time Lock for Mosler Lock Co., Covington, Ky. Movement is 18 size, 15 jewels, open face, Model number 6, serial number 4,576,540. Note 72 hour dial. Strong arm rooms first used vault time locks in the 1870s.

Grade or Name — Description	Avg	Ex-Fn	Mint
Stuart, 17J, M#3, 5th Pinion ......★★	$300	$400	$475
Stuart, 17J, M#3, 5th Pinion, ADJ ......★★	375	425	500
Transition Models, 17J, OF......	100	125	155
Time King, 17J, OF, LS, FULL, NI......	150	170	250
Time King, 21J, OF, LS, FULL......	175	200	275
Vault Time Lock for Mosler, 15J, 72 hr......	100	125	155
🖙 Washington W. Co. (See Army & Navy, Liberty Bell, Lafayette, Senate)			
Ward's Special, 15J, NI, FULL, LS,	95	110	130
George Washington,11J, HC......	100	125	165
65, 15J, HC, LS, M#2......	75	100	135
101, 11J, FULL, SW, KW, OF......	75	100	135
101, 11J, SW, KW, Silveroid......	40	60	85
101, 11J, SW, KW, HC......	75	100	150
102, 13J, SW, KW, Silveroid......	40	60	85
102, 13J, SW, KW, OF......	75	100	135
102, 13J, FULL, SW, KW, HC......	100	125	155
104, 15J, M#2, HC......★★	250	300	375
104, 17J, M#3, OF......★★★	300	350	425
105, 17J, M#3, OF......★★★	300	350	425
105, 15J, M#2, GJS, ADJ, FULL, KW, KS, HC ......★★	275	325	400
106, 15J, ADJ, FULL, KW, KS......	100	125	155
444, 17J, OF, NI, ADJ, FULL......	55	75	135
445, 19J, GJS, 2-Tone, HC......★★	1,000	1,200	1,500
1905 Special, 21J, OF, NI, Adj.5P	300	400	550

🖙 NOTE: Watches listed in this book are priced at the retail level, as complete watches having an original 14k goldfilled case, an original white enamel single sunk dial, and with the entire original movement in good working order with no repairs needed, unless otherwise noted.

ILLINOIS
16 SIZE

Note: Bunn Special original cases were marked Bunn Special except for Elinvars (Hamilton cased).

Grade or Name — Description	Avg	Ex-Fx	Mint
Adams Street, 17J, 3/4, SW, NI, DMK, HC	$175	$225	$300
Adams Street, 21J, 3F brg, NI, DMK	250	300	375
Ak-Sar-Ben (Nebraska backward), 17J, OF, GCW	150	175	225
Ariston, 11J, OF	50	75	125
Ariston, 15J, OF	50	75	125
Ariston, 17J, 3F brg, HC	175	225	300
Ariston, 17J, Adj.3P, OF	150	175	225
Ariston, 19J, Adj.3P, OF	150	175	225
Ariston, 21J, GJS, Adj.6P, OF	300	375	450
Ariston, 23J, GJS, Adj.6P, OF	500	600	750
Ariston, 23J, GJS, Adj.6P, HC ★★	700	800	1,000
Arlington Special, 17J, OF	75	100	135
Arlington Special, 17J, OF, Silveroid	50	75	125
Army & Navy, 19J, GJS, Adj.5P, NI, 1F brg	200	250	325
Army & Navy, 21J, GJS, Adj.5P, 1F brg	250	300	375
B & M Special, 17J, BRG, Adj.4P	200	250	325
B & O Standard, 21J	350	400	525
Benjamin Franklin, 17J, ADJ, DMK,	300	325	400
Benjamin Franklin, 21J, GJS, Adj.5P, DR, GT,	500	550	625
Benjamin Franklin, 25J, GJS, Adj.6P, DR, GT, OF ★★	3,000	3,500	4,000
Benjamin Franklin, 25J, GJS, Adj.6P, DR, GT, HC ★★★	3,500	4,000	4,500
Bunn, 17J, LS, OF, NI, 3/4, GJS, Adj.5P	100	125	155
Bunn, 17J, LS, NI, 3/4, Adj.5P, HC ★★★	650	800	1,000
Bunn, 19J, LS, OF, NI, 3/4, GJS, Adj.5P	100	125	155

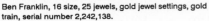

Ben Franklin, 16 size, 25 jewels, gold jewel settings, gold train, serial number 2,242,138.

Bunn Special, Model 163, 16 size, 23J., gold jewel settings, gold train, 60 hour movement, serial # 5,421,504.

☞ Note: Some grades or styles are not included. Their values can be determined by comparing with similar age, models, styles and grades listed.

Left: Standard style escapement. Right: DeLong style escapement.

Illinois Watch Co., 16 size, 25J., three-fingered bridge, gold train, hunting, note serial number S731,870.

Grade or Name — Description	Avg	Ex-Fn	Mint
Bunn, 19J, LS, NI, 3\4, Adj.5P, HC ....★★★	$800	$1,000	$1,500
Bunn, 19J, LS, OF, NI, 3/4, GJS, Adj.5P, 60 hour.......................	300	350	425
Bunn, 19J, marked Jeweled Barrel	175	200	250
Bunn Special, 19J, LS, OF, NI, 3/4, Adj.6P, GT...........................	125	150	200
Bunn Special, 19J, LS, OF, NI, 3/4, Adj.5P, GT, 60 hour	300	350	425
Bunn Special, 21J, NI, GJS, HC.................................★	400	450	525
Bunn Special, 21J, LS, OF, NI, 3/4, GJS, Adj.6P, GT	125	150	175
Bunn Special, 21J, LS, OF, NI, 3/4, GJS, Adj.6P, GT, 60 hour...	200	225	275
Bunn Special, 21J, LS, OF, NI, 3/4, GJS, Adj.6P, GT, 60 hr. Elinvar..	275	300	375
Bunn Special, 21J, 60 hr., 14K, OF, Bunn Special case .... ★	675	725	800
Bunn Special, 23J, LS, OF, NI, 3/4, GJS, Adj.6P, GT	300	375	425
Bunn Special, 23J, LS, OF, NI, 3/4, GJS, Adj.6P, GT, 60 hour...	350	425	475
Bunn Special, 23J, LS, OF, NI, 3/4, GJS, Adj.6P, GT, with 23J, 60-hour on dial..	450	475	525
Bunn Special, 23J, LS, NI, GJS, ...★★★★	1,200	1,500	1,800
161 Bunn Special, 21J, 3/4, Adj.6P, 60 hour	250	300	375
161A Bunn Special, 21J, 3/4, Adj.6P, 60 hour (Elinvar signed under balance or on top plate)	325	375	450
161 Elinvar Bunn Special, 21J, 3/4, Adj.6P, 60 hour (Elinvar signed at bottom of bridge)	375	425	500
161B, Bunn Special, 21J, 60 hour, pressed jewels ....★★★★	4,000	5,000	6,500
163 Bunn Special, 23J, GJS, Adj.6P, 3/4, 60 hour..........................	400	475	575
163 Elinvar Bunn Special, 23J, GJS, Adj.6P, 60 hour (Elinvar signed at bottom of cock, uncut balance)......... ★	900	950	1,050

Grade or Name — Description	Avg	Ex-Fn	Mint
163A Elinvar Bunn Special, 23J, GJS, Adj.6P, 3/4, 60 hour (Elinvar signed under balance)	$800	$850	$950
163A Elinvar Bunn Special, 23J, Adj.6P, 3/4, 60 hour (Elinvar signed on top plate)	800	850	950
Burlington, 15J, OF	50	75	125
Burlington, 15J, HC	125	150	200
Burlington, 17J, OF	50	75	125
Burlington, 17J, HC	125	150	200
Burlington W. Co., 19J, 3/4, NI, Adj.3P	75	100	135
Burlington W. Co., 19J, BRG, NI, Adj.3P	75	100	135
Burlington W. Co., 19J, 3/4, HC	125	150	200
Burlington W. Co., 19J, 3F brg, NI, Adj.3P	75	100	125
Burlington W. Co., 21J, 3/4, NI, Adj.3P	125	150	175
Burlington W. Co., 21J, Adj.6P, GJS ★★	200	225	275
Burlington, Bull Dog, 21J, SW, LS, GJS, GT	200	275	350
C & O Special, 21J, 3/4, NI, ADJ ★	600	700	900
Capitol, 19J, OF, 3/4, NI, Adj.5P	100	125	150
Central, 17J, SW, PS, OF	50	75	125
Commodore Perry special,21J,Adj.6P,GT,OF	185	200	285
Craftsman, 17J, OF	50	75	125
DeLong Escapement, 21J, GJS, Adj.6P, 14K OF ★★★	1,500	1,600	1,800
Dependon, 17-21J, (J.V.Farwell)	125	155	225
Diamond, Ruby, Sapphire, 21J, GJS, GT, Adj.6P, NI, BRG, DR ★	800	900	1,100
Diamond, Ruby, Sapphire, 23J, GJS, GT, Adj.6P, NI, BRG, DR ★★★	1,500	2,000	2,200
Diamond, Ruby, Sapphire, 23J, GJS, GT, Adj.6P, NI,DR, 3/4 plate ★★★	1,200	1,400	1,600
Dispatcher, 19J, Adj.3P	50	75	125
Fifth Ave.,19J,Adj.3P,GT,OF	95	110	150
Franklin Street, 15J, 3/4, NI, ADJ	75	100	150
Getty Model, 21J	150	175	225
Getty Model, 17J	75	100	135

Interstate Chronometer, 16 size, 23 jewels, one-fingered bridge, serial number 2,327,614.

A. Lincoln, 16 size, 21 jewels, gold jewel settings, gold train, Adj5p, serial number 2,237,406.

Grade or Name — Description	Avg	Ex-Fn	Mint
Great Northern Special, 17J, BRG, ADJ	$250	$275	$325
Great Northern Special, 19J, BRG, ADJ	275	300	350
Great Northern Special, 21J, BRG, ADJ, Adj.3P........................	300	325	375
Greenwich, 23J, Washington W. Co. GT,GJS, ADJ.6P......★★★	1,500	1,700	2,000
Illinois Central, 17J, 2-Tone, GT	100	125	150
Illinois Watch Co., 7J, M#1-2-3..	50	75	125
Illinois Watch Co., 11J, M#1-2-3..	80	75	125
Illinois Watch Co., 11J, 3/4, OF...	50	75	125
Illinois Watch Co., 11J, M#7, 3/4, OF	50	75	125
Illinois Watch Co., 11J, M#6, 3/4, HC	100	125	175
Illinois Watch Co., 15J, M#2, OF..	50	75	125
Illinois Watch Co., 15J, M#1, HC...	100	125	175
Illinois Watch Co., 15J, M#3, OF..	50	75	125
Illinois Watch Co., 15J, 3/4, ADJ	50	75	125
Illinois Watch Co., 15J, 3F brg, GJS...	50	75	125
Illinois Watch Co., 17J, 14K, HC..	400	450	525
Illinois Watch Co., 17J, M#2-3, SW, OF	50	75	125
Illinois Watch Co., 17J, M#6, SW, HC	100	125	175
Illinois Watch Co., 17J, M#7, OF..	75	100	135
Illinois Watch Co., 17J, M#5, 3\4, ADJ, HC	100	125	150
Illinois Watch Co., 17J, M#4, 3F brg, GJS, Adj.5P, HC	100	125	150
Illinois Watch Co., 19J, M#1, 3/4, GJS, Adj.5P	75	100	135
Illinois Watch Co., 19J, 3/4, BRG, Adj.3P.................................	75	100	135
Illinois Watch Co., 21J, ADJ, OF..	175	200	250
Illinois Watch Co., 21J, GJS, HC..	150	175	225
Illinois Watch Co., 21J, 3/4, GJS, Adj.5P..................................	125	150	175
Illinois Watch Co., 21J, 3F brg, GJS, Adj.5P.............................	125	150	200
Illinois Watch Co., 23J, GJS	250	300	375
Illinois Watch Co., 25J, 3F brg, GJS, Adj.5P ....★★★	3,000	3,500	4,000
Imperial Sp, 17J, SW, LS, Adj.4P, OF...	75	100	135
Interstate Chronometer, 17J, GCW, Adj.5P, HC	275	300	325
Interstate Chronometer, 17J, GCW, Adj.5P, OF.........................	250	275	300
Interstate Chronometer, 23J, 1F brg, ADJ, OF	600	700	850
Interstate Chronometer, 23J, 1F brg, ADJ, HC..........................	900	1,000	1,150
Lafayette, 23J, Washington W.Co., GJS, Adj.5P, GT, OF ....★★	750	850	1,000
Lafayette, 23J, Washington W.Co., GJS, Adj.5P, GT, HC.★★★	1,000	1,200	1,500
Lakeshore, 17J, OF	75	100	135
Lakeshore, 17J, HC..	150	175	225
Landis W. Co., 15J...	75	100	135
Liberty Bell, 17J, OF..	100	125	150
Liberty Bell, 17J, HC ....★★★	600	700	800
A. Lincoln, 21J,3/4, GJS, Adj.5P..	125	150	200
Marvel, 19J, GT, GJS, Adj.3P, Of	75	95	120
Marine Special, 21J, 3/4, Adj.3P..	250	275	325
Monroe, 17J, NI,3/4, OF (Washington W. Co.)............................	100	125	150
Monroe, 15J, 3/4, OF (Washington W. Co.)	75	100	150
Montgomery Ward, 17J, LS, Thin Model , OF............................	75	95	135
Our No. 1, 15J, HC, M#1...	150	200	275
Paillard Non-Magnetic Watch Co., 11J, 3/4	75	100	135
Paillard Non-Magnetic Watch Co., 15J, 3/4	75	100	135
Paillard Non-Magnetic Watch Co., 17J, 3/4, Adj.5P, DMK	100	125	175

Sangamo, 16 size, 21 jewels, Adj.6p, gold jewel settings, gold train, serial number 2,222,797.

Sangamo Special, 16 size, 23J., 60 hour movement, Adj.6p, gold jewel settings, gold train, serial number 4,720,522.

Grade or Name Description	Avg	Ex-Fn	Mint
Paillard Non-Magnetic Watch Co., 21J,3/4, GJS, Adj.5P, DMK .	$300	$400	$500
Pennsylvania Special, 23J,3/4, GJS, Adj.5P................................. ★	1,200	1,400	1,600
Plymouth W. Co., 15-17J, OF (Add $25 for HC)	75	100	125
Precise, 21J, OF, LS, Adj.3P..	125	150	200
Quincy Street, 17J,3/4, NI, DMK, ADJ	75	100	125
Railroad Dispatcher, 11J, HC..	150	175	225
Railroad King, 17J, HC..	200	225	275
Railroad Official, 23J, 3F brg ....★★	800	900	1,200
Railway King, 17J, OF..	150	175	225
Sangamo, 21J, GJS, Adj.6P, HC	275	300	350
Sangamo, 21J, GJS, Adj.6P, EXTRA or SPECIAL, HC........ ★	500	600	750
Sangamo, 21J, GJS, Adj.6P, EXTRA or SPECIAL, OF .... ★	500	600	750
Sangamo, 21J, GJS, Adj.5P, OF...	150	175	225
Sangamo, 21J,3/4, GJS, DR, Adj.6P, OF.....................................	160	185	245
Sangamo, 23J,3/4, GJS, DR, Adj.6P, OF.....................................	250	275	325
Sangamo, 23J,3/4, GJS, DR, Adj.6P, HC.....................................	425	475	550
Sangamo, 25J, M#5, 3/4, GJS, DR, Adj.6P ....★★★	4,000	5,000	6,500
Sangamo, 26J, M#5, 3/4, GJS, DR, Adj.6P ....★★★	5,000	6,000	7,500
Sangamo Special, 19J, BRG, GJS, GT, Adj.6P	350	375	425
Sangamo Special, 19J, BRG, GJS, GT, Adj.6P, HC...........★★★	1,200	1,500	1,800
Sangamo Special, 21J, M#7, OF	325	375	450
Sangamo Special, 21J, M#8, BRG, HC ....★★★	1,400	1,600	1,900
Sangamo Special, 21J, M#9, BRG, GJS, GT, Adj.6P, OF	325	375	450
Sangamo Special, 21J, BRG, GJS, GT, Diamond end cap	350	400	475
Sangamo Special, 23J, M#9-10, BRG, GJS, GT, Adj.6P,			
Sangamo Special case	400	450	525

Grade or Name — Description	Avg	Ex-Fn	Mint
Sangamo Special, 23J, BRG, GJS, GT, Adj.6P, Diamond end stone, screw back, Sangamo Special case	$400	$450	$525
Sangamo Special, 23J, BRG, GJS, GT, Adj.6P, marked 60 hour, rigid bow, Sangamo Special case	750	850	900
Sangamo Special, 23J, BRG, GJS, GT, Adj.6P, not marked 60 hour, rigid bow, Sangamo Special case	450	550	575
Sangamo Special, 23J, M#8, GJS, GT, Adj.6P, HC ★★★	1,500	1,800	2,000
Santa Fe Special, 17J, BRG, Adj.3P	150	175	225
Santa Fe Special, 21J, 3/4, Adj.5P, OF	175	225	275
Santa Fe Special, 21J, 3/4, Adj.5P, HC	200	250	300
Sears, Roebuck & Co. Special, 15-17J, ADJ	75	100	135
Senate, 17J, OF, NI, 3/4	75	100	135
Standard, 15J	50	75	125
Sterling, 17J, SW, PS, Adj.3P, OF	50	75	115
Sterling, 19-21J, SW, PS, Adj.3P, OF	60	80	125
Stewart, 17J	50	75	125
Stewart Special, 17J	50	75	125
Time King, 17J, OF	75	100	135
Time King, 19J, Adj.3P, M#p	80	100	145
Union Pacific,17J, Adj.,DR, 2 — tone, DMK, OF ★	300	350	400
Victor, 21J, 3/4, Adj.5P	75	100	135

Grade 163, 16 size, 23 jewels, adjusted to 6 positions, motor barrel, 60 hour model, serial number 5,421,504.

Grade 187, 16 size, 17 Ruby jewels, three-fingered bridge model, gold jewel settings, gold train, Adj5p, serial number 2,487,510.

Grade or Name — Description	Avg	Ex-Fn	Mint
161 through 163A — See Bunn Special			
167L, 17J, marked	$125	$150	$175
167, 17J	50	75	125
169, 19J, Adj.3P, OF	100	125	150
174, 23J, LS, GJS, Adj.5P, OF, marked ★★	675	725	800
175, 17J, RR grade with a (RR inspectors name on dial &mvt.)	200	245	300
177, 19J, SW, LS, 60 hour, Adj.5P, OF ★	400	500	650

Grade or Name — Description	Avg	Ex-Fn	Mint
179, 21J, HC, 3F brg, marked Ruby Jewels .... ★	$300	$400	$550
184, 17J, LS, OF..	100	125	155
187, 17J, 3F brg, Adj.5P, GJS, GT, HC................................	225	275	350
189, 21J, 3F brg, Adj.6P, GJS, GT, DR, marked Ruby Jewels, HC	400	450	525
333, 15J, HC...	100	125	175
555, 17J, 3/4, ADJ	75	100	135
777, 17J, 3/4, ADJ	75	100	135
900, 19J, LS, Adj.3P...	100	125	150

Illinois Watch Co., 14 size, 16 jewels, Adj5p.

Illinois Watch Co., 14 size, 21J., adjusted, nickel movement, gold jewel settings, serial number 1,029,204.

ILLINOIS
14 SIZE

Grade or Name — Description	Avg	Ex-Fn	Mint
Illinois Watch Co., 7J, M#1-2-3, SW, OF	$40	$50	$65
Illinois Watch Co., 11J, M#1-2-3, SW, OF	50	60	75
Illinois Watch Co., 15J, M#1-2-3, SW, OF	60	70	90
Illinois Watch Co., 16J, M#1-2-3, SW, OF	75	80	115
Illinois Watch Co., 21J, M#1-2-3, SW, OF .... ★	200	275	375
Illinois Watch Co., 21J, Silveroid .... ★	175	250	350

NOTE: Add $25 for above watches in hunting case.

ILLINOIS
12 SIZE and 13 SIZE

Grade or Name — Description	Avg	Ex-Fn	Mint
Accurate, 21J, GJS, OF	$60	$75	$125
Aristocrat, 19J, OF..	40	50	70
Ariston, 11-17J, OF..	60	70	85
Ariston, 19J, OF..	75	100	150
Ariston, 21J, OF..	85	110	160
Ariston, 23J, OF.. ★	200	250	300

Ben Franklin, 12 size, 17 jewels, open face, gold train, serial number 2,366,286.

Illini, 12 size, 21 jewels, bridge model, serial number 3,650,129. Note five tooth click.

Grade or Name — Description	Avg	Ex-Fn	Mint
Autocrat, 17J, Adj.3P, 3/4	$60	$70	$85
Autocrat, 19J, Adj.3P, 3/4	65	75	95
Banker, 17-21J, Adj.3P, OF	60	70	90
Benjamin Franklin, 17J, OF	200	250	325
Burlington Special, 19J, GT, OF	50	60	75
Burlington Special, 19J, GT, HC	75	95	135
Burlington W. Co., 21J, GT, OF	60	70	85
Burlington W. Co., 21J, GT, HC	85	100	150
Criterion, 21J, OF	50	60	75
Central, 17J, OF, 2-Tone	40	50	70
Dependon, 17, (J.V.Farwell), OF HC,	100	125	185
Diamond Ruby Sapphire, 21J, Adj.5P, GJS ★	300	350	425
Elite, 19J, OF.	60	75	85
Garland, 17J, Adj.,GT, OF	60	70	80
Illini, 13 Size, 21J, Adj.5P, 14K, HC	275	325	400

Example of Illinois Thin Model, 12 size, 17 jewels, adjusted to 3 positions.

Maiden America, 12 size, 17 jewels, serial number 2,820,499.

Santa Fe Special, 12 size, 21 jewels, three-quarter plate, serial number 3,414,422.

Grade or Name — Description	Avg	Ex-Fn	Mint
Illini, 13 Size, 21J, Adj.5P, BRG, GJS	$75	$100	$135
Illini Extra, 13 Size, 21J, Adj.5P, OF	75	100	135
Illini, 13 Size, 23J, Adj.5P, BRG, GJS	125	150	200
Illinois Watch Co., 15J, OF	40	50	70
Illinois Watch Co., 17J, OF, 14K	250	275	325
Illinois Watch Co., 17J, OF, GF	65	90	120
Illinois Watch Co., 17J, HC, GF	75	100	135
Illinois Watch Co., 19J, OF	60	70	85
Illinois Watch Co., 21J, OF	70	80	95
Illinois Watch Co., 21J, HC	100	125	150
Interstate Chronometer, 21J, GJS, OF	150	175	225
Interstate Chronometer, 21J, GJS, HC ★	200	225	275
A. Lincoln, 19J, Adj.5P, GJS, DR, 3/4, marked on mvt.	60	70	85
A. Lincoln, 21J, Adj.5P, DR, GJS	70	80	95
Maiden America, 17J, ADJ	60	70	85
Marquis Autocrat, 17J, OF	60	70	85
Master, 21J, GT, GJS, OF	70	80	95
Masterpiece, 19J, Adj.3P, OF	65	75	100
A. Noton, 21J, OF	55	65	75
Plymouth Watch Co., 15-17J, OF, HC	50	60	75
Railroad Dispatch Special, 17J, SW, GT	70	80	95
Roosevelt, 19J, Adj.3P, Of	70	80	90
Santa Fe Special, 21J	75	100	135
Sterling, 17J, OF	40	50	65
Sterling, 19-21J, OF	45	55	70
Stewart Special, 17J, SW, Adj.3P	50	60	75
Stewart Special, 19J, SW, OF, GT	55	65	80
Time King, 19J, SW, Adj.3P	60	70	85
Time King, 21J, SW, Adj.3P	70	80	95
Transit, 19J, OF, PS	60	70	85
Vim, 17J, ADJ, BRG, GJS, DR, OF	50	60	75
Washington W. Co., 11J, HC	100	125	150
Washington W. Co., Army & Navy, 19J	100	125	150
Washington W. Co., Senate, 17J, M#2, PS, HC	60	70	85

Grade or Name — Description	Avg	Ex-Fn	Mint
121, 21J, Adj.3P	$70	$85	$95
127, 17J, ADJ	60	70	85
129, 19J, Adj.3P	60	70	85
219, 11J, M#1	50	60	75
403, 15J, BRG	60	70	85
405, 17J, BRG, ADJ, OF	60	70	85
409, 21J, BRG, Diamond, Ruby, Sapphire, Adj.5P, GJS .... ★	275	325	450
410, 23J, BRG, GJS, Adj.6P, DR	150	200	275
410, 23J, BRG, GJS, Adj.6P, DR, 14K, OF	250	300	375

ILLINOIS
8 SIZE

Grade or Name — Description	Avg	Ex-Fn	Mint
Arlington, 7J, ... ★	$125	$150	$200
Rose LeLand, 13J, ★★	225	250	300
Stanley, 7J, ★★★	250	300	350
Mary Stuart, 15J, ★★	200	250	300
Sunnyside, 11J, ★	150	200	250
151, 7J, 3/4	40	50	65
152, 11J, 3/4	50	60	75
155, 11J, 3/4	60	70	85
155, 11J, 3/4, Coin	30	40	55

Note: Add $10 more for above watches in hunting case.

Illinois Watch Co., 8 size, 7 jewels

Grade 144, 6 size, 15 jewels, serial number 5,902,290.

ILLINOIS
6 SIZE

Grade or Name — Description	Avg	Ex-Fn	Mint
Illinois W. Co., 7J, LS, HC, 14K	$200	$225	$300
Illinois W. Co., 7J, HC	50	75	125

Grade or Name — Description	Avg	Ex-Fn	Mint
Illinois W. Co., 7J, OF, Coin	$35	$45	$60
Illinois W. Co., 11J, OF, HC	50	75	125
Illinois W. Co., 15J, OF, HC, 14K	200	250	325
Illinois W. Co., 17J, OF, HC	50	75	125
Illinois W. Co., 19J, OF, HC	75	100	150
Plymouth Watch Co., 17J, OF HC	50	60	75
Washington W. Co., 15J, HC, Liberty Bell	125	150	200

ILLINOIS
4 SIZE

Grade or Name — Description	Avg	Ex-Fn	Mint
Illinois W. Co., 7J, LS, HC	$50	$55	$95
Illinois W. Co., 11J, LS, HC	50	75	125
Illinois W. Co., 15J, LS, HC	50	75	125

ILLINOIS
0 SIZE

Grade or Name — Description	Avg	Ex-Fn	Mint
Burlington Special, 15-17J, 3/4, OF	$75	$95	$150
Illinois W. Co., 7J, LS, HC, 14K	175	225	300
201, 11J, BRG, NI	75	100	150
203, 15J, BRG, NI	75	100	150
204, 17J, BRG, NI	75	100	150
Interstate Chronometer, 15J, HC, SW	175	200	275
Interstate Chronometer, 17J, HC, SW	185	210	285
Plymouth Watch Co., 15-17J, HC	50	60	75
Washington W. Co., Liberty Bell, 15J, ADJ	150	175	250
Washington W. Co., Mt. Vernon, 17J, ADJ	160	185	275

Grade 201, 0 size, 11 jewels, originally sold for $8.10.

Grade 203, 0 size, 15 jewels, originally sold for $10.40

Grade 204, 0 size, 17 jewels, originally sold for $12.83.

ILLINOIS SPRINGFIELD WATCH CO.
IDENTIFICATION OF MOVEMENTS
BY MODEL NUMBER

How to Identify Your Watch: Compare the movement of your watch with the illustrations in this section. Upon matching the movement exactly, the model number and size can be determined. While comparing, note the location of the balance, jewels, screws, gears, and type of back plate (Full, 3/4, Bridge) which will be clues in identifying the movement you have. Having determined the size and model number, you can now find your watch in the main price listing by name or number (which is engraved on the movement).

THE ILLINOIS WATCH CO. GRADE AND MODEL CHART

Size	Model	Plate Design	Setting	Hunting or Open Face	Type Barrel	Started w/ Serial No.	Remarks
18	1	Full	Key	Htg	Reg	1	Course train
	2	Full	Lever	Htg	Reg	38,901	Course train
	3	Full	Lever	OF	Reg	46,201	Course train, 5th pinion
	4	Full	Pendant	OF	Reg	1,050,001	Fast train
	5	Full	Lever	Htg	Reg	1,256,101	Fast train, RR Grade
	6	Full	Lever	OF	Reg	1,144,401	Fast train, RR Grade
16	1	Full	Lever	Htg	Reg	1,030,001	Thick model
	2	Full	Pendant	OF	Reg	1,037,001	Thick model
	3	Full	Lever	OF	Reg	1,038,001	Thick model
	4	¼ & brg	Lever	Htg	Reg	1,300,001	Getty model
	5	¼ & brg	Lever	OF	Reg	1,300,601	Getty model
	6	¼ & brg	Pendant	Htg	Reg	2,160,111	DR & Improved RR model
	7	¼ & brg	Pendant	OF	Reg	2,160,011	DR & Improved RR model
	8	¼ & brg	Lever	Htg	Reg	2,523,101	DR & Improved RR model
	9	¼ & brg	Lever	OF	Reg	2,522,001	DR & Improved model
	10	Cent brg	Lever	OF	Motor	3,178,901	Also 17S Ex Thin RR gr 48 hr
	11	¼	Lever & Pen	OF	Motor	4,001,001	RR grade 48 hr
	12	¼	Lever & Pen	Htg	Motor	4,002,001	RR grade 48 hr
	13	Cent brg	Lever	OF	Motor	4,166,801	Also 17S RR grade 60 hr
	14	¼	Lever	OF	Motor	4,492,501	RR grade 60 hr
	15	¼	Lever	OF	Motor	5,488,301	RR grade 60 hr Elinvar
14	1	Full	Lever	Htg	Reg	1,009,501	Thick model
	2	Full	Pendant	OF	Reg	1,000,001	Thick model
	3	Full	Lever	OF	Reg	1,001,001	Thick model
13	1	brg	Pendant	OF	Motor		Ex Thin gr 538 & 539
12 Thin	1	¼	Pendant	OF	Reg	1,685,001	
	2	¼	Pendant	Htg	Reg	1,748,751	
	3	Cent brg	Pendant	OF	Reg	2,337,011	Center bridge
	4	Cent brg	Pendant	Htg	Reg	2,337,001	Center bridge
	5	Cent brg	Pendant	OF	Motor	3,742,201	Center bridge
	6	Cent brg	Pendant	Htg	Motor	4,395,301	Center bridge
12T	1	True Ctr brg	Pendant	OF	Motor	3,700,001	1 tooth click, Also 13S
	2	True Ctr brg	Pendant	OF	Motor	3,869,301	5 tooth click
	3	¼	Pendant	OF	Motor	3,869,201	2 tooth click
8	1	Full	Key or lever	Htg	Reg	100,001	Plate not recessed
	2	Full	Lever	Htg	Reg	100,101	Plate is recessed
6	1	¼	Lever	Htg	Reg	552,001	
4	1	¼	Lever	Htg	Reg	551,501	
0	1	¼	Pendant	OF	Reg	1,815,901	
	2	¼	Pendant	Htg	Reg	1,749,801	
	3	Cent brg	Pendant	OF	Reg	2,644,001	
	4	Cent brg	Pendant	Htg	Reg	2,637,001	

Model 1, 18 size, hunting, key wind & set.

Model 2, 18 size, hunting, lever set, coarse train.

Model 3, 18 size, open face, lever set, coarse train, with fifth pinion.

Model 4, 18 size, open face, pendant set, fine train.

Model 5, 18 size, hunting, lever set, fine train.

Model 6, 18 size, open face, lever set, fine train.

Model 1, 16 size, hunting, lever set.

Model 2, 16 size, open face, pendant set.

Model 3, 16 size, open face, lever set

Model 4, 16 size, three-quarter plate, hunting, lever set.

Model 4, 16 size, three-quarter plate, bridge, hunting, lever set.

Model 5, 16 size, three-quarter plate, open face, lever set.

Model 5, 16 size, three-quarter plate, bridge, open face, lever set.

Model 6, 16 size - Pendant set
Model 8, 16 size - Lever set
hunting, three-quarter plate

Model 6, 16 size - Pendant set
Model 8, 16 size - Lever set
hunting, bridge model

Model 7, 16 size - Pendant set
Model 9, 16 size - Lever set
open face, three-quarter plate

Model 7, 16 size - Pendant set
Model 9, 16 size - Lever set
open face, bridge model

Model 10, 16 size, bridge, extra thin, open face, lever set, motor barrel.

Model 11, 16 size, three-quarter plate, open face, pendant set, motor barrel.

Model 12, 16 size, three-quarter plate, hunting, pendant set, motor barrel.

Model 13, 16 size, bridge, open face, lever set, motor barrel.

Model 14, 16 size, three-quarter plate, open face, lever set, 60-hour motor barrel.

Model 15, 60 Hr. Elinvar.

Model B, 16 size, hunting case.

Model C, 16 size, open face

Model D, 16 size, open face

Model 1, 14 size, hunting, lever set.

Model 2, 14 size, open face, pendant set.

Model 3, 14 size, open face, lever set.

Model 1, 13 size, bridge, extra thin, open face, pendant set, motor barrel.

Model 1, 12 size, three-quarter plate, open face, pendant set.

Model 1, 12 size, three-quarter plate, bridge, open face, pendant set.

Model 2, 12 size, three-quarter plate, hunting, pendant set.

Model 2, 12 size, three-quarter plate, bridge, hunting, pendant set.

Model 3, 12 size, **Model 4**, 12 & 14 size, bridge, open face, pendant set.

Model 4, 12 size, bridge, hunting, pendant set.

Model 5, 12 size, bridge, open face, pendant set, motor barrel.

Model 1, 12 size, extra thin, bridge, open face, pendant set, motor barrel.

Model 2, 12 size, extra thin, bridge, open face, pendant set, motor barrel.

Model 3, 12 size, extra thin, three-quarter plate, open face, pendant set, motor barrel.

Model A, 12 size, bridge, open face.

Model 1, 8 size, hunting, key or lever set.

Model 2, 8 size, hunting, lever set.

Model 1, 6 size, hunting, lever set.

Model 1, 4 size, hunting, lever set.

Model 1, 0 size, three-quarter plate, open face, pendant set.

Model 2, 0 size, three-quarter plate, hunting, pendant set.

Model 3, 0 size, bridge, open face, pendant set.

Model 4, 0 size, bridge, hunting, pendant set.

Model 3, 3/0 size, bridge, open face, pendant set.

Model 4, 3/0 size, bridge, hunting, pendant set.

Model 1, 6/0 size, three-quarter plate, open face, pendant set.

Model 2, 6/0 size, bridge, open face, pendant set.

INDEPENDENT WATCH CO.

Fredonia, New York
1880 - 1885

The California Watch Company was idle for two years before it was purchased by brothers E. W. Howard and C. M. Howard. They had been selling watches by mail for sometime and started engraving the Howard Bros. name on them and using American-made watches. Their chief supply came from Hampden Watch Co., Illinois, U. S. Watch Co. of Marion, and Cornell Watch Co. The brothers formed the Independent Watch Co. in 1880, but it was not a watch factory in the true sense. They had other manufacturers engrave the Independent Watch Co. name on the top plates and on the dials of their watches. These watches were sold by mail order and sent to the buyer C. O. D. The names used on the movements were "Mark Twain," "Howard Bros.," "Independent Watch Co.," "FredoniaWatch Co.," and "Lakeshore Watch Co., Fredonia, N. Y."

The company later decided to manufacture watches and used the name Fredonia Watch Co. But they found that selling watches two different ways was no good. The business survived until 1885 at which time the owners decided to move the plant to a new location at Peoria, Illinois. Approximately 350,000 watches were made that sold for $16.

CHRONOLOGY OF THE DEVELOPMENT OF INDEPENDENT WATCH CO.:

Independent Watch Co.	1880–1883
Fredonia Watch Co.	1883–1885
Peoria Watch Co.	1885–1895

18 SIZE

Grade or Name — Description	Avg	Ex-Fn	Mint
18S, 7J, KW, KS, OF, by U.S. W. Co. Marion, with butterfly cutout .... ★	$450	$550	$675
18S, 11J, KW, KS, by Hampden...	200	250	325
18S, 11J, KW, KS, Coin...	150	175	225
18S, 11J, KW, KS	150	175	225
18S, 15J, KW, KS	160	185	235

Independent Watch Co., 18 size, 11 jewels, key wind & set, made by Hampden Watch Co. (Model Number 1), serial number 170,844.

Independent Watch Co., 18 size, 15 jewels, key wind, made by U.S. Marion Watch Co., note butterfly cuttout, serial number 192,661.

Grade or Name — Description	Avg	Ex-Fn	Mint
18S, Howard Bros., 11J, KW, KS	$250	$300	$375
18S, Independent W. Co., 11J................................	150	175	225
18S, Lakeshore W. Co., 15J, KW, HC, by N.Y. W. Co.	200	250	325
18S, Mark Twain, 11J, KW, KS................................★★	500	650	800

ROBERT H. INGERSOLL & BROS.

New York, New York
1892 - 1922

In 1892 this company published a catalog for the mail order trade. It listed men's watch chains and a "silverine" watch for $3.95. It was not a true Ingersoll but a "Universal," introduced that same year to the dealers. The first $1 watches were jeweled; "Reliance" had seven jewels. In 1916, Ingersoll's production was 16,000 a day. The slogan was "The Watch that Made the Dollar Famous." The first 1,000 watches were made by Waterbury Clock Co. By 1922 the Ingersoll line was completely taken over by Waterbury. U. S. Time Corp. acquired Waterbury in 1944 and continued to use the Ingersoll name on certain watches.

ESTIMATED SERIAL NUMBERS
AND PRODUCTION DATES

Date	Serial No.	Date	Serial No.	Date	Serial No.
1892	150,000	1905	10,000,000	1918	47,500,000
1893	310,000	1906	12,500,000	1919	50,000,000
1894	650,000	1907	15,000,000	1920	55,000,000
1895	1,000,000	1908	17,500,000	1921	58,000,000
1896	2,000,000	1909	20,000,000	1922	60,500,000
1897	2,900,000	1910	25,000,000	1923	62,000,000
1898	3,500,000	1911	30,000,000	1924	65,000,000
1899	3,750,000	1912	38,500,000	1925	67,500,000
1900	6,000,000	1913	40,000,000	1926	69,000,000
1901	6,700,000	1914	41,500,000	1927	70,500,000
1902	7,200,000	1915	42,500,000	1928	71,500,000
1903	7,900,000	1916	45,500,000	1929	73,500,000
1904	8,100,000	1917	47,000,000	1930	75,000,000
				1944	95,000,000

Ingersoll Back Wind & Set , patent date Dec. 23, 1890 and Jan. 13, 1891, c. late 1890s.

Ingersoll Blind Man's Watch.

INGERSOLL
DOLLAR TYPE

NOTE: Prices are for complete watch in good running order. In some specialty markets, the comic character watches may bring higher prices in top condition.

Grade or Name — Description	Avg	Ex-Fn	Mint
Ingersoll Back Wind	$100	$125	$175
Admiral Dewey, "Flagship Olympia" on back of case	150	175	250
American Pride	75	100	125
Are U My Neighbor	35	45	65
B. B. H. Special, Backwind	65	75	95
Blind Man Pocket Watch	50	75	95
Buck	25	30	40
Champion (many models)	50	75	125
Chancery	50	75	125
Chicago Expo. 1933	200	250	325
Climax	40	45	65
Clock Watch, pat. 1878-90-91	75	85	125
Cloverine	60	70	85
Colby	20	25	35
Columbus	45	60	85
Columbus (3 ships on back of case), 1893 ★	250	300	450
Connecticut W. Co.	30	40	50
Cord	20	30	45
Crown	20	25	35
Dan Dee	35	45	75
Defiance	30	40	55
Delaware W. Co.	25	30	40
Devon Mfg. Co.	20	25	35

Scout watch (Be prepared)

Yankee watch with bicycle on dial.

Ingersoll Premium, early back wind & set.

Ingersoll Triumph, note pin for setting.

Grade or Name — Description	Avg	Ex-Fn	Mint
Eclipse (many models)	$25	$30	$40
Eclipse Radiolite	30	35	40
Ensign	30	35	40
Escort	25	30	40
Fancy Dials (unfaded to be mint)	100	145	200
Freedom	30	35	40
Gotham	15	20	35
Graceline	45	50	65
Gregg	15	25	35
Junior (several models)	15	25	35
Junior Radiolite	35	40	55
Kelton	10	15	25
Lapel Watches	35	55	75
Leeds	15	20	25
Liberty U.S.A., backwind	75	100	150
Liberty Watch Co.	35	45	75
Limited, lever set	40	50	60
Major	25	40	60
Maple Leaf	25	30	40
Master Craft	10	15	20
Midget (several models)	35	50	75
Midget , 6 size, "patd. Jan. 29 01," Damaskeened, fancy case	75	100	150
Monarch	20	25	30
New West	30	45	65
New York World's Fair, 1939	150	175	200
Overland	35	40	50
Pan American Expo., Buffalo, 1901	200	275	350
Paris World Expo., 1900	150	175	225
Patrol	35	45	65
Perfection	35	45	55
Pilgram	40	50	55
Premier, back wind, eagle on back, c. 1894 ★	95	125	200

Left: Ingersoll Back Wind, c. 1895. Right: Yankee Back Wind, c. 1893.

Grade or Name — Description	Avg	Ex-Fn	Mint
Premium Back Wind and Set	$50	$75	$100
Progress, 1933 World's Fair Chicago	200	275	350
Puritan	35	50	75
Quaker	40	45	60
Radiolite	30	35	45
Reliance, 7J	50	70	95
Remington W. Co. USA	60	75	95
Rotary International, c. 1920	50	65	80
Royal	10	15	25
St. Louis World's Fair (two models)	250	300	400
St. Louis World's Fair, 1904	150	200	275
The Saturday Post	150	175	225
Senator	35	40	50
Senior	25	30	40
Sir Leeds	25	30	40
Solar	25	30	40
Souvenir Special	50	75	100
Sterling	35	40	50
Ten Hune	60	70	85
Traveler with Bed Side Stand	35	45	65
Triumph	100	125	150
Triumph Penset	150	175	225
True Test	25	30	40
Trump	35	45	55
USA (two models)	50	75	100
Universal, 1st model	200	250	300
Uncle Sam	40	50	60
George Washington	150	175	225
Waterbury (several models)	40	60	90

Grade or Name — Description	Avg	Ex-Fn	Mint
Waterbury Back Wind, 35 Size	$100	$150	$200
Winner	30	40	50
Winner with S.B.B.	40	45	55
Yankee Backwind	85	95	150
Yankee Bicycle Watch (sold for $1.00 in 1896)	175	195	250
Yankee Radiolite	40	55	75
Yankee Radiolite with S.B.B.	45	50	60
Yankee Special (many models)	75	100	150
Yankee, Perpetual calendar on back of case	75	100	150

Example of an Ingersoll moveable calendar for years 1929-1951 located on back of case.

Example of an Ingersoll watch made in Great Britain.

INGERSOLL LTD.
(GREAT BRITAIN)

Grade or Name — Description	Avg	Ex-Fn	Mint
Ingersoll Ltd. (many models)	$50	$75	$100
Coronation, Elizabeth II on watch	175	200	250
Coronation, June 2, 1953 on dial	175	200	250
16S, 7J, 3F Brg	55	60	85
16S, 15J, 3F Brg	75	85	110
16S, 17J, 3F Brg, ADJ	115	145	175
16S, 19J, 3F Brg, Adj5P	250	300	375
12S, 4J	35	40	65

Example of an Ingraham movement.

New York to Paris, airplane model commemorating Lindbergh's famous flight.

E. INGRAHAM CO.

Bristol, Connecticut

1912 - 1968

The E. Ingraham Co. purchased the Bannatyne Co. in 1912. They produced their first American pocket watch in 1913. A total of about 65 million American-made pocket watches and over 12 million wrist watches were produced before they started to import watches in 1968.

Grade or Name — Description	Avg	Ex-Fn	Mint
Ingraham W. Co. (many models)	$25	$35	$50
Aristocrat Railroad Sp	35	40	50
Autocrat	15	20	25
Beacon	15	20	25
Biltmore	10	15	20
Biltmore Radium	10	15	20
Bristol	15	20	25
Clipper	25	35	45
Comet	15	20	25
Companion, sweep second hand	25	30	40
Cub	15	20	25
Demi–hunter style cover	30	40	55
Dixie	10	15	20
Dot	10	20	25
Endura	10	15	20
Everbrite (all models)	15	25	30
Ingraham USA	10	15	20

Grade or Name — Description	Avg	Ex-Fn	Mint
Jockey	$15	$20	$25
Laddie	25	30	40
Laddie Athlete	40	45	55
Lady's Purse Watch, with fancy bezel	45	50	65
Lendix Extra	25	30	40
Master	10	15	20
Miss Ingraham	25	30	40
New York to Paris	200	250	300
Overland	30	35	45
The Pal	20	30	45
Pastor, stop watch	45	50	65
Pathfinder, compass on pendant	65	75	95
Patriot	125	150	250
Peerless	30	35	55

Example of Path Finder showing compass in crown.   Printed on dial, "Unbreakable crystal," ca. 1924.

Grade or Name — Description	Avg	Ex-Fn	Mint
Pilot	$30	$40	$55
Pocket Pal	15	20	25
Pony	25	30	40
Pride	20	25	35
Princess	20	30	45
Pup	25	30	40
Reliance	45	50	65
Rex	15	20	25
Rite Time	25	30	40
St. Regis	15	20	25
Secometer	20	25	35
Sentinel	15	20	25
Sentinel Click	20	25	35
Sentinel Fold Up Travel	45	50	65
Sentry	25	30	35
Seven Seas, 24 hr. dial & nautical dial	45	50	65
Silver Star	15	25	30
Sterling	20	25	35
Sterling W. Co. Stop Watch, fly back to zero	45	50	65
Sturdy	10	15	20

E. INGRAHAM CO. (continued)

Grade or Name — Description	Avg	Ex-Fn	Mint
Target	$10	$15	$20
Time Ball	25	30	40
Time & Time	30	40	55
Top Flight	20	25	35
Top Notch	35	45	50
Tower	15	20	25
Trail Blazer	175	225	300
Unbreakable Crystal	45	50	65
Uncle Sam (all models)	50	75	95
Uncle Sam Backwind & Set	125	150	190
Viceroy	20	25	35
Victory	25	30	55
Zep, (Zepplin)	175	250	350

Left: Example of a basic International Watch Co. movement with patent dates of Aug. 19, 1902, Jan. 27, 1903 & Aug. 11, 1903. Right: Example of a Highland.

INTERNATIONAL WATCH CO.

Newark City, New Jersey
1902 - 1907

This company produced only non-jeweled or low-cost production type watches that were inexpensive and nickel plated. Names on their watches include: Berkshire, Madison, and Mascot.

Grade or Name — Description		Avg	Ex-Fn	Mint
18 Size, skeletonized, pinlever escape., first model	★★	$100	$125	$175
Berkshire, OF	★	75	100	150
Highland	★	65	90	140
Madison, 18S, OF	★	75	100	150
Mascot, OF	★	50	75	125

KANKAKEE WATCH CO.

Kankakee, Illinois
1900

This company reportedly became the McIntyre Watch Co. Little other information is available.

Grade or Name — Description		Avg	Ex-Fn	Mint
16S, BRG, NI..★★★		$5,500	$6,000	$7,000

Kelly Watch Co., 16 size, aluminum movement, straight line lever, quick train, porcelain dial, stem set, reversible ratchet stem wind, originally sold for $2.20, c. 1900.

KELLY WATCH CO.

Chicago, Illinois
c. 1900

Grade or Name — Description		Avg	Ex-Fn	Mint
16S, aluminum movement and OF case....................................★★		$125	$150	$250

KEYSTONE STANDARD WATCH CO.

Lancaster, Pennsylvania
1886 - 1890

Abram Bitner agreed to buy a large number of stockholders' shares of the Lancaster Watch Co. at 10 cents on the dollar; he ended up with 5,625 shares out of the 8,000 that were available. Some 8,900 movements had been completed but not sold at the time of the shares purchase. The company Bitner formed assumed the name of Keystone Standard Watch Co. as the trademark but in reality existed as the Lancaster Watch Co. The business was sold to Hamilton Watch Co. in 1891. Total production was 48,000.

Grade or Name — Description	Avg	Ex-Fn	Mint
18S, 20J, 3/4, LS, HC..★★	$600	$700	$900
18S, 7-15J, OF, KW	55	75	125
18S, 15J, dust proof, ADJ..	125	150	200
18S, 15J, dust proof, OF	100	125	175
18S, 15J, dust proof, HC...	150	175	225
18S, West End, 15J, HC...	75	125	175
18S, 11J, dust proof...	100	125	175
18S, 7-15J, OF, SW, 3/4, LS......................................	55	75	125
6S, 7-10J, HC...	100	125	175

Keystone Watch Co., dust proof model, 18 size, 15 jewels, serial number 352,766.

Example of a basic Knickerbocker movement, 16-18 size, 7 jewels, duplex escapement.

KNICKERBOCKER WATCH CO.

New York, New York

1890 - 1930

This company imported and sold Swiss and low-cost production American watches.

Grade or Name — Description	Avg	Ex-Fn	Mint
18S, 7J, OF, PS, NI, duplex escapement	$60	$75	$95
16S, 7J..	45	55	75
12S, 7J, OF...	45	55	85
10S, Barkley "8 Day"..	75	100	125
6S, Duplex..	50	60	75

LANCASTER WATCH CO.

Lancaster, Pennsylvania
1877 - 1886

Work commenced on Sept. 1, 1877, at the Lancaster Watch Co. The watches produced there were designed to sell at a cheaper price than normal. They had a solid top, 3/4 plate, and a pillar plate that was fully ruby-jeweled (4 pairs). They had a gilt and nickel movement and a new stem-wind device, modeled by Mosly & Todd. By mid-1878 the Lancaster Watch Co. had produced 150 movements. Four grades of watches were made: Keystone, Fulton, Franklin, and Melrose. In September 1879 the company had made 334 movements. In 1880 the total was up to 1,250 movements, and by mid-1882 about 17,000 movements had been produced. All totaled, about 20,000 watch movements were made.

About 75 8-size ladies' watches were also made.

CHRONOLOGY OF THE DEVELOPMENT OF THE LANCASTER WATCH CO.:

Adams and Perry Watch Mfg. Co. — 1874-1876
Lancaster Watch Co. — 1877-1878
Lancaster Pa. Watch Co. — 1878-1879
Lancaster Watch Co. —1879-1886
Keystone Standard Co.— 1886-1890
Hamilton Watch Co. — 1892-1958

LANCASTER
18 SIZE
(All 3/4 Plate)

Grade or Name — Description	Avg	Ex-Fn	Mint
Chester, 7J, KW, gilded	$125	$150	$200
Comet, 7J, NI	125	150	200
Delaware, 20J, ADJ, SW, gilded	300	375	450
Denver, 7J, gilded	75	100	125
Denver, 7J, gilded, Silveroid	40	50	65
Elberon, 7J, dust proof	125	150	200
Ben Franklin, 7J, KW, gilded	250	300	375
Ben Franklin, 11J, KW, gilded	300	350	425
Fulton, 7J, ADJ, KW, gilded	125	150	200
Fulton, 11J, ADJ, KW, gilded	125	150	200
Girard, 15J, ADJ, gilded	100	150	200
Hoosac, 11J, OF	125	175	225
Keystone, 15J, ADJ, gilded, GJS, dust proof	100	125	175
Keystone, 15J, ADJ, gilded, GJS, Silveroid	50	60	75
Lancaster, 7J, SW	40	50	65
Lancaster, 15J, SW, Silveroid	50	60	75
Lancaster, 15J, OF	75	100	150
Lancaster Pa., 20J, ADJ, NI ★★	400	500	650

Lancaster Watch Co., 18 size, 20 jewels, gold jeweled settings, stem wind & pendant set, serial number 1747.

Stevens Model, 18 size, 15 jewels, adjusted, dust proof model, swing-out movement, c.1886.

Grade or Name — Description	Avg	Ex-Fn	Mint
Lancaster Watch, 20J, DR, ADJ, NI, GJS, 14K HC ....★★	$800	$1,000	$1,200
Malvern, 7J, gilded	50	60	75
Melrose, 15J, NI, ADJ, GJS	100	125	175
Nation Standard American Watch Co., 7J, HC............................	200	225	275
New Era, 7J, gilded, KW, HC.....................................	75	100	150
New Era, 7J, gilded, KW, Silveroid...............................	40	60	90
Paoli, 7J, NI	50	75	125
Wm. Penn, 20J, ADJ, NI, dust proof.................................	400	500	650
Radnor, 7J, gilded...	100	125	175
Record, 7J, Silveroid	40	50	65
Record, 15J, NI	75	100	150

West End, 18 size, 15 jewels, key wind & set, serial number 158,080, c. 1878.

Example of a basic Lancaster movement, 8-10 size, 15 jewels, serial number 317,812.

Grade or Name — Description	Avg	Ex-Fn	Mint
Ruby, 16J, NI	$275	$325	$400
Sidney, 15J, NI	100	125	150
Stevens, 15J, ADJ, NI, dust proof	150	175	225
West End, 19J, HC, KW, gilded	450	500	550
West End, 15J, HC, KW, KS	175	200	250
West End, 15J, SW	175	200	250
West End, 15J, SW, Silveroid	40	60	85

8 SIZE

Grade or Name — Description	Avg	Ex-Fn	Mint
Flora, gilded	$75	$100	$150
Lady Penn, 20J, GJS, ADJ, NI	300	350	425
Lancaster W. Co., 7J	75	100	125

Manhattan Watch Co., stop watch, 16 size, note the escapement uses upright "D"—shaped pallets (steel), serial number 117,480.

Manhattan Watch Co., 16 size, stop watch. Note two buttons on top; one sets hands, the other starts and stops watch.

MANHATTAN WATCH CO.

New York, New York
1883 - 1891

The Manhattan Watch Co. made mainly low cost production watches. A complete and full line of watches was made, and most were cased and styled to be sold as a complete watch. The watches were generally 16S with full plate movements. The patented winding mechanism was different. These watches were in both in hunter and open-face cases and later had a sweep second hand. Total production was 160,000 or more watches.

16 SIZE

Grade or Name — Description		Avg	Ex-Fn	Mint
OF, with back wind, base metal case	★	$250	$300	$400
OF, 2 button stop watch, screw back & bezel, **enamel dial**, **gold-filled** case	★★	200	250	350
OF, 2 button stop watch, snap back & bezel, paper dial, base metal case	★	100	125	150
HC, 2 button stop watch, snap back & bezel, paper dial, base metal case	★	200	250	300
OF, 1 button, sweep sec., base metal case , paper dial	★	125	175	225
HC, 1 button, sweep sec., base metal case, paper dial	★	200	250	300
Stallcup, 7J, OF	★	150	200	250

12 SIZE

Grade or Name — Description		Avg	Ex-Fn	Mint
12S	★	$125	$200	$275

MANISTEE WATCH CO.

Manistee, Michigan
1908 - 1912

The Manistee watches, first marketed in 1909, were designed to compete with the low-cost production watches. Dials, jewels, and hairsprings were not produced at the factory. The first movement was 18S, 7J, and sold for about $5. Manistee also made 5J, 15J, 17J, and 21J watches in cheap cases in sizes 16 and 12. Estimated total production was 60,000. Most were sold by Star Watch Case Co.

18 TO 12 SIZE

Grade or Name —Description		Avg	Ex-Fn	Mint
18S, 7J, 3/4, LS, HC	★	$325	$375	$425
18S, 7J, 3/4, LS, OF	★	275	325	375
18S, 7J, 3/4, LS, OF, gold train	★★	375	400	450
16S, 7J, OF	★	200	250	325
16S, 15J, OF	★	225	250	325
16S, 15J, HC	★	250	275	350

Manistee movement, 18 size, 7 jewels, 3/4 plate, open face, serial number 919.

Manistee movement, 16 size, 17 jewels, three-quarter plate, open face, serial number 39,052.

Grade or Name —Description		Avg	Ex-Fn	Mint
16S, 17J, OF	★	$225	$250	$325
16S, 19J, HC	★	300	350	425
16S, 21J, OF	★	325	375	450
2S, 15J	★	150	175	225

McIntyre Watch Co., 16 size, 25 jewels, adjusted to 5 positions with wind indicator, with equidistant escapement, manufactured about 1909. Above illustration taken from a blue print.

McINTYRE WATCH CO.

Kankakee, Illinois

1905 - 1911

This company probably bought the factory from Kankakee Watch Co. In 1908 Charles DeLong was made master watchmaker, and he designed and improved the railroad watches. Only a few watches were made, estimated total production being about eight watches.

Grade or Name — Description		Avg	Ex-Fn	Mint
16S, 21J, BRG, NI, WI	★★★	$4,500	$5,000	$6,500
16S, 25J, BRG, NI, WI, Adj.5P, equidistant escapement	★★★	5,500	6,000	7,500
12S, 19J, BRG	★★★	2,000	2,500	3,500

MELROSE WATCH CO.

Melrose, Massachusetts
1866 - 1868

Melrose Watch Co. began as Tremont Watch Co. and imported the expansion balances and escapements. In 1866 the Tremont Watch Co. moved, changed its name to Melrose Watch Co., and started making complete watch movements, including a new style 18S movement engraved "Melrose Watch Co." About 3,000 were produced. Some watches are found with "Melrose" on the dial and "Tremont" on the movement. Serial numbers start at about 30,000.

Example of a basic Melrose Watch Co. movement, 18 size, 15 jewels, key wind & set.

Grade or Name — Description		Avg	Ex-Fn	Mint
18S, 7J, KW, KS .... ★★		$300	$350	325
18S, 11J, KW, KS, OF .... ★★		325	370	450
18S, 15J, KW, KS .... ★★		350	400	475
18S, 15J, KW, KS, Silveroid .... ★★		250	300	375

☞ Note: Add $25.00 to values of above watches in hunting case.

MOZART WATCH CO.

Providence, Rhode Island
Ann Arbor, Michigan
1864 - 1870

In 1864 Don J. Mozart started out to produce a less expensive three-wheel watch in Providence, R. I. Despite his best efforts, the venture was declared a failure by 1866. Mozart left Providence and moved to Ann Arbor, Mich. There, again, he started on a three-wheel watch and succeeded in producing thirty. The three-wheel watch was not a new idea except to American manufacturers. Three-wheel watches were made many decades before Mozart's first effort, but credit for the first American-made three-wheel watch must go to him. The size was about 18 and could be called a 3/4 or full plate movement. The balance bridge was screwed on the top plate, as was customary. The round bridge partially covered the opening in the top plate and was just large enough for the balance to oscillate. The balance was compensated and somewhat smaller in diameter than usual. Mozart called it a chronolever, and it was to function so perfectly it would be free from friction. That sounded good but was in no way true. The watch was of the usual thickness of the American watches of 18S. The train had a main wheel with the usual number of teeth and a ten-leaf center pinion, but it had a large center wheel of 108 teeth and a third wheel of 90 teeth, with a six-leaf third (escape) pinion. The escape wheel had 30 teeth and received its impulse directly from the roller on the staff, while the escape tooth locked on the intermediate lever pallet. The escape pinion had a long pivot that carried the second hand, which made a circuit of the dial, once in 12 seconds. The total number of Mozart watches produced was 165, and about 30 of these were the three-wheel type.

Grade or Name — Description		Avg	Ex-Fn	Mint
18S, 3/4, KW, KS, 3-wheel .... ★★★★★		$11,000	$15,000	$20,000
18S, 3/4, KW, KS... ★★★★		6,000	7,000	8,000

Example of a basic Mozart Watch Co. movement, 18 size, three-quarter plate, key wind & set, three-wheel train, "Patent Dec. 24th, 1868" engraved on back plate.

Nashua Watch Co. (marked), 20 size, 19 jewels, key wind & set from back, serial number 1,057.

NASHUA WATCH CO.

Nashua, New Hampshire

1859 - 1862

One of the most important contributions to the American Watch industry was made by the Nashua Watch Co. of Nashua, New Hampshire. Founded in 1859 by B. D. Bingham, the company hired some of the most innovative and creative watchmakers in America and produced an extremely high grade American pocket watch.

His company included N. P. Stratton, C. V. Woerd, Charles Moseley, James H. Gerry, and James Gooding, among others. Most of the people connected with the Nashua Watch Company became famous for various advances in watch manufacture, at one time or another. Many had extremely important American patents on various inventions that came to be regarded as a benchmark of the best watches America was capable of making at the time.

The Nashua Watch Co. is important for many reasons. It was the first American company to produce a truly superior high grade movement; the 3/4 plate design used by Nashua became the standard for over 40 years in the American marketplace. Perhaps most importantly, the watches designed by the Nashua Watch Co., and later by the Nashua division of the American Watch Co., became the leaders in the production of the highest quality watches made in America and forced the entire Swiss watch industry to change their technology to compete with the Nashua designs.

Nashua continually won awards for their various models of watches both here and in Europe. By virtue of their sheer technical superiority and classical elegance, Nashua became known universally as the most innovative producer of watches America ever knew.

The original Nashua company produced material for about 1,000 movements but, except for a handful, almost the entire production was finished by the American Watch Company at Waltham, Mass., after R. E. Robbins took over Nashua in 1862 when the company was in grave financial difficulty. Robbins was very happy about the arrangement since he got back almost all the watchmaking geniuses who had left him in 1859 to join Nashua. Robbins incorporated the Nashua Division into the American Watch Company as its high grade experimental division.

Over the years, many of the major advances were made by the Nashua division of Waltham, including the 1860 model 16-size keywind keyset, the 1862 model 20-size key wind keyset, the 1870 model 18-size keywind keyset, pin set, and lever set (which became the first American advertised Railroad watch), the 1868 model 16-size stem wind, and the 1872 model 17-size stemwind. The Nashua division also greatly influenced the 1888 model and the 1892 model by Waltham.

Since almost all the production material made by Nashua from 1859 until its incorporation into the American Watch Co. in 1862 was unfinished by Nashua, only about four examples of the 20-size keywind keyset from the back signed Nashua Watch Co. are known to exist.

Grade or Name — Description	Avg	Ex-Fn	Mint
Nashua (marked), 19J, KW, KS, 3/4, 18K .... ★★★★	$18,000	$22,000	$28,000
Nashua (marked), 15J, KW, KS, 3/4, silver case .... ★★★	9,000	11,000	13,000

NEWARK WATCH CO.

Newark, New Jersey
1864 - 1870

Arthur Wadsworth, one of the designers for Newark Watch Co., patented an 18 Size full plate movement. The first movements reached the market in 1867. This company produced only about 4,000 watches before it was sold to the Cornell Watch Co.

CHRONOLOGY OF THE DEVELOPMENT OF NEWARK WATCH CO.:
Newark Watch Co. 1864-1870; S#s 6,501 to 12,000;
Cornell Watch Co., Chicago, Ill. 1870-1874; S#s 12,001 to 25,000;
Cornell Watch Co., San Francisco, Calif. 1874-Jan. 1876; S#s 25,001 to 35,000;
California Watch Co., Jan. 1876-mid 1876.

Newark Watch Co. Robert Fellows movement, 18 size, 15 jewels, key wind & set, serial number 12, 044.

Grade or Name — Description		Avg	Ex-Fn	Mint
18S, 15J, KW, KS, HC	★★	$350	$400	$500
18S, 15J, KW, KS, OF	★★	300	350	425
18S, 7J, KW, KS	★★	300	350	425
J. C. Adams, 11J, KW, KS	★★	350	400	475
J. C. Adams, 11J, KW, KS, Coin	★★	350	400	475
Edward Biven, 11-15J, KW, KS	★★	350	400	475
Robert Fellows, KW, KS	★★	400	450	525
Keyless Watch Co., 15J, LS, SW	★★	300	350	425
Newark Watch Co., 7-15J, KW, KS	★★	350	400	475
Arthur Wadsworth, SW	★★★	400	500	600
Arthur Wadsworth, 18S, 15J, 18K, HC ("Arthur Wadsworth, New York" on dial; "Keyless Watch, Patent #3655, June 19, 1866" engraved on movement)	★★★	1,000	1,200	1,500

NEW ENGLAND WATCH CO.

Waterbury, Connecticut

1898 - 1914

The New England Watch Co., formerly the Waterbury Watch Co., made a watch with a duplex escapement, gilt, 16S, open faced. Watches with the skeletonized movement are very desirable. The company later became Timex Watch Co.

Grade or Name — Description		Avg	Ex-Fn	Mint
16S, OF, duplex, skeleton, good running order	★	$250	$300	$350
12S, 16S, 18S, OF, pictures on dial: ladies, dogs, horses, trains, flags, ships, cards, etc.		150	175	225
12S, 16S, 18S, OF, duplex escapement, good running order		50	65	95
12S, 16S, 18S, OF, pin lever escapement, good running order		25	35	60

Front and back view of a skeletonized New England Watch Co. movement. This watch is fitted with a glass back and front, making the entire movement and wheels visible, 4 jewels, silver hands, black numbers, originally sold for $10-13.

Grade or Name — Description	Avg	Ex-Fn	Mint
6S, duplex	$35	$40	$55
Addison, (all sizes)	35	40	55
Alden	35	40	55
Ambassador, 12S, duplex	25	30	40
Americus, duplex	20	25	30
Avour, duplex escapement	35	40	55
Berkshire, duplex, 14K, GF	60	70	85

New England Watch co., 16 size, 7 jewels, open face, double roller, Dan Patch stop watch.

New England Watch Co., Scout, about 16 size, 4 jewels, duplex escapement, New England base metal case.

New England Watch Co., multi-colored paper dials, showing an assorted selection. Watches complete with these type dials bring $125 - $175.00.

Grade or Name — Description	Avg	Ex-Fn	Mint
Cadish, duplex escapement	$35	$40	$55
Cavour	45	50	60
Columbian	15	20	30
Cruiser, duplex	45	50	69
Dan Patch, 7J ★	275	350	425
Excelsor, 7J	65	70	95
Fancy dial, "unfaded"	100	145	200
Gabour	65	70	85
General	20	30	45
Hale, 7J	25	30	45
Jockey, duplex	55	60	75
Oxford	15	20	30
Padishah, duplex	45	50	65
Putnam	65	70	85
Rugby, stop watch	65	70	85
Scout, 12 Size, duplex escapement, HC	40	45	60
Senator, duplex escapement	40	45	55
Trump, duplex	15	20	30
Tuxedo	15	20	35

NEW HAVEN CLOCK AND WATCH CO.

New Haven, Connecticut
1853 - 1956

The company started making watches in early 1880 in New Haven and produced the regular 16S, lever watch. These sold for $3.75. The company soon reached a production of about 200 watches per day, making a total of some 40 million watches.

New Haven Clock & Watch Co., Angelus, with rotating dials, patented Jan 23, 1900.

Example of a New Haven movement.

Grade or Name – Description	Avg	Ex-Fn	Mint
Always Right	$45	$55	$75
Angelus, 2 rotating dials	65	80	100
Beardsley Radiant	45	50	65
Buddy	35	40	45
Bull Dog	40	45	60
Captain Scout	85	100	150
Chronometer	45	85	100
Elite	40	50	65
Fancy dials, no fading	100	145	200
Football Timer	65	75	95
Ford Special	75	85	100
Hamilton	35	45	60
Handy Andy	50	60	75
Jerome USA	35	40	50
Kaiser Wilhelm ★★	200	275	350

☞ Note: Some grades or styles are not included. Their values can be determined by comparing with similar age, models, styles and grades listed.

Example of Kaiser Wilhelm.　　　　　Example of Traveler.

Grade or Name – Description	Avg	Ex-Fn	Mint
Kermit	$40	$45	$55
Laddie	25	30	40
Leonard Watch Co.	25	40	50
Leonard	25	35	45
Mastercraft Rayolite	35	45	60
Miracle	25	30	40
Nehi	50	70	85
New Haven, pin lever, SW	50	75	100
New Haven, back wind	100	135	200
Panama Official Souvenir, 1915	200	250	350
Pastor Stop Watch	65	85	100
Pedometer, 14 size, OF	25	30	35
Playing cards on dial	100	175	300
Ships Time & Franklin dial	50	60	75
Sports Timer	65	75	95
Surity	15	20	30
Tip Top	20	30	50
Tip Top Jr.	20	30	50
Tommy Ticker	30	35	40
Traveler, with travel case	40	45	60
True Time Teller Tip Top	40	45	60
USA	30	35	40

NEW HAVEN WATCH CO.

New Haven, Connecticut
1883 - 1887

This company was organized October 16, 1883 with the intention of producing W. E. Doolittle's patented watch; however, this plan was soon abandoned. They did produce a "Model A" watch, the first was marketed in the spring of 1884. Batch or lot numbers were used instead of serial numbers, and watches can be found bearing the same batch number. Estimated total production was 2,000 to 3,000. The original capital became absorbed by Trenton Watch Co.

Example of a basic New Haven Watch Co. movement with batch or lot number 65. Note this is not a serial number.

Grade or Name – Description	Avg	Ex-Fn	Mint
"A" Model, about 18S, pat. Dec. 27, '81 ....★★★	$200	$275	$475
Alpha Model, pat. Dec. 27, '81 ....★★★	200	275	475

NEW YORK WATCH CO.

and

NEW YORK CITY WATCH CO.
New York, New York
1890 - 1897

This company manufactured the Dollar-type watches, which had a pendant-type crank. The watch is wound by cranking the pendant, and has a pin lever escapement. The patent number 526,871, is engraved on movement dated October 1894, and was held by S. Schisgall. The New York City Watch Co., 20 size watch has the words "Lever Winder" printed the on dial.

Grade or Name – Description	Avg	Ex-Fn	Mint
20S, no jewels, "Lever Winder" .... ★★★★	$450	$600	$850

New York City Watch Co., 20 size, "Lever Winder" on dial. This watch is wound by cranking the pendant, pin lever escapement, patent number 526,871.

NEW YORK CHRONOGRAPH WATCH CO.
NEW YORK, NEW YORK
1883 -1886

This company sold about 18,000 watches marked "New York Chronograph Watch Co." The 18 size stop watch was manufactured by Manhattan Watch Co.

Grade or Name –Description	Avg	Ex-Fn	Mint
18S, 7J, stop watch, HC .... ★	$125	$150	$200
18S, 7J, stop watch, OF..	100	125	175
16S, 7J, SW, time only, OF... ★	100	175	250
16S, 9J, SW, time only, OF... ★	100	175	250
16S, 9J, SW, time only sweep sec., OF......................... ★	100	175	250
16S, 11J, SW, CHRONOGRAPH,OF................................★★★	200	250	300

N.Y. Chronograph Watch Co., dial and movement, 16 size, 7 jewels, open face, sweep second hand.

New York Chronograph Watch Co. dial and movement, 7 jewels, open face, buttons at the top of case set hands and stop watch.

NEW YORK STANDARD WATCH CO.

Jersey City, New Jersey
1885 - 1929

The first watch reached the market in early 1888 and was a 18S. The most interesting feature was a straight line lever with a "worm gear escapement." This was patented by R. J. Clay. All watches were quick train and open-faced. The company also made its own cases and sold a complete watch. A prefix number was added to the serial number after the first 10,000 watches were made. Estimated total production was 7,000,000.

Chronograph, 16-18 size, 7 jewels, stem wind, second hand start-stop and fly back, three-quarter plate, serial number 5,334,322.

Example of a basic New York Standard movement, 18 size, 7 jewels, stem wind, serial number 296,893.

N. Y. STANDARD
16 AND 18 SIZE

Grade or Name – Description	Avg	Ex-Fn	Mint
18S, 7J, N. Y. Standard, KW, KS...............................	$250	$300	$375
18S, 7J, N. Y. Standard, SW...................................	40	60	85
18S, 15J, N. Y. Standard, SW, LS, HC	100	125	175
Chronograph, 7J, 3/4, NI, DMK, SW, fly back hand	125	175	250
Chronograph, 10J, (marked 10J), fly back hand.................... ★	135	185	275
Chronograph, 13J, sweep sec., stop & fly back hand	135	185	260
Chronograph, 15J, 3/4, NI, DMK, SW, fly back hand, ...	150	200	275
Columbus, 7J	40	60	85
Convertible,15J.,16 Size, HC or OF ....★★	300	425	600
Crown W. Co., 7J, OF or HC...................................	40	60	85
Crown W. Co., 15J, HC..	50	75	100
Dan Patch, 7J, stop watch(pat. DEC. 22 '08).................... ★	275	350	425
Dan Patch, 17J, stop watch(pat. DEC. 22 '08).................★★	375	450	525
Edgemere, 7J, OF & HC..	40	60	85
Excelsior, 7J, OF or HC.......................................	40	60	85

New York Standard, with worm gear (located under cutout star), 18 size, 7 jewels, there was two runs of the worm-drive model 52,000 made, serial number 31,138.

Remington W. Co. (marked on movement & case), 16 size, 11 jewels, 2-tone damaskeening, serial number CC021,331.

Grade or Name – Description	Avg	Ex-Fn	Mint
Harvard W. CO.7–11J., ...	$30	$40	$50
Hi Grade	40	60	85
Ideal	40	60	85
Jefferson, 7J.,...	40	50	60
La Salle, 7J.,..	35	45	55
New Era, 7J., OF or HC, skeletonized (Poor Man's Dudley)	250	275	325
New Era,7–11J.	30	40	55
New York Standard W. Co., 11J, 3/4	50	75	100
New York Standard, 7J, 3/4	50	75	100
New York Standard, 15J, BRG	75	100	125
N. Y. Standard, with (" WORM GEAR") .... ★	300	350	425

Grade or Name – Description	Avg	Ex-Fn	Mint
Pan American, 7J, OF	$50	$75	$100
Perfection, 7J, OF or HC	40	60	85
Perfection, 15J, OF or HC, NI	50	75	100
Remington W. Co., 11J, marked mvt. & case	75	100	135
Solar W. Co., 7J	40	60	85
Special USA, 7J	35	45	55
18S Tribune USA, 23J, HC or OF, Pat. Reg. Adj.	150	175	225
Washington, 7 "11J.,	40	50	65
William Penn, 7 "11J.,	40	50	65
Wilmington	40	60	85

☞ Note: For watches with O'Hara Multi-Color Dials, add $75 to value in mint condition; add $5 for Hunting Cases.

12 SIZE

Grade or Name – Description	Avg	Ex-Fn	Mint
N. Y. Standard, 7J, OF	$25	$30	$45
N. Y. Standard, 7J, HC, Multi-Color dial	100	125	175

New York Standard Watch Co., 12 size, 7 jewels, open face, serial number 1021224.

6 SIZE AND 0 SIZE

Grade or Name – Description	Avg	Ex-Fn	Mint
American,7J.,	$35	$40	$55
Empire State W. Co., 7J	40	50	65
Standard USA, 7J	40	50	65
6S, Columbia, 7J, HC	60	70	85
6S, N. Y. Standard, 7J, HC	60	70	85
6S, Orient, SW	30	40	55
6S, Progress, 7J, YGF	40	50	65
0S, Ideal, 7J, HC	60	70	85
0S, N. Y. Standard, 7J, HC	60	70	85

☞ NOTE: Watches listed in this book are priced at the retail level, as complete watches having an original 14k gold filled case, an original white enamel single sunk dial, and with the entire original movement in good working order with no repairs needed, unless otherwise noted.

NEW YORK STANDARD WATCH CO.
IDENTIFICATION OF MOVEMENTS

How to Identify Your Watch: Compare the movement of your watch with the illustrations in this section. Upon matching the movement exactly, the model number and size can be determined. While comparing, note the location of the balance, jewels, screws, gears, and type of back plate (Full, 3/4, Bridge) which will be clues in identifying the movement you have. Having determined the size and model number, you can now find your watch in the main price listing by name or number (which is engraved on the movement).

18 size, 5th model, hunting

18 size, 6th model, open face

18 size, No. 80

18 size, No. 64

18 size, No. 360

18 size, No. 60

18 size, No. 165

18 size, 4th Model

16 size, No. 94

16 size, No. 91

16 size, 1st Model,
converts to open
or hunting

16 size, No. 1516

16 size, No. 390

12 size, No. 170

12 size, No. 1570

12 size, hunting

12 size, No. 1512

12 size, No. 370

6 size, No. 146

6 size, No. 44

0 size, No. 300

3/0 size, No. 730

10/0 size, No. 1015

NEW YORK SPRINGFIELD WATCH CO.
Springfield, Massachusetts
1866 - 1876

The New York Watch Co. had a rather difficult time getting started. The name of the company was changed from the Mozart Watch Co. to the New York Watch Co., and it was located in Rhode Island. Before any watches had been produced, they moved to Springfield, Mass., in 1867. A factory was built there, but only about 100 watches were produced before a fire occurred on April 23, 1870. Shortly after the fire, in 1870, a newly-designed watch was introduced. The first movements reached the market in 1871, and the first grade was a fully-jeweled adjusted movement called "Frederick Billings." The standard 18S and the Swiss Ligne systems were both used in gauging the size of these watches. The New York Watch Co. used full signatures on its movements. The doors closed in the summer of 1876.

In January 1877, the Hampden Watch Co. was organized and commenced active operation in June 1877.

CHRONOLOGY OF THE DEVELOPMENT OF NEW YORK WATCH CO.

The Mozart Watch Co., Providence, R. I. 1864-1866
New York Watch Co., Providence, R. I. 1866-1867
New York Watch Co., Springfield, Mass. 1867-1875
New York Watch Mfg. Co., Springfield, Mass. 1875-1876
Hampden Watch Co., Springfield, Mass. 1877-1886
Hampden-Dueber Watch Co., Springfield, Mass. 1886-1888
Hampden Watch Co., Canton, Ohio 1888-1923
Dueber Watch Co., Canton, Ohio 1888-1923
Dueber-Hampden Watch Co., Canton, Ohio 1923-1931
Amtorg, U.S.S.R. 1930-

NEW YORK WATCH CO. SPRINGFIELD
ESTIMATED SERIAL NUMBERS
AND PRODUCTION DATES

Date	Serial No.	Date	Serial No.
1866	1,000	1871	20,000
1867	3,000	1872	30,000
1868	5,000	1873	40,000
1869	7,000	1874	50,000
1870	10,000	1875	60,000

N. Y. W. SPRINGFIELD
18 TO 20 SIZE

Grade or Name – Description		Avg	Ex-Fn	Mint
Aaron Bagg, 7J, KW, KS	★	$200	$250	$325
Frederick Billings, 15J, KW, KS	★	200	250	325
E. W. Bond, 15J, 3/4	★★★	450	600	700
J. A. Briggs, 11J, KW, KS, from back	★★	300	350	425

E.W. Bond movement, 18 size, 7 jewels, three-quarter plate.

Chas. F. Hayward, 18 size, 15 jewels, key wind & set, serial number 18,733.

Grade or Name – Description	Avg	Ex-Fn	Mint
Albert Clark, 15J, KW, KS, from back, 3/4 ....★★	$300	$350	$425
Homer Foot, 15J, KW, KS, from back, 3/4 ....★★	300	350	425
Herman Gerz, 11J, KW, KS...★	200	250	325
John Hancock, 7J, KW, KS...	100	200	275
John Hancock, 7J, KW, KS, Silveroid	75	100	125
John Hancock, 7J, KW, KS, Coin..	150	200	275
Chas. E. Hayward, 15J, KW, KS, long balance cock	150	200	275
Chas. E. Hayward, 15J, KW, KS, Coin	150	200	275
John L. King, 15J, KW, KS, from back, 3/4 ....★★	400	500	600
New York Watch Co., 7J, KW, KS..★	150	200	275
New York Watch Co., 15J, KW, KS, (Serial #s below 75)	1,300	1,500	1,800
New York Watch Co., 15J, KW, KS, Wolf's Teeth winding, all original..★★★	1,000	1,200	1,500
New York Watch Co., 11J, KW, KS...★★	300	350	375
H. G. Norton, 15J, KW, KS, from back, 3/4 ....★★	300	350	425

H.G. Norton, 18 size, 15 jewels, three-quarter plate, gold escape wheel, serial number 6592.

New York Watch Co., 18 size, 15-19 jewels, stem wind, hunting case, note wolf teeth winding, serial number 978.

State Street movement, 18 size, 11 jewels, three-quarter plate.

Theo E. Studley movement, 18 size, 15 jewels, key wind & set, full plate.

Grade or Name – Description	Avg	Ex-Fn	Mint
J. C. Perry, 15J.. ★	$150	$200	$275
J. C. Perry, 15J, Silveroid............................ ★	100	125	175
Railway, 15J, KW, FULL, Coin...................★★	600	650	725
Railway, 15J, KW, KS, FULL ....★★	600	650	725
William Romp,15J,KW,KS from back,3/4 ....★★	500	650	950
Geo. Sam Rice, 7J, KW, KS .... ★	300	350	425
Springfield, 19J, KW, KS, from back, ADJ, Wolfsteeth wind, serial Nos. below 1,000 ....★★★	1,300	1,500	1,800
State Street, 11J, 3/4, SW ....★★	325	400	500
State Street, 11J, 3/4, SW, Silveroid ....★★	325	425	550
Theo E. Studley, 15J, KW, Coin......................	100	125	175
Theo E. Studley, 15J, KW, KS	100	125	175
George Walker, 17J, KW, 3/4, ADJ................... ★	300	400	500
Chester Woolworth, 15J, KW, KS.....................	100	125	175
Chester Woolworth, 11J, KW, KS.....................	100	125	175
Chester Woolworth, 11J, KW, KS, Silveroid........	50	65	95
Chester Woolworth, 11J, KW, KS, ADJ...............	150	175	225
#4, 15J, ADJ, KW, KS	125	150	200
#5, 15J, KW, KS...	100	125	175
#6, 11J, KW, KS...	100	125	175
#6, 11J, KW, KS, Silveroid.............................	50	65	95

☞ NOTE: Some KW, KS watches made by the New York Watch Co. have a hidden key. If you unscrew the crown, and the crown comes out as a key, add $100 to the listed value.

☞ NOTE: Watches listed in this book are priced at the retail level, as complete watches having an original 14k gold-filled case, an original white enamel single sunk dial, and with the entire original movement in good working order with no repairs needed, unless otherwise noted.

NON-MAGNETIC WATCH CO.
Geneva and America
1887 - 1905

The Non-Magnetic Watch Co. sold and imported watches from the Swiss as well as contracted watches made in America. Geneva Non-Magnetic marked watches appear to be the oldest type of movement. This company sold a full line of watches, high grade to low grade, as well as repeaters and ladies watches. An advertisement appeared in the monthly journal of "Locomotive Engineers" in 1887. The ad states that the "Paillard's patent non-magnetic watches are uninfluenced by magnetism of electricity." Each watch contains the Paillard's patent non-magnetic, inoxydable compensation balance and hairspring. An ad in 1888 shows prices for 16 size Swiss style watches as low as $15 for 7 jewels and as high as $135 for 20 jewels.

18 SIZE
(must be marked Paillard's Patent)

Grade or Name – Description	Avg	Ex-Fn	Mint
Elgin, 17J, FULL, SW, LS, OF	$100	$125	$175
Elgin, 17J, FULL, SW, LS, HC	125	150	225
Elgin, 15J, FULL, SW, LS, OF	75	100	150
Elgin, 15-17J, FULL, SW, LS, HC	100	125	175
Illinois, 24J, GJS, NI, Adj.5P, OF	800	850	925
Illinois, 24J, GJS, NI, Adj.5P, HC ★	900	1,100	1,300
Illinois, 23J, GJS, NI, Adj.5P, OF	700	750	925
Illinois, 23J, GJS, NI, Adj.5P, HC ★★★	1,600	1,800	2,100
Illinois, 21J, GJS, NI, Adj.5P, OF	200	250	325
Illinois, 21J, GJS, NI, Adj.5P, HC	250	300	325
Illinois, 17J, NI, ADJ, OF	100	125	175
Illinois, 17J, NI, ADJ, HC	125	150	225
Illinois, 15J, NI, OF	75	100	150
Illinois, 15J, NI, HC	100	125	175
Illinois, 11J, OF	75	100	150

Non-Magnetic Watch Co., 18 size, 15 jewels, gold jewel settings, Adj.5p, by Peoria Watch Co.

Non-Magnetic Watch Co., 18 size, 21 Ruby jewels, Adj.5p, note "Paillard" engraved on movement.

Non-Magnetic Watch co., 18 size, 16J., plate, hunting, note "Geneva" engraved on movement, serial # 6113.

Non-Magnetic Watch Co., 18 size, 16 jewels, bridge model, example of a Swiss Ebauche.

Grade or Name – Description	Avg	Ex-Fn	Mint
Illinois, 11J, HC	$100	$125	$175
Peoria, 17J, FULL, SW, LS, OF	325	350	400
Peoria, 15J, FULL, SW, LS, OF	300	325	375
Peoria, 15J, FULL, SW, LS, HC	400	425	475
Peoria, 11J, FULL, SW, LS, OF	100	125	175
Peoria, 11J, FULL, SW, LS, HC	175	200	250
Swiss, 16J, plate, SW, LS, OF	60	70	85
Swiss, 16J, plate, SW, LS, HC	75	100	150
Swiss, 15J, bar bridge, SW, LS, OF	55	65	80
Swiss, 15J, bar bridge, SW, LS, HC	75	100	150
Swiss, 11J, plate, SW, LS, OF, HC	75	100	150
Swiss, 11J, bar bridge, SW, LS, OF, HC	75	100	150

Magnetic Watch Co., 16 size, 21 Ruby jewels, adjusted, made by Illinois Watch Co.

Non-Magnetic Watch Co., 16 size, 20J., in gold jewel settings, stem wind, open or hunting. Swiss made.

16 SIZE
(must be marked Paillard's Patent)

Grade or Name – Description	Avg	Ex-Fn	Mint
Illinois, 21J, GJS, 3/4, DR, Adj.6P, OF	$200	$250	$325

Non-Magnetic Watch Co., 16 size, three-quarter plate, 15 jewels, adjusted.

Non-Magnetic Watch Co., 16 size, three-quarter plate, 15 jewels, note "Paillard's Patent, Balance And Spring" engraved on movement.

Grade or Name – Description	Avg	Ex-Fn	Mint
Illinois, 21J, GJS, 3/4, DR, Adj.6P, HC	$300	$350	$425
Illinois, 17J, 3/4, DR, ADJ, OF	75	100	150
Illinois, 17J, 3/4, DR, ADJ, HC	100	125	175
Illinois, 15J, HC	75	100	125
Illinois, 15J, OF	55	80	135
Illinois, 11J, OF	50	75	125
Illinois, 11J, HC	75	100	150
Swiss, 20J, GJS, DR, Adj.6P, NI, 1/2 ,OF	75	100	150
Swiss, 20J, GJS, DR, Adj.6P, NI, 1/2, HC	100	125	175
Swiss, 18J, GJS, DR, Adj.6P, NI, 1/2, OF	75	100	150
Swiss, 18J, GJS, DR, Adj.6P, NI, 1/2, HC	100	125	175
Swiss, 16J, GJS, DR, Adj.6P, NI, 1/2, OF	75	100	150
Swiss, 16J, GJS, DR, Adj.6P, NI, 1/2, HC	75	100	150
Swiss, 15J, DR, NI, 3/4, OF	75	100	150
Swiss, 15J, DR, NI, 3/4, HC	100	125	175
Swiss, 11J, NI, 3/4, OF	60	70	95
Swiss, 11J, NI, 3/4, HC	100	125	175
Swiss, 7J, OF & 3/4, HC	50	60	85

OTAY WATCH CO.

Otay, California

1889 - 1894

This company produced about 1,000 watches with a serial number range of 1,000 to 1,500 and 30,000 to 31,000. The company was purchased by a Japanese manufacturer in 1894. Names on Otay movements include: Golden Gate, F. A. Kimball, Native Sun, Overland Mail, R. D. Perry, and P. H. Wheeler.

Otay Watch Co. Dial; note hunting case style and lever for setting hands.

Otay Watch Co., F.A. Kimball, 18 size, 15 jewels, lever set, hunting, serial number 1,264.

18 SIZE

Grade or Name – Description		Avg	Ex-Fn	Mint
California, 15J., LS, HC, N	★★★	$2,000	$2,200	$2,500
Golden Gate, 15J, LS, HC, OF, NI	★★★	2,000	2,200	2,600
F. A. Kimball, 15J, LS, HC, Gilt	★★	1,200	1,400	1,700
Native Son, 15J, LS, HC, NI	★★	1,600	1,800	2,100
Overland Mail, 15J, LS, HC, NI	★★★	2,200	2,600	2,800
R. D. Perry, 15J, LS, HC, Gilt	★★	1,200	1,400	1,700
P. H. Wheeler, 15J, LS, HC, Gilt	★★	1,200	1,400	1,700

D. D. PALMER WATCH CO.

Waltham, Massachusetts

1864 - 1875

In 1858, at age 20, Mr. Palmer opened a small jewelry store in Waltham, Mass. Here he became interested in pocket chronometers. At first he bought the balance and jewels from Swiss manufacturers. In 1864 he took a position with the American Watch Co. and made the chronometers in his spare time (only about 25 produced). They were 18S, 3/4 plate, gilded, key wind, and some were nickel. At first they were fusee driven, but he mainly used going barrels. About 1870, Palmer started making lever watches and by 1875 he left the American Watch Co. and started making a 10S keywind, gilded movement, and a 16S, 3/4 plate, gilt and nickel, and a stem wind of his own invention (a vibrating crown wheel). In all he made about 1,500 watches. The signature appearing on the watches was "Palmer W. Co. Wal., Mass."

He basically had three grades of watches: Fine-Solid Nickel; Medium-Nickel Plated; and Medium-Gold Gilt. They were made in open-face and hunter cases.

D.D. Palmer Watch Co., 18 size, 15 jewels, "Palmer's Pat. Stem Winder" on movement, serial number 1,007.

Grade or name – Description	Avg	Ex-Fn	Mint
10-14S, 15-17J, 3/4 plate, KW, spring detent chronometer.★★★	$4,000	$4,500	$6,000
16-18S, 17J, NI, OF, 18K..★★	1,500	1,800	2,200

PEORIA WATCH CO.
Peoria, Illinois
1885 - 1895

The roots of this company began with the Independent Watch Co. (1880 - 1883). These watches marked Marion and Mark Twain were made by the Fredonia Watch Co. (1883 - 1885) Peroia Watch Co. opened Dec. 19, 1885, and made one model of railroad

Peroia Watch Co., 18 size, 15 jewels, nickel damaskeening plates, hunting, note patented regulator, serial number 11,532.

watch in 1887. They were 18S, quick train, 15 jewel, and all stem wind. These watches are hard to find, as only about 3,000 were made. Peoria also made railroad watches for A. C. Smith's Non-Magnetic Watch Co. of America, from 1884-1888. The 18S watches were full plate, adjusted, and had whiplash regulator.

The Peoria Watch Co. closed in 1889, having produced about 47,000 watches.

Grade or Name – Description	Avg	Ex-Fn	Mint
18S, 11J, SW, OF..	$150	$200	$250
18S, 15J, SW, personalized name.....................................	175	225	275
18S, Peoria W. Co., 15J, SW, OF	200	250	300
18S, Peoria W. Co., 15J, SW, HC.....................................	225	250	325
18S, Peoria W. Co., 15J, SW, low S#.................................	325	350	400
18S, Anti-Magnetic, 15J, SW	325	350	400
18S, Non-Magnetic Watch Co. of America, 15J, NI, SW, GJS, Adj.5P, OF..	350	375	425
18S, 15J, Non-Magnetic Watch Co. of America, NI, SW, GJS, Adj.5P, HC..	400	425	475
18S, Made for Railway Service, 15J, NI, GJS, Adj.5P, OF	300	350	425
18S, Made for Railway Service, NI, GJS, Adj.5P, HC	350	400	475

PHILADELPHIA WATCH CO.
Philadelphia, Pennsylvania
1874 - 1886

Eugene Paulus organized the Philadelphia Watch Co. about 1874. Most all the parts were made in Switzerland, and finished and cased in this country. The International Watch Co. is believed to have manufactured the movements for Philadelphia Watch Co. Estimated total production of the company is 12,000 watches.

Philadelphia Watch Co., 16 size, 15 jewels, gold jewel settings, hunting case model. "Paulus Patents 1868. Aug. 25th, Nov. 3rd" on movement, serial number 5,751.

☞ Note: Watches listed in this book are priced at the retail level, as complete watches having an original 14k gold-filled case, an original white enamel single sunk dial, and with the entire original movement in good working order with no repairs needed.

Grade or Name – Description		Avg	Ex-Fn	Mint
18S, 15J, SW, HC	★	$350	$450	$575
18S, 15J, KW, KS	★	275	375	500
18S, 15J, SW, OF	★	325	425	525
18S, HC, KW, KS, 18K original case marked				
Philadelphia Watch Co.	★★	1,200	1,400	1,800
18S, 11J, KW, KS	★	150	175	225
16S, 15J, KW, KS	★	150	175	225
16S, 19J, KW, KS, GJS	★	375	475	600
8S-6S, 11J, HC	★	150	175	225
8S-6S, 15J, HC	★	150	175	225
8S-6S, Paulus, 19J, KW, KS	★	225	300	400
000/S, 7J, HC, PS	★	125	200	300

JAMES & HENRY PITKIN

Hartford, Connecticut
New York, New York
1838 - 1852

Henry Pitkin was the first to attempt to manufacture watches by machinery. The machines were of Pitkin's own design and very crude, but he had some brilliant ideas. His first four workers were paid $30 a year plus their board. After much hardship, the first watches were produced in the fall of 1838. The watches had going barrels, not the fusee and chain, and the American flag was engraved on the plates to denote they were American made and to exemplify the true spirit of American independence in watchmaking.

The first 50 watches were stamped with the name "Henry Pitkin." Others bore the firm name "H & J F Pitkin." The movements were about 16S and 3/4plate. The plates were rolled brass and stamped out with dies. The pinions were lantern style with eight leaves. The movement had a slow train of 14,400 beats per hour. Pitkin's first plan was to make the ends of the pinions conical and let them run in the ends of hardened steel screws, similar to the Marine clock balances. A large brass setting was put in the plates and extended above the surface. Three screws, with small jewels set in their ends, were

Example of a basic Henry Pitkin movement, 16 size, key wind & set.

inserted so that they closed about the pivot with very small end shake. This proved to be too expensive and was used in only a few movements. Next, he tried to make standard type movements extend above the plates with the end shake controlled by means of a screw running down into the end of the pivots, reducing friction. This "capped jewel train" was used for a while before he adopted the standard ways of jeweling. The escape wheels were the star type, English style. The balance was made of gold and steel. These movements were fire gilded and not interchangeable. The dials, hands, mainsprings and hairsprings were imported. The rounded pallets were manufactured by Pitkin, and the cases for his watches were made on the premises. As many as 900 watches could have been made by Pitkin.

Grade or Name – Description	Avg	Ex-Fn	Mint
Henry Pitkin S#1-50 .... ★★★★	$15,000	$20,000	$25,000
H. & J. F. Pitkin & Co., S#50-377 .... ★★★	10,000	15,000	20,000
Pitkin & Co., New York, S#378-900 .... ★★★	4,500	6,000	7,500
W. Pitkin, Hartford, Conn., S# approx. 40,000, fusee lever, KW, Coin .... ★★	600	700	800

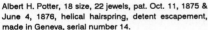

Albert H. Potter, 18 size, 22 jewels, pat. Oct. 11, 1875 & June 4, 1876, helical hairspring, detent escapement, made in Geneva, serial number 14.

A.H. Potter Watch Co., Boston, 18 size, about 6 jewels, detent escapement, note similarity to E.H. Howard & Co. early watches, serial number 5.

ALBERT H. POTTER WATCH CO.

New York, New York

1855 - 1875

Albert Potter started his apprenticeship in 1852. When this was completed he moved to New York to take up watchmaking on his own. He made about 35 watches in all that sold for $225 to $350. Some were chronometers, some were lever escapements, key wind, gilded movements, some were fusee driven, both bridge and 3/4 plate. Potter was a contemporary of Charles Fasoldt and John Mulford, both horological inventors from Albany, N. Y. Potter moved to Cuba in 1861 but returned to New York in 1868. In 1872 he worked in Chicago and formed the Potter Brothers Company with his brother William. He moved to Geneva about 1876. His company produced a total of about 600 watches, but only about 40 of those were made in the U. S.

Grade or Name – Description	Avg	Ex-Fn	Mint
18S, 29J, 18K HC, 1 min. repeater, Geneva ....★★★	$8,500	$10,000	$13,000
18S, BRG lever, Chronometer, signed A. H. Potter, New York, 18K Potter case, U.S. mfg. ....★★★★	10,000	12,000	16,000
18S, BRG lever with wind indicator, 18K Potter case ....★★★	6,500	8,500	9,500
18S-20S, Tourbillion, signed A. H. Potter, Boston, gilded, 18K Potter case, U.S. mfg. ....★★★★	15,000	17,000	20,000
16S-18S, 22J, helical spring, detent chronometer escapement, Geneva, 18K..................	4,000	5,000	6,500
4S, 21J, hour repeater, Geneva, 18K Potter HC	3,000	3,500	4,500

George P. Reed, 18 size, 15 jewels, key & stem wind, key & lever set, lever escapement, 48 hour up and down wind indicator, serial number 262.

George P. Reed, 18 size, 15 jewels, key & stem wind, key & lever set, lever escapement, 48 hour up and down wind indicator, serial number 5.

GEORGE P. REED

Boston, Massachusetts
1865 - 1885

In 1854, George P. Reed entered the employment of Dennison, Howard and Davis, in Roxbury, Mass., and moved with the company to Waltham, Mass. Here he was placed in charge of the pinion finishing room. While there he invented and received a patent for the mainspring barrel and maintiming power combination. This patent was dated February 18, 1857. Reed returned to Roxbury with Howard who purchased his patented barrel. He stayed with the Howard factory as foreman and adjuster until 1865, when he left for Boston to start his own account.

He obtained a patent on April 7, 1868, for an improved chronometer escapement which featured simplified construction. He made about 100 chronometers with his improved escapement, to which he added a stem-wind device. His company turned out about 100 watches the first three years. Most, if not all, of his watches run for two days and have up and down indicators on the dial. They are both 18S and 16S, 3/4 plate, nickel, and are artistically designed. Reed experimented with various combinations of lever and chronometer escapements. One was a rotary watch he made in 1862 and called the "Monitor." It was the first rotary watch made in America. In all, Reed made a total of about 550 watches, and these are valuable to collectors.

Grade or Name – Description		Avg	Ex-Fn	Mint
18S, 15J, LS, OF or HC, Wind Indicator, chronometer escapement, 18K case ★★★★		$9,000	$11,500	$15,000
16S, 15J, LS, OF or HC, not chronometer, 18K case ★★★		6,500	7,000	9,000
16S, 15J, LS, OF, 31 day calendar, 18K case ★★★		6,500	7,000	9,000

ROCKFORD WATCH CO.

Rockford, Illinois

1873 - 1915

The Rockford Watch Company's equipment was bought from the Cornell Watch Co., and two of Cornell's employees, C. W. Parker and P. H. Wheeler, went to work for Rockford. The factory was located 93 miles from Chicago on the Rock River. The first watch was placed on the market on May 1, 1876. They were key wind, 18S, full plate expansion balance. By 1877 the company was making 3/4 plate nickel movements that fit standard size cases. Three railroads came through Rockford, and the company always advertised to the railroad and the demand was very popular with them. The company had some problems in 1896, and the name changed to Rockford Watch Co. Ltd. It closed in 1915.

ROCKFORD ESTIMATED SERIAL NUMBERS AND PRODUCTION DATES

Date	Serial No.	Date	Serial No.	Date	Serial No.	Date	Serial No.
1876	5,000	1886	110,000	1896	290,000	1906	620,000
1877	15,000	1887	125,000	1897	320,000	1907	650,000
1878	25,000	1888	140,000	1898	350,000	1908	690,000
1879	35,000	1889	150,000	1899	385,000	1909	730,000
1880	50,000	1890	165,000	1900	415,000	1910	765,000
1881	60,000	1891	175,000	1901	450,000	1911	820,000
1882	70,000	1892	195,000	1902	480,000	1912	850,000
1883	80,000	1893	200,000	1903	515,000	1913	880,000
1884	90,000	1894	230,000	1904	550,000	1914	930,000
1885	100,000	1895	260,000	1905	580,000	1915	1,000,000

(See Rockford Watch Co. Identification of Movements section located at the end of the Rockford price section to identify the movement, size, and model number of your watch.)

(Prices are with gold filled cases except where noted.)

☞ NOTE: Some grades are not included. Their values can be determined by comparing with similar models or grades listed.

ROCKFORD

18 SIZE

Grade or Name – Description	Avg	Ex-Fn	Mint
Belmont USA, 21J, LS, OF, NI, M#7	$200	$250	$325
Chronometer, 17J, ADJ, OF, G925	275	350	500
Dome Model, 9J, brass plates ★	150	175	225

Rockford Watch Co., 18 size, 11 jewels, hunting, Model number 6, exposed escapement, serial number 190,564.

Special Railway, 18 size, 17 jewels, hunting, Model number 8, serial number 344,551.

Grade or Name – Description	Avg	Ex-Fn	Mint
King Edward, Plymouth W. Co., 21J, 14K HC	$700	$800	$975
King Edward (Sears), 21J, GJS, ADJ, NI, OF	275	350	475
King Edward (Sears), 21J, GJS, ADJ, NI, HC	300	325	500
Pennsylvania Special, 25J, LS, Adj.6P, tu-tone, OF ★★★	3,000	4,000	6,000
Railway King, 21J, OF	475	600	750
The Ramsey Watch, 11J, NI, KW or SW	100	125	150
The Ramsey Watch, 15J, NI, KW or SW	100	125	150
The Ramsey Watch, M#7, 21J, OF, NI, ADJ	350	375	450
Rockford Early KW-KS, M#1-2, with low Serial #s less than 500 ★	400	500	675
Rockford Early KW-KS, M#1-2, with low Serial #s less than 500, Coin ★	400	500	675
Rockford Early KW-KS, M#1-2, with reversible case	275	325	400
Rockford Early,19J, KW-KS, M#1-2, S# less than 100 ★★	1,000	1,400	2,000
Rockford, 7!9J, SW, FULL, OF	70	85	135
Rockford, 7J, KW, FULL, OF	70	85	135
Rockford, 7J, KW, FULL, Silveroid	50	60	85
Rockford, 9J, SW, FULL, HC	100	125	175
Rockford, M#1, 9J, KW, FULL, HC	150	175	225
Rockford, 11J, SW, FULL, OF	75	100	150
Rockford, M#1-2, 11J, KW, FULL	150	175	225
Rockford, M#1-2, 11J, transition case, FULL	100	125	175
Rockford, 11J, KW, Coin HC	150	175	225
Rockford, 9J, KW, M#5, 3/4 Plate, HC Coin ★	225	300	450
Rockford, 11J, KW, M#5, 3/4 Plate, HC Coin ★	250	325	500
Rockford, 15J, KW, M#5, 3/4 Plate, HC Coin ★	275	350	550
Rockford, 13J, HC	100	125	175
Rockford, 15J, SW, FULL	75	100	150
Rockford, 15J, KW, FULL, multi-color dial	275	350	425
Rockford, 15J, SW, 2-Tone movement	100	125	175

Rockford movement, 18 size, 7 jewels, model 5, hunting, lever set, three-quarter plate.

Grade 900, 18 size, 24J., Adj5p. Warning: 24J. fakes have been made from 21J movements. The fakes are missing the eliptical jewel setting on the barrel bridge.

Grade or Name – Description	Avg	Ex-Fn	Mint
Rockford, 15J, KW, FULL, ADJ	$175	$225	$350
Rockford, 15J, KW/SW	100	150	200
Rockford, 15J, KW/SW, Silveroid	70	90	110
Rockford, 15J, M#6, exposed escapement wheel, FULL, HC, LS, nickel mvt.	275	300	350
Rockford, 15J, M#6, exposed escapement wheel, FULL, HC, LS, gilded mvt.	175	200	250
Rockford, 15J, M#6, exposed wheel, nickel mvt., Coin	175	200	250
Rockford, M#1, 15J, KW, FULL	100	125	175
Rockford, 16J, GJS, NI, DMK, SW	75	100	150
Rockford, 16J, GJS, NI, DMK, SW, Silveroid	50	60	90
Rockford, 16J, GJS, NI, DMK, SW, Coin	75	100	150
Rockford, 17J, NI, DMK, SW, OF	75	100	150
Rockford, 17J, GJS, NI, DMK, SW, Adj.5P	100	125	175
Rockford, 17J, GJS, NI, SW, 2-Tone, OF	125	150	200
Rockford, M#1-2, 19J, KW, FULL, GJS, ADJ ★★★★	1,500	1,700	2,200
Rockford, 19J, transition, HC, GJS ★	400	500	650
Rockford, 21J, SW, Silveroid	125	150	175
Rockford, 21J, GJS, OF, Adj.5P, wind indicator ★★	2,500	3,000	3,500
Rockford, 21J, SW, DMK, ADJ, HC	275	325	400
Rockford, 21J, NI, DMK, ADJ, OF	175	225	300
Rockford, 21J, GJS, NI, DMK, Adj.5P, marked "RG"	200	250	325
Rockford, 24J, GJS, SW, LS, Adj.5P, marked "RG," OF	800	1,000	1,200
Rockford, 24J, GJS, SW, LS, Adj.5P, marked "RG," HC ★	1,200	1,400	1,600
Rockford, 25J, GJS, SW, LS, Adj.5P, NI, DMK ★★	3,500	5,000	6,500
Rockford, 26J, GJS, SW, LS, Adj.5P, NI, DMK ★★★	8,000	10,000	16,000

Rockford Watch Co., 18 size, 15 jewels, model # 5, 3/4 plate, key & stem wind.

Rockford Watch Co., 18 size, 15 jewels, model 4, open face, lever set, serial number 227,430.

Grade or Name – Description	Avg	Ex-Fn	Mint
Special Railway, 17J, ADJ, 2-tone, SW, HC	$300	$400	$550
The Syndicate Watch Co., M#7, 15J, LS, NI, HC	150	200	275
Winnebago, 17J, LS, GJS, Adj.5P, DR, NI, DMK	150	175	225
Winnebago, 17J, LS, GJS, Adj.5P, DR, NI, DMK, Silveroid	100	125	175
24 Hour Dial, 15J, SW or KW	150	170	225
40, 15J, M#3, HC ★★	250	300	375
43, 15J, M#3, HC, 2-Tone	100	125	175
66, 11J, M#7, OF	75	100	150
66, 11J, M#7, OF, Silveroid	40	50	65
66, 11J, M#7, HC	75	100	150
72, 15J, KW-SW, exposed escapement, HC ★	600	700	850
81, 9J, M#3, HC, Gilt	100	125	175
82, Special, 21J, SW ★★	400	500	650
83, 15J, M#8, HC, 2-Tone	125	150	200
86, 15J, M#7, OF, NI	55	75	125
93, 9J, M#8, HC, Gilt	100	125	175
94, 9J, M#7, OF	55	75	125
200-205, 17J, M#9, OF, NI, LS	75	100	150
245, 19J, HC, GJS, 2-Tone ★	1,000	1,200	1,400
800, 24J, GJS, DR, Adj.5P, DMK, HC ★	1,200	1,400	1,600
805, 21J, GJS, Adj.5P, NI, DMK, HC, marked "RG"	200	250	325
810, 21J, NI, DMK, ADJ, HC	250	300	375
820, 17J, HC, SW ★★	300	350	425
825, 17J, HC, FULL	125	150	200
830, 17J, HC, FULL	100	125	175
835, 17J, HC, FULL	100	125	175
835, 17J, HC, FULL, Silveroid	50	75	125
845, 21J, HC, GJS, FULL ★	400	475	550
870, 7J, HC, FULL	75	100	150

Grade or Name – Description	Avg.	Ex-Fn	Mint
900, 24J, GJS, DR, Adj.5P, OF, NI, DMK ....★★	$1,000	$1,200	$1,500
900, 24J, GJS, DR, Adj.5P, 14K, OF case ....★★	1,400	1,600	1,900
905, 21J, GJS, DR, Adj.5P, OF, NI, DMK	250	275	350
910, 21J, NI, DMK, 1 ADJ, OF..	150	175	250
912, 21J, OF..★★	425	475	600
915, 17J, M#9, OF, SW...★★★	450	500	625
918, 21J, OF, NI, GJS, Adj.5P, DR......................................	150	175	225
918, 21J, OF, NI, GJS, Adj.5P, DR, Silveroid..............................	150	200	250
918, 21J, OF, NI, GJS, Adj.5P, DR, Coin	125	175	225
930, 17J, OF...	175	225	275
935, 17J, OF...	75	100	135
945, 21J, M#9, OF, SW..	150	175	225
950, 21J, OF, NI, GJS, Adj.5P, DR, Wind Indicator ....★★	2,500	3,000	4,000
970, 7J, OF...	60	70	90
970, 7J, OF, Silveroid	40	50	70

16 SIZE

Grade or Name – Description	Avg	Ex-Fn	Mint
Commodore Perry, 21J, OF, GJS, GT, marked "RG"	$350	$450	$600
Cosmos, 17J, OF, GJS, LS, DMK, marked dial & mvt.	225	350	500
Doll Watch Co., 23J, marked dial & mvt. ....★★★	1,000	1,200	1,500
Dome Model, 15J	60	75	100
Dome Model, 17J	65	80	120
Dome Model, 17J, 2-tone, HC..	200	250	325
Herald Square, 7J, 3/4, OF..	75	100	125
Iroquois, 17J, DR, 14K, HC..	525	575	675
Iroquois, 17J, DR..	150	175	225
Peerless, 17J, OF, NI, LS, DMK	75	100	125
Pocahontas, 17-21J, GJS, Adj.5P, DR....................................★	225	250	375
Prince of Wales (Sears), 21J...	225	250	375
Prince of Wales (Sears), 21J, 14K.......................................	525	550	675

Grade 103, 16 size, 17 jewels, model 1, hunting.

Example of a Cosmos movement, 16 size, 17 jewels, open face, gold jewel settings.

Example of a Rockford movement, 16 size, 21 jewels, three-quarter plate, serial number 842,520.

Grade 500-HC, 505-OF, 16 size, 21 jewels, gold jewel settings, gold train, Adj6p, marked "RG," originally sold for $100.00

Grade or Name – Description	Avg	Ex-Fn	Mint
Rockford 7J, 3/4, HC..	$100	$125	$175
Rockford, 9J, 3/4, SW, OF...	40	60	85
Rockford, 9J, SW, Silveroid......................................	30	40	60
Rockford, 9J, SW, HC..	100	125	175
Rockford, 11J, SW, Silveroid.....................................	40	60	85
Rockford, 11J, 3/4, HC...	100	125	175
Rockford, 15J, 3/4, ADJ, OF	75	100	135
Rockford, 15J, 3/4, ADJ, Silveroid	40	60	85
Rockford, 15J, 3/4, ADJ, HC......................................	100	125	175
Rockford, 16J, 3/4, SW, Silveroid	40	60	85
Rockford, 16J, 3/4, ADJ, NI, DMK.............................	75	100	135
Rockford, 17J, 3/4	75	100	135
Rockford, 17J, 3/4, 2-Tone, marked "RG"	125	150	200
Rockford, 17J, BRG, Adj.3P, DR	100	125	175
Rockford, 17J, GJS, Adj.5P, DR, Wind Indicator.......	400	450	525
Rockford, 17J, BRG, Silveroid	40	60	85
Rockford, 17J, 3/4, Silveroid	40	60	85
Rockford, 21J, 3/4, SW, Silveroid..............................	75	100	135
Rockford, 21J, BRG, SW, Silveroid............................	75	100	135
Rockford, 21J, 3/4, GJS, Adj.5P................................	125	150	200
Rockford, 21J, BRG, GJS, Adj.5P, GT, DR	150	175	225
Rockford, 21J, GJS, Adj.5P, DR, Wind Indicator.......	500	600	750
Winnebago, 17J, BRG, GJS, Adj.5P, NI.....................	150	175	225
Winnebago, 21J, BRG, GJS, Adj.5P, NI.....................	200	250	300
100, 16J, M#1, HC, 3/4, 2-Tone	175	200	250
100S, 21J, Special, HC, 3/4, LS................................	200	250	325
102, 15J, HC, M#1...★	125	150	200
103, 17J, HC, M#1..★★	250	300	375
104, 11J, HC, M#1...	50	60	75
110, 17J, 2 tone dome style mvt.,HC.........................	300	350	400
115-125, 17J, Special, HC ....★★★	500	600	750
120-130, 17J, HC ....★★★	400	500	650

Pocahontas, 16 size, 21 jewels, hunting case, bridge model, Adj.5pserial number 670,203.

Rockford movement, 16 size, 17 jewels, 3/4 plate, hunting, lever set, serial number 556,064.

Grade or Name – Description	Avg	Ex-Fn	Mint
400 & 405, 17J, NI, Adj.5P, GJS, DR, BRG	$100	$125	$175
445, 19J, HC, GJS, BRG...★★	850	1,000	1,200
500, 21J, BRG, NI, GJS, Adj.5P, GT, HC ....★★	500	550	625
501, 21J, GJS, HC..★★★	900	1,100	1,250
505, 21J, BRG, NI, GJS, Adj.5P, GT, OF ....★★	400	500	650
510, 21J, BRG, NI, GJS, Adj.5P, GT, HC .... ★	300	400	550
515 & 525, 21J, OF, 3/4...	150	175	225
520, 21J, HC, 3/4...	200	250	325
520, 21J, BRG, NI, GJS, Adj.5P, HC..	400	450	525
525, 21J. M#5, GT, Adj.5P .... ★	250	300	350
530, 21J, HC, GJS, Adj.5P, marked "RG".............................. ★	300	350	425
535, 21J, OF, 3/4.. ★	225	275	350
537, 21J, OF, GJS, Adj.5P ....★★	500	600	775
545, 21J,GT,BRG, Adj.5P, OF	150	175	225
561, 17J, BRG..	125	150	200
566, 17J, BRG..	125	150	200
572, 17J, BRG, NI, GJS, Adj.5P	85	110	150
573, 17J, BRG, NI...	75	100	135
578-579, 17J, PS, GJS..★★	300	350	475
584 & 585, 15J, 3/4 NI..	40	60	85
620-625, 21J, HC, 3/4.. ★	300	400	525
655, 21J, OF, Wind Indicator, marked 655 .... ★	500	600	750

12 SIZE
All 3/4 Bridge

Grade or Name – Description	Avg	Ex-Fn	Mint
Iroquois, 17J, BRG, DR, ADJ...	$60	$70	$100
Pocahontas, 21J, GJS, Adj.5P, BRG, DR......................................	100	125	150

Rockford Watch co., 12 size, 15 jewels, model 1, hunting, pendant set.

Rockford Watch Co., 12 size, 15 jewels, model 2, open face, pendant set.

Grade or Name – Description	Avg	Ex-Fn	Mint
Rockford, 15J, BRG	$35	$40	$55
Rockford, 17J, BRG, NI, DR, ADJ	50	60	75
Rockford, 21J, BRG, NI, DR, ADJ	70	80	110
Rockford, 21J, BRG, NI, DR, ADJ, Silveroid	40	60	85
Winona, 15J, BRG	45	55	80
300, 23J, 3/4, HC, GJS, Adj.5P ★★★	300	350	425
305, 23J, BRG, NI, GJS, Adj.5P, GT, OF ★★★	300	350	425
310(HC)-315(OF), 21J, BRG, NI, GJS, Adj.5P	75	100	150
320(HC)-325(OF), 17J, BRG, NI, ADJ, DR	40	60	85
330, 17J, BRG, NI, DR, OF	40	60	85
335, 17J, BRG, NI, DR, HC	40	60	85
340(HC)-345(OF), 21J, M#1 ★	200	225	300
350, 17J, OF	40	60	85
355, 17J, HC	50	65	95

Note: Add $10 to above watches with hunting case.

8 SIZE

Grade or Name – Description	Avg	Ex-Fn	Mint
15J, 3/4, HC, LS, 14K, 40 DWT	$375	$400	$475
9–15J, 3/4, KW or SW, LS, OF or HC,	100	125	175

6 SIZE

Grade or Name – Description	Avg	Ex-Fn	Mint
9J, HC, NI	$60	$70	$85

Rockford movement, 6 size, 17 jewels, quick train, straight line escapement, compensating balance, adjusted to temperature, micrometric regulator, three-quarter damaskeened plates.

Grade or Name – Description	Avg	Ex-Fn	Mint
15J, 3/4, NI	$40	$60	$85
16J, 3/4, NI	70	90	115
17J, 3/4, ADJ, NI	80	100	125

0 SIZE

Grade or Name – Description	Avg	Ex-Fn	Mint
Plymouth Watch Co., 15-17J, HC	$200	$225	$275
7J, BRG, HC	100	120	155
11J, BRG, NI, DR, HC	110	130	165
15J, BRG, NI, DR, HC	125	135	175
17J, BRG, NI, DR, HC	180	200	250
17J, BRG, NI, DR, in marked Rockford HC in dust cover ring	325	350	375

ROCKFORD WATCH CO.
IDENTIFICATION OF MOVEMENTS
BY MODEL NUMBER

How to Identify Your Watch: Compare the movement of your watch with the illustrations in this section. Upon matching the movement exactly, the model number and size can be determined. While comparing, note the location of the balance, jewels, screws, gears, and type of back plate (Full, 3/4, Bridge) which will be clues in identifying the movement you have. Having determined the size and model number, you can now find your watch in the main price listing by name or number (which is engraved on the movement).

Model 1, 18 size, full plate, hunting, key wind & set.

Model 2, 18 size, full plate, hunting, lever set.

Model 3, 18 size, full plate, hunting, lever set.

Model 4, 18 size, full plate, open face, lever set.

Model 5, 18 size, three-quarter plate, hunting, lever set.

Model 6, 18 size, full plate, hunting, lever set, exposed escapement.

Model 7, 18 size, full plate, open face, lever set.

Model 8, 18 size, full plate, hunting, lever set.

Model 9, 18 size, full plate, open face, lever set.

Model 10, 18 size, full plate, hunting, lever set.

Model 1, 16 size, three-quarter plate, hunting, lever set.

Model 2, 16 size, three-quarter plate, open face, pendant & lever set.

Model 3, 16 size, three-quarter plate, hunting, pendant & lever set.

Model 4, 16 size, three-quarter plate, bridge, hunting, pendant & lever set.

Model 5, 16 size, three-quarter plate, bridge, open face, pendant & lever set.

Model 1, 12 size, three-quarter plate bridge, hunting, pendant set.

Model 2, 12 size, three-quarter plate bridge, open face, pendant set.

Model 1, 6 & 8 size, three-quarter plate, hunting, lever set.

Model 2, 6 size, three-quarter plate, hunting, lever set.

Model 1, 0 size, three-quarter plate, bridge, hunting, pendant set.

Model 2, 0 size, three-quarter plate, bridge, open face, pendant set.

SAN JOSE WATCH CO.
California
1891

Very few watches were made by the San Jose Watch Co., and very little is known about them. The company purchased the Otay Watch Company and machinery and remaining watch movements. The San Jose Watch Co. produced about a dozen watches. Engraved on a San Jose Watch Co. movement S# 30,656 (First watch manufactured by San Jose Watch Co. November 1891).

Grade or Name – Description		Avg	Ex-Fn	Mint
18S, 15J,LS,SW .... ★★★★		$1,500	$2,000	$2,500

Example of a basic SAN JOSE WATCH CO. movement 18 size 15 jewels, Otay W.Co. material and machinery used to produce movement,

Example of a basic M.S. Smith & Co. movement, 18 size, 19 jewels, three-quarter plate, key wind & set.

M. S. SMITH & CO.
Detroit, Michigan
1870 - 1874

Eber B. Ward purchased the M. S. Smith & Co. which was a large jewelery firm. These watches carried the Smith name on them. A Mr. Hoyt was engaged to produce these watches and about 100 were produced before the Freeport Watch Co. purchased the firm.

Grade or Name – Description	Avg	Ex-Fn	Mint
18S, 19J, 3/4, KW, KS, 18K case	$2,500	$3,000	$3,600
18S, 19J, 3/4, KW, KS	1,200	1,500	2,300
6S, 15J, SW, 18K case	700	800	1,000
6S, 15J, SW	400	500	700

SOUTH BEND WATCH CO.

South Bend, Indiana
March 1903 - December 1929

Three brothers, George, Clement and J. M. Studebaker, purchased the successful Columbus Watch Co. The first South Bend watches were full plate and similar to the Columbus watches. The serial numbers started at 380,501 where as the Columbus serial numbers stopped at about 500,000. The highest grade watch was a "Polaris," a 16S, 3/4 plate, 21 jewels, and with an open face. This watch sold for about $100. The 227 and 229 were also high grade. The company identified its movements by model numbers 1, 2, and 3, and had grades from 100 to 431. The even numbers were hunting cases, and the odd numbers were open-faced cases. The lowest grade was a 203, 7J, that sold for about $6.75. The company closed on Dec. 31, 1929.

SOUTH BEND ESTIMATED SERIAL NUMBERS
AND PRODUCTION DATES

Date	Serial No.	Date	Serial No.	Date	Serial No.	Date	Serial No.
1903	380,501	1910	620,000	1917	865,000	1924	1,110,000
1904	410,000	1911	655,000	1918	900,000	1925	1,145,000
1905	445,000	1912	690,000	1919	935,000	1926	1,180,000
1906	480,000	1913	725,000	1920	970,000	1927	1,215,000
1907	515,000	1914	760,000	1921	1,005,000	1928	1,250,000
1908	550,000	1915	795,000	1922	1,040,000	1929	1,275,000
1909	585,000	1916	825,000	1923	1,075,000		

SOUTH BEND
18 SIZE (Lever set)

Grade or Name – Description	Avg	Ex-Fn	Mint
South Bend, 15J, OF	$75	$100	$150
South Bend, 15J, HC	100	125	175
South Bend, 17J, OF	75	100	150
South Bend, 17J, HC	100	125	175
South Bend, 21J, OF	150	175	225
South Bend, 21J, HC, 14K	550	600	675
South Bend, 21J, OF, HC, Silveroid	125	150	175
South Bend, 21J, SW, HC	200	225	275
The Studebaker, G#323, 17J, OF, GJS, NI, Adj.5P	200	250	325
The Studebaker, G#328, 21J, HC, GJS, NI, FULL, Adj.5P .. ★	375	425	575
The Studebaker, G#329, 21J, OF, GJS, NI, FULL, Adj.5P	225	275	350
304, 15J, HC	100	125	175

South Bend movement, 18 size, 17 jewels, stem wind, hunting, serial number 426,726.

The Studebaker, 18 size, 21 jewels, gold jewel settings, stem wind.

Grade or Name – Description	Avg	Ex-Fn	Mint
305, 15J, OF	$75	$100	$150
305, 15J, OF, Silveroid	40	50	65
309, 17J, OF	75	100	150
312, 17J, HC, NI, ADJ	100	125	175
313, 17J, OF, NI, ADJ, marked 313 ★	200	250	325
315, 17J, OF, NI, Adj.3P	75	100	150
G#s 323, 328 & 329 " see The Studebaker			
327, 21J, OF, Adj.5P	150	175	250
327, 21J, OF, Adj.5P, Silveroid	125	150	175
330, 15J, M#1, LS, HC	100	135	200
331, 15J, M#1, LS, OF	75	100	150
332, 15J, HC	175	225	300
333, 15J, OF	75	100	150
337, 17J, OF	75	100	150
340, 17J, M#1, Adj.3P, NI, HC	125	150	200
341, 17J, M#1, ADJ, NI, Adj.3P, OF	100	125	175
342, 17J, M#1, LS	75	100	150
343, 17J, M#1, LS, OF	75	100	150
344, 17J, HC, NI, Adj.3P ★★	300	350	425
345, 17J, OF, NI, Adj.3P ★★	275	325	400
346, 17J, HC, NI ★★	300	350	425
347, 17J, OF, NI	75	100	125
355, 19J, GJS, 2-Tone, HC ★★	1,000	1,200	1,500

(Prices are with gold filled cases except where noted.)

☞ NOTE: Some grades are not included. Their values can be determined by comparing with similar models or grades listed.

Grade 211, 16 size, 17 jewels, three-quarter plate, serial number 703,389.

Grade 295, 16 size, 21 jewels, first model, gold jewel settings, gold train, open face, serial number 518,022.

16 SIZE
M#1 Lever set

Grade or Name – Description	Avg	Ex-Fn	Mint
Polaris, 21J, M#1, Adj.5P, 3/4, NI, DR, GJS, GT, 14K South Bend case with Polaris dial ....★★	$1,500	$1,800	$2,200
South Bend, 7J, OF	50	75	125
South Bend, 7J, HC	75	100	150
South Bend, 9J, OF	50	75	125
South Bend, 9J, HC	75	100	150
South Bend, 15J, OF	50	75	125
South Bend, 15J, HC	75	100	150
South Bend, 15J, OF, Silveroid	40	60	85
South Bend, 17J, OF	50	75	125
South Bend, 17J, HC, ADJ	100	125	175
South Bend, 17J, 14K HC	475	500	575
South Bend, 21J, OF	125	150	185
South Bend, 21J, HC, ADJ	200	250	325
The Studebaker 223,17J, M#2, Adj.5P, BRG, GJS, DR, GT	275	300	375
The Studebaker 229, 21J, M#2, Adj.5P, BRG, GJS, DR, GT ...	300	325	400
Studebaker, 21J, OF, PS, Adj.5P	125	150	200
203, 7J, 3/4, NI, OF	50	75	125
204, 15J, 3/4, NI, HC	75	100	150
207, 15J, OF, PS	50	75	125
209, 9J, M#2, OF, PS	50	75	125
211, 17J, M#2, 3/4, NI, OF	50	75	125
212, 17J, M#2, HC, LS, heat & cold	100	125	175
215, 17J, M#2, OF, LS, heat & cold	50	75	125

☞ Note: Watches listed in this book are priced at the retail level, as complete watches having an original 14k gold-filled case, an original white enamel single sunk dial, and with the entire original movement in good working order with no repairs needed.

South Bend Watch Co. Polaris, 16 size, 21 jewels, model number 1, Adj5p, gold jewel setting, gold train, open face, serial number,518,236.

Grade 227, 16 size, 21 jewels, RR approved, gold jewel settings, Adj5p, serial number 1,222,843.

Grade or Name – Description	Avg	Ex-Fn	Mint
215, 17J, M#2, OF, SILVEROID	$40	$50	$65
217, 17J, M#2, OF, NI, BRG, DR, GT, ADJ.3P	75	100	150
219, 19J, OF, NI, PS, BRG, DR, ADJ.4P	125	150	200
233, 17J, M#2, OF, LS, ADJ.5P	50	75	125
227, 21J, M#2, BRG, NI, LS, DR, ADJ.5P, OF	175	225	275
229, 21J, M#2, BRG, GJS, ADJ. OF ★★	300	350	425
245, 19, GJS, BRG, HC ★★	600	700	850
260, 7J, M#1, HC	75	100	125
261, 7J, M#1, OF	50	75	100
280, 15J, M#1, HC	80	100	150
281, 15J, M#1, OF	50	75	125
290, 17J, M#1, LS, ADJ.3P, HC ★★	200	250	325
291, 17J, M#1, OF, ADJ.3P ★★	175	200	275
292, 19J, M#1, HC, 3/4, GJS, NI, DR, ADK.5P ★	250	300	375
293, 19J, M#1, OF, 3/4, GJS, NI, DR, ADJ.5P ★	175	225	275
294, 21J, M#1, ADJ.5P, GJS, GT, HC, marked 294 ★★	300	350	475
295, 21J, M#1 OF, LS, ADJ.5P, GJS, GT, marked 295 ★	350	400	475
298, 17J, M#1, HC, ADJ.3P ★★	200	250	325
299, 17J, M#1, OF, ADJ.3P ★★	175	225	275

12 SIZE
(OF Only)

Grade or Name – Description	Avg	Ex-Fn	Mint
Chesterfield, 15J, BRG, NI, DR, G#407	$50	$60	$75
Chesterfield, 17J, BRG, NI, DR, GJS, ADJ.3P,G#419	60	70	85
Chesterfield, 21J, BRG, NI, DR, GJS, ADJ.5P,G#431 ★	100	125	150
Digital,Studebaker, 21J, BRG, NI, DR, GJS, ADJ.5P, ★★	200	250	325

Grade 411, 12 size, 17 jewels, open face, double roller.

Chesterfield, 12 size, 21 jewels, open face only, bridge, gold jewel settings, pendant set, double roller, Adj5p.

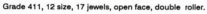

Grade or Name – Description	Avg	Ex-Fn	Mint
South Bend, 15J	$35	$45	$60
South Bend, 17J	40	50	65
South Bend, 17J, Silveroid	30	40	55
South Bend, 19J	60	70	85
South Bend, 21J	70	80	95
Studebaker, 21J, PS, 3/4, NI, Adj.5P, GJS	125	150	225
407, 15J, Silveroid	30	35	45
407, 15J	35	45	60
411, 17J, DR, GJS	40	50	65
415, 17J, ADJ to temp. ★★	125	150	200
419, 17J, Adj.3P ★★	125	150	200
429, 19J, Adj.4P, GT, GJS ★	100	125	175
431, 21J, Adj.5P, DR, GJS ★★	125	150	200
431, 21J, Adj.5P, Silveroid	40	50	65

6 SIZE

Grade or Name – Description	Avg	Ex-Fn	Mint
South Bend, 11J, G#160, HC ★	$75	$85	$150
South Bend, 15J, G#170, HC ★	100	125	200
South Bend, 17J, G#180, HC ★★	100	125	200
South Bend, 17J, G#180, 14K ★★	200	250	325

South Bend, 6 size, grade # 170, 15 jewels.

Grade 120-HC, 121-OF, 0 size, 17 jewels, bridge, nickel, double roller, pendant set.

0 SIZE

Grade or Name – Description	Avg	Ex-Fn	Mint
South Bend, 15J, M# 1 & 2, OF, PS..	$50	$60	$75
Grade 100 HC & 101 OF, 7J, PS..	75	100	150
Grade 110 HC & 111 OF, 15J, 3F Brg, DR................................ ★	100	125	150
Grade 120 HC & 121 OF, 17J, BRG, NI, DR, PS ....★★	125	150	200
Grade 150 HC & 151 OF, 17J, M# 3, BRG, NI, PS ....★★	125	150	200

☞ Note: Add $20 to above watches with hunting case; add $40 for hunting cases marked South Bend.

SOUTH BEND WATCH CO.
IDENTIFICATION OF MOVEMENTS
BY MODEL NUMBER

How to Identify Your Watch: Compare the movement of your watch with the illustrations in this section. Upon matching the movement exactly, the model number and size can be determined. While comparing, note the location of the balance, jewels, screws, gears, and type of back plate (Full, 3/4, Bridge) which will be clues in identifying the movement you have. Having determined the size and model number, you can now find your watch in the main price listing by name or number (which is engraved on the movement).

18 SIZE—MODEL 1
Open Face and Hunting. Lever Set
Grade Numbers and Description of Movements

No. 341 – Open Face, 17 Jewels, Lever Set, Adjusted to Temperature & 3 Positions.
No. 340 – Hunting, 17 Jewels, Lever Set, Adjusted to Temperature & 3 Positions.
No. 343 – Open Face, 17 Jewels, Lever Set.
No. 331 – Open Face, 15 Jewels, Lever Set.

Model 1, Full Plate, Open face.   **Model 1** , Full Plate, Hunting

18 SIZE—MODEL 2
Open Face and Hunting. Lever Set
Grade Numbers and Description of Movements

No. 329—21J, Open Face, "Studebaker," Adjusted to Temperature and 5 Positions.
No. 328—21J, Hunting, Adjusted to Temperature and 5 Positions.
No. 327—21J, Open Face, Adjusted to Temperature and 5 Positions.
No. 323—17J, Open Face, "Studebaker," Adjusted to Temperature and 5 Positions.
No. 345—17J, Open Face, Adjusted to Temperature and 3 Positions.
No. 344—17J, Hunting, Adjusted to Temperature and 3 Positions.
No. 313—17J, Open Face, Adjusted to Temperature.
No. 312—17J, Hunting, Adjusted to Temperature.

Model 2, Full Plate, Open face.   **Model 2**, Full Plate, Hunting.

Nos. 309, 337, 347—17J, Open Face.
No. 346—17J, Hunting.
Nos. 333, 305—15J, Open Face.
Nos. 332, 304—15J, Hunting.

16 SIZE—MODEL 1
Open Face and Hunting. Lever Set
Grade Numbers and Description of Movements

No. 295—Open Face, 21 Jewels, Adjusted to Temperature and 5 Positions.
No. 294—Hunting, 21 Jewels, Adjusted to Temperature and 5 Positions.
No. 293—Open Face, 19 Jewels, Adjusted to Temperature and 5 Positions.
No. 292—Hunting, 19 Jewels, Adjusted to Temperature and 5 Positions.
No. 299—Open Face, 17 Jewels, Adjusted to Temperature and 3 Positions.
No. 298—Hunting, 17 Jewels, Adjusted to Temperature and 3 Positions.
No. 291—Open Face, 17 Jewels, Adjusted to Temperature and 3 Positions.
No. 290—Hunting, 17 Jewels, Adjusted to Temperature and 3 Positions.
No. 281—Open Face, 15 Jewels.
No. 280—Hunting, 15 Jewels.
No. 261—Open Face, 7 Jewels.
No. 260—Hunting, 7 Jewels.

Model 1, ¼ Plate, Open Face.   **Model 1, ¼ Plate, Hunting.**

16 SIZE—MODEL 2
Open Face and Hunting. Pendant and Lever Set.
Grade Numbers and Description of Movements

No. 229—21J, Open Face, Lever Set, "Studebaker," Adjust. to Temp. and 5 Positions.
No. 227—21J, Open Face, Lever Set, Adjusted to Temperature and 5 Positions.
No. 219—19J, Open Face, Pendant Set, Adjusted to Temperature and 4 Positions.
No. 223—17J, Open Face, Lever Set, "Studebaker," Adjust. to Temp. and 5 Positions.

No. 217—17J, Open Face, Lever Set, Adjusted to Temperature and 3 Positions.
No. 215—17J, Open Face, Pendant Set, Adjusted to Temperature.
No. 212—17J, Hunting, Lever Set, Adjusted to Temperature.
No. 211—17J, Open Face, Pendant Set.
No. 207—15J, Open Face, Pendant Set.
No. 204—15J, Hunting, Lever Set.
No. 209— 9J, Open Face, Pendant Set.
No. 203— 7J, Open Face, Pendant Set.

Model 2, ¾ Plate, Hunting.

Model 2, ¾ Plate, Open Face.

Model 2, Bridges, Open Face.

12 SIZE—MODEL 1
Chesterfield Series
and Grade 429 Special

Made in Pendant Set, Open Face Only
Grade Numbers and Description of Movements

No. 431—21J, Adjusted to Temperature and 5 Positions.
No. 429—19J, Adjusted to Temperature and 4 Positions.

No. 419—17J, Adjusted to Temperature and 3 Positions.
No. 415—17J, Adjusted to Temperature.
No. 411—17J.
No. 407—15J.

Model 1, Bridges, Open Face

Model 1, Lower Plate, Dial Side

6 SIZE—MODEL 1
Hunting
Grade No. 180, 17 Jewels
Grade No. 170, 15 Jewels
Grade No. 160, 11 Jewels

Serial Number Range
380,501 to 389,900

Model 1, ¾ Plate, 6
size

0 SIZE—MODEL 1
Open Face, No second hand, Hunting has second hand

Model 1, Open Face, ¾ Plate, 7 jewels.

Model 1, Hunting, Bridges, 15-17 jewels.

Model numbers 1 & 2 serial numbers under 659,700. All open face and hunting parts for this model except dial and fourth pinion are interchangeable.

0 SIZE—MODEL 2
Open Face, No second hand, Hunting has second hand

No. 100, 7 Jewels, Hunting, ¾ Bridge.
No. 101, 7 Jewels, Open Face, ¾ Plate.
No. 110, 15 Jewels, Hunting, ¾ Bridge.
No. 111, 15 Jewels, Open Face, ¾ Plate.
No. 120, 17 Jewels, Hunting, ¾ Bridge.
No. 121, 17 Jewels, Open Face, ¾ Plate.

Model 2, Open Face, ¾ Plate.   Model 2, Hunting, ¾ Bridge.

0 SIZE—MODEL 3
Both Open Face and Hunting have second hand
Grade Numbers and Description of Movements

No. 151—21J, Open Face, Bridge Model.
No. 150—21J, Hunting, Bridge Model.
No. 121—17J, Open Face, Bridge Model.
No. 120—17J, Hunting, Bridge Model.

Model 3, Open Face, Bridges.   Model 3, Hunting, Bridges.

Example of a basic original J. P. Stevens movement, 18 size, 15 jewels, note patented eccentric style regulator, serial number 65.

J.P. Stevens Watch Co. movement by Waltham, 18 size, 11 jewels, serial number 1,240,058.

J. P. STEVENS & CO.

Atlanta, Georgia
1882 - 1887

In mid-1881 J. P. Stevens bought part of the Springfield Watch Co. of Massachusetts; and some unfinished watch components from E. F. Bowman. He set up his watchmaking firm above his jewelry store in Atlanta, Ga., and started to produce the Bowman unfinished watches which were 16 size and 18 size, to which was added the "Stevens Patent Regulator." This regulator is best described as a simple disc attached to the plate which has an eccentric groove cut for the arm of the regulator to move in. This regulator is a prominent feature of the J. P. Stevens, and only the top is jeweled. These watches were 16S, 3/4 plate, stem wind and had a nickel plate with damaskeening. The pallets were equidistant locking and needed greater accuracy in manufacturing. About 50 of these watches were made. A line of gilt movements was added. The pallet and fork are made of one piece aluminum. The aluminum is combined with 1/10 copper and formed an exceedingly tough metal which will not rust or become magnetized. The lever of this watch is only one-third the weight of a steel lever. The aluminum lever affords the least possible resistance for overcoming inertia in transmitting power from the escape wheel to the balance. In 1884, the company was turning out about ten watches a day at a price of $20 to $100 each. In the spring of 1887 the company failed. Only 174 true Stevens watches were made, but other watches carried the J. P. Stevens name.

16 TO 18 SIZE

Grade or Name – Description		Avg	Ex-Fn	Mint
Original Model, Serial Nos. 1 to 174,(recased) ....★★★		$2,000	$2,500	$3,000

Grade or Name – Description	Avg	Ex-Fn	Mint
Original Model, Serial Nos. 1 to 174 with original J. P. Stevens dial & 18K case ★★★★	$7,000	$8,000	$9,500
Aurora, 17J ★	350	400	525
Chronograph, 17J, Swiss made ★	500	600	700
Columbus W. Co., 17J ★	400	450	575
Elgin, 17J ★	300	350	425
Hamilton, 17J ★	400	450	525
Hampden, 17J	300	350	425
Illinois, 17J ★	600	650	725
N. Y. W. Co., 17J, Full Plate, S#s range in 500s ★	700	750	825
N. Y. W. Co. "Bond" Model, S#s range in 500s ★★	850	950	1,100
A. Potter, 14K case, Swiss made ★★	2,000	3,000	4,000
Rockford, 15J, Full Plate, HC ★	400	450	625
16S Swiss, 17J, Longines ★	175	200	250
Waltham, 17J ★	400	450	625

J.P. Stevens movement made by Hampden, 18 size, 17 jewels, note eccentric style regulator, serial number 1695.

J.P. Stevens Watch Co., 6 size, 11 jewels, exposed winding gears.

6 SIZE

Grade or Name – Description	Avg	Ex-Fn	Mint
Ladies Model, 15J, LS, HC, 14K	$500	$575	$650
Ladies Model, 15J, LS, GF case, HC	225	275	350
Ladies Model, 15J, LS, GF cases, OF	200	250	325
Ladies Model, 15J, LS, GF cases, Swiss made	175	225	325

SUFFOLK WATCH CO.

Waltham, Massachusetts

c. 1899 - 1901

The Suffolk Watch Company officially succeeded the Columbia Watch Company in March 1901. However, the Suffolk 0-size, 7-jewel nickel movement with lever escapement was being manufactured in the Columbia factory before the end of 1899. More than 25,000 movements were made. The factory was closed after it was purchased by the Keystone Watch Case Company on May 17, 1901. The machinery was moved to the nearby factory of the United States Watch Company (purchased by Keystone in April 1901), where it was used to make the United States Watch Company's 0-size movement,introduced in April 1902.

Both the Columbia Watch Company and the Suffolk Watch Company made 0-size movements only.

Suffolk Watch Co., 0 Size, 7 jewels, serial number 216,841.

Grade or Name – Description	Avg	Ex-Fn	Mint
0S, 7J, NI, HC .... ★	$100	$150	$175

SETH THOMAS WATCH CO.

Thomaston, Connecticut
1883 - 1915

Seth Thomas is a very prominent clock manufacturer, but in early 1883, the company made a decision to manufacture watches. The watches were first placed on the market in 1885. They were 18S, open face, stem wind, 3/4 plate, and the escapement was between the plates. The compensating balance was set well below the normal. They were 11J, 16,000 bpm train, but soon went to 18,000 or quick train. In 1886, the company started to make higher grade watches and produced four grades: 7J, 11J, 15J, and 17J. That year the output was 100 watches a day.

SETH THOMAS ESTIMATED SERIAL NUMBERS AND PRODUCTION DATES

Date	Serial No.	Date	Serial No.	Date	Serial No.	Date	Serial No.
1885	5,000	1893	510,000	1901	1,230,000	1909	2,500,000
1886	20,000	1894	600,000	1902	1,320,000	1910	2,725,000
1887	40,000	1895	690,000	1903	1,410,000	1911	2,950,000
1888	80,000	1896	780,000	1904	1,500,000	1912	3,175,000
1889	150,000	1897	870,000	1905	1,700,000	1913	3,490,000
1890	235,000	1898	960,000	1906	1,900,000	1914	3,600,000
1891	330,000	1899	1,050,000	1907	2,100,000		
1892	420,000	1900	1,140,000	1908	2,300,000		

S. Thomas movement, 18 size, 17 jewels, Molineux model, 2 tone yellow gold, heavy damaskeening, H. C.

SETH THOMAS 18 size, "Molineux" 17 J., 2 tone yellow gold gilt & nickel heavy damaskeening model #2, HC

18 SIZE

Grade or Name – Description	Avg	Ex-Fn	Mint
Century, 7J, OF	$50	$75	$125
Century, 7J, HC	75	100	150
Century, 15J, OF	50	75	125
Century, 15J, HC	75	100	150
Chautauqua, 15J, GJS, M#5	125	150	225
Eagle Series, No. 36, 7J, OF	75	100	125
Eagle Series, No. 37, 7J, HC	100	125	150
Eagle Series, No. 106, 11J, OF	75	100	125
Eagle Series, No. 107, 11J, HC	100	125	150
Eagle Series, No. 206, 15J, OF	75	100	125

Liberty, 18 size, 7 jewels, hunting or open face, eagle on movement.

Maiden Lane, 18 size, 28 jewels, gold jewel settings, Adj5p, engraved dated as = 8,1,99. No serial number.

Henry Molineux, 18 size, 17 jewels, "Corona W. Co. USA" on dial, open face, serial number 54,951.

Seth Thomas, 18 size, 23 jewels, gold jewel settings, adjusted, serial number 298,333.

Grade or Name – Description	Avg	Ex-Fn	Mint
Eagle Series, No. 207, 15J, HC	$125	$150	$175
Eagle Series, 15J, M# 2, HC	100	125	175
Eagle Series, No. 210, 17J, OF	100	125	150
Eagle Series, No. 211, 17J, HC	150	175	225
Eagle Series, 17J, NI, 3/4, OF	100	125	150
Edgemere, 11J	55	75	125
Edgemere, 17J	75	100	150
Keywind M#2, 7J, 11J, & 15J, 3/4	150	200	300
Keywind M#4, 7J, 11J, & 15J, 3/4	150	200	300
Lakeshore, 17J, GJS, ADJ, NI	200	250	300
Liberty, 7J, 3/4, eagle on back plate	75	100	125
Maiden Lane, 17J, GJS, DR, Adj.6P, NI, marked ★★	900	1,100	1,400
Maiden Lane, 19J, GJS, DR, Adj.6P, NI, marked ★★★	1,000	1,200	1,500
Maiden Lane, 21J, GJS, DR, Adj.6P, NI, marked ★	1,000	1,200	1,500
Maiden Lane, 24J, GJS, DR, Adj.6P, marked ★★★	1,500	1,700	2,000
Maiden Lane, 25J, GJS, DR, Adj.6P, NI, marked ★★	2,400	2,500	3,000
Maiden Lane, 28J, GJS, DR, Adj.5P, NI, marked ★★★★	15,000	18,000	25,000
Henry Molineux, M#3, 17J, 3/4, GJS, ADJ ★★	500	550	650
Henry Molineux, M#2, 17J, GJS, ADJ ★★	500	550	650
Henry Molineux, M#2, 20J, GJS, ADJ ★★★	1,000	1,200	1,500
Monarch Watch Co., 7-15J, 2-tone	75	100	150
Republic USA, 7J, OF	55	75	125
S. Thomas, 7J, 3/4, multi-color dial	150	200	275
S. Thomas, 7J, 3/4	55	75	125
S. Thomas, 11J, 3/4, HC	75	100	150
S. Thomas, 11J, 3/4, OF	55	75	125
S. Thomas, 15J, 3/4, HC	100	125	175
S. Thomas, 15J, 3/4, gilded, OF	55	75	125
S. Thomas, 15J, 3/4 , OF	55	75	125
S. Thomas, 16J, 3/4	75	100	150
S. Thomas, 17J, 3/4, OF, nickel	100	125	175

Grade or Name – Description	Avg	Ex-Fn	Mint
S. Thomas, 17J, 3/4, 2-Tone	$125	$150	$200
S. Thomas, 17J, 3/4, OF, gilded	75	100	150
S. Thomas, 17J, 3/4, HC	125	150	175
S. Thomas, 21J, GJS, DR, Adj.5P	275	325	400
S. Thomas, 23J, GJS, DR, Adj.5P ★★	800	1,000	1,300
Special Motor Service,17J, 2 tone, LS, OF	275	300	350
20th Century (Wards), 11J	75	100	150
20th Century (Wards), 11J, 2-Tone	100	125	175
Wyoming Watch Co., 7J, OF	125	150	200
33, 7J, 3/4, gilded, OF	50	75	125
37, 7J, 3/4, NI, HC	75	100	150
44, 11J, 3/4, gilded, OF	55	75	125
47, 7J, gilded, FULL, OF	55	75	125
58, 11J, FULL, gilt, OF	55	75	125
70, 15J, 3/4, gilded, OF	55	75	125
80, 17J, 3/4, gilded, ADJ, HC	75	100	150
101, 15J, 3/4, gilded, ADJ, OF	55	75	125
149, 15J, gilded, FULL, OF	55	75	125
159, 15J, NI, FULL, OF	55	75	125
169, 17J, NI, FULL, OF	75	125	150
170, 15J, 3/4, NI, OF	55	75	125
179, 17J, 3/4, NI, ADJ, OF	75	125	150
180, 17J, 3/4, NI, HC	75	125	150
182, 17J, DR, NI, FULL, OF	100	125	175
201, 15J, 3/4, NI, ADJ, OF	75	100	150
245, 19J, GJS, 2-Tone, HC	1,000	1,200	1,500
260, 21J, DR, Adj.6P, NI, FULL, OF	225	275	350
281-282, 17J, OF, LS, FULL, DR, Adj.3P, OF, 2-tone	150	175	225
382, 17J, OF, LS, FULL, DR, Adj.5P, OF, 2-tone	150	175	225

Centennial, 16 size, 7 jewels, three-quarter nickel plate.

Grade 36, 16 size, 7 jewels, open face, three-quarter nickel plate.

16 SIZE
(OF Only)

Grade or Name – Description	Avg	Ex-Fn	Mint
Centennial, 7J, 3/4, NI, OF..	$50	$60	$75
Locust, 7J, NI, 3/4, OF	50	60	75
Locust, 17J, NI, ADJ, 3/4, OF	75	100	175
Republic USA, 7J, OF	50	60	75
25, 7J, BRG, OF..	50	60	75
26, 15J, BRG, GJS, OF	50	60	75
27, 17J, BRG, GJS, OF	50	60	75
28, 17J, BRG, Adj.3P, GJS, OF......................................	75	100	150
326, 7J, 3/4, NI, OF...	50	60	75
328, 15J, 3/4, NI, OF	50	60	75
332, 7J, 3/4, NI, OF	50	60	75
334, 15J, NI, ADJ,3/4, DMK, OF....................................	75	100	150
336, 17J, ADJ, 3/4, DMK, OF...	100	125	150

Seth Thomas, 12 size, 7 jewels, open face, pendant set.   Seth Thomas, 12 size, 17 jewels, gold jewel settings, gold center wheel, open face, Adj3p.

12 SIZE
(OF Only)

Grade or Name – Description	Avg	Ex-Fn	Mint
Republic USA, 7J, OF	$40	$50	$65
25, 7J, BRG, OF..	40	50	65
26, 15J, BRG, GJS, OF	45	55	70
27, 17J, BRG, GJS, OF	50	60	75

Grade or Name – Description	Avg	Ex-Fn	Mint
28, 17J, OF, BRG, Adj.3P, GJS	$55	$65	$80
326, 7J, OF, 3/4, NI	40	50	65
328, 15J, OF, 3/4, NI	45	55	70

Example of a basic Seth Thomas movement, 6 size, 7 jewels, serial number 441,839. Sometimes appears in a 12 size case.

Grade 45, 6 size, 7 jewels, open face, three-quarter nickel plate.

6 SIZE

(Some 6 Size were used to fit 12 Size cases)

Grade or Name – Description	Avg	Ex-Fn	Mint	
Century, 7J, NI, 3/4		$45	$50	$65
Eagle Series, 7J, No. 45, 3/4, NI, DMK, OF		55	60	75
Eagle Series, 7J, No. 205, 3/4, HC		75	100	150
Eagle Series, 15J, No. 35, 3/4, NI, DMK, OF		65	70	85
Eagle Series, 15J, No. 245, 3/4, HC		75	100	150
Edgemere, 7-11J,		55	60	75
Republic USA, 7J		45	50	65
Seth Thomas, 7J, 3/4, HC, 14K, 26 DWT		250	275	325
Seth Thomas, 11J, 3/4, HC		75	100	150
Seth Thomas, 11J, 3/4, OF		45	55	65
35, 7J, HC, NI, DMK,3/4		45	55	65
119, 16J, HC, GJS, NI, DMK, 3/4		100	125	175
205, 15J, HC		75	100	150
320, 7J, OF, NI, DMK, 3/4		50	65	85
322, 15J, OF		55	60	70

NOTE: Add $25 for HC.

0 SIZE

Grade or Name – Description	Avg	Ex-Fn	Mint
Seth Thomas, 7J, OF, No. 1	$60	$70	$85
Seth Thomas, 7J, HC, No. 1	75	100	150
Seth Thomas, 15J, OF, GJS, No. 3	60	70	85
Seth Thomas, 15J, HC, No. 3	75	100	150
Seth Thomas, 17J, OF, GJS, PS, No. 9	60	70	85
Seth Thomas, 17J, HC, GJS, PS, No. 9	75	100	150

NOTE: Add $25 for HC.

SETH THOMAS WATCH CO.
IDENTIFICATION OF MOVEMENTS
BY MODEL NUMBER

How to Identify Your Watch: Compare the movement of your watch with the illustrations in this section. Upon matching the movement exactly, the model number and size can be determined. While comparing, note the location of the balance, jewels, screws, gears, and type of back plate (Full, 3/4, Bridge) which will be clues in identifying the movement you have. Having determined the size and model number, you can now find your watch in the main price listing by name or number (which is engraved on the movement).

Model 1, 18 size, Open Face

Model 2, 18 size, Hunting

Model 3, 18 size, Open Face

Model 4, 18 size, Key Wind

Model 5, 18 size, Maiden Lane Series, Open Face.

Model 6, 18 Size, Open Face

Model 7 & 9, 18 size

Model 8, 18 size

Model 10, 18 size, Open Face

Model 11, 18 size, Hunting

Model 13, 18 size, Hunting

16 Size

16 Size, Open Face

12 Size, Open Face

6 Size, Open face

Model 14, 6 size

Model 16 & 17, 6 size

TREMONT WATCH CO.

Boston, Massachusetts
1864 - 1866

In 1864 A. L. Dennison thought that if he could produce a good movement at a reasonable price, there would be a ready market for it. Dennison went to Switzerland to find a supplier of cheap parts, as arbors were too high in America. He found a source for parts, mainly the train and escapement and the balance. About 600 sets were to be furnished. Dials were first made by Mr. Gold and Mr. Spear, then later by Mr. Hull and Mr. Carpenter. Tremont had hoped to produce 600 sets of trains per month. In 1865, the first movements were ready for the market. They were 18S, key wind, fully jeweled, and were engraved "Tremont Watch Co." In 1886, the company moved from Boston to Melrose. Another 18S was made, and the company made its own train and escapement. The watches were engraved "Melrose Watch Co., Melrose, Mass." The Tremont Watch Co. produced about 5,000 watches before being sold to the English Watch Co.

Tremont Watch Co., with "Washington Street Boston" engraved on movement, 18 size, 15 jewels, key wind and set, serial number 5,264.

Example of a basic Tremont movement, 18 size, 15 jewels, key wind & set, serial number 8,875.

Grade or Name – Description	Avg	Ex-Fn	Mint
18S, 7J, KW, KS .... ★	$250	$275	$350
18S, 11J, KW, KS	250	275	350
18S, 15J, KW, KS, Silveroid, recased............................	150	200	250
18S, 15J, KW, KS, gilded	250	275	350
18S, 15J, KW, KS, HC, 14K...	650	675	750
18S, 15J, KW, KS, gilded, Washington Street ....★★	450	550	700
18S, 17J, KW, KS, gilded	300	325	400
18S, 15J, KW, KS from back, 3/4 plate ....★★★	1,500	1,700	2,000

☞ NOTE: Watches listed in this book are priced at the retail level, as complete watches having an original 14k goldfilled case, an original white enamel single sunk dial, and with the entire original movement in good working order with no repairs needed, unless otherwise noted.

TRENTON WATCH CO.
Trenton, New Jersey
1885 - 1908

Trenton watches were marketed under the following labels: Trenton, Ingersoll, Fortuna, Illinois Watch Case Company, Calumet U.S.A., Locomotives Special, Marvel Watch Co., and Reliance Watch Co.

Serial numbers started at 2,001 and ended at 4,100,000. Total production was about 1,934,000.

CHRONOLOGY OF THE DEVELOPMENT OF TRENTON WATCH CO.:
New Haven Watch Co., New Haven, Conn. 1883-1887
Trenton Watch Co., Trenton, N. J. 1887 -1908
Sold to Ingersoll 1908-1922

TRENTON MODELS AND GRADES
With Years of Manufacture and Serial Numbers

Date	Numbers	Size	Model	Date	Numbers	Size	Model
1887-1889	2,001- 61,000	18	1	1900-1903	2,000,001-2,075,000	6	2
1889-1891	64,001- 135,000	18	2	1902-1905	2,075,001-2,160,000	6	3 LS
1891-1898	135,001- 201,000 *¹	18	3			12	2 LS
1899-1904	201,001- 300,000	18	6	1905-1907	2,160,001-2,250,000	6	3 PS
1891-1900	300,001- 500,000	18	4			12	2 PS
1892-1897	500,001- 600,000	6	1	1899-1902	2,500,001-2,600,000	3/0	1
1894-1899	650,001- 700,000	16	1	ca. 1906	2,800,001-2,850,000	6	3 PS
1898-1900	700,001- 750,000	6	2			12	2 PS
1900-1904	750,001- 800,000 *²	18	4	1900-1904	3,000,001-3,139,000	16	2
1896-1900	850,001- 900,000	12	1	1903-1907	3,139,001-3,238,000	16	3 OF
1898-1903	900,001-1,100,000	18	5	1903-1907	3,500,001-3,600,000	16	3 HC
1902-1907	1,300,001-1,400,000	18	6	1905-1907	4,000,001-4,100,000	0	1

1—7 jewel grades made only during 1891; 9 jewel chronograph made 1891-1898.

2—A few examples are KWKS for export to England.

Trenton movement, 18 size, 4 jewels, serial number 4,744.   Trenton movement, 18 size, 7 jewels, 4th model, serial number 788,313.

18 SIZE

Grade or Name – Description	Avg	Ex-Fn	Mint
M#1-2, gilded, OF.. ★	$150	$175	$250
M#3, 7J, 3/4..	50	75	125
M#3, 9J, 3/4..	50	75	125
M#4, 7J, FULL...	50	75	125
M#4, 11J, FULL..	50	75	125
M#4, 15J, FULL..	50	75	125
M#4-5, FULL, OF, NI	50	75	125
New Haven Watch Co. style, M#1, 4J .... ★★★	250	325	450
Trenton, 7J, KW, KS... ★	225	300	425

Note: Add $25 to value of above watches in hunting case.

Trenton movement, 18 size, 7 jewels, serial number 148,945.

Chronograph, 16 size, 9 jewels, third model; start, stop & fly back, sweep second hand.

16 SIZE

Grade or Name – Description	Avg	Ex-Fn	Mint
M#1-2, 7J, 3/4, NI, OF..	$50	$75	$125
M#3, 7J, 3F BRG	50	75	125
M#3, 11J, 3F BRG	50	75	125
M#3, 15J, 3F BRG	50	75	125
7,11,15J, 3F BRG, NI	50	75	125
Chronograph, 9J, start, stop, & fly back	150	175	225
Convertible Model, 7J, OF	100	125	175
Grade #30 & 31, 7J..	50	75	125
Grade #35, 36 & 38, 11J......................................	50	75	125
Grade #45, 16J..	75	100	150
Grade #125, 12J..	50	75	125
Ingersoll Trenton, 7J, 3F BRG...............................	50	75	125

Ingersoll Trenton movement, 16 size, 19 jewels, three fingered bridge, adjusted, serial number 3,419,771.

Ingersoll Trenton movement, 16 size, 12 jewels; "Edgemere" engraved on movement.

Grade or Name – Description	Avg	Ex-Fn	Mint
Ingersoll Trenton, 15J, 3F BRG, NI, ADJ	$75	$100	$150
Ingersoll Trenton, 17J, 3F BRG, NI, ADJ	75	100	150
Ingersoll Trenton, 19J, 3F BRG, NI, Adj.5P .... ★	150	250	300
Peerless, 7J, SW, LS	50	65	80
Reliance, 7J	50	65	80

Note: Add $25 to value of above watches in hunting case.

Reliance, 16 size, 7 jewels, serial number 241,265.

Trenton movement, convertible model, 16 size, 7 jewels.

12 SIZE

Grade or Name – Description	Avg	Ex-Fn	Mint
"Fortuna," 7J, BRG	$40	$50	$65

Grade or Name – Description	Avg	Ex-Fn	Mint
M#1, 7J, 3/4	$40	$50	$65
Monogram, 7J, SW	30	40	55

Note: Add $25 to value of above watches in hunting case.

Example of a basic Trenton Watch Co. movement, 6 size, 7 jewels, open face & hunting, nickel damaskeened.

6 SIZE

Grade or Name – Description	Avg	Ex-Fn	Mint
7J, 3/4, NI	$30	$40	$55
7J, 3F BRG	30	40	55
15J, 3F BRG	40	50	65

Note: Add $25 to value of above watches in hunting case.

0 SIZE

Grade or Name – Description	Avg	Ex-Fn	Mint
7J, 3F BRG	$40	$50	$65
15J, 3F BRG	50	60	75

Note: Add $25 to value of above watches in hunting case.

UNITED STATES WATCH CO.

Marion, New Jersey
1865 - 1877

The United States Watch Company was chartered in 1865, and the factory building was started in August 1865 and was completed in 1866. The first watch, called the "Frederic Atherton," was not put on the market until July 1867. It was America's first mass produced stem winding watch. This first grade was 18S, 19J, full plate and a gilt finish movement. A distinctive feature of the company's full plate movements was the butterfly shaped patented opening in the plate which allowed escapement inspection. That same year a second grade called the "Fayette Stratton" was introduced. It was also a gilt finish, full plate movement. Most of these were 15J, but some of the very early examples have been noted in 17J. In 1868 the "George Channing," "Edwin Rollo," and "Marion Watch Co." grades were introduced. All were 18S, 15J, full plate movements in a gilt finish. In February 1869 the gilt version of the "United States Watch Co." grade was introduced. It was 18S, 19J, full plate and was the company's first entry into the prestige market. Later that year the company introduced their first nickel grade, a 19J, 18S, full plate movement called the "A. H. Wallis." About this same time, in December 1869, they introduced America's most expensive watch, the first nickel, 19J, 18S, full plate "United States Watch Co." grade. Depending on case weight, these prestige watches retailed between $500 and $600, more than the average man earned in a year at that time. The company also introduced damaskeening to the American market; first on gilt movements and later on the nickel grades. The United States and Wallis 19J prestige grades were beautifully finished with richly enameled engraving including a variety of unique designs on the balance cock. It is significant to note that no solid gold trains have been seen with these prestige items in the extant examples presently known.

Example of a FREDERICK ATHERTON & CO. movement, 18 size, 19 jewels, gold jewel settings, key wind & pin set. Note butterfly cut-out.

In 1870 the company introduced their first watch for ladies, a 10S, 15J, plate, cock & bridge movement which was made to their specifications in Switzerland. This model was first introduced in two grades, the "R. F. Pratt" and "Chas. G. Knapp," both in a 15J, gilt finish movement. Later it was offered in a high grade, 19J "I. H. Wright" nickel finish movement. During 1870 and 1871 several other full plate grades in both gilt and nickel finish were introduced. In 1871 development on a new line of full plate, 3/4, plate, and plate & bridge was started but not introduced to the market until late in 1872 and early in 1873. The 10S and 16S new grades in plate and bridge were probably delayed well into 1873 and were not available long before the "Panic of 1873" started in September; this explains their relative scarcity.

By July 1874 the "Panic" had taken its toll and it was necessary for the company to reorganize as the Marion Watch Company, a name formerly used for one of their grades. At this time jewel count, finish standards, and prices were lowered on the full plate older grades, but this proved to be a mistake. That same year they introduced a cased watch called the "North Star" their cheapest watch at $15 retail. The year of 1875 hit the watch industry the hardest; price cutting was predatory and the higher priced watches of the United States Watch Co. were particulary vulnerable. Further lowering of finish standards and prices did not help and in 1876 the company was once again reorganized into the Empire City Watch Co. and their products were displayed at the Centennial that year. The Centennial Exhibition was not enough to save the faltering company and they finally closed their doors in 1877. The Howard brothers of Fredonia, New York (Independent and Fredonia Watch Co.) purchased most of the remaining movement stock and machinery. In the ten year period of movement production, current statistical studies indicate an estimated production of only some 60,000 watches, much smaller than the number deduced from the serial numbers assigned up to as high as 289,000.

NOTE: The above historical data and estimated production figures are based on data included in the new NAWCC book **MARION, A History of the United States Watch Company,** by William Muir and Bernard Kraus. This definitive work is available from NAWCC, Inc., 514 Poplar St., Columbia, PA. (Courtesy, Gene Fuller, MARION book editor.) This book is recommended by Mr. Shugart and Mr. Gilbert for your library.

EMPIRE CITY W. CO. & EQUIVALENT U.S.W. CO. GRADES

Empire City W. Co.	United States W. Co.
W. S. Wyse	A. H. Wallis
L. W. Frost	Henry Randel
Cyrus H. Loutrel	Wm. Alexander
J. L. Ogden	S. M. Beard
E. F. C. Young	John W. Lewis
D. C. Wilcox	George Channing
Henry Harper	Asa Fuller
Jesse A. Dodd	Edwin Rollo
E. C. Hine	J. W. Deacon
New York Belle	A. J. Wood
The Champion	G. A. Read
Black Diamond	Young America

NOTE: Courtesy Gene Fuller, NAWCC "MARION" book editor.

☞Note: Watches listed in this book are priced at the retail level, as complete watches having an original 14k gold-filled case, an original white enamel single sunk dial, and with the entire original movement in good working order with no repairs needed.

United States Watch Co. movement, 18 size, 19 jewels, gold jewel settings, key wind. Their highest grade watch.

United States Watch Co. double sunk dial, hunting, note pin setting at 4 o'clock.

MARION
18 SIZE
(All with Butterfly Cutout Except for 3/4 Plate)

Grade or Name – Description	Avg	Ex-Fn	Mint
Wm. Alexander, 15J, NI, KW, HC	$275	$350	$425
Wm. Alexander, 15J, NI, KW, OF	200	250	325
Wm. Alexander, 15J, NI, SW, OF	225	275	350
Frederic Atherton & Co., 15J, SW, gilded	250	325	400
Frederic Atherton & Co., 17J, KW, gilded, HC	300	350	425
Frederic Atherton & Co., 17J, KW, gilded, OF	250	300	375
Frederic Atherton & Co., 17J, SW, gilded, HC	300	350	425
Frederic Atherton & Co., 17J, SW, gilded, OF	250	325	400

U.S. Watch Co., dial and movement, 18 size, 20 jewels, hunting case, 3/4 plate, engraved on movement "N.D. Godfrey," serial number 72,042. Painted on the dial "New York 1873." The dial consists of day-date-month and moon phases.

Grade or Name – Description		Avg	Ex-Fn	Mint
Frederic Atherton & Co., 19J, SW, gilded,	★★★★	$800	$1,000	$1,300
Frederic Atherton & Co., 19J, KW, gilded	★★	600	700	850
BC&M R.R., 11J, KW	★★★★	1,600	1,800	2,100
BC&M R.R., 15J, gilded, KW	★★★★	1,600	1,800	2,100
S. M. Beard, 15J, KW, NI, OF		250	300	375
S. M. Beard, 15J, SW, NI, OF		250	300	375
S. M. Beard, 15J, SW or KW, HC		300	350	425
Centennial Phil., 11-15J, SW or KW, NI	★★★★	1,800	2,000	2,300
George Channing, 15J, KW, NI		250	300	375
George Channing, 15J, KW, gilded		225	275	325
George Channing, 15J, KW, NI, 3/4 Plate	★★	350	400	475
George Channing, 17J, KW, NI		275	325	400
J. W. Deacon, 11-13J, KW, gilded		175	225	300
J. W. Deacon, 15J, KW, gilded		175	225	300
J. W. Deacon, 11-15J, KW, 3/4 Plate	★	275	325	400
Empire City Watch Co., 11J, SW, no cutout		175	225	300
Empire City Watch Co., 15J, SW, NI, no cutout		200	250	325
Empire Combination Timer, 11J, FULL, time & distance on dial	★★	400	500	650
Empire Combination Timer, 15J, 3/4, time & distance on dial	★★	600	750	1,000
Fellows, 15J, NI, KW		400	450	525
Benjamin Franklin, 15J, KW		400	450	525
Asa Fuller, 7-11J, gilded, KW		200	225	275
Asa Fuller, 15J, gilded, KW		200	225	275
Asa Fuller, 15J, gilded, KW, 3/4 Plate	★★	300	325	350
N. D. Godfrey, 20J, NI, 3/4 plate, day date month, moon phases, c. 1873, HC, 18K	★★★★	4,000	5,000	6,000
John W. Lewis, 15J, NI, KW		225	275	350
John W. Lewis, 15J, NI, SW		250	300	375

Edwin Rollo, 18 size, 15 jewels, gilded, key wind & set, note butterfly cut-out, serial number 110,214.

Marion Watch Co. personalized Watch, 18 size, about 15J., pin set, note butterfly cut-out, serial # 106,761.

Empire City Watch Co. on movement, U.S. Marion Watch Co. on dial, 18 size, 15 jewels, note no butterfly cut-out on this model.

United States Watch Co., 18 size, 19 jewels, gold jewel settings, key wind & pin set, serial number 24,054.

Grade or Name – Description	Avg	Ex-Fn	Mint
John W. Lewis, 15J, NI, 3/4 Plate ★★	$350	$400	$475
Marion Watch Co., 11J, KW, gilded	200	250	325
Marion Watch Co., 15J, KW, gilded	200	250	325
Marion Watch Co., 15J, SW, gilded, 3/4 Plate ★★	300	350	425
Marion Watch Co., 17-19J, KW, gilded ★	300	350	425
N.J. R.R.&T. Co., 15J, gilded, KW ★	1,200	1,400	1,700
Newspaper Special Order, 11-15J, gilded, SW or KW	325	375	450
North Star, 7J, KW, NI case	300	350	425
North Star, 7J, SW, KS	300	350	425
North Star, 7J, 3/4 Plate	325	375	450
Pennsylvania R.R., 15J, NI, KW ★★★★	2,500	2,800	2,900
Personalized Watches, 7-11J, KW, 3/4 Plate ★	250	300	375
Personalized Watches, 11J, KW, gilded ★	250	300	375
Personalized Watches, 15J, KW, gilded ★	250	300	375
Personalized Watches, 15J, KW, NI ★	275	325	400
Personalized Watches, 15J, KW, 3/4 Plate ★	300	350	425
Personalized Watches, 19J, KW, Full Plate ★	400	450	525
Henry Randel, 15J, KW, NI	250	300	375
Henry Randel, 15J, SW, NI	250	300	375
Henry Randel, 15J, 3/4 Plate ★★	350	400	475
Henry Randel, 17J, KW, NI ★	275	325	400
G. A. Read, 7J, gilded, KW	200	250	325
G. A. Read, 7J, 3/4 Plate	300	350	425
Edwin Rollo, 11J, KW, gilded	200	250	325
Edwin Rollo, 15J, KW, gilded	200	250	325
Edwin Rollo, 15J, SW, gilded	200	250	325
Edwin Rollo, 15J, 3/4 Plate ★	300	350	425
Royal Gold, 11J, KW	200	250	300
Royal Gold, 15J, KW	300	350	425
Royal Gold, 15J, 3/4 Plate ★★	400	450	525

A.H. Wallis on movement, Empire City Watch Co. on dial, 18 size, 19 jewels, three-quarter plate, hunting. This combination timer has listed on the dial, 16 cities showing the time of day and distance in comparison with New York City, serial number 54,409.

Grade or Name – Description	Avg	Ex-Fn	Mint
Rural New York, 15J, gilded..	$250	$300	$375
Fayette Stratton, 11J, gilded	250	300	375
Fayette Stratton, 15J, KW, gilded	250	300	375
Fayette Stratton, 15J, SW, gilded	250	300	325
Fayette Stratton, 17J, KW, gilded	275	325	400
Fayette Stratton, 17J, SW, gilded	300	350	425
Union Pacific R.R., 15J, KW, gilded .... ★★★	1,800	2,000	2,300
United States Watch Co., 15J, NI, KW	500	550	625
United States Watch Co., 15J, NI, SW	600	650	725
United States Watch Co., 15J, 3/4 Plate, NI.................	600	650	725
United States Watch Co., 15J, 3/4 Plate, gilded	600	650	725
United States Watch Co., 19J, GJS, Adj.5P, 18K HC, dial mvt. & case all marked, Pin Set, SW .... ★★★	3,500	4,000	4,500
United States Watch Co., 19J, NI, KW .... ★★	750	950	1,200
United States Watch Co., 19J, NI, SW........................ ★★	900	1,100	1,350
A. H. Wallis, 15J, KW, NI	250	300	375
A. H. Wallis, 15J, SW, NI	250	300	375
A. H. Wallis, 17J, KW, NI	275	325	400
A. H. Wallis, 17J, SW, NI	300	350	425
A. H. Wallis, 19J, KW, NI .... ★★★	600	650	725
A. H. Wallis, 19J, SW, NI .... ★★★	650	700	775
D. C. Wilcox, 15J, SW, no butterfly cutout....................	250	300	375
I. H. Wright, 11J, KW, gilded	225	275	350
I. H. Wright, 15J, KW, gilded	225	275	350

☞ Note: 18S, 3/4 plate are scarce. Add $25 to $50 for listed open face watches with hunting cases.

☞ NOTE: Watches listed in this book are priced at the retail level, as complete watches having an original 14k gold filled case, an original white enamel single sunk dial, and with the entire original movement in good working order with no repairs needed, unless otherwise noted.

16 SIZE
1/4 Plate

Grade or Name – Description		Avg	Ex-Fn	Mint
S. M. Beard, 15J, NI, KW,	★★★★	$400	$450	$525
John W. Lewis, 15J, NI, KW	★★★★	400	450	525
Personalized Watches, 15J, NI, SW	★★★★	400	450	525
Edwin Rollo, 15J, , KW	★★★★	400	450	525
United States Watch Co., 15J, NI, SW	★★★★	600	700	850
A. H. Wallis, 19J, NI, SW,	★★★★	600	700	850

Note: 16S, 1/4 plate are the scarcest of the U.S.W.Co.–Marion watches.

Asa Fuller, 16 size, 15 jewels, stem wind, one-quarter plate, serial number 280,018.

United States Watch Co., 14 size, 15 jewels, three-quarter plate, engraved on movement "Royal Gold American Watch, New York, Extra Jeweled."

14 SIZE
3/4 Plate

Grade or Name – Description		Avg	Ex-Fn	Mint
Centennial Phil., 11J, KW, gilded		$400	$500	$750
J. W. Deacon, 11J,	★★	250	300	375
Asa Fuller, 15J,	★★	350	400	475
John W. Lewis, 15J, NI	★★	300	350	400
North Star, 15J,		250	300	375
Personalized Watches, 7-11J,	★★	350	400	475
Edwin Rollo, 15J,	★	300	350	425
Royal Gold, 15J,	★	350	400	475
Young America, 7J, gilded		300	350	425

10 SIZE
1/4 Plate

Grade or Name – Description	Avg	Ex-Fn	Mint
Wm. Alexander, 15J, KW, NI	$200	$250	$325
S. M. Beard, 15J, KW, NI, Plate...................................	200	250	325
Empire City Watch Co., 15J, KW.............................. ★	200	250	325
Chas. G. Knapp, 15J, Swiss, Plate, KW	100	150	225
Personalized Watches, 11-15J, Plate	200	250	325
R. F. Pratt, 15J, Swiss, Plate, KW.............................	100	150	225
Edwin Rollo, 11-15J, Plate .... ★	250	300	375
A. H. Wallis, 17-19J, KW, Plate	225	275	350
A. J. Wood, 15J, Plate, KW .... ★★★★	300	350	425
I. H. Wright, 19J, Swiss, NI, Plate, KW .... ★★★	500	550	625

S. M. Beard, 10 size, 15 jewels, key wind, quarter plate, serial number 248,407.

Chas. G. Knapp, 10 size, 15 jewels, Swiss, quarter plate, key wind.

U. S. WATCH CO.
OF WALTHAM
Waltham, Massachusetts
1884 - 1905

The business was started as the Waltham Watch Tool Co. in 1879. It was organized as the United States Watch Co. in 1884. The first watches were 16S, 3/4 plate pillar movement in three grades. They had a very wide mainspring barrel (the top was thinner than most) which was wedged up in the center to make room for the balance wheel. These watches are called dome watches and are hard to find. The fork was made of an aluminum alloy with a circular slot and a square ruby pin. The balance was gold at first, as was the movement which was a slow train, but the expansion balance was changed when they went to a quick train. The movement required a special case which proved unpopular. By 1887, some 3,000 watches had been made. A new model was then produced, a 16S movement that would fit a standard case. These movements were quick train expansion balance with standard type lever and 3/4 plate pillar movement. The company had a top production of ten watches a day. It was sold to the E. Howard Watch Co. in 1903. The United States Watch Co. produced some 802,000 watches total. Its top grade watch was the "President."

U. S. WATCH CO. OF WALTHAM
ESTIMATED SERIAL NUMBERS AND PRODUCTION DATES

Date	Serial No.	Date	Serial No.
1887	3,000	1896	300,000
1888	6,500	1897	350,000
1889	10,000	1898	400,000
1890	30,000	1899	500,000
1891	60,000	1900	600,000
1892	90,000	1901	700,000
1893	150,000	1902	750,000
1894	200,000	1903	800,000
1895	250,000		

U.S. Watch Co. of Waltham, The President , 18 size, 17 jewels, hunting, serial number 150,000.

U.S. Watch Co. of Waltham, The President, 18 size, 17 jewels, open face, 2-tone, adj., note regulator, serial number 150,350.

18 SIZE

Grade or Name – Description	Avg	Ex-Fn	Mint
Express Train, 15J, OF, ADJ	$275	$325	$400
Express Train, 15J, HC, ADJ	375	425	500
The President, 17J, HC ★★	500	550	625
The President, 21J, GJS, Adj.6P, DR, 14K ★★	900	950	1,025
The President, 17J, GJS, Adj.6P, DR, NI, DMK, OF ★	500	550	625
U. S. Watch Co., 15J, OF, 2-tone, stem attached ★	250	300	375
Washington Square, 15J, HCH ★	150	200	275
39 (HC) & 79 (OF), 17J, GJS, ADJ, NI, DMK, Adj.5P, BRG ..	100	125	175
40 (HC) & 80 (OF), 17J, GJS	100	125	175
48 (HC) & 88 (OF), 7J, gilded, FULL	100	125	175
48 (HC) & 88 (OF), 7J, gilded, FULL, Silveroid	55	60	75
52 (HC)	125	150	200
92 (OF), 17J, Silveroid	55	60	75

Grade or Name – Description	Avg	Ex-Fn	Mint
52 (HC) & 92 (OF), 17J..	$100	$125	$175
53 (HC) & 93 (OF), 15J, NI, FULL, DMK...............................	100	125	175
54 (HC) & 94 (OF), 15J..	100	125	175
56 (HC) & 96 (OF), 11J..	100	125	175
57 (HC) & 97 (OF), 15J..	100	125	175
58 (HC) & 98 (OF), 11J, NI, FULL, DMK...............................	100	125	175

☞ (Prices are with gold filled cases except where noted; add $25 to value of above watches with hunting case.)

☞ NOTE: Some grades are not included. Their values can be determined by comparing with similar models or grades listed.

U.S. Watch Co. of Waltham, 16 size, 7 jewels, guilded, note raised dome on center of movement, engraved on movement "Chas. V. Woerd's Patents," serial number 3,564.

U.S. Watch Co. of Waltham, 16 size, 7 jewels, "A New Watch Company At Waltham, Est'd 1885" on movement, serial number 770,771.

16 SIZE

Grade or Name – Description	Avg	Ex-Fn	Mint
Dome Plate Model, 7J, gilded	$125	$150	$200
Early KW-KS, 7J, S# below 100......................................	500	700	1,000
103, 17J, NI, 3/4, ADJ	50	75	125
104, 17J, NI, 3/4	50	75	125
104, 17J, NI, 3/4, Silveroid..	40	50	65
105, 15J, NI, 3/4, HC..	125	150	200
105, 15J, NI, 3/4, OF..	50	75	125
105, 15J, NI, 3/4, Silveroid..	40	65	115
106, 15J, gilded,3/4, Silveroid......................................	40	65	115
106, 15J, gilded,3/4..	50	75	125
108, 11J, gilded, 3/4	50	75	125
109, 7J, NI, 3/4	50	75	125
110, 7J, 3/4, HC	65	75	125
110, 7J, 3/4, OF...	50	60	75

Note: Add $20 to value of above watches in hunting case.

U.S. Watch Co., 16 size, 15 jewels, three-quarter plate.

6 SIZE

Grade or Name – Description	Avg	Ex-Fn	Mint
60, 17J, GJS, NI, 3/4, Adj.3P	$40	$60	$85
60, 17J, GJS, NI, 3/4, Adj.3P, HC, 14K	225	275	350
62, 15J, NI, 3/4	40	60	85
63, 15J, gilded	40	60	85
64, 11J, NI	40	60	85
65, 11J, gilded	20	30	40
66, 7J, gilded	20	30	40
66, 7-11J, NI, 3/4	40	60	85
68, 16J, GJS, NI, 3/4	50	75	125
69, 7J, NI, HC	75	100	150
69, 7J, NI, OF	20	30	40

Note: Add $10 to value of above watches in hunting case.

Grade 64, 6 size, 11 jewels

U.S. Watch Co. of Waltham, 0 size, 7 jewels, serial number 808,231.

0 SIZE

Grade or Name – Description	Avg	Ex-Fn	Mint
Betsy Ross, HC, GF case	$125	$150	$200
U. S. Watch Co., 15J, HC, GF case	100	125	175
U. S. Watch Co., 7-11J, HC, GF case	100	125	175

THE WASHINGTON WATCH CO.

Washington, D. C.

1872 - 1874

J. P. Hopkins, though better known as the inventor of the Auburndale Rotary Watch, was also connected with the Washington Watch Co. which made about 50 watches. They were 18S, key wind, 3/4 plate and had duplex escapements. Before Hopkins came to Washington Watch Co. he had handmade about six fine watches. Most of the materials used to produce the watch movements were purchased from the Illinois Watch Co. The company had a total production of 45 movements with duplex escapements.

Grade or Name – Description		Avg	Ex-Fn	Mint
18S, 15J, 3/4, KW, KS	★★★★	$3,500	$4,500	$5,500

Waterbury Watch Co., skeletonized movement; "A poor man's tourbillon," c. 1890.

Waterbury Watch Co., long wind movement. Note six spokes on dial.

WATERBURY WATCH CO.
Waterbury, Connecticut
1880 - 1898

The Waterbury Watch Co. was formed in 1880, and D. A. Buck made its first watch. The watches were simple and had only 50 parts. The mainspring was about nine feet long and coiled around the movement. It had a two-wheel train rather than the standard four-wheel train. The Waterbury long wind movement revolved once every hour and had a duplex escapement. The dial was made of paper, and the watch was priced at $3.50 to $4.00. Some of these watches were used as give aways.

CHRONOLOGY OF THE DEVELOPMENT OF THE WATERBURY WATCH CO.:

Waterbury Watch Co., Waterbury, Conn. — 1880-1898
New England Watch Co. — 1898-1912
Purchased Ingersoll — 1914
Became U. S. Time Corp. (maker of Timex) — 194

Example of a basic Waterbury Watch Co. movement, Series C.

Series L, Waterbury W. Co. Duplex Escapement, about 16 size.

18 TO 0 SIZES

Grade or Name – Description		Avg	Ex-Fn	Mint
35S, 1890-1891, back wind		$100	$150	$200
Long wind, skeletonized, 3 spokes	★	350	400	550
Long wind, skeletonized, 4 spokes	★★	600	750	1,000
Long wind, skeletonized, 6 spokes	★	400	450	700
Long wind, skeletonized, 6 spokes, **celluloid case**	★	500	600	750
Series A, long wind, skeletonized	★	350	400	550
Series B, long wind		200	225	300
Series C, long wind		200	225	300
Series D, long wind		225	250	350
Series E, long wind (discontinued 1890)		275	300	400
Series F, Duplex escapement		75	85	100

Series I, The Trump, about 18 size, no jewels, pin lever escapement.

Series T, Oxford Duplex Escapement, about 18 size, no jewels.

Grade or Name – Description	Avg	Ex-Fn	Mint
Series G, 3/4 lever escapement ★	$200	$225	$300
Series H, Columbian Duplex ★★	250	275	350
Series I, Trump, duplex,	85	95	110
Series I, Trump, 3/4	85	95	110
Series J, Americus Duplex	85	95	110
Series K, Charles Benedict Duplex	125	150	200
Series L, Waterbury W. Co. Duplex	85	100	125
Series N, Addison Duplex	60	80	95
Series P, Rugby Duplex	100	125	150
Series R, Tuxedo Duplex	80	100	125
Series S, Elfin	65	75	85
Series T, Oxford Duplex	65	75	85
Series W, Addison	85	125	135
Series Z	65	85	95
Free Press Watch, Series E	200	225	250
Oxford	55	80	95
The Trump	50	75	90
Waterbury W. Co., 7J, 3/4, low Serial No.	300	375	500

☞ NOTE: Dollar watches must be in running condition to bring these prices.

E. N. WELCH MFG. CO.

Bristol, Connecticut
1834 - 1897

Elisha Welch founded this company about 1834. His company failed in 1897, and the Sessions Clock Co. took over the business in 1903. E. N. Welch Mfg. Co. produced the large watch which was displayed at the Chicago Exposition in 1893. This watch depicted the landing of Columbus on the back of the case.

E.N. Welch Mfg. Co., 36 size, back wind & set, made for the Chicago Exposition in 1893. Die debossed back depicting the landing of Columbus in America, Oct, 12th, 1492.

Grade or Name – Description	Avg	Ex-Fn	Mint
36S, Columbus Exhibition watch	$275	$375	$475

WESTCLOX
United Clock Co.
Westclox & Western Clock Co.
General Time Corp.
Athens, Georgia
1899 - Present

The first Westclox pocket watch was made about 1899; however, the Westclox name did not appear on their watches until 1906. In 1903 they were making 100 watches a day, and in 1920 production was at 15,000 per day. This company is still in business today in Athens, Georgia.

Grade or Name – Description	Avg	Ex-Fn	Mint
M#1, SW, push to set, GRO	$75	$100	$125
M#2, SW, back set, GRO	50	60	75
18S, Westclox M#4, OF, GRO	50	60	75
1910 Models to 1920, GRO	35	45	60
Anniversary	35	45	60
Antique	20	30	45
Boy Proof	45	50	75
Bingo	30	40	55
Bulls Eye (several models)	15	20	25
Country Gentleman	40	50	60
Dax (many models)	10	15	20

Boy Proof Model, about 16 size, designed to be tamper proof.

Example of a basic Westclox movement, stem wind, back set.

Grade or Name – Description	Avg	Ex-Fn	Mint
Elite..	$25	$35	$40
Everbrite (several models)......................	15	20	30
Explorer.......................................	225	275	325
Farm Bureau	65	85	100
Glo Ben	65	85	100
Ideal	30	35	40
Lighted Dial...................................	25	30	40
Mark IV.......................................	35	45	55
Maxim...	30	40	50
Military Style, 24 hour........................	65	85	100

Example of a basic Westclox movement, about 16 size, stem wind, lever escapement.

Explorer, back of case and dial, "Wings Over The Pole, The Explorer" on back of case.

Example of a basic Westclox movement, stem wind & set.   Zep, about 16 size with radiant numbers and hands, c. 1929.

Grade or Name – Description	Avg	Ex-Fn	Mint
Mustang	$40	$45	$60
NAWCC, ETP 1,000	40	45	50
Pastor Stop Watch, (fly back hand)	65	75	90
Pocket Ben (many models)	20	35	60
Ruby	25	30	45
Scotty (several models)	15	20	25
Smile	25	30	40
Sterling Watch Co. (see **Pastor Stop Watch**)			
Sun Mark	30	35	40
Team Mate (various major league teams)	25	35	40
Tele Time	25	35	45
Texan	35	45	65
Tiny Tim	150	200	275
Victor	80	100	130
Vote	25	35	45
Westclox	15	20	25
Zep	225	275	375

WESTERN WATCH CO.

Chicago, Illinois
1880

Albert Trotter purchased the unfinished watches from the California Watch Co. Mr. Trotter finished and sold those watches. Later he moved to Chicago and, with Paul Cornell and others, formed the Western Watch Company. Very few watches were completed by the Western Watch Co.

Grade or Name – Description		Avg	Ex-Fn	Mint
Western Watch Co., 18S, FULL .... ★★★		$2,500	$3,000	$4,000

Example of a Western Watch Co. movement, 18 size, 15 jewels, key wind & set.

WICHITA WATCH CO.

Wichita, Kansas
July, 1887 - 1888

This company completed construction of their factory in Wichita, Kansas in June 1888, and only a half dozen watches were produced during the brief period the company was in operation. The president was J. R. Snively. These watches are 18S, half plate, adjusted, 15 jewels.

Grade or Name – Description		Avg	Ex-Fn	Mint
18S, 15J, plate, ADJ .... ★★★★		$3,500	$4,500	$5,500

☞ NOTE: Watches listed in this book are priced at the retail level, as complete watches having an original 14k gold-filled case, an original white enamel single sunk dial, and with the entire original movement in good working order with no repairs needed, unless otherwise noted.

COMIC AND CHARACTER WATCHES

When discussing the topic of watches and someone mentions Comic Character Watches, we immediately picture a watch with Mickey Mouse. Isn't Mickey Mouse the most famous of all watches in the world? Before Mickey appeared in the 1930's there were a handful of lesser known comic watches with characters like Skeezix, Smitty and Buster Brown, but it was the Mickey Mouse Watch that paved the way for all other comic character watches. As a collaboration between Walt Disney (the creator of Mickey Mouse) and Robert Ingersoll and his brother the founders of the Ingersoll-Waterbury Watch Company. The Mickey Mouse Watch was one of this century's greatest marketing concepts. In a two year period Ingersoll had sold nearly 2.5 million Mickey Mouse wrist and pocket watches. Throughout the 1930's they also introduced other watches with Disney characters such as Big Bad Wolf in 1934, as well as, the Donald Duck wrist watch. The Donald Duck pocket watch was produced several years later in 1939. The Mickey Lapel and Mickey Deluxe Wrist were produced in the late 1930's.

Ingersoll dominated the character watch market in the early 1930's due to the incrediable popularity of the Disney characters, however by the mid 1930's other companies mainly Ingraham and New Haven secured the rights to other popular characters. Throughout the 1930's kids fell in love with these watches featuring their favorite comic character or hero, such as, Popeye, Superman, Buck Rogers, Orphan Annie, Dick Tracy and The Lone Ranger. There was also a couple of other well known characters, Betty Boop and Cowboy Tom Mix produced but for some reason these watches did not become popular like all the others, so very small quantities were produced.

During World War II production of comic watches ceased, but after the war comic watches came back stronger than ever. Once again Disney was the overall leader. The Ingersoll name only appeared on some of the watches to keep the trade name still familiar, as Ingersoll was sold to U.S. Time Watch Company.

The late 1940's was very good to the character watch market and proof being the many character watches produced as the Twentieth Birthday Series for Mickey in 1948 that included with Mickey, Donald Duck, Pinocchio, Pluto, Bambi, Joe Carioca, Jiminy Cricket, Bongo Bear and Daisy Duck. Other watches from this time include Porky Pig, Puss-N-Boots, Joe Palooka, Gene Autry, Captain and Mary Marvel and others featuring characters of the comic and cartoons, space and western heroes.

The early to mid 1950's was also a vibrant time for character watch production with more Disney characters, western heroes and comic characters than ever before, but by 1958 manufacturing of character watches had almost completely stopped as manufacturing costs went up, popularity of some characters faded and many other circumstances led to a complete stop of any of these watches until the late 1960's. The watches were never the same again.

In the 1970's the Comic Character Watch once again made it's come back with the Bradley Watch Company (Elgin W. Co.) leading the way just as Ingersoll did in the first years of comic watches.

Today there are hundreds of character watches to choose from, Disney Super Hero movie characters like E.T., and Roger Rabbit and a wealth of others, but today's facination is not just with the new but with the old as we see in the re-issue of the original Mickey watches. There is a growing awareness and appreciation for all the originals. It is a very unusual attraction that draws people to love and collect the character watches of the past. Collectors appreciate the original boxes (that are facinating works of art) and the face of the watch that features the character that we love. The manufacturing method of these simple pin lever movements were not the best of timekeepers, but were solidly constructed.

All in all, when you put together the watches and boxes they are pieces of functional art and history that brings back memories of our youth. Something that no other kind of watch can do.

Babe Ruth, by Exact Time, ca. 1948.

Betty Boop, by Ingraham, ca. 1934.

Style or Grade – Description	Avg	Ex-Fn	Mint	Mint +Box
Alice in Wonderland, WW, c. 1951, by U.S. Time	$20	$30	$45	$325
Alice, Red Riding Hood, & Marjory Daw, WW, c. 1953, by Bradley	20	30	55	150
Alice in Wonderland, WW, c. 1958, by Timex	15	25	40	250
Alice in Wonderland & Mad Hatter, WW, c. 1948, by New Haven	50	85	125	250
Annie Oakley, WW, "Action Gun," c. 1951, by New Haven	125	175	250	375
Babe Ruth, WW, c. 1948, by Exact Time, box baseball pledge card	★ 150	250	375	1,200
Bambi, WW, c. 1949, by U.S. Time, Birthday series	100	175	250	450
Barbie, WW,c.1964 (blue dial),by Bradley	20	30	40	100
Batman, WW, c. 1970 by Gilbert (band in shape of bat)	75	125	200	350
Batman, WW, c. 1978, by Timex	35	60	75	120
Betty Boop, PW, c. 1934, by Ingraham (with diedebossed back)	★★★★ 350	600	900	1,600
Big Bad Wolf & 3 Pigs, PW, c. 1936, by Ingersoll	300	500	700	1,200
Big Bad Wolf & 3 Pigs, WW, c. 1936, by Ingersoll	300	550	850	1,800
Big Bad Wolf & Little Red Riding Hood, Wolf eyes move	150	200	300	600
Boy Scout,PW, c.1937, by Ingersoll, be prepaired hands	250	275	350	600
Boy Scout,WW,c.1938,,by New Haven	50	60	75	125
Buck Rogers, PW, c. 1935, by Ingraham (lightning bolt hands)	300	400	650	1,000
Bugs Bunny, WW, c. 1951, Swiss, (carrot shaped hands)	75	150	250	525
Bugs Bunny, WW, c. 1951,Swiss, (without carrot hands)	60	100	175	400
Bugs Bunny, WW, c. 1970, Swiss, (standing bugs)	30	40	50	65

Note: To be mint condition, character watches must have unfaded dials, and boxes must have all inserts. (PW = Pocket Watch; WW = Wrist Watch)

Big Bad Wolf & 3 Pigs, Ingersoll, ca. 1936.   **Buck Rogers,** Ingraham, ca. 1935.

Bugs Bunny, Exact Time, ca. 1949.   **Buster Brown,** Ingersoll, ca. 1925.

Dick Tracy, New Haven, ca. 1948.   **Dick Tracy,** New Haven (six shooter action arm), ca. 1952.

Note: To be mint condition, character watches must have unfaded dials, and boxes must have all inserts. (PW = Pocket Watch; WW = Wrist Watch)

Style or Grade – Description	Avg	Ex-Fn	Mint	Mint +Box
Buster Brown, PW, c. 1928, by Ingersoll	$125	$175	$250	$450
Buster Brown, PW, c. 1928, by Ingersoll (Buster inside circle)	125	175	300	450
Buzz Corey, WW, c. 1952, by U.S. Time	75	100	200	450
Buzzy the Crow, in red hat	25	30	35	55
Captain Liberty, WW, c. 1950, by U.S. Time	50	75	150	450
Captain Marvel, PW, c. 1945, by New Haven	175	250	400	700
Captain Marvel, WW, c. 1948, by New Haven (small watch, plastic box)	40	70	140	300
Captain Marvel, WW, c. 1948, by New Haven (larger size watch)	50	90	170	450
Captain Marvel, WW, c. 1948, Swiss made	95	140	225	350
Captain Midnight, PW, c. 1948, by Ingraham	250	300	400	600
Cinderella, WW, c. 1950, by U.S. Time (slipper box)	25	35	50	250
Cinderella, WW, c. 1955, by Timex (box with imitation cel)	15	25	50	250
Cinderella, WW, c. 1958, by Timex (box with plastic statue)	15	25	50	250
Cinderella, WW, c. 1958, by Timex (box with porcelain statue)	15	25	60	200
Coca Cola, PW, c. 1948, by Ingersoll	125	150	200	350
Daisy Duck, WW, c. 1947, by Ingersoll (tonneau style)	100	175	250	500
Daisy Duck, WW, c. 1948, by U.S. Time (fluted bezel, birthday series)	100	175	250	450
Dale Evans, WW, c.1949, by Ingraham, Dale standing	80	100	125	250
Dale Evans, WW, c. 1950, by Bradley (western style leather band & necklace &lucky horseshoe)	30	50	65	250
Dale Evans, WW, c. 1960, by Bradley (round)	30	50	65	150
Dan Dare, PW, c. 1950, by Ingersoll Ltd. (made in England) (action arm)	200	350	400	600
Davy Crockett, WW, c. 1951, by Bradley (round dial)	30	50	90	250
Davy Crockett, WW, c. 1955, by U.S. Time (came with powder horn)	25	45	85	300
Davy Crockett, WW, c. 1956, by Bradley (watch barrel shaped dial)	30	65	100	225
Dennis the Menace, WW, c. 1970, by Bradley	20	35	55	75
Dick Tracy, PW, c. 1948, by Ingersoll	250	350	500	800
Dick Tracy, WW, c. 1948, by New Haven (round dial)	75	100	125	275
Dick Tracy, WW, c. 1948, by New Haven (small tonneau)	75	100	150	275
Dick Tracy, WW, c. 1935, by New Haven (large)	150	225	300	500
Dick Tracy, WW, c. 1951, by New Haven (six shooter action arm)	175	250	325	500
Dizzy Dean, PW, c. 1935, by Ingersoll ★★	200	350	500	1,000
Dizzy Dean, WW, c. 1938, by Ingersoll ★★	200	300	500	1,000

Note: To be mint condition, character watches must have unfaded dials, and boxes must have all inserts. (PW = Pocket Watch; WW = Wrist Watch)

Dizzy Dean, Ingersoll, ca. 1935

Donald Duck, Ingersoll, ca. 1940.

Style or Grade – Description	Avg	Ex-Fn	Mint	Mint +Box
Donald Duck, PW, c. 1939, by Ingersoll (Mickey on back) .... ★	$200	$400	$700	$1,500
Donald Duck, WW, c. 1935, by Ingersoll (Mickey on second hand) ....★★	500	800	1,200	2,800
Donald Duck, WW, c. 1948, by U.S. Time (tonneau style, silver tone)	100	150	250	500
Donald Duck, WW, c. 1948, by U.S. Time (tonneau style, gold tone)	150	200	300	500
Donald Duck, PW, , c. 1954, Swiss made	75	150	250	400
Donald Duck, WW, c. 1948, by Ingersoll (fluted bezel, birthday series)	150	175	250	450
Donald Duck, WW, c. 1955, by U.S. Time, (plain bezel, pop-up in box)	40	70	125	400
Dopey, WW, c. 1948, by Ingersoll (fluted bezel, birthday series)	100	150	250	450
Dudley Do-Right, WW, 17J (Bullwinkle & Rocky)	55	75	150	225
Flash Gordon, PW, c. 1939, by Ingersoll	350	475	650	950
Flash Gordon, WW, c.1970, Precision	100	225	350	500
From Outer Space, PW, Igersoll G.Briten, ...	100	220	325	450
Garfield, WW, (The Cat Jumped Over The Moon)	20	25	30	45
Gene Autry, WW, c. 1939, by Ingersoll (Gene and Champion on dial)	85	125	200	350

Donald Duck, Ingersoll, ca. 1947.

Gene Autry (Swiss made), ca. 1956.

Above: Hopalong Cassidy, U.S. Time, ca. 1950s. Left: Hopalong Cassidy, Ingersoll, ca. 1958.

Style or Grade – Description	Avg	Ex-Fn	Mint	Mint +Box
Gene Autry, WW, c. 1939, by Ingersoll	$85	$115	$175	$375
Gene Autry, WW, c. 1950, by New Haven, (action gun)	125	200	300	450
Gene Autry, WW, c. 1956, Swiss made	45	55	75	200
Goofy, WW, c. 1972, by Helbros, 17J (watch runs backward)	350	450	650	900
Hopalong Cassidy, WW, by U.S. Time (metal watch, box with saddle)	15	25	45	200
Hopalong Cassidy, WW, by U.S. Time (plastic watch, box with saddle)	5	20	35	200
Hopalong Cassidy, WW, by U.S. Time (small watch, leather Western band, flat rectangular box)	25	45	75	300
Hopalong Cassidy, WW, by U.S. Time (regular size watch, black leather cowboy strap)	15	35	65	300
Hopalong Cassidy, PW, c. 1950, by U.S. Time (rawhide strap and fob)	100	200	275	400
Howdy Doody, WW, c. 1954, by Ingraham (with moving eyes)	100	125	175	400
Howdy Doody, WW, c. 1954, by Ingraham (with friends)	75	100	150	550
Jamboree, PW, c. 1951, by Ingersoll, Ltd.	75	100	250	425

Howdy Doody, Ingraham, ca. 1954.

Li'l Abner, New Haven, waving flag, ca. 1948.

Lone Ranger, New Haven, ca. 1939.

Lone Ranger, New Haven, ca. 1939.

Mickey Mouse, Ingersoll, ca. 1933.

Mickey Mouse, Ingersoll, ca. 1933.

Mickey Mouse, Ingersoll, birthday series, ca. 1948.

Mickey Mouse, Ingersoll (U.S. Time), ca. 1950.

Note: To be mint condition, character watches must have unfaded dials, and boxes must have all inserts. (PW = Pocket Watch; WW = Wrist Watch)

Style or Grade – Description	Avg	Ex-Fn	Mint	Mint +Box
James Bond 007, WW, c. 1972, by Gilbert	$60	$125	$200	$300
Jeff Arnold, PW, c. 1952, by Ingersoll (English watch with moving gun)	150	200	325	550
Joe Carioca, WW, c. 1948, by U.S. Time (fluted bezel, birthday series)	95	150	250	450
Joe Palooka, WW, c. 1948, by New Haven	100	150	250	500
Li'l Abner, WW, c. 1948, by New Haven (waving flag)	150	175	250	500
Li'l Abner, WW, c. 1948, by New Haven (moving mule)	150	175	200	400
Little King, WW, c. 1968, by Timex	35	100	200	400
Little Pig Fiddler, WW, c.1947, by Ingersoll	125	250	400	700
Lone Ranger, PW, c. 1939, by New Haven (with fob)	150	250	400	600
Lone Ranger, WW, c. 1938, by New Haven (large)	75	150	250	450
Lone Ranger, WW, c. 1948, New Haven, (Fluted lugs)	75	125	200	400
Mary Marvel, WW, c. 1948, by U.S. Time (paper box)	35	65	100	300
Mary Marvel, WW, c. 1948, by U.S. Time (plastic box)	35	65	100	300
Mickey Mouse, PW, c.1933, by Ingersoll, #1&2 (tall stem)	285	350	450	650
Mickey Mouse, PW, c. 1936, by Ingersoll, #3&4 (short stems)	200	275	400	650
Mickey Mouse, PW, c. 1938, by Ingersoll (Mickey decal on back)	275	400	700	1,000
Mickey Mouse, PW, c. 1933, by Ingersoll Ltd. (English)	300	450	750	1,400
Mickey Mouse, PW, c.1976, by Bradley (bicentennial model)	35	50	75	125
Mickey Mouse, PW, c. 1974, by Bradley (no second hand)	25	40	50	85
Mickey Mouse, PW, c. 1974, by Bradley ("Bradley" printed at 6)	15	20	30	55

MICKEY MOUSE, Ingersoll, model no.3 on the left.   Right: Model no.4 is shown with lapel button

Style or Grade – Description	Avg	Ex-Fn	Mint	Mint +Box
Mickey Mouse, WW, c. 1933, by Ingersoll (metal band with 3 Mickeys' on seconds disc)	$125	$250	$325	$750
Mickey Mouse, WW, c. 1938, by Ingersoll (one Mickey for second hand)	100	200	275	900
Mickey Mouse, WW, c. 1938, by Ingersoll (girl's watch, 1 Mickey for second hand)	175	200	275	900
Mickey Mouse, WW, c. 1948, by Ingersoll (fluted bezel, birthday series)	150	175	200	450
Mickey Mouse, WW, c. 1946, by U.S. Time (10k gold plated)	100	125	200	300
Mickey Mouse, WW, c. 1947, by U.S. Time (tonneau, plain, several styles)	50	75	125	300
Mickey Mouse, WW, c. 1947, by U.S. Time (same as above, gold tone)	50	75	125	250
Mickey Mouse, WW, c. 1950s, by U.S. Time (round style)	25	35	55	275
Mickey Mouse, WW, c. 1958, by U.S. Time (statue of Mickey in box)	15	25	45	250
Mickey Mouse, WW, c. 1965, by Timex (Mickey Mouse electric)	75	100	125	200
Mickey Mouse, WW, c. 1965, Timex (manual wind)	35	55	75	125
Mickey Mouse, WW, c. 1970s, by Bradley	10	15	35	80
Mickey Mouse, WW, c. 1980, by Bradley (colored min. chapter)	50	65	85	150
Mickey Mouse, WW, c. 1983, by Bradley (limited commemorative model)	50	75	100	150

Mickey Mouse, Bradley, ca. 1955.   Mickey Mouse, with wide bezel, Ingersoll, ca. 1948.

Note: To be mint condition, character watches must have unfaded dials, and boxes must have all inserts. (PW = Pocket Watch; WW = Wrist Watch)

Left: Mary Marvel, Swiss made, ca. 1948. **Center: Minnie Mouse**, U.S. Time, ca. 1961. **Right: Orphan Annie**, New Haven, ca. 1939.

Orphan Annie, New Haven, ca. 1940.

Popeye, New Haven, ca. 1938.

Popeye, New Haven (with friends), ca. 1935.

Popeye, New Haven, ca. 1940.

Note: To be mint condition, character watches must have unfaded dials, and boxes must have all inserts. (PW = Pocket Watch; WW = Wrist Watch)

Style or Grade – Description	Avg	Ex-Fn	Mint	Mint +Box
Mickey Mouse, WW, c. 1985, by ETA (clear plastic bezel and band)	$15	$20	$35	$75
Minnie Mouse, WW, c. 1958, by U.S. Time (statue of Minnie in box)	20	40	60	200
Moon Mullins, PW, c. 1930, by Ingersoll	★ 200	300	500	750
Orphan Annie, WW, c. 1939, by New Haven (fluted bezel)	50	75	100	300
Orphan Annie, WW, c. 1935, by New Haven (large style)	100	125	155	400
Orphan Annie, WW, c. 1948, by New Haven smaller model)	50	75	100	300
Orphan Annie, WW, c. 1968, by Timex	35	45	65	95
Peter Pan, PW, c. 1948, by Ingraham	150	225	300	600
Pinocchio, WW, c. 1948, by Ingersoll (fluted bezel, birthday series)	125	160	250	450
Pinocchio, WW, c. 1948, by U.S. Time (Happy Birthday cake box)	125	150	250	450
Pluto, WW, c. 1948, by U.S. Time(birthday series)	85	135	250	450
Popeye, PW, c. 1935, by New Haven (with friends on dial)	★ 275	450	650	1,100
Popeye, PW, c. 1936, by New Haven (plain dial)	200	350	450	1,000
Popeye, WW, c. 1936, by New Haven (tonneau style, with friends on dial)	★ 250	375	650	1,200
Popeye, WW, c. 1966, by Bradley (round style)	75	100	125	200
Popeye, WW, c. 1948, Swiss, Olive Oyl at 3	75	150	250	400
Porky Pig, WW, c. 1948, by Ingraham (tonneau)	100	175	250	450
Porky Pig, WW, c. 1949, by U.S. Time (round)	75	175	250	450
Puss-N-Boots, WW, c. 1959, by Bradley	100	175	250	400
Quarterback, WW, c.1965, Swiss, (Football action arm)	65	75	85	125
Robin, WW, c. 1978, by Timex	25	35	50	75
Robin Hood, WW, c. 1955, by Bradley (tonneau style)	75	100	175	350
Robin Hood, WW, c. 1958, by Viking (round)	75	150	200	400
Rocky Jones Space Ranger, WW, c. 1955, by Ingraham	100	200	300	700
Roy Rogers, WW, c. 1954, by Ingraham (Roy and rearing Trigger)	50	75	100	225

Robin Hood, Bradley, ca. 1955.

Roy Rogers, Ingraham, ca. 1954.

Roy Rogers, Ingraham, ca. 1960.

Roy Rogers, Ingraham (large), ca. 1951.

Roy Rogers, Ingraham, ca. 1951.

Skeezix, Ingraham, ca. 1936.

Left: Smitty, New Haven, ca. 1936. Center: Superman, New Haven, ca. 1939. Right: Superman, New Haven, ca. 1939.

Style or Grade – Description	Avg	Ex-Fn	Mint	Mint +Box
Roy Rogers, WW, c. 1954, by Ingraham (Roy and Trigger) ..	$50	$75	$100	$250
Roy Rogers, WW, c. 1954, by Ingraham (expansion band)......	50	75	100	250
Roy Rogers, WW, c. 1956, by Ingraham (round dial)	50	75	100	200
Rudy Nebb, PW, c. 1930, by Ingraham	150	200	275	500
Shirley Temple, PW, c.1958, by Westclox ....★★	275	375	450	550
Skeezix, PW, c. 1928, by Ingraham...	225	275	350	650
Smitty, PW, c. 1928, by New Haven	225	275	350	650
Smitty, WW, c. 1936, by New Haven	150	200	300	550
Smokey Stover, WW, c. 1968, by Timex	75	100	150	225
Snoopy, WW, c. 1958 (tennis racket)......................................	20	30	45	75
Snoopy, WW, c. 1958 (Woodstock)	20	30	45	75
Snow White, WW, c. 1938, by Ingersoll (tonneau).................	100	125	200	400
Snow White, WW, c. 1952, by U.S. Time (round)	25	35	50	350
Snow White, WW, c. 1956, by U.S. Time (statue in box)	25	35	50	250
Snow White, WW, c. 1962, by U.S. Time (plastic watch)	25	35	50	250
Spiro Agnew, WW,c.1970s, Swiss...	20	25	35	45
Superman, PW, c. 1956, by Bradley	150	250	350	600
Superman, WW, c. 1938, by New Haven	200	250	325	600
Superman, WW, c.1946, by Ingraham(lightning bolt hands)	150	175	250	450
Superman, WW, c. 1978, by Timex (large size)........................	45	65	95	150
Superman, WW, c. 1978, by Timex (small size)	45	65	75	125
Superman, WW, c.1975, Dabs & Co., yellow min. chapter	40	65	75	150
Superman, WW, c.1965, Swiss, rotating superman	50	75	125	225
Superman, WW, c.1976, Timex, sweep sec. hand	40	65	75	125
Three Little Pigs, PW, c. 1936, by Ingersoll.......................★★	400	600	850	1,200
Tom Corbett, WW, c. 1954, by New Haven	75	100	150	450
Tom Mix, PW, c. 1936, by Ingersoll (with fob) ....★★★	450	750	1,000	2,500
Tom Mix, WW, c. 1936, by Ingersoll...............................★★★	400	600	900	3,000
Winnie the Pooh Bear, c.1970s, Swiss	20	25	30	45
Wizzard of Oz, c.1972, swiss, ...	25	50	70	120
Wonderwomen,WW, c.1975, Timex, stars at 1,2,4,5,7,8,10,11 .	40	65	75	130
Wonderwomen,WW, c.1975, Dabs & Co.	40	65	75	130
Woody Woodpecker, WW, c. 1948, by Ingersoll (town)..........	85	125	250	450
Woody Woodpecker, WW, c. 1952, by Ingraham (round dial)	100	125	175	400
Yogi Bear, WW, c. 1964, by Bradley...	35	45	60	75
Zorro, WW, c. 1956, by U.S. Time...	40	50	75	250

Left: Tom Corbett, Space Cadet, New Haven, ca. 1936. Center: Tom Mix, Ingersoll, ca. 1936. Right: Woody Woodpecker, U.S. Time, ca. 1948.

Moon Mullins, by Ingersol, ca. 1928

Rudy Nebb, by Ingersoll, ca. 1928

ABOVE:Gene Audtry, by New Haven with action six gun
LEFT: Shirley Temple, by Westclox, ca. 1958

CUB SCOUT by Timex   BOY SCOUT by New Haven   DAVY CROCKETT, by Ingraham

MOVEMENTS STYLES AND TYPES

INGERSOLL – US TIME

INGERSOLL

INGRAHAM

INGRAHAM MODEL # L

NEW HAVEN

WESTCLOX

TIMEX

TIMEX#21

NEW HAVEN (SWISS)

EARLY ANTIQUE WATCHES

The early antique watches looked quite similar to small table clocks. These drum-shaped watches were about two inches in diameter and usually over one-half inch thick. The drum-shaped watch lost popularity in the late 1500s. The earliest portable timepieces did not carry the maker's name, but initials were common. The cases generally had a hinged lid which covered the dial. This lid was pierced with small holes to enable ready identification of the position of the hour hand. They also usually contained a bell. The dial often had the numbers "I" to "XII" engraved in Roman numerals and the numbers "13" to "24" in Arabic numbers with the "2" engraved in the form of a "Z." Even the earliest of timepieces incorporated striking. The oldest known watch with a date engraved on the case was made in 1548. A drum-shaped watch with the initials "C. W.," it was most likely produced by Casper Werner, a protege of Henlein.

Early pocket watches were designed to run from 12 to 16 hours. The pinions usually bore five leaves, the great wheel 55 teeth, the second wheel 45 teeth, the third wheel 40 teeth, and the escape wheel 15 teeth. With one less pinion and wheel the escape wheel ran reverse to a standard four-wheel watch. During the 1500s, 1600s, and much of the 1700s, it was stylish to decorate not only the case and balance cock but all parts including the clicks, barrel, studs, springs, pillars, hands, and stackfreed. The plates themselves were decorated with pierced and engraved metal scrolls, and in some instances the maker's name was engraved in a style to correspond with the general decoration of the movement. During these periods the most celebrated artists, designers, and engravers were employed. The early watches were decorated by famous artists such as Jean Vauquier 1670, Daniel Marot 1700, Gillis l'Egare 1650, Michel Labon 1630, Pierre Bourdon 1750, and D. Cochin 1750. Most of the artists were employed to design and execute pierced and repouse cases.

THE MID-1700s

In the mid-1700s relatively minor changes are noticed. Decoration became less distinctive and less artistic. The newer escapements resulted in better timekeeping, and a smaller balance cock was used. The table and foot became smaller. The foot grew more narrow, and as the century and the development of the watch advanced, the decoration on the balance cock became smaller and less elaborate. About 1720 the foot was becoming solid and flat. No longer was it hand pierced; however, some of the pierced ones were produced until about 1770. Thousands of these beautiful hand pierced watch cocks have been made into necklaces and brooches or framed. Sadly, many of the old movements were destroyed in a mad haste to cater to the buyers' fancy.

THE 1800s

As the 1800s approached the balance cocks became less artistic as the decoration on movements gradually diminished. Breguet and Berthoud spent very little time on the beauty or artistic design on their balance cocks or pillars. But the cases were often magnificient in design and beauty, made with enamels in many colors and laden with precious stones. During this period the movements were plain and possessed very little artistic character.

As early as 1820 three-quarter and one-half plate designs were be ing used with the balance cock lowered to the same level as the other wheels. The result was a slimmer watch.

Exposed illustration of an early watch movement, c. 1800-1850. Note that movement is key wind and set from the dial side. The illustrated example is a chain driven fusee with a verge escapement: a-Main spring barrel and chain. b-Fusee. c -Verge escapement. d-Balance wheel. e-Dial. f -Hour hand. g-Minute hand. h-Winding arbor. i-Setting arbor.

CLUES TO DATING YOUR WATCH

To establish the age of a watch there are many points to be considered. The dial, hands, pillars, balance cock and pendant, for example, contain important clues in determining the age of your watch. However, no one part alone should be considered sufficient evidence to draw a definite conclusion as to age. The watch as a whole must be considered. For example, an English-made silver-cased watch will have a hallmark inside the case. It is quite simple to refer to the London Hallmark Table for hallmarks after 1697. But this hallmark will reveal the age of the case only. This does not fix the age of the movement. Many movements are housed in cases made years before or after the movement was produced. An informed collector will note that a watch with an enamel dial, for instance, could not have been made before 1635. A pair of cases indicates it could not have been made prior to 1640. The minute hand was introduced in 1687. The presence of jewels would indicate it was made after 1700. A dust cap first appeared in 1774. Keyless winding came into being after 1820 but did not gain widespread popularity until after 1860. All of these clues and more must be considered before accurately assessing the age of a watch.

Example of an early pocket watch with a stackfreed design to equalize power much as a fusee does. Note dumbbell shaped foliot which served as a balance for verge escapement, and the tear shaped cam which is part of the stackfreed.

PILLARS

Pillars are of interest and should be considered as one of the elements in determining age. Through the years small watches used round pillars, and the larger watches generally used a square type engraved pillar.

(*Illus.* 1) This pillar is one of the earliest types and used in the 1800s as well. This particular pillar came from a watch which dates about 1550. It is known that this type pillar was used in 1675 by Gaspard Girod of France and also in 1835 by James Taylor of England.

(*Illus*. 2) This style pillar is called the tulip pattern. Some watchmakers preferred to omit the vertical divisions. This style was popular between 1660 and 1750 but may be found on later watches. It was common practice to use ornamentation on the tulip pillar.

(*Illus*. 3) The ornament shown was used by Daniel Quare of London from 1665 to 1725 and by the celebrated Tompion, as well as many others.

(*Illus*. 4) This type pillar is referred to as the Egyptian and dates from 1630 to the 1800s. The squared Egyptian pattern was introduced about 1630 and some may be found with a wider division with a head or bust inserted. This style was used by D. Bouquet of London about 1640 and by many other watchmakers.

Illus. 1   Illus. 2   Illus. 3   Illus. 4

(*Illus*. 5) This pillar was used by Thomas Earnshaw of London about 1780. The plain style was prominent for close to two hundred years 1650 to 1825.

Illus. 5   Illus. 6   Illus. 7   Illus. 8

(Illus. 6) This style was popular and was used by many craftsmen. Nathaniel Barrow of London put this in his watches about 1680.

(Illus. 7) This pillar may be seen in watches made by Pierre Combet of Lyons, France, about 1720. It was also used by many others.

(Illus. 8) This style pillar and the ornament were used by John Ellicott of England and other watchmakers from 1730 to 1770.

These illustrations represent just a few of the basic pillars that were used. Each watchmaker would design and change details to create his own individual identity. This sometimes makes it more difficult to readily determine the age of watches.

BALANCE COCKS OR BRIDGES

The first balance cocks or bridges used to support the balance staff were a plain "S" shape. The cocks used on the old three-wheel watches were very elaborate; hand-pierced and engraved. At first no screws were used to hold the cock in place. It is noteworthy that on the three wheel watch the regulator was a ratchet and click and was used on these earlier movements to adjust the mainspring. About 1635 the balance cock was screwed to the plate and pinned on its underside, which helped steady the balance. The first cock illustrated is a beautifully decorated example made by Josias Jeubi of Paris about 1580. Note that it is pinned to a stud which passes through a square cut in the foot of the cock. Next is a balance cock made by Bouquet of London about 1640. The third balance cock is one made by Jean Rousseau and dates around 1650. The fourth one dates around 1655.

The next two bridges are supported on both sides of the balance cock by means of screws or pins. They are strikingly different and usually cover much of the plate of the movement. This style of balance cock was used around 1675 and was still seen as late as 1765.

The beautiful balance cock below at left, with the ornate foot, dates about 1660. The next illustrated balance cock with the heavy ornamentation was used from about 1700 to 1720 or longer. By 1720 a face was added to the design. The face shows up where the table terminates on most balance cocks.

1680–1700 NOTE wavy edge to the foot and two ears.

1750–1780 NOTE Helmet shape.

1780–1850

1810–1830

1850 NOTE under-sprung

Cylinder escapement

Invented in 1695

Virgule Escapement

Rack and lever escapement

Invented in 1722

Duplex escapement

Invented in 1750

EARLY EUROPEAN WATCHMAKERS

Note abbreviations used:
enamel = enamel case painter or artist
pat. = patent or inventor
ca. = circa or about
since = founded to present

Achard, J. Francois (Geneva, ca. 1750)
Addison, J. (London, 1760-1780)
Adamson, Gustave (Paris, 1775-1790)
Alfred, W. Humphreys (London, ca. 1905)
Alibut (Paris, ca. 1750s)
Allier, Bachelard & Teron Co. (French, ca. 1830)
Amabric, Abraham (Geneva, ca. 1750-1800)
Amabric, Freres (Geneva, ca. 1760-1795)
Amon (Paris, 1913)
Andre, Jean (enamel) (Geneva, 1660-1705)
Anthony, Willams (London, 1785-1840)
Antram, J. (London, ca. 1700-1730)
Appleby, Edward (London, ca. 1675)
Appleby, Joshua (London, 1720-1745)
Ardin, Coppet (ca. 1710)
Arland, Benjamin (London, c. 1680)

Arlaud, Louis (Geneva, ca. 1750)
Arnold & Frodsham, Charles (London, 1845)
Arnold, Henery (London, ca. 1770-1780)
Arnold, John (London, ca. 1760-1790)
Arnold, John Roger (London, ca. 1800-1830)
Arnold, Nicolas (ca. 1850)
Arnold & Lewis, Lote Simmons (Manchester, ca. 1860)
Arnold & Son (London, ca. 1787-1799)
Assman, Julius (Glasshutte, 1850-1885)
Auber, Daniel (London, ca. 1750)
Aubert, D. F. (Geneva, ca. 1825)
Aubert, Ferdinand (1810-1835)
Aubert & Co. (Geneva, ca. 1850)
Aubry, Irenee (Geneva, 1885-1910)
Audebert (Paris, 1810-1820)

Audemars, Freres (Swiss, 1810 until company splits in 1885)
Audemars, Louis-Benjamin (Swiss, 1811-1867)
Aureole (Swiss, 1921)
Auricoste, Jules (Paris, ca. 1910)
Bachhofen, Felix (Swiss, 1675-1690)
Badollet, Jean-Jacques (Geneva, 1779-1891)
Baillon, Jean-Hilaire (Paris, ca. 1727)
Baird, Wm. (London, 1815-1825)
Balsiger & Fils (ca. 1825)
Barberet, J. (Paris, ca. 1600)
Barbezat, Bole (Swiss, 1870)
Baronneau, Jean-Louis (France, 1675-1700)
Barraud & Lunds (1812-1840)
Barraud, Paul-Philip (London, 1752-1820)
Barrow, Edward (London, ca. 1650-1710)
Barrow, Nathaniel (London, 1653-1689)
Barry, M. (French, ca. 1620)
Bartholony, Abraham (Paris, 1750-1752)
Barton, James (London, 1760-1780)
Barwise (London, 1800)
Bassereau, Jean-Hilaire (Paris, ca. 1800-1810)
Bautte, Jean-Francois (Geneva, 1800-1835)
Bautte & Moynier (Geneva, ca. 1825)
Beaumarchais, Caron (Paris, 1750-1795)
Beauvais, Simon (London, ca. 1690)
Beckman, Daniel (London, 1670-1685)
Beckner, Abraham (London, ca. 1640)
Beliard, Dominique (Paris, ca. 1750)
Bell, Benj. (London, 1650-1668)
Bennett, John (London, 1850-1895)
Benson, J. W. (London, 1825-1890)
Benson, J. W. (London, 1850-1900)
Bergstein, L. (London, ca. 1840)
Bernard, Nicholas (Paris, 1650-1690)
Bernoulli, Daniel (Paris, 1720-1780)
Berrollas, J. A. (Denmark, 1800-1830)
Berthound, Augusta-Louis (Paris, ca. 1875)
Berthound, Ferdinand (Paris, 1750-1805)
Beihler & Hartmann (Geneva, ca. 1875)
Blanc, Henri (Geneva, ends 1964)
Blanc, Jules (Geneva, 1929-1940)
Blanc & Fils (Geneva, 1770-1790)
Bock, Johann (German, 1700-1750)
Bockel (London, ca. 1650)
Bolslandon, Metz (ca. 1780)
Bolviller, Moise (Paris, 1840-1870)
Bommelt, Leonhart (Nuremburg, Ger., ca. 1690)
Bonney (London, ca. 1790)
Bonniksen, Bahne (England, 1890-1930)
Booth, Edward (name change to Barlow)
Bordier, Denis (France, ca. 1575)
Bordier, Freres (Geneva, 1787-1810)
Bordier, Jacques (enamel) (ca. 1670)
Bornand, A. (Geneva, 1895-1915)
Boubon (Paris, 1810-1820)
Bouquet, David (London, ca. 1630-1650)
Bovet, Edouard (Swiss, 1820-1918)
Bovier, G. (enamel painter) (Paris, c. 1750)
Brandt, Iacob (Swiss, ca. 1700)
Brandt, Robert & Co. (Geneva, ca. 1820)
Breitling, "Leon" (Swiss, since 1884)
Brockbank (London, 1776-present)
Brocke (London, ca. 1640)
Brodon, Nicolas (Paris, 1674-1682)

Bronikoff, a Wjatka (Russia, 1850 "watches of wood")
Bruguier, Charles A. (Geneva, 1800-1860)
Bull, Rainulph (one of the first British) (1590-1617)
Burgis, Eduardus (London, 1680-1710)
Burgis, G. (London, 1720-1740)
Burnet, Thomas (London, ca. 1800)
Busch, Abraham (Hamburg, Ger., ca. 1680)
Buz, Johannes (Augsburg, Bavaria, ca. 1625)
Cabrier, Charles (London, ca. 1690-1720)
Capt, Henry Daniel (Geneva, 1802-1880)
Caron, Augustus (Paris, ca. 1750-1760)
Caron, Francois-Modeste (Paris, 1770-1788)
Caron, Pierre (Paris, ca. 1700)
Caron, Pierre Augustin (Paris, 1750-1795) (pat. virgule escapement)
Carpenter, William (London, 1750-1800)
Carte, John (England, 1680-1700)
Champod, P. Amedee (enamel) (Geneva, 1850-1910)
Chapponier, Jean (Geneva, 1780-1800)
Charman (London, 1780-1800)
Charrot (Paris, 1775-1810)
Chartiere (enamel) (France, ca. 1635)
Chaunes (Paris, ca. 1580-1600)
Chavanne & Pompejo (Vienna, 1785-1800)
Cheneviere, Louis (Geneva, 1710-1740)
Cheneviere, Urbain (Geneva, 1730-1760)
Cheriot or Cherioz, Daniel (ca. 1750-1790)
Cheuillard (Blois, France, ca. 1600)
Chevalier & Co. (Geneva, 1795-1810)
Cisin, Charles (Swiss, 1580-1610)
Clark, Geo. (London, 1750-1785)
Clerc (Swiss, ca. 1875)
Clouzier, Jacques (Paris, 1690-1750)
Cochin, D. (Paris, ca. 1800)
Cocque, Geo. (ca. 1610)
Cogniat (Paris, ca. 1675)
Coladon, Louis (Geneva, 1780-1850)
Cole, James Ferguson (London, 1820-1875)
Cole, Thomas (London, 1820-1864)
Collins, Clement (London, ca. 1705)
Collins, John (London, ca. 1720)
Collins, R. (London, ca. 1815)
Colondre & Schnee (ca. 1875)
Combet, Pierre (Lyons, France, ca. 1610-1625)
Cotton, John (London, ca. 1695-1715)
Coulin, Jaques & Bry, Amy (Paris & Geneva, 1780-1790)
Court, Jean-Pierre (ca. 1790-1810)
Courvosier, Freres (Swiss, 1810-1852)
Courvoisier & Houriet (Geneva, ca. 1790)
Cox, James (London, 1760-1785)
Csacher, C. (Prague, Aus., ca. 1725)
Cumming, Alexander (London, 1750-1800)
Cummins, T. (London, 1820)
Cuper, Barthelemy (French, 1615-1635)
Curtis, John (London, ca. 1720)
Cusin, Charles (Geneva, ca. 1587)
Darling, William (British, ca. 1825)
De Baghyn, Adriaan (Amsterdam, ca. 1750)
Debaufre, Peter (French, 1690-1720) (Debaufre escapement)
Debaufre, Pierre (Paris, London, Geneva, 1675-1722)
De Bry, Theodore (German, 1585-1620)

De Charmes, Simon (London, France, 1690-1730)
De Choudens (Swiss & French, 1760-1790)
Decombaz, Gedeon (Geneva, 1780-1820)
Degeilh & Co. (ca. 1880-1900)
De Heca, Michel (Paris, ca. 1685)
De L Garde, Abraham (Paris, "Blois," ca. 1590)
Delynne, F. L. (Paris, ca. 1775)
Dent, Edward John (London, 1815-1850)
Derham, William (English, ca. 1677-1730)
Deroch, F. (Swiss, 1730-1770)
Des Arts & Co. (Geneva, 1790-1810)
Desquivillons & DeChoudens (Paris, ca. 1785)
Destouches, Jean-Francois-Albert (Holland, ca. 1760)
Devis, John (London, 1770-1785)
Dimier & Co. (Geneva, 1820-1925)
Dinglinger (enamel) (Dresden, Ger., ca. 1675)
Ditisheim & Co. "Maurice" (Swiss, 1894)
Ditisheim, Paul (Swiss, 1892)
Dobson, A. (London, 1660-1680)
Droz, Daniel (Chaux-de-Fonds, Sw., ca. 1760)
Droz, Henri (Chaux-de-Fonds, Sw., ca. 1775)
Droz, Pierre Jacquet (Chaux-de-Fonds, Sw., 1750-1775)
Droz, Pierre (Swiss, 1740-1770)
Droz & Co. (Swiss, ca. 1825)
Dubie (enamel) (Paris, ca. 1635)
Dubois & Fils (Paris, ca. 1810)
Duchene & Co. "Louis" (Geneva, 1790-1820)
Ducommun, Charles (Geneva, ca. 1750)
Duduict, Jacques (Blois, France, ca. 1600)
Dufalga, Philippe (Geneva, 1730-1790)
Dufalga, P. F. (Geneva, ca. 1750)
Dufour, Foll & Co. (Geneva, 1800-1830)
Dufour, J. E. & Co. (ca. 1890)
Dufour & Ceret (Ferney, Fr., ca. 1770-1785)
Dufour & Zentler (ca. 1870)
Duhamel, Pierre (Paris, ca. 1680)
Dupin, Paul (London, 1730-1765)
Dupont (Geneva, ca. 1810-1830)
Dupont, Jean (enamel) (Geneva, 1800-1860)
Duru (Paris, ca. 1650)
Dutertre, Baptiste (ca. 1730) (pat. duplex escapement)
Dutton, William (London, 1760-1840)
Earnshaw, Thomas (London, 1760-1842)
East, Edward (London, 1630-1670)
Edmonds, James (London to U.S.A., 1720-1766)
Edward, George & Son (London, ca. 1875)
Ekegren, Henri-Robert (Geneva, 1860)
Ellicott, John (London, 1728-1810)
Emery, Josiah (Geneva, 1750-1800)
Esquivillon & De Choudens (Paris, 1710-1780)
Ester, Jean Henry (Geneva, 1610-1665)
Etherlington, George (London, 1680-1730)
Etienne Guyot & Co. (Geneva, ca. 1880)
Facio De Duillier, Nicholas (British, 1665-1710)
Fallery, Jacques (Geneva, ca. 1760)
Farmer, G. W. (wooden watches) (Germany, ca. 1650-1675)
Fatio, Alfred (Geneva, 1920-1940)
Fatton, Frederick Louis (London, ca. 1822)
Favre Marius & Fils (Geneva, 1893)
Fenie, M. (ca. 1635)
Ferrero, J. (ca. 1854-1900)
Fiacre, Clement (Paris, ca. 1700)

Fitter, Joseph (London, ca. 1660)
Fontac (London, ca. 1775)
Forfaict, Nicolas (Paris, 1573-1619)
Fowles, Allen (Kilmarnock, Scot., ca. 1770)
French (London, 1810-1840)
Fureur (Swiss, 1910)
Gallopin "Henri Capt" (Geneva, 1875)
Gamod, G. (Paris, ca. 1640)
Garnier, Paul (Paris, 1825) (pat. Garnier escapement)
Garrault, Jacobus (Geneva, ca. 1650)
Garty & Constable (London, ca. 1750)
Gaudron, Antoine (Paris, 1675-1707)
Gaudron, Pierre (Paris, 1695-1740)
Geissheim, Smod (Augsburg, Ger., ca. 1625)
Gent, James & Son (London, 1875-1910)
Gerbeau, V. (Paris, 1900-1930)
Gerrard (British, 1790-1820)
Gibs, William (Rotterdam, ca. 1720)
Gibson & Co., Ltd. (Ireland, ca. 1875-1920)
Gidon (Paris, ca. 1700)
Gillespy, Charles (Ireland, 1774-1171)
Girard, Perregaux (Swiss, 1856)
Girard, Theodore (Paris, 1623-1670)
Girardier, Charles (Geneva, 1780-1815)
Girod, B. (Paris, ca. 1810)
Girod, Gaspard (Paris, ca. 1670-1690)
Godod, F. (Paris, ca. 1790)
Godon, F. L. (Paris, ca. 1787)
Golay, A. Leresche & Fils (Geneva, 1844-1857)
Golay, H. (Swiss, 1969-1911)
Golay, Stahl & Fils (1878-1914)
Gollons (Paris, ca. 1663)
Gounouilhou, P. S. (Geneva, 1815-1840)
Gout, Ralph (London, 1790-1830)
Graham, George (London, 1715-1750)
Grandjean, Henri (Swiss, 1825-1880)
Grandjean, L. C. (Swiss, 1890-1920)
Grant, John & Son (English, 1780-1867)
Grantham, William (London, ca. 1860)
Grasset, Isaac (Geneva, ca. 1896)
Gray & Constable (London, ca. 1750)
Grazioza (Swiss, ca. 1901)
Grebauval, Hierosme (ca. 1575)
Gregory, Jermie (London, ca. 1652-1680)
Gregson, Jean P. (Paris, 1770-1790)
Griblin, Nicolas (French, 1650-1716)
Griessenback, Johann G. (Bavaria, ca. 1660)
Grignion "family" (London, 1690-1825)
Grignion, Daniel & Thomas (London, 1780-1790)
Grosclaude, Ch. & Co. (Swiss, ca. 1865)
Grosjean, Henry (French, ca. 1865)
Gruber, Hans (Nurnberg, Ger., ca. 1520-1560)
Gruber, Michel (Nurnberg, Ger., ca. 1605)
Gruet (Geneva, Sw., ca. 1664)
Gubelin, E. (Lucern, Switzerland, ca. 1832)
Guillaume, Ch. (pat. Invar, Elinvar)
Haas Nevevx & Co. (founder B. J. Haas) (Geneva, 1828-1925)
Hagen, Johan (German, ca. 1750)
Haley, Charles (London, 1781-1825)
Hallewey (London, 1695-1720)
Hamilton & Co. (London, 1865-1920)
Harper, Henry (London, ca. 1665-1700)
Harrison, John (England, 1710-1775) (pat. comp. balance)
Hasluck Brothers (London, ca. 1695)

Hautefeuille, Jean (Paris, 1670-1722)
Hautefeuille, John (Paris, 1660-1700)
Hawley, John (London, ca. 1850)
Hebert, Juliette (enamel) (Geneva, ca. 1890)
Helbros (Geneva, since 1918)
Hele or Henlein, Peter (Nurnberg, 1510-1540)
Heliger, J. (Zug, Sw., ca. 1575)
Henner, Johann (Wurtzburg, Ger., ca. 1730)
Henry, F. S. (Swiss, ca. 1850)
Hentschel, J. J. (French, ca. 1750)
Hess, L. (Zurich, Sw., ca. 1780)
Hessichti, Dionistus (ca. 1630)
Higgs & Evans (London, 1775-1825)
Hill, Ben. (London, 1640-1670)
Hoguet, Francois (Paris, ca. 1750)
Hooke, Robert (England, 1650-1700)
Hoseman, Stephen (London, ca. 1710-1740)
Houghton, James (England, ca. 1800-1820)
Houghton, Thomas (Chorley, England,
    ca. 1820-1840)
Houriet, Jacques Frederic (Paris 1810-1825)
Huaud, Freres (enamel) (Geneva, ca. 1685)
Huber, Peter (German, ca. 1875)
Hubert, David (London, 1714-1747)
Hubert, Oliver (London, ca. 1740)
Hubert, Etienne (French, 1650-1690)
Hues, Peter (Augsburg, Ger., ca. 1600)
Huguenin, David L. (Swiss, 1780-1835)
Humbert-Droz, David (Swiss, ca. 1790)
Huygens, Christian (Paris, 1657-1680)
Iaquier or Jacquier, Francois (Geneva,
    1690-1720)
Ilbery, William (London, 1800-1835)
Ingold, Pierre-Frederic (Swiss, Paris, London,
    1810-1870)
Invicta ("R. Picard") (Swiss, 1896)
Jaccard, E. H. & Co. (Swiss, ca. 1850)
Jacot, Charles-Edouard (Swiss, 1830-1860)
    (pat. Chinese duplex)
Jaeger, Edmond (Paris, 1875-1920)
Jaeger Le Coultre & Co. (Swiss, since 1833)
Jamison, Geo. (London, 1786-1810)
Janvier, Antide (Paris, 1771-1834)
Japy, Frederic & Sons "family" (French, Swiss,
    ca. 1776)
Jaquet, Pierre (Swiss, 1750-1790)
Jean Richard, Daniel (Swiss, 1685-1740)
Jean Richard, Edouard (Swiss, 1900-1930)
Jeannot, Paul (ca. 1890)
Jefferys & Gildert (London, 1790)
Jesop, Josias (London, 1780-1794)
Jeubi, Josias (Paris, ca. 1575)
Joly, Jacques (Paris, ca. 1625)
Jovat (London, ca. 1690)
Jones, Henry (London, ca. 1665-1690)
Jump, Joseph (English, ca. 1827-1850)
Junod, Freres (Geneva, ca. 1850)
Jurgensen, Urban & Jules (Copenhagen, Swiss,
    1745-1912)
Just & Son (London, 1790-1825)
Juvet, Edouard (Swiss, 1844-1880)
Juvet, Leo (Swiss, 1860-1890)
Keates, William (London, ca. 1780)
Keely, W. (London, ca. 1790)
Kendall, Larcum (London, ca. 1786)
Kendall, James (London, 1740-1780)
Kessels, H. J. (Holland, 1800-1845)
Kirkton, R. (London, ca. 1790)
Klein, Johann Heinr (Copenhagen, Den., ca.

1710)
Klentschi, C. F. (Swiss, 1790-1840)
Koehn, Edward (Geneva, 1860-1908)
Kreizer, Conard (German, 1595-1658)
Kuhn, Jan Hendrik (Amsterdam, 1775-1800)
Kullberg, Victor (Copenhagen to London,
    1850-1890)
Lamy, Michel (Paris, 1767-1800)
Lang & Padoux (ca. 1860)
Larcay (Paris, ca. 1725)
Lardy, Francois (Geneva, ca. 1825)
Larpent, Isacc & Jurgensen (Copenhagen,
    1748-1811)
Laurier, Francois (Paris, 1654-1675)
Le Baufre (Paris, ca. 1650)
Lebet (Geneva, ca. 1850)
Lebet & Fils (Swiss, 1830-1892)
Le Coultre, Ami (Geneva, ca. 1887)
Le Coultre, Eugene (Geneva, ca. 1850)
Leekey, C. (London, ca. 1750)
Leeky, Gabriel (London, ca. 1775-1820)
Lepaute, Jean-Andre (Paris, 1750-1774)
Lepine, Jean-Antoine (Paris, 1744-1814)
Le Puisne, Huand (enamel) (Blois, Fr., ca. 1635)
Leroux, John (England, 1758-1805)
Le Roy & Co. (Paris, ca. 1853)
Le Roy, Charles (Paris, 1733-1770)
Le Roy, Julien (Paris, 1705-1750)
Le Roy, Pierre (French, 1710-1780)
    (improved duplex escapement)
Levy, Hermanos (Hong Kong, "Swiss,"
    1880-1890)
L'Hardy, Francois (Geneva, 1790-1825)
Lichtenauer (Wurzberg, Ger., ca. 1725)
Lindesay, G. (London, ca. 1740-1770)
Lindgren, Erik (England, 1735-1775) (pat. rack
    lever)
Litherland, Peter (English, 1780-1876)
Loehr, (Von) (Swiss, ca. 1880)
Long & Drew (enamel) (London, ca. 1790-1810)
Losada, Jose R. (London, 1835-1890)
Lowndes, Jonathan (London, ca. 1680-1700)
MacCabe, James (London, 1778-1830)
Maillardet & Co. (Swiss, ca. 1800)
Mairet, Sylvain (Swiss, 1825-1885) (London,
    1830-1840)
Malignon, A. (Geneva, ca. 1835)
Marchand, Abraham (Geneva, 1690-1725)
Margetts, George (London, 1780-1800)
Markwick Markham, "Perigal" "Recordon"
    (London, 1780-1825)
Marshall, John (London, ca. 1690)
Martin (Paris, ca. 1780)
Martin, Thomas (London, ca. 1870)
Martineau, Joseph (London, 1765-1790)
Martinot, "family" (Paris, 1570-1770)
Martinot, James (London, ca. 1780)
Mascarone, Gio Batt (London, ca. 1635)
Massey, Edward (England, 1800-1850)
Massey, Henry (London, 1692-1745)
E. Mathey-Tissot & Co. (Swiss, 1886-1896)
Matile, Henry (Swiss, ca. 1825)
Maurer, Johann (Fiessna, Ger., ca. 1640-1650)
May, George (English, 1750-1770)
Mayr, Johann Peter (Augsburg, Ger., ca. 1770)
McCabe, James (London, 1780-1710)
McDowall, Charles (London, ca. 1820-1860)
Meak, John (London, ca. 1825)

Mecke, Daniel (ca. 1760)
Melly, Freres (Geneva, Paris, 1791-1844)
Mercier, A. D. (Swiss, 1790-1820)
Mercier, Francois David (Paris, ca. 1700)
Meuron & Co. (Swiss, ca. 1784)
Meylan, C. H. "Meylan W. Co." (Swiss, ca. 1880)
Michel, Jean-Robert (Paris, ca. 1750)
Miller, Joseph (London, ca. 1728)
Milleret & Tissot (ca. 1835)
Miroir (London, ca. 1700-1725)
Mistral (Swiss, ca. 1902)
Mobilis (Swiss, ca. 1910)
Modernista (Swiss, ca. 1903)
Moillet, Jean-Jacques (Paris, 1776-1789)
Molina, Antonio (Madrid, Spain, ca. 1800)
Molinie (Swiss, ca. 1840)
Molyneux, Robert (London, ca. 1825-1850)
Montandon, Chs. Ad. (Swiss, 1800-1830)
Morand, Pierre (Paris, ca. 1790)
Moricand & Co. (Swiss, ca. 1780)
Moricand & Desgranges (Geneva, 1828-1835)
Moricand, Christ (Geneva, 1745-1790)
Morin, Pierre (English, French & Dutch style, ca. 1700)
Morliere (enamel) (Blois, Fr., ca. 1636-1650)
Moser, George Michael (London, ca. 1716-1730)
Motel, Jean Francois (French, 1800-1850)
Moulineux, Robert (London, 1800-1840)
Moulinier, Aine & Co. (Swiss, 1828-1851)
Moulinier, Freres & Co. (Swiss, ca. 1822)
Mudge, Thomas (London, 1740-1790)
Mulsund (enamel) (Paris, ca. 1700)
Munoz, Blas (Madrid, Spain, ca. 1806-1823)
Mussard, Jean (Geneva, 1699-1727)
Musy Padre & Figlo (Paris, 1710-1760)
Myrmecide (Paris, ca. 1525)
Nardin, Ulysse (Swiss, ca. 1846)
Nelson, W. (London, 1777-1818)
Nocturne (ca. 1920)
Noir, Jean-Baptiste (Paris, 1680-1710)
Norris, J. (Dutch, 1680-1700)
Nouwen, Michael (1st English, 1580-1600)
Noyean (ca. 1850)
Oldnburg, Johan (German, ca. 1648)
Oudin, Charles (Paris, 1807-1900)
Owen, John (English, ca. 1790)
Palmer, Samuel (London, ca. 1790-1810)
Panier, Iosue "Josue" (Paris, ca. 1790)
Papillon (ca. 1690)
Papillon, Francesco (Florence, ca. 1705)
Parr, Thomas (London, ca. 1735-1775)
Payne, H. & John (London, ca. 1735-1775)
Pellaton, Albert (Swiss, ca. 1873)
Pellaton, James (Swiss, 1903) (Tourbillon)
Pendleton, Richard (London, 1780-1805)
Pennington, Robert (English, 1780-1816)
Perigal, Francis (English, 1770-1790)
Pernetti, F. (Swiss, ca. 1850)
Perrelet, Abram (Swiss, 1780) (self wind)
Perret, Edouard (Swiss, 1850)
Perrin, Freres (Swiss, 1810)
Phillips, Edouard (Paris, ca. 1860)
Phleisot (Dijon, Fr., ca. 1700)
Piaget, George (Swiss, ca. 1881)
Picard, James (Geneva, ca. 1850)
Piguet & Capt (Geneva, 1802-1811)

Piguet & Meylan (Geneva, 1811-1828)
Piguet, Victorin-Emile (Geneva, 1870-1935)
Plairas, Solomon (Blois, Fr., ca. 1640)
Plumbe, David (ca. 1730)
Poitevin, B. (Paris, 1850-1935)
Poncet, J. F. (Dresden, 1750)
Poncet, Jean-Francois (Swiss, 1740-1800)
Potter, Harry (London, 1760-1800)
Pouzait, Jean-Moise (Geneva, 1780-1800)
Poy, Gottfrey (London, ca. 1725-1730)
Prest, Thomas (English, 1820-1855)
Prevost, Freres (ca. 1820)
Prior, Edward (London, 1825-1865)
Prior, George (London, 1800-1830)
Pyke, John (English, 1750-1780)
Quare, Daniel (London, 1700-1724)
Quarella, Antonio (ca. 1790)
Racine, Cesar (Swiss, ca. 1902)
Racine, Charles Frederic (Chaux-de-Fonds, Sw., ca. 1810-1832)
Raillard, Claude (Paris, 1662-1675)
Raiss (1890-1910) (enamel)
Rait, D. C. (German, ca. 1866)
Ramsay, David (Scotland, France, London, 1590-1654)
Ramuz, Humbert U. & Co. (Swiss, ca. 1882)
Ratel, Henri (Paris, 1850-1900)
Recordon, Louis (London, 1778-1824)
Redier, Antoine (Paris, 1835-1883)
Renierhes (London, ca. 1850)
Rey, Jn. Ante, & Fils (Paris, 1790-1810)
Reynaud, P. & Co. (1860)
Rich, John (Geneva, London, 1795-1825)
Richard, Daniel Jean (1685-1740)
Richter, Jean Louis (enamel) (Geneva, 1786-1840)
Rigaud, Pierre (Geneva, 1750-1800)
Rigot, Francois (Geneva, ca. 1825)
Robert & Courvoisier & Co. (Paris, 1781-1832)
Robin, Robert (Paris, 1765-1805)
Robinet, Charles (Paris, ca. 1640)
Robinson, Olivier & Fredmahn (Naples, 1727-1790)
Rogers, Isaac (London, 1770-1810)
Romilly, Sieur (Geneva, ca. 1750-1775)
Rooker, Richard (London, 1790-1810)
Rose, Joseph (London, 1752-1795)
Rosier, John (Geneva, ca. 1750)
Roskell, Robert (London, 1798-1830) (rack-lever)
Roskopf, G. (German to Swiss, 1835-1885)
Rosselet, Louis (Geneva, 1855-1900) (enamel)
Rousseau, Jean (Paris, 1580-1642)
Roux, Bordier & Co. (Geneva, ca. 1795)
Ruegger, Jacques (ca. 1800-1840)
Ruel, Samuel (Rotterdam, ca. 1750)
Rugendas, Nicholas (Augsburg, Ger., ca. 1700-1750)
Rundell & Bridge (London, ca. 1772-1825)
Sailler, Johann (Vienna, Aus., ca. 1575)
Sanchez, Cayetano (Madrid, Spain, c. 1790-1800)
Sandoz, Henri F. (Tavannes W. Co.) (ca. 1840)
Savage, George (London, 1808-1855) (Inv. pin lever)
Savage, William (London 1800-1850)
Savile, John (London, ca. 1656-1679)
Schatck, Johann Engel (Prague, ca. 1650)

Schultz, Michael (ca. 1600-1650)
Schuster, Caspar (Nunburg, ca. 1570)
Sermand, J. (Geneva, ca. 1640)
Sherman De Neilly (Belfort, ca. 1910)
Sherwood, J. (London, ca. 1750-1775)
Solson (London, 1750)
Soret (Geneva, ca. 1810)
Soret, Frederic II (1735-1806)
Soret, Isaac & Co. (1690-1760)
Spencer & Perkins (London, 1790-1808)
Stadlin, Francois (Swiss, 1680-1735)
Staples, James (1755-1795)
Stuffer, M. T. (Swiss, 1830-1855)
Stauffer "Stauffer Son & Co." (London, 1880)
Strasser & Rohde (Glashutte, 1875)
Sudek, J. (ca. 1850)
Sully, Henry (French, London, 1700-1725)
Swift, Thomas (London, ca. 1825-1865)
Tavan, Antoine (Geneva, 1775-1830)
Tavernier, Jean (Paris, 1744-1795)
Tempor Watch Co. (1930) (Masonic watch)
Terond, Allier & Bachelard (ca. 1805-1830)
Terrot & Fazy (ca. 1767-1775)
Terrot, Philippe (Geneva, ca. 1732)
Terroux (ca. 1776)
Theed & Pikett (ca. 1750)
Thierry, J. (London, ca. 1760)
Thierry, Niel (ca. 1810)
Thiout, Antoine (Paris, 1724-1760)
Thorne, Robert (London, 1850)
Thoroton, James (London, 1860)
Thuret, Jacques (Paris, ca. 1695)
Thompion, Thomas (English, 1671-1713)
Timing & Repeating W. Co. (Geneva, 1900)
Tonkin, Tho. (London, ca. 1760)
Toutaia, Henri (French, 1650) (enamel)
Toutin, Jean (enamel) (Blois, Fr., ca. 1630)
Treffler, Sebastain (ca. 1750)
Tregent, J. (English, 1765-1800)
Truitte, Louis & Mourier (Geneva, ca. 1780)
Tyrer, Thomas (London, ca. 1782)

Uhren Fabrik Union (Glashutte, 1893-1970)
Ullman, J. & Co. (Swiss, 1893)
Ulrich, Johann (London, 1820-1870)
Upjohn, W. J. (London, 1815-1824)
Vacheron, Abraham Girod (German, 1760-1843)
Valere (Paris, 1860)
Vallier, Jean (Lyons, Fr., ca. 1630)
Valove, James (London, ca. 1740)
Vanbroff, James (Germany, ca. 1600)
Van Ceule, J. (ca. 1799-1725)
Vandersteen (ca. 1725)
Vaucher, C. H. (Geneva, ca. 1835)
Vaucher, Daniel (Paris, 1767-1790)
Vaucher, Freres (Swiss, 1850)
Vauquer, Robert (French, ca. 1650) (enamel)
Veigneur, F. I. (ca. 1780)
Vernod, Henriette (Paris, ca. 1790)
Vigne, James (London, ca. 1770)
Vrard, L., & Co. (Pekin, 1860-1872)
Vulliamy, Justin (London, ca. 1830-1854)
Vully, Jaques (1890-1900)
Vuolf (Swiss, ca. 1600)
Waldron, John (London, 1760)
Wales, Giles & Co. (Swiss, ca. 1870)
Waltrin (Paris, ca. 1820)
Weston, D. & Willis (enamel) (London, ca. 1800-1810)
Whitthorne, James (Dublin, since 1725)
Willats, John (London, ca. 1860)
Williamson, Timothy (London, 1770-1790)
Wilter, John (London, ca. 1760)
Winckles, John (London, 1770-1790)
Winnerl, Joseph Thaddeus (Paris, 1829-1886)
Wiss, Freres & Menu (Swiss, ca. 1787-1810)
Wiss, G. (Geneva, ca. 1750)
Wright, Charles (London, 1760-1790)
Wright, Thomas (English, ca. 1770-1790)
Young, Richard (London, 1765-1785)
Zech, Jacob (Prague, Aus. 1525-1540)
Zolling, Ferdinand (Frankfurt, Ger. ca. 1750)

Tambour style case, probably Nuremburg, ca. 1575, hinged cover, pierced to reveal engraved Roman chapter I-XII and Arabic 13-24 Central chapter, 60mm.

HALLMARKS OF LONDON

Hallmarks were used on gold and silver cases imported from England. These marks, when interpreted, will give you the age of the case and location of the assay office.

The date-marks used 20 letters of the alphabet, A-U, never using the letters W, X, Y, or Z. The letters J & I or U & V, because of their similarity in shape, were never used together within the same 20-year period. A total of four marks can be found on English cases, which are:

The Maker's Mark The Standard Mark

The Assay Office Mark The Date Letter Mark

1822-up   1478 to 1821

The **Maker's Mark** was used to denote the manufacturer of the case.

The **Standard Mark** was used to denote a guarantee of the quality of the metal.

The **Assay Office Mark** (also known as the town mark) was used to denote the location of the assay office.

The **Date Letter Mark** was a letter of the alphabet used to denote the year in which the article was stamped. The stamp was used on gold and silver cases by the assay office.

SWISS HALLMARKS

18k .750   14k .585   Platinum

Sterling Silver   Silver .800

Lucerne.   Neuchatel.
Poinçons d'essai
de décembre 1852.

.800

LONDON HALLMARKS

Letter	Year
O	1551
P	1552
Q	1553
R	1554
S	1555
T	1556
V	1557
A	1558
b	1559
C	1560
D	1561
E	1562
F	1563
G	1564
h	1565
I	1566
k	1567
l	1568
m	1569
n	1570
o	1571
p	1572
q	1573
r	1574
S	1575
t	1576
u	1577
A	1578
B	1579
C	1580
D	1581
E	1582
F	1583
G	1584
H	1585
I	1586
K	1587
L	1588

Letter	Year
M	1589
N	1590
O	1591
P	1592
Q	1593
R	1594
S	1595
T	1596
V	1597
X	1598
B	1599
C	1600
D	1601
E	1602
F	1603
G	1604
h	1605
I	1606
K	1607
L	1608
M	1609
N	1610
O	1611
P	1612
Q	1613
R	1614
S	1615
T	1616
V	1617
a	1618
b	1619
C	1620
d	1621
e	1622
f	1623
g	1624
h	1625
i	1626

Letter	Year
k	1627
l	1628
m	1629
n	1630
o	1631
p	1632
q	1633
r	1634
s	1635
t	1636
u	1637
A	1638
B	1639
C	1640
g	1641
E	1642
F	1643
O	1644
b	1645
g	1646
B	1647
C	1648
D	1649
E	1650
b	1651
P	1652
S	1653
U	1654
O	1655
d	1656
B	1657
T	1658
B	1659
C	1660
D	1661
E	1662
F	1663
G	1664
H	1665

Letter	Year
I	1666
K	1667
L	1668
M	1669
N	1670
O	1671
P	1672
Q	1673
R	1674
S	1675
Z	1676
A	1677
a	1678
b	1679
c	1680
d	1681
e	1682
f	1683
g	1684
h	1685
i	1686
k	1687
j	1688
m	1689
n	1690
o	1691
p	1692
q	1693
r	1694
s	1695
t	1696
u	1697
v	1698
s	1699
A	1700
ff	1701
O	1702
b	1703
d	1704
k	1705
t	1706
v	1707
O	1708

Letter	Year
O	1709
F	1710
Q	1711
B	1712
S	1713
U	1714
h	1715
A	1716
B	1717
C	1718
D	1719
E	1720
F	1721
G	1722
H	1723
I	1724
K	1725
L	1726
M	1727
N	1728
O	1729
P	1730
Q	1731
R	1732
S	1733
T	1734
V	1735
a	1736
b	1737
c	1738
d	1739
d	1739
e	1740
f	1741
g	1742
h	1743
i	1744
k	1745
l	1746
m	1747
n	1748
o	1749
p	1750
q	1751

Letter	Year
r	1752
f	1753
t	1754
u	1755
a	1756
b	1757
c	1758
D	1759
e	1760
f	1761
g	1762
h	1763
i	1764
k	1765
l	1766
m	1767
n	1768
o	1769
p	1770
q	1771
r	1772
s	1773
t	1774
u	1775
a	1776
b	1777
c	1778
d	1779
e	1780
f	1781
g	1782
h	1783
i	1784
k	1785
l	1786
m	1787
n	1788
o	1789
p	1790
q	1791
r	1792
s	1793
t	1794
u	1795
A	1796

Letter	Year
B	1797
C	1798
D	1799
E	1800
F	1801
G	1802
H	1803
I	1804
K	1805
L	1806
M	1807
N	1808
O	1809
P	1810
Q	1811
R	1812
S	1813
T	1814
U	1815
a	1816
b	1817
c	1818
d	1819
e	1820
f	1821
g	1822
h	1823
i	1824
k	1825
l	1826
m	1827
n	1828
o	1829
p	1830
q	1831
r	1832
s	1833
t	1834
u	1835
E	1836
B	1837
C	1838
B	1839
C	1840

Letter	Year
f	1841
G	1842
H	1843
J	1844
J	1845
L	1846
M	1847
A	1848
O	1849
P	1850
Q	1851
R	1852
S	1853
T	1854
U	1855
a	1856
b	1857
c	1858
D	1859
e	1860
f	1861
g	1862
h	1863
i	1864
k	1865
l	1866
m	1867
n	1868
o	1869
p	1870
q	1871
r	1872
s	1873
t	1874
u	1875
A	1876
B	1877
C	1878
D	1879
E	1880
F	1881
G	1882
H	1883

Letter	Year
I	1884
K	1885
L	1886
M	1887
N	1888
O	1889
P	1890
Q	1891
R	1892
S	1893
T	1894
U	1895
a	1896
b	1897
c	1898
d	1899
e	1900
f	1901
g	1902
h	1903
i	1904
k	1905
l	1906
m	1907
n	1908
o	1909
p	1910
q	1911
r	1912
s	1913
t	1914
u	1915
a	1916
b	1917
c	1918
d	1919
e	1920
f	1921
g	1922
h	1923
i	1924
k	1925
l	1926

EUROPEAN WATCHES
COLLECTED IN AMERICA

Auguste Agassiz of Saint Imier and Geneva started manufacturing quality watches in 1832. They later became interested in making a flat style watch which proved to be very popular. Some of these movements can be fitted inside a $20 gold piece.

The company was inherited by Ernest Francillion who built a factory called Longines. The Longines factory continued the Agassiz line until the Great Depression.

Agassiz, 43mm, 17 jewels, stem wind, 14 carat case, open face, serial number 39,863.

Julius Assmann began producing watches with the help of Adolf Lange in 1852. His watches are stylistically identical to those produced by Lange. Later on he adopted his own lever style. Assmann made highly decorative watches for the South American market which are highly regarded by German collectors.

Audemars, Piguet & Cie. was founded in 1875 by Jules Audemars and Edward Piguet, both successors to fine horological families. This company produced many fine high grade and complicated watches, predominantly in nickel and, with a few exceptions, fully jeweled. Their complicated watches are sought after more than the plain timepieces. They also produced some very handsome wrist watches.

The Swiss company of **Blancpain** was founded in 1735 by **Jean-Jacques Blancpain**. The company still produces mechanical watches of the greatest craftsmanship, but does not make a quartz-type watch.

Abraham-Louis Breguet, one of the worlds most celebrated watchmakers.

Abraham-Louis Breguet was born at Neuchatel in 1747 and died in 1823. He was perhaps the greatest horologist of all time in terms of design, elegance, and innovation. He is responsible for the development of the tourbillon, the perpetual calendar, the shock-proof parachute suspension, the isochronal overcoil, and many other improvements. It is difficult to include him in this section because of the complexity surrounding identification of his work which was frequently forged, and the fact that so many pieces produced by his shop were unique. Suffice it to say that the vast majority of watches one encounters bearing his name were either marketed only by his firm or are outright fakes made by others for the export market. Much study is required for proper identification.

As early as 1884 **Leon Breitling** made chronographs using his own name. The Swiss company made chronographs during World War I for different governments, gaining important acceptance in this field. One such model is the "Chronomat."

Breitling Watch Co., about 16-18 size, 16 jewels, open face, stem wind, chronograph.

Henry Daniel Capt of Geneva was an associate of Isac Daniel Piguet for about 10 years from 1802 to 1812. Their firm produced quality watches and specialized in musicals, repeaters, and chronometers. By 1844 his son was director of the firm, and around 1880 the firm was sold to Gallopin.

Cartier was a famous artisan from Paris who first made powder flasks. By the mid-1840s the family became known as the finest goldsmiths of Paris. Around the turn of the century the Cartier firm was designing watches and in 1904 the first wrist watches were being made. In 1917 Cartier created a watch design that was to become known as the tank-style case. The tank-style case was made to look like tank caterpillars of the U. S. This style is still popular today.

The **Chopard** family made and crafted many fine watches as early as 1860 and by the 1920s were making watches for the Swiss Railway. The company was sold to a German company in 1960 and still produces very fine watches.

Edward John Dent worked with Vulliamy and Barraud separately before joining J. R. Arnold in 1830. After 10 successful years in that association, he established his own firm, **E. Dent & Co.**, which continued after his death in 1853. His name is associated with Big Ben, although his successor is responsible for the execution of that contract. Dent's chronometers and complicated watches are particularly desirable, whereas the later products of the company are less so.

Paul Ditisheim founded his company in 1892 at La Chaux de Fonds in Switzerland. He made extremely small watches, some as small as 6.75 millimeters. The company later became Vulcain et Volta, Ditisheim & Co.

Henry Robert Ekegren, a Swiss maker of quality watches, started in business around 1870. The firm specialized in flat watches, chronometers, and repeaters. Ekegren became associated with F. Koehn in 1891.

John Ellicott, an Englishman, made watches from 1706 to 1772. One of his most notable developments was the cylinder escapement. After Ellicott's death the company was named John Ellicott & Son.

J. Girard and A. Schild started a small company in the mid-1800s making movements only, and by 1906 the name was changed to **Eterna**. The company was well known for its precision pocket watches. By 1930 the company decided to make a small wrist watch, which they call the "baguette," and an eight-day alarm. Both proved to be very popular. A movement named the "Eterna-Matic" was being produced by 1948, and their first electronic watch was made in 1974, followed by the quartz "Kontiki" produced in 1976. This Swiss company still produces quality watches, both jeweled and electronic.

Charles Frodsham followed in the footsteps of his father William, whose father was close with Earnshaw. Charles became the most eminent of the family, producing very fine chronometers and some rare tourbillons and complicated watches. He died in 1871. The following code was used to denote the year in which the watch was made:

F R O D S H A M Z   Thus, FMHZ = 1860
1 2 3 4 5 6 7 8 0

Charles Frodsham, 55mm, jeweled through center wheel, engraved on movement "By appointment to the king, A.D. FMSZ" [5] 1850. Note Karrusel at top of movement. Included within the Karrusel are the balance and escape wheel. The whole mechanism revolves about once every 60 minutes.

In 1856 the Constant Girard and Henry Perragaux families founded the Swiss firm of **Girard-Perregaux**. About 1880 the firm made a tourbillion with three golden bridges. A replica of this watch was made in 1982. Both were a supreme expression of horological craftsmanship. In 1906 the company purchased the Hecht factory in Geneva. Girard-Perregaux has been recognized many times and still makes prestigious quartz and mechanical watches.

Jacques Edouard Gubelin joined the firm of Mourice Brithschmid in Lucerne around 1854. By 1919 Edouard Gubelin headed the firm. In 1921 they opened an office in New York and produced fine jewelry and watches for five generations.

The founder of the prestigious Swiss **International Watch Co.** was an American engineer F. A. Jones from Boston. The company began in 1868 and in 1879 was sold to Mr. J. Rauschenbach. The company today is still making precision, handcrafted watches. IWC is well known for its super-light watch constructed of titanium.

E. Gubelin, 54mm, 33 jewels, minute repeater, split second chronograph.

Right: Jules Jurgensen example of his famous bow setting feature.

The firm of **Jules Jurgensen** was an extension of the earlier firm of Urban Jurgensen & Sons, which was located, at various times, in Copenhagen and Le Locle. Jules ultimately established his firm in Le Locle after his father's death in the early 1830s. From that time forward the company produced, generally speaking, very fine watches that were high grade and complicated. It appears that by 1850 the company had already established a strong market in America, offering beautiful heavy 18k gold watches of exemplary quality. Until around 1885 most stem-winding watches exhibited the bow-setting feature. Almost any collectable Jurgensen watch will be fully signed on the dial and movement, with an impressively embossed "JJ" stamping on all covers of the case. Watches not so marked should be examined carefully; and untypical or inelegant stampings should be viewed suspiciously, as there has been some forgeries of these fine watches. Frequently one finds the original box and papers accompanying the watch, which exhances the value. After 1885, as the firm started to buy movements from other companies, we begin to see variations in Jurgensen watches. By 1930, Jurgensen watches barely resembled the quality and aesthetics of the early period, and they are not particularly desirable to the collector.

Jules Jurgensen, 17 jewels, rectangular 14k case.

Adolf Lange, 49mm, jewel-ed through the center wheel, gold escape and pallet, gold jeweled settings, gold train, diamond end stones, 14k hunting case, serial number 9,524.

A. Lange & Sohne was established with the aid of the German government at Glashutte, Germany in 1845. Lange typically produced ¾ plate lever watches in gilt finish for the domestic market, and in nickel for the export market. High grade and very practical, these watches had a banking system for the pallet that was later used briefly by E. Howard in America. Lange complicated watches are scarce and very desirable.

Le Coultre and Co. was founded by Antoine Le Coultre in 1833. A fine clockmaker, he created a machine to cut pinions from solid steel as well as other machines for manufacturing clocks and watches. By 1900 they were making flat or thin watches. They made parts for Patek Philippe & Co., Tissoy, Vacheron & Constantin, Omega, Paul Ditisheim, Agassiz, Longines and others.

Le Coultre round 18k gold case with sweep center second and date.

Le Roy et Cie. was the final product of a dynasty of great watch-makers, starting with Julien Le Roy and his son Pierre, whose credits are numerous in the development of horology in the 18th century. There is, however, much confusion and hooplah over "Le Roy" watches. Frequently you will see watches signed "Le Roy" that have nothing to do with the original family. These watches are unimportant. You have to distinguish between the works of Julien, of Pierre, of Charles; and of their contemporary namesakes. The modern firm, Le Roy et Cie., established in the late 19th century, contracted and finished some very fine and, in some cases, extremely important complicated watches, using imported Swiss ebauches.

The beautiful **Fabrique des Longines** is situated in St. Imier, Switzerland. The company was founded by Ernest Francillon in 1866. They manufacture all grades of watches.

Meylan Watch Co., founded by C. H. Meylan in 1880, manufactured fine watches, with complications, in Le Brassus, Switzerland.

Movado pocket watch, 42mm, 15 jewels, 8 day with alarm.

L. A. Ditisheim & Freres founded their company in 1881 and the name **Movado** ("always in motion") was adopted in 1905. The Swiss company invented a system of watch making which they called "Polyplan." This was an arrangement of three different angles to the watch movement which produced a curve effect to the case so as to fit the curvature of the arm. Another unusual watch produced by this company in 1926 was the "Ermeto." This watch was designed to be protected while inside a purse or pocket, and each time the cover was opened to view the time, the watch was partially wound.

Ulysse Nardin, 12 & 16 size, 19 jewels, adjusted to heat, cold & six positions. Illustrated example was used as a pocket and deck watch.

Ulysse Nardin was born in 1823. The company he started in 1846 produced many fine timepieces and chronometers, as well as repeaters and more complicated watches. This firm, as did Assmann, found a strong market in South America as well as other countries. Ulysse's son Paul David Nardin succeeded him, as did Paul David's sons after him. The firm also made wrist watches.

Omega Watch Co. was founded by Louis Brandt in 1848. They produced watches of different grades. By 1920 Omega had manufactured about 5,000,000 watches; by 1923, 6,000,000; and by 1931, 10,000,000.

Patek, Philippe & Cie. has produced some of the world's most desirable factory-made watches. Antoine Norbert de Patek began contracting and selling watches in the 1830s, later became partners with Francois Czapek, and generally produced lovely decorative watches for a high class of clientel. In 1845 Adrien Philippe, inventor of the modern stem-winding system, joined the firm of Patek & Cie., and in 1851 the

399

firm established its present name. Between Philippe's talent as a watchmaker and Patek's talent as a businessman with a taste for the impeccable, the firm rapidly established an international reputation which
lasts to this day.

Patek, Philippe & Co., 39 jewels, self wind
movement, 18k case.

Early Patek, Philippe & Cie. watches are generally signed only on
the dust cover, but some are signed on the dial and cuvette. It was not
until the 1880s that the practice began of fully signing the dial, movement and case—perhaps in response to some contemporary forgery,
but more likely a necessity to conform to customs' regulations for their
growing international market. Many early and totally original Patek
watches have suffered from the misconception that all products of this
company are fully signed. Nevertheless, collectors find such pieces more
desirable. It requires more experience, however, to determine the
originality of the earlier pieces. As with Vacheron & Constantin, some
watches were originally cased in America, but this lowers their value
in general.

The Swiss company **Piaget** was founded by Georges Piaget who
has a history of employing master goldsmiths. They have always produced watches in limited amounts, and watch collectors seek out these
watches of *D'art*.

Rolex was founded by Hans Wilsdorf in 1919. In 1926 they made
the first real waterproof wrist watch and called it the "oyster." In 1931,
Rolex introduced a self-wind movement which they called "perpetual."
In 1945 they introduced the "datejust" which showed the day of the

month. The "submariner" was introduced in 1953 and in 1954 the "GMT Master" model. In 1956 a "day-date" model was released which indicates the day of the month (in numbers) and the day of the week (in letters).

In 1837 **Charles Lewis Tiffany** opened a store with John P. Young. They enlarged this operation in 1841, with the help of J. L. Eliss, and imported fine jewelry, watches and clocks from Europe. They incorporated as **Tiffany & Co.** in 1853. Tiffany made clocks, on special order, in New York around the mid-1880s. About 1874 Tiffany & Co. started a watch factory in Geneva but with little success. Four years later Patek, Philippe & Co. assumed the management of their Geneva watch business. The watch machinery was returned to America. Tiffany, Young & Ellis had been a client of Patek, Philippe & Co. since 1849. Tiffany & Co. introduced Patek, Philippe to the American market in 1851. Audemars, Piguet and International Watch Co. also made watches for this esteemed company. Tiffany & Co. sell watches of simple elegance as well as watches with complications such as chronographs, moonphases, repeaters, etc.

Vacheron & Constantin, about 38-39mm, 21 jewels, nickel bridge movement, wolf tooth wind, 18k case, serial number 386,637.

The firm of **Vacheron & Constantin** was officially founded by Abraham Vacheron in 1785, but the association bearing the name today did not come into being until 1819. In these early periods, different grades of watches produced by Vacheron & Constantin bore different names. The firm produced several hundred thousand watches. The association with Leschot, around 1840, catapulted the firm into its position as a top quality manufacturer. Before that time, their watches were typical of Genevese production. Vacheron & Constantin exported many movements to the United States to firms such as Bigelow, Kennard & Co., which were cased domestically, typically in the period 1900-1935. In its early period the firm produced some lovely ladies' enameled watches, later it produced high grade timepieces and complicated watches, and to this day produces fine wrist watches.

Zenith Watch and clock factory was founded in 1865 by George Farvre Jacot. They mass produced watches of different grades in large quantities. By 1920 they had manufactured 2,000,000 watches.

Example of **Split Second & Fly-Back Movement** with a minute repeater, c. 1890.

Example of **English Clock Watch**, 20 size, jeweled through hammers, minute repeater. Note two train movement.

REPEATING WATCHES

Repeating watches or repeaters are those watches which will sound the time at the wish of the user. The repeating mechanism is operated by either a slide, plunger, or button in the case of the watch. There are basically five types of repeating mechanisms, some more common than others:

(1). QUARTER REPEATERS—The quarter repeater strikes the previous hour and quarter hour. In the older watches—usually verge—the striking is on a single bell attached to the inside of the case and the hour and quarter striking uses the same tone. There is first a series of hammer blows on the bell to indicate the hours, followed, after a short pause, by up to three twin strikes to denote the number of quarters elapsed. In later watches the striking is on wire gongs attached to the movement itself. The hours are struck on a single deep gong and the quarters on a higher-pitched gong followed by the deeper gong, producing a "ting-tang" sound.

(2). HALF-QUARTER REPEATERS—These strike the hours, the last quarter (ting-tang) and the previous half-quarter; i.e., seven and a half minutes. Half-quarter repeaters are mostly all verge escapement watches and are rarely seen by the average collector.

(3). FIVE-MINUTE REPEATERS—These fall into two types. One system is similar to the half-quarter repeater but follows the quarter "ting-tang" by a single higher-pitched strike for each five minute interval elapsed since the last quarter. The other system strikes the hours on a deep gong and follows this with a single higher note for each five minute period after the hour, omitting a quarter striking.

(4). MINUTE REPEATERS—This is the most complicated of the repeating mechanisms and is similar to the quarter repeater with the addition of the minutes being struck on the higher-pitched gong after the quarters.

(5). CLOCK WATCHES—The clock watch is essentially a repeater with the features of a striking clock. Whereas the above-mentioned repeaters are all operated by a plunger or slide which winds the repeating function and which runs down after the last strike, the clock watch is wound in the same way as the going train—usually with a key—and is operated by the touch of a button in the case. The repeat function can be operated many times before the watch needs to be rewound. The "clock" part of the name comes from the watch also striking the hours and sometimes the quarters or half hour in passing. The clock watch is easily recognizable by the two winding holes in either the case or the dial.

In addition to the five types described above, the features of striking are sometimes found with not only two but three and even four gongs, this producing a peal of notes. These repeaters are known as "carillons."

At the other end of the scale from the carillon is the "dumb" repeater. This strikes on a block of metal in the case or on the movement and is felt rather than heard. It is said that the idea was to produce a watch that would not embarrass its owner when he wished to know when to slip away from boring company. Although the dumb repeater is less desirable for the average collector, it certainly should not be avoided—Breguet himself made dumb repeaters.

A BIT OF HISTORY

Now that we have seen what repeaters are supposed to do, it might be in order to look briefly at their origins.

Before the days of electric light, it was a major project to tell the time at night, since striking a tinderbox was said to have taken up to fifteen minutes to accomplish. Clocks, of course, had striking mechanisms, but they tended to keep the occupants of the house awake listening for the next strike. The repeating addition to the clock meant that the master of the house could silence the passing strike at night and, at his whim, simply pull a cord over his bed to activate the striking in another part of the house and thus waking everyone. To silence those members of the household who did not appreciate a clock booming out in the early hours of the morning, the horologists of the day turned their thoughts to the idea of a repeating watch.

The first mention of repeating watches is in the contest between Daniel Quare (1649-1724) and the Rev. Edward Barlow (1639-1719) to miniaturize the repeating action of a clock. Barlow, who for some reason had changed his name from Booth, was a theoretical horologist of outstanding ability. Barlow's design—made for him by Thomas Tompion—and Quare's watch were both submitted to King James II and the Privy Council for a decision as to whom should be granted a patent. The King chose Quare's design because the repeating mechanism was operated by a single push-button, whereas Barlow's required two. Quare was granted a patent in 1687. Barlow had had his share of fame earlier, however, with the invention of rack-striking for clocks in 1676.

Quare went into production with his new repeater watches, but changed the design to replace the push-button in the case with a pendant that could be pushed in. The first of these watches showed a fault that is still found on the cheaper repeaters of this century—that is, if the pendant was not pushed fully in, then the incorrect hours were struck. To overcome this problem, he invented the so-called "all-or-nothing" piece. This is a mechanism whereby if the pendant was not pushed fully home, then the watch would not strike at all.

The half-quarter appeared shortly after the all-or-nothing piece, and then by about 1710 the five-minute repeater was on the market. Some five years after this, a "deaf-piece" was often fitted to the watch. This was a slide or pin fitted to the case which, when activated, caused the hammers to be lifted away from the bell and had the same effect as a dumb repeater.

Sometime around 1730, Joseph Graham decided to dispense with the idea of a bell and arranged for the hammers to strike a dust-cover, thus making the watch slimmer and preventing dust from entering the pierced case.

About the middle of the century, the French master Le Roy carried the idea a stage further and dispensed with both bells and dust-covers, and used a metal block which revolutionized the thickness of the repeating watch and introduced the dumb repeater. Breguet used wire gongs around 1789 and the pattern for the modern repeater was set. The minute repeater came into more common use after 1800, and earlier examples are definitely very rare, although it is known that Thomas Mudge made a complicated watch incorporating minute repeating for Ferdinand VI of Spain about 1750.

By the last quarter of the 1700s, Switzerland had gone for the repeater in a big way and the centre of fine craftsmanship for complicated watches was in the Valley of Joux. Here the principle of division of labour was highly refined and whole families were hard at work producing parts for repeating and musical watches. Since one person concentrated only on one part of the watch, it is hardly surprising that parts of excellent quality were turned out. The basic movements were then sold to watchmakers/finishers all over the Continent and even to England, where the principle of one man, one watch, among the stubborn majority eventually led to the downfall of what had once been the greatest watchmaking nation in history.

The greatest popularity of the repeater came, however, in the last quarter of the 1800s, when Switzerland turned them out in the tens of thousands. Although there were many different names on the dials of the watches, most seem to have been produced by the company "Le Phare" and only finished by the name on the dial. The production of repeaters in quantity seems to have ground to a finish in about 1921 due to (a) the invention of luminous dials and universal electric or gas lighting, and (b) a lack of watchmakers willing to learn the highly demanding skills. The interest in horology over the past decade has, however, revived the idea of the repeater and several companies in Switzerland are now producing limited editions of expensive models.

BUYING A REPEATER

Since so many repeaters seem to have been repaired at some time in the past by incompetent watchmakers, it is often too expensive a purchase if the buyer does not know what he is doing.

Rule One should be: if it does not work perfectly, avoid it like the plague unless a competent repairer first gives you an estimate which suits your pocket. All too often in the past the repairer was under the impression that metal grows with age and he has filed the teeth of a rack in order to get the full striking to work again. When it dawned on him that the problem was a worn bearing, the tooth was stretched with a punch and refiled, making it weak. It was then goodbye to a fine piece of craftsmanship.

A better quality repeater is usually one which is "jewelled to the hammers." This simply means that the hammers have jewelled bearing—which can be seen by searching the movement for the hammers, locating the pivots around which they swing, and looking for the jewelled bearing in which they sit.

All repeaters have some system for regulating the speed of the repeating train. On the older fusee types, there was usually a rather primitive arrangement of a pinion in an eccentric bushing which could be turned to increase or decrease the depth of engagement of the pinion with the next wheel. Another system, a little better, uses an anchor and a toothed wheel as in an alarm clock. This system is usually located under the dial but can be detected by the buzzing sound it makes when the train is operated. The far superior system is the centrifugal governor which can be seen whizzing around in the top plate of the watch when the repeating action is operated. On the whole, the watch with the centrifugal governor is more desirable, although it must be mentioned that the Swiss turned out some inferior watches with this system.

If possible—and it should be possible if you are investing a lot of money—have a watchmaker look under the dial to see if the watch is jewelled throughout. Many are only jewelled in the places the owner can see and leave much to be desired in the "blind" places.

Test the watch by operating the repeating train over a full hour, seeing that the quarters and minutes function correctly, then test each individual hour. Finally, set the hands to just before 1 o'clock and test the striking. Any defect due to dirt or worn bearings will show up by the final blow(s), being either sluggish or not striking at all. If there is incorrect striking, have an expert look at it before you buy.

Try a partial operation of the slide or push-piece. If the watch has an all-or-nothing piece (as a reasonable grade movement should have), then the watch will not strike. Partial striking indicates either a low-grade watch or a non-functioning all-or-nothing piece.

   Additional features such as chronograph functions, calendar, moon phase, etc., will obviously affect the price of the watch and one must be guided by current price listings from reputable dealers.

   Remember Rule One, though—if any function does not work, BEWARE!

Example of a 33 minute karrusel by **Russell & Son**, makers to the Queen (London), 55mm, 16 jewels, open face.

Tourbillon

A. Fixed fourth wheel
B. Third wheel
C. Carriage (one revolution per minute)
D. Carriage pinion
E. Escape Wheel & pinion
F. Arbor for seconds hand
G. Escape cock
H. Lever & pallets

TOURBILLON

Breguet invented the tourbillon in 1795. A tourbillon is a device designed to reduce the position errors of a watch. This device has the escape wheel, lever and balance wheel all mounted in a carriage of light frameworks. This carriage makes one complete turn every minute. The fourth wheel is fixed and is concentric with the carriage pinion and arbor. The escape wheel pinion meshes with the fourth wheel and will roll around the fixed fourth wheel. The escape wheel and lever are mounted on the carriage, and the third wheel drives the carriage pinion, turning the carriage once every minute. This rotation of the escapement will help reduce the position errors of a watch. One of the major objections is that the carriage and escapement weight mass must be stopped and started at each release of the escapement. The tourbillon design requires extreme skill to produce and is usually found on watches of high quality. Somewhat similar to the tourbillon is the karrusel, except it rotates about once per hour and the fourth wheel is not fixed. It also takes less skill to produce.

MUSICAL WATCHES
(Three basic types)

Stacked Tooth

Disc Type with individual teeth

Pinned Cylinder & Comb

PRODUCTION TOTALS

PATEK PHILIPPE

1840	100
1845	1,200
1850	3,000
1855	8,000
1860	15,000
1865	22,000
1870	35,000
1875	45,000
1880	55,000
1885	70,000
1890	85,000
1895	100,000
1900	110,000
1905	125,000
1910	150,000
1915	175,000
1920	190,000
1925	200,000
1950	700,000
1955	725,000
1960	750,000
1965	775,000
1970	795,000

1920	800,000
1925	805,000
1930	820,000
1935	824,000
1940	835,000
1945	850,000
1950	860,000
1955	870,000
1960	880,000
1965	890,000
1970	895,000
1940	900,000
1945	915,000
1950	930,000
1955	940,000
1960	960,000
1965	975,000
1970	995,000
1960	1,100,000
1965	1,130,000
1970	1,250,000
1975	1,330,000
1980	1,400,000

A. LANGE

1870	5,000
1875	10,000
1880	20,000
1885	25,000
1890	30,000
1895	35,000
1900	40,000
1905	50,000
1910	60,000
1915	70,000
1920	75,000
1925	80,000
1930	85,000
1935	90,000
1940	100,000

LONGINES

1870	20,000
1880	200,000
1890	600,000
1900	1,200,000
1910	2,000,000
1920	3,000,000
1930	5,000,000
1940	6,000,000

The above list is provided for determining the approximate age of your watch. Match serial number with date.

Brevet — French word for "patented"
✚ SWISS — symbol

ASHLAND

Over the past 25 years, the internationally recognized firm of ASHLAND has been building a clientele of astute collectors and investors. As a major buyer in the field of horology and vertu, ASHLAND possesses the expertise and purchasing power to acquire and offer to you the finest timepieces available. An in depth view of some of the extraordinary watches currently available may be obtained by sending for our most recent wrist or pocket watch catalog.

If you wish to receive these important publications free of charge, please send your name and address as soon as possible. Please specify if you are interested in pocket watches or wrist watches. Catalogs are already on reserve for our current customers. Keep ASHLAND in mind if the time comes to liquidate your investment. As a major force in the industry we are able to offer you top dollar for your valued collection.

ASHLAND

1819 Main Street, Suite 720
Sarasota, Florida 34236
1 (813) 957-3760   1 (800) 424-5353

LEFT: SWATCH "HAPPY FISH" Model # SDN 101, with green rotating Bezel, clear light blue green case, dark blue bracelet with transparent & colored fish, red skeletonized dial.
RIGHT: SWATCH "WHITE HORSES" Model # SCW 100, Chronograph with quartz movement, water resistant to 100 feet, 3 registers, Multi-colored 1/5 sec. Tachymeter dial, Stop Start & Reset round steel metal pushers, White case & bracelet.

LEFT: SWATCH, ART Collection limited series, 700 years Confoederatio Helvetica (1991), "FLACK" Model # GZ 117, green case, note the face of a Cow on dial and Bracelet, made in 2 Editions Ca. 1991.
RIGHT: SWATCH, "IBISKUS", Model # GL 101, Light green Case, Dark Blue dial with a red flora l leaf, Bracelet multi-colored dark red, blue, yellow and green, Ca. (1991) Spring / Summer.

From the Renaissance...to the wristwatch
Experience and Expertise

LEFT: PAIR OF GOLD MINATURE ENAMEL AND LAPIS HARPS, one harp open to reveal a keywind musical movement with a circular pin barrel and a stacked steel comb. The watch form harp has a verge fusee movement, the enamel dial is about 22mm, Ca.1830s.
RIGHT: GOLD and ENAMEL 1/4 HOUR REPEATER, 52mm, colorful scene of a lady and gentleman, decorated with Seed Pearls, The pendant activates the 1/4 repeater, ca. 1790.

LEFT: BALL WATCH CO. Form style 14 K Gold case 21 jeweled watch, in line gold train with gold jewel settings, parts made by WALTHAM, printed on dial BALL WATCH CO. CLEVELAND, OHIO.
RIGHT: GENE AUTRY COMIC CHARACTER WATCH, has a SIX SHOOTER ACTION GUN, made by New Haven Watch Co., Ca.1950s.

LEFT: WALTHAM MASONIC, 45mm, Enamel Triangular dial with multi-color Masonic Emblems for Numbers, signed WALTHAM on dial & " Love your fellow man lend him a helping hand ", engraved chain on bezel, with Masonic Emblem at top.
RIGHT: CARTIER LADIES WATCH, with 40 diamonds on Platinum bezel, 18k yellow gold back, 19 jewel E.W.C. Nickel movement, ca. 1920s.

LEFT: AUDEMARS PIGUET, "Moon Phase", 18K yellow gold case, Gold Audemars buckle, white enamel dial, stem wind movement signed Audemars Piguet, ca. 1970s.
RIGHT: PATEK PHILIPPE ASTRONOMIC, 18K white gold chronograph, with perpetual calendar day, date & month, moon phases, auxiliary dials for date of the month and the seconds + 24 hours, also 30 minutes register showing the leap year, 24 jewel movement, REF. # 3970, Cal. # 27-70-Q, Dial, Case and Movement signed, Ca. 1990s.

LEFT: SWATCH " RUFFLED FEATHERS", Model # GF 100, transparant copper tone color bracelet, feathers on orange & black dial, blue hands, Ca. Fall/Winter 1986.
RIGHT: SWATCH "COLORED LOVE", Model # GB 122, left half of dial with man over orange and right side lady over yellow, multi-colored bracelet with man and lady repeated also decorative acanthus floral leaf designs, Ca. Fall/ Winter 1988.

LEFT: SWATCH " NINE TO SIX", Model # GB 117, buckle side of bracelet is deep Red and the other side is deep Blue, dial is yellow and white, Ca. Fall/ Winter 1987.
RIGHT: SWATCH " HARAJUKU", Model # GB 124, dial is black with a Oriental design and Red Hands, the case is black, the bracelet is multi-colored with Oriental designs, Ca. Spring/ Summer 1989.

EUROPEAN POCKET WATCH LISTINGS
Pricing at Retail Level
(Complete Watches Only)

Unless otherwise noted, watches listed in this section are priced at the retail level and as complete watches having an original 14k goldfilled case with an original white enamel single sunk dial, and the entire original movement in good working order with no repairs needed. Watches listed as 14k and 18k are solid gold cases. Coin or silveroid type and stainless steel cases will be listed as such. Keywind and keyset pocket watches are listed as having original coin silver cases. Dollar type watches, or low cost production watches, are listed as having a base metal type case and a composition dial.

Many of the watch manufacturers were commissioned to put jewelers' or jobbers' names on their movements in place of their own. Because of this practice, the true manufacturers of these movements are difficult to identify. These watch models are listed under the original manufacturer and can be identified by comparison with the model sections under each manufacturer. See "Personalized Watches" for more detailed information.

The prices shown were averaged from dealers' lists just prior to publication and are an indication of the retail level or what collectors will pay. Prices are provided in three categories: average condition, extra fine, and mint condition, and are shown in whole dollar amounts only. The values listed are a guide for the retail level and are provided for your information only. Dealers will not necessarily pay FULL RETAIL PRICE. Prices listed are for watches with *original cases and dials*.

Note: Descriptions and serial number ranges listed for early watches cannot be considered 100 percent accurate due to the manner in which records were kept by these companies.

INFORMATION NEEDED–We are interested in any facts and information you might have that should possibly be considered for future editions. Documented facts are needed. Please send photo or sources of information to: **COOKSEY SHUGART, P.O.BOX 3147, CLEVELAND, TENNESSEE 37320-3147.** *(WHEN CORRESPONDING, PLEASE INCLUDE A SELF-ADDRESSED, STAMPED ENVELOPE.)*

AGASSIZ
Swiss

Agassiz, 43mm, 18 jewels, serial number 44,844.

Agassiz, 43mm, 21 jewels, 3/4 plate, serial number 39,863.

Size and Description	Avg	Ex-Fn	Mint
52mm, split sec. chronograph, 14K, OF, register	$800	$950	$1,200
50mm, art deco, "Cartier," 1925, 19J, Adj.5P, 18K	1,200	1,600	2,000
43mm, 18J, nickel mvt., 14K, OF..	425	475	575
43mm, 21J, nickel mvt., 18K, OF, WI, 8 day................................	750	900	1,100
43mm, 19J, World Time, 32 Cities, 14K, OF..............................	4,800	5,800	7,000
43mm, 19J, World Time, 32 Cities, 18K, OF..............................	5,600	6,600	8,000
37mm, 21J, 8 day, wind indicator, OF, 18K	750	875	1,000
Lady's, 40mm, HC, 18K, white enamel dial................................	225	275	375

Agassiz, 43mm, 17 jewels, World Time, 42 towns, ca. 1940.

Assmann, 44mm, 21 jewels, serial number 19,539, ca. 1914.

ASSMANN
GLASSHUTTE

Size and Description	Avg	Ex-Fn	Mint
50mm, 19J., Bridge Model, diamond end stone, GJS, 18K..........	$3,250	$3,750	$4,500
50mm, 19J., diamond end stone, GJS, gold lever, 18K...............	3,000	3,500	4,500
44mm, 21J., elaborate chasing, fancy dial, for South American market, 18K, HC........................	3,750	4,500	5,500
42mm, SW, Timepiece, OF, 18K	1,800	2,250	2,750

Assmann, 50mm, 19 jewels, diamond cap jewels, gold jewel settings, gold lever escapement, serial number 3,086, BRIDGE MODEL, ca. 1855.

Assmann, 50mm, 19 jewels, diamond cap jewels, gold jewel settings, gold lever escapement, serial number 3,739, ca. 1857.

AUDEMARS, PIGUET
SWISS

Size and Description	Avg	Ex-Fn	Mint
48mm, 30J., min. repeater, 18K OF	$3,000	$3,600	$4,250
46mm, 20J., min. repeater, chronograph, register, 18K HC	3,800	4,500	5,200

Audemars, Piguet, 46mm, 20 jewels, minute repeater. Note governor at right-hand side of balance bridge.

Audemars, Piguet, 48mm, 30 jewels, minute repeater, serial number 4,155, ca. 1890.

Size and Description	Avg	Ex-Fn	Mint
46mm, OF, min. repeater, split chronograph, register, 18K	$4,800	$5,500	$6,500
46mm, min. repeater, 18K, HC..	3,500	4,200	5,000
46mm, 20J, 1/4 repeater, OF, 18K..	1,500	1,800	2,200
44 - 45mm, OF, timepiece, 18K	600	700	850
44mm, OF, min. repeater	2,600	3,200	3,800
44mm, OF, 5-min. repeater..	2,000	2,400	3,000
43mm, 18J., Jump hour, day date month, 18K	6,000	8,000	10,000
40mm, 31J, min. repeater, 18K, OF, c. 1875	2,600	3,200	4,000

Audemars, Piguet, 46mm, 36 jewels, minute repeater, split-second chronograph, serial number 3853, ca. 1888.

Audemars, Piguet, 43mm., 18 jewels, adj.6P, jumping hour, day-date-month windows, ca. 1925.

J. W. BENSON
LONDON

Size and Description	Avg	Ex-Fn	Mint
58mm, Grande & Petite Sonnerie, min. repeater, perpetual calendar, moonphases	$55,000	$60,000	$70,000
40mm, KW, KS, fusee, lever, wind indicator, free sprung, 18K, HC..	1,400	1,600	1,950

ABRAHAM LOUIS BREGUET
PARIS

Date	Serial No.	Date	Serial No.
1795	150	1815	2700
1800	600	1820	3500
1805	1600	1825	4500
1810	2000	1830	5000

61mm. Example of Breguet souscription style face and movement. Gilt movement with central winding arbor, balance with parachute suspension, HANGING ruby cylinder escapement. White enamel dial with secret signature at 12 o'clock.

Size and Description	Avg.	Ex-Fn	Mint
61mm, Hanging ruby cylinder, souscription, enamel dial, gold case..	$14,000	$16,000	$22,000
60mm, ruby cylinder, souscription, secret signature , silver case	7,500	9,000	11,000
60mm, ruby cylinder, souscription, back wind, gold case recased	4,000	5,000	6,000
58mm, clock watch, verge, ting-tang on hour, silver case signed Breguet & Fils but is a ebauche by F. Japy	1,000	1,200	1,500
56mm, two train ruby cylinder, 1/4 repeater, 18K gold case	8,000	6,000	12,000
55mm, ruby cylinder, parachute suspension, gold case	5,000	6,000	7,500
55mm, Jacquemarts, 1/4 repeater, 2 automatons, gold case	3,500	4,200	5,000
55mm, Jacquemarts, 1/4 repeater, verge escap., push pendant....	3,500	4,200	5,000

Example of a typical souscription style Breguet movement. Dial side shown. Note the HANGING ruby cylinder escapement below finger bridge.

Abraham Breguet repeater, 55mm; a verge repeating watch with two jacquemarts with push pendant to repeat, serial number 23,592.

Abraham Louis Breguet, repeating, ruby cylinder watch. Left: gilt movement with standing barrel. Note jeweled parachute suspension. Right: Dial side of movement, repeating train with exposed springs.

Size and Description	Avg	Ex-Fn	Mint
55mm, montre simple, secret signature on enamel dial	$5,500	$6,000	$6,800
54mm, ruby cylinder, 1/4 repeater, standing barrel, gold dial	9,000	11,000	14,000
54mm, repeater, verge escapement, push pendant, gold case	1,500	1,800	2,200
54mm, horologer de la marine royale, repeater, gold case	14,000	17,000	21,000
53mm, min. repeater, split sec. chronograph, two tone gold case, c. 1948.................	12,000	16,000	20,000
52mm, ruby cylinder, 1/4 repeater, push pendant, gold case	8,000	10,000	12,500
52mm, ruby cylinder, 1/4 repeater, push piece, gold case	8,000	10,000	12,000
51mm, min. repeater, chronograph, WI, day, month, moon phase, 18K case, c. 1932.............	40,000	50,000	65,000
49mm, ruby cylinder, parachute suspension, gold case	5,000	6,500	8,500
47mm, thin, perpetual calendar, moon ph., platinum case	8,000	10,000	12,500

Important repeater Horloger De La Marine by Breguet. Left: Guilloche silver dial with roman numberals and typical Breguet hands. Right: Gilt brass movement with ruby cylinder escapement and triple arm balance.

Breguet "montre a tact" or touch time watch, 36mm. Case embellished with 12 pearls for tactile hours (Braille style watch). The arrow on case revolves. Souscription movement with 6 jewels, central barrel, ruby cylinder escapement.

Size and Description	Avg	Ex-Fn	Mint
45mm, thin digital watch, perpetual calendar, 18K case	$9,000	$11,000	$14,000
43mm, thin art deco, jump hours & rotary window, 18K	5,500	6,500	8,500
36mm, pearls tactile braille watch, 18K enamel case	22,000	27,000	32,500
18mm, small keyless watch, platinum balance, gold case	20,000	25,000	32,000

Breguet, 51mm, chronograph with perpetual calendar and minute repeater. Note sector style wind indicator.

Breguet, 53mm, minute repeating, split-second chronograph. Chronograph activated by crown and button on band. Repeater activated by slide.

BREITLING
SWISS

Size and Description	Avg	Ex-Fn	Mint
43mm, 16J., chronograph, OF	$200	$250	$375
43mm, 16J., chronograph, 14K OF	325	375	500

BULOVA
SWISS AND U.S.A.

Size and Description	Avg	Ex-Fn	Mint
40mm, 18J, "Phantom," c. 1920, OF platinum case	$650	$750	$950

HENRY CAPT
GENEVE

Size and Description	Avg	Ex-Fn	Mint
52mm, min. repeater, perpetual calendar, moon phases, 18K hunting case	$22,000	$26,000	$32,000
Lady's, OF, 1 min. repeater, 18K	3,000	3,600	4,500

Henry Capt, 52mm, 32 jewels, minute repeater, serial number 34,711, ca. 1900.

Cartier, 52mm, 40 jewels, triple complicated-perpetual calendar, minute repeater, split-second chronograph

CARTIER
PARIS

Size and Description	Avg	Ex-Fn	Mint
52mm, 40J, triple complication moon phase astronomical min. repeater, perpetual calendar, day-date-month, split sec. chron. with min. recorder, signed European Watch & Clock Co., 18K case, c. 1930	$100,000	$120,000	$150,000
49mm, 19J, art deco, black onyx, gold, enamel & diamonds on case	4,500	6,500	9,500

H. R. EKEGREN
GENEVE

Size and Description	Avg	Ex-Fn	Mint
55mm, min. repeater, jeweled to hammers, 18K case, OF	$3,400	$3,800	$4,500
43mm, min. repeater, 18K, HC, jeweled to hammers	3,200	3,600	4,250
42mm, 18K, OF, fully jeweled, SW, LS	600	750	950
39mm, min. repeater, jeweled to hammers, OF, 18K	2,600	3,000	3,600

H.R. Ekegren, 39mm, minute repeater, slide activated, jeweled through hammers, open face, serial number 78,268.

H.R. Ekegren, 43mm, minute repeater, jeweled through hammers, hunting case.

Frodsham, 44mm, jeweled through center wheel., Ca. 1895, serial number 04172.

Frodsham, 55mm, 60 minute karrusel, 15 jewels, stem wind, open face, 18k gold case, c. 1896.

FRODSHAM
LONDON

Size and Description	Avg	Ex-Fn	Mint
55mm, min. repeater, jeweled thru hammers, DES, 18K, HC ...	$4,600	$5,250	$6,250
55mm, 16J, 59 min., Karrusel, 18K case	4,400	5,000	5,600
54mm, one min., tourbillon, 3/4 plate, signed, 18K, OF ...★★★	26,000	32,000	38,000
44mm, detent escapement, 18K, HC	2,400	2,800	3,400
42mm, 17J, 3/4 plate, GJS, DES, 18K, HC	800	1,000	1,250
42mm, KW, KS, wind indicator, free sprung, 18K, OF	1,300	1,500	1,750
35mm, 1/4 & 5 min. repeater, by Thomas Frodsham, 18K, HC	3,500	4,000	4,500

GIRARD PERRAGAUX
SWISS

Size and Description	Avg	Ex-Fn	Mint
55mm, 3 gold bridges, c. 1884, silver case	$4,000	$5,000	$6,000

Girard Perragaux, 55mm, three golden bridge movement, patented March 25th, 1884.

GRUEN
SWISS AND U.S.A.

Size and Description	Avg	Ex-Fn	Mint
45mm, 14K, HC, by D. Gruen & Son, 21J, GJS, gold escape wheel, "Dresden," by Assman	$1,000	$1,200	$1,500
45mm, 23J, wind indicator, ADJ. 5P, OF, 18k	1,500	2,000	2,600
44mm, made for R.R. Service, GF	125	150	200
40mm, 19J, "Precision," SW, LS, YGF	100	120	145
40mm, 50th Anniversary, 21J, including 2 diamonds, 18K, OF...	2,000	2,400	2,850
40mm, "Detrich Gruen," marked Extra Precision, 31J, min. repeater, 18K, OF	2,800	3,000	3,500
38mm, 17J, pentagon case, veri thin style, YGF	75	85	95
38mm, 17J, pentagon case, veri thin style, 14K	200	250	325
38mm, 17J, pentagon case, veri thin style, 18K	300	375	450

D. Gruen & Son, 44mm, jeweled through center wheel, made for railroad service, serial number 62,428.

Gruen 50th Anniversary Watch, 40mm or 10 size, 21 jewels, (two diamonds) placed in a five-sided pentagon case, solid gold bridges.

Size and Description	Avg	Ex-Fn	Mint
38mm, 21J, RGJ, GT, Adj.5P, YGF	$75	$110	$145
38mm, 19J, GT, Adj.5P	65	95	110
38mm, 15J, ADJ	50	60	75
36mm, 17J, ultra veri thin, GF	50	60	75

E. GUBELIN

SWISS

Size and Description	Avg	Ex-Fn	Mint
54mm, min. repeater, 33J, split sec. chronograph, GT	$4,000	$4,500	$5,250
54mm, 28J, min. repeater, OF, 18K	2,600	2,900	3,400
50mm, min. repeater, chronograph, day-date-month, moon phase, 18K, HC	4,800	5,600	6,500
38mm, 21J, deco style, Adj.5P, perpetual calendar, 18K, OF	6,500	7,500	8,500

E. Gubelin, 50mm, 29 jewels, minute repeater, chronograph, day-date-month-moon phase.

C.L. Guinand, 50mm, split-second chronograph, serial number 44,109.

C. L. GUINAND

SWISS

Size and Description	Avg	Ex-Fn	Mint
50mm, 34J, min. repeater, split sec. chronograph, 18K, OF	$3,800	$4,300	$4,800

HAAS, NEVEUX & CO.

SWISS

Size and Description	Avg	Ex-Fn	Mint
42mm, 18K, HC, cover wind..	$2,200	$2,600	$3,200
40mm, 31J, min. repeater, 18K hunting case................................	2,800	3,200	3,800
40mm, 31J, min. repeater, 18K, OF..	2,300	2,600	3,250
34mm, $20 gold piece form watch...	1,100	1,300	1,650

Haas, Neveux & Co., 40mm, 31 jewels, minute repeater, 18k open face case, serial number 11,339.

Hebdomas novelty watch, 8-day movement, balance can be seen from dial side. Made about 1920. This style watch is now being made by Aenex Time Corp.

HEBDOMAS

SWISS

Size and Description	Avg	Ex-Fn	Mint
50mm, 7J, 8 day, balance seen from dial (old stock c.1920s).......	$75	$100	$145

INTERNATIONAL WATCH CO.

SWISS

Size and Description	Avg	Ex-Fn	Mint
54mm, 17J, lever escapement, GJS, 14K, HC	$475	$550	$650
42mm, early mvt., 18K, HC	550	700	850
42mm, OF, 14K case...	350	425	500

International Watch Co., 42mm, 18 size, 15 jewels, serial number 7,609.

International Watch Co., 54mm, 17 jewels, adj.6P, serial number 741,073.

JULES JURGENSEN
SWISS

Size and Description	Avg	Ex-Fn	Mint
55mm, OF, detent chronometer, KW, 18K	$3,200	$3,600	$4,200
55mm, OF, detent chronometer, SW, 18K	5,500	6,500	8,000
55mm, HC, detent chronometer, SW, 18K	6,000	7,200	8,500
50mm, OF, timepiece, enamel dial, 18K	2,000	2,400	2,850
49mm, 1/4 repeater, c. 1880, nickel mvt., gold train, 18K HC	3,000	3,600	4,200
46mm, OF, min. repeater, chronograph, register, 18K	7,200	8,200	9,800
46mm, OF, min. repeater, split chrono., register, 18K	8,500	9,500	11,500
46mm, HC, min. repeater, 18K	6,500	7,500	8,500
46mm, HC, min. repeater, chronograph, 18K	7,000	8,000	9,500
46mm, HC, min. repeater, split chronograph, register, 18K	10,000	12,000	14,500
46mm, OF, chronograph, timepiece, register, 18K	2,400	2,800	3,600

JULES JURGENSEN, 1 minute repeater, popular bow set, triple signed case, movement & dial, 18k hunting case, serial number 13,824.

JULES JURGENSEN, 46mm, 21 jewels, hand-setting by inclination of pendant ring, serial number 14,492, ca. 1890.

Size and Description	Avg	Ex-Fn	Mint
46mm, OF, split chronograph, timepiece, register	$3,200	$3,800	$4,600
46mm, HC, chronograph, timepiece, register.............................	2,800	3,250	4,000
46mm, HC, split chronograph, timepiece, register	4,800	5,400	6,200
45mm, OF, timepiece, enamel dial	1,700	2,000	2,400
45mm, HC, timepiece, enamel dial	2,000	2,500	3,000
45mm, OF, KW, timepiece, enamel dial	700	900	1,100
45mm, OF, min. repeater, enamel dial...	4,200	4,800	5,500
44mm, OF, 5-min. repeater...	3,200	3,800	4,400
40mm, OF, timepiece, enamel dial	1,200	1,400	1,800
40mm, HC, timepiece, enamel dial	1,500	1,700	2,200

A. LANGE

GERMANY

Size and Description	Avg	Ex-Fn	Mint
55mm, min. repeater, 18K, HC, jeweled thru hammers, GJS, NI, GT, gold escape & pallet, DES, 1st quality mvt.	$17,000	$19,000	$22,000
55mm, 1/4 repeater, NI, DES, 1st quality mvt., HC	7,500	8,500	10,000
54mm, 1/4 repeater, DES, jeweled thru hammers, OF	6,800	7,800	9,000
53mm, 18K case, c. 1885, GJS, GT, DES, gold pallet and escape wheel..	2,400	2,900	3,400
52mm, World War II model, WI, OF, silver case	1,200	1,400	1,800
49mm, 18K case, 17J, GJS, GT, gold escape wheel & pallet, c. 1914, OF...	1,550	1,800	2,200
49mm, 18K case, HC, gild mvt., 17J, GJS, DES, gold lever and escape wheel..	1,850	2,200	2,600
49mm, min. repeater, 3rd grade mvt., gilt, 14K, triple sized HC	8,500	9,500	11,500
48mm, 3/4 plate, Deutsche Uhren Fabrikation, silver	450	550	700

A. Lange & Sohne, 52mm, wind indicator, World War II model, open face.

A. Lange & Sohne, 48mm, three-quarter plate, engraved on movement "Deutsche Uhren Fabrikation-Glashutte," serial number 58,398.

LE COULTRE & CO.
SWISS

Le Coultre & Co., 57mm, 32 jewels, minute repeater, exposed winding gears, 14k hunting case.

Le Coultre & Co., 55mm, 31 jewels, day, date, month and moon phases, 18k hunting case, minute repeater.

Style or Grade Description	Avg	Ex-Fn	Mint
57mm, 32J, min. repeater, slide repeat, 14K, HC..........................	$2,300	$2,600	$3,000
57mm, 32J, min. repeater, slide repeat, 18K, HC	3,000	3,400	4,000
55mm, 31J, min. repeater, day-date-month, moon ph., 18K, HC	4,600	5,200	6,200
55mm, 30J, min. repeater, 2 automatons, c. 1900, 18K case	6,300	7,500	9,000
54mm, min. repeater, gilt, lever escapement, 14K, HC	1,600	2,000	2,500
52mm, 1/4 repeater, double dial, calendar, moon ph., 18K, HC.	2,800	3,300	4,000
49mm, nickel mvt., 18K, OF...	500	650	800

Le Coultre, 55mm, 30 jewels, minute repeater, two automatons.

Le Phare, 56mm, minute repeater, chronograph & calendar with moon phases.

LE PHARE
SWISS

Size and Description	Avg	Ex-Fn	Mint
56mm, min. repeater, day-date-month, moon phase, 18K case...	$3,200	$3,600	$4,200

LE ROY
SWISS

Size and Description	Avg	Ex-Fn	Mint
55mm, musical, plays on demand, repeater, 18Kcase	$2,800	$3,400	$4,250
50mm, min. repeater, 2 train, jumpcenter sec., 18K HC	4,500	5,500	6,850
20mm,1/4 repeater, exposed repeat work on back plate, pearl bezel, 18Kcase	2,600	3,200	3,800

LE ROY, 50mm, minute repeater, two train, tandem winding wheels, jump center seconds.

LONGINES, 45mm, 13—15 jewels lever escapement, stem wind, ca. 1900's

LONGINES
SWISS

Size and Description	Avg	Ex-Fn	Mint
59mm, 30J, min. repeater, chronograph, calendar & moon moon phases, 18K HC	$4,000	$4,800	$6,000
59mm, 26J, min. repeater, chronograph, 2 registers, 18K	2,800	3,200	3,800
55mm, OF, 18K, split chronograph, 2 registers	1,200	1,450	1,750
50mm, chronograph with register, nickel mvt., silver case	150	175	225
50mm, 8 day, wind indicator, 15J, Adj.3P, silver	325	425	550
46mm, 21J, "Express Monarch," R.R. approved, Adj.5P	125	145	175
46mm, rectangular case, 30 small diamonds on case, 15J	700	900	1,200
45mm, 13-15J., lever escapement,ADJ.	100	125	175
44mm, 15J, 3 ADJ, 8 day, WI, 14Kcase	650	750	900
44mm, "U. S. Army," sweep sec. hand, WI, Adj.5P	300	350	425
26mm, lady's pendant, 18K, OF, enamel & diamonds	600	700	850

Longines, 44mm, 21 jewels, U.S. Army AC, adjusted to temp. & 5 positions, World War II model, serial number 5,939,626.

Longines, 59mm, 26 jewels, minute repeater, chronograph, one register, ca. 1910.

MATHEY-TISSOT
SWISS

Size and Description	Avg	Ex-Fn	Mint
52mm,1/4 jump sec. chronograph, tandem wind, 2 train, 18K ...	$2,600	$3,000	$3,600
48mm, min. repeater, 14K, OF..	2,000	2,400	2,800

Mathey-Tissot, 52mm, 27 jewels, quarter jump sweep-second chronograph, two train, 18k hunting case.

C.H. Meylan, 44mm, 21 jewels, straight line lever escapement.

C. H. MEYLAN
SWISS

Style or Grade — Description	Avg	Ex-Fn	Mint
50mm, min. repeater, OF, 18K, jeweled to hammers	$2,400	$2,700	$3,200

Style or Grade Description	Avg	Ex-Fn	Mint
50mm, min. repeater, HC, 18K, chronograph, fully jeweled	$3,200	$3,500	$4,200
48mm, split sec. chronograph, register, OF, 18K	1,000	1,200	1,500
48mm, chronograph, register, OF, 14K....................................	550	700	900
46mm, platinum & sapphire dress watch, c. 1925.........................	1,000	1,400	1,850
44mm, min. repeater, 14K, OF....................................	1,800	2,250	2,750
44mm, timepiece, 18K, thin model............................	350	450	550

Ulysse Nardin, 53mm, 52 minute karrusel, free sprung balance, ca. 1905.

Ulysse Nardin Chronometer, 45mm, 21 jewels, ultra-high grade movement, c. 1878, serial number 7,685.

ULYSSE NARDIN

SWISS

Size and Description	Avg	Ex-Fn	Mint
Deck chronometer w/mahogany box, detent mvt., silver dial	$1,400	$1,600	$2,000
53mm, 17J, 52 1/2 min. karrusel, free sprung regulator, silver	5,500	7,000	9,500
50mm, 15J, made for Corps of Engineers, U.S.A., WWI	195	245	295
50mm, min. repeater, jeweled thru hammers, HC, 18K	3,450	4,000	4,800
45mm, split chronograph, 2 registers, 14K, 18K OF....................	1,050	1,250	1,500
45mm, 21J., detent chronometer, SW, 18K OF.............................	3,500	4,500	5,500
45mm, detent chronometer, KW, KS, 18K OF.............................	700	825	1,000
45mm, SW, timepiece only, 18K, OF.................................	550	675	800
45mm, SW, timepiece only, 14K....................................	350	400	475
42mm, perpetual calendar, moon phases, OF, 18K	7,200	8,200	9,500
42mm, moon phases, perpetual calendar, 18K, HC.....................	9,000	12,000	14,000
40mm, 29J, min. repeater, Adj.5P, 18K, OF................................	2,800	3,200	3,800

NICOLE, NIELSEN & CO.

SWISS

(Made ebauche for Dent, Frodsham & Smith)

Size and Description	Avg	Ex-Fn	Mint
64mm, tourbillon min. repeater, made for Frodsham, free sprung, c. 1918, 18K case..	$75,000	$85,000	$100,000

Nicole, Nielsen, 52mm, minute repeater & split-second chronograph, made for Dent.

Nicole, Nielsen, 64mm, minute repeater, split-second chronograph tourbillon, free sprung escapement.

Size and Description	Avg	Ex-Fn	Mint
52mm, half 1/4 repeater, chronograph, slide repeat, 18K case ..	$4,000	$4,500	$5,000
52mm, min. repeater, split sec. chronograph, made for Dent, 1882, 18K case	7,500	8,500	10,000
50mm, min. repeater, chron., made for Dent, c. 1885, 18K	4,500	5,000	6,000

OMEGA
SWISS

Size and Description	Avg	Ex-Fn	Mint
45mm, 15J, lever escapement, silver	$55	$75	$95
45mm, 17J, OF, 14K	275	325	375
45mm, 17J, HC, 14K	325	375	450
38mm, 15J, OF	55	75	95

Omega pocket watch, 38mm, 15 jewels, serial number 9,888,934.

Patek Philippe & Co., 38-39mm, 18 jewels, deco bridge movement, 8 adj., 18k open face case, serial number 196,051.

Patek, Philippe dial and movement, minute repeater with split second chronograph, 29 jewels, perpetual calendar, day, date, month, moon phase, adjusted to 5 positions, 18k solid gold case.

PATEK, PHILIPPE & CO.

SWISS

(All must be triple signed case, dial, movement, Patek Philippe)

Size and Description	Avg	Ex-Fn	Mint
56mm, 22J, "Chronometro Gondolo," 24 hr. dial, 18K, OF, c. 1890s	$2,000	$2,500	$3,000
55mm, astronomic, perpetual calendar, min. repeater, 1897, white enamel dial, 3 registers, split sec. chronograph, moon phases, 38J, slide repeat, original box and papers ★★★★	80,000	90,000	105,000
54mm, split sec. chronograph, 18K, HC	5,500	7,000	9,000
52mm, split sec. chronograph, 18K, OF, Tiffany & Co., register	4,000	5,000	6,000
51mm, 22J, independent dead seconds, 2 train, heavy 18K HC, c. 1890 ★★★	18,000	24,000	32,000
51mm, 18K, HC, gilt, lever mvt.	1,800	2,200	2,800
50mm, 25J, pulsometer chronograph, c. 1923, 18K case	4,500	5,500	7,000
50mm, 22J, "Chronometer Gondolo," c. 1890, 18K, OF	2,000	2,400	2,800
48mm, 18J, chronometer with one min. tourbillon, awarded first prize 1933-34, platinum case ★★★★	110,000	130,000	160,000
48mm, 18K, HC, nickel mvt.	2,200	2,600	3,200
48mm, early chronograph, fly back sec. hand, 18K, OF, wolf's teeth winding	2,400	2,900	3,400
47mm, 1 min. tourbillon, by James Pellaton, c. 1920, 18K case ★★★	75,000	85,000	100,000
46mm, OF, timepiece, enamel dial	1,400	1,600	2,000
46mm, two train, min. repeater, Tiffany & Co.	13,000	16,000	20,000
46mm, "Gondolo," OF, timepiece, enamel dial	1,700	2,100	2,500
46mm, 18K, OF, 18J, Adj.5P, cam regulator	1,400	1,600	2,000
46mm, OF, min. repeater, split chronograph, registers	15,000	19,000	24,000

Patek Philippe & Co., 38-39mm, 18 jewels, nickel bridge movement, wolf tooth wind, cam regulator, serial number 124,348.

Patek, Philippe & Co., 50mm, 25 jewels, Chronograph & Pulsometer, ca. 1923.

Size and Description	Avg	Ex-Fn	Mint
46mm, HC, min. repeater, split chronograph, reg.	$16,000	$21,000	$27,000
46mm, HC, min. repeater, split chronograph, perpetual calendar, moon phase .... ★★★	75,000	85,000	100,000
45mm, 18J, 18K, OF, Tiffany & Co.	1,200	1,400	1,800
45mm, 18K, HC, 1860, SW & set, wolf tooth wind	1,400	1,700	2,200
45mm, OF, split chronograph, timepiece, register	5,000	6,000	7,200
45mm, OF, perpetual calendar, timepiece, metal dial	18,000	22,000	27,000
45mm, OF, perpetual calendar, timepiece, enamel dial	22,000	27,000	32,000
45mm, OF, timepiece, gilt dial, 18K	1,400	1,600	1,800
45mm, HC, min. repeater, chronograph	13,000	15,000	18,000
45mm, HC, chronograph, timepiece, register	3,600	4,200	5,200
45mm, HC, split chronograph, timepiece, register	5,800	6,800	8,200
45mm, HC, min. repeater, split chronograph, perpetual calendar, register + moon phases	70,000	80,000	95,000
44mm, OF, timepiece, gilt, enamel dial, 18K	1,200	1,400	1,600
44mm, OF, timepiece, nickel, enamel dial, 18K...........................	1,400	1,600	1,800
44mm, HC, min. repeater..	12,000	14,000	17,000
44mm, OF, 5 min. repeater	4,500	5,500	7,000
44mm, OF, 5 min. repeater, chronograph	6,000	7,000	8,200
44mm, OF, min. repeater	8,000	9,000	10,500
44mm, OF, min. repeater, chronograph	10,000	12,000	14,500
44mm, OF, min. repeater, split chrono., register	15,000	19,000	25,000
42mm, 14K, OF, chronometer on dial, USA cased	800	900	1,000
39mm, 18J, wolf tooth wind, 14K, OF, NI. mvt. USA cased........	800	900	1,000
39mm, 18J, Adj.5P, enamel on bezel & back	1,800	2,100	2,400
38mm, "Gondolo," OF, timepiece, enamel dial, 16 Size	1,800	2,100	2,400
35mm, 29J, min. repeater, very thin, 18K, OF..............................	8,000	9,000	10,000
32mm, 18K, HC, early bridge mvt., Tiffany & Co.	1,100	1,400	1,700
30mm, lady's, 18K, gold & enamel + diamonds, lapel watch	4,000	5,000	6,000

Style or Grade Description	Avg	Ex-Fn	Mint
30mm, lady's, 18K, multi color gold, enamel & diamonds, matching chain & pin, OF, art nouveau	$5,500	$6,500	$7,500
29mm, lady's, 18K, OF	750	900	1,250
26mm, lady's, 18K, OF, gold, seed pearls & enamel, lapel watch, matching pin	4,500	5,500	6,500

ALBERT H. POTTER & CO.

GENEVA

Style or Grade Description	Avg	Ex-Fn	Mint
45mm, 29J, min. repeater, 18K, HC	$5,500	$6,500	$8,000
43mm, 22J, helical hairspring, detent chronometer escapement 18K, HC	8,000	10,000	12,500
33mm, 21J, 1/4, repeater, 18K, HC	2,500	3,000	4,000

Albert Potter, 22 jewels, hunting case, helical hair spring, detent escapement.

Rolex, 42-43mm, 17 jewels, three adjustments, cam regulator, exposed winding gears.

ROLEX

SWISS

Size and Description	Avg	Ex-Fn	Mint
43mm, 3 ADJ, cam regulator, 14K, OF	$550	$750	$950

THOMAS RUSSEL & SONS

ENGLAND

Size and Description	Avg	Ex-Fn	Mint
52mm,1/2 1/4 repeater, rachet tooth escapement, 18K, OF	$2,600	$3,000	$3,600
46mm, min. repeater, 3/4 plate, 18K, HC	3,500	4,000	4,500
46mm, karrusel, 59 min., chronometer, free sprung, 18K, OF	3,500	4,000	5,000

TIFFANY & CO.
U.S.A.

Size and Description	Avg	Ex-Fn	Mint
50mm, 25J., split sec. chronograph, by Ekegren, 14K	$1,800	$2,200	$2,600
49mm, 5 min. repeater, c. 1900, 18K, HC	3,000	3,500	4,200
49mm, 1 min. repeater, 18K, OF	3,600	4,200	4,800
49mm, 1 min. repeater, 18K, HC	3,800	4,400	5,250
48mm, nickel mvt., wolf's tooth wind, 18K, OF	750	850	1,000
48mm, nickel mvt., chronograph, 18K, OF	900	1,100	1,250
48mm, nickel mvt., split sec. chronograph, 18K, OF	1,200	1,400	1,800
48mm, min. repeater, split sec. chronograph, day-date month, moonphase, perpetual, 18K, OF, mvt. by Vacheron & Constantin	34,000	38,000	45,000
48mm, min. repeater, split sec. chronograph, day-date month, moonphase, 18K, OF, mvt. by Patek Philippe	75,000	85,000	100,000
48mm, timepiece, 18K, HC, enamel dial	900	1,100	1,200
48mm, timepiece, 18K, OF, by Patek, Philippe & Co.	1,200	1,400	1,600
47mm, 5 min. repeater, 18K, OF	3,200	3,700	4,400
45mm., 29J., min. repeater, by Patek, Philippe & Co. 18k	6,000	7,000	8,000
45mm, 18K, OF, by Longines	300	425	575
44mm, 18K, HC, timepiece	850	900	1,100
42mm, OF, 18K, timepiece	575	650	750

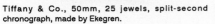

Tiffany & Co., 50mm, 25 jewels, split-second chronograph, made by Ekegren.

Tiffany & Co., flat minute repeater, 45mm, 29 jewels, made by Patek, Philippe & Co., ca. 1911.

☞ NOTE: Watches listed in this book are priced at the retail level, as complete watches having an original 14k gold filled case, an original white enamel single sunk dial, and with the entire original movement in good working order with no repairs needed, unless otherwise noted.

Touchon & Co., 47mm, 29 jewels, minute repeater, open face, jeweled through hammers.

Touchon & Co., 47mm, 29 jewels, split-second chronograph and minute repeater, ca. 1910.

TOUCHON & CO.

SWISS

Size and Description	Avg	Ex-Fn	Mint
47mm, 29J, min. repeater, thin model, 1925, 18K, OF	$2,200	$2,600	$3,000
47mm., 29J., split sec. chronograph, min. repeater, 18K.............	3,600	4,400	5,500
46mm, min. repeater, jeweled thru hammers, wolf tooth wind, 18K, HC..	2,600	3,000	3,600
45mm, 23J, min. repeater, 14K, OF...	1,800	2,000	2,250
44mm, OF, 18K, timepiece...	350	425	525
40mm, 28J, min. repeater, 14K, OF...	1,700	1,900	2,100

50 pesos 900 fine gold coin with Vacheron & Constantin watch inside. The left view shows the movement inside the coin which was hollowed out to receive the Vacheron & Constantin watch.

VACHERON & CONSTANTIN
SWISS

Size and Description	Avg	Ex-Fn	Mint
59mm, chronometer escapement, with silver deck case, c. 1920.	$1,700	$1,900	$2,250
55mm, min. repeater, 18K, OF, ultra high grade, nickel mvt.	4,600	5,000	5,500
51mm, 14K, HC, nickel mvt., c. 1890	600	750	1,000
50mm, min. repeater, chronograph mvt., 18K, OF, gilt	3,800	4,200	5,000
47mm, 14K, OF, c. 1900, nickel mvt..	400	500	650
43mm, 18K, OF, c. 1920, nickel lever mvt., Adj.5P	575	700	850
42mm, 14K, OF, 17J, Adj.5P, c. 1915...	375	475	600

Vacheron & Constantin , 40mm, wolf tooth winding, 18k open face.

Vacheron & Constantin, 40mm, 31 jewels, minute repeater, slide repeat, wolf tooth wind, 18k open face, serial number 340,949.

Style or Grade Description	Avg	Ex-Fn	Mint
41mm case size, 24mm mvt. size, skeletonized, c. 1930, 18J	$2,200	$2,600	$3,200
40mm, 21J, NI, BRG, wolf tooth wind, 18K, OF·..........................	650	750	900
40mm, 19J, high quality mvt., 14K, OF	375	475	600
40mm, 17J, wolf tooth wind, GF, HC..	100	150	225
40mm, min. repeater, slide repeat, jeweled thru hammers, OF..	3,200	3,600	4,200
40mm, 31J, min. repeater, 18K, OF, slide activated	3,200	3,800	4,200
40mm, 21J, observatory time trial, 3rd place winner, 18K	2,000	2,400	3,000
30mm, lady's, jeweled to center wheel, 18K, OF	200	300	450
50 PESOS 900 fine gold coin, V.&C. movement inside coin.......	3,000	3,500	4,000

MISC. ENGLISH

Size and Description	Avg	Ex-Fn	Mint
120mm, 1/4 repeating coach watch with alarm, verge, fusee, by Charles Clay, c. 1730, silver respousse case (illo.1)	$8,000	$9,000	$11,000
70mm, silver & horn triple cased, for Turkish market, by G. Charles, c. 1810, verge, & pierced cock, enamel dial	650	800	1,000

1/4 repeating coach watch, with alarm,120mm diameter, verge fusee, silver repousse case, ca.1730-40.   (illo. 1)

Size and Description	Avg	Ex-Fn	Mint
60mm, pair cased, silver c. 1800, hand painted battle scene on dial...	$550	$650	$775
60mm, 1/4 repeater, pair cased, push repeat, pierced cock, 18K, repousse case	2,500	2,650	3,250
58mm, silver pair case, winged pierced cock, c.1700-20, (illo.2)..	1,400	1,800	2,250
56mm, winged pierced cock, verge fusee with calendar, (illo.3) .	1,000	1,200	1,600
56mm, by Robert Roskell, pair cased, 18K, full plate, dust cover, rack & lever escapement.....................................	850	1,100	1,400
55mm, min. repeater, by John Barwise, jeweled thru hammers, duplex escapement, heavy 18K case.....................	4,400	5,000	5,600
55mm, reversible case, KW, KS, cylinder escapement, 18K	1,000	1,200	1,600
55mm, fusee, lever escapement, KW, KS, by W. Chance & Sons, 18K pair cased, repousse case (illo.4).........................	1,300	1,600	2,000
55mm, diamond end stone, lever escape., KW, c.1840-60, (illo.5)	65	75	125
54mm, min. repeater, by H. C. Boddington, 18K, 3/4 plate, HC.	2,500	2,900	3,250
52mm, full plate, 14K, HC, by Johnson...	400	475	650
52mm, by Arnold & Dent, chronometer, fusee, KW, KS, OF, silver	1,400	1,700	2,000

58mm, Early silver pair case watch, Impressively pierced winged single-footed balance cock, Egyptain style pillars, gilt verge and fusee movement, ca. 1700-30s, (illo.2).

English watch 56mm, winged hand pierced single footed cock, verge and fusee, ca.1720-60, (illo.3).

English watch, 55mm, with repousse case. (illo.4)

Liverpool, 55mm, lever escapement, diamond end stone, ca. 1840 - 1860, (illo.5)

John Creed, 50mm, Edinburgh, c. 1820. (illo6.)

Tobias (Liverpool), 51mm, captain's watch, gold dial engraved with leaf and flower patterns, KW KS, 18K case, Ca.1860, (illo.7).

Size and Description	Avg	Ex-Fn	Mint
52mm, demi-hunter, by Robert Roskell, resilient lever, silver case	$850	$950	$1,100
52mm, gold & enamel + pearls, by John Page, c. 1800, cylinder	2,500	2,900	3,400
51mm, by Dent, OF, lever movement, 18K	500	600	750
51mm, Tobias, captains watch, double train,18K case, (illo.7)	1,000	1,250	1,600
51mm, Tobias, captain's watch, single train, 18k case, (illo.7)	650	850	1,100
50mm, c. 1872, WI, with resilient banking, KW, KS, 18K,HC	1,250	1,500	1,800

Cooper, 48mm, bar detached lever movement, key wind & set, parachute system at end stone, 18k open face, serial number 6631. (illo.8)

Wm. Hopetown, 48mm, chain driven fusee, verge escapement, dust cover, c. 1842, made in London, pair case, serial number 3865. (illo.9)

Size and Description	Avg	Ex-Fn	Mint
50mm, by William Jones, pierced cock, chain driven fusee, c. 1842, pair cased	$125	$175	$250
50mm, 1/4 repeater, silver & enamel, by Weill & Harburg, c.1886	700	800	950
50mm, gold & enamel + pearls, by John Page, c. 1800, cylinder	2,000	2,400	2,800
50mm, gold & gems, set in OF watch, by James McCabe, c.1820, cylinder, pierced cock, DES, gold dial, 18K, diamond on back	2,800	3,200	3,700
50mm, by Robert Gellatly, of Edinburgh, 18K, OF, free sprung, c. 1870	750	900	1,100
50mm, 1/4 repeater, 18K, OF, by John Barwise, c. 1830, 3/4 plate	1,200	1,400	1,800
50mm, 11J, lever escapement, fusee, gold balance, by Yates, 16K case	400	500	650
50mm, by J.Creed, Edinburgh,c.1820, silver pair cased (illo.6)	150	175	250
48mm, bar movement, by Cooper, KW, KS, 18K, OF, with parachute, gold dial, (illo.8)	275	350	450
48mm, pair case, verge, fusee, pierced cock, silver	125	175	250
48mm, by M. I. Tobias & Co., Liverpool, lever, fusee, KW, KS, 18K, OF, multi-color gold dial	500	700	900
48mm, by William Hopetown, London, silver pair case, chain driven, fusee, verge escapement (illo.9)	125	150	200
48mm, 18K, OF, c. 1896, 3/4 plate, GJS	400	475	575

LEFT: 48mm, winged pierced cock, verge fusee,18k pair case, ca.1790, (illo.10). CENTER: 45mm, Repousse 20k pair case, verge fusee, c.1750 (illo.11). RIGHT: 40-42mm, TOBIAS, multi-color gold dial & case, made of thin gold for case (illo.12)

Size and Description	Avg	Ex-Fn	Mint
48mm, Tarts (London), Verge Fusee, REPOUSSE Silver case.	$700	$800	$900
48mm, winged pierced cock ,ca.1790, pair case, fusee, 18k(illo.10)	1,000	1,200	1,400
46mm, KW, KS, c. 1865, by McPherson, lever gilt mvt., silver case	55	75	95
46mm, KW, KS, fusee, dust cover, pinned plates	55	75	95
46mm, KW, KS, fusee, dust cover, Scotland	65	85	110
45mm, KW, KS, c. 1865, dust cover, lever, gilt	45	55	65
45mm, KW, KS, c. 1880, fusee, dust cover, HC	65	75	85
45mm, Repousse 20kpair case, verge fusee, ca.1750, 20K (illo.11)	2,000	2,500	3,500
44mm, KW, KS, silver case, lever movement	45	55	65
44mm, fusee, lever, KW, KS, 18K, OF	400	475	575
44mm, repousse, 18K, by Williamson, pierced cock, enamel dial	1,000	1,400	2,000
40-42mm, Tobias, multi-color gold dial & thin gold case, (illo.12)	400	500	750
23mm, small triple 18K case translucent pink enamel, for Turkish market, by Edward Prior, c.1815, pierced cock ...	5,500	7,000	8,500

MISC. FRENCH

Size and Description	Avg	Ex-Fn	Mint
58mm, 1/4repeater, musical 23 vibrating blades, signed "Berthound," sweep sec., c. 1880, 18K (illo.13)	$5,000	$6,000	$7,500
55mm, 2 figure automaton, min. repeater, 18K HC, (illo.14)	4,800	5,400	6,500
55mm, 3 figure automaton, 1/4 repeater, 18K, c. 1830	4,200	5,000	6,000
54mm, 2 figure automaton, 1/4 repeater, 18K	2,800	3,200	3,800
50mm, chain driven fusee, two-foted bridge, silver case, (illo.15)	100	150	200
50mm, chain driven fusee, two-foted bridge, 18K case, (illo.15)	550	700	875
50mm, 1 figure automaton, 1/4 repeater, silver	1,600	1,800	2,200
50mm, 1/4 repeater, repeat on bell, c. 1780, 18K	1,100	1,400	1,700
50mm, 1/4 repeater, by L'Epine, parachute, cylinder escape, gold & enamel, champleve	1,650	1,950	2,400
49mm, repousse gold pair case, 1/4 repeater on bell, (illo.16)....	3,500	4,500	5,500
47mm, by La Cloche, ultra thin, 18K, OF, gilt movement	250	350	475

Berthoud, 58mm, 1/4 repeater, center seconds, musical watch striking hours on request, with 25 vibrating blades showing dial side of movement, ca. 1820, (illo.13)

Father & Baby Time, automated minute repeater, 54mm, note animated bell striking by father and baby time, 18k hunting case. (illo.14)

French made movement, 50mm, chain driven fusee, verge escapement, note hand pierced two-footed cock attached on both sides. (illo.15)

Above 49mm, 1/4 hour verge repeater, 22K gold repousse pair case, repeating on an inner bell, repeat mechanism is activated from the pendant, ca. 1750-1780, (illo.16)

Size and Description	Avg	Ex-Fn	Mint
46mm, time, calendar & mobile sunrise & sunset, virgule escapement, c. 1795, silver, (illo.17)	$950	$1,100	$1,500
45mm, gold champleve enamel, by LeRoy, c. 1840, cylinder escapement	1,200	1,400	1,700
44mm, by Robin, gold enamel portrait, parachute, KW, KS	3,000	3,500	4,000
42mm, musical and 1/4 repeater, KW, OF, (illo.18)	2,750	3,150	3,750
41mm, 1/4 repeater, c.1820, cylinder escapement, KW,KS silver	450	575	750
40mm, ROULETTE WHEEL, marked roulette france	100	120	150
39mm, skeletonized, diamond bezel, ca.1790 , 18K, (illo.19)	2,000	2,400	2,800
38mm, gold & champleve enamel, by A. Verdiere, c. 1830, cylinder	900	1,100	1,400
36mm, 1/4 repeater, ladies, by LeRoy et Fils, HC	1,500	1,700	2,200
32mm, gold enamel, "acorn form," by Ch. Oudin, Palais Royal, c. 1880, cylinder	3,200	3,800	4,500
32mm,1/4 repeater, 18K, lever mvt., slide to repeat, KW	1,000	1,200	1,500
29mm, gold & enamel with pearls, by Bovet Flevrier, c. 1810, duplex movement	2,000	2,200	2,700

46mm, Time, calendar, mobile sunrise & sunset, virgule escapement, ca. 1795. (illo.17)

French watch, 42mm, musical, plays music on the hour or on demand. (illo.18)

Skeletonized French watch with diamond bezel, 39mm, ca. 1780. (illo.19)

MISC. SWISS

Size and Description	Avg	Ex-Fn	Mint
62mm, min. repeater, calendar & moon phases, split sec., chronograph, 30 min. register, GJS, 18K, HC	$5,200	$6,200	$7,500
60mm, heavy 14K HC, spring detent, by Ulysse Breting, c. 1880, nickel mvt., gold train & escape wheel	1,400	1,700	2,200
56mm,1/4 repeater, chronograph, by R. Picard, 18K, HC	1,200	1,400	1,800
56mm, 1/4 repeating musical, 2 barrels, music on hour or at will, c. 1820, 18K case	2,700	3,200	4,000
55mm, min. repeater, by Paul Henri Mathey, 18K, heavy HC, gold train	3,000	3,400	4,000
55mm, detent, chronometer, by Emile Perret, KW, KS, 18K, HC, nickel mvt.	800	1,100	1,400
55mm, split sec. chronograph, by James Picard, fully jeweled, 18K, HC, min. repeater................	3,800	4,400	5,200
55mm, 1/4 repeater, 2 jacks, gilt case, (illo.20)	2,200	2,500	3,000
54mm, min. repeater, moon ph., triple date, 18K HC	4,000	4,500	5,500
54mm, min. repeater, jeweled thru hammers, 18K, HC(illo.21)	2,400	2,700	3,200
54mm, by Piguet & Meylan, 1/4 musical repeater, c. 1815, 18K..	3,500	4,200	5,000
54mm, min. repeater, 18K, HC, chronograph with calendar and moon phases................	4,200	4,700	5,400
54mm, automated min. repeater, Father & Cherub, 18K, HC....	4,600	5,200	6,000
54mm, visible poor man's tourbillon, c.1905, silver, (illo.22)....	1,200	1,400	1,800
53mm, 35J, min. repeater, 1900, 18K, HC, "Zenith"	2,800	3,200	3,800
52mm, moon phase, triple date, massive 18K OF case, by Henri Grandjean	2,250	2,750	3,400

55mm, 1/4 repeater, 2 Jacquemarts, gilt case, (illo.20)

Swiss minute repeater, 54mm, jeweled through hammers, 18k case. (illo.21)

54mm Swiss, One minute so called "Poor Man's Tourbillon", center seconds silver watch with decentred dial & visible system. (illo.22)

World Time 52mm Watch, giving time in London, Singapore, Madras, Rangoon, Bombay & Calcutta. (illo.23)

Size and Description	Avg	Ex-Fn	Mint
52mm, captain's watch, KW, KS, OF, 18K, 2 train, independent sec., gold dial	$1,050	$1,350	$1,750
52mm, Time Zone or Captain's watch, KW, KS, 18K, HC	750	850	1,050
52mm, by L'Epine, c.1869, cylinder escap., KW, KS, 18K, OF	350	450	600
52mm, min. repeater, by J. Barth, 14K, HC	1,600	2,000	2,400
52mm, min. repeater, by Ernest Duval, 18K, OF	2,000	2,400	3,000
52mm, musical 1/4 repeater, KW, KS, silver case	2,100	2,400	2,800
52mm, world time, 6 time zones, c. 1900, silver, (illo.23)	500	600	800
52mm, double dials front & back, c.1910, 18k HC, (illo.24)	1,000	1,250	1,500
52mm, 20J., triple date moon ph., 18K HC, (illo.25)	1,000	1,400	1,800
51mm, 15J., enamel dial, jump hr. & min. (illo.26), 18k case	1,000	1,300	1,700
51mm, 15J., enamel dial, jump hr. & min. (illo.26), silver case	350	450	600
50mm, 1/4 repeater, by Leresche & Fils, c. 1900, 18K, OF, slide repeat	1,000	1,200	1,500
50mm, 18K, OF, by Duchene Peyrot & Co., c. 1840, gilt, lever, parachute	450	550	750
50mm, min. repeater, Carillon chime, 18K, HC, top grade	3,800	4,200	4,800

52mm, 20J., day date month, moon phase, 18K HC, (illo.25)

51mm, 15J., jump hr & min., enamel dial, ca. 1905, (illo.26)

52mm, double dials, back side opens to reveal calendars, front open to reveal the time and moon phase, ca.1910, Hunting style case, (illo. 24).

Size and Description	Avg	Ex-Fn	Mint
49mm, 18K, pocket chonometer, by Breting, Frers, c. 1840, spring detent, 15J., KW, KS......	$1,100	$1,300	$1,500
49mm, OF, c.1800-75, by common maker, pierced cock, silver .	85	125	175
48mm, 8 day, enamel dial, visible balance on dial, (illo.27).........	350	450	550
45mm, 15J, OF, HCI4P....................	55	60	75
45mm, 21J, LS, SW, Railway Special, OF......................	85	95	110
45mm, CHATELAINE, ca. 1750, 22K pair case, (illo.28)..........	2,400	2,900	3,500
44mm, ROSKOPK, 4J., 3 wheel train, base metal, (illo.29)........	65	85	110
44mm, ROSKOPK, 4J., 3 wheel train, multi-color dial, multi-color enamel on base metal case (illo.29)...................	100	125	200
44mm, Waltham Swiss mvt., 17J, "Incabloc"	55	65	75
44mm, 7J, SW, gold filled	50	55	60
44mm, multi-color, verge, pierced cock	800	1,000	1,400
44mm, min. repeater,15-21J, GUN metal HC	1,000	1,200	1,500
44mm, 1/4 repeater, 28J, by Bernard Reber, multi-color dial, gold train, 14K, HC	1,350	1,550	2,000

48mm, 8 day watch, visible balance wheel from dial side, enamel scene, (illo.27)

44mm, ROSKOPH, 3 wheel train, (4 wheel is standard), nail set, (illo.29)

45mm, CHATELAINE, with a 22K pair case watch, verge & fusee, (illo.28).

Size and Description	Avg	Ex-Fn	Mint
43mm, Automaton, blacksmith with hammered gun metal, pen set	$350	$450	$550
42mm, gold & enamel, 18K, HC	650	700	950
42mm, self wind by Von Loehr, wind indicator, silver	750	850	1,050
42mm, 21J, "Dueber" chronometer, helical hairspring, OF	800	1,000	1,400
41mm, gold champleve enamel, floral design, 18K, c. 1830	800	900	1,200
40mm, self wind, by Von Loehr, gun metal	500	650	900
40mm, 15J, moon phase, day, date, month, calendar, gun metal	165	200	250
40mm, 31J, min. repeater, split sec. chronograph, register, 18K	2,800	3,200	3,700
40mm, gilt metal & enamel, verge	300	400	550
40mm, 18K, gold & enamel + diamonds, HC, KW, KS	1,000	1,400	1,800
40mm, 18K, HC, enamel landscape scene on each side, c. 1860..	1,100	1,400	1,800
40mm, 1/4 repeater, gold enamel + diamonds, verge, fusee movement	2,600	3,000	3,500
38mm, 15J, 3/4 plate, c. 1930, YGF	50	70	95
37mm, 20K gold skeleton, entirely pierced, verge fusee, c.1770 .	3,500	4,200	5,000
36mm, self wind, cylinder escapement, gun metal case, (illo.30)	350	450	550
30mm, 18K, enamel, OF, blue & white champleve enamel, cylinder movement	400	550	650

Swiss, self wind, 36mm, cylinder escapement with wind indicator, gun metal case. (illo.30)

18mm, RING watch, enamel dial, diamond bezel, ca. 1900, 18K, (illo.31)

Size and Description	Avg	Ex-Fn	Mint
25mm, gold & enamel watch, matching enamel chain..................	$1,200	$1,450	$1,750
25mm, 18K gold & enamel, ladies, 17J, lever mvt.	700	900	1,200
25mm, 18K, OF, gold & 7 pearls, lapel watch	400	500	650
21mm, min. repeater, by Henri Grand Jean....................	2,000	2,400	3,000
21mm, 5 min. repeater, by James Freres, c. 1890, 18K, HC slide repeat........................	1,600	2,000	2,600
18mm, Ring watch, enamel dial, diamond bezel, 18K, (illo.31) ..	1,100	1,300	1,600

OTHER MISC. WATCHES

Size and Description	Avg	Ex-Fn	Mint
58mm, gilt verge oignon, a false pendulum, c.1700 , (illo.32).....	$1,800	$2,200	$2,700
57mm, 14J., 52 min.Karrusel, by Carley, ca.1895, (illo.33)...........	2,750	3,200	3,750
56mm, VIRGULE escapement, ca.1770-1800, gold case	1,200	1,500	1,850
56mm, 14K, HC, min. repeater, chronograph, calendar & moon phases........................	3,800	4,200	4,800
56mm, 18K, HC, by Union Watch Co., GJS, DES, gold pallet & escape wheel	600	700	850
53mm, 14K, 1/4 repeater, chronograph, "Invicta," c. 1900, push button repeat, HC........................	1,000	1,200	1,500
50mm, 1/4 hour repeater, by J. R. Losada, c. 1870, 18K, slide repeat, HC........................	1,700	2,100	2,600
50mm, scarab form watch, by Goering Watch Co., enamel & diamond	3,400	4,000	4,800
50mm, German dollar watch, (illo.34)	30	40	55
46mm, musical hour repeater, KW, KS, 18K	2,800	3,100	3,500
46mm, min. repeater, by J. Ullman & Co., 14K, slide repeat, c. 1900, OF........................	1,600	1,800	2,200

58mm, A gilt metal verge oignon watch with false pendulum, 58mm, ca. 1700-20. (illo.32)

57mm, 14J., a 52 minute KARRUSEL, by Geo. Carley & Co., silver case, ca.1895, (illo.33)

Size and Description	Avg	Ex-Fn	Mint
45mm, min. repeater, 18K HC, case very fancy & high grade	$2,800	$3,200	$4,000
45mm, chronometer, 15J, 14K, OF	400	450	550
45mm, lever, bar, Geneve, by Gilbert, 18K	275	325	425
44mm, 1/4 repeater, 21J, recased	250	350	450
43mm, 15J, 9K, demi-hunter case	150	200	275
42mm, 1/4 repeater, by Denand, 14K, OF	700	800	1,000
38mm, square-cut corners case, 44 diamonds on bezel, chronometer, platinum, (illo.35)	1,200	1,600	2,200

German Dollar Watch, 50mm, no jewels, 3 adjustments, "Gebruder, thiel, Ruhla Germany" engraved on back plate. (illo.34)

Chronometer, 38mm, 44 diamonds on bezel, platinum case. (illo.35)

SPECIALIZED & TECHNICAL WATCHES

Size and Description	Avg	Ex-Fn	Mint
65mm, world time, double dial in multi-color, 14K, OF	$2,400	$3,000	$3,800
60mm, calendar, triple date, moon phase, gun metal, (illo.36) ..	150	200	250
58mm, 2 train, 2 time zones, captain's watch, c.1860, 18K, (illo.37)	1,400	1,600	2,000
58mm, min. repeater, perpetual calendar, moon phases, day-date-month, chronograph, 18K, HC	12,000	14,000	17,000
55mm, 52 min. karussel, c. 1920, 3/4 plat., signed T. A. Pimblett, 18K, OF	3,200	3,600	4,400
55mm, 40J, grand sonnerie clockwatch, carillion strike, 2 train min. repeater, 18K, HC	7,500	8,200	9,500
55mm, grand & petite sonnerie clockwatch, min. repeater, 2 train, jeweled thru hammers, exposed tandem winding wheels, signed Marcks & Co., 18K, HC	8,500	10,000	12,000
54mm, musical 1/4 repeater, Piguet & Meylan, c. 1815, 18K	3,800	4,200	4,800
54mm, musical watch, with pinned cylinder, c. 1800, 18K	3,500	4,000	4,500
53mm, virgule escapement, by Lepine (inventor), c.1780, 18K ..	1,400	1,600	2,000
53mm, 2 train, clockwatch, hour repeater, signed Bourguin Le Jeune, c. 1800, 18K, OF	1,400	1,800	2,400
53mm, 13J, visible tourbillon system, c. 1913, silver, (illo.38)	1,200	1,500	1,850

Perpetual Calendar Watch, Swiss, 60mm, triple date, moon phases, gold hands, gun metal case. (illo.36)

Time Zone or Captain's Watch, 58mm, key wind & set, note separate registers for two time zones, 18k hunting case. (illo.37)

Size and Description	Avg	Ex-Fn	Mint
52mm, duplex with trapelozoidal weights, c. 1830, KW, KS, deck box, silver case	$1,300	$1,600	$2,000
52mm, deck watch, resilient lever, free sprung, c. 1880	800	1,000	1,250
51mm, 15J, helical mainspring, by Isaac Gasset & Co., Geneva, 1910 (unusual winding) (illo.39)	1,000	1,600	2,200
50mm, detent escapement, helical hairspring, 17J, 14K, HC	600	800	1,000
50mm, ruby duplex, min. repeater, signed J. R. Lund, 18K OF, 4 color of gold	4,000	4,500	5,500
50mm, 1/4 repeater, cylinder escapement, parachute shock, c. 1800, 18K, OF, (illo.40)	850	1,000	1,200
50mm, carillon chimes, triple repeat gongs, repeater, chronograph, 14K, HC	2,500	2,800	3,400
48mm, gold digital repeater, parachute shock, c. 1820	1,600	1,800	2,250
45mm, detent escapement, gold escape wheel, GF case, OF	225	275	350
45mm, chronometer escapement, wind indicator, by A. P. Walsh, 18K, OF	3,500	4,200	5,000

Visible Tourbillon, 53mm, 13 jewels, tourbillon system is visible from dial side, ca. 1913. (illo.38)

Helical Mainspring, 51mm, 15 J., rare winding system, cylindrical spring replaces standard mainspring. (illo.39)

Size and Description	Avg	Ex-Fn	Mint
44mm, reverse fusee, helical hairspring, detent escapement, by J. Penlinston 18K case	$2,000	$2,300	$2,600
44mm, circuit breaker, made by Ulysee Nardin	350	400	495
41mm, 2 train, min. repeater, 18K (Wittnauer)	3,600	4,000	4,800

Swiss 1/4 Repeater, 50mm, cylinder escapement, note parachute shock on balance bridge. (illo.40)

Early French watch movement with hour and minute hand, striking bell each hour, hand pierced case & gilt brass movement, catgut fusee, c. 1600s. (illo.41)

EARLY WATCHES

Size and Description	Avg	Ex-Fn	Mint
172mm, 4 train, coach watch, grand sonnerie, alarm, repeat, repousse case, c. 1700	$12,000	$14,000	$18,000
103mm, 3 train, coach watch, alarm, by Higgs Evans, c.1790	4,000	4,500	5,500
60mm, early French watch, catgut fusee, bell strikes the hours, hand pierced silver case, (illo.41)	14,000	18,000	24,000
Crucifix form 1/4 repeater, early French original Crystal case, ca.1600-50, (illo.42)	15,000	20,000	28,000
Crucifix form 1/4 repeater, Viennese made case, ca.1780-1800, (illo.42)	4,500	5,500	6,500
60mm, pair case, by Richard Vick, champleve dial, c. 1700	1,000	1,200	1,500
50mm, pair case, verge fusee, by Clayton, silver, c. 1730	250	300	425
50mm, rack & lever, fusee, by Ganthony of London, KW, KS	200	250	350
50mm pair case, verge fusee, pierced cock, by J. A. Freeman, c. 1790, silver	145	185	275
50mm, repeater, pair case, silver repousse scene	1,000	1,400	1,800
50mm, detached lever, fusee, DES, compensating balance by Marshall, 18K	650	750	900
48mm, pair case, repousse, by Robert Allan, c. 1760, 20K	1,600	1,900	2,600
47mm, pair case, verge, pierced cock, Benjamin Lamb, silver	450	575	650
46mm, pair case, verge fusee, by Hallifax, c.1785, 18K, repousse	1,200	1,600	2,200
45mm, repousse, fancy matching chatelaine, pierced cock, by Grantham, c. 1750, 18K	2,800	3,700	4,600
45mm, multi-color enamel case watch, by Berthoud, c.1780, 18K	1,800	2,400	2,950
45mm, multi-color gold, verge, KW, KS, by Louis Roch	1,200	1,600	2,000
43mm, pair cased, chatelaine, tortoise shell pique, by Cornelius Horbert, London, c. 1695, silver	1,800	2,600	3,500

CRUCIFIX Form 1/4 hour repeater and musical watch, Crystal and silver form case, verge fusee, original French form circa 1600 - 1660, Viennese form circa 1780 - 1800, (illo.42)

43mm, Early Drum Clock, iorn plates, 4 wheel train, brass fusee on a steel great wheel, steel contrate wheel with brass teeth, steel verge and foliot balance with T-shaped ends . The cylindrical gilt brass case is finely engraved and is 34mm high. (illo.43)

42mm, Small Lady's style pendent watch, signed Claude Raillard, French maker, ca. 1660, (illo.44)

Size and Description	Avg	Ex-Fn	Mint
43mm, Drum Clock, 34mm high, Iron plates, ca.1550s, (illo.43)	$28,000	$35,000	$45,000
42mm, early 22K watch, by Claude Raillard, ca.1160, (illo.44)....	10,000	12,000	15,000
41mm, multi-color gold case, verge, pierced cock, by Romilly, KW, KS	700	1,000	1,400
40mm, 3 colors gold, portrait of lady, diamonds, c. 1760	1,600	1,800	2,250
40mm, 3 colors gold & diamonds, repeater, by Mallet	2,400	2,700	3,400
40mm, pearls & enamel on gold, verge, pierced cock	2,800	3,000	3,200
39mm, pair cased, Freres Esquivillons, porcelain back 18K........	1,300	1,600	1,900
39mm, pair cased, adj., hour dial, for Japanese market, silver....	4,800	5,400	6,000

NOVELTY WATCHES

Rare wooden works by Bronnikoff of Russia, 60-50mm, wooden wheels, balance bridge and movement, no jewels, cylinder type escapement, c. 1890. (illo.45)

Chinese Duplex, 59mm, made for Chinese market with Chinese symbols, key wind & set. (illo.46)

Centennial Watch, 55mm, Chronograph, 17 jewels, engraved on movement "Henry O. Stauffer, Ponts Martel, pat. May 9th, 1882." (illo.47)

52mm, Eight day watch, by Hebdomas , with exposed escapement, gun metal case, (old stock look out for new style watches), (illo.48)

NOVELTY WATCHES

Size and Description	Avg	Ex-Fn	Mint
67mm, barometer watch, silver case	$500	$600	$750
60mm, bar movement, day, date, month, moon phase, gun metal, pin set	95	150	225
60mm, wooden works & case, no jewels , c.1890, (illo.45)	∽1,400	1,800	2,400
59mm, Chinese duplex, for Chinese market, silver, (illo.46)......	175	225	295
55mm, 17J, "Commemorative 1776," chronograph dial, for American mkt , 14K HC, (illo.47)	1,400	1,600	2,000
52mm, 8 day watch, balance seen from dial, GF OF, (illo.48)....	75	100	125
51mm, "Mysterieuse," mystery watch, crescent mvt., (illo.49)...	900	1,200	1,600
51mm, "Mysterieuse," mystery watch, min. repeater, crescent mvt., silver	3,500	4,000	4,500
51mm, repeater, slide repeat, gun metal..	250	300	400
50mm, digital jump hour & min., silver	150	225	300
50mm, 15J, visible tourbillon style escapement, c. 1915, gun metal	1,200	1,400	1,750
49x34mm, sector watch (fan shaped), fly back hour & min., by Record W. Co., GF, (illo.50)	1,200	1,400	1,700
46mm, gambling devices (roulette, horse racing, & dice)	85	120	175
46mm, blinking eye, silver case, (illo.51)..	250	300	375
46mm, blinking eye, gun metal case..	175	225	275
45mm, double time watch, single train, OF, silver	250	300	425
44mm, skeletonized, open numbers, open back plates, 18K	550	650	850
42mm, plates in form of bird, 22J, KW, KS, silver	95	110	150
40mm, "Shell Oil Co." watch, 7-17J, skeletonized, (illo.52).......	90	125	150
40mm, grasshopper alarm, (cricket sound), silver case	750	900	1,200
40mm, digital watch, engraved dial, silver, c. 1900	225	300	395
40mm, compass watch, KW, KS, silver case	125	175	225
30mm, ball form watch, silver & enamel, c. 1870	150	225	350
25mm, ball form watch, rim wind & set, 18K, (illo.53)...............	900	1,000	1,200
25mm, skull form watch, cylinder escapement, silver, (illo.54)..	550	700	950
20mm, ball form watch, Juvenia W. Co., silver & enamel, c.1900	125	175	225
Lock form watch, cylinder escap., 18K & enamel, (illo.55)	1,400	1,700	2,100
Masonic, triangular shape, by Tempor W. Co., 15J, Adj.3P, Swiss, (illo.56)...	1,100	1,300	1,700

Mysterieuse on watch, 51mm, note hands are set with finger, silver case. (illo.49)

Sector watch, by Record Watch Co., hour and minute hand moves to the right, then returns to home. (illo.50)

Blinking Eyes, 46mm, pin set, animated eyes. (illo.51)

Lock form watch, cylinder escap., 18K & enamel, (illo.55)

Ball Lapel Watch, rim wind & set, 18k with diamonds & sapphires. (illo.53)

Shell, 40mm, made for Shell Oil Co. through Girard Perregaux as advertising premium Ca. 1943. (illo.52)

25mm, Miniature skull form watch, cylinder escapement, chain driven fusee, silver, (illo.54)

Masonic, triangular shape, by Tempor W. Co., 15J, Adj.3P, Swiss, (illo.56)

ENAMELLED WATCHES

Floral enamel watch. Bouquet of flowers within a champleve border of scrolls enclosing panels of flowers. (illo.E-2)

Floral enamel watch. Finely painted floral enamel panel within border of seed pearls, signed Bovet. (illo.E-1)

Size and Description	Avg	Ex-Fn	Mint
58mm, harbor scene enamel, duplex, 18k, c. 1790, (illo.E-10) .	$20,000	$26,000	$32,000
57mm, floral enamel, duplex, (Bovet), pearls, 18K, (illo.E-9) ...	9,000	11,000	13,000
56mm, transfer painted lovers, c. 1761, gilt case, (illo.E8.)	500	600	700
55mm, gold fine floral enamel, pearl set, 1/4 repeating	1,500	1,800	2,200
musical, (Piguet-Meylan)	20,000	32,000	40,000
55mm, finely painted floral, seed pearls, (Bovet),18K, (illo.E.1)	6,000	7,500	9,000
55mm, Viennese enamelled verge, enamel on gilt, (illo.E-13)....	1,800	2,000	2,500
54mm, 29J., 1/4 repeater, pearls & enamel, silver case, (illo.E-14)	2,200	2,800	3,500
53mm, repeater, enamel portrait of Napoleon, gold case..........	4,500	5,500	6,500
52mm, gold enamel portrait, 3/4 plate lever mvt., c. 1910	1,200	1,500	2,000
52mm, gold fine enamel chatelaine, three formed plaques bordered in seed pearls..	10,000	12,000	15,000
48mm, painted transfer of man & women, painted border, gilt case, (illo.E.4)	650	950	1,400
47mm, gold fine enamel 1/4 repeater, by Le Roy, with a brequet style ruby cylinder..	12,000	15,000	18,000
47mm, gold enamel repeater, with chatelaine of pierced gold links & enamel plaques with enamel key & fob seals, (illo.E.2),	3,500	4,500	5,500
46mm, flowers & scrolls on green on white , gilt case, (illo.E.3)	600	750	950

Painted Floral Garlands, (illo.E-3)

Transfer Painted with scene of shepard, (illo.E-4)

Painted with scrolls and fans, (illo.E-5)

Painted with flowers within border of scrolls, (illo.E-6)

Transfer painted scene of boy and lamb. (illo.E-7)

Transfer painting with couple before alter, (illo.E-8)

VIENNESE enamelled watch, the front cover shows a lady and gentleman in a scene, the back cover pictures three boys in a scene, 55mm, (illo.E13)

VIENNESE enamelled watch, same watch as above, two-footed balance bridge, the inner lids are decorated with polychrome enamelled scenes, (illo.E-13A)

54mm, 29J., 1/4 hour repeater, Pearls and enamel on a silver case, ca. 1885, (illo.E-14

VIENNESE Lapis Lazuli enamel watch, verge fusee, top and bottom covers are finely cut solid lapis stone, champleve enamelled dial, ca. 1800, (illo.E15)

Floral enamel watch, 57mm, bouquet of flowers within a gold case set with split pearls. (illo.E.9)

Enamel scene watch, 58mm, finely painted scene of ships in harbor. (illo.E.10)

Size and Description	Avg	Ex-Fn	Mint
45mm, painted boy & lamb, gilt case, (illo.E.7)	$600	$700	$800
43mm, basket form champleve enamel, 18k, c.1800, (illo.E.11).	2,400	2,800	3,500
42mm, champleve border, finely painted flowers, (Le Roy), gold case & chain	2,500	3,000	3,500
37mm, rose gold guilloche enamel demi-hunter	400	500	600
36mm, gold enamel & champleve enamel, verge, c. 1800	1,800	2,200	2,800
35mm, gold champleve enamel, (L'Epine), cylinder	800	1,000	1,200
35mm, gold enamel & seed pearls, rose cut diamonds	400	500	600
35mm, painted flowers & painted border, gilt case, (illo.E.6)	400	500	700
34mm, gold egg-shaped form enamel, verge, (Austrian)	2,000	2,200	2,500
30mm, painted fans & scrolls, gilt case, (illo.E.5)	350	450	600
30mm, gold miniature enamel, verge, seed pearls, c. 1800	2,000	2,400	2,800
27mm, gold enamel lapel brooch with seed pearls & rose cut diamonds, c. 1890	700	800	900
27mm, gold fine enamel lapel brooch with cut diamonds by C. H. Meylan, (illo.E.12)	1,400	1,600	2,200
Enamel Form, Viennese style, verge fusee, ca.1800, (illo.E15) ..	1,500	1,700	2,000

Enamel form tapered oval basket with rising rope handle, inhanced with panels of flowers, 18K case. (illo.E.11)

A chased enamelled gold lady's pendant watch. Enamel portrait of a lady. (illo.E.12)

(ILLO. A)   (ILLO. B)   (ILLO. D)

Size and Description	Avg	Ex-Fn	Mint
27mm, Art Noveau design, multi-colored flowers gold & diamond pendant watch & pin, 18K, OF, C.1890, (illo. A)	$1,000	$1,200	$1,400
25mm, Enamel & pearls & diamonds, star shaped gold settings , pendant and pen, 18K, OF, c.1890, (illo. B)	800	900	1,000
25mm, enamel pendant with pin, golden frame of vines around a scene of a lady , 14K, OF, C.1900, ...	900	1,100	1,400
24mm, pearl pendant watch with pin, seed pearls also on classic fleur-de-lis designed pin, 14K OF, C.1885, (illo. C)	800	1,000	1,200
24mm, enamel and gold pendant watch with a starburst gold and pearl pin, 10 J. cylinder movement, 18K OF, C.1900, (illo. D) ..	1,100	1,300	1,600
22mm, ball-shaped enamel & pearl pendant watch, exposed balance, lever escapement can been seen back crystal, (illo. E)	1,400	1,700	2,200
20mm, 17J., three-finger bridge miniature movement, Adj.5P, by Didsheim platinum OF case, C.1930s, (illo. F)	1,500	1,600	1,800

(ILLO. C)   (ILLO. E)   (ILLO. F)

ROMANCING THE WRIST WATCH

The wrist watch is considered by many watch collectors to be "today's collectable." This phenomenon is due, in part, to the development of the quartz movement which began about 20 years ago and virtually revolutionized the watch market. Although these quartz watches are quiet, accurate timekeepers, and are inexpensive to manufacture, the watches of the past hold a special fascination in the heart of the collector. They enjoy collecting the timepieces with jeweled and moving parts that produce a rhythmic heartbeat inside their gold cases.

The watch collector has seen the prices of wrist watches soar in the past 10 years, as wrist watches have become more and more in demand as an object of fashion, function and jewelry. Prices have climbed highest in just the last two or three years. This year a Patek, Philippe man's platinum minute repeater wrist watch sold for the record price of 345,000 Swiss francs, about $250,000 U.S. Not far behind this record-setting sale was a Patek, Philippe "Calatrava" that brought $198,000. A Patek, Philippe enameled white gold "World Time" man's wrist watch sold for about $130,000. Some collectors have seen the values of their wrist watches double and, in many cases, triple in recent years. For example, in the early 1980s, a Patek, Phillipe perpetual calendar chronograph watch would have sold for $10,000. In 1987, the same watch would have sold for $50,000, and in 1988 for $80,000. In 1989, the price could conceivably be $100,000. Such dramatic increases in values have brought about a feverish demand for wrist watches. The Swiss wrist watch has the attention of the wealthiest collectors, with Patek, Philippe & Co. at the top of their list and Audemars Piguet, Cartier, Rolex, and Vacheron & Constantin close behind. Other wrist watches showing appreciable value are Ebel, A. Lange, Gubelin, International Watch Co., Le Coultre, Ulysse Nardin, and Piaget. Next are Jules Jurgensen, Baume & Mercier, Gerard Perregaux, Movado, and Omega; then Benrus, Bulova, Agassiz, Elgin, Gruen, Hamilton, Illinois, Longines, and Waltham, the character watches, chronographs, and complicated watches.

Many wrist watch collectors have focused on fashion and take pride in wearing their unique watches. Women have been buying high fashion men's watches to wear, making women candidates for collecting. Young men appear to enjoy collecting wrist watches rather than pocket watches. The intense competition within their increasing numbers has influenced the rising prices. European and Japanese collectors are making the biggest impact on the wrist watch market with their volume of buying, as well as the higher prices being paid. The American collector has been inspired by the heated market which has been, in part, fueled by the weakened U.S. dollar. The general appearance of a wrist watch seems to be the main factor in the price of the watch, but high mechanical standards, along with the various functions of the watch, also determine the price. Some of these features include repeaters, chronographs, duo-dials, bubble backs, curvex, flip-up tops, reverso, day-date-month moon phase, jump hour, diamond dial, world time, sector, skeletonized, character, first versions as early autowinds, very early electronics, unusual shapes, and enamel bezels.

Ebel Watch Co., chronograph with day-date-month & moon phases, outside chapter shows tachymetre, 18k gold.

Today's watches are a "mixed bag," ranging from gold luxury watches priced at $10,000, and mid-priced watches at $1,000, to the low-end plastic quartz watches at $30, and all keep time equally well. The gold watch is still a status symbol today; a mark of affluence and of appreciation for the finer things in life. The Swiss control about 85 percent of the luxury watch market, while the Japanese have about the same percentage of the market for more moderately-priced watches. The predominant companies producing the "top of the line" watches are Patek, Phillipe & Co., Cartier, Gubelin, Audemars Piguet, Piaget, Vacheron Constantin. Just below in price, but higher in volume, are names like Rolex, International Watch Co., Girard Perregaux, and Le Coultre. Collectors are also wearing high grade new watches by Ebel, Blancpain, Gerald Genta, Hublot, Raymond Weil, and watches produced for and bearing the names of Chanel, Christian Dior, and Dunhill. Prices of Ebel watches start at about $1,000 and go upward to $24,000. This company also manufactures watches for Cartier. Patek, Philippe watches range in price from $3,000 to $100,000. Audemars

Piguet produces a tourbillon wrist watch that retails for about $28,000. Blancpain, owned by Omega, produces only about 100 ultra-thin hand-made watches per year. Rolex is the most recognizable name in today's luxury wrist watch market. The Rolex 18k gold President with fluted bezel, champagne cabochon dial, and 18k gold bracelet, sells for $9,400, while the same watch with diamond bezel and dial sells for $14,400. Rolex makes the Oyster Quartz day-date, 18k gold, pave diamond dial with sapphire, bezel case, and bracelet set with 107 diamonds totaling 8.06 carats, which bears a price tag of $100,000.

The Warhol collection, which included about 200 watches, was sold on April 27, 1988 at Sotheby's for a reported price of $461,000. The artist collected watches of various styles and types. A set of three vinyl quartz character watches brought the price of $2,400. A stainless steel Gene Autry watch listed and pre-determined to bring about $100 sold for $1,700. The so-called "heavy weight" wrist watches such as Patek Philippe, Cartier, Rolex, and Vacheron Constantin sold for two to three times the estimated prices.

The trend or vogue for older watches has motivated some watch companies to reproduce favorite watches from their past models. Companies have searched their archives to find older models that sold well, and are now marketing replicas of those watches. Hamilton Classics—Authentic Reproductions From America's Past—include the Ventura (1957), Wilshire City (1939), Cabot (1935), and Ardmore (1934). Jaeger-LeCoultre's Reverso has been reintroduced, as well as Longines' hour angle watch developed and worn by Charles Lindbergh. Also, the Lorus Company has marketed a close look-a-like to the Mickey Mouse wrist watch first sold by Ingersoll in the early 1930s.

The romancing of the wrist watch is moving at a steady upward pace. Price adjustments may be needed, but should hold for a few more years. The quality American movements may still be undervalued, and the novelty or comic character wrist watches may still be a good value for the investor.

Ebel Watch Co., time only, waterproof, self winding, date, white enamel dial, bracelet and case made of stainless steel and 18k gold.

A SHORT HISTORY OF WRIST WATCHES

In the late 1700s, Queen Elizabeth adorned her wrist with a watch heavily decorated with jewels and gold. While no one is sure who invented the wrist watch Queen Elizabeth was wearing, or even the first wrist watch ever, as few appeared around 1790. Small miniature watches had been made earlier than this, however. David Rosseau made a watch which was about 18mm in diameter (the size of a dime) in the late 1600s.

Miniaturized wrist watch by Waltham. Model 400. Note size comparison to dime.

Miniaturization was a great challenge to many of the famous watch-makers including Louis Jaquet, Paul Ditisheim, John Arnold and Henri Capt. The smallest watch in semi-mass production was 12mm by 5mm. In early 1930, the American Waltham Watch Co. made a 9mm by 20mm Model 400 watch.

Wrist watches were at first thought to be too small and delicate to be practical for men to wear. However, during World War I a German officer was said to have strapped a small pocket watch to his wrist with a leather webbed cup. This arrangement freed both hands and proved to be most useful. After the war, the wrist watch gained in popularity. Mass production of wrist watches was started around 1880 by the Swiss industry. The Swiss introduced them to the United States around 1895, but they did not prove to be very popular at first. Around 1907 the Elgin and Illinois watch companies were manufacturing wrist watches and by 1912 Hampden and Waltham had started. By 1920 the

Breguet self-winding pocket watch, c.1785.   **Rotor** for self winding wrist watch.   **Harwood** self-winding wrist watch, c. 1928.

round styles were being replaced with square, rectangular and tonneau shapes and decorated with gems. By 1928 wrist watches were outselling pocket watches, and, by 1935, over 85 percent of the watches being produced were wrist watches.

Self-wind pocket watches were first developed by Abraham Louis Perrelet in 1770 and by Abraham Louis Breguet about 1777. Louis Recordon made improvements in 1780, but is was not until 1923 that the principle of self-winding was adapted to the wrist watch by John Harwood, an Englishman who set up factories to make his patented self-wind wrist watches in Switzerland, London, France, and the United States. His watches first reached the market about 1929. The firm A. Schild manufactured about 15,000 watches in Switzerland. Mr. Harwood's watch company removed the traditional stem or crown to wind the mainspring, but in order to set the hands it was necessary to turn the bezel. The Harwood Watch Co. failed around 1931 and the patent expired.

Early in 1930 the Rolex Watch Co. introduced the Rolex Oyster Perpetual, the first waterproof and self-winding wrist watch. By 1940 wrist watches came in all shapes and types including complicated chronographs, calendars, and repeaters. Novelties, digital jump hour and multi-dial were very popular, as well.

A dramatic change occurred in 1957 when the Hamilton Watch Co. eliminated the mainspring and replaced it with a small battery that lasted well over one year. In 1960 the balance wheel was removed in the Accutron by Bulova and replaced by a tuning fork with miniature pawls.

1. Case number. 2. Movement serial number. 3. Caliber number. 4. Caliber number.

Some wrist watches have a grade or caliber number engraved on the movement. For example, Patek, Phillipe & Co. has a caliber number 27-460Q. The '27' stands for 27mm; the '460Q' is the grade; the 'Q' designates Quantieme (Perpetual calendar and moon phases).

AUTOMATIC WINDING

The self-winding watch uses the movements of the body in order to wind up the mainspring slowly and nearly continuously. The first pocket self-winding watches were executed by a watchmaker from Le Locle, Abraham-Louis Perrelet, around 1770.

Early self wind pocket watch by Breguet.

Eterna-Matic Automatic Winding Mechanism. 1—Oscillating weight. 2—Oscillating gear. 3—Upper wheel of auxiliary pawl-wheel. 4—Lower wheel of auxiliary pawl-wheel. 5—Pawl-wheel with pinion. 6—Lower wheel of pawl-wheel with pinion. 7—Transmission-wheel with pinion. 8—Crown-wheel yoke. 9—Winding pinion. 10—Crown-wheel. 11—Ratchet-wheel. 12—Barrel. 13¢Driving runner for ratchet-wheel. 14—Winding stem. 15-Winding button.

They were improved soon after by Abraham-Louis Breguet. In the case of the pocket watch, the movements causing the winding of the watch were essentially the result of walking. This system of winding was never widely adopted. The watch was a fancy model and not a really useful one. Herman von der Heydt was the only maker in America to work with the self-winding pocket watch. However, inventors always kept the idea of the self-winding watch in mind.

In 1923, the British firm Harwood took up once again the solution of the problem of automatic winding, for wrist watches. This was the spark which rapidly resulted in research to improve and simplify this type of mechanism. A company was formed in London to manufacture Harwood's watch, and before long over 500 jewelers in the United Kingdom were selling his automatic watch. A second company was formed in France, and a third in the United States. The business flourished about two and one-half years. Then, in 1931, these companies were liquidated.

HOW TO READ THE TACHY-TELEMETER DIAL

Tachometer

The spiral scale around center of dial indicates miles per hour, based on a trial over one mile. It indicates speeds from 400 to 20 miles per hour on three turns. Each turn of spiral corresponds to one minute (scale for first 8 seconds being omitted), the outer turn from 400 to 60 (0 to 1 minute) and the center turn from 30 to 20 miles per hour (2 to 3 minutes).

When passing the first marker of mile zone, start chronograph hand by pressing push piece. When passing following mile marker, press push piece again. The chronograph hand now indicates the speed in miles per hour on the spiral. If a mile has been made in less than one minute the speed will be indicated on outside turn of spiral; from 1 to 2 minutes on middle turn and 2 to 3 minutes on center turn.

EXAMPLE: If a mile has been made in 1 minute and 15 seconds the chronograph hand indicates 48 miles per hour on middle turn of spiral.

Telemeter

The Telemeter scale around margin of dial is based on the speed of sound compared with the speed of light. Each small division is 100 meters. The scale is read in kilometers and hundreds of meters. Approximately 16 divisions equal 1 mile.

TO DETERMINE THE DISTANCE OF A STORM: When you see the flash of lightning press push piece of chronograph. When hearing thunder press again, the chronograph hand will indicate on the Telemeter scale the distance in kilometers and hundreds of meters. One kilometer equals 5/8 of a mile.

Dial No. 1 is a simple stop watch dial. Graduated into fifths of seconds.

Dial No. 2 is used to time a car over a quarter-mile track and read the numbers of miles per hour directly from dial.

Dial No. 3 is used to measure speed in kilometers per hour over a course of one fifth of a kilometer.

Dial No. 4 used by physicians to count the pulse beats of a patient.

Dial No. 5 is used by artillery officers for determining distance by means of sound in kilometers.

Dial No. 6 shows a tachometer: many watches are made with several scales on the same dial in order to cover a greater range of functions. The figures are sometimes grouped in a spiral form or in several circles, thus the hand may make more than one complete revolution.

WRIST WATCH CASE AND DIAL STYLES

Barrel

Maxine

Square

Round

Square Cut Corner

Cushion

Rectangle

Flared

Tank

Round
(Ladies style; converts to lapel or wrist)

Curved or Curvex

Rectangle Cut Corner

Tonneau

Baguette

Oval

Caliber number

Coded number

Coded symbol

Company name

MERCEDES

TRYLON

BATON (RECTILINE)

BATON

MOON

REGATE

POINTEX

LEAF

HOUR and MINUTE HANDS

ALPHA

DAUPHINE

DAUPHINE PITCHED

DIAMOND

FILS

RADIUM

INDEX

MODERN

FUSEAUX

LANCE

RADIUM DAUPHINE

SECOND HANDS

ALPHA   DAUPHINE   INDEX   MODERN

FILS

(REGULAR)

CHRONOGRAPH

The term chronograph is derived from the Greek words *chronos* which means "time" and *grapho* which means "to write." The first recording of intervals of time was around 1822 by the inventor Rieussec. His chronograph made dots of ink on a dial as a measure of time. Around 1862 Adolph Nicole introduced the first chronograph with a hand that returned to zero. The split second chronograph made its appearance around 1879. Today a chronograph can be described as a timepiece that starts at will, stops at will, and can return to zero at will. A mechanical chronograph had a sweep or center second hand that will start, stop, and fly back to zero. The term chronometer should not be confused with chronograph. A chronometer is a timepiece that has superior timekeeping qualities at the time it is made.

A. Day window. **B.** Split second hand. **C.** Calendar pusher. **D.** Register for seconds. **E.** Calendar pusher. **F.** Date hand. **G.** Register for total hours. **H.** Sweep center second hand. **I.** Month window. **J.** Start/stop pusher. **K.** Register for total minutes. **L.** Return pusher. **M.** Day of month.

SWISS CODE INITIALS

Some Swiss watches have three initials on the balance bridge. These initials are **not** model identification but are for house identification. Following is a list of import initials with the name of the Swiss company maker.

AOC—Roamer
AOL—Adolph Schwarcz & Son
AOX—Alstate W. Co.
AXA—Wittnauer
AXZ—Benrus
BOL—Bernard S. Lipman
BXC—Avia
BXJ—Midland
BXN—Benrus
BXP—Imperial, Bayer, Pretzfelder & Mills
BXW—Bulova
COC—Crawford
COW—Croton
CXC—Concord
CXD—Cypres
CXH—Clinton
CXV—Cort
CXW—Central; Benrus
DOB—Dreffa W. Co.
DOW—Deauville
EOE—Elrex
EON—Avalon
EOP—Harvel
EOT—Lavina
EXC—Everbrite
FXE—Provis
FXU—Louis Aisenstein & Bros.
FXW—Louis
GXC—Gruen
GXI—Gotham (Ollendorff)
GXM—Girard-Perregaux
GXR—Grant
GXW—Gothic
HOM—Homis
HON—Tissot; A. Hirsch

HOR—Lanco; Langendorf
HOU—Oris
HOX—Patek, Philippe
HXF—Harman
HXM—R. H. Macy & Co.
HXN—Harvel
HXO—Harold K. Oleet
HXW—Helbros
JXE—Normandie
JXJ—Jules Jurgensen
KOT—Landau
KXJ—Wm. J. Kappel
KXV—Louis
KXZ—Kelton; Benrus, Central
LOA—Emil Langer
LOD—Latham
LOE—Packard
LXA—Laco, Winton, Elbon
LXE—Evkob
LXJ—LeCoultre
LXW—Longines
MOG—Mead & Co.; Boulevard
MOU—Tower; Delbana
MXE—Monarch
MXH—Seeland
MXI—Movado
MXT—Mathey-Tissot
NOS—Heritage
NOU—Louvic
NXJ—National Jewelers Co.
NXO—Oris
OXG—Omega
OXL—Wyler
OYT—Shriro (Sandoz)
POY—Camy; Copley
PXA—Pierce
PXP—Patek, Philippe

PXT—Paul Breguette
PXW—Parker
PYS—Langel
QXO—Kelbert
ROC—Raleigh
ROL—Ribaux
ROP—Rodania
ROW—Rolex
RXG—R. Gsell & Co.
RXM—Galmor
RXW—Rima
RXY—Liengme
RYW—Ritex
SOA—Felca
SOE—Semca
SOW—Seeland
SOX—Cortebert, Orvin
SXE—Savoy; Banner
SXK—S. Kocher & Co.
SXS—Franco
UOA—Actua
UOB—Aero
UOW—Universal
UXM—Medana
UXN—Marsh
UYW—Stanley W. Co.
VOS—Sheffield
VXN—Vacheron & Constantin
VXT—Kingston
WOA—Tower
WOB—Wyler
WOR—Creston
WXC—Buren
WXE—Welsbro
WXW—Westfield
ZOV—Titus
ZYV—Hampden (new company)

☞ To determine your wrist watch band size use the above gauge and measure between the lugs. The band sizes are listed on each side of the gauge.

WRIST WATCH LISTINGS
Pricing at Retail Level
(Complete Watches Only)

Unless otherwise noted, wrist watches listed in this section are priced at the retail level and as complete watches having an original 14k gold-filled case with an original dial, and the entire original movement in good working order with no repairs needed. They are also priced as having a watch band made of leather except where bracelet is described. Watches listed as 14k and 18k are solid gold cases. Coin or silveroid-type and stainless steel cases will be listed as such. Dollar-type watches, or low cost production watches, are listed as having a base metal type case and a composition dial.

Many of the watch manufacturers were commissioned to put jewelers' or jobbers' names on their movements in place of their own. Because of this practice, the true manufacturers of these movements are difficult to identify. These watch models are listed under the original manufacturer and can be identified by comparison with the model sections under each manufacturer. See "Personalized Watches" and "Swiss Code Initials" for more detailed information.

The prices shown were averaged from dealers' lists just prior to publication and are an indication of the retail level or what collectors will pay. **Prices** are provided in three categories: **average condition, extra fine,** and **mint condition,** and are shown in whole dollar amounts only. The values listed are a guide for the retail level and are provided for your information only. Dealers will not necessarily pay full retail price. Prices listed are for watches with **original** cases and dials.

Note: Descriptions and serial number ranges listed for early watches cannot be considered 100 percent accurate due to the manner in which records were kept by these companies.

WARNING: There are currently fake wrist watches being sold on the worldwide market. These watches have the appearance of authenticity but are merely cheap imitations of prestigious companies such as Rolex (all types), Gucci, Cartier, and Piaget.

INFORMATION NEEDED — We are interested in any facts and information you might have that should possibly be considered for future editions. Documented facts are needed, so please send photo or sources of information. Send to: Cooksey Shugart, P. O. BOX 3147, Cleveland, Tennessee 37320 – 3147. (When corresponding, please include a self-addressed, stamped envelope.)

ABERCROMBIE & FITCH,17J.,chronog.by Valj.,3 reg.
s.steel.. $400 $500 $600

ABERCROMBIE & FITCH, 17J., "Sea Farer," chronog.,
waterproof
s. steel.. $300 $350 $450

ABRA, 17J.,step design case, c.1930s
base metal................................. $40 $45 $55

ABRA, 17J.,step case, c.1930s
base metal................................. $30 $35 $45

ABRA,17J.,carved case, c.1930s
base metal $30 $35 $45

ABRA, 17J.,engraved case
base metal $30 $35 $45

ABRA,15J.,curved case, c.1930s
base metal $30 $35 $45

ABRA,15J.,engraved case, c.1930s
gold plate..................................... $30 $35 $45

ABRA,17J., jump hour,
s. steel.......................................$200 $250 $300

ACRO W. CO., 17 jewels, hinged back,
18k $600 $700 $800

ADMES, 17 jewels, self wind, waterproof, center sec.,
gold filled $25 $30 $40

AGASSIZ, 17 jewels, World Time,
18k $7,000 $8,000 $9,000

AGASSIZ, 17 jewels, fancy bezel,
18k $2,000 $2,500 $3,000

AGASSIZ 18 jewels, for Tiffany & Co., 48mm,
18k $1,000 $1,200 $1,400

AGASSIZ, 17J., C. 1940s
18K(W) $600 $700 $800

AGASSIZ, 18 jewels, barrel shaped dial, 40mm,
18k $700 $800 $900

AGASSIZ, 17 jewels, for Tiffany & Co., 45mm
18k $1,000 $1,200 $1,400

ALPHA, 17J.,chrono. 2 reg., cal.48, c.1950s
s.steel $150 $175 $200

ALPHA, 17J., sweep sec., c. 1948
18k $250 $300 $350

ALPINA, 15 jewels, automatic, water proof, center sec.
gold filled $30 $40 $50

ALTUS, 17 jewels, ref. 827
18k..$150 $175 $200

ALPINA, 17 jewels, automatic, water proof, aux. sec.
18k $200 $250 $300

AM. WALTHAM, 17J., c.1930s
14k..$150 $175 $250

ALSTA, 17 jewels, wrist alarm
gold filled................................. $100 $125 $150

AM. WALTHAM, 17J., aux. sec. c.1930s
14k..$150 $175 $250

ALTON, 17J., fancy lugs, c.1950s
14K $125 $150 $175

AM. WALTHAM, 17J., aux. sec., c.1930s
14k..$140 $165 $240

AM. WALTHAM, 21J., cal. 750B, GJS, c.1950s
14k..$150 $175 $250

AM. WALTHAM, 17J.,cal.750B, c.1951
gold filled $75 $85 $150

AM. WALTHAM, 17 jewels, "Cromwell"
gold filled $65 $80 $150

AM. WALTHAM, 15J.,"Ruby "model, c.1918
14k $165 $185 $230

AM. WALTHAM, 17 jewels, "Oberlin"
gold filled $65 $80 $150

AM. WALTHAM, 17J, "Premier"model, c.1940s
gold filled $65 $75 $150

AM. WALTHAM, 15 jewels, engraved bezel
gold filled $65 $80 $125

AM. WALTHAM, 17J, "ruby"model, G#714, c.1950s
gold filled $65 $75 $150

AM. WALTHAM, for Tiffany & Co.
14k $400 $450 $550

AM. WALTHAM, 17 J, barrel shaped dial, c. 1920
14k $400 $500 $600

AM.WALTHAM, 19J.,enamel dial, C. 1905
silver $200 $250 $300

AM. WALTHAM, 17 jewels, wire lugs
14k $300 $400 $500

AM. WALTHAM, 17 jewels, "Duxbury"
gold filled $65 $80 $150

AM. WALTHAM, 21 jewels, curved back
14k $250 $300 $425

AM. WALTHAM, 17 jewels, wandering sec., c. 1930
gold filled $200 $250 $300

AM. WALTHAM, 17 jewels, "Fairmont"
gold filled $75 $100 $200

AM. WALTHAM, 17 jewels, "Stan Hope"
gold filled $65 $80 $150

AM. WALTHAM, 17 jewels, "Winfield"
gold filled $65 $80 $150

AM. WALTHAM, wandering min., jumping hr., c. 1933
gold filled $600 $900 $1,200

AM. WALTHAM, 15J., aux. sec.
gold filled $100 $150 $200

AM. WALTHAM, 21 jewels, "Albright"
14k $100 $125 $150

AM. WALTHAM, 21 jewels, "Sheraton"
14k $125 $150 $175

AM. WALTHAM, 17 jewels, center sec.
gold filled................................... $40 $50 $65

AM. WALTHAM, 21J.,"Riverside"model, enamel dial
gold filled.................................... $75 $100 $175

AM. WALTHAM, 15 jewels, wire lugs, c. 1916
silver $200 $250 $300

AM. WALTHAM, 7J.,pulsations,c.1925
silver.. $225 $250 $350

AM. WALTHAM, 15 J., case by Rolland Fischer
silver $225 $275 $350

AM. WALTHAM, 17J.,"riverside",GJS, c.1918
silver..$400 $450 $600

AM. WALTHAM, 7J.,oxidized case,c.1930s
gold filled................................... $65 $75 $150

AM. WALTHAM, 15J., enamel dial, single lugs,c.1915
silver $225 $274 $375

AM. WALTHAM, 7-15J., c.1930s
gold filled................................$70 $80 $175

AM. WALTHAM, 15J., oxidized case, c. 1930s
gold filled $75 $100 $175

AM. WALTHAM, 15J., engraved case
gold filled $75 $85 $150

AM. WALTHAM, 15J., case by Rolland Fischer,
silver $400 $500 $600

AM. WALTHAM, 15 jewels, "Depollier," early water
proof, (tin can style), c. 1917
silver $400 $500 $600

AM. WALTHAM, 15 jewels, protective grill, c. 1907
14k.. $1,000 $1,200 $1,500

AM. WALTHAM, 17 jewels, military with hack set
s. steel.. $75 $100 $175

AM. WALTHAM, 17 jewels, cut-corner dial
14k.. $250 $350 $500

AM. WALTHAM, 17 jewels, luminus dial
14k.. $250 $350 $500

AM. WALTHAM, 17 jewels, wire lugs
gold filled.................................. $125 $175 $250

AM. WALTHAM, 17 jewels, center lugs
14k... $125 $150 $175

AM. WALTHAM, 17 jewels, "Allen"
gold filled.................................. $65 $80 $150

AM. WALTHAM, 17 jewels, "Penton"
gold filled.................................. $65 $80 $125

AM. WALTHAM, 9-17 jewels, "side-wrist"
gold filled.................................. $125 $150 $200

AM. WALTHAM, 17 jewels, curvex, 42mm
14k... $300 $350 $400

AM. WALTHAM, 17 jewels, curvex, 52mm
14k...$400 $500 $700

AM. WALTHAM, 17 jewels, curvex, 42mm
gold filled...................................$100 $125 $175

AM. WALTHAM, 17-21 jewels, curved
14k...$175 $225 $300
gold filled...................................$65 $75 $125

AM. WALTHAM, 17 jewels, curved, aux. sec.
gold filled...................................$65 $80 $150

AM. WALTHAM, 17 jewels, curved
gold filled...................................$65 $75 $120

AM. WALTHAM, 21 jewels, C.1938
14K $150 $200 $250

AM. WALTHAM, 17 jewels, curved
gold filled $60 $70 $100

AM. WALTHAM, 17 jewels, curved
gold filled $65 $75 $125

AM. WALTHAM, 17 jewels, enamel bezel
14k $800 $1,000 $1,500
14k (w) $600 $800 $1,000
gold filled $200 $300 $400

AM. WALTHAM, 17J., enamel bezel,"ruby" model,c.1928
14k(w) $350 $400 $550

AM. WALTHAM,17J., stepped case,
gold filled $100 $150 $200

AM. WALTHAM, 17 jewels, "Jeffrey"
gold filled $65 $80 $150

AM. WALTHAM, 21 jewels, "Tulane"
gold filled $40 $50 $75

AM. WALTHAM, 17J., triangular, masonic symbols,
fancy hands, c. 1950
gold filled $900 $1,100 $1,500

AM. WALTHAM, 7-15J.,luminous dial, c.1928
base metal $60 $70 $100

AM. WALTHAM, 7-15J., cushion case, c.1928
gold filled.................................... $65 $75 $150

AM. WALTHAM, 17J.,luminous dial, c.1929
14k(w)......................................$175 $225 $325

AM. WALTHAM, 7-15J., tonneau case, c. 1928
gold filled.................................... $65 $75 $150

AM. WALTHAM, 17J.,aux. sec., c. 1928
14k(w)..$175 $225 $325

AM. WALTHAM, 7J., luminous dial, c.1928
base metal.................................. $60 $70 $120

AM. WALTHAM,7-15J., lugless case, c.1928
gold filled.................................... $60 $75 $125

AM. WALTHAM, 7J., luminous dial, c. 1928
gold filled.................................... $75 $85 $150

AM. WALTHAM,15J., luminous dial, c.1928
14k..$175 $225 $375

AM. WALTHAM,15J., brush finish, c.1928
14k..$175 $225 $375

AM. WALTHAM, 7J., luminous dial, c.1928
gold plate $75 $85 $135

AM. WALTHAM, 17J., GJS, ca.1940
14K $150 $175 $250

AM. WALTHAM, 7-15J., cut corner case, c.1929
gold filled $75 $85 $95

AM. WALTHAM, 7-15J., Butler finish, c.1928
gold filled $85 $95 $185

AM. WALTHAM, 15J., fluted case, GJS, c.1925
14k(w) $95 $110 $150

AM. WALTHAM, 7-15., engraved case, etched dial, c.1929
14k(w).. $65 $75 $120
gold filled...................................... $30 $40 $80

AM. WALTHAM, 15J., engraved case, etched dial, c.1928
14K(W) $65 $75 $120
gold filled...................................... $30 $40 $90

AM. WALTHAM, 7-15J., enamel case, c. 1928
14k(w).. $80 $95 $155

AM. WALTHAM, 15J., enamel case, c.1929
gold filled (w) $30 $40 $90

AM. WALTHAM, 15J., enamel case, c.1929
gold filled (w) $30 $40 $90

AM. WALTHAM, 15J., engraved case, c.1928
14k(w).. $65 $75 $120
gold filled (w) $30 $40 $90

AM. WALTHAM, 15J., oxidized engraved case, c.1928
gold filled (w) $35 $45 $95

AMERICAN WALTHAM WATCH CO. IDENTIFICATION BY MOVEMENT

Model 1900, 0 size

Model 1907, 0 size

Jewel Series

Model 1900, 0/3 size, open face

Model 1907, 0/3 size, hunting

Model 1898 & 1912, 0/6 size, hunting

Model 1898 & 1912, 0/6 size, open face

10½ ligne

10 ligne

7½ ligne

5¼ ligne

Model 400

Model 450

Model 650

Model 675

Model 750

AMERICUS, 17 jewels, 8 day movement, c. 1933
18k $1,000 $1,200 $1,500
gold filled $400 $500 $600

ANGELUS, 17J., day, date, moon ph.,C. 1949
s. steel $100 $150 $200

AMERICUS, 7 jewels, c.1935
gold filled $100 $125 $150

ANGELUS, 17 jewels, chrono., 2 reg., water proof
s. steel $200 $250 $300

ANGELUS, 17 jewels, chronog., 2 reg., c. 1943
18k $700 $900 $1,100
14k $400 $500 $600
gold filled $150 $200 $250

ANGELUS, 17J.,date and alarm, c.1955
s. steel $100 $125 $150

ANGELUS, 17J.,chronog.,triple date, C. 1949
s. steel $200 $250 $300

ANGELUS, 27 jewels, quarter repeater
s. steel $2,500 $2,700 $3,000

ARAMIS, 15 jewels, early self wind, lug action winding by back & forth motion of watch case, c. 1933
s. steel.................................. $600 $700 $900

ARDATH, 17J., chrono, triple date, c.1947
s. steel $250 $300 $350

ARBU, 17 jewels, triple date, moon phase
18k $800 $1,000 $1,200
s. steel...$300 $350 $400

ARISTO, 17 jewels, chronog., water proof
s. steel...$150 $175 $225

ARBU, 17 jewels, chronog., 3 reg., day-date-month
s. steel...$200 $250 $300

ARISTO, 17J., chronog, 3 reg., triple date
s. steel $300 $400 $550

ARBU, 17 jewels, split sec. chronog.
18k $2,000 $2,500 $3,000

ARISTO, 17 jewels, day-date-month, moon phase
s. steel $100 $135 $185

ARSA, 17 jewels, day-date-month, moon phase
18k....................................$700 $800 $900
s. steel...................................$200 $250 $300

ARSA, 15 jewels, day-date-month, moon phase
18k................................$700 $800 $900
s. steel...................................$200 $250 $300

ASPREY, 16 jewels, curved hinged back
9k $300 $400 $500

ASPREY, 17J., date, ca. 1930s
gold filled. $150 $200 $275

ASPREY, 15 jewels, duo dial
18k $1,200 $1,400 $1,600

ASPREY, 17 jewels, enamel dial, center lugs
9k................................$200 $250 $300

AUDEMARS PIGUET, 29 J., min. repeater, c. 1907
18k..$60,000 $70,000 $80,000

AUDEMARS PIGUET, 29 J., min. repeater, c. 1925
platinum $70,000 $80,000 $90,000

AUDEMARS PIGUET, 19 J., tourbillon, self-winding
tourbillon can be seen from dial side
18k..$8,000 $9,000 $10,000

AUDEMARS PIGUET, 36 J., octogonal shaped case,
triple date, moon phase
18k C&B $12,000 $13,000 $14,000

AUDEMARS PIGUET, 33J., day date, moon ph. c.1989
18k $3,000 $3,200 $3,400

AUDEMARS PIGUET, 17 J., chronog., 3 reg., c. 1945
18k.......................................$20,000 $25,000 $30,000

AUDEMARS PIGUET, day date, moon ph., C. 1980s
18k $3,000 $3,500 $4,000

AUDEMARS PIGUET, 22 jewels, chronog., 2 reg.,
18k.......................................$18,000 $20,000 $22,000

AUDEMARS PIGUET, chronog.,triple date, moon ph.,
c. 1940s
18k $20,000 $25,000 $39,000

AUDEMARS PIGUET, 18 J., triple date, moonphase
18k...$8,000 $9,000 $10,000

AUDEMARS PIGUET, 36 jewels, gold rotor, day-date
month, moon phase
18 C&B $9,000 $10,000 $11,000

AUDEMARS PIGUET, skeletonized, triple date,
moon phase, C. 1980s
platinum $12,000 $14,000 $16,000

AUDEMARS PIGUET, 18 J., "Le Brassus," chronog. skeletonized
18k C&B............................ $20,000 $22,000 $25,000

AUDEMARS PIGUET, 17 J., center lugs,skeletonized
18k...$7,000 $7,500 $8,500

AUDEMARS PIGUET, 18 jewels, skeletonized
18k $7,000 $8,000 $10,000

AUDEMARS PIGUET, 17J., Dodecagonal, black dial
18k...$1,200 $1,400 $1,600

AUDEMARS PIGUET, 17 jewels, thin skeletonized
18k $5,000 $6,000 $7,000

AUDEMARS PIGUET, 17J., diamond dial, c. 1970
18k...$2,000 $2,200 $2,500

AUDEMARS PIGUET, 36 jewels, skeletonized
18k $5,500 $6,500 $8,000

AUDEMARS PIGUET, 12 diamond dial c.1960
platinum $2,000 $2,200 $2,500

AUDEMARS PIGUET, 11 diamond dial
18k...$1,600 $1,800 $2,000

AUDEMARS PIGUET, 12 sapphire dial, c.1950
18k $2,500 $2,700 $3,000

AUDEMARS PIGUET, 17J., diamond bezel, ctr. lugs
18k................................$2,000 $2,200 $2,400

AUDEMARS PIGUET, 17 jewels, 12 diamond dial
18k (w) $2,500 $2,700 $3,000

AUDEMARS PIGUET, 20J.,rope style bezel, c. 1980s
18k case 14k band................$1,000 $1,100 $1,200

AUDEMARS PIGUET, 36 jewels, self-winding
18k $1,400 $1,600 $1,800

AUDEMARS PIGUET, 20J., "Le Brassus," c. 1970
18k C&B $2,000 $2,200 $2,400

AUDEMARS PIGUET, 17 jewels, adj. to 5 positions
18k C&B................................ $1,200 $1,400 $1,600

AUDEMARS PIGUET, fancy shaped, c.1960s
18k..$2,500 $3,000 $3,500

AUDEMARS PIGUET, 17 jewels, rope style bezel
18k C&B................................ $1,500 $1,800 $2,000

AUDEMARS PIGUET, 36 jewels, self-winding
18k $1,800 $2,000 $2,400

AUDEMARS PIGUET, 36 jewels, lazuli dial
18k C&B................................. $2,200 $2,400 $2,800

AUDEMARS PIGUET, 17 jewels, thin style
18k C&B................................. $2,000 $2,200 $2,500

AUDEMARS PIGUET, 17 jewels, fancy bezel, c. 1950
18k $1,500 $2,000 $2,500

AUDEMARS PIGUET, 17J., "Philosopher", hour hand
18k $2,200 $2,500 $2,800

AUDEMARS PIGUET, 20 jewels, thin model
18k...$900 $1,000 $1,200

AUDEMARS PIGUET, 17J., engraved bezel, c. 1963
18k...$900 $1,000 $1,250

AUDEMARS PIGUET, 17J., wide bezel, thin model
14k C&B $1,500 $1,600 $1,800

AUDEMARS PIGUET, 21J., auto wind, center sec.
18k...$1,500 $1,600 $1,800

AUDEMARS PIGUET, world time, fancy lugs
s. steel $10,000 $12,000 $15,000

AUDEMARS PIGUET, world time , c. 1940s
14k $12,000 $14,000 $17,000

AUDEMARS PIGUET, 18 jewels, gold train
18k $2,500 $3,000 $3,500

AUDEMARS PIGUET, 18J., adj. to 8 pos., c. 1940
18k $1,500 $1,600 $1,700

AUDEMARS PIGUET, 18 jewels, aux. sec. c. 1940
18k $2,000 $2,200 $2,500

AUDEMARS PIGUET, 17 jewels, for Tiffany & Co.
18k C&B $1,500 $1,600 $1,800

AUDEMARS PIGUET, 18 jewels, aux. sec.
18k $1,500 $1,800 $2,000

AUDEMARS PIGUET, 18 jewels, tank style, c. 1960
18k (w) $1,500 $1,600 $1,800

AUDEMARS PIGUET, 18 jewels, hooded lugs
18k $2,500 $2,800 $3,200

AUDEMARS PIGUET, 17J., engraved bezel, c.1966
18k $1,500 $1,700 $2,000

AUDEMARS PIGUET, 18 J., curved back, c. 1940
18k $1,500 $1,800 $2,000

AUDEMARS PIGUET, 18 jewels, center sec., c. 1950
18k $1,500 $1,800 $2,200

AUDEMARS PIGUET, 18 J., straight line lever escape.
18k $1,200 $1,400 $1,700

AUDEMARS PIGUET, 17 jewels, mid-size
18k $500 $600 $700

AUDEMARS PIGUET, gold textured dial, c. 1960s
18k $1,000 $1,100 $1,200

AUDEMARS PIGUET, 18j., aux. sec., c. 1950s
18k $1,200 $1,500 $1,800

AUDEMARS PIGUET, 18j., auto wind, waterproof
18k $1,600 $1,800 $2,000

AUDEMARS PIGUET, 18 jewels, painted dial, c. 1970
18k $800 $900 $1,100

AUDEMARS PIGUET, 21 jewels, 18k gold rotor
18k $1,700 $1,900 $2,300

AUDEMARS PIGUET, 19j.,center sec.
18k $1,500 $2,000 $2,500

AUDEMARS PIGUET, 18J., screw back, waterproof
18k $1,600 $1,800 $2,000

AUDEMARS PIGUET, 17 jewels, gold train
18k $1,000 $1,200 $1,500

AUDEMARS PIGUET, triple date,moon ph., c.1930s
18k $30,000 $35,000 $40,000

AUDEMARS PIGUET, 18 jewels," top hat", aux. sec., c.
1950
platinum................................... $3,000 $3,500 $4,000

AUDEMARS PIGUET, 17J., gold train, 2 tone case in
platinum & gold
18k (w) C&B $2,500 $2,700 $3,000

AUDEMARS PIGUET, large bezel, c.1940s
18k C&B $3,000 $3,500 $4,000

AUDEMARS PIGUET, 17 jewels, gold train
14k C&B $1,600 $1,800 $2,200

AUDEMARS PIGUET, 18 J., textured bezel, c. 1950
18k..$2,000 $2,200 $2,600

AUDEMARS PIGUET,2 tone dial, c.1930s
18k...$2,500 $3,000 $3,500

AUDEMARS PIGUET, 17 jewels, gold train, c. 1960
18k (w) $1,500 $1,600 $1,800

AUDEMARS PIGUET, 18J, curvex, large bezel, c. 1950
18k $2,000 $2,200 $2,500

AUDEMARS PIGUET, 18 jewels, tank style
18k $2,000 $2,200 $2,500

AUDEMARS PIGUET, Royal Oak, c.1980s, date
18k C&B............................. $5,000 $6,000 $7,000

AUDEMARS PIGUET, quartz, 12 diamonds, c. 1981
s. steel.................................... $1,200 $1,400 $1,600

AUDEMARS PIGUET, ladys 72 small diamonds, c.30s
plat.case 7 band.................... $1,500 $1,700 $2,000

AUSTIN, 17J., fancy bezel,
gold filled................................... $70 $80 $90

AUTOMATIQUE, 17J., cal.F699, c. 1955
s. steel... $50 $60 $75

AUTORIST, 15 jewels, lug action wind, enamel dial
s. steel...................................... $500 $600 $700

AUTORIST, 15 jewels, lug action, c. 1930
s. steel... $500 $600 $700

AUTORIST, 15 jewels, lug action, c. 1930
gold filled $600 $700 $800

AUTORIST, 15 jewels, lug action (lady's)
s. steel $300 $350 $400

AVALON,17J., aux.sec.
gold filled $30 $35 $50

AVALON,17J., aux.sec.
gold filled $50 $60 $70

BALL W. CO., 25 jewels, adj. to 5 pos., E.T.A.
10k $375 $400 $450

BALL W. CO., 25 jewels, adj. to 5 pos., E.T.A.
gold filled $275 $300 $325

BALL W. CO., 25 jewels, adj. to 5 pos., E.T.A.
s. steel $225 $250 $275

BAUME & MERCIER, 18J., triple date, moon phase
s. steel $300 $350 $400

BAUME & MERCIER, 17j.,chronog. 2 reg.,c.1949
gold filled $200 $250 $300

BAUME & MERCIER, 17j.,chronog. 2 reg.,c.1950s
18k $600 $700 $800

BAUME & MERCIER, 18J., chronog., 3 reg. & dates
s. steel...................................... $700 $800 $900

BAUME & MERCIER, 18 J., chronog., 3 reg. & dates
18k $800 $900 $1,000

BAUME & MERCIER, 18 jewels, tachymeter, c. 1960
s. steel.. $500 $600 $700

BAUME & MERCIER, 17J., triple date,chronog.
moon ph. c.1950s
18k.......................................$1,200 $1,500 $1,800

BAUME & MERCIER, 18 J., chronog., fancy lugs
18k..$1,800 $2,200 $2,600

BAUME & MERCIER, 17J., chronog., triple date
18k..$800 $900 $1,000

BAUME & MERCIER, 18J., triple date, moon phase
18k..$800 $900 $1,000

BAUME & MERCIER, 17J., 2 dials, 2 time zones &
2 movements
18k $600 $700 $800

Baume & Mercier, 18 jewels, gold dial, date
14k C&B.................................... $400 $450 $500

BAUME & MERCIER, 18 jewels, thin model
14k C&B.................................... $400 $450 $500

BAUME & MERCIER, 17 jewels, center sec., c. 1956
14k $200 $250 $300

BAUME & MERCIER, 17 jewels, aux. sec., c. 1955
14k..$225 $250 $275

BAUME & MERCIER, 17J., RF#49300, c. 1965
14k..$150 $175 $200

BAUME & MERCIER, 18 J., "Rivira", date, c. 1980s
18k & s. steel $500 $600 $700

BAUME & MERCIER, quartz, enamel dial, tank, c.1990s
14k..$300 $350 $400

BAUME & MERCIER, 17J., curved, c. 1990s
14k C&B $350 $400 $450

BAUME & MERCIER,17J.,sec. window,auto-w., c.50s
base metal................................ $100 $125 $150

BAUME & MERCIER, 17J.,diam. dial, cal#1080, c.50s
14k(W)...................................... $200 $250 $300

BELTONE, 17J., fancy hidden lugs
14k $125 $150 $175

BEMONTOIR, 15J., enamel dial, c.1920
14k $125 $150 $175

BENRUS,17J., day date
base metal $45 $55 $75

BENRUS, 18J., mystery-diamond dial
18k.. $400 $500 $700
gold filled.................................. $150 $200 $250

BENRUS, 15 jewels, date, c. 1948
s. steel.. $50 $60 $70

BENRUS, 15 jewels, quick change date
gold filled.................................... $60 $75 $90

BENRUS,17J.,"Sky Chief", chronog., c.1945
s. steel.......................................$200 $250 $325

BENRUS,17J.,"Sky Chief", chronog., center lugs, c.1945
gold filled...................................$225 $275 $350

BENRUS,17J.,"Sky Chief",triple date,chronog.,c.1940s
s. steel.......................................$300 $400 $500

BENRUS, 15 jewels, date, fancy lugs, c. 1950
14k...$115 $135 $200
gold filled.....................................$60 $75 $90

BENRUS,17J., jumping hour, wandering min.
gold filled..................................$100 $125 $160

BENRUS,17J., dial-0-rama, direct read, c. 1958
gold filled....................................$85 $95 $155

BENRUS, 15 jewels, jumping hour, wandering min.
gold filled..................................$100 $120 $140
s. steel.......................................$60 $70 $85

BENRUS,17J., rhine stone dial,
s. steel...$60 $70 $110

BENRUS, 17J., fancy lugs
gold filled $60 $70 $120

BENRUS,17J., center sec., heavy lugs,
gold filled $65 $75 $150

BENRUS, 15 jewels, fancy lugs, c. 1948
14k $115 $135 $200
gold filled $60 $75 $90

BENRUS, 15J.,auto-wind, water-proof, c
gold filled $30 $40 $50

BENRUS, 15 jewels, fancy bezel, cal. BB14
14k $120 $150 $175
gold filled $60 $75 $90

BENRUS, 15J.,aux sec.
gold filled $75 $90 $120

BENRUS,17J., flared case, cal.180, c. 1951
gold filled $75 $85 $150

BENRUS, 7J., rhine stone dial, fancy lugs, c. 1948
base metal $60 $70 $90

BENRUS,17J., rhine stone dial, cal. bb1, c. 1945
gold plate $75 $85 $100

BENRUS, 15J.,stepped case
gold filled $80 $100 $120

BENRUS, 15 jewels, 26 diamond bezel
14k (w)......................................$400 $500 $600

BENRUS, 15J.,fancy lugs
14kC&B $400 $500 $600

BENRUS,17J., aux sec.,
gold filled....................................$65 $75 $120

BENRUS, 15J.,fancy bezel
14k $165 $185 $250

BENRUS, 15 jewels, flip-top case, c. 1940
gold filled....................................$150 $200 $250

BENRUS, 15J.,hooded lugs, cal#bb3
gold filled.................................... $75 $100 $150

BENRUS,17J., hooded lugs, c.1948
14k..$100 $125 $160

BENRUS, 15J., enamel bezel, c. 1930
14k (w) $125 $150 $200

BENRUS,17J., hooded lugs, cal.ax11, c. 1950
14k..$150 $175 $225

BENRUS, 15 jewels, hooded lugs
gold filled $65 $80 $125

BENRUS, 15 jewels, cal. AX, fancy bezel
14k $150 $200 $300

BENRUS, 17 jewels, curved, rhine stones , hooded lugs
14k $175 $225 $350

BENRUS, 15 jewels, curved back, c. 1942
gold filled $60 $75 $90

BENSON, 15 jewels, by Landon, aux sec. c.1930s
9k $200 $250 $300

BENSON, 15 jewels, enamel dial, tank style case
9k $300 $400 $500

BENSON, 15 jewels, enamel dial, flared case
9k $400 $450 $600

BLANCPAIN, 23 jewels, day-date-month, moon phase
18k $2,000 $2,500 $3,000

BLANCPAIN, 17J.,hooded lugs, c.1945
14k $200 $300 $400

BOILLAT FRERES, 17 jewels, "Blita," waterproof
s. steel $30 $40 $50

E. BOREL, 17 jewels, chronometer, aux. sec.
18k $200 $300 $400
gold filled $75 $85 $100

E. BOREL, 17 jewels, auto wind, date
gold filled $80 $90 $110

E. BOREL, 17J., cocktail style, c.1960s
gold filled $100 $150 $200
s. steel $75 $85 $100

BOUCHERON, 17J., c.1930s
18k $800 $1,000 $1,200

E. BOREL, 17J., cocktail dial, date, c. 1969
base metal $50 $60 $75

BOVET, 17 jewels, chronog., 2 reg., c. 1940
s. steel $100 $150 $200

E. BOREL, 15J., hour dial, min. dial, center sec., c.1940
s. steel $200 $250 $325

BOVET, 17 jewels, chronog., triple date & 3 reg.
14k $500 $600 $700
gold filled $200 $250 $300

BRADFORD,15J., chronog.,date, c.1980s
silver $100 $125 $150

BREGUET,jump hour, c.1980s, total made =50
18k.. $7,000 $8,000 $9,000

BREGUET, 21 jewels, skeletonized
18k C&B................................. $7,000 $7,500 $8,000

BREGUET,37J., auto-w.,date, moon ph.,60 hr.wind ind.
18k... $12,000 $13,000 $14,000

BREGUET, 17J., chronog., triple date, moon phase
s. steel..................................... $8,000 $9,000 $10,000

BREGUET, 17 jewels, silver dial, thin model
18k... $1,200 $1,400 $1,600

BREGUET,auto-w.,triple date, moon ph., leap year
18k $12,000 $14,000 $16,000

BREGUET, 17 jewels, curvex
platinum $3,000 $4,000 $5,000

P. BREGUETTE, 17J., gold jewel settings, flared case
14k $125 $150 $185

P. BREGUETTE, 17J., gold jewel settings,
gold filled $75 $100 $135

P. BREGUETTE, 17 jewels, diamond dial, c. 1940
14k $300 $400 $500

P. BREGUETTE, 17J., triple date, c.1960s
s. steel $100 $125 $150

Breitling, 17 J., "Chronomat," slide rule bezel
18k $1,500 $1,600 $1,700
gold filled $400 $500 $600
s. steel $300 $400 $500

BREITLING, 17J., chronog., RF#769, sq.button, c.1942
18k $1,000 $1,100 $1,200

BREITLING, 17J., chronog., RF#1199, sq. button, c.1958
s. steel $200 $225 $250

BREITLING, 17 jewels, chronog., "Navitimer," 3 reg.
18k $3,000 $3,500 $4,000
s. steel $500 $600 $700

BREITLING, 17 jewels, split sec. chronog., 2 reg.
s. steel.................................... $3,000 $4,000 $5,000

BREITLING, 17 J., chronog., "Cosmonaute," date
s. steel....................................$200 $250 $300

BREITLING, 18J. date, moon ph., split chronog. 3 reg.
18k $7,000 $8,000 $9,000

BREITLING, 17 J., chronog., "Chronomat," 3 reg.
s. steel....................................$200 $250 $300

BREITLING, 17 jewels, chronog., "Navitimer," date
s. steel....................................... $200 $250 $300

BREITLING, 17 J., telemeter, 1 button, hinged lugs
s. steel......................................$700 $800 $900

BREITLING, 17 J., chronog., mid size,
gold filled $200 $225 $325

BREITLING, 17 jewels, tachymeter, wire lugs
s. steel.................................... $1,000 $1,100 $1,200

BREITLING, 17 jewels, tachymeter, hinged lugs
s. steel...................................... $700 $800 $900

BREITLING, 17 jewels, chronog., pulsations
s. steel.. $500 $600 $700

BREITLING, 17J., chronog., RF#765, c.1960
s. steel...................................... $300 $350 $400

BREITLING, 17 J., telemeter, hinged lugs, 1 button
s. steel.. $800 $900 $1,000

BREITLING, 17 jewels, chronog., Toptime
s. steel.. $200 $300 $400

BREITLING, 17 jewels, chronog., 2 reg.
s. steel.................................... $1,000 $1,100 $1,200

BREITLING, 17 jewels, chronog., 2 reg. RF#790
18k.. $700 $800 $900

BREITLING, 17J., chronog., 2 reg., "Premier", RF#790
18k $1,200 $1,300 $1,400

BREITLING, 17 jewels, chronog., 2 reg.
s. steel $200 $250 $300

BREITLING, 17J., chronog., 3 reg., RF#787, c.1942
14k C&B $800 $900 $1,000

BREITLING, 17 jewels, chronog., 2 reg.
s. steel $200 $250 $300

BREITLING, 17 jewels, chronog., "Premier," 3 reg.
s. steel $300 $400 $500

BREITLING, 17 J., split sec. chronog., "Duograph"
18k $6,000 $7,000 $8,000
s. steel $3,000 $4,000 $5,000

BREITLING, 17 J., chronog., day-date-month, 3 reg.
18k $1,800 $2,000 $2,400
s. steel $800 $700 $1,000

BREITLING, 17J., chronog., 3 reg., RF#815, c.1968
gold filled $200 $250 $300

BREITLING, 17J., chronog., RF#2009-33, c. 1975
s. steel..................................$100 $125 $150

BREITLING, 17J., chronog., Toptime, RF#810, c.1968
s. steel.......................$300 $350 $400

BREITLING, 17J., chronog., RF#2110, c. 1970
s. steel..................................$100 $125 $150

BREITLING, 17J., chronog., auto w., date, c. 1969
s. steel..................................$80 $90 $100

BREITLING, 17J., chronog., Datora,RF#2031, c.1970
s. steel..................................$100 $125 $150

BREITLING, 17J., chronog., RF#1450, 3 reg., c.1970
s. steel..................................$80 $90 $100

BREITLING, 17J., chronog., RF#2110, c.1970
s. steel..................................$100 $125 $150

BREITLING, 17J., day date month,
18k...............................$400 $500 $600

BUCHERER, 17 jewels,
18k $300 $400 $500

BUCHERER, 17 jewels, chronog., 2 reg.
18k $600 $700 $800

BUCHERER, 17J., chronog., 2 reg., C.1959
s. steel $300 $400 $500

BUCHERER, 25 J., triple date moon ph., cal.693, c.1950
18k $700 $800 $900

BUCHERER, 21 J., 3 dates, moon ph., diamond dial
18k $2,000 $2,200 $2,400

BUCHERER, 15 jewels, 8 day movement
18k $1,200 $1,400 $1,600
gold filled $600 $700 $800

BUECHE-GIROD, 17 J., day-date-month, moon ph.
s. steel $200 $250 $300

BUECHE-GIROD, 17J., by Piguet, cal.99, c.1975
18k $400 $500 $600

BUECHE-GIROD, 17J., dual time movements,
18k $500 $600 $700

BUECHE-GIROD, 17 jewels, tank style case
18k $600 $700 $850

BUECHE-GIROD, 17 jewels
18k C&B.............................. $600 $700 $800

P. BUHRE, 17 jewels, aux. sec.
gold filled $70 $80 $100

P. BUHRE, 17J., alarm, C.1956
s. steel.. $60 $80 $100

BULGARI, 7J., quartz, RF#1023, c.1987
s. steel......................................$700 $900 $1,000

BULOVA, Accutron, "Spaceview"
s. steel......................................$150 $200 $250

BULOVA, Accutron, cal. 214, c.1963
gold filled...................................$125 $150 $225

BULOVA, Accutron, cal. 214, c. 1963
s. steel......................................$120 $150 $225

BULOVA, Accutron, "Spaceview," c. 1960
14k $400 $450 $600
gold filled $175 $225 $275
s. steel $150 $200 $250

BULOVA, Accutron, "Spaceview," Alpha, waterproof
14k $500 $600 $700
gold filled $200 $300 $400
s. steel $150 $200 $250

BULOVA, Accutron, "Spaceview"
s. steel $150 $200 $250

BULOVA, Accutron, "Spaceview," center lugs
s. steel $200 $250 $300

BULOVA, Accutron, "Spaceview"
18k $600 $700 $800
s. steel $150 $200 $250

BULOVA, Accutron, center lugs,
gold plate (w) $125 $150 $225

BULOVA, Accutron, "Spaceview," c. 1967
gold filled $225 $275 $350
s. steel $125 $175 $250

BULOVA, Accutron, two tone, date, cal. 418
14k 2 tone $400 $450 $550

BULOVA, Accutron, two tone, date
14k 2 tone.................................. $225 $250 $350

BULOVA, Accutron, "Spaceview,"
s. steel...................................... $150 $200 $250

BULOVA, Accutron, 2 tone
G.F. & s. steel.......................... $125 $150 $200

BULOVA, Accutron, oval, spaceview,
s. steel...................................... $125 $150 $225

BULOVA, Accutron, "Spaceview,"
s. steel...................................... $150 $200 $250

BULOVA, Accutron, "Spaceview," gold bezel
s. steel gold bezel.....................$200 $250 $300

BULOVA, Accutron, railroad approved, C. 1960s
s. steel...................................... $100 $125 $150

BULOVA, Accutron, RR approved, 24 hr. dial
gold filled................................. $125 $150 $200

BULOVA, Accutron, quartz, RR approved, day date,
gold plate................................... $75 $85 $150

☞ NOTE: BULOVA, some cases are stamped with a
year code number.L=1950s, M=1960s, N=1970s,
example: L3=1953, M4=1964, N5=1975, etc.

BULOVA, Accutron, cal. 214, c. 1966
14k $500 $550 $600

BULOVA, Accutron, cal. 214, diamond dial
14k $450 $550 $700

BULOVA, Accutron, sweep sec. hand
gold filled $80 $100 $150

BULOVA, Accutron, masonic dial
14k $400 $450 $500

BULOVA, Accutron, asymmetric
14k $600 $700 $800

BULOVA, Accutron, ASTRONAUT, 24 hour dial
14k $800 $1,000 $1,200
gold filled $200 $250 $350
s. steel $150 $175 $250

BULOVA, Accutron, astronaut II, time zone,
s. steel $150 $175 $240

BULOVA, Accutron, astronaut II, time zone,
s. steel $165 $185 $250

BULOVA, Accutron, cushion spaceview, c.1973
s. steel.......................... $175 $200 $300

BULOVA, Accutron, day date, gold filled bezel
s. steel.......................... $65 $75 $150

BULOVA, Accutron, asymmetric, day date
s. steel.......................... $125 $150 $250

BULOVA, Accutron, cal.2181, date
gold filled.......................... $65 $75 $150

BULOVA, Accutron, octagonal case
gold filled.......................... $125 $150 $250

BULOVA, (Accu- quartz), quartz & tuning fork, day date
gold filled.......................... $90 $130 $200

BULOVA, Accutron, model 2183,
s. steel.......................... $60 $70 $120

BULOVA, Accutron, day date
base metal $65 $75 $150

BULOVA, Accutron, faceted crystal, day date
gold filled................................... $75 $85 $160

BULOVA, Accutron, numbered bezel, day date
14k..$250 $275 $375

BULOVA, Accutron, day date
gold filled................................... $85 $95 $165

BULOVA, Accuquartz, diamond bezel, day date
14k..$350 $400 $500

BULOVA, Accutron, wood bezel, day date
gold filled................................ $150 $175 $250

BULOVA, Accutron, day date
14k C&B $450 $475 $575

BULOVA, Accutron, red dial, date
gold filled................................... $125 $150 $225

BULOVA, Accutron, note band with accutron symbol
18k C&B $900 $1,000 $1,200

BULOVA, Accutron, day date, c. 1970
s. steel.. $75 $90 $120

BULOVA, Accutron, divers 660 ft.depth, 24 hr.dial,
rotating out side chapter, day date
s. steel $175 $200 $300

BULOVA, Accutron, model 2186, direct read
gold filled $175 $200 $300

BULOVA, Accutron, day date,
14k C&B $450 $500 $700

BULOVA, Accutron, cut corner, day date
gold filled $85 $95 $150

BULOVA, Accutron, date.
14k C&B $450 $500 $700

BULOVA, Accutron, diamond on bezel
14k(w) C&B............................. $700 $800 $1,000

BULOVA, Accutron, fancy bezel
14k C&B $500 $550 $650

BULOVA, Accutron, lady accutron
14k $100 $125 $175

BULOVA, Accutron, cal. #221, textured bezel
sterling & 14k $450 $500 $650

BULOVA, Accutron, note links in accutron band
gold plate $125 $150 $200

BULOVA, Accutron, quartz
gold filled..................................... $75 $85 $150

BULOVA, Accutron, date
gold filled..................................... $75 $85 $150

BULOVA, Accutron, pendent style watch
14k..$350 $400 $600

BULOVA, Accutron, wide oval bezel
gold filled..................................... $75 $85 $150

BULOVA, digital,
s. steel...$65 $80 $135

BULOVA, Accutron, 32 small diamond bezel
14k(w) $350 $400 $550

☞ NOTE: BULOVA, some cases are stamped with a
year code number .L=1950s, M=1960s, N=1970s,
example: L3=1953, M4=1964, N5=1975, etc.

BULOVA, enamel bezel
s. steel... $100 $125 $150

BULOVA, 15J., one button chronog.,1/5 sec.,C.1946
gold filled.................................. $250 $300 $350

BULOVA, 17J., chronog., cal.890, Sky Chief, c.1940
s. steel.. $200 $225 $325

BULOVA, 16 jewels, military style
s. steel.. $200 $250 $300

BULOVA, 17J., auto-wind, rotating outside chapter
s. steel.. $100 $125 $175

BULOVA, 17J., Alarm, cal.11aerc, c.1967
s. steel.. $100 $125 $175

BULOVA, self winding, c. 1960
14k.. $100 $125 $175
gold filled.................................... $40 $50 $60

BULOVA, 17J., fancy lugs
gold filled..................................... $95 $110 $175

BULOVA, 23 jewels, waterproof
14k $125 $150 $200

BULOVA, fancy long lugs, c. 1942
gold filled.................................... $65 $80 $100

BULOVA, 23 jewels, date, 6 adj., c. 1951
gold filled.................................... $75 $85 $110

BULOVA, cal. 700, canteen style, c. 1946
s. steel $200 $300 $400

BULOVA, 17 jewels, center sec., c. 1935
gold filled.................................... $100 $125 $200

BULOVA, 15J., military style, cal.10bnch, c.1940
s. steel $75 $85 $120

BULOVA, 17 jewels, center sec., cal.9arc, ca.1952
14K $150 $175 $250

BULOVA, 17J., 20 diamond dial
14k(w)...................................$150 $185 $275

BULOVA, 17J., one button chronog., cal.10BK, c.1947
gold filled $175 $200 $275

BULOVA, 23J., 12 diamond dial, c. 1959
14k(w) $100 $175 $250

BULOVA, 30J., diam. dial, cal#10B2AC, C.1960s
14k(w) $200 $250 $300

BULOVA, early auto wind movement by Champ,

BULOVA, early auto wind, by Champ, c. 1930
gold filled $500 $600 $700

BULOVA, diamond dial, c. 1939
14k (w)...................................... $400 $500 $600

BULOVA, 21 jewels, hidden lugs, diamond dial, c. 1935
14k.. $400 $500 $600

BULOVA, hidden lugs, diamond dial, c. 1945
14k.. $400 $500 $600

BULOVA, 21 jewels, diamond dial, long lugs, c. 1941
14k (w)...................................... $200 $235 $270

BULOVA, 17J., 3 diamond dial, cal.8ae, c.1949
14k.. $165 $180 $225

BULOVA, 17 jewels, curved, cal. 7AP, c. 1939
14k $200 $250 $350

BULOVA, 17J., 5th ave., cal.6am, engraved bezel, c.1935
gold filled $90 $110 $175

BULOVA, 21J., stepped bezel, curved,
gold filled $100 $125 $225

BULOVA, 21J., plain bezel, curved,
gold filled $75 $120 $200

BULOVA, 17J., cal. 7ap, c.1937
gold filled $100 $125 $225

BULOVA, 17J., curved, cal.7ap, c.1936
gold filled $85 $95 $175

BULOVA, 17J., cal.13al,c.1935
14k $165 $185 $275

BULOVA, 17J., cal.9af, c.1929
s. steel $65 $75 $125

BULOVA, 17J., cal.7ap, c.1934
gold filled $100 $125 $225

BULOVA, 15J., cal.10ae, c.1938
gold filled $65 $75 $150

BULOVA, 17 jewels, curved, c. 1939
gold filled $85 $100 $150

BULOVA, 21 jewels, curved, c. 1939
gold filled $85 $100 $165

BULOVA, 17 J., stepped case, wandering sec., c. 1942
gold filled $200 $250 $300

BULOVA, 21J., cal# 6AE,
14k $200 $300 $500

BULOVA, 17 jewels, cal. 10GM, fancy lugs, c. 1953
14k $200 $225 $250

BULOVA, 17 jewels, duo dial, c. 1935
s. steel $300 $350 $400

BULOVA, 17J., fancy lugs, cal. 8an, c. 1951
gold filled $110 $135 $240

BULOVA, 17 jewels, 2 tone duo dial
s. steel $300 $350 $400

BULOVA, 17J., cal. 8ad, fancy lugs, c. 1939
gold plate $70 $90 $170

BULOVA, 17 jewels, 2 tone dial, fancy bezel
s. steel $75 $85 $100

BULOVA, 21J., cal. 7ak, c. 1945
gold filled $75 $85 $175

BULOVA, 21J., c.1950s
gold filled.................................. $75 $85 $175

BULOVA, 21J., cal.7ak, engraved case, c.1948
14k...$150 $175 $250

BULOVA, 21J., c.1950s
gold filled.................................. $75 $85 $175

BULOVA, 21J., cal.7ak, c.1945
gold filled..................................$75 $85 $150

BULOVA, 7J., c.1945
gold filled.................................. $65 $75 $150

BULOVA, 17J., cal.8ae, fancy hidden lugs, c.1941
gold filled..................................$70 $90 $150

BULOVA, 17J., fancy lugs, c.1950 code on case= (LO)
gold filled.................................. $65 $75 $150

BULOVA, 21J., hooded lugs, c.1945
14k...$125 $150 $250

BULOVA, 21J., fancy "U" style lugs,
14k C&B.................................. $500 $550 $650

BULOVA, 21 jewels, hooded lugs, cal. 8AC, c. 1952
14k...$250 $300 $400

BULOVA, 17 jewels, fancy long lugs, c. 1942
14k $225 $300 $400

BULOVA, 15 jewels, engraved bezel, c. 1925
gold filled $100 $125 $175

BULOVA, 17J., cal. 8AC, photo watch, c. 1940
14k $175 $200 $225

BULOVA, 15 jewels, wandering hr. min. sec., c. 1928
s. steel $125 $150 $175

BULOVA, 17J., right angle, cal. 8AZ, c. 1938
14k $300 $400 $500

BULOVA, 17 jewels, aux. sec.
14k $150 $175 $250

BULOVA, 17 jewels, fancy bezel
gold filled $100 $120 $140

BULOVA, 17 jewels, bell shaped lugs
14k $225 $300 $400

BULOVA, 17 jewels, fancy lugs
14k $175 $200 $250

BULOVA, 30 jewels, date, autowind,
s. steel $50 $60 $80

BULOVA, 23 jewels, autowind,adj.6 pos.
s. steel.............................. $60 $70 $80

BULOVA, 17J., engraved bezel only
base metal;................................ $60 $70 $110

BULOVA, 17J., center sec., cal.10bac, c.1935
gold filled $90 $100 $175

BULOVA, 15J., cal.11ac, c.1958
gold filled.................................. $65 $75 $150

BULOVA, 17J., cal.8ac, fancy lugs, c.1940
gold plate $65 $75 $150

BULOVA, 15J., cal.10ae, c.1935
gold filled.................................. $65 $75 $150

BULOVA, 17J., flared top of case & sides,
gold filled $70 $90 $150

BULOVA, 7J., cal.10bc, c.1949
gold filled.................................... $60 $70 $120

BULOVA, 17J., engraved lugs & bevel, cal.10an, c.1928
s. steel.. $65 $75 $140

BULOVA, 15J., cal.10an, c.1929
base metal $60 $70 $120

BULOVA, 17 jewels, cal#11AF
10k $100 $125 $150

BULOVA, 17 jewels, "The Ambassador"
gold filled.................................$50 $60 $75

BULOVA, 17 jewels , engraved bezel
gold filled $100 $125 $175

BULOVA, 17 jewels, "The Curtis," tank style
gold filled................................$100 $125 $150

BULOVA, 17 jewels, engraved, tank style, hinged case
chrome plate $60 $75 $150

BULOVA, 15 jewels, "The Athelete"
gold filled................................$100 $115 $125

BULOVA, 17 jewels, engraved bezel,
gold filled $75 $100 $150

BULOVA, 15 jewels, engraved, tank style, hinged case
gold filled....................................$95 $110 $135

BULOVA, 17 jewels, "The Governor"
14k $200 $225 $300

BULOVA, 17 jewels, "The Lone Eagle," fancy bezel
gold filled................................$200 $250 $350

BUREN, 17 jewels, day-date-month, moon phase
s. steel.. $150 $185 $245

BUREN, 17 jewels, long lugs
14k $150 $170 $200

BUTEX, 17J., triple date, moon ph.
gold filled $200 $250 $300

CARLTON, 15 jewels, stepped case, c. 1939
14k $200 $250 $300

CARTIER, 18 J., 8 day Mvt., tank style, by E. W. Co.
18k $30,000 $35,000 $40,000

CARTIER, 18 J., sapphire crown & bezel, c. 1970
18k..$2,000 $2,200 $2,500

CARTIER, 18 jewels, curved, tank style
18k..$7,000 $8,000 $9,000

CARTIER, 18 jewels, curved, signed E. W. Co.
18k..$6,000 $7,000 $8,000

CARTIER, 18 J., tank style, platinum case & band
platinum C&B....................$10,000 $12,000 $14,000

CARTIER, 18 jewels, tank style case
18k..$1,200 $1,400 $1,600

CARTIER, 20 jewels, tank style case, c. 1950
18k..$1,000 $1,100 $1,200

CARTIER, Must de, quartz, tank style case, c.1980s
Vermeil =(gold over sterling)
G.P. vermeil $200 $250 $300
SAME STYLE CASE AS ABOVE
CARTIER, Must de, Mechanical, tank style case, c.1980s
Vermeil =(gold over sterling)
G.P. vermeil $200 $250 $300

CARTIER, 18 jewels, tank style, European W. Co.
18k C&B............................... $5,000 $5,500 $6,000

CARTIER, 18 jewels, by Movado
14k $1,200 $1,600 $2,200

CARTIER, 18 jewels, duo plan, European W. Co.
18k C&B............................... $3,000 $3,500 $4,000

CARTIER, 18J., by Le Coultre, long lugs
18k $900 $1,000 $1,100

CARTIER, 18 jewels, curved, hidden lugs
18k $4,000 $5,000 $6,000

CARTIER, 18 jewels, by Universal, c. 1960
18k.. $1,200 $1,400 $1,600

CARTIER, 18 jewels, center lugs, c. 1930
18k.. $1,200 $1,400 $1,600

CARTIER, 18 J., Prince, by Lecoultre, C.1930
18k.. $25,000 $30,000 $35,000

CARTIER, 18 J., reversible to view 2nd dial & 2nd
time zone
18k.. $25,000 $30,000 $35,000

CARTIER, 18 jewels, c. 1960
18k.. $1,000 $1,100 $1,200

CARTIER, 18 J., early E.W.Co., C. 1928
18k.. $6,000 $7,000 $8,000

CARTIER, 18 J., lady's watch by European W. Co.
18kC&B.............................$1,200 $1,500 $1.800

CARTIER, 18 J., sovonnette H.C.style, C. 1928
18k $10,000 $12,000 $14,000

CARTIER,18 J., guichet tank, jump hr. & min. by E.W.Co.
18k $25,000 $30,000 $35,000

CARTIER, 18 J., jump hr. & min., E. W. Co. c. 1930
platinum...............................$25,000 $30,000 $35,000

CARTIER, 18 J.,"Santos", cal.21
mens18k.................................$1,500 $1,700 $1,900
ladies 18k $1,000 $1,200 $1,400

CARTIER, 18 J., "Santos," 18k & s. steel case, band
platinum & 18k C&B........$12,000 $14,000 $16,000
18k & s. steel C&B.............$1,000 $1,200 $1,400

CARTIER, 18 jewels, "Santos," date
18k & s. steel C&B.................$800 $1,000 $1,200

CARTIER, 18 jewels, "Santos," octagonal, date
18k & s. steel C&B.................$600 $800 $1,000

CARTIER, 18 jewels, "Santos," lady's, date
18k & s. steel C&B.................$500 $600 $700

CARTIER, 25 jewels, chronog., European W. Co.
18k.......................................$50,000 $60,000 $70,000

CARTIER, 29 jewels, min. repeater, c. 1925
18k $80,000 $90,000 $100,000

CARTIER, 18 J., bamboo style bezel, C.1970s
18k $3,500 $4,000 $4,500

CARTIER, 18 jewels, c. 1925
18k $3,000 $3,500 $4,000

CARTIER, 18 J., large cut conner bezel, C.1970s
18k... $2,500 $3,000 $3,500

CARTIER, 18 jewels, asymmetric, E. W. Co., c. 1928
18k $8,000 $9,000 $10,000

CARTIER, 18 J., "Helm", single lug, C. 1950s
18k $12,000 $14,000 $16,000

CARTIER, 18 J., oval maxi, C. 1968
18k $10,000 $12,000 $14,000

CARTIER, 18 jewels, by Le Coultre
18k $2,000 $2,500 $3,000

CARTIER, 18 J., by E.W.CO., single lug, C. 1949
18k... $10,000 $12,000 $14,000

CARTIER, 29 J., min. repeater, by Le Coultre, c. 1930
platinum.............................. $80,000 $90,000 $100,000

CARTIER, 18 J., by ESKA,
18k(w) C&B........................ $1,000 $1,200 $1,500

CARTIER, 18 jewels, date chapter, by Le Coultre
14k $1,000 $1,200 $1,400

CARTIER, 18 J., lady's, E.W.CO., c.1948
18k $2,000 $2,200 $2,400

CARTIER, 7J., quartz, MUST, c.1985
G.P. vermeil $200 $250 $300

CARTIER, 18 J., lady's, E.W.Co., C.1949
14k(w) C&B $400 $500 $600

CENTTRAL, 7J., cal.39, c.1937
gold filled..................................... $75 $85 $110

CHEVROLET, 6J., in form of car radiator, C. 1927
silver..$400 $500 $600

CHOPARD, 18 J., 2 dial , 2 time zones, diam.bezel
18k C&B $2,000 $2,500 $3,000

CHOPARD, 18 J., skeletonized, diamond dial &hands
18k...$4,000 $4,500 $5,000

CHOPARD, 28J., triple date moon ph., cal.900, c.1980
18k $800 $900 $1,000

CLEBAR, 17 jewels, chronog., 3 reg. c.1950s
s. steel $250 $300 $350

CHOPARD, 20 J., RF#2113, c.1978
18k $300 $400 $500

CLEBAR, 17J., chronog.,triple date, moon ph.
s. steel $500 $600 $700

CHOPARD, 17J., RF#2134, c.1978
18k $300 $400 $500

CLEBAR, 17 jewels, chronog., c. 1938
s. steel $75 $85 $100

CLEBAR, 17 jewels, chronog., 2 reg., cal.2248, c.1952
base metal $400 $450 $500

CONCORD, 17J., aux. sec., ca. 1947
14k $250 $300 $400

CONCORD, 17 jewels, center sec.
14k $125 $150 $175

CONCORD, 17 jewels, chronog. 2 reg., c.1940s
s. steel..................................... $300 $350 $400

CONDAL, 15J. hunter style, flip top, C. 1928
silver $400 $500 $600

CONTINENTAL, 17J. 3 diamond dial
14k $150 $175 $200

CORNAVIN, 17J., day date, c. 1960
gold filled................................. $100 $125 $150

CORNAVIN, 17J., date, auto, RF#1243, C.1963
gold filled................................. $100 $120 $175
s. steel $50 $75 $100

CORONET, 17J., chronog.
s. steel..................................... $300 $350 $400

CORTEBERT, 15 jewels, c. 1940s
gold filled..................................... $60 $80 $100

CORTEBERT, 15 jewels, c. 1941
gold filled..................................... $60 $70 $85

CORTEBERT, 17 J., "Sport," triple date, moon phase
18k $600 $700 $800
gold filled.................................. $200 $240 $300

CORUM, 17 J., twenty dollar gold piece
18k & 22k $2,400 $2,600 $2,800

CORTEBERT, 17 jewels, center sec.
s. steel.. $40 $45 $60

CORUM, 24k gold ingot, GR.15
24k...$1,000 $1,200 $1,400

CORUM, 17 J., in form of Rolls-Royce car radiator
18k...$1,800 $2,000 $2,200

CORTEBERT, quartz, U.K. military, (CWC)
s. steel.. $150 $175 $200

CORUM, 17 jewels, peacock feather dial
18k..$700 $800 $900

CORTEBERT, (CWC), chronog., by Valjoux, c.1971
s. steel.. $300 $350 $400

CORUM, 17 jewels, rope style bezel
18k C&B $700 $800 $900

CORUM, 17 jewels, in form of book
18k $600 $700 $900

CRAWFORD, 17J., hooded lugs, c. 1940
14k $100 $125 $150

CORUM, 21 jewels, gold dial
18k $400 $500 $600

CRAWFORD, 17J., pendant watch
base metal $40 $50 $75

CRAWFORD, 17J., triple date, c. 1942
s. steel $50 $60 $70

CROTON, 17 jewels, day date
gold filled.................................... $40 $50 $60

CROTON, 17 jewels, diamond bezel & dial
14k (w).. $500 $600 $700

CRAWFORD, 17J., chronog.engraved bezel
base metal................................. $125 $150 $175

CROTON, 17 jewels, chronog., c. 1948
s. steel $250 $300 $350

CROTON, 17 jewels, chronog., c. 1946
s. steel.. $100 $125 $150

CROTON, 17 jewels, cal.630, c.1943
gold filled.................................... $30 $40 $55

CROTON, 17 jewels, fancy lugs
14k $150 $175 $200

CROTON, 17 jewels, fancy lugs
14k $200 $250 $300

CROTON, 7 jewels, drivers style, c.1938
gold filled.................................... $150 $175 $200

CROTON, 17 jewels, swinging lugs, cal.f3x, c.1940
14k.............................$125 $150 $175

CROWN, 7J., luminous dial
base metal $30 $40 $55

CROWN, 7J., luminous dial
gold filled.................................... $50 $75 $100

CRYSLER, 17J., aux. sec., ca. 1950s
gold filled.................................... $50 $70 $90

CYMA,7J.,enamel dial, wire lugs,(signal corp.USA),c.1928
silver...$250 $300 $350

CYMA, 17 jewels, aux. sec.

18k	$200	$250	$300
14k	$175	$200	$250
gold filled	$65	$75	$85

DAU, 15J., wire lugs, c.1915

14k	$125	$150	$175

DAYNITE, 7 jewels, 8 day movement, c. 1925

s. steel	$250	$300	$400

DELBANA, 17J., fancy hooded lugs, c.1951

14k	$100	$125	$150

DIDISHEIM, 15J., "Winton", enamel art deco bezel, c.1927

14k(w)	$250	$300	$350

P. DITISHEIM, 17 J., "Solvil," diamond dial, c. 1947

18k	$400	$500	$600

P. DITISHEIM, 17 J., "Solvil," diamond dial, c. 1947

platinum	$700	$800	$900

P. DITISHEIM, 17 J., "Solvil," diamond dial, c. 1948

platinum	$700	$800	$900

P. DITISHEIM, 17 J., "Solvil," curved, diamond dial

platinum	$1,200	$1,400	$1,600

P. DITISHEIM, 17 jewels, diamond dial, curved

platinum	$1,200	$1,400	$1,600

P. DITISHEIM, 17 J., baguette diamonds, fancy bezel
platinum.................................. $1,400 $1,600 $1,800

P. DITISHEIM, 17 jewels, hinged lugs, enameled bezel
14k $700 $800 $900

DOME, 25 jewels, triple dates, auto wind
18k $500 $600 $700

DORIC, 17J., fancy lugs, two tone case, c.1935
gold filled $60 $70 $85

DOXA, 17 jewels, aux sec.
gold filled $40 $50 $60

DOXA, 17 jewels, center sec., fancy lugs
14k $150 $200 $250

DOXA, 17 jewels, chronog., fluted lugs
14k $300 $350 $400

DOXA, 17J., chronog. 3 reg. by Valjoux,
14k $600 $700 $800

DOXA, 17 jewels, chronog., triple dates, moon phase
14k $1,100 $1,200 $1,500

DOXA, 17 jewels, chronog, 2 reg., c. 1942
gold filled.................................. $200 $250 $300

DOXA, 17 jewels, chronog., cal. 1220, c. 1940
s. steel.. $125 $150 $175

DOXA, 17 jewels, center sec
s. steel.. $50 $75 $100

DOXA, 17 jewels, center sec., c. 1949
gold filled.................................. $100 $125 $150

DOXA, 17J., "Grafic" date,
14k..$150 $175 $200

DOXA, 17J., cal. 1361, c.1948
14k..$150 $175 $200

DRIVA, 15 jewels, repeater, repeats on gong, repeater
wound by bolt above hand, c. 1930
s. steel.....................................$3,000 $4,000 $5,000

DRIVA, 15 jewels, 5 min. repeater
14k...$2,500 $3,000 $3,500

DRIVA, 17 jewels, fancy lugs, c.1945
14k..$300 $350 $400

DUGENA, 17J., cal.985, c.1960
14k $250 $300 $375

DUNHILL, 17J., date, alarm by Le Coultre, c. 1965
s. steel $300 $350 $400

DUNHILL, 15J., by Bulwark W.Co., engraved bezel, c.1930
gold filled $75 $125 $185

DUODIAL, 15 jewels, c. 1934
9k $700 $800 $900

EBEL, 21 jewels, chronog., self winding, perpetual cal.
18k $7,000 $8,000 $9,000

EBEL, 18 jewels, applied gold numbers, c. 1950
18k $400 $450 $500

EBEL, 17 jewels, slide open to wind
leather $200 $250 $300

EBEL, 17 jewels, chronog., 2 reg., enamel dial
s. steel $200 $250 $300

EBEL, 17 jewels, chronog., c. 1955
gold filled $250 $350 $400

EBEL, 17 jewels, chronog., "pulsation", c. 1943
s. steel...................................... $300 $350 $400

EBEL, 17 jewels, chronog, 3 reg., c. 1941
s. steel...................................... $250 $300 $350

EBEL, 17J., "sport", c.1949
gold filled.................................. $60 $70 $80

EBEL, 17J., cal.119, auto-wind, c.1950
s. steel...................................... $100 $125 $155

EBEL, 17J., cal.93, center sec., c.1950
18k..$300 $350 $400

EBEL, 17J., lady's watch, c.1948
14k C&B $200 $225 $250

EBERHARD, 18 jewels, split sec. chronog., 3 reg.
18k..$5,000 $6,000 $7,000

EBERHARD, 17 J., tele-tachymeter, enamel dial, c. 1930
18k..$2,000 $2,500 $3,000

EBERHARD, 17 jewels, chronog., 2 reg,
18k $1,500 $1,700 $2,000

EBERHARD, 17 J., chronog., center lugs, 1 button,
enamel dial
s. steel $400 $500 $600

EBERHARD, 17 J., wire lugs, enamel dial, c.1928
early waterproof case
silver $700 $800 $900

EKEGREN, 17 jewels, jumping hr., min. hand, c. 1920
platinum $10,000 $11,000 $12,000

EKEGREN, 18 jewels, jumping hr., c. 1920
18k $8,000 $9,000 $10,000

ELECTRA W. Co., 17J, chronog., 1 button, hinged back,
enamel dial
silver $500 $600 $700

ELECTION, 17J., cal.4019, c.1940
s. steel $100 $125 $150

ELGIN, 21J., Lord Elgin, extended lugs,
gold filled $125 $150 $225

ELGIN, 23J., fancy bezel, Lord Elgin
gold filled $85 $95 $175

ELGIN, 19J., fancy bezel, c.1950s
gold filled $90 $110 $160

ELGIN, 19J., U shaped lugs
gold filled $85 $95 $150

ELGIN, 21J., Lord Elgin, hinged lugs
gold filled $100 $120 $200

ELGIN, 17J., auto-wind, hooded lugs
gold filled $70 $90 $150

ELGIN, 17J., Shockmaster, auto-wind,
gold filled $85 $95 $150

ELGIN, 21J., Lord Elgin, 3 diamonds, cal.626, c.1950
14k(w) $175 $200 $300

ELGIN, 17J., stepped hooded lugs, c.1925
gold filled $90 $100 $200

ELGIN, 17J., chamfered lugs,
gold filled $65 $75 $125

ELGIN, 15J., stepped case,
gold filled $65 $75 $125

ELGIN, 15J., hinged case, engraved bezel, c.1928
gold filled(w) $75 $90 $135

ELGIN, 21J., bevelled lugs,
14k $140 $160 $250

ELGIN, 19J., flared case
gold filled $65 $75 $125

ELGIN, 7J., tear drop lugs,
gold filled $65 $75 $125

ELGIN, 17J., long fluted lugs,
gold filled $65 $75 $125

ELGIN, 21J., Lord Elgin,
gold filled $75 $85 $135

ELGIN, 17J., carved lugs
gold filled $65 $75 $125

ELGIN, 21J., Lord Elgin, carved lugs
14k $150 $175 $275

ELGIN, 21J., Lord Elgin, cal.625, c.1950
14k $150 $175 $275

ELGIN, 21J., Lord Elgin, cal. 713, GJS, c.1958
14k $140 $160 $260

ELGIN, 17J., carved case,
gold filled $65 $75 $125

ELGIN, 21J., Lord Elgin, cal.559, c.1942
gold filled.................................. $75 $85 $135

ELGIN, 21J., Lord Elgin, GJS, c. 1936
14k $150 $175 $250

ELGIN, 21J., Lord Elgin, GJS, cal.626, c.1940
14k $150 $175 $250

ELGIN,15J., fancy bezel, G#554
gold filled $60 $70 $85

ELGIN, 17 jewels, raised numbers
14k $175 $220 $350

LORD ELGIN, 21 jewels, curved, raised numbers
14k $200 $225 $275

ELGIN, 17 jewels, embossed dial
14k... $150 $175 $250

LORD ELGIN, 21 jewels, curved
gold filled.................................... $75 $90 $140

ELGIN, 17 jewels, curved, "Streamlined"
gold filled.................................. $100 $120 $140

ELGIN, 17 jewels, raised numbers
gold filled.................................... $75 $90 $140

ELGIN, 15 jewels, curved, fancy bezel
gold filled.................................... $75 $90 $140

LORD ELGIN, 21 jewels, curved
platinum $450 $575 $700

LORD ELGIN, 21 jewels, curved
14k.. $175 $200 $275

ELGIN, 17 jewels, curved
gold filled................................... $75 $90 $140

ELGIN, 17 jewels, curved
gold filled................................... $80 $100 $165

ELGIN, 15 jewels, drivers style
gold filled................................... $250 $300 $400

ELGIN, 17 jewels, "Ristflo"
gold filled................................... $225 $275 $350

ELGIN, 17 jewels
gold filled................................... $75 $90 $135

ELGIN, 17 jewels, hidden lugs
gold filled................................... $100 $110 $120

ELGIN, 17 jewels, embossed dial
gold filled................................... $75 $90 $125

ELGIN, 17 jewels, curved, thin model
gold filled................................... $70 $85 $120

ELGIN, 17 jewels, stepped case
gold filled................................... $75 $90 $120

ELGIN, 17J., cal.11553, c.1928
gold filled................................... $100 $125 $225

ELGIN, 15 jewels, "William Osler" recess crown
gold filled................................... $150 $200 $250

ELGIN, 7 jewels, center sec., recess crown
gold filled................................... $125 $150 $200

ELGIN, 17J., engraved case, c.1928
gold filled.................................. $90 $110 $175

ELGIN, 15J., curved engraved case, c. 1928
gold filled.................................$160 $175 $250

ELGIN, 15J., 2 tone case, recessed crown
gold filled.................................... $70 $85 $135

ELGIN, 15J., engraved case, c.1928
gold filled.................................$70 $90 $140

ELGIN, 7-15J., engraved case, c. 1928
14K...$150 $175 $250
gold filled.................................. $70 $90 $140

ELGIN, 15J., engraved case, hooded lugs, c.1928
gold filled..................................$75 $85 $135

ELGIN, 15J., engraved mermaid design case, c.1928
gold filled.................................. $90 $100 $175

ELGIN, 15 jewels, center lugs
gold filled..................................$80 $90 $100

ELGIN, 15J., engraved case, c. 1928
gold filled.................................. $165 $185 $275

ELGIN, 7 jewels, fancy bezel
s. steel...$50 $60 $70

ELGIN, 7 jewels, fancy bezel
gold filled $60 $70 $80

ELGIN, 17 jewels, "Crusade"
gold filled $100 $120 $140

ELGIN, 7 jewels
gold filled $40 $45 $60

ELGIN, 7 jewels, stepped bezel
s. steel.. $60 $70 $90

ELGIN, 15J., wire lugs, stem at "12", c.1920s
silver $100 $120 $200

ELGIN, 7J., engraved case, c.1920s
base metal $65 $75 $125

ELGIN, 15J., engraved case, c.1925
gold filled.................................... $80 $90 $130

ELGIN, 21j., Lord Elgin, stepped case, c.1930
gold filled.................................... $75 $90 $135

ELGIN, 21J., Lord Elgin, stepped case, c.1930
gold filled.................................... $85 $95 $150

ELGIN, 7J., stepped case, c.1925
gold filled.................................... $65 $75 $125

ELGIN, 15J., stepped case, c.1930
gold filled.................................... $65 $75 $125

ELGIN, 17 jewels, c. 1927
14k...$150 $200 $275

ELGIN, 21J., Lord Elgin, GJS, c.1937
14k $150 $175 $250

LORD ELGIN, 21 jewels, diamond dial
14k (w).....................................$135 $155 $195

ELGIN, 17J., stepped case, c.1930
gold filled.................................... $65 $75 $125

Elgin, 19 jewels, c. 1947
14k..$140 $165 $220
gold filled...................................$80 $95 $145

ELGIN, 17J., curved, stepped case, c.1927
gold filled.................................... $70 $80 $125

LORD ELGIN, 21 jewels, diamond dial
14k (w).......................................$125 $150 $200

ELGIN, 17 jewels, raised numbers
gold filled.................................... $75 $90 $135

LORD ELGIN, 21 jewels, aux. sec., fancy lugs
14k...$175 $200 $275

ELGIN, 21J., Lord Elgin, cal.670, c.1948
14k $175 $200 $275

ELGIN, 15J., pierced shield, wire lugs, c.1918
silver..$350 $450 $600

LORD ELGIN, 21 jewels, flared case
14k $200 $250 $300

ELGIN, 15J., pierced shield, c.1918
silver...$325 $425 $600

ELGIN, 19 jewels, fancy lugs
14k $175 $200 $250

ELGIN, 15J., canteen style case, wire lugs, c.1919
nickel $150 $175 $235

ELGIN, 7J., cushion case, c.1930
gold filled $60 $80 $125

ELGIN, 15J., military style, 24 hr. dial, c.1942
s. steel $135 $150 $250

ELGIN, 7-15J., cushion case, c.1930
chromium $40 $45 $60

ELGIN, 15J., military style, cal.539, c.1940
s. steel.. $75 $95 $145

ELGIN, 15 jewels, "Official Boy Scout" model
s. steel...................................... $100 $125 $175

ELGIN, 7 jewels, "Official Boy Scout" model
s. steel...................................... $70 $85 $120

ELGIN, 15 jewels, enamel dial, wire lugs, c. 1915
silver $175 $250 $350

ELGIN, 15 jewels, enamel dial, wire lugs, c. 1915
silver $150 $175 $200

ELGIN, 15 jewels, center lugs
gold filled................................$125 $150 $225

ELGIN, 15 jewels, center lugs, c. 1922
silver...................................$175 $200 $235

ELGIN, 15J., case by Rolland Fischer, c. 1928
silver...$175 $200 $225

ELGIN, 17J., center sec., c.1950
base metal $40 $45 $60

ELGIN, 30J., center sec., cal. 760 auto-wind, c.1960
gold filled.................................... $65 $75 $125

ELGIN, 21J., water-proof, c.1952
s. steel... $50 $60 $80

ELGIN, 17J., center sec.,
base metal.................................... $50 $60 $80

ELGIN, 17J., aux. sec., center lugs
gold filled....................................$85 $100 $150

ELGIN, 21J., center sec., cal. 680, c.1952
gold filled.................................... $75 $90 $135

ELGIN, 21J., Lord Elgin, aux. sec., cal.688, c.1948
gold filled....................................$90 $110 $165

ELGIN, 23J.,B.W Raymond, RR approved, c.1952
gold filled................................ $150 $175 $250

ELGIN, 23 J., "B. W. Raymond," R.R. approved
14k..$300 $350 $400
gold filled....................................$150 $200 $250
s. steel $125 $150 $175

LORD ELGIN, 21 jewels, diamond dial, c. 1958
14k (w) $250 $300 $400

LORD ELGIN, 21 jewels, mystery dial, c. 1957
14k (w) $150 $200 $250

LORD ELGIN, 21J., direct reading, cal#719, C.1957
gold filled $250 $350 $450

ELGIN, 17 J., in form of golf ball, rotating hr. & min.
gold filled $250 $300 $350

LORD ELGIN, 21 jewels, applied numbers, c. 1946
14k $200 $250 $300

LORD ELGIN, 21 jewels, curved, applied numbers
14k $250 $300 $450

LORD ELGIN, 21 jewels, diamond dial, faceted crystal
14k $300 $350 $475

ELGIN, 17 jewels, hinged back
14k (w) $200 $250 $375

ELGIN, 17 jewels, enamel bezel
14k (w) $500 $600 $800

ELGIN, 15 jewels, Art Deco bezel, c. 1935
gold filled $100 $125 $150

ELGIN, 15 jewels, 2 tone, c. 1930
gold filled $80 $100 $120

ELGIN, 15 jewels, enamel bezel, c. 1920
14k (w) $600 $700 $850

ELGIN, 17 jewels, raised numbers
gold filled $95 $125 $180

ELGIN, 21 jewels, enamel bezel, 2 tone, c. 1931
14k $700 $800 $1,000
gold filled $150 $200 $300

ELGIN, 7 jewels, fancy bezel
s. steel $50 $60 $70

ELGIN, 7 jewels, engraved bezel
s. steel $45 $55 $80

ELGIN, 17 jewels, aux. sec., curved
gold filled $75 $95 $140

ELGIN, 17 jewels, curved
gold filled $75 $90 $125

ELGIN, 17 jewels, curved
gold filled $90 $100 $110

ELGIN, 21 jewels, blue enamel bezel, c. 1920
14k $1,000 $1,100 $1,500

ELGIN, 21 jewels, enamel bezel
18k $1,000 $1,100 $1,500

LORD ELGIN, 21J, model 670, large lugs, anniversary of
50,000,000th watch (small run of watches), c. 1953
18k $1,600 $2,000 $2,400

LORD ELGIN, 21 jewels, wandering hr. & min., curved
gold filled $200 $250 $300

ELGIN, 17 jewels, double dial
gold filled $450 $550 $700

LORD ELGIN, 21 jewels, hooded lugs, c. 1952
14k $225 $250 $275

LORD ELGIN, 21 jewels, curved, c. 1957
14k $175 $225 $300

LORD ELGIN, 21 jewels, hooded lugs, c. 1950s
14k $175 $200 $250

ELGIN, 15 jewels, waterproof
s. steel $30 $40 $50

ELGIN, 15 jewels, center sec.
gold filled $35 $45 $55

ELGIN, 7 jewels, aux. sec.
gold filled $30 $40 $55

LORD ELGIN, 21 jewels, stepped case
18k $375 $425 $500

LORD ELGIN, 21 jewels, stepped case, curved
14k $200 $250 $350

ELGIN, 17 jewels, stepped case
14k $175 $200 $250

LORD ELGIN, 21 jewels, curved
gold filled $125 $150 $200

ELGIN, 17 jewels, curved, fancy bezel
gold filled $100 $120 $140

ELGIN, 17 jewels, curved, stepped case
gold filled $100 $120 $140

ELGIN, 17 jewels, curved, stepped case
gold filled $100 $120 $140

ELGIN, 17 jewels, curved
gold filled $90 $110 $150

ELGIN, 19 jewels, stepped case
gold filled $100 $120 $140

ELGIN, 15 jewels
gold filled $80 $90 $125

ELGIN, 7 jewels, fancy bezel
s. steel $40 $45 $70

ELGIN, 7 jewels, fancy bezel
gold filled $80 $90 $120

LORD ELGIN, 21 jewels, curved, c. 1938
14k $200 $250 $350

ELGIN, 15 jewels, fancy bezel
gold filled $100 $110 $150

ELGIN, 21 jewels, curved
gold filled $100 $110 $140

LORD ELGIN, 21 jewels, raised numbers
14k $150 $200 $300

LORD ELGIN, 21 jewels, curved
14k $200 $220 $275

LORD ELGIN, 21 jewels, curved
14k $200 $225 $300

LORD ELGIN, 21 jewels, aux. sec.
gold filled $90 $110 $140

LORD ELGIN, 21 jewels, curved
14k $200 $275 $300

ELGIN, 17 jewels, curved
gold filled $100 $120 $140

ELGIN, 17 Jewels, raised numbers
14k $200 $225 $250

LORD ELGIN, 15jewels, electric, c. 1962
(sold for $89.50, July of 1962)
s. steel $100 $125 $200

LORD ELGIN, 15 jewels, electric,c.1962
(back–set)
s. steel.. $100 $125 $200

LORD ELGIN, 15 jewels,"electric",c.1962
(grade 725, 6 adj.)
gold filled.................................. $150 $200 $275

ELGIN, 17 Jewels, Lady Elgin, flader case, cal. 650, c.1950
14k $75 $90 $130

ELGIN, 15 Jewels, art deco, c.1925
gold filled.................................... $30 $45 $75

ELGIN, 15 Jewels, art deco, c.1928
14k $60 $70 $90

ELGIN, 17 Jewels, art deco, c.1928
18k(w) $75 $90 $140

ELGIN, 15 Jewels, art deco, c.1928
gold filled.................................... $25 $30 $45

ELGIN, 15 Jewels, art deco, c.1928
gold filled.................................... $25 $30 $45

ELGIN, 15 Jewels, art deco engraved case, c.1928
gold filled.................................... $25 $30 $45

ELGIN, 15 Jewels, sport model, c.1928
14k.. $60 $70 $80

ELGIN, 17J., 20 diamonds, art deco engraved case, c.1928
18k.. $225 $250 $350

ELGIN, 15 J., 2 diamonds, art deco engraved case, c.1928
gold filled.................................... $75 $85 $135

Model 3, 3-0 size, three-quarter plate, open face, pendant set, first serial number 18,179,001, Grade 414, March, 1915.

Model 1, 5-0 size, three-quarter plate, hunting, pendant set, first serial number 14,699,001, Grade 380, Feb., 1910.

Model 2, 5-0 size, three-quarter plate, open face, pendant set, first serial number 17,890,001, Grade 399, Feb., 1914.

Model 2, 8-0 size, Grade 532, 539, sweep second.

Model 7, 8-0 size, Grades 554, 555,

Model 20, 8-0 size, Grades 681, 682.

Model 1, 10-0 size, three-quarter plate, open face

Model 2, 15-0 size, Grades 623, 624, 626.

15-0 Size, movement, Grades 670, 672, 673.

15-0 size, movement. Grade 674.

15-0 size, movement, Grades 557, 558, 559.

Model 2, 21-0 size, Grade 541, 533, 535.

Model 3, 21-0 size, Grade 547, sweep second.

Model 4, 21-0 size, Grades 617, 617L, 619, 619L.

Model 9, 21-0 size, Grades 650, 651.

Model 9, 21-0 size, Grades 655, 656.

GRADE 725, 15 jewels,"electric" model movement

"ELECTRIC", case showing back—set

Grade 607, self wind.

Grade 630, sweep second.

Grade 641, 642

Grade 643, self wind.

Grades 644, 645, self wind.

Grade 647, sweep second.

Grade 661

Grade 666, sweep second.

Grade 668, sweep second.

Grade 685

Grade 687

Grade 700

Grade 710

Grade 716

ENICAR, 17 jewels, center sec.
s. steel.................................$10 $20 $30

ELOGA, triple calendar,
base metal...................................$50 $60 $70

ENICAR, 17 jewels, triple date, moon phase
gold filled..................................$150 $200 $250

EMERSON, 17J., hooded lugs,
gold filled....................................$60 $70 $80

ENICAR, 15 jewels, egg shaped with compass, c. 1918
silver...$400 $450 $500

ENICAR, 17 jewels, center sec.
18k..$250 $300 $350

ENICAR, 17J. autow., date, 24 hour dial, C.1970
s. steel......................................$100 $125 $150

ENICAR, 7 jewels, enamel dial, higged case, c.1929
sw. steel......................................$75 $100 $125

ESKA, 17J.,chronog., triple date, moon phase
14k..$1,200 $1,400 $1,600

ESKA, 17 jewels, chronog., 2 reg., C. 1950s
s. steel.. $200 $250 $300

ETERNA, 19 jewels, day-date-month
18k..$350 $400 $450

ESKA, 17 jewels, chronog., 2 reg., c. 1940
s. steel.................................... $1,000 $1,200 $1,400

ETERNA, 17 jewels, chronog., triple date, 3 reg.
18k..$800 $900 $1,000

ESKA, 17 jewels, multi-colored enamel dial
18k $2,500 $2,700 $3,000

ETERNA, 21 jewels, date, cal. 14390, c.1960
18k..$250 $300 $350

ETERNA, quartz, date, by ETA, cal#954, C.1975
s. steel...$75 $100 $125

ETERNA, 19 jewels, c.1944
14k..$150 $175 $200

ETERNA, 19 jewels, c.1938
gold filled $75 $100 $125

EVANS, 17 jewels, rhinestone on bezel, c. 1948
gold plate $70 $80 $95

EVANS, 17 jewels, chronog., 2 reg., c. 1940
18k $300 $400 $500

EXACTUS, 17 J., chronog.,triple-date, moon ph.
s. steel.. $500 $600 $700

EXCELSIOR, 17 jewels, chronog., 2 reg.
gold filled................................$150 $200 $250

EXCELSIOR, 17 jewels, chronog.
s. steel....................................... $200 $225 $250

FAIRFAX, 6J, engraved case, c.1929
base metal $40 $50 $65

FAIRFAX, 6J, engraved case, c.1929
base metal $100 $125 $150

FAIRFAX, 6J, butler finish case, c.1929
base metal $50 $60 $75

FAIRFAX, 6J, engraved case, c.1929
gold filled $100 $125 $150

FRAMONT, 17J, timer, date, cal. 290, c.1970
s. steel $100 $125 $150

FAITH, 17J, flip top case, by Hyde Park, c.1950
gold filled $140 $150 $165

FERRARI, quartz, chronog., c.1988
base metal $250 $300 $375

FREY, 25J., rotating outside chapter, c.1970
s. steel $75 $100 $125

FELCA, 17 jewels, auto wind
18k $100 $150 $200

FREY,17J., GJS, c.1970
s. steel $30 $40 $55

FONTAINEMELON, S. A., 17 J., gold train, digital
14k $1,500 $1,600 $1,800

FREY,15J., engraved case, c.1933
base metal $30 $40 $55

FREY,15J., engraved stepped case, c.1933
base metal.................................... $40 $50 $65

FREY,15J., engraved case, c.1933
base metal.................................... $50 $60 $70

FRIEDLI, 17 jewels, auto wind, center sec.
18k.. $150 $200 $250

GALLET, 15 jewels, waterproof, auto wind
s. steel.. $50 $60 $70

GALLET, 17 jewels, chronog., single button, c. 1950
s. steel...................................... $300 $350 $400

GALLET, 17J., chronog., by Racine, US air force, c. 1978
s. steel...................................... $100 $150 $200

GALLET, 17 jewels, chronog., 3 reg., c. 1945
s. steel......................................$300 $350 $400

GALLET, 17 jewels, chronog., 3 reg., c. 1942
gold filled..................................$350 $400 $475

GALLET, 17J., chronog., 2 reg.,single button, C.1925, small size
silver $800 $1,000 $1,200

GALLET, 17 jewels, day-date-month, c. 1941
gold filled.................................. $400 $500 $600

GALLET, 17J., chronog., 3 reg.,triple date, moon ph.
18k $2,000 $2,500 $3,000

GALLET, 17 jewels, chronog., 2 reg.
s. steel.. $100 $150 $200

GALLET, 17J., chronog., 3 reg.,triple date,
s. steel.. $400 $500 $600

GALLET, 17 jewels, chronog., mid size, c. 1940
s. steel.. $400 $450 $500

GALLET, 17 jewels, chronog., 3 reg., c. 1955
s. steel.. $300 $350 $400

GALLET, 17J., chronog., flying officer, cal.149, c. 1958
s. steel.. $400 $500 $600

GALLET, 17 jewels, chronog., waterproof
s. steel........................ $300 $400 $500

GALLET, 17 jewels, chronog., 2 reg.
s. steel........................$100 $150 $200

GALLET, 17 jewels, chronog., 2 reg.
s. steel........................ $200 $300 $400

GALLET, 17 jewels, chronog., 2 reg., c. 1939
s. steel........................$200 $300 $350

GALLET, 17 jewels, oval, chronog., 2 reg.
s.steel........................ $300 $400 $500

GALLET, 17 jewels, time dial at 12 , chronog.
s. steel........................$300 $300 $400

GALLET, 17 jewels, chronog., 2 reg.
gold filled.................... $125 $175 $225

P. GARNIER, 17 jewels, minu-stop, c. 1965
s. steel........................ $75 $100 $125

P. GARNIER, 17 jewels, world time, c. 1968
s. steel... $60 $70 $85

GARLAND, 17J., center sec., water-proof.
s. steel... $30 $40 $50

GENEVE, 15 jewels, dual dial, c. 1939
s. steel... $300 $350 $400

GENEVE, 15 jewels, dual dial, c. 1937
s. steel... $300 $350 $400

GERMINAL, 17 J., "Voltaire"
14k $150 $175 $200

GERMINAL, 15 J., early auto wind, lug action, c. 1933
s. steel....................................... $500 $600 $700

GERALD GENTA, 29J., skeletonized, auto wind,
perpetual calendar
18k C&B $20,000 $25,000 $30,000

GIRARD-PERREGAUX, 17J., autowind, C.1951
s. steel $60 $80 $100

GIRARD-PERREGAUX, 17J., alarm, c.1960
gold filled.................................... $100 $125 $150

GIRARD-PERREGAUX, 39J., center sec. c.1955
14k $200 $225 $255

GIRARD-PERREGAUX, 17J., center sec., c.1948
18k $250 $275 $300

GIRARD-PERREGAUX, 17J., center sec., c.1960
s. steel $60 $70 $85

GIRARD-PERREGAUX, 17J., cal.47ae, c.1953
14k $250 $300 $350

GIRARD-PERREGAUX, 17J., Sea Hawk., c.1960
gold filled $50 $60 $75

GIRARD-PERREGAUX, 17J., aux. sec., c.1958
gold filled $50 $60 $75

GIRARD-PERREGAUX, 17J., aux. sec., c.1950
s. steel $80 $90 $110

GIRARD-PERREGAUX, 17J., date, c.1960
gold filled $50 $60 $75

GIRARD-PERREGAUX, 39J., auto-matic, date, c.1960
18k $275 $300 $325

GIRARD-PERREGAUX, 39J., chronometre HF, c.1970
s. steel.. $70 $80 $95

GIRARD-PERREGAUX,17J.,"Gyromatic",date
gold filled $60 $70 $80

GIRARD-PERREGAUX, 17J.,"Gyromatic",date
18k $200 $250 $300

GIRARD-PERREGAUX, 39 J., auto wind, c. 1960
18k...$300 $350 $400

GIRARD-PERREGAUX, 17J., triple date, autow.
s. steel......................................$100 $125 $150

GIRARD-PERREGAUX, 39 jewels, center sec.
14k...$200 $250 $300

GIRARD-PERREGAUX, 17J., chronog, 2 reg.
s. steel $300 $350 $400

GIRARD-PERREGAUX, 17J., by Valjoux cal.72, c.1955
s. steel.....................................$500 $550 $600

GIRARD-PERREGAUX, 17J., chronog., triple date,
moon phase
18k.............................$1,500 $1,800 $2,000

GIRARD-PERREGAUX, 17J., chronog cal.285, c.1940
gold filled $300 $350 $400

GIRARD-PERREGAUX, 17J., aux. sec., fancy lugs
14k................................$300 $350 $400

GIRARD-PERREGAUX, 17J., pulsations, c.1948
14k $500 $550 $600

GIRARD-PERREGAUX, 17J., enamel dial, c.1960
14k...............................,$200 $225 $265

GIRARD-PERREGAUX, 17J., RF#2459, c.1970
14k................................$150 $175 $200

GIRARD-PERREGAUX, 17 J., chronog., 3 reg., c. 1952
s. steel...................................$350 $400 $500

GIRARD-PERREGAUX, 17J., cal.a6 3606, GJS, c.1955
14k...................................$150 $175 $200

GIRARD-PERREGAUX, 17J., recess crown, GJS, c.1954
14k $200 $225 $250

GIRARD-PERREGAUX, 17J., cal. 86ae, GJS, c.1942
s. steel $50 $60 $75

GIRARD-PERREGAUX, 17J., cal.86, GJS, c.1948
14k $100 $125 $165

GIRARD-PERREGAUX, 17J., recess crown, GJS, c.1947
gold filled.................................. $50 $60 $75

GIRARD-PERREGAUX, 17J., cal.86ae, GJS, c.1940
s. steel.................................. $50 $60 $75

GIRARD-PERREGAUX, 17J., "1791", GJS, c.1942
s. steel $100 $125 $150

GIRARD-PERREGAUX, 17J., two tone case,GJS, c.1942
14k $300 $350 $400

GIRARD-PERREGAUX, 17J., cal.91ae220, GJS, c.1948
gold filled.................................. $60 $70 $85

GIRARD-PERREGAUX, 17J., GJS, c.1953
14k $150 $175 $200

GIRARD-PERREGAUX, 17J., GJS, c.1936
gold filled.................................$80 $90 $110

GIRARD-PERREGAUX, 17J., cal.86ae, GJS, c.1942
14k $50 $60 $75

Girard-Perregaux, 17 jewels, aux. sec.
14k $250 $300 $350

Girard-Perregaux, 17 jewels, aux. sec.
gold filled $100 $125 $150

Girard-Perregaux, 17 jewels, tank style, c. 1948
14k $200 $250 $300

GIRARD-PERREGAUX, 17 J., C. 1948
14k $250 $300 $350

GIRARD-PERREGAUX, 17 J., date, stepped case,
14k $600 $700 $800

GLASHUTTE, 17J., 2 reg., fluted bezel, c.1942
s. steel $800 $900 $1,100

GLYCINE, 17J., airman sst,auto-wind, 24hr., date, c.1970
s. steel $75 $100 $125

GLYCINE, 17J., 15 diamond dial, cal. 4645, c.1945
14k $800 $900 $1,000

GLYCINE, 17J., 3 diamond dial, c.1950
14k(w) $200 $300 $350

GLYCINE, 17 jewels, airman, 24 hr. dial, date, C.1960s
s. steel.......................................$250 $300 $350

GLYCINE, 17 jewels, curved, c. 1938
18k $350 $400 $500

GOERING W. Co., 15J., center sec., C.1935
base metal $50 $60 $75

GLYCINE, 17 jewels, aux. sec., c. 1934
14k (w) $125 $150 $175

GOERING W. Co., 15J., engraved case, C.1935
gold filled..................................$50 $60 $75

GLYCINE, 18 jewels, faceted crystal & bezel
gold filled $90 $100 $130

GOERING W. Co., 15J., engraved case, C.1935
gold filled..................................$80 $90 $110

GOERING W. Co.,jump hr., wandering sec.,C.1935
14k $800 $1,000 $1,200

GOERING W. Co., 15J., engraved case, C.1935
gold filled....................................$80 $90 $110

GOERING W. Co., 15J., rectangular, C.1935
gold filled $70 $80 $95

GOERING W. Co., 15J., ladies engraved case, C.1935
gold filled $30 $40 $55

GOLAY, 18 jewels, aux. sec., c. 1928
18k & platinum $2,500 $3,000 $3,500

GOLAY, 32 jewels, min. repeater, adj. to 5 positions
18k $20,000 $25,000 $30,000

GOTHAM, 17J., 12 diamond dial, "Aristocrat", center sec.
14k $100 $125 $150

GRANA, 16J., GJS, ca. 1948
14k $125 $150 $175

GRUEN, 15J., enamel dial, wire lugs, c. 1915
silver $100 $125 $200

GRUEN, 17J.,driver's watch, winds at 12, cal.400, c.1938
gold filled $450 $475 $550

GRUEN,17J., curved, drivers, cal.401, RF#352, c.1932
gold filled $450 $500 $650

GRUEN, 17J., extremely curved, drivers, c. 1932, and
side view of watch
gold filled $500 $600 $750

GRUEN, 17 J., extremely curved, driver's watch
gold filled $550 $650 $800

GRUEN, 17J., driver's watch , flexible long lugs
gold filled $600 $700 $850

GRUEN, 17 jewels, curvex, c. 1949
gold filled $225 $250 $300

GRUEN, 17 jewels, curvex, 35mm long
gold filled $250 $300 $400

GRUEN, 17 jewels, curvex, 55mm long, C.1937
14k $800 $900 $1,000

GRUEN, 17J.,curvex, precision, C. 1930s
14k $400 $500 $650

GRUEN, 17 jewels, curvex, c. 1937
gold filled $250 $300 $400

GRUEN, 17 jewels, curvex, c. 1945
gold filled $300 $350 $400

GRUEN, 17 jewels, curvex, 50mm long, c. 1937
gold filled $400 $500 $650

GRUEN, 17 jewels, curvex, c. 1937
s. steel $175 $200 $250

GRUEN, 17 jewels, curvex, aux. sec.
gold filled $275 $350 $450

GRUEN, 17J., note bezel,curvex, ca.1936
gold filled $250 $300 $400

GRUEN, 17 jewels, curvex
gold filled $250 $300 $400

GRUEN, 17 jewels, curvex
gold filled $175 $200 $250

GRUEN, 17J., curvex, RF#266, cal.165c. 1935
gold filled $100 $120 $200

GRUEN, 17 jewels, curvex
gold filled $175 $200 $250

GRUEN, 17J., curvex, RF#280, cal.330, c. 1934
gold filled $250 $300 $400

GRUEN, 17J., curvex, RF#202, cal.311, c. 1936
gold filled $250 $300 $400

GRUEN, 17J., curvex, stepped case, RF#280, c. 1937
gold filled $250 $300 $400

GRUEN, 15J., curvex, RF#226, c. 1936
gold filled $175 $200 $300

GRUEN, 17J., precision, RF#292, cal.330, c. 1937
gold filled $250 $300 $400

GRUEN, 15J., curvex, stepped case, RF#278c. 1936
s. steel.. $250 $300 $400

GRUEN, 15J., curvex, RF#324, cal.500, c. 1936
gold filled $125 $150 $225

GRUEN, 15J., curvex, RF#255, cal.500c. 1936
gold filled $250 $300 $400

GRUEN, 17J., curvex, RF#308, cal.330, c. 1936
gold filled $250 $300 $400

GRUEN, 17J., curvex, RF#339, cal.330, c. 1939
gold filled $250 $300 $400

GRUEN, 17 jewels, jumping hr., double dial
14k.................................$2,000 $2,500 $3,000

GRUEN, 17J., curvex, aux. sec.
gold filled $200 $250 $350

GRUEN, 17 jewels, double dial
gold filled.................................. $500 $600 $700

GRUEN, 17J., curvex, cal#440, hooded lugs, ca.1943
14k $200 $235 $300

GRUEN, 17 jewels, double dial, curved, c.1930s
gold filled..................................$400 $450 $550

GRUEN, 17 jewels, curvex, fancy lugs
14k $300 $350 $400

GRUEN, 17 jewels, curved, c. 1938
gold filled.................................. $400 $450 $550

GRUEN, 17 jewels, curvex, long lugs
14k $300 $350 $450

GRUEN, 17 jewels, double dial
gold filled.................................. $500 $550 $600

GRUEN, 17 jewels, double dial, c. 1935
gold filled $600 $700 $800

GRUEN, 17 jewels, double dial, c. 1932
gold filled.................................. $500 $550 $600

GRUEN, 15 jewels, in form of car radiator, curved
nickel.. $800 $900 $1,000

GRUEN, 17J., curvex, diamond dial, faceted crystal
14k..$375 $450 $500

GRUEN, 17 jewels, curvex, diamond dial, c. 1946
14k $250 $350 $500

GRUEN, 17 jewels, veri thin model, fancy lugs
14k............................$300 $350 $450

GRUEN, 17J., curvex, 3 diam., RF#568, cal.440, c. 1945
14k(w) $200 $250 $350

GRUEN, 17 jewels, auto wind, cal. 840, c. 1952
18k................................$350 $400 $450

GRUEN, 17J., curvex, 5 diam., RF#615, cal.370c. 1945
14k(w) $225 $275 $400

GRUEN, 17 jewels, curvex, fancy lugs
gold filled................................$200 $250 $400

GRUEN, 17J., stepped case, 3 diam., RF#798, c. 1950
14k(w) $250 $300 $425

GRUEN, 17 jewels, curvex, diamond dial, fancy lugs
14k (w)..$200 $250 $300

GRUEN, 21 jewels, diamond dial, fancy center lugs
14k $400 $500 $600

GRUEN, 21 jewels, fancy lugs, c. 1945
14k $350 $400 $500

GRUEN, 17 jewels, curvex, fancy lugs, c. 1943
14k $300 $350 $450

GRUEN, 17 jewels, curvex, diamond dial, c. 1945
14k $400 $500 $650

GRUEN, 17J., flared, diamond dial,
14k(w) $400 $500 $600

GRUEN, 17 jewels, curvex, diamond dial, c.1945
14k.................................$350 $450 $625

GRUEN, 17 jewels, curvex, c.1951
14k.................................$300 $350 $450

GRUEN, 17 jewels, curvex, diamond dial, c. 1943
14k(w)..............................$300 $350 $400

GRUEN, 17 jewels, curvex, diamond dial, c. 1951
14k(w)..............................$550 $650 $800

GRUEN, 17 jewels, curved
gold filled...............................$125 $150 $250

GRUEN, 17 jewels, curvex
14k.................................$350 $450 $600

GRUEN, 21J., veri-thin, precision, swinging lugs
gold filled.................................. $200 $250 $300

GRUEN, 15J., RF#467, cal.431, c. 1948
gold filled.................................. $85 $100 $150

GRUEN, 15J., RF#93, cal.179, c. 1925
gold filled.................................. $85 $95 $150

GRUEN, 17J., precision, RF#498, cal.440, c. 1945
gold filled.................................. $85 $100 $150

GRUEN, 17J., stepped lugs, RF#449, cal.440, c. 1945
gold filled.................................. $110 $125 $200

GRUEN, 17J., curvex, RF#498, cal.440, c. 1945
gold filled.................................. $95 $110 $175

GRUEN, 17J., large lugs, RF#449, cal.440, c. 1945
gold filled.................................. $200 $250 $350

GRUEN, 17J., curvex, RF#530, cal.335, c. 1948
gold filled.................................. $110 $125 $200

GRUEN, 17J., RF#449, cal.440, c. 1943
gold filled.................................. $150 $175 $250

GRUEN, 17J., veri-thin, RF#530, cal.430, c. 1945
14k.................................. $175 $195 $275

GRUEN, 17J., curvex, RF#544, cal.440, c. 1942
gold filled.................................. $150 $175 $275

GRUEN, 17J., fancy lugs, curvex, RF#610, c. 1945
14k.. $400 $450 $575

GRUEN, 17J., veri-thin 3 diam., RF#558, cal.335, c. 1945
14k(w) $185 $200 $300

GRUEN, 17J., curvex, RF#610, cal.1370, c. 1945
14k.. $375 $400 $500

GRUEN, 17J., curvex, RF#576, cal.440, c. 1942
14k $300 $350 $475

GRUEN, 17J., 3 diam., curvex, RF#615, cal.370, c. 1945
14k.. $200 $250 $400

GRUEN, 17J., 3 diam.curvex, RF#587, cal.430, c. 1948
gold filled.................................. $100 $120 $200

GRUEN, 17J., curvex, RF#642, cal.370, c. 1945
gold filled.................................. $125 $150 $225

GRUEN, 17J., curvex, RF#607, cal.370, c. 1943
gold filled.................................. $175 $200 $350

GRUEN, 17J., curvex, cal.370, c. 1948
gold filled.................................. $130 $160 $220

GRUEN, 17J., twisted bezel, RF#657, cal.335, c. 1953
gold filled.................................. $125 $150 $225

GRUEN, 17J., curvex, faceted crystal, cal.440, c. 1947
14k.. $175 $200 $300

GRUEN, 21J., precision, RF#674, cal.430, c. 1947
gold filled.................................. $100 $125 $200

GRUEN, 21J., precision, RF#801, cal335., c. 1953
14k.. $175 $200 $300

GRUEN, 21J., precision, RF#738, cal.335, c. 1948
14k $175 $200 $300

GRUEN, 17J., veri-thin, large lugs, c. 1950
14k.. $200 $235 $350

GRUEN, 17J., curvex, RF#750, cal.370, c. 1940
gold filled.................................. $125 $150 $250

GRUEN, 17J., center wheel not jeweled, c. 1938
gold filled.................................. $90 $110 $175

GRUEN, 17J., curvex, RF#773, cal.370, c. 1945
gold filled.................................. $150 $175 $275

GRUEN, 17J., stepped case, ca.1930
gold filled..................................$100 $125 $150

GRUEN, 19 jewels, precision, c. 1920
14k $500 $600 $700

GRUEN, 17J., curvex, RF#450, cal.440, c. 1938
gold filled.................................. $200 $250 $350

GRUEN, 17 jewels, curvex
14k $400 $500 $650

GRUEN, 17J., curvex, RF#450, cal.440, c. 1938
14k.. $200 $250 $300

GRUEN, 17J., curvex, cal#440, ca.1940s
gold filled.................................. $125 $150 $200

GRUEN, 17J., curvex, RF#450, cal.440, c. 1942
14k.. 125   150   225

GRUEN, 17 jewels, curvex, c. 1943
14k $300 $350 $450

GRUEN, 17J., curvex, RF#364, cal.400, c. 1935
gold filled.................................. $175 $200 $250

GRUEN, 17J., veri-thin, cal.405, c. 1946
gold filled.................................. $85 $100 $150

GRUEN, 17J., precision, RF#271, cal., c. 1936
gold filled.................................. $125 $150 $200

GRUEN, 17J., curvex, RF#448, cal.440, c. 1941
gold filled.................................. $200 $250 $350

GRUEN, 17J., curvex, RF#602, cal.370, c. 1943
14k... $325 $350 $475

GRUEN, 17J., curvex, RF#879, cal.370, c. 1942
14k $350 $375 $500

GRUEN, 17J., curvex, RF#449, cal.440, c. 1945
14k... $300 $335 $450

GRUEN, 17J., curvex, RF#448, cal.440, c. 1944
14k $350 $375 $500

GRUEN, 17J., veri-thin, cal.420, c. 1948
gold filled.................................. $85 $95 $150

GRUEN, 17J., curvex, RF#293, cal.330, c. 1940
gold filled.................................. $150 $175 $275

GRUEN, 17 jewels, curvex, c. 1936
gold filled..................................$300 $350 $400

GRUEN, 17J., fluted bezel, RF#240, cal.335, c. 1935
14k $175 $200 $300

GRUEN, 17 jewels, precision, fancy lugs
14k..$350 $450 $600

GRUEN, 17 jewels, curvex, c. 1947
14k $300 $350 $450

GRUEN, 17 jewels, curvex, c. 1937
gold filled................................. $175 $200 $250

GRUEN, 17 jewels, curvex, fancy lugs
14k $350 $400 $500

GRUEN, 17 jewels, curvex, c. 1939
gold filled................................. $350 $400 $500

GRUEN, 17 jewels, curvex, fancy lugs, c. 1961
14k $550 $600 $700

GRUEN, 17J., pulsemeter,
s. steel $400 $500 $600

GRUEN, 17 jewels, physicians chronog., screw back
18k..$1,500 $1,700 $2,000

GRUEN, 17J., jump 24 hour, c. 1970
s. steel $90 $110 $150

GRUEN, 17J., alarm, date, c. 1964
s. steel $150 $175 $250

GRUEN, 17J., triple date, cal.415, c. 1953
gold filled $135 $150 $225

GRUEN, 17 jewels, rope style bezel with diamonds
14k $300 $350 $400

GRUEN, 17J., center sec., cal.n510, c. 1960
base metal $55 $65 $85

GRUEN, 17 jewels, day-date-month, c. 1948
s. steel $120 $160 $200

GRUEN, 17 jewels, veri thin model, fancy lugs
14k $250 $300 $400

GRUEN, 17J., mystery dial, cal#215, ca.1965
gold filled $200 $250 $300

GRUEN, 17J., veri thin model, fancy lugs, 24 hr. dial
14k $400 $500 $600

GRUEN, 17 jewels, jumping dial, c. 1960
gold filled $150 $180 $250

GRUEN, 17J., engraved case, cal.117, c. 1929
14k(w) $200 $225 $325

GRUEN, 15J., cushion, luminous dial, c. 1930s
gold filled .... $$85 $95 $150

GRUEN, 15J., veri-thin, c. 1930s
gold filled $100 $125 $200

GRUEN, 17J., veri-thin, stepped lugs, c. 1930s
gold filled $75 $85 $125

GRUEN, 17J., precision, oval wide bezel, recess crown
14k $150 $175 $250

GRUEN, 17J., fluted center lugs, cal.343, c. 1936
gold filled.......................................

GRUEN, 17J., nurse style double dial, ca.1937
s. steel $200 $250 $300

E. GUBELIN, 17 jewels, chronog. 3 reg., Valj.72, c. 1950
18k............................ $1,200 $1,500 $1,700

E. GUBELIN, 19 jewels, chronog., day-date-month
18k.. $1,500 $1,800 $2,000

E. GUBELIN, 19J., chronog.by Valjoux, waterpf, 3 reg.
18k............................... $2,500 $3,000 $3,500

E. GUBELIN, 29 jewels, min. repeater
18k C&B............................. $25,000 $30,000 $35,000

E. GUBELIN, 17J., ca. 1970s
18k...$200 $250 $300

E. GUBELIN, 25J., ipso-matic, triple date, moon ph.
18k $2,000 $2,500 $3,000

E. GUBELIN, 17J., cal#F690, center sec., ca. 1950s
s. steel $100 $150 $200

E. GUBELIN, 15J., triple date, c.1945
s. steel..$400 $450 $500

E. GUBELIN, 17J., ca. 1952
s. steel..$150 $200 $250

E. GUBELIN, 19 jewels, 18k case, 14k band
18k & 14k C&B $500 $700 $900

E. GUBELIN, 25J., ipso-matic, c.1955
14k..$300 $350 $400

E. GUBELIN, 17J., alarm, ipso-vox, c.1960
18k $600 $650 $700

E. GUBELIN, 17J., ipso-vox, date, alarm, c.1960
s. steel.. $350 $400 $450

E. GUBELIN, 17J., carved lugs, center sec., c.1944
18k $400 $450 $500

E. GUBELIN, 17J., 8 baguettes 3 diamonds, c.1948
platinum.................................... $500 $550 $600

E. GUBELIN, 15J., duoplan, c.1935
s. steel.. $150 $200 $250

E. GUBELIN, 15J., ca. 1935
18k(W) $800 $1,000 $1,200

E. GUBELIN, 19 J., hunter style pop-up lid, c. 1930
18k (w)................................... $6,000 $7,000 $8,000

E. GUBELIN, 17jewels, jumping hr., c. 1924
14k.. $8,000 $9,000 $10,000

E. GUBELIN, 25J., triple date, moon phase, c. 1950
18k.. $2,500 $3,000 $3,500

E. GUBELIN, 19 jewels, fancy bezel, enamel dial
18k.. $1,500 $1,600 $1,800

E. GUBELIN, 19 jewels, fancy lugs, center sec.
18k $500 $600 $800

E. GUBELIN, 19 jewels, fancy hooded lugs
18k $1,000 $1,200 $1,500

E. GUBELIN, 19 jewels, curvex, 2 tone
18k $1,500 $1,700 $2,000

E. GUBELIN, 19J. center sec., flared case, c. 1950
18k $350 $450 $550

E. GUBELIN, 21 jewels, center sec.
18k $300 $325 $375

E. GUBELIN, 17 jewels, by Vacheron & Constantin
18k $2,500 $3,000 $3,500

E. GUBELIN, 18 jewels, curved, stepped case, c. 1940
18k $1,000 $1,200 $1,500

GUINAND, 17J., chronog., day-date-month, 3 reg.
18k $600 $700 $800
s. steel $300 $350 $400

GUINAND, 17 J.s, chronog., triple date, moon phase
18k $1,000 $1,200 $1,400
s. steel $600 $700 $800

HAFIS, 15J., center sec., cushion style
gold plate $50 $60 $75

HAFIS, 15J., luminous dial
gold plate $50 $60 $75

HAFIS, 15J., engraved case
gold plate.................................$60 $70 $85

HAFIS, 15J., engraved case
gold plate $70 $80 $95
14k $150 $200 $275

HAFIS, 15J., engraved case
gold plate.................................$60 $70 $85

HAFIS, 15J., engraved case
gold plate $50 $60 $75

HAFIS, 15J., engraved case
gold plate.................................$60 $70 $85

HAFIS, 15J., engraved case
gold plate $60 $70 $85

HAFIS, 15J., luminous dial
gold plate..................................... $50 $55 $65

HAFIS, 15J., engraved case
gold plate $50 $60 $75

HAFIS, 15J., curved case
gold plate...................................$50 $60 $75
14k...$125 $150 $200

HAFIS, 15J., engraved case, curved
gold plate $60 $70 $85
14k $150 $175 $200

HAFIS, 17J., 'Queen Druga", 52 diamonds
Platinum $350 $400 $450

HAFIS, 15J., "Queen Marie", 26 diam. 12 synthic emeralds
18k $200 $250 $300

HAFIS, 15J., "Queen Charlotte", 22 diamonds
18k $175 $200 $225

HALLMARK, 17 jewels, day-date-month, auto wind
gold filled $100 $125 $150

HAMILTON, electric, "Altair"
gold filled $700 $800 $900

HAMILTON, electric, "Aquatel B"
gold filled.................................$100 $125 $150

HAMILTON, electric, "Clearview"
s. steel $100 $125 $175

HAMILTON, electric, "Converta"
gold filled.................................$100 $125 $150

HAMILTON, electric, "Everest"
gold filled.................................$125 $150 $175

HAMILTON, electric, "Meteor," c. 1959
gold filled.................................$300 $350 $400

HAMILTON, electric, "Nautilus" 200
14k $200 $250 $325
gold filled $65 $75 $100

HAMILTON, electric, "Nautilus" 400–404
gold filled................................. $100 $125 $200

HAMILTON, electric, engraved bezel
gold filled................................. $80 $90 $110

HAMILTON, electric, "Nautilus" 401
gold filled................................. $90 $100 $165

HAMILTON, electric, "Polaris
14k..$300 $350 $400

HAMILTON, electric, "Nautilus" 605
gold filled................................. $70 $80 $150

HAMILTON, electric,"Polaris", diamond dial
14k..$400 $450 $500

HAMILTON, electric, "Regulus"
s. steel......................................$200 $300 $400

HAMILTON, electric, "Pacer," 2 tone
gold filled................................. $175 $200 $250

HAMILTON, electric, "R. R. Special", model 50 =s. steel
model 51 = s.steel case 10k bezel,
model 52 =10k gold filled case
#52 10k GF case......................$150 $200 $250
#51 GF bezel............................$85 $100 $150
#50 s. steel...............................$75 $85 $120

HAMILTON, electric, "Saturn"
14k $400 $500 $600
gold filled $125 $150 $250

HAMILTON, electric, "Skip Jack"
gold filled $70 $80 $90

HAMILTON, electric, "Savitar"
14k $350 $400 $450

HAMILTON, electric, "Spectra"
14k $300 $400 $500
gold filled $120 $150 $200

HAMILTON, electric, "Savatar 11", ca.1966
gold filled $175 $200 $250

HAMILTON, electric, "Summit"
10k $150 $175 $200
gold filled $100 $125 $150

HAMILTON, electric, "Sea-Lectric I"
s. steel $100 $125 $150

HAMILTON, electric, "Taurus"
gold filled $100 $125 $150

HAMILTON, electric, "Sea-Lectric II"
s. steel $100 $125 $150

HAMILTON, electric, "Titan"
gold filled $100 $125 $175

HAMILTON, electric, "Titan II"
gold filled.................................. $100 $125 $150

HAMILTON electric, Ventura
18k...$1,000 $1,200 $1,500
14k...$650 $850 $1,000

HAMILTON, electric, "Titan III"
gold filled.................................. $125 $150 $200

HAMILTON electric, Ventura, diamond dial
14K...$800 $1,000 $1,200

HAMILTON, electric, "Uranus"
gold filled.................................. $125 $150 $175

HAMILTON, electric,"Victor", ca.1958
gold filled.................................. $100 $125 $200

HAMILTON, electric, Vantage , ca.1959
gold filled.................................. $150 $200 $250

Hamilton, electric, "Victor II"
gold filled..................................$150 $200 $250

HAMILTON, electric, "Vega"
14k $350 $400 $450
gold filled.................................. $175 $200 $275

HAMILTON, 17 jewels, "Seckron," dual dial
gold filled..................................$500 $600 $700

HAMILTON, 17 jewels, dual dial
gold filled................................. $500 $600 $700

HAMILTON, 17 jewels, "Flint Ridge," flip top
14k $1,800 $2,000 $2,200

HAMILTON, 17 jewels, "Cross Country," c. 1962
14k $250 $300 $400
gold filled................................. $100 $150 $250

HAMILTON, 17 jewels, "Flight II"
14k $1,500 $1,700 $2,000
gold filled................................. $500 $600 $700

HAMILTON, 17J., chronog., by Valjoux cal.7733, c.1971
s. steel....................................... $175 $200 $300

HAMILTON, 17J., chronog., DATE, by Valjoux cal.7732,
s. steel...$200 $250 $350

HAMILTON, 17J., auto-wind, c.1971
s. steel...$40 $50 $80

HAMILTON, 17J., auto-wind, day date, c.1971
s. steel...$45 $55 $95

HAMILTON, 17J., hinged lugs, cal., c.1940
gold filled.................................$125 $150 $200

HAMILTON, 17J., hinged lugs, cal., c.1940
gold filled.................................. $125 $150 $200

HAMILTON, 17J., drivers, cal.907, c.1938
gold filled.................................. $125 $150 $200

HAMILTON,17J., drivers winds at 12, ca. 1942
gold filled $400 $450 $500

HAMILTON, 19 jewels, "Otis," reversible, c. 1946
gold filled $850 $1,000 $1,200

HAMILTON, 19 J., "Coronado," black enamel bezel
14k $900 $1,000 $1,200

HAMILTON, 19 jewels, "Piping Rock," enamel bezel
14k..................................$850 $1,000 $1,200

HAMILTON, 19 jewels, blue enamel bezel, grade 986
14k..................................$900 $1,000 $1,400

HAMILTON, 19 jewels, "Spur," enamel bezel
14k..................................$2,000 $2,500 $3,200
14k(w)..................................$1,500 $2,000 $3,000

HAMILTON, 15J."Oval", c. 1920s
14k..................................$350 $400 $600

HAMILTON, 19 jewels, "Andrews"
14k..................................$200 $250 $350

HAMILTON, 17 jewels, "Alan"
gold filled..................................... $90 $125 $195

HAMILTON, 19 jewels, "Allison"
14k $300 $400 $550

HAMILTON, 17J.," Austin "
gold filled................................... $100 $125 $200

HAMILTON, 17 jewels, "Bagley," applied numbers
gold filled................................... $125 $125 $200

HAMILTON, 19J.," Bailey ", c.1951
gold filled $100 $150 $200

HAMILTON, 17J.," Barton' ", tu tone dial, c.1951
14k $250 $300 $425

HAMILTON,17J.,"Beldon", 2 tone dial, sealed case, c.1951
gold filled................................... $100 $125 $200

HAMILTON, 17-21J.," Blake ", c.1951
gold filled................................... $100 $125 $185

HAMILTON, 19 jewels, "Boulton"
gold filled................................... $100 $125 $200

HAMILTON, 17J.,"Boyd", c.1951
gold filled................................... $100 $135 $185

HAMILTON, 17J., Brandon, swing lugs
gold filled................................... $110 $135 $165

HAMILTON, 17 jewels, "Brandon"
gold filled.................................$100 $125 $150

HAMILTON, 19 jewels, "Cameron"
14k...$200 $250 $400

HAMILTON, 19J.,"Brent ", faceted crystal, c.1951
gold filled..................................$100 $125 $200

HAMILTON, 17J.," Carlton ", c.1951
gold filled..................................$100 $125 $200

HAMILTON, 19 jewels, "Brock"
gold filled.....................................$90 $115 $150

HAMILTON, 19J.," Cedil ", c.1951
gold filled..................................$100 $125 $200

HAMILTON, 19 jewels, "Brock"
gold filled..................................$100 $125 $175

HAMILTON, 17J.," Clinton ", c.1951
s. steel...$75 $90 $135

HAMILTON, 19 jewels, "Byrd"
14k $300 $350 $450

HAMILTON, 19J.," Cambridge ", c.1951
platinum...................................$700 $800 $1,000

HAMILTON, 17J.," Clyde ", c.1951
gold filled..................................$100 $125 $200

HAMILTON, 17J.," Craig ", c.1951
gold filled.................................. $100 $125 $200

HAMILTON, 17J.," Dennis ", c.1951
gold filled.................................. $100 $150 $200

HAMILTON, 17J., Darrell, cal#747
10k $120 $160 $220

HAMILTON, 17J.," Dewitt ", c.1951
gold filled.................................. $100 $125 $200

HAMILTON, 17J.," Dexter ", c.1951
gold filled.................................. $100 $125 $200

HAMILTON, 17 jewels, "Dodson"
gold filled.................................. $150 $175 $210

HAMILTON, 19J.," Donald ", c.1951
14k.................................. $275 $325 $450

HAMILTON, 17J.," Dunham ", c.1951
gold filled.................................. $100 $150 $200

HAMILTON, 19 jewels, "Dunkirk"
14k.................................. $250 $350 $400

HAMILTON, 17 jewels, "Dyson"
gold filled.................................. $75 $100 $150

HAMILTON, 17J.," Eaton ", c.1951
gold filled.................................. $100 $150 $200

HAMILTON, 17J.," Emery ", c.1951
gold filled.................................. $100 $125 $200

HAMILTON, 17 jewels, "Eric"
gold filled.................................. $75 $100 $140

HAMILTON, 17 jewels, "Ericsson"
14k $250 $325 $450

HAMILTON, 17 jewels, "Emerson"
gold filled.................................. $100 $125 $175

HAMILTON, 17 jewels, "Endicott
gold filled.................................. $80 $125 $150

HAMILTON, 17 jewels, "Essex"
gold filled.................................. $125 $150 $175

HAMILTON, 18J.,"Fleetwood ", c.1951
14k...$150 $175 $250

HAMILTON, 17 jewels, "Forbes"
gold filled.................................$125 $150 $185

HAMILTON, 19 jewels, "Foster"
14k...$300 $400 $550

HAMILTON, 17J.," Franklin ", c.1951
gold filled.................................$100 $125 $200

HAMILTON, 17J.," Gary ", c.1951
gold filled.................................$150 $175 $200

HAMILTON, 19J.," Gilbert ", c.1951
14k $225 $275 $400

HAMILTON, 19 jewels, "Gilman"
14k $250 $300 $500

HAMILTON, 17J.,"Gladstone", cal.981, c.1951
gold filled $75 $90 $150

HAMILTON, 17J.," Glendale ", engraved case,
14K $350 $400 $600

HAMILTON, 17J.," Glenn ", c.1951
14k $275 $300 $425

HAMILTON, 19 jewels, "Glenn Curtis"
14k $300 $400 $600

HAMILTON, 19J.," Gordon ", c.1951
18k $475 $575 $675

HAMILTON, 17 jewels, "Grant"
gold filled $100 $125 $150

HAMILTON, 17 jewels, "Greenwich"
gold filled $100 $125 $175

HAMILTON, 17J.," Grover ", c.1951
gold filled $100 $125 $200

HAMILTON, 17J.," Hastings ", cal.987
gold filled $100 $125 $200

HAMILTON, 19J.," Hayden ", c.1951
gold filled.................................. $125 $175 $225

HAMILTON, 17J., " Howard", on dial & movement
gold filled.................................. $400 $500 $600

HAMILTON, 17J.," Jeffrey ", c.1951
gold filled.................................. $100 $125 $200

HAMILTON, 19 jewels, "Judson"
gold filled.................................. $100 $125 $200

HAMILTON, 19J.," Keith ", c.1951
14k $250 $275 $400

HAMILTON, 19J.," Kirby ", c.1951
gold filled.................................. $100 $125 $200

HAMILTON, 17J.," Kirk ", c.1951
14k.................................$150 $175 $250

HAMILTON, 17J.,"Lambert ", c.1951
gold filled.................................$100 $125 $200

HAMILTON, 17J.,(Lange is =14k), Langdon is =G. filled
14k...$150 $175 $200
gold filled......................................$75 $100 $150

HAMILTON, 17 jewels, "Langley"
14k...$450 $550 $700

HAMILTON, 17 jewels, "Lee"
gold filled..................................$125 $150 $175

HAMILTON, 19 jewels, "Linwood"
gold filled.................................. $125 $150 $200

HAMILTON, 19 jewels, "Livingston"
14k $250 $300 $450

HAMILTON, 17 jewels, "Martin"
gold filled.................................. $100 $120 $150

HAMILTON, 19 jewels, "Midas," hidden lugs
14k $250 $300 $400

HAMILTON, 19J.," Milton ", c.1951
gold filled.................................. $100 $125 $200

HAMILTON, 17J.," Myron ", c.1951
gold filled.................................. $100 $125 $200

HAMILTON, 17J.," Neil ", c.1951
gold filled.................................. $100 $125 $200

HAMILTON, 17J, <u>Norde is 14k</u>, Nordon is gold filled
14k $175 $200 $250
gold filled.................................. $75 $100 $150

HAMILTON, 19 jewels, "Norman"
14k $175 $200 $250
gold filled.................................. $100 $125 $195

HAMILTON, 19 jewels, "Oakmont"
14k $300 $350 $550

HAMILTON, 19 jewels, "Paige"
gold filled.................................. $80 $100 $150

HAMILTON, 17 jewels, "Perry"
gold filled.................................. $100 $125 $150

HAMILTON, 17J.," Raleigh, plain "
14k...$200 $250 $325

HAMILTON, 19J.," Perry ", c.1951
gold filled................................. $100 $125 $200

HAMILTON, 17 jewels, "Reagan"
gold filled....................................$90 $125 $195

HAMILTON, 17J.," Pinehurst "
14k $300 $350 $450

HAMILTON, 19 jewels, "Ross"
gold filled....................................$75 $95 $150

HAMILTON, 17 jewels, "Putnam"
14k $200 $225 $250

HAMILTON, 17 jewels, "Russell
gold filled.................................. $125 $150 $250

HAMILTON, 17 jewels, "Putnam"
gold filled................................. $100 $125 $150

HAMILTON, 19 jewels, "Rutledge"
platinum $750 $850 $1,000

HAMILTON, 19J.," Scott ", GJS, 982, c.1951
14k $275 $325 $450

HAMILTON, 22J.," Sherwood R", dial is made of wood,
(dial is American walnut) c.1961
14k $800 $900 $1,000

HAMILTON, 18J.,"Sectometer B ", c.1951
gold filled $75 $90 $140

HAMILTON, 17J.," Sheryll ", small size, c.1951, also
matched styling to the Sherwood
gold filled $140 $160 $250

HAMILTON, 18J.," Sectometer C ", c.1951
14k $150 $175 $250

HAMILTON, 17 jewels, "Sidney"
gold filled $125 $175 $225

HAMILTON, 17 jewels, "Sentinel," hack setting
gold filled $100 $120 $140

HAMILTON, 17J.," Spencer ", c.1951
10k $140 $160 $250

HAMILTON, 19J.," Sherwood", c.1951
gold filled $100 $125 $200

HAMILTON, 17 jewels, "Steeldon"
s. steel $50 $60 $90

HAMILTON, 17 jewels, "Stanford"
gold filled................................. $100 $125 $200

HAMILTON, 19 jewels, "Stanley"
gold filled................................. $100 $125 $175

HAMILTON, 19J.," Stuart ", c.1951
gold filled................................. $100 $125 $200

HAMILTON, 19 jewels, "Sutton"
gold filled................................. $125 $150 $175

HAMILTON, 17J.," Todd ", c.1951
gold filled................................. $75 $90 $140

HAMILTON, 19 jewels, "Touraine"
14k $175 $200 $235

HAMILTON, 17J.," Raymon ", c.1951
s. steel... $60 $70 $100

HAMILTON, 17J.," Vardon ", sealed. c.1951
s. steel... $60 $70 $100

HAMILTON, 17 jewels, "Vincent"
gold filled................................. $125 $150 $175

HAMILTON, 17 jewels, "Webster"
gold filled................................. $125 $175 $250

HAMILTON, 19J.," Wesley ", c.1951
14k.. $225 $265 $350

HAMILTON, 17 jewels, "Whitman"
gold filled $100 $125 $200

HAMILTON, 17 jewels, "Whitney"
gold filled .... ★★★$300 $400 $500

HAMILTON, 19 jewels, "Wilshire"
gold filled $125 $150 $225

HAMILTON, 17 jewels, "Winthrop"
14k $200 $250 $300

HAMILTON, 17 jewels, "Yorktown"
gold filled $125 $145 $200

HAMILTON, 17 jewels, aux. sec.
14k... $150 $200 $250

HAMILTON,17J., 6 diamond dial
14k... $250 $285 $350

HAMILTON,18J., cal.735 , c.1960
gold filled.................................. $125 $150 $200

HAMILTON,18J., cal.748 , c.1950
gold filled................................... $85 $95 $150

HAMILTON, 17J., pierced lugs
14k $250 $225 $350

HAMILTON, 22J., medallion series "cld"
gold filled.................................... $80 $90 $120

HAMILTON, 17J., center sec.
gold filled...................................... $75 $85 $150

HAMILTON, 17J., "Master-Piece"
10k.. $125 $150 $250

HAMILTON, 17J., center sec.,
gold plate $60 $70 $95

HAMILTON, 17J., center sec.
gold filled...................................... $75 $85 $120

HAMILTON, 25J., crab leg lugs
14k $175 $200 $300

HAMILTON, 17J., "Cushion Engraved" cal.987
14k..$150 $175 $265
gold filled...................................... $85 $95 $165

HAMILTON, 17J., center sec.
10k $125 $150 $250

HAMILTON, 17 jewels, "Cushion B"
gold filled...................................... $80 $100 $120

HAMILTON, 17 jewels, " Cushion "
14k $175 $200 $300
gold filled $80 $100 $150

HAMILTON, 17 jewels, 2 tone dial, engraved fancy
14k $200 $250 $300
gold filled $100 $125 $150

HAMILTON, 17 jewels, tonneau engraved
14k $175 $200 $300
gold filled $85 $100 $140

HAMILTON, 17 jewels, 2 tone dial, aux. sec.
14k $150 $175 $225

HAMILTON, 17J., "Tonneau"
gold filled(W) $100 $125 $165

HAMILTON, 17J., cal.986, c.1928
gold filled $100 $125 $200

HAMILTON, 17J., " Square " cal.986
gold filled $100 $125 $165
14k $150 $175 $250

HAMILTON, 17J., cal.987, c.1930
gold filled $125 $150 $200

HAMILTON, 17J., Square cut corner, engraved lugs
gold filled $100 $125 $165

HAMILTON, 17J., cal.987f, c.1925
14k $200 $225 $300

HAMILTON, 17J., GJS
gold filled $100 $125 $200

HAMILTON, 17J., aux. sec.,
14k $200 $225 $325

HAMILTON, 19J., gold seal on movement, cal.982
14k $250 $275 $350

HAMILTON, 19J., cal.982, c.1938
14k $225 $250 $350

HAMILTON,17J., cal.980 , c.1938
gold filled $200 $250 $350

HAMILTON,17J., GJS, cal.980 , c.1937
gold filled $175 $225 $325

HAMILTON, 17J., cal.980 , c.1938
gold filled $100 $125 $200

HAMILTON,17J., cal.989E , c.1936
gold filled $100 $125 $200

HAMILTON,17J., cal. 989E, c.1938
gold filled $100 $125 $200

HAMILTON, 17 jewels, engraved bezel, hinged back
18k.. $500 $600 $700

HAMILTON,17J., fluted lugs
gold filled $85 $95 $110

HAMILTON, 22J., c.1970
14k.. $225 $250 $350

HAMILTON, 22J., hooded lugs, cal.770 , c.1955
14k $400 $500 $650

HAMILTON, 17 jewels, hidden lugs
14k $350 $450 $550

HAMILTON, 17 jewels, long lugs
14k $250 $300 $350

HAMILTON, 17 jewels, engraved bezel, c. 1920
14k $300 $350 $400

HAMILTON, 17 jewels, "Hamilton Illinois" on dial
gold filled $100 $150 $225

HAMILTON, 19 jewels
platinum $700 $800 $1,000

HAMILTON, 19 jewels
platinum C&B $1,100 $1,200 $1,400

HAMILTON, 19 jewels, applied numbers
platinum $700 $800 $1,100

HAMILTON, 19 jewels, "Gordon," masterpiece
18k $450 $550 $700

HAMILTON, 17 jewels, curved, c. 1938
14k $350 $450 $550

HAMILTON, 19 jewels, "Chattam"
14k $250 $300 $375

HAMILTON, 15 jewels, center lugs
14k $300 $400 $500

HAMILTON, 19 jewels, "Barton," hidden lugs
14k $425 $525 $675

HAMILTON, 17 jewels, "Mount Vernon," c. 1932
gold filled $175 $225 $325

HAMILTON, 19J., heavy art deco style
14k $450 $550 $700

HAMILTON, 19J.,"bomb timer", c.1944
base metal $300 $350 $400

HAMILTON, 15 J., military frogman style, waterproof
(USN BU SHIPS on dial), canteen style
s. steel $225 $300 $400

HAMILTON, 21 J., military issue, hack setting, c.1960s
base metal $65 $70 $80

HAMILTON, 17-19 jewels, top hat, diamond dial
14k $700 $800 $1,000

HAMILTON, 17-19 jewels, Top Hat, diamond dial
14k $600 $700 $800

HAMILTON, 17-19 jewels, diamond dial, hooded lugs
14k $800 $900 $1,000

HAMILTON, 17-19 jewels, diamond dial
14k(w) $800 $900 $1,000

HAMILTON, 17-19 jewels, diamond dial, hooded lugs
14k $800 $900 $1,000

HAMILTON, 17-19 jewels, diamond dial , curved
14k $1,000 $1,100 $1,250

HAMILTON, 17-19 jewels, diamond dial, c. 1940
14k $1,000 $1,100 $1,250

HAMILTON, 17-19 jewels, diamond dial
14k $400 $500 $600

HAMILTON, 17-19 jewels, diamond dial, c. 1945
14k $600 $700 $800

HAMILTON, 17-19 jewels, diamond dial, hooded lugs
14k(w) $600 $700 $800

HAMILTON, 17-19 jewels, diamond dial, hooded lugs
14k $800 $900 $1,000

HAMILTON, 17-19 jewels,diamond dial
14k $800 $900 $1,000

HAMILTON, 17-19 jewels, diam. dial, c.1948, top hat
14k (w) $1,100 $1,200 $1,300

HAMILTON, 17-19 jewels, diamond dial
14k (w) $400 $500 $600

HAMILTON, 17-19 jewels, diamond dial, hooded lugs
14k (w) $600 $700 $800

HAMILTON, 17-19 jewels, diamond dial
14k (w) $600 $700 $800

HAMILTON, 17-19 jewels, diamond dial
14k (w) $500 $600 $700

HAMILTON, 17-19 jewels, diamond dial, hooded lugs
14k $500 $600 $700

HAMILTON, 17-19 jewels, diamond dial,
14k (w) $600 $700 $800

HAMILTON, 17-19 jewels, mystery dial with diamonds
18k $500 $600 $750
14k $400 $500 $600

HAMILTON, 17-19 jewels, diamond dial
14k $250 $300 $350

HAMILTON, 17-19 jewels, diamond dial
14k (w) $225 $250 $300

HAMILTON,17J., " Ladies' Tonneau "cal.987 , c.1933
gold filled.................................... $50 $60 $75

HAMILTON,17J., " Belmont ", cal.955 , c.1933
gold filled.................................... $40 $45 $60

HAMILTON,17J., "Bianca", diamond & sapphire, c.1933
18k(w) $150 $175 $250

HAMILTON,17J., " Chevy Chase C ", cal. , c.1933
14k(w)..$80 $90 $130

HAMILTON,17J., " Bryn Mawr ", c.1933
14k $70 $90 $130

HAMILTON,17J., " Chevy Chase E ", c.1933
14k(w)..$80 $90 $130

HAMILTON,17J., " Briarcliffe ", c.1933
gold filled $80 $90 $130

HAMILTON,17J., " Diane ", c.1933
14k..$60 $70 $85

HAMILTON,17J., " Caroline ", cal.955, c.1933
gold filled $40 $45 $60

HAMILTON,17J., " Drexel ", cal.955 , c.1933
14k..$50 $60 $80

HAMILTON,17J., " Cedarcrest ", cal.955, c.1933
14k $70 $90 $130

HAMILTON,17J., " Edgewood ", c.1933
gold filled................................$40 $45 $60

HAMILTON,17J., " Chevy Chase A ", cal. , c.1933
14k(w) $60 $70 $85

HAMILTON,17J., " Eugenie ", 44 diamonds, c.1933
platinum $350 $400 $550

HAMILTON,17J., " Chevy Chase B ", cal.989 , c.1933
14k $80 $90 $130

HAMILTON,17J., " Glenwood ", cal.955, c.1933
gold filled.....................................$40 $45 $60

HAMILTON,17J., " Linden Hall ", c.1933
gold filled $40 $45 $60

HAMILTON,17J., " Quadrille ", cal.955, c.1933
14k.. $80 $90 $130

HAMILTON,17J.," Maritza ", 8 diamonds, cal.955 , c.1933
18k(w) $95 $125 $150

HAMILTON,17J., " Rondeau ", cal.955 , c.1933
14k.. $80 $90 $130

HAMILTON,17J., " Mayfield ", cal.955, c.1933
gold filled $40 $45 $60

HAMILTON,17J., " Sargent ", cal.955, c.1933
gold filled.................................. $40 $45 $60

HAMILTON,17J., " Newcomb ", cal.989, c.1933
gold filled.................................. $40 $45 $60

HAMILTON,17J., " Suffolk ", cal.955, c.1933
silver.. $50 $60 $75

HAMILTON,17J., " Nightingale ", 40 diamonds, c.1933
18k(w) $300 $350 $450

HAMILTON,17J., " Wellesley ", cal.989, c.1933
gold filled.................................. $45 $55 $85

HAMILTON,17J., " Portia ", 8 diamonds, c.1933
18k(w) $200 $250 $350

HAMILTON,17J., " Virginia ", cal.955, c.1933
14k.. $70 $80 $100

Grade 986A, 6/0 size
Open face, ¾ plate movt., 17 jewels, double roller

Grade 987, 6/0 size
Hunting, ¾ plate movt., 17 jewels, double roller

Grade 987A, 6/0 size
Open face, ¾ plate movt., 17 jewels, double roller

Grade 987S, 6/0 size
Hunting, ¾ plate movt., 17 jewels, double roller

Grade 747, 8/0 size
Open face, ¾ plate movt., 17 jewels, double roller

Grade 980, 14/0 size
Open face, ¾ plate movt., 17 jewels, double roller

Grade 982, 14/0 size
Open face, ¾ plate movt., 19 jewels, double roller

Grade 982M, 14/0 size
Open face, ¾ plate movt., 19 jewels, double roller

Grade 989, 18/0 size
Open face, ¾ plate movt., 17 jewels, double roller

Grade 997, 20/0 size
Open face, ¾ plate movt., 17 jewels, double roller

Grade 721, 21/0 size
Open face, ¾ plate movt., 17 jewels, double roller

Grade 995, 21/0 size
Open face, ¾ plate movt., 17 jewels, double roller

Grade 911, 22/0 size
Open face, ¾ plate movt., 17 jewels, double roller

Grade 911M, 22/0 size
Open face, ¾ plate movt., 17 jewels, double roller

Grade 780, 21/0 size
17 jewels

Grade 770, 12/0 size
22 jewels

Grade 761, 21/0 size
22 jewels

Grade 757, 21/0 size
22 jewels

Grade 753, 12/0 size, 19 jewels
Grade 752, 12/0 size, 17 jewels

Grade 754, 12/0 size, 19 jewels
Grade 770, 12/0 size, 17 jewels

Grade 750 & 751, 21/0 size
17 jewels

Grade 748, 8/0 size
18 jewels

Grade 747, 8/0 size
17 jewels

Grade 735, 8/0 size
18 jewels

Grade 730, 8/0 size
17 jewels

Grade 679, 17 jewels
Grade 692, 694 - calendar

Grade 666 & 663, 17 jewels
Grade 668 - calendar

Grade 658, 661, 667, 17 jewels
Grade 665, 23J, **Grade 664,** 25J
Grade 662, 690 - calendar, 17J

Grade 623 & 624, 17 jewels

Grade 505, electric, 11 jewels

HAMPDEN, 17J., art deco style, c. 1936
14k $120 $150 $225

HAMPDEN, 15 jewels, c. 1928
14k.................................$150 $175 $200
gold filled....................................$50 $60 $70

HAMPDEN, 17J., by Lonville W. Co., c. 1936
gold filled.................................. $100 $125 $200

HAMPDEN, 11J., Molly Stark, c. 1928
base metal $70 $80 $100

HAMPDEN, 17 jewels, double dial, c. 1930
gold filled.................................. $125 $150 $175

HAMPDEN, 7J., tonneay shaped, c. 1928
gold filled....................................$60 $70 $90

HAMPDEN, 15 jewels, c. 1928
14k $150 $175 $200
gold filled.................................... $60 $70 $80

HARMAN,7J.,doctor style duo-dial,
gold filled....................................$200 $250 $300

HAMPDEN,11J., "LEVER SET" , 3/0 size, c.1928
silver $250 $300 $400

HARMAN,17J.,one button chronog., mid size, c.1940s
s. steel...$150 $200 $250

HARVARD, 17 jewels, chronog., tach-telemeter
s. steel..................................... $250 $300 $350

HARVARD, 17 jewels, 1/5 sec. chronog.
s. steel..................................... $200 $300 $350

HARVEI, 17 jewels, date-o-graph
s. steel.. $50 $60 $70

HARVEL, 17J., center sec.
gold filled................................. $30 $40 $55

HARWOOD, 15 jewels, early self winding, c. 1928
18k (w)................................ $700 $800 $900
14k..................................... $600 $650 $700
gold filled............................ $300 $350 $400
s. steel................................. $200 $250 $300

HARWOOD, 15 J., rim set by turning bezel clockwise
9k.. $500 $550 $600

HARWOOD, 15 jewels, back set, c. 1925
18k... $600 $700 $800

HASTE, 17J., triple calendar moon ph.
gold filled................................. $200 $250 $300

HAYDEN, 7J., by Solomax W.Co., hinged case
gold filled..................................... $60 $70 $85

HEBDOMAS, 7 J., visible escapement, 8 day movement
s. steel.................................... $500 $700 $900

HELBROS, 17 jewels,
14k.................................$150 $175 $200

HELBROS, 17 jewels, aux.sec., alarm
gold filled.................................. $30 $40 $50

HELBROS, 7J., " Falcon ", c. 1929
base metal $40 $50 $65

HELBROS, 7 jewels, fancy bezel, curvex
gold filled................................ $100 $150 $200

HELBROS, 7J., " Fairfax ", c. 1929
base metal $40 $50 $65

HELBROS, 7 jewels, aux. sec., ca. 1962
gold filled.................................. $30 $40 $50

HELBROS, 7J., " Federal ", c. 1929
base metal $40 $50 $65

HELBROS, 17 jewels, aux. sec.
gold filled.................................. $30 $40 $50

HELBROS, 7J., " Filmore ", c. 1929
base metal $40 $50 $65

HELBROS, 7J., " Fletcher ", c. 1929
base metal..................$40 $50 $65

HELBROS, 7J., " Franklin ", c. 1929
base metal $40 $50 $65

HELBROS, 7J., " Flint ", c. 1929
gold plate $50 $60 $75

HELBROS, 7J., " Frigate ", c. 1929
base metal $40 $50 $65

HELBROS, 7J., " Forbes ", c. 1929
base metal..................$40 $50 $65

HELBROS, 7J., " Fulton ", c. 1929
base metal $40 $50 $65

HELBROS, 7J., " Forrest ", c. 1929
base metal..................................$40 $50 $65

HELBROS,17J., 24 hour dial
base metal 50   60 $75

HELBROS, 7J., " Fortress ", c. 1929
gold plate $40 $50 $65

HENDA, 15J., direct read, c. 1930
nickel $200 $250 $300

HERMES, 17J., U shaped lugs, enamel dial
14k $400 $450 $500

HEUER, 17 J., chronog., 3 reg., "Carrera, c.1960
s. steel.................................$250 $300 $350

HELVETIA, 21 jewels, auto wind
gold filled................................... $30 $40 $50

HEUER, 17 jewels, chronog., 3 dates, 3 reg. c.1948
s. steel......................................$300 $350 $400

HEUER, 15 jewels, chronog., 2 reg, one button,
14k $800 $900 $1,000

HEUER, 17 jewels, "Carrera," chronog., 2 reg., c.1960s
s. steel.......................................$200 $250 $300

HEUER, 17J., chronog, 3 reg, 3 dates, moon phase
18k $2,000 $2,500 $3,000
s. steel..................................... $700 $800 $1,000

HEUER,1 7J., " Seafarer ", by Valjoux # 72, c. 1972
s. steel....................................$400 $450 $500

HEUER,17J., "Camro ", by Valjoux #7730, c. 1965
s. steel....................................... $100 $150 $200

HEUER,17J., " Autavia ", cal.72, micro rotor, c. 1972
s. steel....................................... $100 $125 $150

HEUER,17J., " Monaco ", date, c. 1974
base metal................................. $150 $175 $200

HEUER,17J., split sec., date, 600 ft., new $1895.00, c.1991
s. steel & 14k $600 $700 $850

HEUER, 17 jewels, day-date-month, moon phase
s. steel....................................... $150 $200 $250

HEUER, 17 jewels, day-date-month
s. steel....................................... $100 $125 $150

HILTON W. Co.,1 7J., chronog. by Venius W.Co.
18k..$300 $350 $400

HIRCO, 17J., center sec. auto-w.
gold filled $30 $40 $50

HOWARD, 17J. engraved on movement, (Howard
Watch USA, Lancaster, PA, HW138, 17J. H980)

☞ .. (see HAMILTON W. CO.)

E. HUGUENIN, 17 jewels, "Black Star," c. 1940
14k $600 $700 $800

HUGEX, 17J., chronog., 2 reg.
gold filled $150 $200 $250

HYDEPARK, 17 jewels, flip up top
14k $400 $500 $600

ILLINOIS, 15 jewels, wind at 12
silver $400 $500 $600

ILLINOIS, 17 jewels, "Aviator"
gold filled $150 $200 $250

ILLINOIS, 21J., " BARONET ", GJS, cal.601, c.1925
gold filled $300 $350 $450

ILLINOIS, 19 jewels, "Beau Brummel"
gold filled $200 $250 $300

ILLINOIS, 17J., " Beau Brummel ", c.1929
gold filled $200 $250 $350

ILLINOIS, 17J., " Beau Monde ", RF#212, c.1929
gold filled.................................. $200 $225 $300

ILLINOIS, 21 jewels, "Consul"
14k...$250 $350 $500

ILLINOIS, 17 jewels, "Champion"
gold filled................................. $125 $150 $200

ILLINOIS, 15 jewels, Ensign
gold filled..................................$235 $275 $325

ILLINOIS, 15 jewels, "Chatham"
gold filled................................. $150 $175 $200

ILLINOIS, 15 jewels, "Ensign"
gold filled..................................$225 $275 $325

ILLINOIS, 17 jewels, "Chieftain"
gold filled................................. $300 $400 $500

ILLINOIS, 17J., "Guardsman ", cal.307, c.1929
gold filled..................................$175 $225 $300

ILLINOIS, 19 jewels, "Consul"
14k $250 $350 $500

ILLINOIS, 17 jewels, "Jolly Roger"
gold filled..................................$250 $300 $400

ILLINOIS, 19 jewels, "Major"
gold filled..................................$175 $225 $275

ILLINOIS, 17 jewels, Major,
gold filled $250 $300 $350

ILLINOIS, 17 jewels, "Major"
gold filled $175 $225 $275

ILLINOIS, 17J., " Manhatten ", c.1929
14k(w) $225 $300 $400

ILLINOIS, 19 jewels, "Marquis"
gold filled $225 $275 $350

ILLINOIS, 17J., hand engraved,"Mate"
gold filled..................................$200 $225 $300

ILLINOIS, 17 jewels, "Maxine", wire lugs
14k...$250 $300 $350

ILLINOIS, 17J., " Medalist ", curved back, c.1929
gold filled..................................$150 $175 $225

ILLINOIS, 17 jewels, "New Yorker",aux. sec. at 9
14k...$275 $325 $400

ILLINOIS, 17 jewels, "Piccadilly"
gold filled..................................$650 $750 $900

ILLINOIS, 17 jewels, "Pilot"
gold filled $150 $200 $250

ILLINOIS, 15 jewels, "Sangamo"
gold filled $100 $150 $200

ILLINOIS, 17 jewels, "Prince"
gold filled $150 $175 $200

ILLINOIS, 17J., " Special ", c.1929
silver $250 $300 $450

ILLINOIS, 17J., "Ritz", white bezel & yellow center case
also called "Valedictorian"
gold filled $300 $350 $450

ILLINOIS, 17 jewels, "Speedway"
gold filled $200 $250 $300

ILLINOIS, 15 jewels, "Rockingham"
gold filled $200 $300 $400

ILLINOIS, 15 jewels, "Standish"
gold filled $100 $155 $200

ILLINOIS, 17J., " Rockliffe ", cal.805, c.1925
14k $300 $350 $450

ILLINOIS, 17J., " Sterling ", direct   read, c.1929
gold filled $200 $225 $325

ILLINOIS, 15 jewels, "Urbana"
gold filled................................... $100 $125 $195

ILLINOIS, 17 jewels, engraved bezel, grade 807, c. 1920
14k $300 $350 $425

ILLINOIS, 17 jewels, wandering sec., wire lugs, c. 1926
gold filled................................... $175 $200 $300

ILLINOIS, 15 jewels, aux. sec. at 9 o'clock, c. 1925
gold filled................................... $125 $150 $175

ILLINOIS, 19 jewels, aux. sec at 9,
14k(W)...................................... $400 $450 $500

ILLINOIS, 17 jewels, hand engraved, wire lugs
14k (W)..................................... $250 $300 $350

ILLINOIS, 17J., maxine style, hand engraved, wire lugs,
14k (W)..................................... $200 $250 $300

ILLINOIS, 15J., seconds at "9" c.1929
gold filled................................... $200 $250 $300

ILLINOIS, 17J., engraved case, c.1929
gold filled................................... $150 $175 $225

ILLINOIS, 17J., art deco, cal.207, c.1925
gold filled................................... $150 $175 $200

ILLINOIS, 17J., double hinged, GJS, c.1929
gold filled $150 $175 $225

ILLINOIS, 17J., Tonneau style, 0 size Ill. movement
base metal $100 $125 $155

ILLINOIS, 15J., contract case, gold train, c.1929
14k $225 $250 $300

ILLINOIS, 19J., large lugs, wide bezel, c.1929
gold filled $150 $175 $225

ILLINOIS, 17J., recent case, c.1929
gold filled $100 $120 $150

ILLINOIS, 15-17 jewels, lady's watch
14k $100 $120 $140
gold filled $30 $40 $50

ILLINOIS, 15J., " Antoinette ", c.1929
gold filled $50 $60 $75

ILLINOIS, 17J., Shock-Proof Model,
nickel $100 $125 $175

ILLINOIS, 17J., " Babette ", c.1929
14k $80 $90 $120

ILLINOIS, 17J., " Bar Harbor ", c.1929
14k $85 $95 $130

ILLINOIS, 17J., engraved case
gold filled 125 $150 $200

ILLINOIS, 17J., " Beverly=14k, Biloxi=gold filled ",c.1929
14k $80 $90 $120
gold filled $50 $60 $85

ILLINOIS, 17J., " Lynette ", c.1929
gold filled $50 $60 $75

ILLINOIS, 17J., " Coronado ", c.1929
14k $85 $95 $130

ILLINOIS, 17J., " Mariette ", c.1929
gold filled $50 $60 $75

ILLINOIS, 17J., " Daytona ", c.1929
14k $90 $100 $140

ILLINOIS, 17J., " Marionette ", c.1929
gold filled $50 $60 $75

ILLINOIS, 17J., " Debette ", c.1929
gold filled $55 $65 $90

ILLINOIS, 17J., " Marlette ", c.1929
gold filled $50 $60 $75

ILLINOIS, 17J., " Del Monte ", c.1929
gold filled $55 $60 $75

ILLINOIS, 16J., " Mary Todd ", c.1929
18k(w) $150 $175 $250

ILLINOIS, 17J., " Eliza ", c.1929
gold filled $65 $75 $90

ILLINOIS, 16J., " Mary Todd ", c.1929
18k(w) $150 $175 $250

ILLINOIS, 17J., " Long Beach ", c.1929
gold filled $55 $65 $80

ILLINOIS, 16J., " Mary Todd ", c.1929
18k $150 $175 $250

ILLINOIS, 17J., " Mateel ", c.1929
14k(w) $90 $100 $140

ILLINOIS, 17J., " Miami ", c.1929
gold filled $55 $65 $85

ILLINOIS, 17J., " Narragansett ", c.1929
14k $85 $95 $125

ILLINOIS, 17J., " Newprt ", engraved case, c.1929
gold filled $55 $65 $95

ILLINOIS, 16J., " Queen Wilhelmina ", 22 diamonds and
8 synthetic sapphires
18k(w) $200 $225 $350

ILLINOIS, rectangular, Grade 207,17 jewels

ILLINOIS, rectangular, 1st, 2nd & 3rd model

ILLINOIS, Model #4, 3/0 size, bridge, hunting,movement.

IMPERIAL,17J.,fancy lugs
14k(W) $250 $300 $350

IMPERIAL, 17J., center sec.
s. steel $30 $40 $55

INGERSOLL, 2 J.," Rist-Arch", stepped case
base metal $10 $15 $25

INGERSOLL, "Swagger",
base metal $10 $15 $25

INGERSOLL, 7 jewels
base metal..................................... $5 $10 $15

INTERNATIONAL W. CO., 16J., cal.53, c. 1920
18k..$400 $450 $500

INGERSOLL, 7 jewels, radiolite dial
base metal.................................. $10 $20 $30

INTERNATIONAL W. CO., 17 jewels, c. 1920
18k...$500 $600 $700

INGERSOLL, 7 J., military style, protective grill cover
base metal.................................. $75 $100 $150

INTERNATIONAL W. CO., 17 jewels, curved
14k..$800 $900 $1,000

INGRAHAM, 7 jewels, "Wristfit"
base metal..................................... $5 $10 $15

INTERNATIONAL W. CO., 17 jewels, c. 1925
18k..$500 $600 $700

INTERNATIONAL W. CO., 16J., enamel dial, c. 1920
silver $300 $350 $400

INTERNATIONAL W. CO., 17 jewels
14k..$400 $500 $600

INTERNATIONAL W. CO., 21 J., center sec., c. 1920
18k $600 $700 $800

INTERNATIONAL W. CO., 21 jewels, auto wind, date
18k $600 $700 $800

INTERNATIONAL W. CO., 17 jewels
14k C&B $700 $800 $900

INTERNATIONAL W. CO., 17 jewels, c. 1940
18k $500 $600 $700

INTERNATIONAL W. CO., 17J., c. 1945
14k $350 $400 $459

INTERNATIONAL W. CO., 17J., Tiffany on dial, c. 1942
14k $600 $650 $700

INTERNATIONAL W. CO., 17 jewels, hidden lugs
14k $700 $800 $900

INTERNATIONAL W. CO., 17J., aux. sec.
14k $400 $500 $600

INTERNATIONAL W. CO., 17J., c. 1946
18k $350 $400 $459

INTERNATIONAL W. CO., 17J., c. 1926
s. steel $350 $400 $450

INTERNATIONAL W. CO., 17 J., on dial "Yard"
18k $1,000 $1,200 $1,400

INTERNATIONAL W. CO., 21 jewels, auto wind, date
18k...................................$900 $1,000 $1,200

INTERNATIONAL W. CO., 17 J., curved, on dial, "Yard"
platinum................................ $1,800 $2,000 $2,200

INTERNATIONAL W. CO., 17 jewels, center sec.
18k...$600 $700 $800

INTERNATIONAL W. CO., 17 jewels, hinged back
14k $600 $700 $800

INTERNATIONAL W. CO., 17 jewels, center sec.
18k...$600 $700 $800

INTERNATIONAL W. CO., 17 jewels, curved
14k $700 $800 $900

INTERNATIONAL W. CO., 17 J., cen. sec., date,
platinum $1,200 $1,400 $1,600

INTERNATIONAL W. CO., 17J, date, auto-wind,
waterproof
18k $1,000 $1,200 $1,400

INTERNATIONAL W. CO., 17J., RF#802a, cal. 8541, c. 1920
s. steel $300 $350 $400

INTERNATIONAL W. CO., 21J., date, c. 1976
s. steel................................ $500 $550 $600

INTERNATIONAL W. CO., 21J., cal.853, c. 1958
18k.................................... $500 $550 $600

INTERNATIONAL W. CO., 21J., date, c. 1960
18k.................................... $600 $650 $700

INTERNATIONAL W. CO., 17J., center sec.cal.89, c.1957
18k.................................... $400 $450 $500

INTERNATIONAL W. CO., 21J., cal.853, c. 1961
18k.................................... $500 $550 $600

INTERNATIONAL W. CO., 17J., wide lugs, c. 1960
18k.................................... $450 $500 $550

INTERNATIONAL W. CO.,17J.,fancy lugs,cal.C89, c.1952
18k $600 $650 $700

INTERNATIONAL W. CO., 21J., cal.C852, c. 1952
18k.................................... $500 $550 $600

INTERNATIONAL W. CO., 17J., cal.89, c. 1962
s. steel.. $300 $350 $400

INTERNATIONAL W. Co., 18 jewels, center sec.
18k..$600 $700 $800

INTERNATIONAL W. CO., 17J., ca.1960s
18k C & B $900 $1,000 $1,100

INTERNATIONAL W. CO., 17 jewels, center sec.
18k..$600 $700 $800

INTERNATIONAL W. CO., 17J., center sec.
18k $700 $800 $900

INTERNATIONAL W. CO., 17 jewels
18k..$500 $600 $700

INTERNATIONAL W. CO., 17J., fancy lugs, cen. sec.
18k $600 $700 $800

INTERNATIONAL W. CO., 36J., "Da Vinci," chronog.
auto wind, triple date, moon ph., center lugs
18k..$6,500 $7,500 $9,000

INTERNATIONAL W. CO., 17J, for Royal Navy, ca.1950
s. steel...................................... $400 $500 $600

INTERNATIONAL W. CO., 17 jewels, c. 1948
18k... $600 $700 $800

INTERNATIONAL W. CO., 17J., winds at 12 o;clock
s. steel...................................... $400 $450 $500

INTERNATIONAL W. CO., 17J., aux sec., cal.83, c.1938
14k... $500 $550 $600

INTERNATIONAL W. CO., 17 jewels, c. 1953
18k $500 $600 $700

INTERNATIONAL W. CO., 17J., aux. sec., cal., c.1948
s. steel...................................... $300 $350 $400

INTERNATIONAL W. CO., 17 jewels, aux. sec.
18k.. $500 $600 $700

INTERNATIONAL W. CO., 17J., cal.461, c.1962
18k.. $400 $450 $500

INTERNATIONAL W. CO., 17J., date, 30 ATM 1,000 ft.
s. steel $300 $400 $450

INTERNATIONAL W. CO., 17J., ca.1940s
18k $500 $600 $700

INTERNATIONAL W. CO., 17J., 36 small diamonds
platinum................................$600 $700 $800

INVICTA, 15 jewels, chronog., min. reg. at 6 o'clock,
decimal aperture for sec. at 12 o'clock
18k $5,000 $6,000 $7,500

INVICTA, 17 jewels, date, center sec.
18k $200 $250 $300
s. steel................................$75 $100 $125

INVICTA, 17 jewels, day-date, waterproof
18k................................$150 $175 $225
s. steel................................$60 $70 $80

INVICTA, 17 jewels, day-date-month
18k................................$200 $250 $300
s. steel................................$70 $80 $95

INVICTA, 17 jewels, day-date-month, moon phase
18k................................$300 $350 $400
s. steel................................$100 $120 $140

INVICTA, 17 jewels, waterproof
18k................................$150 $200 $250
s. steel................................$40 $50 $60

INTERNATIONAL WATCH CO.
MOVEMENT IDENTIFICATION

Caliber 51N

Caliber 51

Caliber 41

Caliber 93, Baguette

Caliber 92

Caliber 431

Caliber 91

Caliber 90

Caliber 96

Caliber 94

Caliber 84

Caliber 44

Caliber 85

Caliber 852
Calendar - 8521

Caliber 853
Calendar - 8531

Caliber 401

Caliber 60

Caliber 62

Caliber 61

Caliber 86

Caliber 75 & 76

Caliber 87

Caliber 89

Caliber 88

Caliber 70

Caliber 83

Caliber 64

Caliber 63

Caliber 64

INVICTA, 17 jewels, auto wind, waterproof
18k $150 $200 $250
s. steel $50 $60 $70

JUNGHANS W. CO., 17J., cal.J88, c.1980
s. steel $100 $125 $150

JARDUR W. CO., 17J., RF#29840, c.1950
s. steel $200 $250 $300

J. JURGENSEN, 31J, 5 min. repeater, enamel bezel, c.1906
18k $25,000 $30,000 $35,000

JAEGER W. CO., 15J., duoplan, backwind, c.1935
s steel $400 $450 $500

J. JURGENSEN, 15J, jumping hr., revolving min., c.1930s
18k $5,000 $6,000 $7,000

JEAN LOUIS, 17 jewels, double dial, c. 1930
14k $300 $350 $425

J. JURGENSEN,17J., large lugs, recess crown, c.1950
14k $300 $350 $400

J. JURGENSEN,17J., long lugs, c.1948
18k $150 $175 $200

J. JURGENSEN,17J., recess crown, fancy lugs, c.1952
14k $200 $225 $250

J. JURGENSEN,17J., 2 tone, center lugs, c.1940
14k $400 $450 $500

J. JURGENSEN, 17 jewels, fancy lugs, ca.1949
14k $400 $500 $600

J. JURGENSEN, 17 jewels, fancy lugs
14k $300 $400 $500

J. JURGENSEN, 17 jewels, extra fancy lugs, c. 1946
18k $500 $600 $700

J. JURGENSEN, 17 jewels, c. 1950
18k $250 $300 $350

J. JURGENSEN, 17 jewels
18k $175 $200 $225

J. JURGENSEN,17J., center sec., c.1946
14k $150 $175 $200

J. JURGENSEN,17J., aux. sec., c.1948
14k $150 $175 $200

J. JURGENSEN,17J., aux. sec., c.1940
14k $150 $175 $200

J. JURGENSEN,17J., textured bezel, c.1960
14k $125 $150 $175

J. JURGENSEN,17J., hidden lugs, c.1948
14k $175 $200 $225

J. JURGENSEN,17J., hidden lugs, c.1940
14k $150 $175 $200

J. JURGENSEN,17J., hidden lugs, c.1952
14k $300 $350 $400

J. JURGENSEN,17J., hidden lugs, c.1950
14k $300 $350 $400

J. JURGENSEN,17J., hidden lugs, c.1948
14k $150 $175 $200

J. JURGENSEN, 17 J., small size chronog., ca. 1945
14k..................................$1,200 $1,400 $1,800

J. JURGENSEN,17J., 21mm, chronog., c.1944
s. steel.....................................$600 $700 $800

J. JURGENSEN, 17 J., auto-w., cen. sec., ca. 1954
14k $250 $300 $350

J. JURGENSEN,17J., cal.8273, extended lugs, c.1958
14k..$250 $275 $300

J. JURGENSEN,17J., extended bezel, c.1950
14k $350 $375 $400

J. JURGENSEN,17J., 12 diamond dial, date, c.1960
14k(w) $250 $275 $300

J. JURGENSEN,17J., cal.1139, c.1950
18k $250 $275 $300

J. JURGENSEN,17J., 40 diamond bezel, c.1960
14k(w) $350 $375 $400

J. JURGENSEN,17J., center sec., date, c.1960
14k $150 $175 $200

J. JURGENSEN, 17 J., 12 diamond dial, ca. 1960s
14k(W) $200 $250 $300

J. JURGENSEN,17J., center sec., mid size, c.1940
14k $150 $175 $200

JEWEL, 15 jewels, dual dial, c. 1938
gold filled $200 $250 $300

JOHNSON-MATTHEY, 15 J., 5 gram ingot 24k gold
24k $200 $250 $300

JUVNENIA,17J.,3 dates, moon ph., screw on back c. 1950s
18k $500 $600 $700

JUVNENIA, 21 jewels, gold movement
18k $400 $450 $600

JUVNENIA, 17J.,
s. steel.. $60 $75 $100

JUVNENIA, 17J.,
s. steel.. $75 $100 $125

JUVNENIA, 17J.,
s. steel.. $150 $175 $200

JUVNENIA, 17J.,
s. steel.. $125 $150 $175

JUVNENIA, 17J.,
s. steel.. $100 $125 $150

JUVNENIA, 17J.,
s. steel.. $100 $120 $145

KELBERT, 17J., triple date, moon ph., ca.1945
s. steel.. $300 $325 $350

KELBERT (continued)

KELBERT, 17 jewels, fancy lugs, c. 1949
gold filled.................................... $70 $80 $100

KINGSTON, 17 jewels, day-date-month, moon phase
gold filled................................. $150 $200 $250

KELEK, 17J., tachymeter, auto-wind, c.1970
s. steel......................... $40 $50 $65

KINGSTON,17J., cal.G10, hidden lugs, c.1943
gold filled................................. $60 $70 $85

Kelton, 7 jewels, curved, stepped case
gold filled.................................... $30 $35 $40

KORD, day date month, moon ph.
s. steel....................................... $200 $250 $300

KELTON, 7 jewels, "Drake"
gold filled.................................... $30 $35 $40

KURTH, 17 jewels, "Certina"
gold filled.................................... $30 $40 $50

KENT W. CO.,17J., Continental W.Co.(french),chronog.
s. steel........................... $100 $125 $150

LANCEL (Paris),17J., by Nicolet, c.1960
gold filled..................................$125 $150 $175

LANGENDORF, 17J., "Lanco-Matic," waterproof
gold filled....................................$50 $60 $70

A.LANGE & SOHNE,17J., 55mm., c.1940
s. steel....................................$1,000 $1,200 $1,400

LE COULTRE, 18J., skeletonized,
18k..$1,200 $1,400 $1,600

LANGE "UHR" (Glashutte),17J., , c.1937
s. steel...................................... $600 $700 $800

LE COULTRE, 19 jewels, alarm
18k...$700 $800 $900
gold filled................................$200 $275 $350
s. steel $100 $125 $150

LANGE, 17J, (Glashutte), date, auto wind, waterproof
18k $1,500 $1,600 $1,800

LE COULTRE, 19 jewels, alarm, c. 1950
18k...$700 $800 $900
gold filled................................$200 $275 $350
s. steel $100 $125 $150

LE COULTRE, 17J., , alarm, cal.815, c.1960
gold filled $250 $300 $350

LE COULTRE, 17J., RF#3025, wrist-alarm, c.1948
gold filled $200 $250 $300

LE COULTRE, 17J., ruby dial, alarm, c.1960
gold filled $350 $400 $450

LE COULTRE, 17J., cal.489, memvox alarm, c.1949
gold filled $250 $300 $350

LE COULTRE, 17J.,cal.814, memovox, alarm, c.1960
gold filled $200 $250 $300

LE COULTRE, 17J., date, memvox, c.1955
gold filled $300 $350 $400

LE COULTRE, 17J., cal.p815, alarm, c.1960
gold filled $200 $250 $300

LE COULTRE, 17J.,memvox, alarm, c.1973
14k & s.s. $350 $400 $450

LE COULTRE, 17J., RF#2676, cal.911, memvox, c.1960
gold filled.................................... $200 $250 $300

LE COULTRE, 19J., alarm, date,
14k..$800 $900 $1,000

LE COULTRE, 17J., date, memvox, c.1975
s. steel... $150 $175 $200

LE COULTRE, 19 jewels, alarm, date, c. 1950
18k...$900 $1,000 $1,200
gold filled..................................$300 $350 $400
s. steel $125 $150 $175

LE COULTRE, 17J., RF#2051, wrist alarm, c.1952
gold filled $250 $300 $350

LE COULTRE, 15 jewels, wire lugs, c. 1919
silver...$200 $225 $250

LE COULTRE, 19J., date, Memovox, ca. 1959
18k $900 $1,000 $1,200
gold filled....................................$300 $350 $400
s. steel $125 $150 $175

LE COULTRE, 17J., powermatic, auto-wind, c.1950
gold filled..................................$250 $300 $350

LE COULTRE, 17J., cal 481, auto-wind, c.1954
gold filled................................. $175 $200 $225

LE COULTRE, 17J., cal.p478, center sec.c.1947
s. steel..$200 $225 $250

LE COULTRE, 17J., auto wind, wind indicator
14k $400 $500 $600

LE COULTRE, 17J., Master Mariner, c.1952
14k..$250 $300 $350

LE COULTRE, 17 jewels, screw back
18k $500 $600 $700

LE COULTRE, 17J., Master Mariner, auto-wind, c.1960
s. steel.......................................$100 $125 $150

LE COULTRE, 17J., "Master Mariner, c.1960
14k $250 $300 $350

LE COULTRE, 17J., auto-wind, cal.p812, c.1955
gold filled.................................$100 $125 $150

LE COULTRE, 17J., cal.818, aux. sec., c.1962
gold filled $100 $125 $155

LE COULTRE, 17J.,"Coronet", cal.480cw, c.1951
gold filled $300 $350 $400

LE COULTRE, 17J., RF#2013, cal.480cw, c.1950
14k $300 $325 $350

LE COULTRE, 17J., cal.480, wide bezel, c.1958
gold filled $100 $125 $155

LE COULTRE, 17J., RF#555-149, c.1955
14k $200 $250 $300

LE COULTRE, 17J., cal.480, c.1955
14k $250 $300 $350

LE COULTRE, 17J., cal812, auto-wind, c.1952
s. steel $100 $125 $155

LE COULTRE, 17J., RF#7534, c.1960
14k $300 $350 $400

LE COULTRE, 17J., 11 diamond dial, RF#197, c.1955
14k(w) $200 $225 $250

LE COULTRE, 17 jewels, fancy lugs, c. 1952
14k..$300 $400 $500

LE COULTRE, 17 jewels, center lugs, c. 1960
18k $300 $350 $400

LE COULTRE, 17 jewels, fancy bezel & lugs
14k..$700 $800 $900

LE COULTRE, 17 jewels, fancy lugs, c. 1950
14k $400 $450 $500

LE COULTRE, 17J., auto wind, textured bezel, c. 1950
18k..$250 $350 $450

LE COULTRE, 17J., fancy lugs
14k $400 $450 $500

LE COULTRE, 17 jewels, center sec., c. 1949
18k..$400 $500 $600

LE COULTRE, 17J., fancy lugs, ca. 1950s
18k $600 $700 $800

LE COULTRE, 17J., cen. sec., 24 hr dial, c. 1940
s. steel..................................... $200 $250 $300

LE COULTRE, 17J., date alarm, c.1975
gold filled................................$100 $125 $150

LE COULTRE, 17J., center sec., ca. 1930s
silver $350 $400 $450

LE COULTRE, 17 jewels, alarm, date, auto wind
14k...$400 $450 $500

LE COULTRE, 17J., alarm, date, ca.1964
s. steel.................................... $100 $175 $200

LE COULTRE, 17J., chronog., 2 reg.
s. steel $500 $600 $700

LE COULTRE, 17J., quartz, cal.352, c.1970
gold filled $50 $60 $75

LE COULTRE, 17J., chronog., cal.281, c.1940
s. steel $400 $450 $500

LE COULTRE, 17J., chronog., FR#2644, blue dial,
s. steel.................................. $600 $650 $700

LE COULTRE, 17J., chronog. 3 reg, ca. 1958
s. steel.................................. $700 $800 $900

LE COULTRE, 17 jewels, chronog., 3 reg.
18k $3,000 $3,500 $4,000

LE COULTRE, 17 jewels, mystery dial, c. 1955
14k $300 $350 $400

LE COULTRE, 17J., diamond mystery dial & bezel
14k(W) C&B...................... $1,200 $1,400 $1,600

LE COULTRE, 17J., diamond mystery dial,
14k.. $300 $400 $500

LE COULTRE, 17J., diamond mystery dial, waterp.
14k.. $900 $1,000 $1,200

LE COULTRE, 17J., diamond dial, textured bezel, c.60s
14k (w)...................................... $300 $350 $400

LE COULTRE, 17J., date, cal.810, c.1952
14k $400 $450 $500

LE COULTRE, 17J., date, center sec., c.1950
14k $400 $450 $500

LE COULTRE, 15 jewels, triple-date, c. 1945
s. steel $300 $400 $500

LE COULTRE, 17J, astronomic ,moon ph., c. 1940s
18k $1,800 $2,000 $2,200
gold filled $600 $700 $800

LE COULTRE, 17J., triple date, moon ph., fancy lugs
gold filled $1,000 $1,200 $1,400

LE COULTRE, 17J., time in 24 cities, c.1960
14k $1,000 $1,100 $1,200

LE COULTRE, 17J., weems style, cal.450, c.1942
s. steel $800 $900 $1,000

LE COULTRE, 17J., rotating chapters, date, c.1960
s. steel $300 $350 $400

LE COULTRE, 17J., "Futurematic", cal.817, c.1952
14k $600 $650 $700

LE COULTRE, 17J., auto-w., date
14k..$300 $350 $400

LE COULTRE, 17 jewels, "Futurematic"
18k $600 $650 $800
14k $500 $550 $650

LE COULTRE, 17J., day date, mid size, ca. 1940s
gold filled...................................$600 $700 $800

LE COULTRE, 17J, auto wind,power reserve window
gold filled $250 $300 $350
s. steel...................................... $200 $250 $300

LE COULTRE, 17J., fancy lugs, aux. sec., ca. 1948
14k $400 $500 $600

LE COULTRE, 23 J., auto-w., date cen. sec.
14k $300 $350 $400

LE COULTRE, 17J., auto-w., ca. 1950s
14k..$250 $300 $350

LE COULTRE, 17J., fancy lugs
14k $300 $350 $400

LE COULTRE, 17J., aux. sec. ca.1950s
14k $200 $250 $300

LE COULTRE, 17 jewels, fancy wide bezel, ca.1955
14k (W) $400 $500 $600

LE COULTRE, 17J., alarm, date,
14k $400 $500 $600

LE COULTRE, 15J., drivers style wind at 12, c.1960s
s. steel $400 $500 $600

LE COULTRE,17J.,drivers style crown at 6, cal.,
RF#9041
s. steel $250 $300 $350

LE COULTRE, 17J.,RF#9041, cal.818, c.1960s
18k $400 $450 $500

LE COULTRE, 17 jewels, "Reverso," c. 1930
18k $6,000 $7,000 $8,000
s. steel $2,000 $2,200 $2,500

LE COULTRE, 17 jewels, "Reverso," c. 1940s
18k $6,000 $7,000 $8,000
s. steel $2,000 $2,200 $2,500

LE COULTRE, 17 jewels, fancy hooded lugs, c. 1952
14k $600 $650 $700

LE COULTRE, 17 jewels, fancy lugs
14k $500 $600 $700

LE COULTRE, 17 jewels, fancy lugs
14k $800 $900 $1,000

LE COULTRE, 17J., curvex,
14k $500 $600 $700

LE COULTRE, 17J., curvex, ca. 1940s
14k $700 $800 $900

LE COULTRE, 17J., stepped lugs, ca. 1944
gold filled.................................. $150 $200 $250

LE COULTRE, 17J., aux. sec., ca. 1940s
gold filled.................................. $300 $350 $400

LE COULTRE, 17J., square lugs, ca. 1948
14k.. $500 $600 $700

LE COULTRE, 17J., extended lugs, c.1938
gold filled.................................. $100 $125 $150

LE COULTRE, 17J., aux. sec., c.1940
14k.. $250 $300 $350

LE COULTRE, 17J., tu tone dial, c.1940
gold filled.................................. $100 $125 $150

LE COULTRE, 17J., large lugs, c.1938
gold filled.................................. $100 $125 $150

LE COULTRE, 17J.,hidden lugs, c.1942
14k $400 $450 $500
gold filled.................................. $175 $225 $300

LE COULTRE, 17J., hooded lugs, ca. 1940s
14k $500 $600 $700

LE COULTRE, 17J., swing lugs, cen. sec.
s. steel.. $300 $350 $400

LE COULTRE, 17J., fancy bezel, ca. 1940s
14k $800 $900 $1,000

LE COULTRE, 17J.,fancy textured bezel, ca. 1960s
gold filled.................................. $200 $250 $300

LE COULTRE, 17J., cal.438.4cw, c.1957
gold filled.................................$300 $350 $400

LE COULTRE, 17J., diamond dial, RF#2406, c.1960
14k...$300 $350 $400

LE COULTRE, 17 jewels, long lugs, c. 1944
18k...$300 $350 $400

LE COULTRE, 17 jewels, uniplan, c. 1938
14k (w).....................................$400 $500 $600

LE COULTRE, 15 jewels, duoplan, c. 1940
14k...$1,500 $1,700 $2,000

LE COULTRE, 17 jewels, fancy lugs, c. 1948
14k $400 $450 $600

LE COULTRE, 17J., fancy lugs, cal.438-4cw, c.1951
18k $500 $600 $700

LE COULTRE, 17 jewels, fancy lugs
14k $400 $500 $600

LE COULTRE, 17 jewels, diamond dial, fancy lugs
14k $600 $700 $800

LE COULTRE, 17J., diamond dial, ca. 1940s
14k $500 $600 $700

LE COULTRE, 17J., 12 diamond dial, cal.4870cw, c.1958
14k(w) $150 $175 $200

LE COULTRE, 17J., diamond mystery dial ca.1940s
14k..$800 $900 $1,000

LE COULTRE, 15J., hinged case, c.1920
14k..$400 $450 $500

LE COULTRE, 17J., stepped case & lugs, cal., c.1950
gold filled....................................$100 $125 $150

LE COULTRE, 17J., aux. sec., c.1940
14k..$125 $150 $175

LE COULTRE, 17J., cal.493, c.1955
10k..$150 $200 $250

LE COULTRE, 17J., cal. 438-4cw, wide bezel, c.1950
14k $400 $450 $500

LE COULTRE, 17J., textured bezel, cen. sec.
18k..$700 $800 $900

LE COULTRE, 17J., textured bezel, c.1952
14k $400 $450 $500

LE COULTRE, 17J., aux. sec., ca. 1930s
14k..$300 $400 $500

LE COULTRE, 17J., textured bezel, c.1950
14k $400 $450 $500

LE COULTRE, 17J, triple date, moon ph., fancy bezel
18k...............................★★★$5,000 $6,000 $7,000
gold filled.............................$2,000 $2,200 $2,500

LE COULTRE, 17J., RF#7540, engraved bezel, cal., c.1960
14k $300 $350 $400

Le Coultre, 17 jewels, c. 1945
18k..$300 $350 $400

LE COULTRE, 17J., cal. p812, c.1948
gold filled $150 $200 $250

LE COULTRE, 17 jewels, fancy lugs, c. 1948
14k..$400 $500 $600

LE COULTRE, 17 jewels, center lugs, c. 1945
14k $400 $500 $600

LE COULTRE, 17 jewels, center lugs, c. 1945
14k $400 $500 $600

LE COULTRE, 17 jewels, c. 1950s
14k $400 $500 $600

LE COULTRE, 17 jewels, 18k case & band
18k C&B $1,000 $1,200 $1,400

LE COULTRE, 17 jewels, date cal. 810, c. 1952
14k $600 $700 $800

LE COULTRE, quartz, date, waterproof, c. 1960s
18k $300 $350 $400

LE COULTRE, electric, digital calendar
silver & gold $300 $400 $500

LE COULTRE, 17 jewels, c. 1953
gold filled................................... $400 $500 $600

LE COULTRE, 17 jewels, small, c. 1953
gold filled.................................. $300 $350 $400

LE COULTRE, 15J., lady's
14k(W) $250 $300 $350

LE COULTRE, 15J., lady's art deco, by Blancpain, c.1925
silver $350 $400 $450

LE COULTRE, 15J., lady's REVERSO, c.1940
s. steel..................................... $600 $700 $800

LE COULTRE, 17J., lady's, cal.490bw, c.1950
gold filled..................................... $40 $50 $65

LE COULTRE, 17J., lady's MYSTERY dial, c.1959
gold filled................................. $100 $125 $150

LE JOUR, 17J., by Valjoux cal.7750, c.1973
s. steel....................................... $100 $150 $200

LEMANIA, 17 jewels, auto wind
s. steel.. $50 $60 $70

LEMANIA,17J., chronog., 3 reg., c.1946
14k...$500 $600 $700

LEMANIA, 17 jewels, chronog., c. 1950
18k..$600 $700 $900

LEMANIA, 17 jewels, chronog., waterproof
s. steel......................................$300 $350 $400

LEMANIA, 17 jewels, chronog., military, ca.1970s
s. steel.. $300 $350 $400

LEONIDAS,17J., chronog., triple date, c.1945
gold filled................................. $500 $550 $600

LEONIDAS, 17 jewels, triple date, 3 reg.
18k $800 $900 $1,000
s. steel...................................... $400 $500 $600

LEONIDAS, 17 jewels, auto wind, triple date, moon phase
s. steel...................................... $200 $250 $300

LEONIDAS, 17 jewels, chronog., 2 reg.
s. steel....................................... $200 $250 $300

LE PHARE, 17 jewels, chronog., triple date, 3 reg.
18k.. $700 $800 $900

LE PHARE, 17 jewels, chronog., 2 reg.
18k.. $400 $500 $600
14k.. $300 $400 $500
s. steel $100 $150 $200

LE PHARE, 17J., triple date, moon ph., waterproof
18k.. $500 $600 $700
gold filled................................... $250 $300 $350

LEVRETTE,17J., chronog., (fly back), center lugs, c.1935
18k $700 $800 $900

LONGINES, 15 J., center lugs, enamel dial, ca.1923
silver..$250 $275 $350

LIBELA,7J., direct read, c.1952
base metal.................................. $150 $200 $250

LONGINES,15J., enamel dial, pierced shield , c.1923
silver..$325 $350 $475

LIP,15J., chronog., tu-tone, center lugs, (French), c.1940
gold filled & s.s. $400 $500 $600

LONGINES,15J., , GJS, c.1925
14k...$200 $250 $350

LIP, electric, bulbous crown, (French)
s. steel....................................... $200 $250 $335

LONGINES, 18 J.,wire lugs, ca.1928
14k...$400 $500 $600

LONGINES, 15 J., wire lugs, ca. 1930s
silver $250 $300 $350

LONGINES,17J., tu-tone, GJS, c.1936
14k & s.s. $175 $200 $325

LONGINES,17J., cal.932, c.1937
s. steel.. $600 $700 $900

LONGINES,17J., large & curved, GJS,
gold filled $150 $175 $300

LONGINES,15J., GJS, c.1922
silver $225 $275 $350

LONGINES,17J., GJS, cal.940, c.1931
18k... $500 $550 $700

LONGINES,17J., GJS, cal.1086, c.1928
14k... $400 $500 $700

LONGINES,17J., cal.101, c.1947
14k.. $200 $225 $325

LONGINES, 17 J., large Lindberg model, moveable
bezel & center dial, c. 1930s
18k............................★★★$35,000 $40,000 $45,000
silver.................................$5,000 $6,000 $7,000
nickel $3,000 $4,000 $5,000

Longines, 17 jewels, small Lindberg model, c. 1930s

18k	★★ $15,000	$18,000	$20,000
14k	$10,000	$12,000	$15,000
gold filled	$3,000	$3,500	$4,000
s. steel	$2,500	$3,000	$3,500

LONGINES,17J., 1 button chronog., c.1946

14k	$2,000	$2,200	$2,400

LONGINES,17J., "Admiral", auto-wind, GJS, c.1960

14k	$325	$350	$450

LONGINES, 15J., Weems U.S. Patent 200B734, c.40s

s. steel	$200	$300	$400

LONGINES,17J., 1 button chronog., RF#5034, c.1940

gold filled	$400	$450	$500

LONGINES, 17J., chronog. 2 reg, tach.,

14k	$1,800	$2,000	$2,200

LONGINES,17J., 1 button, fly back hand, c.1945

s. steel	$500	$600	$700

LONGINES, 17 jewels, chronog, 1 button, c. 1923

silver	$1,000	$1,100	$1,200

LONGINES, 17J., chronog, one button
14k $1,000 $1,100 $1,200

LONGINES,17J., RF#6474, c.1955
s. steel $1,000 $1,200 $1,400

LONGINES, 17J. chronog., ref. 1333, enamel dial
silver $1,200 $1,400 $1,600

LONGINES, 17 jewels, chronog., 2 reg.
18k $1,200 $1,400 $1,600

LONGINES, 17 jewels, chronog, 2 reg.
18k $1,800 $2,000 $2,200

LONGINES, 17 jewels, chronog., 2 reg.
s. steel $600 $700 $800

LONGINES,17J., chronog., c.1942
s. steel $800 $900 $1,000

LONGINES, 17J., chronog., ca. 1945
gold filled $300 $350 $400

LONGINES, 17 jewels, chronog. 1 button
14k $900 $1,000 $1,100

LONGINES,17J., GJS, cal.23z, c.1958
gold filled.................................. $150 $175 $300

LONGINES,17J., chronog., cal.539, c.1969
s. steel.................................. $175 $250 $350

LONGINES,17J., GJS, cal.194, c.1963
gold filled.................................. $100 $125 $200

LONGINES,17J., Valjoux 726, cal.332, c.1972
s. steel.................................. $200 $250 $350

LONGINES,17J., GJS, cal.352, c.1960
14k.................................. $225 $250 $350

LONGINES, 16J., military issue, waterpr., ca. 1940s
s. steel.................................. $500 $600 $700

LONGINES,17J., GJS, cal., c.1960
14k.................................. $225 $250 $350

LONGINES,17J., textured dial
gold filled.....................$125 $150 $225

LONGINES,17J., one lug at 11 & one at 5, GJS, 1955
14k.................................$450 $500 $700

LONGINES,17J., wide bezel
14k.................................$225 $250 $350

LONGINES,17J., RF#2021, GJS, cal.23z, c.1955
14k.................................$600 $750 $900

LONGINES,17J., RF#2033p, GJS, cal., c.1958
14k.................................$225 $250 $350

LONGINES,17J., large fluted lugs, GJS, c.1940
14k.................................$250 $300 $450

LONGINES,17J., GJS, cal.23z, c.1955
14k.................................$250 $275 $400

LONGINES,17J., GJS, cal.18LN, c.1952
14k.................................$275 $300 $400

LONGINES,17J., GJS, cal.10L, c.1952
14k.................................$300 $350 $475

LONGINES,17J., large lugs, GJS, c.1952
18k.................................$450 $500 $700

LONGINES, 17J., GJS, cal.23z, c.1954
18k $275 $300 $400

LONGINES, 17 jewels, fancy lugs, c. 1949
14k $350 $400 $450

LONGINES, 15 jewels, c. 1940s
18k $400 $450 $500
14k $300 $350 $400
s. steel $100 $125 $150

LONGINES, 19J.,"conquest", auto-wind,
14k $300 $350 $400

LONGINES, 17J.,fancy lugs, diamond dial,
14k $400 $450 $500

LONGINES,17J., GJS, cal.22ls, c.1950
14k $325 $375 $550

LONGINES, 17 jewels, fancy lugs, c. 1954
14k $350 $400 $450

LONGINES,17J., "Flagship", GJS, cal.340, c.1960
18k $225 $250 $350

LONGINES,17J., center sec., GJS, c.1948
14k $175 $200 $300

LONGINES,17J., center sec., GJS, cal., c.1940
14k $175 $200 $300

LONGINES,17J., GJS, cal.19as, c.1955
gold filled $90 $120 $200

LONGINES,17J., auto-wind, date,"Ultra-Chron"
gold filled.................................$100 $125 $200

LONGINES,17J., GJS, cal.340, c.1960
14k $150 $175 $275

LONGINES,17J., RF#9003, GJS, cal.19asd, c.1958
18k................................... $375 $425 $500

LONGINES,17J., RF#3759, GJS, cal.22as, c.1949
14k $225 $275 $350

LONGINES,17J., 36,000 train(beat)"Ultra-Chron, cal.431
14k................................$175 $200 $300

LONGINES,17J., auto-wind, Grand Prize, cal.341, c.1960
gold filled $90 $110 $175

LONGINES, 21 jewels, "Grand Prize," c. 1946
s. steel $100 $125 $150

LONGINES,17J., oval textured bezel, cal.506, c.1965
14k $175 $200 $300

LONGINES, 17 jewels, center seconds
14k..$200 $250 $350

LONGINES, 17 jewels
14k..$125 $150 $200

LONGINES,17J., high frequency, date, c.1972
s. steel... $60 $70 $95

LONGINES, 17 J., "Ultra Chrono," date, auto wind
14k...$300 $350 $425

LONGINES, 17 jewels, "Flagship"
14k $200 $250 $300

LONGINES, 19J., conquest, auto-w., date, ca.1962
s. steel...$150 $200 $250

LONGINES, 17J., grand prize, auto-w., date
14k $150 $175 $200

LONGINES, 17J., conquest, auto-w., date
s. steel.. $150 $200 $250

LONGINES, 17J., date, ca. 1940s
14k $175 $225 $275

LONGINES,17J., mystery dial, cal.232 c.1960
gold filled $175 $200 $300

LONGINES,17J., mystery dial,
gold filled.................................... $175 $200 $300

LONGINES, 17 jewels, mystery hand, ca.1962
gold filled................................... $100 $125 $200

LONGINES, 17 jewels, mystery hand,
14k.. $200 $250 $350

LONGINES, 17 jewels, mystery hand, 12 diamond dial
14k.................................... $600 $700 $800

LONGINES,17J., mystery 39 diamond dial, RF#1017
14k(w).. $575 $675 $800

LONGINES, 17 jewels, diamond dial, center lugs
14k $600 $700 $800

LONGINES, 17 jewels, "Ultra Chrono," diamond dial
14k $250 $300 $475

LONGINES, 17 jewels, "Ultra Chrono," date, c.1949
14k $300 $350 $450

LONGINES, 17J., auto-w., aux. sec.
14k $175 $225 $300

LONGINES, 17J., auto-w., aux. sec.
14k $175 $225 $300

LONGINES, 17J., aux sec.
14k $150 $200 $250

LONGINES, 17J., diamond dial
14k(W) $275 $325 $400

LONGINES, 17J., diamond bezel
gold filled $150 $200 $250

LONGINES, 17J.,3 diamond dial
gold filled $175 $200 $275

LONGINES, 17J., diamond dial,
14k(W) $200 $250 $300

LONGINES, 17 jewels, cocktail style, 36 diamond dial
14k(W) $200 $250 $300

LONGINES, 17 jewels, 12 diamond dial
14k (w) $300 $350 $425

LONGINES,17J., GJS, 34 diamond dial, date, c.1962
14k $400 $450 $575

LONGINES,17J., 36 diamonds, GJS, cal.194, c.1955
14k(w) $300 $350 $450

LONGINES,17J., 14 diamonds,GJS, cal.370, c.1960
14k $250 $275 $400

LONGINES,17J., 4 diamonds, cal.194, c.1958
gold filled $200 $250 $325

LONGINES,17J., 37 diamonds on bezel 24 0n dial, c.1958
14k(w) $300 $350 $450

LONGINES, 17J., 4 diamonds, GJS, cal.23z, c.1948
14k $250 $300 $400

LONGINES, 17J., 5 diamonds, GJS, cal.8ln, c.1940
14k(w) $200 $235 $300

LONGINES, 17J., 8 diamonds, GJS, cal.22L, c.1958
14k $275 $300 $425

LONGINES,17J., 4 diamonds, textured bezel,cal.194, c.1955
gold filled $125 $150 $225

LONGINES, 17J., 6 diamonds, GJS
14k $275 $300 $400

LONGINES, 17J., 5 diamonds, GJS, c.1953
gold filled.................................$150 $175 $275

LONGINES, 17J., 17 diamonds, GJS, c.1951
14k...$500 $600 $750

LONGINES, 17J., 15 diamonds, GJS, cal.9L, c.1945
14k...$500 $600 $725

LONGINES, 17J., 18 diamonds, RF#176, GJS, c.1950
14k(w)..$500 $600 $725

LONGINES, 17J., 16 diamonds, cal.9LT, c.1958
14k(w)..$400 $475 $575

LONGINES, 17J., 4 diamonds, GJS, cal.L8474, c.1960
gold filled $125 $150 $250

LONGINES, 17 jewels, diamond dial, hidden lugs, c. 1938
s. steel $300 $400 $500

LONGINES, 17J., 6 diamonds, RF#2763, GJS, c.1955
14k $250 $300 $400

LONGINES, 17 jewels, fancy hidden lugs, diamond dial
14k (w)................................... $600 $700 $800

LONGINES, 17J., 8 diamonds, GJS, cal.9LT, c.1958
14k(w) $375 $450 $550

LONGINES, 17 jewels, diamond dial, c. 1944
14k.. $500 $600 $700

LONGINES, 17J., 5 diamonds, GJS, c.1945
14k C&B.................................... $550 $600 $750

LONGINES, 17 jewels, diamond dial, c. 1949
14k.. $450 $500 $550

LONGINES, 17J., 5 diamonds, GJS, cal.9L, c.1952
14k $400 $450 $550

LONGINES, 17 jewels, diamond dial, c. 1935
14k.. $750 $850 $1,000

LONGINES, 17 jewels, diamond dial, c. 1944
14k $400 $450 $500

LONGINES, 17 jewels, 18 diamond dial
14k (w)...................................... $300 $350 $425

LONGINES, 17 jewels, flared, 6 diamond dial
14k $600 $700 $800

LONGINES, 17 jewels, diamond bezel, c. 1960
14k $800 $900 $1,000

LONGINES, 17 jewels, 4 diamond dial
14k $225 $255 $350

LONGINES, 17 jewels, 12 diamond dial
s.steel.. $500 $550 $600

LONGINES, 17 jewels, c. 1923
gold filled $175 $225 $300

LONGINES, 17 jewels, flared, c. 1959
14k $450 $500 $600

LONGINES, 17 jewels, flared
14k C&B $600 $700 $800

LONGINES, 17 jewels, fancy lugs, c. 1943
14k.. $300 $350 $400

LONGINES, 17 jewels, torpedo shaped numbers
14k.. $250 $300 $350

LONGINES, 17 jewels, curved, fancy lugs, c. 1939
14k.. $350 $400 $500

LONGINES, 17 jewels, center lugs, c. 1937
14k.. $250 $275 $350

LONGINES, 17 jewels, hooded lugs, diamond dial
14k(w).. $700 $800 $950

LONGINES, 17 jewels, hooded lugs
14k $275 $325 $400

LONGINES, 17 jewels, diamond dial, c. 1930s
platinum $800 $900 $1,000

LONGINES, 17 jewels, diamond dial, fancy lugs
14k $500 $600 $700

LONGINES, 17 jewels, diamond dial
14k(W) $550 $600 $800

LONGINES, 17 jewels, diamond dial, c. 1944
14k $275 $325 $400

LONGINES, 17J.,curved,
14k.. $325 $375 $450

LONGINES, 17 jewels, fancy lugs
14k $400 $450 $575

LONGINES, 17J., stepped case,
14k.. $450 $500 $600

LONGINES, 17 jewels, c. 1930
18k $800 $900 $1,000
14k $450 $550 $700
gold filled $200 $250 $350

LONGINES, 17J., curvex, ca. 1930
gold filled....................................$600 $700 $800

LONGINES, 15J., tonneau, GJS, c.1925
silver $275 $325 $400

LONGINES, 17J., stepped case, GJS, cal.9L, c.1939
14k $300 $350 $450

LONGINES, 17J., extended lugs, GJS, cal.9L, c.1942
14k $300 $350 $450

LONGINES, 17J., cut corner, cal.94w, c.1929
gold filled $125 $150 $250

LONGINES, 17J., , tonneau, cal.9L, c.1948
gold filled $250 $300 $400

LONGINES, 17J., carved bezel, GJS, cal.9LT, c.1950
gold filled $125 $150 $175

LONGINES, 17J., butler finish, GJS, cal., c.1951
gold filled $250 $300 $400

LONGINES, 17J., beveled bezel, GJS, cal., c.1935
gold filled $125 $150 $225

LONGINES, 17J., aux. sec., GJS, cal.9L, c.1948
gold filled $125 $150 $225

LONGINES, 17J., carved case, GJS, cal.9LT, c.1950s
14k $225 $275 $350

LONGINES, 17J., butler finish, GJS, cal.9LT, c.1957
14k $250 $300 $400

LONGINES, 17J., fluted lugs, GJS, cal.9L, c.1949
gold filled.................................$150 $175 $275

LONGINES, 15J., butler finish, c.1926
gold filled................................. $125 $150 $250

LONGINES, 17J., carved case, GJS, cal.9LT, c.1959
gold filled.................................$150 $175 $275

LONGINES, 17J., stepped case, GJS, cal.9LT, c.1958
14k $250 $300 $400

LONGINES, 17J., spur lugs, GJS, cal., c.1948
gold filled.................................$150 $175 $275

LONGINES, 17J., stepped case, GJS, curved, c.1938
s. steel....................................... $275 $325 $450

LONGINES, 17J., extended lugs, GJS, cal.9LT, c.1955
14k..$300 $350 $450

LONGINES, 17J., fancy lugs, GJS, cal.9LT, c.1957
14k $225 $275 $350

LONGINES, 17J.,extended lugs, GJS,
14k..$300 $350 $450

LONGINES, 17J., fluted sides, GJS, cal.9LT, c.1950
gold filled $150 $175 $275

LONGINES, 17J., RF#3327, GJS, cal.,10L c.1948
14k.................................$350 $400 $500

LONGINES, 17J., carved case, GJS, cal.9LT, c.1955
14k $325 $375 $475

LONGINES, 17J., extended lugs, GJS, cal.9LT, c.1951
14k.................................$275 $300 $400

LONGINES, 17J., U shaped lugs, GJS
14k $400 $450 $600

LONGINES, 17J., aux. sec., GJS, cal., c.1951
14k.................................$275 $300 $425

LONGINES, 17J., GJS, curved lugs
14k $250 $275 $375

LONGINES, 17J., butler finish, GJS, cal.9L, c.1955
14k.................................$220 $250 $350

LONGINES, 17J., RF#8475, GJS, cal.10L, c.1948
14k $350 $400 $500

LONGINES, 17J., aux. sec., GJS, cal.9LT, c.1950
14k.................................$275 $300 $425

LONGINES, 17J., butler finish, GJS, cal.8LN, c.1942
14k.. $200 $250 $325

LONGINES, 17J., GJS, cal.23z
gold filled................................... $85 $95 $150

LONGINES, 17J., beveled lugs, GJS, cal.8LN, c.1947
14k $175 $225 $300

LONGINES, 17J., bezeled case, GJS, cal.9LT, c.1955
gold filled................................... $150 $175 $275

LONGINES, 17J., wide bezel, GJS, cal.23z, c.1950
gold filled $150 $175 $275

LONGINES, 17J., curly lugs, GJS, cal.23z, c.1950
gold filled................................... $150 $175 $275

LONGINES, 17J., tank style, GJS, cal.23z, c.1957
14k $200 $250 $350

LONGINES, 17J., checked dial, GJS, cal.22L, c.1957
14k.. $225 $275 $375

LONGINES, 17J., crab leg lugs, GJS, cal.10L, c.1951
gold filled $150 $175 $275

LONGINES, 17J., RF#1050, mystery dial, cal.23z, c.1960
14k.. $275 $325 $425

LONGINES, 17J., stepped lugs, GJS, cal.10L, c.1948
gold filled $150 $175 $275

LONGINES, 17J., RF#2288, hidden lugs, GJS, c.1955
14k $450 $500 $650

LONGINES, 17J., textured bezel, GJS, cal.22L, c.1950
14k $400 $450 $600

LONGINES, 17J., hidden lugs
14k $700 $800 $900

LONGINES, 17J., stepped case, GJS, cal.23z, c.1955
14k $225 $275 $400
gold filled $150 $200 $300

LONGINES, 17J., extended lugs,
14k $800 $1,000 $1,200

LONGINES, 17J., extended lugs, GJS,
gold filled $200 $225 $325

LONGINES, 17 jewels
14k (w) $300 $400 $500

LONGINES, 17J., hooded lugs, GJS, cal.8LN, c.1942
gold filled $150 $175 $275

LONGINES, 17 jewels, fancy lugs
14k $450 $550 $700

LONGINES, 17 jewels, c. 1939
14k $400 $500 $600

LONGINES, 17 jewels, curvex, slanted lugs
14k (w) $250 $300 $375

LONGINES, 17 jewels, fancy lugs, c. 1942
14k $450 $550 $675

LONGINES, 17 jewels, fancy lugs, c. 1947
14k $350 $400 $450

LONGINES, 17 jewels, curved, flared
14k $300 $350 $475

LONGINES, 15 jewels, chased bezel
14k $600 $700 $900

LONGINES, 15 jewels, engraved bezel, c. 1928
14k (w) $450 $500 $650

LONGINES, 17J., faceted crystal,
14k $200 $250 $300

LONGINES, 17J., fancy lugs & diamond bezel
14k(W) $500 $600 $700

LONGINES, 17J., stepped case,
14k $250 $300 $400

LONGINES, 17J., fancy lugs
14k $400 $450 $500

LONGINES, 17J., fancy lugs,
14k $300 $350 $450

LONGINES, 17J., center sec., fancy lugs, ca.1946
14k.................................$350 $400 $450

LONGINES, 17J., cal#232, ca. 1948
14k $250 $300 $400

LONGINES, 17J., fancy lugs, cal#10L
14k.................................$300 $350 $400

LONGINES, 17J., aux. sec.
14k $275 $325 $400

LONGINES, 17J., aux. sec.
14k.................................$250 $300 $350

LONGINES, 17J., ca. 1952
14k $225 $275 $350

LONGINES, 17J., offset lugs
14k.................................$250 $300 $350

LONGINES, 17J., cal#10L, center sec.,
14k $325 $375 $450

LONGINES, 17J., fancy lugs, ca. 1951
14k.................................$500 $600 $700

LONGINES, 17J., fancy bezel
14k $200 $250 $300

LONGINES, 17J., flared case, GJS, cal.9LT, c.1950
gold filled $200 $250 $350

LONGINES, 17J., flared, textured dial
14k $450 $550 $675

LONGINES, 17J., Flared
14k $400 $500 $650

LONGINES, 17 jewels, enameled bezel, c. 1928
14k $400 $450 $500

LONGINES, 17 jewels, formed case
14k $350 $400 $475

LONGINES, 17J.,antimagnetic
s. steel $175 $225 $300

LONGINES, 17J., "COMET", cal.702, c.1972
s. steel $100 $135 $200

LONGINES, 17J., lady's style centert lugs, c.1948
14k C&B $300 $350 $425

LONGINES, 15J., lady's style,
14k C&B $200 $250 $300

LORTON, 17 jewels, chronog., c. 1950
s. steel...................................... $150 $200 $250

LOUIS, 17J., center sec.,
14k.. $100 $125 $150

LOVIC, 17J., mystery dial, long triangular case, c.1950
base metal.................................... $75 $100 $125

LOUVIC, 17J., hunter style case, ca. 1965
s. steel $100 $125 $150

LOUVIC, 17J., mystery diamond dial, ca.1960
s. steel.. $60 $70 $80

LUCERNE, 17 jewels, 14k case & band
14k C&B $350 $400 $450

LUCIEN PICCARD, 17J., movement by Ditisheim
14k.. $200 $250 $300

LUCIEN PICCARD, 17 jewels, gem set bezel
gold filled.................................... $300 $400 $500

LUCIEN PICCARD, 17 jewels, "Seahawk," auto wind
18k C&B $400 $450 $500

LUCIEN PICCARD, 17 jewels, wind indicator, c. 1958
s. steel.. $75 $85 $100

LUCIEN PICCARD, 17 jewels, skeletonized
18k $1,200 $1,400 $1,600

LUSINA, 17 jewels, aux. sec., fancy lugs
gold filled $80 $100 $120

LYCEUM, 17J., beveled case, aux. sec.
14k $125 $150 $175

MAPPIN, 15 jewels, duo dial, c. 1930
9k $1,000 $1,200 $1,500

MARS, 17 jewels, "Dateur," hinged back, c. 1934
gold filled.................................. $300 $400 $500

MARVIN, 17J., center sec., cal.520s, c.1943
14k... $100 $125 $150

MARVIN, 17J., non magnetic,
gold filled.................................... $60 $70 $80

MASTER, 17J., engraved case, c.1943
gold plate...................................... $40 $45 $55

MASTER, 17J., tonneau case, c.1943
gold plate...................................... $40 $45 $55

MASTER, 17J., stepped case, c.1943
gold plate $50 $55 $65

MEYLAN, 17 jewels, c. 1940s
18k $700 $800 $900

MEYLAN, 18 jewels, jumping hr., c. 1920
18k $10,000 $11,000 $12,000

MEYLAN, 16 jewels, wire lugs
14k $1,000 $1,200 $1,500

MEYLAN, 27 jewels, 1 button chronog., 2 reg.
18k $2,500 $3,000 $3,500

C.H. MEYLAN, 18J., Octagon case, c.1917
platinum $400 $500 $600

J.E. MEYLAN, 15J., one button chronog., ca. 1937
s. steel $300 $350 $400

J.E. MEYLAN,17J., stop watch,
s. steel... $175 $200 $250

MIDO, 15 jewels, in form of car radiator, c. 1940s
silver... $2,000 $2,500 $3,000

MIDO, 17 jewels, chronog., c. 1952
s. steel... $500 $600 $700

MIDO, 17 jewels, chronog., multi-center chrono
s. steel... $500 $600 $700
Telemeter dial.......................... $600 $700 $800

MIDO, 17J., choronog., cal.1300, c.1954
18k $1,000 $1,250 $1,500

MIDO, 17J., choronog., pulsations, c.1955
18k $1,000 $1,200 $1,500

MIDO, 17J., carved case, cal.2m, c.1947
14k $150 $200 $250

MIDO, 17 jewels, diamond dial
14k..$250 $300 $350

MIDO, 17 jewels "Multifort," diamond dial
s. steel $175 $200 $250

MIDO, 17 jewels, fancy lugs, c. 1945
14k..$250 $300 $350

MIDO, 15 jewels, mystery dial, c. 1935
s. steel $1,000 $1,200 $1,400

MIDO, 17J., multifort grand luxe, date, ca. 1950s
18k C&B $400 $500 $600

MIDO, 17J., RF#7204, cal.d917b, c.1958
s. steel.................... $100 $125 $150

MIDO, 17J., RF#228, mid size case, c.1943
s. steel....................................... $100 $125 $150

MIDO, 17J., mid size case, c.1940
gold filled.................................. $75 $100 $125

MIDO, 17J., mid size case, cal.917r, c.1949
s. steel....................................... $100 $125 $150

MIDO, 17J., rotating bezel, c.1960
s. steel....................................... $250 $300 $350

MIDO, 17J., multifort grand luxe, extra-flat
s. steel....................................... $100 $125 $150

MILDIA, 17 jewels
s. steel.. $40 $50 $60

MIMO, 15 jewels, date
gold filled.................................. $200 $225 $250

MIMO, 17J., "De Frece", date, c.1935
14k(w)... $300 $350 $400

MIMO, 17 jewels, jumping hr., wandering min. & sec.
gold filled.................................. $300 $400 $500

MIMO, 17 jewels, 8 day, 6 gear train, c. 1950s
gold filled.................................. $800 $900 $1,000

MIMO, 17 jewels, duo dial
s. steel.. $300 $400 $500

MIMO, 15 jewels, engraved bezel
gold filled.................................. $40 $50 $60

MIMO, 15 jewels, "Mimomatic," c. 1932
s. steel... $45 $55 $75

MINERVIA, 29J., min. repeater, repeats on 2 gongs
18k...$20,000 $30,000 $40,000

MINERVIA, 17 jewels, chronog., 2 reg.
18k...$900 $1,000 $1,400
s. steel.......................................$275 $350 $450

MINERVIA, 17 jewels, 2 reg.
18k...$1,000 $1,200 $1,400

MINERVIA, 17 jewels, waterproof, c. 1950s
s. steel...$300 $350 $400

MINERVIA, 17J., Valjoux cal.723, c.1955
s. steel..................................... $500 $600 $700

MINERVIA, 17 jewels, center sec., auto wind
gold filled.................................... $70 $80 $100

MINERVIA, 19 jewels, chronog., 3 reg.
s. steel..................................... $300 $350 $400

MISC. SWISS, 15J., hunter style, wire lugs, ca. 1926
silver..................................... $300 $400 $500

MINERVIA, 17 jewels, chronog., c. 1942
s. steel..................................... $200 $225 $275

MISC. SWISS, 15J., shield cover, enamel dial, ca. 1927
silver..................................... $450 $550 $650

MINERVIA, 17J., chronog., day-date-month, 3 reg.
18k $1,500 $1,700 $1,900

MISC. SWISS,15J., wire lugs, cal., c.1920
s. steel..................................... $300 $350 $400

MISC. SWISS, 15J., enamel dial, c.1925
s. steel.......................................$300 $350 $400

MISC. SWISS, 17 jewels, hunter "Flip Top"
18k...$1,000 $1,200 $1,500

MISC. SWISS,15J., wire lugs, c.1925
silver $300 $500 $600

MISC. SWISS, 17J., jump hr., wandering min., c. 1930
9k..$800 $1,000 $1,200

MISC. SWISS, 15J., wire lugs, ca. 1925
silver $100 $150 $200

MISC. SWISS, 17J., wandering min., hr. by red mark
s. steel......................................$300 $400 $500

MISC. SWISS, 15J., wire lugs, nail set, ca.1925
silver $250 $300 $350

MISC. SWISS, 17 jewels, fancy bezel
14k..$400 $500 $600

MISC. SWISS, 15J., aux. sec., ca. 1930s
gold filled $100 $125 $150

MISC. SWISS, 17 jewels, masonic symbols, c. 1950s
s. steel & gold filled $1,200 $1,400 $1,600

MISC. SWISS, 15 jewels, early auto wind, c. 1930s
s. steel...$800 $900 $1,000

MISC. SWISS,15J., Caldwell on dial Paul Benton on mvt.,
one button chronog. at 12, center hinged lugs, c.1920s
silver...$900 $1,000 $1,100

MISC. SWISS, 17 jewels, digital hr., min., sec.
s. steel...$500 $600 $700

MISC. SWISS, 15 jewels, 8 day movement
silver $300 $400 $500

MISC. SWISS,15J., 1 button chronog. wire lugs, c.1923
silver..$400 $500 $600

MISC. SWISS, 29 jewels, repeater, 2 jacquemart
18k $4,000 $4,500 $5,000

MISC. SWISS, 17 jewels, enamel dial, chronog.
s. steel $400 $500 $600

MISC. SWISS, 17J.,early chronog., ca.1929
18k...$1,500 $2,000 $2,500

MISC. SWISS, 15J., one button chronog., ca. 1925
silver $600 $700 $800

MISC. SWISS, 17J, chronog., 2 reg.
gold filled.................................$200 $300 $400

MISC. SWISS, 17 jewels, chronog., 1 button, 2 reg.
s. steel.. $400 $500 $600

MISC. SWISS,17J., "chronographe" on dial, c.1940
base metal $125 $150 $175

MISC. SWISS, 17J., chronog., ca. 1950
gold filled $200 $300 $400

MISC. SWISS,17J., by Venus
18K..$250 $300 $350

MISC. SWISS, 17J., 2 reg chronog.,
s. steel.. $150 $200 $250

MISC. SWISS,17J., triple date, chronog., 2 reg., c.1955
s. steel... $200 $250 $300

MISC. SWISS,17J, chronog., triple date, moon ph., c. 1945
s. steel.. $400 $500 $600

MISC. SWISS, 17 jewels, split sec. chronog., 2 reg.
s. steel.................................... $2,000 $2,500 $3,000

MISC. SWISS, 18 jewels, Jaeger,chronog., c. 1930s
18k $600 $700 $900

MISC. SWISS, 17J., triple date, moon ph., ca. 1967
gold filled $250 $300 $350

MISC. SWISS, 17 jewels, early auto wind, c. 1930s
14k..$400 $500 $600

MISC. SWISS, 17J., nail set, 31 X 43mm, ca.1915
14k...$1,200 $1,400 $1,600

MONARCH, 7 jewels, stepped case
crome..$40 $45 $50

MONARCH, 7 jewels, stepped case
gold filled....................................$40 $50 $60

MONARCH, 7 jewels,
gold filled....................................$40 $50 $60

MONARCH (continued)

MONARCH, 7 jewels, engraved bezel, curved
gold filled $50 $60 $70

H. MOSER & CO., 17J, "Signal Corps USA", ctr. lugs
silver..$500 $600 $700

MONARCH, 7 jewels , curved.
gold filled................................. $100 $150 $200

MOVADO, 15J., polyplan, winds at 12 o'clock, 46mm,
curved, c. 1910
18k..$4,000 $5,000 $6,000

MONTBRILLANT, 15J., one button chronog. ca 1925
18k $1,500 $2,000 $2,500

MOVADO, 15J., polyplan, winds at 12 o'clock,
14k...$3,000 $4,000 $5,000

MOVADO, 15J., polyplan, winds at 12 o'clock, c. 1910
14k...$3,500 $4,500 $5,500

MORIVA,17J., auto-w. with wind indicator,
s. steel.. $100 $125 $150

MOVADO, 17J., 50mm long,Calendarmeto, moon ph.
leather $800 $900 $1,000

MOVADO, 15J., "Chronometre", c.1930
14k $350 $400 $450

MOVADO, 17J., date, kingmatic,
14k(w) $250 $300 $350

MOVADO, 17J., day date month, "Sportsman"
14k $400 $500 $600

MOVADO, 17J., month date, ca. 1950s
14k $300 $400 $500

MOVADO, 17J., day date month, snap back
18k $600 $700 $800

MOVADO, 17 jewels, day-date-month, c. 1945
18k $700 $800 $900
gold filled $300 $350 $400
s. steel $250 $300 $350

MOVADO, 17J., triple date, snap back, "calendomatic"
18k $1,000 $1,200 $1,400

MOVADO, 15 jewels, day-date-month, center sec.
18k $700 $800 $900

MOVADO, 17 jewels, auto wind, waterproof
14k $600 $700 $800

MOVADO, 17J., 3 reg. chronog.,
s. steel.. $800 $900 $1,200

MOVADO, 17J., 1 button chronog., c.1948
s. steel.. $500 $600 $700

MOVADO, 17J., 3 reg. chronog., date
s. steel..$200 $300 $400

MOVADO, 17J., chronog., 2 reg., c.1940
14k $1,200 $1,400 $1,600

MOVADO, 17J., El Primero date at 5, c.1972
s. steel..$300 $350 $400

MOVADO, 17J., 3 reg. chronog.
s. steel.. $800 $1,000 $1,200

MOVADO,17J., RF#2652, rotating chapter,cal.352, c.1958
s. steel..$200 $250 $300

MOVADO, 17J., center sec., cal.261, c.1948
18k $300 $350 $400

MOVADO, 15J., aux. sec., cal.75, c.1946
s. steel $150 $200 $250

MOVADO, 17J., center sec., c.1942
14k $250 $300 $350

MOVADO, 17J., aux. sec., cal.135, c.1955
s. steel $100 $125 $150

MOVADO, 17J., center sec., c.1948
14k $400 $450 $500

MOVADO, 17J., auto-wind, cal.8577, c.1957
14k $200 $250 $300

MOVADO, 17J., water-tight case,
14k $250 $300 $350

MOVADO, 17J., center sec.,
14k $300 $350 $400

MOVADO, 20J., auto-w.,
14k $250 $300 $350

MOVADO, 17J., center sec.
14k $250 $300 $350

MOVADO, 17., center sec
s. steel $100 $150 $200

MOVADO, 20J., auto-wind,
14k $250 $300 $350

MOVADO, 28J., center sec.," Kingmatic",
14k $250 $300 $350

MOVADO, 17J., aux. sec.
18k $300 $400 $500

MOVADO, 17J., auto-w., ca. 1949
14k $300 $350 $400

MOVADO, 17J., nonmagnetic
s. steel $150 $200 $250

MOVADO, 15 jewels, center lugs, c. 1930
18k $500 $600 $700

MOVADO, 17., textured 18k dial
18k $400 $500 $600

MOVADO, 17 jewels, date at 12 o'clock
14k C&B $400 $500 $600

MOVADO, 15 jewels, aux. sec.
14k C&B $300 $400 $500

MOVADO, 15 jewels, fancy lugs
18k $500 $600 $700

MOVADO, 17 jewels, aux. sec., center lugs
14k $400 $500 $600

MOVADO, 17J., wide bezel, c.1958
gold filled................................... $150 $175 $200

MOVADO, 17J., cal. 7025, GJS, c.1964
18k $250 $300 $350

MOVADO, 17J., diamond bezel,
18k $300 $350 $400

MOVADO, 17J., hidden lugs, tu-tone dial, c.1960
18k $450 $550 $600

MOVADO, 17J., RF#621, c.1932
gold filled................................... $200 $250 $300

MOVADO, 17J., stepped case, curviplan, GJS, c.1942
14k $600 $700 $800

MOVADO, 17J., tu-tone case, RF#13906c.1948
14k..$300 $350 $400

MOVADO, 17J., aux. sec., c.1940
14k $400 $500 $600

MOVADO, 15 jewels, curved
14k...$600 $700 $800

MOVADO, 17J., extended lugs, c.1945
14k $400 $500 $600

MOVADO, 17J., cal#510, ca.1941
14k...$500 $600 $700

MOVADO, 17J., aux. sec., c.1945
14k $350 $400 $450

MOVADO, 17J., curviplan,
gold filled..................................$300 $400 $500

MOVADO, 17J., curviplan, ca.1941
14k...$600 $700 $800

MOVADO, 17J., extended lugs, GJS, c.1940
14k $300 $350 $400

MOVADO, 17J., fancy lugs, ca.1942
14k...$500 $600 $700

MOVADO, 15 jewels, c. 1929
18k $500 $600 $700

MOVADO, 17 jewels
14k $300 $350 $400

MOVADO, 17 jewels, automatic, tank style
18k $400 $500 $600

MOVADO, 17 jewels, fancy lugs, c. 1947
14k $400 $500 $600

MOVADO, 17 jewels
18k $600 $700 $800

MOVADO, 17 jewels, day date, c. 1948
18k $400 $500 $600

MOVADO, 17J., hidden lugs, c.1940
14k $500 $600 $700

MOVADO, 17J., stepped hidden lugs, GJS, c.1937
14k $500 $600 $700

MOVADO, 17J., lady alarm, c.1950
gold filled.................................. $100 $125 $150

SIDE VIEW

MT VERNON, 15J.&21J, curvex,
gold plate................................... $85 $100 $125

MOVADO MOVEMENT IDENTIFICATION

Caliber 35   Caliber 65   Caliber 575   Caliber25, 27-Sweep Second

Caliber 28   Caliber 575, Ermeto-Baby   Caliber 578, Ermeto Calendine   579, Calendoplan Baby

Caliber 5   Caliber 15   Caliber 50SP   Caliber 105, 107-Center Second

Caliber 190   Caliber 375, 377-Center Second   Caliber 440, 443-Center Second

Caliber 510   Caliber 260M, 261   Caliber 150MN, 157-Sweep Second

Caliber 155, Calendermeto   Caliber 470, 477-Center Second   Caliber 473, 473SC-Calendar/Moon phase

Caliber 475, 475SC-Center Second   Caliber 225, 255M

Caliber 115   Caliber 118   Caliber 220, 220M

Caliber 221, 226   Caliber 223, 228   Caliber 224, 224A

MT VERNON, 15J., curvex,
gold plate $70 $80 $90

MT VERNON, 15J., stepped case,
s. steel... $60 $70 $80

MT VERNON, 17J.,
gold filled $60 $70 $80

MT VERNON, 15J.,
gold filled $35 $45 $55

U. NARDIN, 29 J., "Astrolabium," self wind, waterproof,
local time, equinoctial time, months, signs of zodiac, eleva-
tion & azimuth of sun & moon, aspect in which sun &
moon stand to each other
18k $6,000 $7,000 $9,000

U. NARDIN, 17J., one button pulsations. ca.1920
18k...$1,800 $2,000 $2,200

U. NARDIN, 17J., chronog., "Pulsations," c. 1920
18k...$3,000 $3,500 $4,000

U. NARDIN, 17 jewels, chronog., c. 1950s
18k...$2,500 $2,700 $3,000

U. NARDIN, 17 jewels, split sec. chronog., c. 1910
silver...$7,000 $8,000 $9,000

U. NARDIN, 17 jewels, chronog., 3 reg. c. 1940s
18k $2,800 $3,200 $3,600

U. NARDIN, 17J., center sec., auto-wind c. 1950
14k $250 $300 $350

U. NARDIN, 25 jewels, date
14k $300 $350 $400

U. NARDIN, 17J., center sec., auto-wind c. 1950
18k $250 $300 $350

U. NARDIN, 17 jewels, auto wind, c. 1952
14k $300 $350 $400

U. NARDIN, 21J., auto-wind
18k $300 $350 $400

U. NARDIN, 17J., aux sec.
s. steel $100 $150 $200

U. NARDIN, 17J., center sec., chronometer, c.1950
gold filled $100 $125 $150

U. NARDIN, 17J., aux. sec.
18k $300 $350 $400

U. NARDIN, 17J., fancy lugs
18k $400 $500 $600

U. NARDIN, 17J., aux. sec., carved lugsc.1950
14k $400 $450 $500

U. NARDIN, 17J., aux. sec., chronometer, c.1950
14k $250 $300 $350

U. NARDIN, 17J., aux. sec., chronometer, c.1947
18k $250 $300 $350

U. NARDIN, 17J., aux. sec., chronometer, c.1948
gold filled................................$100 $125 $150

U. NARDIN, 17J., fluted case
14k................................$400 $500 $600

U. NARDIN, 17J., fancy lugs
14k................................$400 $500 $600

U. NARDIN, 17J., aux. sec., chronometer, c.1949
14k................................$250 $300 $350

U. NARDIN, 17J., aux. sec., chronometer, c.1950
18k................................$300 $350 $400

U. NARDIN, 17J., extended side lugs, chronometer, c.1951
14k $250 $300 $350

U. NARDIN, 17 jewels, faceted crystal & bezel
s. steel $200 $250 $325

U. NARDIN, 17 jewels, c. 1920
18k $700 $750 $800

U. NARDIN, 17 jewels, WW I military style
s. steel $400 $500 $600

U. NARDIN, 17J., lady's chronometer, c.1947
14k C&B $500 $550 $600

NATIONAL, 17 jewels, day-date-month
gold filled $100 $110 $125

NATIONAL, 15 jewels
gold filled $40 $50 $60

NATIONAL, 17 jewels, center sec., waterproof
s. steel $30 $40 $50

NATIONAL, 17 J., auto wind, center sec., waterproof
gold filled $35 $45 $60

NEW HAVEN, 7 jewels, engraved bezel
base metal $10 $15 $25

NEW HAVEN, 7 jewels, stepped case
base metal.................................. $10 $15 $25

NEW HAVEN, 7 jewels
base metal.................................. $10 $15 $25

NEW HAVEN, 2 jewels, "Elf" ladies, etched case
base meta.................................. $5 $10 $15

NEW HAVEN, 7 jewels, "Duchess" ladies, etched case
gold plate $5 $10 $15

NEWMARK, 17J., military chronog., c.1979
s. steel.................................. $150 $200 $250

NEW YORK STANDARD, 7 jewels
gold filled.................................. $10 $20 $35
base metal $5 $10 $15

NICOLET W. CO., 17J., chronog., ca. 1960
gold filled.................................. $300 $350 $400

CHARLES NICOLET, 17J., chronog., ca. 1945
18k.................................. $200 $250 $300

MARC NICOLET, 17J., hidden lugs,
14k.................................. $200 $250 $300

NITON, 18J., jump hr., (showing dial and movement)
(made ebauche for P.P.&CO.)
18k(W)..................................... $3,000 $4,000 $5,000

OFAIR, 17J., chronog., cal. Valjoux 72c, c.1948
gold filled.................................. $300 $350 $400

NIVADA, 25 jewels, waterproof, c. 1940
gold filled.................................. $250 $300 $350

OGIVAL, 17 jewels, auto wind
gold filled.................................. $30 $40 $50

NORMANDIE, 17 jewels, compass, c. 1945
s. steel.. $50 $60 $70

OLLENDORFF, 17 jewels, fancy lugs
14k..$400 $450 $500

NORMANDIE, 17J., gold train, hidden lugs, cal.4873
14k $150 $175 $200

OLLENDORFF, 17 jewels, gold movement
14k..$600 $700 $800

OCTO, 17J., fluted lugs,
14k $250 $275 $300

OLLENDORFF, 7J., direct read, stepped case, c.1930
base metal $200 $250 $300

OLLENDORFF, 15J., engraved bevel,
chrome plated............................ $40 $45 $55

OLMA, 17J., auto-wind, by Wyler, c.1932
s. steel... $150 $175 $200

OLMA, 17J., large crab legs,
gold plate $100 $125 $150

OLYMPIA, 15 jewels, double dial, c. 1938
s. steel....................................... $200 $250 $300

OMEGA, 15J., center lugs, enamel dial, ca. 1930,
18k $600 $700 $800

OMEGA, 15J., wire lugs, ca. 1925s
silver.. $250 $300 $425

OMEGA, 15J., wire lugs, ca. 1930s
18k.. $800 $900 $1,000

OMEGA, 15J., wire lugs,
14k.. $350 $425 $450

OMEGA, 17 jewels, center sec.
14k.. $225 $275 $350

OMEGA, 17 jewels, chronog, c. 1935
18k $2,000 $2,500 $3,000

OMEGA, 17J., 2 reg. chronog, ca. 1940s
18k $800 $900 $1,000
s. steel...................................... $300 $400 $500

OMEGA, 17J., 2 reg., chronog, c. 1958
18k $800 $900 $1,000

OMEGA, 17 jewels, chronog., "Seamaster," c. 1963
s. steel.. $500 $600 $700

OMEGA, 17J., "Seamaster", chronog., cal.321, c. 1962
18k..$1,200 $1,400 $1,600

OMEGA, 17J., "Seamaster", chronog., c. 1970
s. steel.. $200 $250 $300

OMEGA, 17J., "Seamaster Pro.", chronog., c. 1969
"the first watch worn on the moon" on back of watch
s. steel.. $300 $350 $400

OMEGA, 17J., "SeamasterPro. Mark 11", chronog., c.1975
s. steel.. $200 $250 $300

OMEGA, 22J., "Seamaster", date, 2 reg., auto-wind, c.1975
s. steel....................................... $100 $150 $200

OMEGA, 17J., "Seamaster", chronostop, cal.865, c.1965
s. steel....................................... $100 $125 $150

OMEGA, 17J., "Seamaster Pro. Mark 111", cal.1040,c.1978
s. steel....................................... $150 $200 $250

OMEGA, 17J., "Seamaster", chronostop., rotating bezel
s. steel....................................... $150 $175 $275

OMEGA, 17J., "Seamaster", auto-wind, chronog., c.1975
s. steel....................................... $200 $250 $300

OMEGA, 17J., "Seamaster", chronog., cal.321, c.1970
s. steel....................................... $150 $200 $250

OMEGA, 17 jewels, chronog., "Seamaster," 3 reg.
14k $500 $600 $700

OMEGA, 17 jewels, chronog., "Flightmaster," 3 reg.
18k $4,000 $5,000 $6,000

OMEGA, 17 jewels, day-date-month, moon phase
18k $1,200 $1,400 $1,600
14k $1,000 $1,100 $1,200

OMEGA, 17J., day-date-month, moon phase, c. 1940
14k $1,000 $1,100 $1,200

OMEGA, 17 J. day-date-month, moon phase, c. 1950s
18k $2,500 $3,000 $3,500

OMEGA, 17J.,date, Constellation, chronometer
14k $400 $500 $600

OMEGA, 24J., "Constellation", auto-wind, c.1960
s. steel $150 $200 $275

OMEGA, 24J., "Constellation", auto-wind, c.1968
gold filled $150 $200 $275

OMEGA (continued)

OMEGA, 24J., "Constellation", auto-wind, c.1969
s. steel.. $125 $150 $200

OMEGA, 17 jewels, "Constellation," auto wind, date
gold filled.................................$150 $200 $250

OMEGA, 7J., "Constellation", quartz, cal.1342, c.1970
18k & s. s. $400 $450 $550

OMEGA, 24 jewels, "Constellation," auto wind
18k C&B $1,200 $1,400 $1,600

OMEGA, 17J., date, seamaster de ville, auto-w.,
14k $300 $350 $400

OMEGA, 24 jewels, "Constellation," c. 1959
18k.................................$650 $700 $850

OMEGA, electronic, "F300," c. 1950s
18k C&B..............................$1,600 $1,800 $2,000

OMEGA, 17 jewels, "Seamaster," date, waterproof
18k.................................$400 $500 $600

OMEGA, 24J., "Constellation", auto-wind, c.1962
s. steel... $100 $125 $200

Omega, 17 jewels, "Seamaster," auto wind
14k...$300 $350 $400

OMEGA, 24J., "Constellation", auto-wind, cal.562, c.1962
gold filled.................................. $100 $125 $200

OMEGA, 17J.,"seamaster",chronometer
18k...$350 $400 $550

OMEGA, 23J., "Constellation", auto-wind, cal.1022, c.1978
s. steel... $85 $100 $150

OMEGA, 17J., "Seamaster Delux",
18k...$325 $400 $550

OMEGA, 17 jewels, automatic, date
14k $200 $225 $275

OMEGA, 20J., "Seamaster", auto-wind, cal.501c.1957
s. steel $100 $125 $200

OMEGA, 17J., "Seamaster", auto-wind, cal.1570c.1955
gold filled $110 $135 $200

OMEGA, 16J., gold train, c.1930
s. steel $100 $125 $200

OMEGA, 17J., "Constellation", chronometer.
18k $700 $800 $900

OMEGA, 16J., center sec., c.1940
s. steel $100 $125 $200

OMEGA, 24J., "Constellation", auto-wind, cal.505, c.1958
18k $500 $550 $650

OMEGA, 16J., U.S. Army, cal., c.1948
s. steel $175 $200 $300

OMEGA, 24J., "Constellation", auto-wind, cal.551, c.1962
14k $375 $425 $525

OMEGA, 16J., center sec., c.1948
s. steel $125 $150 $225

OMEGA, 17J., "Railmaster", center sec.
s. steel......................................$150 $175 $275

OMEGA, 17J., center sec., cal.283,
18k.. $300 $325 $425

OMEGA, 17J., auto-wind, center sec., c.1946
s. steel......................................$100 $125 $200

OMEGA, 17J., Seamaster, diamond dial, cal.563, c.1955
s. steel......................................$150 $175 $275

OMEGA, 17J., 12 diamond dial, center sec.
14k(W)......................................$200 $250 $300

OMEGA, 17J., fancy lugs, ca.1948
14k..$400 $500 $600

OMEGA, 17J., aux.sec., cal.266, c.1956
s. steel......................................$100 $125 $200

OMEGA, 17J., aux. sec., cal.266, c.1945
14k..$250 $275 $375

OMEGA, 17J., aux. sec., cal.360, c.1950
14k $250 $275 $375

OMEGA, 17J., auto-wind, c.1949
18k $325 $350 $450

OMEGA, 17J., auto-wind, cal.342, c.1955
gold filled................................. $100 $125 $200

OMEGA, 17J., seamaster, auto-wind
s. steel... $90 $120 $175

OMEGA, 17J., aux. sec., cal.302, c.1948
gold filled..................................$125 $150 $225

OMEGA, 15J., extended lugs, c.1939
gold filled..................................$125 $150 $225

OMEGA, 15J., aux. sec., c.1937
s. steel..$125 $150 $225

OMEGA, 15J., small lugs, c.1935
gold filled..................................$150 $175 $275

OMEGA, 17J., beveled case, c.1936
s. steel..$150 $175 $275

OMEGA, 15J., small lugs, c.1937
s. steel....................................... $125 $150 $225

OMEGA, 17 jewels, aux. sec.
14k C&B $600 $700 $800

OMEGA, 17J., fancy lugs, ca. 1950s
14k $300 $350 $400

OMEGA, 17J., extended lugs, cal.301, c.1948
14k.. $300 $350 $450

OMEGA, 17J., faceted crystal,
14k(W)..................................... $300 $350 $400

OMEGA, 17J., sculptured lugs, cal.302, c.1953
14k.. $300 $350 $450

OMEGA, 17J., fancy lugs, ca. 1948
14k $400 $450 $500

OMEGA, 17J., hidden lugs, c.1947
14k.. $275 $325 $425

OMEGA, 17J., 9 diamond dial, ca. 1955
14k(W)..................................... $200 $250 $300

OMEGA, 17 jewels, hidden lugs
14k.. $600 $700 $800

OMEGA, 17 jewels, curved center lugs
14k $350 $450 $550

OMEGA, 17 jewels, sculptured lugs
14k $400 $500 $600

OMEGA, 17 jewels, c. 1948
14k $300 $350 $400

OMEGA, 17 jewels, c. 1938
14k $250 $300 $350

OMEGA, 15 jewels, c. 1935
14k $275 $300 $350

OMEGA, 17J., wide bezel, center sec.,cal.470, c.1955
14k $275 $325 $425

OMEGA, 17J., RF#347sc, cal.471, c.1956
18k $275 $300 $400

OMEGA, 17J., wide bezel & lugs, cal.369, c.1947
platinum $700 $800 $950

OMEGA, 17J., "De Ville",
18k $200 $225 $325

OMEGA, 17J., cal.620, c.1960
14k $175 $200 $300

OMEGA, 17 jewels, aux. sec.
18k $350 $450 $550

OMEGA, 17 jewels, c. 1937
s. steel.............................. $200 $225 $300

OMEGA, 17 jewels
14k $300 $350 $450

OMEGA, 15 jewels, hidden winding stem, c. 1930
14k $2,000 $2,500 $3,000
s. steel.............................. $1,500 $1,750 $2,000

OMEGA, "Chrono-quartz, cal.1611, c.1975
s. steel.............................. $150 $175 $250

OMEGA, quartz, marine chronometer
s. steel.............................. $500 $550 $600

OMEGA, 15J., ladies, wire lugs, c.1925
silver.............................. $75 $95 $135

OMEGA, 17J., ladies center sec., c.1938
silver.............................. $200 $250 $325

OMEGA, 17J., ladies flip open, 16 diamonds, c.1955
14k C&B $700 $800 $1,000

OMEGA, 19J., alarm,"Memomatic", c.1975
s. steel.............................. $125 $150 $225

OMEGA, 15J., ladies, non-magnetic, c.1945
s. steel.. $125 $150 $225

OMEGA, 17J., ladies, sapphire stones on lugs, c.1950
14k C&B.................................... $500 $600 $800

OMEGA, 17J., ladies, RF#8065, c.1965
18k C&B.................................... $600 $700 $950

OPEL, 21 jewels, waterproof
gold filled.................................... $75 $100 $125

ORATOR, 17 jewels, auto wind
s. steel.. $50 $60 $70

ORFINA, 17 jewels, triple date, moon phase
gold filled.................................... $200 $250 $300

ORFINA, 17 jewels, triple date, moon phase
gold filled.................................... $200 $250 $300

ORFINA, 17 jewels, day-date-month
gold filled.................................... $70 $80 $100

ORFINA, 17 jewels, date
s. steel... $50 $60 $70

ORVIN, 17 jewels, day-date, c. 1945
s. steel... $70 $80 $90

PABRO, 17J., ladies 76 diamond watch, c.1930
platinum.................................... $700 $800 $900

PARKER, 17J., 2 reg. chronog.,ca.1948
s. steel.. $200 $225 $250

☞ " PATEK PHILIPPE" watches should be signed on
the case, dial & movement to bring the prices listed in this
book. (triple signed P.P.CO.)

PATEK PHILIPPE, 29 jewels, min. repeater, c. 1920
platinum $150,000 $175,000 $200,000

PATEK PHILIPPE, 29J., min. repeater, 30 x 34mm
18k..$200,000 $250,000 $300,000

PATEK PHILIPPE, 39J., auto-wind, min. repeater,
perpetual day date monthcalendars, moon ph., 24 hr. ind.,
leap year ind., RF#3974, 5 year wating list, c.1989
18K.....................................$300,000 $325,000 $350,000

PATEK PHILIPPE, 29, min. repeater, RF#2524
18k..$130,000 $160,000 $180,000

PATEK PHILIPPE, 29 jewels, min. repeater, six watches
finished by E. Gublin, 18k case & band, triple signed
18k C&B............................$135,000 $165,000 $185,000

PATEK PHILIPPE, 18J., designed by Gilbert Albert,
RF#3412, c. 1958
18k...$18,000 $20,000 $22,000

PATEK PHILIPPE, 50 sec. tourbillon, 57 hr. power
reserve 5 gear train, 28 x 38mm, RF#3834
18k $150,000 $170,000 $190,000

PATEK PHILIPPE, 18J., asymmetric case designed by
Gilbert Albert, RF#3413, c. 1958
18k...$20,000 $22,000 $25,000

PATEK PHILIPPE,18J., horizontal case, RF#504, 2 tone
18k $10,000 $11,000 $12,000

PATEK PHILIPPE,18J., fluted hooded lugs, RF#2517
18k...$5,000 $6,000 $7,000

PATEK PHILIPPE,18 J., horizontal case, RF#139
18k $8,000 $9,000 $10,000

PATEK PHILIPPE, 18 J., RF#3497, diamond set case
platinum C&B.....................$12,000 $14,000 $16,000

PATEK PHILIPPE, 18J., RF#3424, asymmetric, c. 1960
18k $12,000 $14,000 $17,000

PATEK PHILIPPE, 18J., asymmetric, diamond set
platinum $15,000 $20,000 $25,000

PATEK PHILIPPE, 18 J., M. 9, hinged back, c. 1920s
18k $3,000 $3,300 $3,600

PATEK PHILIPPE, 18 jewels, M. 9, curved, c. 1926
18k $3,500 $4,000 $4,500

PATEK PHILIPPE, 18 J., M. 10, hinged back, c. 1920s
18k $3,500 $4,000 $4,500

PATEK PHILIPPE, 18 jewels, M. 9, c. 1940s
18k $3,500 $4,000 $4,500

PATEK PHILIPPE, 18 jewels, M. 9, c. 1950s
18k $3,000 $3,500 $4,500

PATEK PHILIPPE, 18J., cal. 990, c. 1936
18K $4,000 $4,250 $4,500

PATEK PHILIPPE, 18J., RF#409, cal. c. 1934
18K $3,500 $3,700 $4,000

PATEK PHILIPPE, 18 jewels, M. 9, c. 1940s
18k $3,000 $3,500 $4,500

PATEK PHILIPPE, 18 jewels, c. 1950s
18k $3,000 $3,500 $4,000

PATEK PHILIPPE, 18 jewels, M. 9
18k $3,000 $3,500 $4,000

PATEK PHILIPPE, 18 jewels, M. 9
18k $3,000 $3,500 $4,000

PATEK PHILIPPE, 18 jewels, c. 1940s
18k $3,500 $4,000 $4,500

PATEK PHILIPPE, 18 jewels, c. 1943
18k $3,500 $4,000 $4,500

PATEK PHILIPPE, 18 jewels, c. 1930s
18k $3,000 $3,500 $4,000

PATEK PHILIPPE, 18 jewels, c. 1945
18k $5,000 $6,000 $7,000

PATEK PHILIPPE, 18 jewels
18k $3,500 $4,000 $4,500

PATEK PHILIPPE, 18 jewels, M. 9, c. 1960s
18k $3,500 $4,000 $4,500

PATEK PHILIPPE, 18 jewels, curved, M. 9
18k $5,000 $6,000 $7,000

PATEK PHILIPPE, 18J., decorated enamel case, c. 1920s
18k $8,000 $9,000 $10,000

PATEK PHILIPPE, 18J., RF#2334,
18K $3,300 $3,500 $3,800

PATEK PHILIPPE, 18J., extended lugs, cal.885, c.1943
18K $4,500 $5,000 $5,500

PATEK PHILIPPE,18J., diamond on dial & case
18K C&B $3,000 $3,500 $4,000

PATEK PHILIPPE, 18J, M.9, fancy lugs
18k...$6,000 $7,000 $8,000

PATEK PHILIPPE, 18 jewels, hidden lugs, c. 1930s
18k $2,000 $2,500 $3,000

PATEK PHILIPPE, 18J., curved, hooded satin lugs
18k...$8,000 $9,000 $10,000

PATEK PHILIPPE, 18 jewels, c. 1940s
18k $4,000 $4,500 $5,000

PATEK PHILIPPE, 18 jewels, "Staybrite," curved case
s. steel $2,800 $3,000 $3,500

PATEK PHILIPPE, 18 jewels, hinged back, c. 1920s
18k $4,000 $4,500 $5,500

PATEK PHILIPPE, 18 jewels, M. 9, hooded lugs
18k...$2,000 $2,500 $3,000

PATEK PHILIPPE, 18 jewels, applied gold numbers
18K $6,000 $7,000 $8,000

PATEK PHILIPPE, 18 jewels, curved
18k...$4,500 $5,000 $6,000

PATEK PHILIPPE,18J.engraved bezel,hinged back,c.1920
18k $5,000 $5,500 $6,500

PATEK PHILIPPE, 18J., ribbed case & fancy lugs
18k $2,500 $3,000 $3,500

PATEK PHILIPPE, 18 jewels, large lugs, c. 1960s
18k $4,000 $4,500 $5,000

PATEK PHILIPPE, 18 jewels, m.9, c.1930
18k $4,000 $5,000 $6,000

PATEK PHILIPPE, 18 jewels, c. 1930s
18k $3,000 $3,500 $4,000

PATEK PHILIPPE, 18J., M. 9, center lugs, c. 1940s
18k $3,500 $4,000 $4,500

PATEK PHILIPPE, 18 jewels, c. 1940s
18k $4,000 $4,500 $5,000

PATEK PHILIPPE, 18J., triple lugs, RF#2471, ca.1951
18k $10,000 $12,000 $14,000

PATEK PHILIPPE, 18 jewels, triple lugs, RF#1482
18k $8,000 $9,000 $10,000

PATEK PHILIPPE, 18 jewels, curved, c. 1940s
18k $3,500 $4,000 $4,500

PATEK PHILIPPE, 18 jewels, M.9, c. 1940s
18k $4,000 $4,500 $5,000

PATEK PHILIPPE, 18 jewels, curved, c. 1950s
18k $3,500 $4,000 $5,000

PATEK PHILIPPE, 18 jewels, hinged back, c. 1920s
18k $3,000 $3,500 $4,500

PATEK PHILIPPE, 18J., hinged back, stepped case
18k $4,000 $4,500 $5,000

PATEK PHILIPPE, 18J., RF#2520, M. 9, extended lugs
18k C&B................................. $8,000 $9,000 $10,000

PATEK PHILIPPE, 18J., fancy lugs, ca.1949
18k $6,000 $7,000 $8,000

PATEK PHILIPPE, 18 jewels, M. 9, concave lugs
18k.. $6,000 $7,000 $8,000

PATEK PHILIPPE, 18 J., M.9, tank model, c.1940
18k.. $3,000 $3,500 $4,000

PATEK PHILIPPE, 18 jewels, moveable lugs
18K.. $6,000 $7,000 $9,000

PATEK PHILIPPE, 18 jewels, lapidated lugs
18k.. $4,000 $4,500 $5,000

PATEK PHILIPPE, 18 jewels, fancy lugs, RF#1480
18k.. $4,000 $4,500 $5,000

PATEK PHILIPPE, 18 jewels, fancy lugs
18k $5,000 $5,500 $6,000

PATEK PHILIPPE, 18 jewels, top hat style, c. 1940s
platinum $7,000 $8,000 $9,000
18k $5,000 $5,500 $6,500

PATEK PHILIPPE, 18j., stylized hooded lugs, RF#2441
18k $5,000 $6,000 $7,000

PATEK PHILIPPE, 18Jewels, top hat style,
18k C&B $5,500 $6,000 $7,000

PATEK PHILIPPE, 18 jewels, M. 9, c. 1940s
18k $4,500 $5,000 $6,000

PATEK PHILIPPE, 18 jewels, hooded & fluted lugs
18k $4,000 $5,000 $6,000

PATEK PHILIPPE, 18J., 2 tone, hooded & stepped lugs
18k $8,000 $9,000 $10,000

PATEK PHILIPPE, 18 jewels, M. 9, curved, tank style
18k $6,000 $7,000 $8,000

PATEK PHILIPPE, 18 jewels, "Reverso"
18k $20,000 $25,000 $30,000
s. steel.................................... $6,000 $8,000 $10,000

PATEK PHILIPPE, 18 jewels, c. 1960s
18k $4,000 $4,500 $5,000

PATEK PHILIPPE, 18 jewels, Adj. to 8 positions
18k $4,000 $4,500 $5,000

PATEK PHILIPPE, 18 jewels, massive flared case
18k..$14,000 $16,000 $18,000
platinum $18,000 $20,000 $22,000

PATEK PHILIPPE, 18 jewels, curvex, c. 1940s
18k $4,000 $4,500 $5,000

PATEK PHILIPPE, 18J., RF#2441, curved, flared case
18k.....................................$8,000 $9,000 $10,000

PATEK PHILIPPE, 18 J., converted to jump hr., recased
18k $4,000 $4,500 $5,000

PATEK PHILIPPE,18J., RF#2441, Eiffel tower, c. 1945
18k......................................$8,000 $9,000 $10,000

PATEK PHILIPPE, 18 jewels, flared case, c. 1940s
18k $6,500 $7,000 $8,000

PATEK PHILIPPE, 18 jewels, flared case
18k..$5,000 $5,500 $6,500

PATEK PHILIPPE, 18 jewels, M. 9, c. 1950s
platinum.............................. $15,000 $16,000 $18,000

PATEK PHILIPPE, 18 jewels, flared case, c. 1950s
18k.................................$6,000 $6,500 $7,000

PATEK PHILIPPE, 18J., M. 9, flared case, c. 1950s
18k $6,500 $7,500 $8,500

PATEK PHILIPPE, 18 jewels, c. 1950s
18k $6,000 $6,500 $7,000

PATEK PHILIPPE, 18J., 16 diamond on bezel, ca.1960
18k C&B.............................. $6,000 $7,000 $8,000

PATEK PHILIPPE, 18 jewels, diamond dial, c. 1945
18k $5,000 $5,500 $6,000

PATEK PHILIPPE, 18 jewels, diamond dial
platinum.................................. $5,000 $5,500 $6,000

PATEK PHILIPPE, 18 jewels, diamond dial, c. 1935
platinum.................................. $5,000 $5,500 $6,000

PATEK PHILIPPE, 18 jewels, diamond dial & bezel
platinum.............................. $7,000 $8,000 $9,000

PATEK PHILIPPE, 18J., hinged back, diamond bezel
18k................................$6,000 $7,000 $8,000

PATEK PHILIPPE, 18 jewels, c. 1940s
18k..$4,000 $4,500 $5,000

PATEK PHILIPPE, 18J., diamond dial, flared case
18k..................................$7,500 $8,000 $9,000

PATEK PHILIPPE, 18J, M. 9, diamond dial, starbritel case
s. steel $3,000 $3,500 $4,000

PATEK PHILIPPE, 30 J., rf#2540, ca. 1957
18k...$2,500 $3,000 $3,500

PATEK PHILIPPE,18J., RF#2493, c.1953
18K $2,000 $2,400 $2,800

PATEK PHILIPPE,18J., stepped lugs, c.1940
18K...................................$2,500 $3,000 $3,500

PATEK PHILIPPE,18J., RF#1431, cal., c.1940
18K $2,000 $2,200 $2,400

PATEK PHILIPPE, 18 J. 18k band & case, c. 1950s
18k C&B $3,000 $3,500 $4,000

PATEK PHILIPPE,18J., RF#2447, c.1950
18K $1,800 $2,000 $2,200

PATEK PHILIPPE, 18 jewels, textured bezel, c. 1940s
18k..$2,000 $2,500 $3,000

PATEK PHILIPPE,18J., carved lugs, RF#2423, c.1949
18K $2,500 $3,000 $3,500

PATEK PHILIPPE, 18 jewels, ogival lugs, thick crystal
18k..$2,500 $3,000 $3,500

PATEK PHILIPPE,18J., RF#2424, c.1951
18K $2,500 $3,000 $3,500

PATEK PHILIPPE, 18 jewels
18k..$2,000 $2,500 $3,000

PATEK PHILIPPE, 18 jewels, M. 9, c. 1963
18k $2,000 $2,500 $3,000

PATEK PHILIPPE, 18 jewels, M. 9, c. 1948
18k................................$3,000 $3,500 $4,000

PATEK PHILIPPE, 18 jewels, c. 1947
18k................................$2,000 $2,500 $3,000

PATEK PHILIPPE, 18 jewels, diamond bezel , tank style
platinum $6,500 $7,500 $8,500

PATEK PHILIPPE, 18 jewels, c. 1960s
18k $1,800 $2,000 $2,200

PATEK PHILIPPE, 18 J., curved, diamond dial, top hat
platinum $8,500 $9,000 $10,000

PATEK PHILIPPE, 18 jewels, oval lugs
18k $3,500 $4,000 $4,500

PATEK PHILIPPE, 18J., M. 9, hidden dial, gold & plat.
18k & platinum $20,000 $22,000 $24,000

PATEK PHILIPPE, 18 jewels
18k $2,000 $2,200 $2,500

PATEK PHILIPPE, 18 jewels, M. 9, c. 1980s
18k C&B $2,500 $3,000 $3,500

PATEK PHILIPPE, 18 jewels, M. 9, c. 1970s
18k C&B............................ $2,000 $2,200 $2,500

PATEK PHILIPPE, 18 jewels
18k (w) $1,500 $1,600 $1,800

PATEK PHILIPPE, 18 jewels
18k C&B............................... $2,200 $2,400 $2,600

PATEK PHILIPPE, 18 jewels, textured dial & bezel
18k $3,000 $3,500 $4,000

PATEK PHILIPPE, 18 jewels, c. 1950s
18k $2,800 $3,000 $3,500

☞ " PATEK PHILIPPE" watches should be signed on
the case, dial & movement to bring the prices listed in this
book. (triple signed P.P.CO.)

PHILIPPE, 18 jewels, center sec., c. 1960s
18k C&B $3,000 $3,500 $4,000

PATEK PHILIPPE, 18 J., rf#2530-1, ca. 1959
18k C&B $3,000 $3,500 $4,000

PATEK PHILIPPE, 18 jewels, M. 9, c. early 1910s
18k C&B $4,000 $5,000 $6,000

PATEK PHILIPPE, 18 jewels, c. 1950s
18k.. $1,800 $2,000 $2,500

PATEK PHILIPPE, 18 jewels, c. 1950s
18k.. $2,000 $2,500 $3,000

PATEK PHILIPPE, 18 jewels, c. 1950s
18k $2,000 $2,500 $3,000

PATEK PHILIPPE, 18 jewels, c. 1960s
18k $3,000 $3,500 $4,000

PATEK PHILIPPE, 18 J., guilloche bezel, thick lugs
18k $3,000 $3,500 $4,000

PATEK PHILIPPE, 18 jewels, hidden lugs, c. 1945
18k $3,000 $3,500 $4,000

PATEK PHILIPPE, 18J. fluted cylindrical hooded lugs
18k $6,000 $7,000 $8,000

PATEK PHILIPPE, 18 jewels, hidden lugs
18k $1,800 $2,000 $2,300

PATEK PHILIPPE, 18 jewels, hooded lugs, c. 1940s
18k $2,000 $2,500 $3,000

PATEK PHILIPPE, 18 jewels, blue sapphire bezel
platinum $7,000 $8,000 $9,000

PATEK PHILIPPE, 18 jewels, overhanging lugs
18k $5,000 $5,500 $6,500

PATEK PHILIPPE, 18 jewels, fluted dropped lugs
18k $4,000 $4,500 $5,000

☞ " PATEK PHILIPPE" watches should be signed on the case, dial & movement to bring the prices listed in this book. (triple signed P.P.CO.)

PATEK PHILIPPE, 18 jewels, c. 1940s
18k $3,000 $3,500 $4,000

PATEK PHILIPPE, 18 jewels, c. 1910
18k $3,000 $3,500 $4,000

PATEK PHILIPPE, 18 jewels, large bezel
18k $2,000 $2,500 $3,000

PATEK PHILIPPE, 18 jewels, c. 1920s
18k $4,000 $4,500 $5,000

PATEK PHILIPPE, 18 jewels, c. 1940s
18k $2,000 $2,200 $2,500

PATEK PHILIPPE, 18 jewels, c. 1920s
18k $3,500 $4,000 $4,500

PATEK PHILIPPE, 15J.,for Baily,Banks & Biddle, ca.1920
18k $5,000 $6,000 $7,000

PATEK PHILIPPE, 18 jewels, enamel dial,c. 1920s
18k $5,000 $5,500 $6,000

PATEK PHILIPPE, 16J., enamel dial, ca.1923
18k $4,000 $5,000 $6,000

PATEK PHILIPPE, 18 jewels, M. 9, c. 1910
platinum $7,000 $8,000 $9,000

PATEK PHILIPPE, 18 jewels, c. 1930s
18k $3,500 $4,000 $5,000

PATEK PHILIPPE, 18 jewels, c. 1930s
18k $4,000 $4,500 $5,500

PATEK PHILIPPE, 18 jewels, contract case
18k (w) $3,000 $3,500 $4,000

PATEK PHILIPPE, 18 jewels, M. 9, c. 1925
18k $3,500 $4,000 $4,500

PATEK PHILIPPE, 18 jewels, M. 9, c. 1920s
18k $5,000 $5,500 $6,000

PATEK PHILIPPE, 18J, diamond dial, curved, 42mm,
c. 1919
platinum $8,000 $9,000 $10,000

PATEK PHILIPPE, 18 jewels
18k $2,500 $3,000 $3,500

PATEK PHILIPPE, 18 jewels, made for E. Gublin
18k $4,000 $4,500 $5,000

PATEK PHILIPPE, 18 jewels, "Chronometro Gondolo"
18k $5,000 $6,000 $7,000

PATEK PHILIPPE, 18J., RF#515, world time zone, 24 hr.
rotating outside chapter, tu-tone case and band
18K C&B $200,000 $250,000 $300,000

PATEK PHILIPPE, 18J., RF#2523, "World Time,"
cloisonne polychrome enamel map on dial, 41 cities
18k $70,000 $80,000 $90,000

PATEK PHILIPPE, 18j., "World Time," 41 cities RF#1415
18k $40,000 $50,000 $60,000

PATEK PHILIPPE, 18 jewels, landscape cloisonne
polychrome enamel dial
18k $20,000 $25,000 $30,000

PATEK PHILIPPE, 18 jewels, 2 hands, 2 time zones
18k $18,000 $20,000 $24,000

PATEK PHILIPPE, 18J., traveling watch, hr. hand moves
forward or backward to time zone, steps 1 hr. at a time
18k $20,000 $25,000 $30,000

PATEK PHILIPPE, 18J., RF#130, chronog., 1940s
18k $20,000 $22,000 $25,000

PATEK PHILIPPE, 18J., RF#530, chronog.
18k $16,000 $18,000 $20,000

PATEK PHILIPPE, 18J., calatrava style,chronog., 2 reg.,
RF#130, c. 1940s
18k $20,000 $22,000 $25,000

☞ " PATEK PHILIPPE" watches should be signed on
the case, dial & movement to bring the prices listed in this
book. (triple signed P.P.CO.)

PATEK PHILIPPE,18J.,chronog., RF#530, fancy lugs
18k $15,000 $17,000 $19,000

PATEK PHILIPPE,18J., chronog., RF#591, 2 reg., c.1943
18k $22,000 $24,000 $26,000

PATEK PHILIPPE,18J., RF#130, chronog.,"2 tone"
18k & s. steel...................... $22,000 $24,000 $26,000

PATEK PHILIPPE, 32J., split sec. chronog.
18k $170,000 $190,000 $210,000

PATEK PHILIPPE,18J. RF#130,split sec. chronog.,c.1958
18k........................$100,000 $115,000 $130,000

PATEK PHILIPPE,18J., RF#1506, chronog., waterproof
18k.......................... $29,000 $32,000 $35,000

PATEK PHILIPPE, 18J., chronog., pulsometer, c. 1965
18k...........................$30,000 $33,000 $36,000

PATEK PHILIPPE, 18J., rf#3970E, chronog,triple date
moon ph., 24 hr. indicator, leap year indicator
18k..........................$50,000 $55,000 $60,000

☞ " PATEK PHILIPPE" watches should be signed on the case, dial & movement to bring the prices listed in this book. (triple signed P.P.CO.)

PATEK PHILIPPE, 18 jewels, chronog., day-date month, moon phase, made for E. Gueblin
18k C&B.............................. $75,000 $85,000 $95,000

PATEK PHILIPPE, 23 J., chronog., triple date, moon ph. perpetual calendar, ref.2499 (2 series)
18K...................................... $70,000 $80,000 $85,000

PATEK PHILIPPE, 18J., chronog., triple date, moon ph. perpetual calendar,ref.1518
18k $75,000 $88,000 $95,000

PATEK PHILIPPE, 23J., chronog., triple date, moon ph. perpetual calendar, ref.2499 (3 series)glass crystal
18k.. $65,000 $70,000 $80,000

PATEK PHILIPPE, 23 J., chronog., triple date, moon ph. perpetual calendar,ref.2499 (1 series) square button
18K $80,000 $85,000 $95,000

PATEK PHILIPPE, 23J., chronog., triple date, moon ph. perpetual calendar,ref.2499 (3 series)only 2 in platinum
platinum $150,000 $170,000 $200,000

PATEK PHILIPPE, 23J., chronog., triple date, moon ph.
perpetual calendar, ref.2499 (4 series)sapphire crystal
18k $60,000 $70,000 $80,000

PATEK PHILIPPE, 18 jewels, date, mid-sized
platinum................................. $7,000 $8,000 $9,000

PATEK PHILIPPE, 18Jewels, auto wind, date, c. 1970s
18k C&B................................ $3,000 $3,500 $4,000

PATEK PHILIPPE,18J., RF#3514/1, date,c.1967
18K C&B............................... $2,000 $2,200 $2,400

PATEK PHILIPPE,18J., date, RF#3445, c.1961
18K..$3,000 $3,300 $3,600

PATEK PHILIPPE,18J., date, RF#3604, textured dial,
c.1977
18K(w)....................................$2,000 $2,200 $2,400

PATEK PHILIPPE,36J., date, c.1970s
18K(w)C&B $2,200 $2,400 $2,600

PATEK PHILIPPE, 18J., RF#3450, day-date-month,
moon phase, waterproof, perpetual date at 3
18k..$25,000 $28,000 $32,000

PATEK PHILIPPE, 37J., RF#3448, cal.27-460q c.1968
18K $30,000 $32,000 $35,000

PATEK PHILIPPE,18J., "Officer", RF#3960, c.1992
18k 2,000 made, 18k(w) 150 made, platinum 50 made
18K.................................$13,000 $14,000 $15,000
18k(w)...........................$15,000 $16,000 $17,000
platinum $30,000 $32,000 $34,000

PATEK PHILIPPE, 37J., triple date, moon ph. RF #3448
platinum.............................. $35,000 $40,000 $45,000

PATEK PHILIPPE, 15J., enamel dial, c. 1910
18k...$6,000 $7,000 $8,000

PATEK PHILIPPE,18J., triple date, moon ph., RF#2438,
c.1962
18k $40,000 $50,000 $60,000

PATEK PHILIPPE, 18 jewels, RF#1461
18k...$2,000 $2,200 $2,500

PATEK PHILIPPE, 15 jewels, enamel dial, c. 1910
18k $6,000 $7,000 $8,000

PATEK PHILIPPE, 18 jewels
18k...$2,000 $2,500 $3,000

PATEK PHILIPPE, 18 jewels, aux. sec.
18k $2,300 $2,700 $3,200

PATEK PHILIPPE, 18 jewels, man's half size, c. 1920
18k $4,000 $4,500 $5,000
s. steel $2,600 $2,800 $3,000

PATEK PHILIPPE, 18J., Amagnetic on dial, ca. 1960
18k $5,000 $6,000 $7,000

PATEK PHILIPPE, 18 jewels, c. 1950s
18k $1,800 $2,000 $2,200

PATEK PHILIPPE, 18J.,"calatrava", aux. sec., c. 1940
18k $2,500 $2,800 $3,200

PATEK PHILIPPE, 18 jewels, aux. sec., c. 1950s
18k $2,500 $2,800 $3,200

PATEK PHILIPPE, 18 jewels, c. 1955
18k $2,200 $2,400 $2,600

PATEK PHILIPPE, 37J., RF#3429, self winding
18k $3,500 $3,800 $4,200

PATEK PHILIPPE, 18J., aux. sec., c. 1950s
18k $2,000 $2,200 $2,400

PATEK PHILIPPE, 18 J., auto wind, RF#2536, c.1950s
18k..$4,000 $4,500 $5,000

PATEK PHILIPPE, 18 jewels, aux. sec., c. 1950s
18k $2,000 $2,200 $2,400

PATEK PHILIPPE,18J., auto wind, RF#1516, c.1950
18K..$3,000 $3,200 $3,400

PATEK PHILIPPE, 18J., aux. sec., enamel dial, ca. 1957
18k $6,000 $7,000 $8,000

PATEK PHILIPPE,18J., aux. sec., RF#2445,
18K..$2,000 $2,200 $2,400

PATEK PHILIPPE, 18J., "Calatrava," rf#96c. 1950s
18k $3,000 $3,500 $4,000

PATEK PHILIPPE,18J., aux. sec., c.1943
18K..$2,500 $2,700 $2,900

PATEK PHILIPPE,37J., auto wind, RF#3429, c.1961
18K $3,500 $3,700 $4,000

PATEK PHILIPPE, 18J., "Calatrava," auto-wind, c. 1950s
18k... $3,500 $4,000 $4,500

PATEK PHILIPPE,18J., aux. sec., RF#96, cal.12-20, c.1937
18K $3,000 $3,200 $3,400

PATEK PHILIPPE, 18 jewels, extra long lugs, c. 1950
18k... $2,300 $2,500 $2,700

PATEK PHILIPPE,18J.,   RF#1543, c.1947
18K $2,600 $2,800 $3,000

PATEK PHILIPPE, 18 jewels, aux. sec., c. 1950s
18k... $2,200 $2,400 $2,600

PATEK PHILIPPE,18J.,   RF#1590, c.1951
18K $2,600 $2,800 $3,000

PATEK PHILIPPE, 18 jewels, auto wind
18k... $2,000 $2,200 $2,400

PATEK PHILIPPE, 18 jewels, waterproof, c. 1940s
18k $2,200 $2,400 $2,600

PATEK PHILIPPE, 18J.,waterproof, "Calatrava," rf#2545
18k..$4,000 $4,500 $5,000

PATEK PHILIPPE, 18J.,"Calatrava" waterproof, c. 1950s
18k $3,500 $4,000 $4,500

PATEK PHILIPPE, 18 jewels, "Calatrava," waterproof
platinum $6,000 $7,000 $8,000

PATEK PHILIPPE, 30 jewels, auto wind, gold rotor
18k $3,500 $4,000 $4,500

PATEK PHILIPPE, 18 jewels, aux. sec., enamel dial
18k C&B $7,000 $8,000 $9,000

PATEK PHILIPPE, 18J., "Calatrava," rf#96, c. 1950s
18k $3,000 $3,500 $4,000

☞ " PATEK PHILIPPE" watches should be signed on
the case, dial & movement to bring the prices listed in this
book. (triple signed P.P.CO.)

PATEK PHILIPPE, 18 jewels, fancy lugs, c. 1940s
18k..$3,500 $4,000 $4,500

PATEK PHILIPPE, 18J., fancy lugs, ca. 1948
18k $7,000 $8,000 $9,000

PATEK PHILIPPE, 18 jewels, curled lugs
18k $3,000 $3,500 $4,000

PATEK PHILIPPE, 18 jewels, "Calatrava," c. 1950s
18k $3,500 $4,000 $4,500

PATEK PHILIPPE, 18 jewels, "Calatrava," c. 1940s
18k-rose $3,500 $4,000 $4,500

PATEK PHILIPPE, 18 jewels, "Calatrava," waterproof
18k..$4,000 $4,500 $5,000

PATEK PHILIPPE, 21J., "Calatrava," Breguet #s, c.1950s
18k..$4,000 $4,500 $5,000

PATEK PHILIPPE, 18J., center sec., rf#2466, ca.1949
18k...$3,000 $3,500 $4,000

PATEK PHILIPPE, 18 jewels, center sec., c. 1950s
18k..$2,000 $2,200 $2,500

PATEK PHILIPPE, 18 jewels, center sec., waterproof
s. steel.................................. $2,500 $2,800 $3,200

PATEK PHILIPPE, 18 jewels, textured dial & bezel
18k..............................$2,200 $2,500 $2,700

PATEK PHILIPPE, 18 jewels, center sec., c. 1950s
18k $2,500 $2,700 $3,000

PATEK PHILIPPE, 18 jewels, center sec., c. 1952
18k................................$2,400 $2,600 $2,800

PATEK PHILIPPE, 18 jewels, conical lugs, center sec.
18k.. $3,000 $3,500 $4,000

PATEK PHILIPPE, 18 jewels, center sec., waterproof
18k...$3,000 $3,500 $4,000

PATEK PHILIPPE, 20 jewels, center sec.
18k $2,500 $2,700 $3,000

PATEK PHILIPPE, 20 jewels, center sec.
18k..................................$2,200 $2,400 $2,700

PATEK PHILIPPE,18J., center sec., RF#3411, c.1960
18K $1,800 $2,000 $2,200

PATEK PHILIPPE, 18 jewels, auto wind,back set
18k..$3,000 $3,500 $4,000

PATEK PHILIPPE, 18 jewels, center sec., c. 1950s
18k $2,200 $2,400 $2,700

PATEK PHILIPPE, 18 jewels
18k..$1,800 $2,000 $2,200

PATEK PHILIPPE,18J., RF#3495, cal.27sc, c.1969
18K $1,500 $1,600 $1,700

PATEK PHILIPPE, 18 jewels, date-month
18k..$2,800 $3,000 $3,200

PATEK PHILIPPE, 18 jewels, center sec., c. 1960s
18k C&B.............................. $3,000 $3,500 $4,000

PATEK PHILIPPE, 18 jewels, "Calatrava," c. 1940s
18k..$3,500 $4,000 $4,500

PATEK PHILIPPE, 36 jewels, auto-w.,c. 1970s
18k $2,800 $3,000 $3,200

PATEK PHILIPPE,18J., RF#3574, c.1960
s. steel $1,000 $1,200 $1,400

PATEK PHILIPPE, 18 jewels
18k C&B $2,500 $3,000 $3,500

PATEK PHILIPPE, 18J., "Calatrava,", rf#2588, c.1940s
18k.. $3,000 $3,500 $4,000

PATEK PHILIPPE,18J., RF#2501, c.1954
18K $1,500 $1,600 $1,700

PATEK PHILIPPE, 18 jewels, unusual shape, c. 1940s
18k.. $6,000 $7,000 $8,000

PATEK PHILIPPE,18J., RF#2592, c.1956
18K $1,500 $1,600 $1,700

PATEK PHILIPPE, 36J., Nautilus, date,gold & steel
18K.................................... $10,000 $11,000 $12,000
18k&s. steel $4,000 $4,500 $5,000
s. steel $2,500 $3,000 $3,500

PATEK PHILIPPE, 36J., "Nautilus," date, large size
s. steel.....................................$2,500 $3,000 $3,500

PATEK PHILIPPE, 18J., Calatrava, diamond dial
platinum $8,000 $9,000 $10,000

PATEK PHILIPPE, 36 J. "Nautilus," diamond bezel
18k $12,000 $13,000 $14,000

PATEK PHILIPPE, 18J., "Calatrava," mid-sized, dia. dial
platinum $8,000 $8,500 $9,000

PATEK PHILIPPE, 36 jewels, diamond dial & bezel
18k $4,000 $4,500 $5,000

PATEK PHILIPPE, 18 jewels, c. 1980s
18k C&B $2,500 $2,800 $3,200

PATEK PHILIPPE, 18J., diamond dial, ca. 1952
platinum.................................$6,000 $7,000 $8,000

PATEK PHILIPPE, quartz, c. 1980s
18k C&B $2,300 $2,500 $2,800

PATEK PHILIPPE, 18 jewels, c. 1960s
18k C&B............................. $3,000 $3,200 $3,500

PATEK PHILIPPE, 18 jewels, c. 1980s
18k C&B............................. $2,500 $2,700 $3,000

PATEK PHILIPPE, 18 jewels, massive lugs
18k $3,500 $4,000 $4,500

PATEK PHILIPPE, 18 jewels, concave & hooded lugs
18k $3,000 $3,200 $3,500

PATEK PHILIPPE, 18 jewels, hooded lugs, c.1930s
18K.......................................$3,000 $3,500 $4,000

PATEK PHILIPPE, 18 jewels, mid-sized, 2 tone
18k (y & w) $8,000 $9,000 $10,000

PATEK PHILIPPE, 18 J., extended lugs, 2 tone, rf#497
18k (y & w) $8,000 $9,000 $10,000

PATEK PHILIPPE, 18 jewels, lady's watch
18k...$1,200 $1,400 $1,700

763

PATEK PHILIPPE,18 J., lady's, hinged lid set in diamonds
18k $3,500 $4,000 $4,500

PATEK PHILIPPE, 18 jewels, lady's watch, c. 1940s
18k C&B $3,500 $4,000 $4,500

PATEK PHILIPPE, 18 jewels, lady's watch
18k C&B................................. $2,500 $3,000 $3,500

PATEK PHILIPPE, 18J., lady's watch, min. repeater
18k...$60,000 $70,000 $80,000

PATEK PHILIPPE, 18 J., lady's watch, diamond bezel
platinum................................. $3,000 $3,500 $4,000

PATEK PHILIPPE, 18 jewels, lady's watch, c. 1950s
18k...$1,800 $2,000 $2,500

PATEK PHILIPPE, 18 jewels, lady's watch, c. 1950s
18k $3,000 $3,500 $4,000

PATEK PHILIPPE, 18 jewels, lady's watch, c. 1940s
18k...$1,000 $1,200 $1,400

☞ " PATEK PHILIPPE" watches should be signed on the case, dial & movement to bring the prices listed in this book. (triple signed P.P.CO.)

PATEK PHILIPPE, 18 jewels, lady's watch, c. 1940s
18k...$1,500 $1,700 $2,000

PATEK, PHILIPPE
MOVEMENT IDENTIFICATION

Caliber 6¾, no. 60
S.no. 865000-869999
(1940-1955)

Caliber 7, no. 70
S.no. 943300-949999
(1940-1960)

Caliber 8, no. 80
S.no. 840000-849999
(1935-1960)

Caliber 8, no. 85
S.no. 850000-859999
(1935-1968)

Caliber 9, no. 90
S.no. 833150-839999
S.no. 970000-979999
(1940-1950)

Caliber 9, no. 90a
830000-833149
(1940-1950)

Caliber 10, no. 105
S.no. 900000-909999
(1940-1945)

Caliber 10, no. 110
S.no. 910000-919999
(1940-1950)

Caliber 10, no. 200
S.no. 740000-759999
(1952-1965)
S.no. 950000-959999
(1945-1955)

Caliber 23, no. 300
S.no. 780000-799999
(1955-1965)

Caliber 12, no. 600AT
S.no. 760000-779999
(1952-1960)

Caliber 12, no. 400
S.no. 720000-739999
(1950-1965)

Caliber 12, no. 120
826900-829999 (1935-1940)

Caliber 12, no. 120A
92000-929999 (1940-1950)
960000-969999 (1946-1952)
938000-939999 (1952-1954)

Caliber 13, no. 130A   **Caliber 13, no. 130B**   **Caliber 13, no. 130C**
Chronograph, no. 862000-863995 (1940-1950); no. 867000-869999 (1950-1970)

Caliber 12-600 AT, S.no. 760,000-779,999 (1960-1970)

PATRIA, 7 jewels, enamel dial, compass
s. steel.. $300 $350 $400

PERFINE, 17 jewels, chronog, 2 reg.
gold filled................................... $100 $125 $150
s.steel... $45 $65 $85

PERPETUAL W. CO., 15J., rim wind & set, and
    sold for "$31.50" in1933
base metal................................. $125 $150 $175

PERPETUAL W. CO., 15 jewels, rim wind & set
14k $700 $800 $900
gold filled.................................. $300 $350 $400
s. steel...................................... $175 $200 $250

PERPETUAL W. CO., 15 jewels, c. 1930s
14k................................$600 $700 $800
gold filled...............................$350 $400 $450

PERPETUAL W. CO., 15J., fluted bezel, and sold for
"$37.50" in1933
base metal $200 $225 $275

PERPETUAL W. CO., 15 jewels, fancy bezel
gold filled.................................$350 $400 $450

PERPETUAL W. CO., 15 J., diamond bezel, c. 1930s
silver...$700 $800 $900

PHILLIPE W. CO., 17J., RF#2501, chronog, c.1950
s. steel..$200 $250 $300

PIAGET,18J., cal.9p2 , c.1980
18k(w) $500 $600 $700

PIAGET,18J., center sec., RF#1176, cal.f1560, c.1952
18k $400 $500 $600

PIAGET,18J., center sec., c.1950
18k $400 $500 $600

PIAGET, 18 jewels, 1904 $20 dollar gold piece, flip top
22k $800 $1,000 $1,400

PIAGET, 18 jewels, 2 movements 2 dials,
18k................................$700 $800 $900

PIAGET, 18 jewels, black dial
18k................................$500 $600 $700

PIAGET, 18 jewels, center sec., auto wind
18k................................$500 $600 $700

PIAGET, 18 jewels, ref. #8177, auto wind
18k................................$500 $600 $800

PIAGET, 18 jewels
18k $400 $500 $600

PIAGET, 30 jewels, auto wind, gold rotor
18k $500 $600 $700

PIAGET, 18 jewels, 18k case, 14k band
18k & 14k C&B $600 $700 $900

PIAGET, 18 jewels, gold train, center lugs, thin model
18k $500 $600 $700

PIAGET, 18J., RF#9821, c.1975
18k C&B $800 $900 $1,000

PIAGET, 18 jewels, oval style
18k C&B $400 $450 $550

PIAGET, 18 jewels, oval style
18k $400 $450 $500

PIAGET, 18 jewels, textured bezel
18k $700 $800 $900

PIAGET, 18 jewels, textured bezel, classic 90 model
18k $1,000 $1,100 $1,200

PIAGET, 30 jewels, textured bezel
18k $600 $700 $800

PIAGET, 18 jewels, tank style
18k $500 $550 $650

PIERCE, 17 jewels, chronog.
s. steel.. $40 $50 $65

PICARD,17J., chronog., reg at 12 ,
base metal.................................... $75 $100 $125

PIERCE, 17 jewels, chronog., c. 1940s
s. steel $50 $60 $75

PIERCE, 17J., early auto wind, "Parashock," c. 1930s
gold filled.................................. $400 $500 $600

PIERCE, 17J., triple date, moon ph.
gold filled.................................... $150 $200 $250

PIERCE, 17 jewels, auto wind, c. 1948
gold filled $40 $50 $60

PONTIAC,17J., center sec., anti-magnetic, c.1955
s. steel $20 $30 $40

PRONTO, 17 jewels, triple date, auto wind, waterproof
s. steel...$60 $70 $85

PONTIFA, 17 jewels, chronog. day-date-month, 3 reg.
s. steel.......................................$300 $350 $400

PRAESENT, 17J., triple date, mid size, c.1948
gold filled................................$150 $200 $250

PULSAR, L.E.D. (light emitting diode), ca.1975
14k..$300 $350 $400
gold filled................................$100 $150 $250

PREXA, 17 jewels, auto wind
gold filled.....................................$40 $50 $60

PULSAR, L.E.D. (light emitting diode)
18k...$400 $450 $500
14k...$300 $375 $450
gold filled................................$125 $150 $185
s. steel...$75 $95 $125

PROVITA, 17J., cal.1525, c.1973
18k...$150 $200 $250

RAPID, 17J., on mvt. PATHE W. CO.
gold filled....................................$75 $85 $100

RECORD, 17J., split sec. chronog., date, moon phase
18k $5,000 $5,500 $6,000

RECORD, 17 jewels, split sec. chronog.
s. steel $2,200 $2,500 $3,000

RECORD, 17 J., triple date, moon ph., auto wind ,
2 reg. chronograph,
18k $1,500 $1,700 $2,000

RECORD, 17 jewels, triple date, moon phase, c. 1940s
18k $800 $900 $1,000

REMBRANT, 17J., chronog., c.1942
s. steel $100 $125 $150

REVUE, 17J., beveled case, cal.54, c.1940
nickel $75 $100 $125

RIMA, 17J., aux. sec.,
14k.. $80 $100 $125

A. RIVALLE, 17J., chronog., c.1970
s. steel $50 $60 $70

RECORD, 17 jewels, day-date-month, moon phase
s. steel..........................$125 $135 $185

RECORD, 17 J., triple date, moon phase, auto wind
18k $1,000 $1,100 $1,200

ROAMER, 17 jewels, date, auto wind
gold filled...................... $40 $50 $60

ROAMER, 17 jewels, auto wind, aux. sec.
gold filled................................... $25 $30 $35

ROAMER, 23 jewels, ref. #4346
gold filled....................................$40 $50 $60

ROAMER, 17 jewels, hidden lugs
gold filled....................................$30 $40 $50

ROCAIL, 15J., auto-wind, c.1930s
s. steel.......................................$300 $350 $400

ROCKFORD,15J., Winona,made in USA, S#761074
gold filled.................................$300 $350 $400
s. steel $150 $200 $275

ROLEX, 15jewels, enamel dial, ca.1920
silver $400 $500 $600

ROLEX, 26 jewels, Milgauss, oyster, perpetual
s. steel.................................$1,000 $1,200 $1,400

ROLEX, 15 jewels, enamel dial, flip top, c. 1918
silver $700 $800 $900

ROLEX, 17 jewels," Century Club", c. 1960s
18k...$1,200 $1,400 $1,600
14k...$1,000 $1,200 $1,400

ROLEX, 17 jewels, ref. #4035
14k C&B................................ $1,000 $1,200 $1,400

ROLEX, 17 jewels, "Precision," center sec.
18k...$400 $450 $650

ROLEX, 26J., "Milgauss", c.1960s
s.steel...................................... $1,200 $1,400 $1,600

ROLEX, 17 jewels, center sec., large lugs
18k...$1,000 $1,200 $1,400

ROLEX, 17J., Precision
s. steel.................................. $350 $400 $450

ROLEX,17J., center sec., RF#9829, cal.1210
s. steel....................................... $250 $300 $350

ROLEX,17J., center sec., RF#9659, c.1960
14k $600 $800 $1,000

ROLEX,17J., "Precision", GJS
18k $700 $800 $900

ROLEX, 17J., Precision, fancy lugs,
9k..$400 $500 $600

ROLEX, 17 jewels, "Precision"
18k..$800 $1,000 $1,200

ROLEX, 15 jewels, wire lugs
9k..$600 $700 $800

ROLEX, 15 jewels, early waterproof, (case within a case)
silver..$1,600 $1,800 $2,000

ROLEX, 17 jewels
14k C&B $1,200 $1,400 $1,600

ROLEX, 17 jewels, ref. #9659
14k C&B.............................. $1,200 $1,400 $1,600

ROLEX, 17 jewels, "Precision"
gold filled................................ $300 $350 $400

ROLEX,15J., wire lugs, c.1925
silver $300 $400 $450

ROLEX, 15J., oyster, royal, c. 1930s
9k $1,000 $1,400 $1,600

ROLEX, 15J., oyster, ca. 1930
silver.. $600 $700 $800

ROLEX, 15 jewels, oyster, center sec.
18k...	$3,000	$3,400	$3,800
14k...	$2,200	$2,600	$3,000
9k...	$1,400	$1,600	$1,800
silver.......................................	$900	$1,000	$1,200
s. steel....................................	$800	$900	$1,000

ROLEX, 17 jewels, oyster, c. 1934
18k...	$3,000	$3,200	$3,400
14k...	$2,200	$2,500	$2,800
9k...	$1,400	$1,600	$1,800
silver.......................................	$800	$900	$1,000
s. steel....................................	$600	$700	$800

ROLEX,15J.,"Aqua", RF#2136, c.1928
s. steel..$300 $350 $400

ROLEX,15J., RF#6071, c.1926
s. steel............................... $400 $450 $500

ROLEX, 17 jewels, graduated bezel, c. 1928
silver.......................................$800 $950 $1,100

OYSTER,15J., by OYSTER W. CO., c. 1927
s. steel....................................... $400 $500 $700

ROLEX, 18J., note dial top half & bottom, RF#3139
s. steel.......................................$400 $450 $500

ROLEX, 17 jewels, oyster, ref. #2081
gold filled $600 $700 $900

ROLEX,17J., RF#4647, c.1948
s. steel.......................................$400 $450 $500

ROLEX, 17 jewels, oyster, center sec.
18k $2,500 $2,700 $3,000
14k $2,000 $2,200 $2,500
9k $1,400 $1,500 $1,700
s. steel...................................... $600 $700 $800

ROLEX, 18J., center sec. ca. 1937
s. steel.......................................$500 $600 $700

ROLEX, 17J., RF#4647, c.1943
s. steel.. $350 $400 $450

ROLEX, 17J., "observatory", RF#3386, c.1940
gold filled..................................... $450 $500 $550

ROLEX, 17J., RF#3139, c.1942
s. steel.. $400 $450 $500

ROLEX, 17J., RF#3116, c.1942
14k.. $1,500 $1,700 $2,000

ROLEX, 17 jewels, oyster, ref. #4547
s. steel.. $600 $700 $800

ROLEX, 17 jewels, oyster, "Viceroy," 2 tone, c. 1943
14k & s. steel $1,000 $1,100 $1,200

ROLEX, 17 jewels, oyster, c. 1930s
18k $2,500 $2,800 $3,400
14k $2,200 $2,400 $2,600

ROLEX, 17J., "Viceroy", RF#3359, c.1943
14k & s. seel.............................. $800 $900 $1,000

ROLEX, 17 jewels, oyster, extra prima Viceroy
18k $2,000 $2,500 $3,000

ROLEX, 26 jewels, Viceroy, center sec.
9k $1,500 $1,700 $1,900

ROLEX,17J., "Skyrocket", RF#, c.1944
gold filled $300 $350 $400

ROLEX,17J., "Royal", RF#3351, c.1936
gold filled $300 $350 $400

ROLEX,15J., RF#3116, c.1940
gold filled $300 $350 $400

ROLEX,17J., split sec. chronog.,12 examples, 43mm,c.1945
s. steel $50,000 $60,000 $70,000

ROLEX, 17 jewels, chronog., flat, tachometer, c. 1940s
18k.. $15,000 $20,000 $25,000

ROLEX, 17J., one button chronog. 2 reg., curved back
18k.. $30,000 $35,000 $40,000

ROLEX, 17 jewels, chronog., center lugs, c. 1940s
18k.. $9,000 $10,000 $12,000
14k.. $6,000 $7,000 $9,500
9k.. $4,000 $5,000 $6,500
s. steel.................................... $3,000 $3,500 $4,500

☞ **Note:** Rolex chronographs must have original dial, deduct 30% for refinished dial.

ROLEX, 17 jewels, chronog., mid-sized, c. 1950s
18k $8,000 $10,000 $12,000
14k $6,000 $8,000 $10,000

ROLEX, 17J., triple date, RF#4767, c.1948
s. steel $8,000 $8,500 $9,000

ROLEX, 17J., Valjoux cal.23, RF#4062, c.1940
18k $5,000 $5,500 $6,000

ROLEX, 17J., chronog., triple-date, diamond style chapter
18k $20,000 $22,000 $25,000
14k $15,000 $19,000 $20,000
s. steel $6,000 $7,000 $8,000

ROLEX, 17 jewels, chronog., 3 reg. oyster,
s. steel $3,000 $3,500 $4,000

ROLEX, 17 J., chronog., pulsations, 3 reg., c. 1960s
18k $10,000 $12,000 $14,000

ROLEX, 17 jewels, chronog., 3 reg.
14k $6,000 $7,000 $8,000

ROLEX, 17J., RF#6238, Valjoux 72bc. 1950
s. steel $3,500 $4,000 $4,500

ROLEX, 17J., chronog., RF#6234, c.1950
s. steel.................................... $3,000 $4,000 $4,500

ROLEX, 17J., Daytona, red outside chapter exotic dial
s. steel.................................... $6,000 $6,500 $7,000

ROLEX, 17J., chronog., 3 reg., c. 1950s, rect. markers
18k $8,000 $9,000 $10,000

ROLEX, 17J., exotic dial, RF#6239, Valjoux 727, c.1965
s. steel.................................... $7,000 $7,200 $7,500

ROLEX, 17J., chronog, 3 reg., tear drop lugs, c. 1940s
18k $10,000 $11,000 $12,000
14k $8,000 $9,000 $10,000
s. steel.................................... $5,000 $6,000 $7,500

ROLEX, 17J., "Daytona", RF#6263, c.1978
s. steel.................................... $3,500 $3,700 $4,000

ROLEX, 17J., triple-date, 3 reg., square markers
s. steel.................................... $5,000 $6,000 $7,000

ROLEX, 17J., screw down pusher 1st used 1976, RF#6265,
s. steel.................................... $3,500 $3,700 $4,000

ROLEX, 17 jewels, "Daytona," chronog., waterproof
18k	$8,000	$9,000	$10,000
14k	$6,000	$7,000	$8,000
s. steel	$1,800	$2,000	$2,500

ROLEX, 17 jewels, tachometer, 3 reg. c. 1960s
18k	$10,000	$12,000	$14,000
14k	$8,000	$9,000	$12,000
s. steel	$2,500	$3,000	$3,500

ROLEX, 17J., triple-date, moon phase, RF#8171, c.1949
18k	$18,000	$20,000	$22,000
14k	$12,000	$14,000	$16,000
s. steel	$6,000	$7,000	$8,500

ROLEX, 17 J., day-date-month, moon phase, oyster
s. steel C&B $6,000 $7,000 $8,000

ROLEX, 17J., STARS on dial, triple date, rf#6062, c. 1945
18k $20,000 $22,000 $25,000

ROLEX, 17J., day-date-month, moon phase, c. 1945
18k $18,000 $20,000 $22,000

ROLEX, 15 jewels, jumping hr., duo dial, c. 1930s
platinum	$14,000	$16,000	$19,000
18k	$12,000	$14,000	$16,000
14k	$10,000	$11,000	$12,000
9k	$7,000	$8,000	$9,000
silver	$6,000	$7,000	$8,000
gold filled	$4,000	$5,000	$6,500
s. steel	$5,000	$6,000	$7,500

ROLEX, 17., jumping hr., duo dial, stepped case, c. 1930s
18k 2 tone	$15,000	$18,000	$22,000
18k	$12,000	$14,000	$16,000
14k	$9,000	$10,000	$12,000
9k	$7,000	$8,000	$10,000
s. steel	$6,000	$7,000	$8,000

ROLEX, 17J., 2 tone case tiger stripe, Adj. to 6 pos.
18k	$12,000	$14,000	$16,000
14k	$10,000	$11,000	$12,500
9k	$7,000	$7,500	$8,500

ROLEX, 17 jewels, "Prince," duo dial
18k C&B	$6,000	$7,000	$8,000

ROLEX, 15 jewels, flared, duo dial, Adj. to 6 pos.
9k	$3,000	$3,200	$3,500

ROLEX, 17 jewels, flared, duo dial, c. 1930s
9k	$1,800	$2,000	$2,400

ROLEX, 15 jewels, "Prince," duo dial, c. 1930s
s. steel	$2,500	$3,000	$3,600

ROLEX, 17 jewels, 2 tone case
18k	$12,000	$14,000	$16,000

ROLEX, 15 jewels, chronometer, duo dial, c. 1930s
s. steel	$3,000	$3,500	$4,000

ROLEX, 17 jewels, "Prince," duo dial, stepped case
18k	$6,000	$7,000	$8,000
14k	$4,500	$5,000	$6,000
9k	$3,500	$4,000	$4,500
silver	$3,500	$4,000	$4,500
s. steel	$3,000	$3,500	$4,000
gold filled	$2,800	$3,200	$3,500

ROLEX, 15 jewels, "Railway," stepped case, c. 1930s
18k 2 tone	$12,000	$14,000	$16,000
18k	$10,000	$12,000	$14,000
14k 2 tone	$9,000	$10,000	$11,000
14k	$7,000	$8,000	$9,000
9k 2 tone	$5,000	$6,000	$7,000
9k	$4,000	$4,500	$5,500
s. steel	$4,000	$4,500	$5,000

ROLEX, 15 jewels, "Prince," center sec., c. 1930s
18k $8,000 $9,000 $10,000

ROLEX, 15 jewels, 1/4 century club,
14k $5,000 $5,500 $6,000

ROLEX, 15 jewels, 1/4 century club,
14k $5,000 $5,500 $6,000

ROLEX, 15 jewels, "Prince," c. 1935
platinum $10,000 $11,000 $12,000
18k $6,000 $7,000 $8,000
14k $5,000 $5,500 $6,500
gold filled $3,000 $3,200 $3,500

ROLEX, 17J., "Observatory", c.1938
gold filled $1,000 $1,100 $1,200

ROLEX, 15 jewels, stepped case
18k $8,000 $9,000 $10,000

ROLEX, 17J., date, mid size,
s. steel $400 $450 $500

ROLEX,17J., date, marked gold bezel, 2 tone case, rf#6305
s. steel $800 $900 $1,000

ROLEX, 17J., date, RF#6964, ca.1953
s. steel $350 $400 $450

ROLEX, 17 jewels, center sec., date just
18k C&B $3,500 $4,000 $4,500

ROLEX, 17 jewels, oyster, perpetual, date
14k $2,000 $2,200 $2,500

ROLEX, 17 jewels, oyster, perpetual
14k C&B $2,500 $2,700 $3,000

ROLEX, 17 jewels, oyster, perpetual, date, c. 1950s
14k $2,000 $2,200 $2,500

ROLEX, 17 jewels, auto wind, center sec., c. 1950s
14k $2,300 $2,800 $3,300

ROLEX, 17 jewels, "Speed King"
s. steel $400 $450 $500

ROLEX, 17 jewels, ref. #4325
14k $800 $900 $1,000

ROLEX, 25 jewels, "Explorer"
s. steel $900 $1,100 $1,400

ROLEX, 17 jewels, oyster, manual wind
18k	$1,000	$1,100	$1,250
14k	$800	$900	$1,000
9k	$500	$550	$700
gold filled	$300	$350	$400
s. steel	$250	$300	$350

ROLEX, 17J., center sec., precision
s. steel.......................... $300 $350 $400

ROLEX, 25J., marked bezel, c.1962
14k & s.s................................ $1,000 $1,100 $1,200

ROLEX, 19J., center sec.,gold & s. steel 2 tone case,
Gold & steel............................. $500 $600 $700

ROLEX, 26J., RF#1002, c.1965
14k.. $1,400 $1,500 $1,600

ROLEX, 17J., marked bezel, rose gold, c.1940s
18k $1,400 $1,500 $1,600

ROLEX, 25J., marked bezel, textured dial, ca. 1949
14k.. $1,000 $1,200 $1,400

ROLEX, 17J., marked bezel 2 tone, ca. 1955
gold & s. steel $400 $500 $600

ROLEX, 25J., RF#1025, c.1960
14k... $1,200 $1,400 $1,600

ROLEX, 25J., "Air King", RF#5500, c.1962
s. steel...$350 $400 $450

ROLEX, 25J., RF#6564, c.1955
s. steel...$450 $400 $450

ROLEX, 25J., "Air King",RF#5504, c.1959
s. steel...$300 $350 $400

ROLEX, 25J., marked bezel, RF#6581, c.1954
14k...$400 $450 $500

ROLEX, 17J., RF#6084, c.1951
14k $1,400 $1,500 $1,600

ROLEX, 25J., RF#6568, c.1956
s. steel...$350 $400 $450

ROLEX, 25J., RF#6084, c.1953
14k $1,800 $2,000 $2,200

ROLEX,17J., "Tudor", auto-wind, RF#7909, c.1955
s. steel...$75 $100 $125

ROLEX, 18J., RF#8405, c.1950
18k $900 $1,000 $1,100

ROLEX,17J., RF#6144, c.1948
18k & s.steel $400 $500 $650

ROLEX, 17J., Linz 1877, oyster, "Bombe"
18k $1,200 $1,400 $1,600

ROLEX, 25J., 12 diamond dial, RF#1030, c.1958
s. steel $500 $550 $600

ROLEX, 17J., center sec.
14k...$700 $800 $900

ROLEX, 17J., precision, center sec.
14k.................................$600 $700 $800

ROLEX, 15J., center sec., ca. 1939
14k $700 $800 $900

ROLEX, 25 jewels, "Bombe", rf. #6593
14k..$1,200 $1,400 $1,600

ROLEX, 19 jewels, "Bombe", center sec., c. 1960s

18k	$1,400	$1,600	$1,800
14k	$1,200	$1,400	$1,600
9k	$800	$900	$1,000
s. steel	$500	$600	$700

ROLEX, 18J., center sec.

| s. steel | $400 | $450 | $500 |

ROLEX, 17 jewels, center sec., gold bezel

| 18k & s. steel | $400 | $500 | $600 |

ROLEX, 18J., aux. sec.

| s. steel | $400 | $450 | $500 |

ROLEX, 17 jewels, center sec., c. 1945

18k	$2,000	$2,200	$2,500
14k	$1,000	$1,200	$1,500
9k	$900	$1,000	$1,100
s. steel	$350	$450	$550

ROLEX, 26 jewels, bubble back, hooded lugs

18k	$6,000	$6,500	$7,500
14k	$5,000	$5,500	$6,500
9k	$3,000	$3,500	$4,000
s. steel	★★$8,000	$9,000	$10,000

ROLEX, 17J., Pall Mall, ca. 1949

| 14k | $500 | $600 | $700 |

ROLEX, 26 jewels, "Bombe", center sec., c. 1945

| 14k | $1,200 | $1,400 | $1,600 |

ROLEX, 17J., "Royal Observatory" , RF#3121, c.1937
s. steel.. $400 $450 $500

ROLEX, 17J., sky-rocket,mid size, ca.1 949,steel back
gold filled................................... $300 $350 $400

ROLEX, 17J., "Record", c.1940
s. steel.. $300 $350 $400

ROLEX, 26 jewels, bubble back, hooded lugs, 2 tone
18k & s. steel $6,000 $7,000 $8,000

ROLEX, 17J., "Neptune", mid size, c.1939
gold filled................................. $300 $350 $400

ROLEX, 26 jewels, bubble back, hooded scalloped lugs
18k & s. steel $5,000 $6,500 $8,000

ROLEX, 17J., RF#2280, c.1951
s. steel..$350 $400 $450

ROLEX, 17J., "Victory", mid size, Tudorc.1940
s. steel.. $200 $250 $300

ROLEX, 15J., RF#2574, c.1940
s. steel.. $800 $900 $1,000

ROLEX, 17J., mid size, RF#6056, c.1952
s. steel.. $300 $350 $400

ROLEX, 17J., mid size, RF#3478, c.1940
gold filled.................................. $200 $250 $300

ROLEX, 17J., mid size, RF#6066, c.1951
s. steel.. $300 $350 $400

ROLEX, 17J., mid size, RF#3478, c.1940
s. steel.. $200 $250 $300

ROLEX, 17J., mid size, RF#6466, c.1957
s. steel.. $300 $350 $400

ROLEX, 17J., mid size, RF#4220, c.1945
s. steel.. $300 $350 $400

ROLEX, 18J., mid size, aux. sec.
s. steel.. $400 $450 $500

ROLEX, 18J., mid size, center sec.
s. steel.. $400 $450 $500

ROLEX, 18J., B.B., not 2 tone
14k.. $2,500 $3,000 $3,500

ROLEX, 18J., B.B., hooded 2 tone yellow gold
G & steel $2,500 $2,800 $3,200

ROLEX, 18J., B.B., marked bezel,
s. steel.. $700 $900 $1,100

ROLEX, 18J., B.B., hooded 2 tone rose gold
G & steel $2,800 $3,200 $3,500

ROLEX, 18J., B.B., marked bezel,
18k... $3,500 $4,000 $4,500

ROLEX, 18J., B.B., center sec.
s. steel.. $600 $800 $1,000

ROLEX, 18J., B.B., chronometer, RF#3131, cal#600
s. steel.. $550 $750 $950

ROLEX, 18J., B.B., cal#600, aux. sec., ca. 1945
s. steel............................... $900 $1,000 $1,200

ROLEX, 17J., BB, RF#2940, B.B.,c.1945
s. steel...................................$700 $800 $900

ROLEX, 18J., B.B., self winding on dial
14k..$3,300 $3,500 $3,900

ROLEX, 17J., BB, RF#3131, B.B., c.1948
14k..$2,800 $3,000 $3,200

ROLEX, 17J., RF#1453, c.1944
14k..$2,500 $2,700 $3,000

ROLEX, 17J., BB, RF#3131, c.1948
14k..$2,500 $2,700 $3,000

ROLEX, 18J., RF#2940, B.B.,marked bezel, 2 tone
G & steel $1,000 $1,200 $1,400

ROLEX, 17J., BB, RF#3133, tu-tone, c.1940
14k &s.s..................................$1,000 $1,200 $1,400

ROLEX, 17J., BB, RF#3372, B.B., marked bezel, c.1954
s. steel.......................... $900 $1,000 $1,100

ROLEX, 17J., BB, RF#3372, B.B., tu-tone, c.1940
14k & s.s. $1,200 $1,300 $1,400

ROLEX, 17J., BB, RF#3725, ROSE GOLD case, c.1945
14k rose $3,000 $3,300 $3,500

ROLEX, 17J., RF#3725, B.B., marked bezel, c.1945
12k $3,200 $3,400 $3,600

ROLEX, 17J., RF#5015, marked bezel, c.1949
s. steel................................... $1,000 $1,100 $1,200

ROLEX, 18J., B.B., center sec. ca. 1940s
14k..$2,600 $2,800 $3,000

ROLEX, 19J., B.B.,ca. 1940s
14k.......................................$2,600 $2,800 $3,000

ROLEX, 26J., bubble back, graduated bezel , aux. sec.
14k..$3,000 $3,500 $4,000

ROLEX, 19 jewels, bubble back, 2 tone
18k & s. steel.........................$1,200 $1,400 $1,600

ROLEX, 26 J., bubble back, mercedes hands, c. 1930s

18k	$3,200	$3,400	$3,800
14k	$2,400	$2,600	$3,000
9k	$1,800	$1,900	$2,200
gold filled	$800	$850	$950
s. steel	$600	$700	$800

ROLEX, 26 jewels, bubble back, Arabic & Roman no.s
14k $3,000 $3,500 $4,000

ROLEX, 26J., bubble back, marked bezel, c. 1940s

18k	$3,500	$4,000	$4,500
14k	$3,000	$3,500	$4,000
9k	$2,000	$2,500	$3,000
gold filled	$900	$1,000	$1,200
s. steel	$700	$800	$900

ROLEX, 26 J., bubble back, aux. sec., c, 1940s

18k	$3,000	$3,500	$4,000
14k	$2,500	$3,000	$3,500
9k	$1,800	$2,000	$2,500
gold filled	$1,000	$1,100	$1,200
s. steel	$600	$700	$850

ROLEX, 26 jewels, bubble back, c. 1940s
14k...............................$2,500 $2,700 $3,000

ROLEX, 26 J., bubble back, mercedes hands, c. 1940s

18k	$3,000	$3,500	$4,000
14k	$2,500	$2,800	$3,000
9k	$1,800	$2,000	$2,200
gold filled	$800	$900	$1,000
s. steel	$700	$750	$850

ROLEX, 26 jewels, bubble back, 2 tone, c. 1940s
18k & s. steel $1,000 $1,100 $1,200

ROLEX, 26 jewels, bubble back, c. 1940s
s. steel...$600 $700 $800

ROLEX, 26 jewels, bubble back, c. 1940s
18k...$3,000 $3,300 $3,800
14k...$2,500 $2,800 $3,200
s. steel...$600 $700 $800

ROLEX, 19 jewels, bubble back, center sec., rf#1453
18k $3,200 $3,400 $3,800
s. steel...$700 $800 $900

ROLEX, 18 jewels, bubble back, c. 1940s
s. steel...$600 $700 $800

ROLEX, 26 jewels, bubble back
18k $3,200 $3,400 $3,800
s. steel...$600 $700 $850

ROLEX, 18 jewels, bubble back, c. 1942
18k...$3,000 $3,200 $3,500
14k...$2,500 $2,700 $3,000
s. steel...$700 $750 $850

ROLEX, 26 jewels, bubble back, c. 1945
14k $2,500 $2,800 $3,200

ROLEX, 18 jewels, bubble back, gold & s. steel band
14k & s. steel C&B..............$1,500 $1,700 $2,000

Rolex, 18 J., bubble back, date, winds at 9 o'clock
18k case & s. steel band $1,200 $1,400 $1,600

ROLEX, 26 jewels, "Presidential," (Tridor), oyster,
daydate, diamond dial, perpetual, oyster
18k (y & w) $8,000 $8,500 $9,000

ROLEX, 26 jewels, "Presidential," 44 diamonds on dial &
bezel, day-date, oyster, perpetual
18k C&B................................ $7,500 $8,500 $9,500

ROLEX, 26J., "Presidential," bark finish, RF#1803, c.1971
18k C&B $5,500 $6,000 $6,500

ROLEX, 26 jewels, day-date, 10 diamond dial, old model
RF#1803
18k C&B..............................$5,000 $5,500 $6,000
18k (w) $4,000 $4,500 $5,000

ROLEX, 26 jewels, "Presidential," day-date, perpetual,
oyster, diamond bezel
18k C&B $7,000 $7,500 $8,500

ROLEX, 26 jewels, "Presidential," diamond dial, day-date,
perpetual, oyster, RF#1804, quick set
18k C&B................................ $6,000 $6,500 $7,000

ROLEX, 26 Jewels, "Presidential," day-date, perpetual,
oyster, old model, RF#1803
18k C&B $4,000 $4,500 $5,000

ROLEX, 26 Jewels, "Presidential," day-date, perpetual,
oyster, sapphire crystal, new quick set model
18k C&B.............................. $5,500 $6,000 $6,500
old molel 18k........................ $4,000 $4,500 $5,000

ROLEX, 26 J., jubilee band, 10 diamond dial, date
18k C&B $4,500 $5,500 $6,500
14k C&B $3,500 $4,000 $5,000
gold & s. steel C&B............ $2,000 $2,500 $3,000

ROLEX, 26J., "Presidential," day-date, perpetual,
note textured dial, rose gold
18k C & B $4,000 $4,500 $5,000

ROLEX, 26 jewels, date, perpetual, oyster
18k...................................... $2,500 $2,700 $3,000
14k...................................... $1,600 $1,800 $2,200
s. steel $450 $550 $650

ROLEX, quartz,
diamond dial & diamond bezel add $1,000-$1,200
18k $4,000 $5,000 $6,000

ROLEX, 26J., quick set, c.1965
14k C&B $2,800 $3,000 $3,200

ROLEX, 21 jewels, date, center sec., c. 1965
18k.. $3,500 $4,000 $5,000

ROLEX, 26 jewels, date, oyster, mid-size
s. steel C&B $500 $600 $700

ROLEX, 26J., perpetual, oyster, date, graduated bezel
14k...$2,400 $2,600 $2,800
s. steel.....................................$600 $700 $850

ROLEX, 17J., RF#6694, c.1961
s. steel.. $300 $350 $400

ROLEX, 26 jewels, oyster, date, ref. #1625
14k & s. steel C&B..............$1,000 $1,200 $1,500

ROLEX, 17J., RF#6426, c.1961
s. steel.. $300 $350 $400

ROLEX, 21 J., "Thunderbird," perpetual, oyster, date just
18k..$3,500 $4,000 $4,500
s. steel.....................................$600 $700 $800

ROLEX, 26 jewels, perpetual, oyster, date just
18k $4,000 $4,500 $5,500
18k & s. steel......................... $1,400 $1,600 $2,000
14k $2,800 $3,200 $4,000
14k & s. steel......................... $1,200 $1,400 $1,600
s. steel....................................... $500 $600 $800

ROLEX, 21 jewels, perpetual, oyster date just, 2 tone
Gold & steel $1,200 $1,400 $1,600

ROLEX, 21 jewels, perpetual, oyster

18k	$1,800	$1,900	$2,000
18k & s. steel	$700	$800	$900
14k	$1,400	$1,500	$1,600
14k & s. steel	$600	$700	$800
s. steel	$300	$400	$500

ROLEX, 26 jewels, "GMT-Master," perpetual, oyster, date ruby & diamond dial

18k	$5,500	$6,500	$7,500

ROLEX, 26 jewels, perpetual, oyster

s. steel	$300	$400	$500

ROLEX, 26 J., "GMT-Master II," perp., oyster, date

18k	$5,000	$6,000	$7,000
s. steel	$700	$800	$900

ROLEX, 26 jewels, "Explorer," perpetual, oyster

s. steel	$800	$900	$1,000

ROLEX, 26 J., "Submariner," perpetual, oyster, date

18k C&B	$7,000	$8,000	$9,000
18k & s. steel C&B	$2,600	$2,800	$3,400
s. steel	$900	$1,000	$1,100

ROLEX, 17J., "Luminor Paneral," for military diving

s. steel	$1,500	$1,700	$2,000

ROLEX, 21 jewels, "Sea-Dweller," up to 4,000 ft., date
s. steel...................................... $1,200 $1,400 $1,700

ROLEX, 21 jewels, "Explorer II," date
s. steel.................................... $1,000 $1,200 $1,500

ROLEX, 26 jewels, "Submariner,"   crown guard, 200M
s. steel...................................... $800 $900 $1,000

ROLEX, 26J., "Submariner", early model,100M,c.1958
s. steel...................................... $500 $600 $800

ROLEX, 15J., ca. 1935
s. steel...................................... $500 $600 $700

ROLEX,18J., hooded lugs
14k.. $1,000 $1,200 $1,400

ROLEX, 18J., stepped case, 2 tone, ca. 1940s
G & steel............................... $1,000 $1,200 $1,400

ROLEX, 15J., ca. 1937
s. steel...$500 $600 $700

ROLEX, 18J., rf#2537,adj.6 pos. 2 tone,ca. 1940s
G & steel $2,000 $2,500 $3,000

ROLEX,15J., stepped case, c.1938
18k $1,500 $1,700 $2,000

ROLEX, 17J., center lug "Standard", c.1940
14k & s.s. $1,000 $1,200 $1,400

ROLEX, 17J., "Standard", c.1940
gold filled $200 $250 $300

ROLEX, 15J., beveled case, c.1927
s. steel...$400 $450 $500

ROLEX, 17J., hidden lugs,
14k..................................$1,200 $1,400 $1,600

ROLEX, 17J., "31 Victories",
18k...$1,000 $1,100 $1,200

ROLEX, 18J., rf#3737,
18k..$800 $900 $1,000

ROLEX, 18J., 3 diamond dial , ca. 1940s
18kC&B $1,500 $1,800 $2,000

ROLEX, 18J., ca. 1940s
s. steel $400 $500 $600

ROLEX, 18J., round movement, ca. 1947
18k $800 $900 $1,000

ROLEX, 17 jewels, hooded lugs, 2 tone
rose & white gold $3,000 $4,000 $5,000

ROLEX, 17 jewels, "Precision"
18k $900 $1,000 $1,200

ROLEX, 17 jewels, curvex
18k C&B $3,000 $4,000 $5,000

ROLEX, 17 jewels, "Standard," c. 1939
14k $2,000 $2,500 $3,000

ROLEX, 17 jewels, curved, c. 1940s
gold filled $400 $450 $500

ROLEX, 17 jewels, "Benvenuto Cellini," thin model
18k $1,000 $1,100 $1,200

ROLEX, 17 jewels, "Ultra Prima," gold train
18k $1,800 $2,000 $2,400

ROLEX, 21 jewels, perpetual, oyster, c. 1945
18k $3,000 $3,500 $4,000

ROLEX, 17 jewels, "Precision," c. 1940s
18k $1,200 $1,400 $1,600
14k $1,000 $1,200 $1,400

ROLEX, 17 J. , "Precision," tank style, faceted bezel
18k $1,200 $1,400 $1,600

ROLEX, 17 jewels, extra flat, c. 1950s
18k $1,000 $1,100 $1,200

ROLEX, 21 jewels, "Cellini"
18k $900 $1,000 $1,200

ROLEX, 21 jewels, "Cellini"
18k $1,000 $1,100 $1,300

ROLEX, 21 jewels, "Cellini"
18k C&B $1,500 $1,800 $2,200

ROLEX, 21 jewels, "Cellini," diamond bezel
18k C&B $2,500 $2,800 $3,200

ROLEX, 17J., "Cellini", RF#4017, c.1988
18k..$1,500 $1,700 $2,000

ROLEX, 21 jewels, "Benvenuto Cellini," diamonds on
bezel & band
18k............................$12,000 $14,000 $16,000

ROLEX, quartz, "Tudor," (Prince)
s. steel $150 $175 $200

ROLEX, quartz, "Tudor," chronog., date
s. steel.. $800 $1,000 $1,200

ROLEX, quartz, "Tudor," date, 2 tone
18k & s. steel........................... $250 $300 $400

ROLEX, 15J., ladies, c.1930s
9k $200 $250 $300

ROLEX, 17J., ladies, 'Oyster",
14k $1,000 $1,200 $1,400

ROLEX, 29J., ladies, 'Oyster", RF#67003
s. steel &14k,C&B $1,000 $1,100 $1,200

ROLEX, 17J., ladies, 'Oyster", RF#4486, c.1957
14k & s.s.case $400 $500 $600

ROLEX, 17J., ladies, 'Oyster", c.1948
18k.. $1,500 $1,700 $2,000

ROLEX, 17J., ladies,"Centregraph,
14k................................... $1,000 $1,100 $1,200

ROLEX, 17J., ladies, 'Oyster", RF#3492
s. steel..................................... $300 $350 $400

ROLEX, 17J., ladies, RF#4593, c.1954
s. steel..................................... $250 $300 $350

ROLEX, 15J., 54 diamonds, 9k band 18k(w) case, c.1930
9k & 18k................................ $1,200 $1,400 $1,600

ROLEX, 17J., ladies, c.1945
gold filled $50 $60 $85

ROLEX, 18J., lady's,
14k $200 $250 $300

ROLEX, 15J., lady's, curved, ca.1925
9k $200 $250 $300

ROLEX, 18J., lady's, ca. 1948
18k $300 $350 $400
14k $150 $200 $250

ROLEX, 15J., lady's, center lugs, ca.1925
9k $200 $250 $300

ROLEX, 18J., lady's,
14k(W) C&B $400 $500 $600

ROLEX, 18J., lady's, ca. 1930s
18k $400 $500 $600

ROLEX, 18J., lady's, bubble back
18k $1,500 $1,700 $2,000

ROLEX, 18J., wire lugs, diamond bezel, ca. 1940s
18k(W) $500 $600 $700

ROLEX, 18J., lady's, large lugs,
18k $400 $500 $600

ROLEX PERPETUAL WATCHES
OF Caliber Numbers
1030, 1035, 1036
1040, 1055, 1065

ROLEX
MOVEMENT IDENTIFICATION

Ref. 90   Ref. 100   Ref. 150   Ref. 160   Ref. 161

(All without seconds)

Ref. 170
without seconds

Ref. 180
without seconds

Ref. 200
without seconds

Ref. 210
sweep seconds

Ref. 250
without seconds

Ref. 270
without seconds

Ref. 300
ordinary seconds

Ref. 310
sweep second

Ref. 350
jump hour

Ref. 360
ordinary second

Ref. 400
ordinary seconds

Ref. 420
ordinary seconds

Ref. 420
rotor

Ref. 500
ordinary seconds

Ref. 510
sweep second

Ref. 520
sweep second

Ref. 520
rotor

Ref. 530
self wind, sweep sec.

Ref. 600
ordinary seconds

Ref. 620
ordinary seconds

Ref. 620
rotor

Ref. 630
self wind, sweep sec.

Ref. 700
ordinary seconds

Ref. 710
sweep seconds

Ref. 720
ordinary seconds

Ref. 720
rotor

Ref. 730
self wind, sweep sec.

Ref. 740
self wind, calendar, sweep sec.

Ref.800
ordinary seconds

Ref. 850
ordinary seconds

Ref. 72
chronograph, 3 registers

Ref. 23
chronograph, 2 registers

Above: Oyster style bracelet. **Below:** Presidential style band with hidden clasp. **Right:** Jubilee style bracelet.

ROLLS, 15J., early auto wind, by Leon Hatot, movement inside case moves back & forth to wind, c. 1920s
s. steel.................................... $600 $700 $900

ROLLS, 15 jewels, early auto wind, c. 1920s
s. steel.. $700 $800 $1,000

ROLLS, 15 jewels, "ATO," flip top
s. steel.. $600 $700 $900

ROLLS, 15 jewels, ladies, "ATO," flip top, by Blancpain
18k... $800 $900 $1,000

ROXY, 8 day, engraved case, ca. 1930s
s. steel.. $200 $250 $300

RULON, ca. 1940s
gold filled.................................... $60 $70 $80

RULON, 17J., 3 diamonds on dial
gold plate...................................$100 $125 $150

SCHULTZ, 17J., diamond dial, c.1930
platinum $1,800 $2,000 $2,200

J. SCHULTZ, 17J., enamel hunter style, ca. 1949
18k...$1,500 $1,800 $2,000

SEELAND, 17J., aux. sec., diamond dial,
14k..$90 $120 $165

SEELAND, 7J., ca. 1950s
gold filled....................................$50 $60 $70

SEIKO, quartz, rope style bezel
14k $175 $200 $225

SEMCA, 17 J. day-date-month, moon phase, c. 1950s
18k $1,000 $1,300 $1,400

SEMCA, 17J., day-date-month, moon phase, c. 1950s
14k $300 $400 $600

SETH THOMAS, day date, moon phases, ca. 1949
s. steel $200 $250 $300

SHEFFIELD, 17J., chronog., by Venus, cal. 189
s. steel $50 $60 $75

SIMGA, 17J., textured dial, c. 1940
18k $200 $250 $300

SPERINA, 7 jewels, day & date on lugs
s. steel $60 $70 $80

SONDOZ, 17J., center sec.
14k $100 $120 $140

STANDARD, 17J., 24 hr. dial, world time, c.1965
s. steel.............................. $70 $80 $95

SUIZO, 17J., one button chronog. ca. 1930s
gold filled................................ $200 $250 $300

SWATCH (see listings at the end of wrist watch section)

TAVANNES, 15J., enamel dial, flip top, c.1915
silver $150 $200 $250

TAVANNES, 17J., chronog., c.1940
s. steel..................................... $125 $150 $175

TAVANNES, 17J., extended lugs, c.1955
gold filled.................................. $50 $60 $75

TAVANNES, 17J., aux. sec., c.1935
14k.. $125 $150 $175

TAVANNES, 17J., GJS, cal.365k, c.1938
14k.. $125 $150 $175

TAVANNES, 17 jewels, hour glass dial, curved
14k.. $200 $250 $300

TAVANNES, 15 jewels, "334," c. 1939
14k (w)....................................... $200 $250 $300

TAVANNES, 17 jewels, aux. sec. ca. 1940s
s. steel...$80 $100 $125

TAVANNES, 17 jewels, aux. sec.
14k $225 $250 $275

TECHNOS, 17J., "Sky Diver", auto-wind, 500m., c.1970
s. steel...$40 $50 $65

TELDA, 17J., chronog.,3 reg, date, moon ph., c.1980s
s. steel...$200 $250 $300

TELDA, 17J., center sec., c.1948
gold filled....................................$50 $60 $75

TEVO, 17J., hidden lugs
14k..$100 $125 $150

NOTE: ☞ Examples of Tiffany made up watches are
listed but were not sold by Tiffany & Co.. These off-brand
watches will be listed but not priced as true Tiffany & Co.
watches. EXAMPLES: Kingston, Emerson, Banner, ETC.

TIFFANY & CO.,17J., wire lugs, c.1920
silver...$400 $500 $600

TIFFANY & CO., 18J., by P.P.& CO., CA. 1920s
18K..$4,000 $5,000 $6,000

TIFFANY & CO., 17J., curved, mvt. by P.P. & Co., c. 1910
18k $6,000 $8,000 $9,000

TIFFANY & CO.,17J., by P.P. & C., wire lugs, c.1915
18k $3,500 $4,000 $4,500

TIFFANY & CO.,17J., by Banner"?", c.1926
18k $300 $400 $500

TIFFANY & CO.,17J., by I.W.C., wire lugs, c.1918
14k...........................$700 $800 $900

TIFFANY & CO.,17J., by Wheeler "?", c.1930
14k $150 $175 $200

TIFFANY & CO., 15J., enamel dial, ca. 1930s
silver...........................$500 $550 $600

TIFFANY & CO., 26Jewels, min. repeater, slide repeat, automaton, 40mm
18k $8,000 $10,000 $12,000

TIFFANY & CO., 18J., by P.P.& CO., CA.1930S
platinum $5,000 $6,000 $7,000

TIFFANY & CO., 15J., wire lugs, ca. 1928
silver $300 $350 $400

TIFFANY & CO., 15 jewels, c. 1926
18k...........................$1,200 $1,400 $1,600

TIFFANY & CO.,17J., by Longines, c.1928
14k $500 $600 $700

TIFFANY & CO.,17J., by Charlin w. Co. "?", GJS, c.1940
14k................................$150 $175 $200

TIFFANY & CO.,17J., aux. sec., c.1926
18k(w) $1,000 $1,100 $1,200

TIFFANY & CO.,17J., by Emerson "?", c.1940
14k................................$100 $125 $150

TIFFANY & CO.,17J., by Fidea "?", c.1930
14k $100 $150 $200

TIFFANY & CO.,17J., by Hampden "?", c.1949
14k................................$100 $135 $175

TIFFANY & CO.,17J., GJS, by Mavado, c.1940
14k $600 $700 $800

TIFFANY & CO.,17J., by I.W.C., c.1942
14k................................$500 $600 $700

TIFFANY & CO.,17J., by Kingston "?", hidden lugs,
c.1943
14k $150 $200 $250

TIFFANY & CO.,17J., by I.W.C., hidden lugs, c.1942
14k................................$500 $600 $700

TIFFANY & CO., 17J., top hat, by I. W. CO.
14K $1,000 $1,200 $1,400

TIFFANY & CO.,15J., one button chronog., by Goering,
V-69 mvt., c.1925
silver $1,000 $1,200 $1,400

TIFFANY & CO.,17J., Valjoux cal.72c., c.1948
gold filled.............................. $1,200 $1,400 $1,600

TIFFANY & CO.,17J., by Mavado, c.1947
14k $2,500 $2,700 $3,000

TIFFANY & CO.,17J., by Bovet"?", c.1940
18k.................................... $600 $700 $800

TIFFANY & CO.,17J., by Tourneau , Valjoux 72c, c.1950
s. steel $600 $700 $800

TIFFANY & CO., 31J., chronog., triple date, moon ph.
screwback, note window for date at 4 & 5
18k.. $2,500 $2,700 $3,000

TIFFANY & CO., 17J., chronog, day-date-month
14k $1,800 $2,000 $2,200

TIFFANY & CO., 21J.s, mvt. by P.P. & Co., c. 1950
18k $800 $900 $1,000

TIFFANY & CO., 17J., curved , ca.1920s
platinum................................... $1,000 $1,200 $1,500

TIFFANY & CO.,15J., engraved bezel, c.1919
18k $1,500 $1,700 $2,000

TIFFANY & CO., 15J., ca. 1920s
14k..$500 $600 $700

TIFFANY & CO.,17J., by Hampden "?", c.1945
14k..$150 $175 $200

TIFFANY & CO.,17J., by Ollendorf "?", c.1945
14k..$200 $250 $300

TIFFANY & CO.,17J., by Crawford "?", c.1947
14k..$150 $175 $200

TIFFANY & CO.,17J., by Tissot, c.1948
14k..$300 $350 $400

TIFFANY & CO., 17J., by Zodiac "?", c.1942
14k $150 $175 $200

TIFFANY & CO.,17J., by Glycine "?", c.1945
14k $150 $200 $250

TIFFANY & CO.,17J., extended bezel, c.1942
14k $400 $500 $600

TIFFANY & CO.,17J., by Wyler "?", c.1950
gold filled $100 $125 $150

TIFFANY & CO., 17J., fancy lugs & bezel, ca.1950s
14k $300 $400 $500

TIFFANY & CO., 17J., applied numbers, ca. 1950s
14k $400 $500 $600

TIFFANY & CO., 17J., flared & stepped, ca.1950s
14k $300 $400 $500

TIFFANY & CO., 17 jewels, c. 1935
18k $1,200 $1,400 $1,600

TIFFANY & CO., 17 jewels, fancy bezel, c. 1942
14k $500 $600 $700

TIFFANY & CO., 17 jewels, sculptured lugs, c. 1948
14k $800 $900 $1,000

TIFFANY & CO.,17J., 3 diamond dial, by Lathin "?",
14k(w) 200 $225 $250

TIFFANY & CO.,17J.,by Tissot,triple date moon ph.,
14k..$800 $900 $1,000

TIFFANY & CO.,15J., rhinestones "?", c.1948
base metal.....................................$40 $50 $75

TIFFANY & CO., 17J., triple date, moon ph.
s. steel..$400 $450 $500

TIFFANY & CO., 17J., "Movado", triple date, center sec.
s. steel...$300 $350 $400

TIFFANY & CO.,17J., by Ardath "?", auto-wind, c.1950
14k...100 $125 $150

TIFFANY & CO.,17J., by Mavado, triple date, c.1948
14k & s.s. $500 $600 $700

TIFFANY & CO.,17J., by Nicolet "?", c.1955
gold filled..........................$65 $75 $100

TIFFANY & CO.,17J., by Helvetia , c.1948
14k $200 $250 $300

TIFFANY & CO.,17J., c.1948
18k $500 $600 $700

TIFFANY & CO.,17J., "?", c.1940
gold filled $75 $100 $125

TIFFANY & CO.,17J., carved lugs, c.1950
18k $300 $350 $400

TIFFANY & CO.,17J., byMepa "?", GJS, c.1949
14k $65 $75 $100

TIFFANY & CO.,17J., ladies, by Longines, c.1920
18k $250 $300 $350

TIFFANY & CO.,17J., by I.W.C., c.1948
18k $300 $400 $500

TIFFANY & CO.,17J., by Zenith, c.1939
14k $200 $250 $300

TIFFANY & CO.,17J., I.W.C., c.1955
18k $200 $250 $300

TIFFANY & CO., 15J., 2 tone , ladies, ca. 1939
18k C&B.................................... $400 $450 $500

TIFFANY & CO., 15J., early ladies, wire lugs ca.1925
14k $400 $450 $500

TIMECRAFT, 17 jewels, c. 1950
s. steel.. $125 $150 $175

TIMEX,stop watch, slide to start, stop & return to zero
base metal................................... $50 $60 $70

TISSOT, 21 jewels, world time, 24 hr. dial, 24 cities
18k $2,500 $3,000 $3,500

TISSOT,17J., world time 24 cities, c.1948
s. steel.. $700 $800 $900

TISSOT, 17 jewels, 1898 USA 20 dollar gold piece
24k.. $1,000 $1,500 $2,000

TISSOT, 21J, world time, 24 hr. dial, 24 cities, mid-size
18k.. $2,500 $3,000 $3,500

TISSOT,17J., military, chronog., Valguox cal.225, c.1955
s. steel.. $250 $300 $350

TISSOT, 17J., Valjoux cal. 726, c.1965
14k $500 $600 $700

TISSOT, 17 jewels, chronog., 3 reg.,
s. steel $250 $300 $350

TISSOT, 17J., auto-wind, "navigator, date, c.1972
s. steel $100 $125 $150

TISSOT, 17 jewels, chronog., 3 reg., c. 1940s
14k $1,000 $1,200 $1,400

TISSOT, 17 jewels, chronog., 3 reg., c. 1956
s. steel $400 $450 $500

TISSOT, 17 jewels, chronog., triple date, moon phase
14k $2,000 $2,200 $2,600

TISSOT, 17 jewels, chronog., 3 reg.,
s. steel $300 $350 $400

TISSOT, 17J., day-date-month, moon phase, ctr. sec.
18k $1,000 $1,200 $1,500

TISSOT,17J., "UHF", date, auto-wind, c.1960
14k $200 $250 $300

TISSOT, 17 jewels, auto wind, aux. sec.
s. steel $60 $70 $85

TISSOT,17J., aux. sec., c.1951
18k $300 $350 $400

TITUS, 17 jewels, chronog., 2 reg.
18k $300 $450 $500
14k $200 $300 $400
s. steel $100 $150 $200

TISSOT,17J., hidden lugs, c.1950
14k $400 $450 $500

TISSOT,17J., aux. sec., c.1942
18k $200 $250 $300

TORNEX-RAYVILLE,17J., military, "SEAL", water-p.
s. steel $100 $150 $200

TISSOT, 17 jewels, large lugs,
14k $250 $300 $350

TOUCHON,17J., tonneau case, c.1928
18k(w) $300 $350 $400

TOUCHON, 17J., jump hr., wandering min., c. 1930s
18k $6,000 $7,000 $8,000

TOURNEAU,17J, triple date, 3 reg., moon ph., c. 1952
s. steel.......................... $600 $700 $800

TOURNEAU,17J.,chronog. by Valjoux cal.886, c.1965
18k $2,500 $2,700 $3,000

TOURNEAU,17J., day date , c.1945
s. steel.......................... $250 $300 $350

TOURNEAU,17J., beveled lugs, c.1945
14k.............................$150 $200 $250

TREBEX, 15 jewels, cut corner dial, c. 1940
gold filled....................................$40 $50 $60

TREBEX, 15 jewels, c. 1940
gold filled....................................$50 $60 $70

TREBEX, 15 jewels, c. 1940s
gold filled....................................$30 $40 $50

TREMONT, 17J., master built, fancy lugs, ca.1945
gold filled....................................$60 $70 $80

TURLER, 17 jewels, chronog., triple date, 3 reg.
18k $700 $800 $900

URANIA, 15 jewels, military style grill, c. 1915
silver.. $200 $300 $400

UHRENFABRIK GLASHUTTE, 17J., chronog., c. 1940s
s .steel.. $400 $500 $600

UNIVER, 17J., triple date , moon ph., chronog.
14k.. $1,000 $1,200 $1,400

ULTIMOR, 17J., chronog., cal.51c.1945
18k $250 $300 $350

UNIVERSAL,17J.,"medico compax", c.1949
18k..$800 $900 $1,000

UNITAS, 17 jewels, triple date, moon phase, c. 1948
s. steel.. $250 $300 $375

UNIVERSAL,17J., "uni compax", c.1942
s. steel..$300 $350 $400

UNIVERSAL, 17J., chronog., triple date, moon phase
14k $2,000 $2,200 $2,400

UNIVERSAL, 17J., chronog., aero compax, diff. meridian
14k $1,800 $2,000 $2,400

UNIVERSAL, 17J. chronog., tri-compax, day date
s. steel $1,000 $1,100 $1,200

UNIVERSAL, 17 jewels, chronog., M. #281, c. 1950s
18k $2,200 $2,500 $2,800

UNIVERSAL, 17J. chronog., tri-compax, moon phase
18k $2,400 $2,600 $2,900

UNIVERSAL, 17 jewels, chronog., aero compax, 4 reg.
18k $2,200 $2,600 $3,200

UNIVERSAL, 17J., tri compax, day date moon ph., c.1955
gold filled $1,200 $1,400 $1,600

UNIVERSAL, 17J., chronog., compax, massive case
18k $2,500 $2,700 $3,000

UNIVERSAL, 17J., chronog, dato-compax, c. 1950s
14k $1,500 $1,800 $2,000
s. steel.. $500 $600 $700

UNIVERSAL,17J., compax, RF#885107, Valj.cal.72,c.1965
s. steel.. $800 $900 $1,000

UNIVERSAL, 17J. chronog, 10 ligne size,uni-compax
s. steel.................................... $1,000 $1,200 $1,400

UNIVERSAL, 17 jewels, c. 1952
14k $125 $150 $175

UNIVERSAL, 17 jewels, day-date-month
14k................................$400 $500 $600

UNIVERSAL,17J., "Polerouter Sub", date, auto-w., c.1960
s. steel.. $200 $250 $300

UNIVERSAL,17J.,"Polerouter Sub",rotating bezel, c.1980s
s. steel.. $100 $125 $150

UNIVERSAl, 17 jewels, "Polerouter", auto wind, day date
18k..$500 $600 $700

UNIVERSAL, 28J., center sec., date, c.1958
18k $400 $450 $500

UNIVERSAL, 17J., m#264, large lugs, c.1957
gold filled.................................... $100 $125 $150

UNIVERSAL, 17J., cal.52, date, c.1965
18k $200 $250 $300

UNIVERSAL, 17J., cal.267g, date, center sec. c.1948
18k... $400 $450 $500

UNIVERSAL, 17J., cal. 138c, date, c.1952
18k $300 $350 $400

UNIVERSAL, 16J., cal#230,ca. 1940s
s. steel $150 $200 $250

UNIVERSAL, 17J., aux. sec. tank style,ca. 1948
14k... $400 $450 $500

UNIVERSAL, 17 jewels, day-date-month, moon phase
18k $1,000 $1,200 $1,400

UNIVERSAL, 17J., fancy lugs
14k... $350 $400 $450

UNIVERSAL, 17 jewels, "Cabriolet," reverso, c. 1930s
s. steel...................................... $3,000 $3,500 $4,000

UNIVERSAL, 17J., aux. sec., , c.1955
s. steel...................................$100 $125 $150

UNIVERSAL,17J., center sec., cal.263, c.1950
18k $300 $350 $400

UNIVERSAL, 17 jewels, auto wind, c. 1955
gold filled.....................................$100 $120 $140

UNIVERSAL,17J., center sec., cal.138, c.1950
s. steel... $50 $75 $100

UNIVERSAL, quartz, day-date, center sec., c. 1960s
18k...$400 $500 $600

UNIVERSAL,17J., center sec., cal.236, c.1955
18k $200 $225 $250

UNIVERSAL, quartz, , c.1981
18k..$300 $350 $400

UNIVERSAL, 17 jewels, auto wind
gold filled.......................................$80 $90 $100

VACHERON, 36J., skeletonized, triple date, moon phase, leap year, gold rotor
18k $13,000 $14,000 $15,000

VACHERON, 17J., triple date, moon phase, c. 1950s
18k... $5,000 $5,500 $6,000

VACHERON, 36J., diamond bezel, triple date, moon ph., leap year, gold rotor
18k C&B............................. $10,000 $11,000 $12,000

VACHERON, 17J., triple date, fancy lugs, moon ph., c. 1940s
18k... $8,000 $9,000 $10,000

VACHERON, 17J., triple date, moon phase, c. 1947
18k $14,000 $16,000 $18,000

VACHERON, 17J., triple date, fancy lugs, c. 1940s
18k... $2,500 $3,000 $3,500

VACHERON, 17J., triple date, moon phase, c. 1945
18k $8,000 $9,000 $10,000

VACHERON, 17 jewels, day-date-month, c. 1940s
18k... $2,000 $2,500 $3,000

VACHERON, 29 jewels, gold rotor, date
18k $1,800 $2,200 $2,600

VACHERON, 29 jewels, center sec., auto wind, date
18k $2,000 $2,200 $2,500

VACHERON, 29 jewels, waterproof, auto-w, c. 1960s
18k $2,000 $2,200 $2,500

VACHERON, 33J., auto-wind 21k rotor cal.1124 , c.1980s
18k & s.s. $1,200 $1,400 $1,600

VACHERON, 29 jewels, auto wind, c. 1960s
18k $1,800 $2,000 $2,200

VACHERON,17J., enamel dial,1 button chronog.,c. 1910s
18k $25,000 $30,000 $35,000

VACHERON, 36 jewels, gold rotor, date
18k $1,600 $1,800 $2,000

VACHERON, 17 jewels, chronog., 2 reg.
18k $8,000 $9,000 $10,000

VACHERON, 19 jewels, chronog, 2 reg, c. 1950s
18k C&B.............................. $8,000 $9,000 $10,000

VACHERON, 17 jewels, chronog., 2 reg., c. 1945
18k $8,000 $9,000 $10,000

VACHERON, 29J., min. repeater, slide repeat, c. 1950
18k $70,000 $80,000 $90,000

VACHERON, 17 jewels, mystery dial with diamonds
18k C&B.............................. $1,200 $1,400 $1,600

VACHERON, 17 jewels, skeletonized
18k..$3,000 $3,500 $4,000

VACHERON, 17 jewels, skeletonized, c. 1960s
18k..$3,000 $3,500 $4,000

VACHERON, 17 jewels, textured bezel
18k..$1,000 $1,100 $1,200

VACHERON, 18 jewels, center sec., c. 1940s
18k..$1,200 $1,400 $1,600

VACHERON, 18J., fancy graduated bezel, c. 1950s
18k..$4,000 $5,000 $6,000

VACHERON, 18 jewels, auto wind, center sec.
18k $1,500 $1,800 $2,200

VACHERON, 18 J., center sec., waterproof, c. 1950s
18k $1,200 $1,400 $1,600

VACHERON, 18 jewels, center sec.
18k $1,000 $1,300 $1,400

VACHERON, 21J., auto wind, gold rotor, center sec.
18k $1,500 $1,700 $2,000

VACHERON, 18 jewels, center sec.
18k $1,200 $1,400 $1,600

VACHERON, 18J., diamond set case, skeletonized
18k(W) $5,000 $5,500 $6,000

VACHERON, 18 jewels, center sec.
14k $1,000 $1,100 $1,200

VACHERON, 29J., min. slide repeater, diamond dial
platinum $80,000 $90,000 $100,000

VACHERON, 29J., min. slide repeater, ca. 1950s
18k $60,000 $70,000 $80,000

VACHERON, 18J., skeletonized, diamond bezel
18k $3,000 $3,500 $4,000

VACHERON, 16J., barrel shaped silver dial, ca. 1916
18k $3,000 $3,500 $4,000

VACHERON, 16J., wire lugs, silver dial, ca.1917
14k $3,000 $3,500 $4,000

VACHERON, 18J., tonneau shaped, ca. 1930s
18k $2,500 $3,000 $3,500

VACHERON, 15J., early chronog.,2 reg.,one button,
ca. 1921, large in size
18k $18,000 $20,000 $22,000

VACHERON, 18J., chronog. 2 reg., ca.1942
s. steel $5,000 $6,000 $7,000

VACHERON, 15J., shutters with center slide to view dial ,
2 tone case, ca. 1933
18k $12,000 $14,000 $16,000

VACHERON, 18J., heavy case,ca.1930s
18k(W) $2,500 $3,000 $3,500

VACHERON, 18J., silver dial, ca.1941
18k $2,000 $2,500 $3,000

VACHERON, 18J., applied numbers, ca.1940
18k $2,000 $2,200 $2,400

VACHERON, 18J., off set lugs,
18k.. $2,000 $2,200 $2,500

VACHERON, 18J., black dial, aux sec.,ca.1937
18k.. $2,200 $2,400 $2,600

VACHERON, 18J., aux .sec.,
s. steel $1,200 $1,400 $1,600

VACHERON, 18J., silver dial, ca.1942
18k $2,000 $2,500 $3,000

VACHERON, 18J., textured dial, large lugs, ca.1951
18k.. $3,500 $4,000 $4,500

VACHERON, 18J., hidden lugs, ca.1940s
18k $2,200 $2,400 $2,800

VACHERON, 18J., fancy lugs,ca.1938
18k.. $2,000 $2,200 $2,500

VACHERON, 18J., off set lugs,
18k $2,000 $2,200 $2,500

VACHERON, 18J., textured bezel,ca.1950s
18k..$2,000 $2,200 $2,500

VACHERON,15J., curvex,wire lugs,33mm long,ca.1923
18k $2,500 $2,700 $3,000

VACHERON, 15J., hinged back, ca. 1930
18k $2,500 $2,700 $3,000

VACHERON, 18J., large 2 tone mans watch, ca.1928
18k $5,000 $6,000 $7,000

VACHERON, 18J.,long curved case, ca.1929
platinum................................. $4,000 $4,500 $5,000

VACHERON, 18J., ca. 1926
18k $2,000 $2,200 $2,500

VACHERON, 18J., ca. 1950s
18k...$1,200 $1,400 $1,600

VACHERON, 15J., early movement, ca.1925
18k...$1,500 $2,000 $2,500

VACHERON, 15J.,2 tone case, ca. 1926
18k..$1,600 $2,000 $2,600

VACHERON, 18J., tank style, ca.1960s
18k..$900 $1,000 $1,100

VACHERON, 18J., no sec. hand,
18k...$900 $1,000 $1,100

VACHERON,17J., RF#6099, cal.1003, c.1960
18k $900 $1,000 $1,100

VACHERON,17J., aux. sec, RF#4073, c.1942
s. steel $600 $700 $800

VACHERON,17J., RF#6335,wide bezel, c.1962
18k $1,000 $1,100 $1,200

VACHERON,17J., aux. sec, tear drop lugs, c.1945
18k........................... $1,200 $1,300 $1,400

VACHERON,17J., diamond bezel, aux. sec., long lugs
18k $2,000 $2,200 $2,500

VACHERON,17J., aux. sec, fluted lugs, c.1950s
18k........................... $1,200 $1,300   #1,400

VACHERON,17J., aux. sec, c.1945
18k $1,100 $1,200 $1,300

VACHERON, 18J.,aux. sec. fancy lugs,ca. 1944
18k..........................$1,400 $1,600 $1,800

VACHERON, 18J., aux. sec.
18k $1,300 $1,500 $1,700

VACHERON, 18J., aux. sec.
18k(W) $800 $900 $1,000

VACHERON, 18J.,fancy lugs
18k $1,400 $1,600 $1,800

VACHERON, 18J., center sec.,fancy lugs, ca.1942
18k..................................$1,000 $1,100 $1,200

VACHERON, 18J., cal#p453/3b,aux.sec.
18k $1,800 $2,000 $2,200

VACHERON, 18J., aux. sec. ca.1951
18k................................$900 $1,000 $1,100

VACHERON, 18J., aux. sec.,
s. steel.. $500 $600 $700

VACHERON, 18J., winds at 12, ca. 1928
18k...$3,000 $3,500 $4,000

VACHERON, 15J., champagne dial, long lugs, ca.1935
18k $1,000 $1,100 $1,200

VACHERON,17J., center sec, c.1940
s. steel $500 $600 $700

VACHERON, 18J., center sec., ca.1940s
18k $1,200 $1,300 $1,400

VACHERON,17J., center sec, large lugs, c.1949
18k... $2,200 $2,400 $2,600

VACHERON, 18J., center sec. ca.1953
18k $1,100 $1,200 $1,300

VACHERON,17J., center sec, c.1940
s. steel $500 $600 $700

VACHERON, 18J., textured dial center sec.
18k $1,000 $1,100 $1,200

VACHERON,17J., center sec, c.1940
18k... $1,200 $1,300 $1,400

VACHERON, 18J., center sec.
s. steel.. $500 $600 $700

VACHERON, 18J., fancy large lugs, center sec. ca.1953
18k...$1,800 $2,000 $2,200

VACHERON, 18J., center sec.
18k $800 $900 $1,000

VACHERON, 18J., rf#4730, fancy lugs, ca. 1950s
18k...$1,200 $1,400 $1,600

VACHERON, 18J.,textured dial, center sec.,ca.1947
18k $2,000 $2,200 $2,400

VACHERON, 18J.,textured dial, fancy lugs
18k...$1,200 $1,400 $1,600

VACHERON, 18J., rf#4824, ca.1950s
18k(W)...................................... $800 $900 $1,000

VACHERON, 18J., center sec., ca.1944
14k..$1,000 $1,100 $1,200

VACHERON, 18J., royal chronometer, ca.1950s
18k $1,200 $1,400 $1,600

VACHERON, 17J., center sec.auto-w., ca.1945
18k $1,100 $1,200 $1,300

VACHERON, 21 J., date, auto-w. ca. 1980s
s. steel.. $800 $900 $1,000

VACHERON, 15J., lady's with wire lugs,ca.1920
18k(W).. $400 $500 $600

VACHERON, 15 J., lady's, wire lugs, ca.1919
18k.. $400 $500 $600

VACHERON, 29J., center sec., auto wind, c. 1950s
18k.. $1,800 $2,000 $2,200

VACHERON, 29 jewels, center sec., auto wind, c. 1949
18k.. $1,800 $2,000 $2,200

VACHERON, 29 jewels, textured dial, c. 1948
18k.. $1,800 $2,000 $2,200

VACHERON, 29 jewels, 2 tone dial, center sec.
18k $1,200 $1,400 $1,600

VACHERON, 29 jewels, center sec., center lugs, c. 1950s
18k $1,400 $1,600 $1,800

VACHERON, 29 jewels, center sec.
18k $1,000 $1,100 $1,200

VACHERON, 17 jewels, aux. sec., fancy lugs
18k $1,400 $1,600 $1,800

VACHERON, 17 jewels, aux. sec., fancy lugs
18k $1,000 $1,200 $1,400

VACHERON, 17 jewels, aux. sec., stepped lugs
18k $1,000 $1,200 $1,400

VACHERON, 17 jewels, 2 tone dial, aux. sec.
18k $1,200 $1,400 $1,600

VACHERON, 17 jewels, aux. sec.
18k $1,200 $1,400 $1,600

VACHERON, 17 jewels, aux. sec.
s. steel $500 $600 $700

VACHERON, 17 jewels, aux. sec.
14k C&B...............................$1,000 $1,200 $1,400

VACHERON, 17 jewels, aux. sec.
18k...$1,000 $1,200 $1,300

VACHERON, 17 jewels, aux. sec., c. 1940s
18k.......................................$1,200 $1,300 $1,400

VACHERON, 17 jewels, aux. sec., c. 1940s
18k...$1,200 $1,400 $1,600

VACHERON, 17 jewels, aux. sec., c. 1940s
18k...$1,200 $1,300 $1,400

VACHERON, 17 jewels, aux. sec.
18k...$1,000 $1,100 $1,200

VACHERON, 17 jewels, aux. sec., large lugs, c. 1950s
18k...$2,000 $2,200 $2,500

VACHERON, 17 jewels
18k C&B.............................$1,000 $1,100 $1,200

VACHERON, 17 jewels, extra thin model
18k...$1,000 $1,100 $1,200

VACHERON, 17 jewels
18k $1,000 $1,100 $1,200

VACHERON, 15 jewels
18k C&B.............................. $2,000 $2,200 $2,600

VACHERON, 17 jewels
18k $2,200 $2,400 $2,600

VACHERON, 36 jewels, auto wind
18k C&B................................. $1,200 $1,400 $1,600

VACHERON, 17J, with shutters, crowns at 3 & 9
18k $15,000 $20,000 $25,000

VACHERON, 17 jewels, hinged back
18k...$1,400 $1,600 $1,800

VACHERON, 17 jewels, aux. sec.
14k...$1,800 $1,900 $2,000

VACHERON, 17 jewels, flat & thin model, c. 1960s
18k...$800 $900 $1,000

VACHERON, 18 jewels, c. 1950s
18k...$1,600 $1,800 $2,000

VACHERON, 17 jewels
18k C&B $1,500 $1,600 $1,700

VACHERON, 18 jewels, textured bezel
18k $1,200 $1,400 $1,600

VACHERON, 17 jewels, applied gold numbers
18k..$1,200 $1,400 $1,600

VACHERON, 18 jewels, aux. sec., c. 1940s
18k $1,200 $1,400 $1,600

VACHERON, 15 jewels, c. 1920s
18k..$1,200 $1,400 $1,600

VACHERON, 17 jewels, aux. sec., c. 1950s
18k $1,200 $1,400 $1,600

VACHERON, 17 jewels, 2 tone, 24mm, c. 1920s
18k..$2,000 $2,200 $2,500

VACHERON, 17J., applied gold numbers, c. 1940s
18k $1,200 $1,400 $1,600

VACHERON, 17 jewels, 68 diamond bezel
18k..$1,400 $1,500 $1,600

VACHERON, 17 jewels, aux. sec., c. 1945
18k $1,400 $1,600 $1,800

VACHERON, 17 jewels, flared, curvex, c. 1940s
18k..$4,000 $4,500 $5,000

VACHERON, 17J., flared,12 diam. dial, aux. sec., c. 1948
platinum................................. $4,000 $4,500 $5,000

VACHERON, 22 jewels, lady's watch, c. 1970s
18k...$1,000 $1,100 $1,200

VACHERON, 17 jewels, flared, c. 1948
18k $3,000 $3,500 $4,000

VACHERON, 17 jewels, aux. sec., ruby dial
18k...$1,800 $2,000 $2,200

VACHERON, 17 jewels, flared, c. 1940s
18k $3,000 $3,500 $4,000

VACHERON, 21 jewels, center sec., c. 1950s
18k...$3,000 $3,500 $4,000

VACHERON, 17 jewels, "Chronoscope," jumping hr.,
revolving ruby min. indicator, c. 1930s
18k $20,000 $22,000 $24,000

VACHERON, 17 jewels, aux. sec., fancy lugs, c. 1947
18k...$2,200 $2,600 $3,000

VACHERON, 20 jewels, Adj. to 5 Pos., c. 1970s
18k $2,000 $2,200 $2,500

VACHERON, 17 jewels
14k...$800 $1,000 $1,200

VACHERON, 17 jewels, fancy lugs
18k $1,200 $1,400 $1,600

VACHERON, 17 jewels, c. 1950s
18k $1,200 $1,400 $1,600

VACHERON, 17 jewels, fancy lugs
14k $1,000 $1,100 $1,200

VACHERON, 17 jewels, stars on dial
18k C&B $1,600 $1,800 $2,000

VACHERON, 17 jewels, aux. sec.
14k $1,200 $1,400 $1,600

VACHERON,17J., aux. sec, hidden lugs, c.1943
14k $1,000 $1,100 $1,200

VACHERON,17J., RF#7252, c.1962
18k $800 $900 $1,000

VACHERON,17J., aux. sec, c.1947
18k $1,500 $1,600 $1,700

VACHERON,17J., aux. sec, c.1942
18k 1,500 $1,600 $1,700

VACHERON,17J., RF#6249, aux. sec, c.1963
18k $1,500 $1,600 $1,700

VACHERON,17J., aux. sec, c.1934
18k $2,200 $2,400 $2,600

VACHERON, 17 jewels, aux. sec. c. 1946
18k $2,200 $2,400 $2,600

VACHERON, 17 jewels, Art Deco bezel, c. 1925
18k $5,000 $5,500 $6,000

VACHERON, 17 jewels, long lugs, applied numbers
18k $2,200 $2,500 $2,800

VACHERON, 17 jewels, aux. sec.,
18k $2,200 $2,500 $2,800

VACHERON, 18 jewels, aux. sec.
18k C&B $2,000 $2,200 $2,400

VACHERON, 15 jewels, heavy bezel, c.1925
18K C&B $3,500 $3,800 $4,200

VACHERON, 17 jewels, curved, hooded lugs, c. 1930s
18k $3,000 $3,200 $3,500

VACHERON,16J., black starr & forst, wire lugs, c.1919
18k $400 $500 $600

VACHERON, 17 jewels, heavy bezel
18k $2,000 $2,200 $2,400

VACHERON,17J., ladies, c.1948
18k $1,000 $1,100 $1,200

VACHERON, 17 jewels, lady's watch, c. 1960s
18k C&B $1,200 $1,400 $1,600

VAN CLEEF & ARPELS,17J., center lugs, c.1970
18k $500 $600 $700

VULCAIN,17J., "Cricket", c.19
s. steel $50 $75 $100

VERNO, 15 jewels, chased bezel
gold filled (w) $75 $100 $125

VULCAIN,17J., "Cricket", c.1960
base metal $40 $45 $55

VULCAIN, 17 jewels, "Cricket," alarm
s. steel $50 $60 $70

VULCAIN,17J., "Cricket", c.1948
s. steel $50 $60 $75

VULCAIN, 17 jewels, "Cricket"
14k $150 $175 $200

VULCAIN,17J., center sec., c.1940
s. steel $50 $60 $75

VULCAIN, 17 jewels, "Cricket"
gold filled $60 $70 $80

WAKMANN, 17J., "Gigandet" Valjoux cal.72, c.1955
18k............................$1,200 $1,400 $1,600

VULCAIN, 17 jewels, "Minstop"
s. steel.. $40 $50 $80

WAKMANN, 17J., chronog., 3 reg., triple date,
14k...$350 $400 $450

WAKMANN,17J., 24 hr. dial, c.1955
s. steel.. $100 $125 $150

WAKMANN,17J., chronog., 3 reg., triple date, sq.buttons
s. steel......................................$100 $125 $150

WAKMANN, 17 jewels, chronog., 3 reg., c. 1958
s. steel.. $150 $200 $250

WAKMANN,17J., chronog., Valjoux cal.188, c.1960
s. steel..$100 $120 $150

WAKMANN,17J., chronog., Valjoux cal.236, c.1968
s. steel.. $80 $100 $125

WAKMANN,17J., chronog., c.1955
s. steel.. $100 $125 $150

WAKMANN,17J., chronog., c.1970s
s. steel.. $60 $70 $85

WARWICK, 6J., hinged back, 1930s
gold plate $40 $50 $65

WARWICK, 15J., 1930s
gold plate.................................... $40 $50 $60

WARWICK, 15J., 1930s
gold plate.................................... $40 $50 $60

WARWICK, 6-15J., 1930s
gold plate.................................... $40 $50 $60

WARWICK, 6-15J., 1930s
gold plate.................................... $40 $50 $60

WARWICK, 6-15J., 1930s
gold plate.................................... $40 $50 $60

WARWICK, 6-15J., 1930s
gold plate $40 $50 $60

WARWICK, 15J., 1930s
gold plate $40 $50 $60

WARWICK, 15J., 1930s
base metal................................. $20 $25 $35

WATEX, 7J., fluted case, c.1940
gold filled $150 $175 $200

WEISCO, 7J., aux. sec., wire lugs, c. 1928
base metal................................. $20 $30 $45

WEST END, 17 jewels, "Keepsake," c. 1925
silver... $300 $400 $500

WEST END, 17 jewels, center lugs
18k... $300 $350 $400

WELDON,17J., aux. sec., large lugs c.1950s
gold filled.................................... $40 $50 $65

WELSBRO ,17J., single button chronog., c.1940
s. steel $75 $100 $125

WHITE STAR, 17J., triple date, moon phase, c. 1948
s. steel.. $200 $250 $300

WITTNAUER, 17 jewels, chronog., c. 1948
s. steel.. $125 $150 $175

WINTON, 17J., hooded lugs
14k $125 $150 $175

WINTON, 16J., curvex, hinged back, c.1930s
silver $125 $150 $200

WITTNAUER,17J., "Professional, RF#6002, c.1955
s. steel.. $150 $175 $275

WITTNAUER, 17 jewels, fancy lugs
14k $250 $275 $375

WITTNAUER,17J., chronog., c.1958
s. steel.. $125 $150 $250

WITTNAUER, 17 jewels, chronog., day-date-month
s. steel.. $175 $200 $275

WITTNAUER,17J., by Venius, c.1955
s. steel.. $125 $150 $250

WITTNAUER, 17 J., chronog., by Valjoux #72, cal.13w1
s. steel.. $125 $150 $225

WITTNAUER, 7 J., "Electronic day date, c.1968
s. steel.. $40 $50 $60

WITTNAUER, 7 J., mid size, stop watch, c.1940
s. steel.. $125 $150 $225

WITTNAUER, 17 J., direct read, c.1970
s. steel.. $60 $70 $85

WITTNAUER, 17 J., day date, set year by button
s. steel.. $75 $100 $125

WITTNAUER, 17 J., Zircon on dial, direct read, c.1970
base metal $65 $75 $95

WITTNAUER, 17 J., perpetual calendar, c.19
base metal.. $75 $100 $125

WITTNAUER, 17 jewels, auto wind, sector, date
s. steel.. $400 $500 $600

WITTNAUER, 17 jewels, c. 1950s
14k $200 $230 $275

WITTNAUER, 17J., aux. sec., GJS, large lugs, c.1950
14k $165 $190 $250

WITTNAUER, 17J., aux. sec., c.1958
gold filled.............................. $100 $125 $200

WITTNAUER, 17J., aux. sec., fancy case, c.1950
gold filled................................ $100 $125 $200

WITTNAUER, 17J., aux. sec., c.1950
14k $150 $175 $250

WITTNAUER, 17J., aux. sec., fluted case
14k.............................. $150 $185 $240

WITTNAUER, 17J., aux. sec., GJS, c.1948
14k $150 $175 $250

WITTNAUER, 17J., aux. sec.,
gold filled.............................. $75 $85 $135

WITTNAUER, 17J., aux. sec., fancy lugs, c.1955
gold filled................................ $100 $125 $200

WITTNAUER, 17 jewels, fancy lugs, c. 1950s
14k................................ $200 $250 $300

WITTNAUER, 17J., aux. sec., GJS, c. 1955
14k $165 $185 $275

WITTNAUER, 17J., aux. sec.,
14k $125 $150 $225

WITTNAUER, 17J., aux. sec., tu-tone dial, c. 1950
gold filled $85 $95 $150

WITTNAUER, 17J., marked bezel
14k $150 $175 $250

WITTNAUER, 17J., aux. sec., c. 1950
gold filled $75 $85 $135

WITTNAUER, 15J., aux. sec., tonneau case, c.1945
gold plate $65 $75 $125

WITTNAUER, 17J., RF#2067, c.1950
gold filled $65 $75 $125

WITTNAUER, 17J., aux. sec.
gold filled $65 $75 $150

WITTNAUER, 17J., auto-wind, c.1960
base metal $40 $50 $75

WITTNAUER, 17J., cal.7630, aux. sec., c.1955
14k $140 $160 $200

WITTNAUER, 17J., "Alarm", c.1960
gold filled $125 $150 $225

WIG WAG, 15 jewels, early auto wind, c. 1932
s. steel.. $600 $700 $800

WYLER, 17 jewels, early auto wind, watch winds by using
the muscular movement of the wrist, back set
gold filled $500 $600 $700

WYLER, 17 jewels, early auto wind, back set
gold filled $500 $600 $700

WYLER, 17 jewels, center sec.
s. steel.. $60 $70 $80

WYLER, 17 jewels, aux. sec.
s. steel.. $60 $70 $80

WYLER, 17 jewels
s. steel.. $60 $70 $85

WYLER, 17 jewels, diamond dial, c. 1946
s. steel.. $60 $70 $85

WYLER, 17J., center sec., c.1945
s. steel.. $75 $90 $135

WYLER, 17J., aux. sec., c. 1938
s. steel.................................. $60 $70 $85

WYLER, 17J., auto-wind, c. 1932
chrome.................................. $70 $85 $125

WYLER, 17J., day date month, c. 1946
gold filled.............................. $150 $175 $250

WYLER, 17 jewels, chronog., c. 1940s
s. steel.................................. $125 $200 $275

YALE, 15 jewels, calendar, c. 1939
gold filled.............................. $100 $125 $175

ZELIA, 17 jewels, chronog.
18k...................................... $600 $700 $800

ZENITH, 15J., signal corps on enamel dial, center lug, 1918
silver.................................... $200 $250 $350

ZENITH, 19 jewels, 33mm, c. 1950s
gold filled.............................. $100 $125 $150

ZENITH, 17 jewels, chronog.
18k...................................... $600 $700 $800

ZENITH, 36 jewels, chronog., auto wind, c. 1969
s. steel.. $450 $500 $600

ZENITH, 36J., chronog., auto-wind, triple date
base metal $200 $250 $300

ZENITH, 36J., "ElPrimero", RF#502, auto wind, c. 1970
18k $1,200 $1,400 $1,600

ZENITH, 17J, "Port Royal" chronometer
18k C&B $400 $450 $550

ZENITH, 17 jewels, fancy bezel
18k.. $250 $350 $500

ZENITH, 36 jewels, "El Primero," chronog., triple date
moon phase, c. 1970s
18k $2,400 $2,600 $2,800

ZENTRA, 24 jewels, ladies, auto wind, c. 1958
14k.. $125 $150 $175

ZODIAC, 17J., chronog, 2 reg, c.1948
gold filled.................................. $200 $250 $300

ZODIAC, 17 jewels, ref. #8088
14k...$125 $150 $175

ZODIAC, 17J., chronog., auto-wind, date, c.1971
s. steel............................ $75 $80 $100

ZODIAC, 17J., auto wind with reserve power indicator
14k...$175 $200 $250
gold filled..................................$85 $100 $120

ZODIAC, 17J., day-date-month, moon phase, c. 1957
14k...$500 $600 $700

ZODIAC, 17J., center sec., auto-wind, c.1959
s. steel..................................... $50 $60 $75

ZODIAC, 17 jewels, 24 hour dial
s. steel....................................... $100 $120 $140

ZODIAC, 17J., center sec., cal. 1094, c. 1959
s. steel $60 $65 $80

SWATCH
1983

NAME & GRADE — Description	N-Mint	New + Box
Tennis Grid — GW-100	$225	$350
Tennis Stripes — GW-101	500	850
Tennis Grid —LW-100	165	285
GB-001	300	500
GB-100	160	280
GB-101	160	280
GB-103	210	350
GB-402	160	280
GB-700	160	280
GB-701	160	280
GB-702	160	280
GB-703, (Classic)	160	280
GC-100	210	350
GC-101	210	350
GC-700	125	210
GG-100	210	350
GG-700	175	290
GG-701	500	840
GG-702	300	500
GM-700	120	200
GN-001	120	200
GN-100	420	700
GN-101	500	840
GN-700	165	270
GN-701	100	175
GR-100	160	280
GR-101	160	280
GR-102	500	840
GR-103	120	200
GR-700	160	280
GT-100	420	700
GT-101	210	350
GT-403	160	280
GT-700	210	350
GT-701	500	840
GT-702	100	170
LB-100	210	350
LM-100	210	350
LN-100	210	350
LR-100	210	350
LR-101	210	350

TENNIS GRID # LW-100

M# LR-101, Ca.1983 (FALL / WINTER)

BLACK DIVERS, M#GB-704, Ca.1984

VALKYRIE, M#LP-101, Ca.1986

TECHNO-SPHERE, M#GK-101, Ca.1985

BLUE NOTE, M#GI-400, Ca.1987

NAUTILUS, M#GK-102, Ca.1986

FOLLOW ME, M#GJ-101, Ca.1987

OSIRIS, M#GM-102, Ca.1986

NAVIGATOR, M#GB-707, Ca.1987

1984

NAME & GRADE — Description	N-Mint	New + Box
Art Deco — LM-103	$125	$200
Beige Arabic — GT-102	175	295
Beige Arabic — LT-100	125	200
Black Divers — GB-704	150	250
Black Magic — GB-101	185	300
Classic — LB-103	120	200
Classique — GB-703	150	250
Classique — LB-103	120	200
Compass — GR-400	160	280
Compass — LR-102	200	345
Compu-Tech — GR-401	550	900
Chrono-Tech — GB-403	175	295
Chrono-Tech — LB-104	80	135
Don't Bee Too Late — GA-100	425	700
4 Flags — GS-100	500	850
4 Flags — LS-100	425	700
12 Flags — GS-101	160	280
12 Flags — LS-101	120	200
Grey Markers — GM-400	195	325
Grey Memphis — GM-100	500	850
Golden Tan — GT-103	245	400
High Tech — GB-002	250	425
High Tech — LB-102	125	220
High Tech II — GA-101	350	600
Mah-Jong — LA-101	80	140
Miss Channel — LA-100	125	210
Navy Roman — GN-702	75	125
Navy Roman — LN-102	65	120
Nicholson — GB-701	180	300
Pirelli — GM-101	425	700
Pirelli — LM-102	210	350
Red 12-3-6-9 — LR-103	120	200
Squiggly — LR-104	120	200
White Memphis — LW-102	120	200
Windrose — GW-103	160	280
Windrose — LW-103	120	200
Yellow Racer — GJ-400	210	350
Yellow Racer — LJ-100	120	200

COMPASS # GR—400, ca. 1984

GREY MEMPHIS # GM—100

1985

NAME & GRADE — Description	N-Mint	New + Box
Banana — LW-106	$120	$200
BC/BG — LT-102	10	30
Black Magic — LB-106	35	60
Black Out — GB-105	210	350
Calypso Diver — GM-701	165	275
Classic — GB-706	110	185
Classic — LB-107	90	150
Dotted Swiss — GW-104	45	75
Dotted Swiss — LW-104	40	65
Golden Tan — LT-101	100	200
Grey Flannel — GM-401	150	270
Grey Flannel —LM-104	70	120
Ice Mint — LW-105	120	200
INC. — GA-103	125	215
Jaegermeister — GB-404	150	275
Jelly Fish — GK-100	225	350
McGregor —GJ-100	195	325
McSwatch — LR-105	125	215
Miss Pinstripe — LA-102	80	135
Neo-Quad — LB-109	90	160
Nicholson — GB-705	120	200
Nicholette — LB-105	90	250
Oxford Navy — GN-401	80	135
Oxford Navy — LN-103	120	200
Pinstripe — GA-102	160	270
Raspberry — LW-107	125	210
Sheherazade — LM-105	20	35
Techno-Sphere — GK-101	165	275
Tri-Color Racer — LS-102	90	150
Velvet Underground — LB-108	75	130
Yamaha Racer — GJ-700	160	285

McGREGOR # GJ-100, ca.1985

YAMAHA RACER # GJ-700, ca.1985

MARMORATA, M#GB-119, Ca.1987

ST. CATHERINE POINT, M#GB-121, Ca.1988

NINE TO SIX, M#GB-117, Ca.1987

TINTARELLA, M#GK-108, Ca. 1988

WAIPITU, M#GB-113, Ca.1987

COLOR WINDOW, M#GB-715, Ca.1989

COLOURED LOVE, M#GB-122, Ca.1988

HANG TWELVE, M#GJ-102, Ca.1989

1986

NAME & GRADE — Description	N-Mint	New + Box
Aqua Dream — LK-100	$75	$125
Black Coral — LK-101	75	125
Carlisle — LG-103	75	125
Chelsea — LB-112	45	75
Club Stripe — GG-401	155	265
Comic Encounter — GS-102	90	150
Emerald Diver — GG-703	80	135
Gambela — LG-102	40	70
Horus — LL-101	30	55
Lancelot — GB-110	120	200
Lion Heart — LK-102	20	35
Little Jelly — LK-103	40	70
Mezza Luna — GB-107	85	140
Nautilus — GK-102	165	275
Osiris — GM-102	90	150
Pink Dots — LL-100	40	70
Ping Pong Blue — GW-106	40	70
Ping Pong White — GW-105	45	75
Pink Flamingo — LP-100	45	75
Radar — LR-106	80	135
Ritz — GA-400	120	200
Rotor — GS-400	90	150
Ruffled Feathers — GF-100	45	75
Running Water — LS-103	20	35
Sir Swatch — GB-111	120	200
Soto — GB-109	120	200
Tonga — GL-100	45	75
Valkyrie — LP-101	20	35
Vasily — LW-111	45	75

COSMIC ENCOUNTER # GS−102, ca.1986

RUFFLED FEATHERS # GF−100, ca.1986

HARAJUKU, M#GB-124, Ca.1989 (MAXI)

TAXI-STOP, M#GB-410, Ca.1989

LUCRETIA, M#GB-126, Ca.1989

WIPEOUT, M#GB-714, Ca.1989

SANDY MOUNTAINS, M#GG-105, Ca.1989

THE BURGLAR, M#GB-717, Ca.1990

SHIBUYA, M#GG-104, Ca.1989

BYZANTHIUM, M#LG-106, Ca.1990

1987

NAME & GRADE — Description	N-Mint	New + Box
Bandos Diver — GB-710	$150	250
Belvedere — LK-105	20	35
Big Eclipse — GW-400	85	145
Black Pearl — LW-114	70	120
Blue Bay — LD-106	20	30
Blue Cassata — LP-103	20	30
Blue Horizon — LF-100	20	35
Blue Note — GI-400	45	75
Blue Racer — LR-107	45	75
Borgo Nuovo — GF-102	240	400
Calafatti — GK-105	55	90
Classic Two — GB-709	45	75
Classic Two — LB-115	20	35
Commander — GB-115	100	175
Follow Me — GJ-101	45	75
Grey Flannel — GA-104	150	250
High Moon — GA-107	100	175
Kasimir — LW-114	70	120
Kir Royale — LW-113	20	35
Lazuli — GF-101	255	425
Little Eclipse — LW-112	70	120
Mackintosh — GB-116	60	100
Marmorata — GB-119	45	80
Nafea — LK-104	40	70
Navigator — GB-707	235	400
New Port — LW-115	70	120
New Port Two — GW-108	75	125
Nikolai — LW-116	45	75
Nine To Six — GB-117	45	75
Pago Pago — GL-400	80	135
Pink Cassata — LL-102	20	35
Pulsometer — GA-106	45	75
Raspberry Shortcake — LP-102	45	75
Silver Circle — GA-105	150	250
Sky Racer — GK-106	85	145
Snowwhite — GK-104	30	50
Speed Limit — LW-117	20	35
Spiga — LF-101	25	40
Trevi — LB-117	40	70
Turquoise Bay — GK-103	75	125
Tutti Frutti — GW-109	75	125
Vulcano — GB-114	150	250
Waipitu — GB-113	45	80
White Out — GW-107	50	80
X-Rated — GB-406	45	75

LOUIS LOUIS, M#GR-106, Ca.1990

TRISTAN, M#GB-135, Ca.1990

SCOOB-A-DOO, M#GV-102, Ca.1990

IBISKUS, M#GL-101, Ca.1991

SOGNO, M#GV-101, Ca.1990

BONDI DIVER, M#GK-115, Ca. 1989(MAXI)

STUCCHI, M#GN-107, Ca.1990

HYPPOCAMPUS, M#SDK-103, Ca.1991 (SCUBA)

1988

NAME & GRADE — Description	N-Mint	New + Box
Albatross — GX-700..	$85	$140
Andromeda — GK-111...	45	75
Antibes — LW-120..	40	70
Backslash — GS-700	45	75
Beauchamps Place — LF-102..............................	20	30
Biarritz — LN-104..	70	120
Black Hawk — GX-702..	85	140
Blue Bay — LK-106...	20	30
Blue Lolly — LP-105...	20	30
Coconut Grove — GB-120...................................	150	259
Coloured Love — GB-122....................................	45	80
Coral Gables — GB-407......................................	45	75
Courier — GX-703...	85	140
Dark Vader — GK-110...	45	75
Deauville — GW-401...	45	75
Disque Bleau — GK-113......................................	45	75
Flamingo Deli — LK-107.....................................	20	30
Flumotions — GN-102..	90	150
Frontloop — LK-117..	20	30
Frozen Dreams — LB-120....................................	20	30
Golden Sphere — GX-102....................................	20	35
Green Wave — GW-402..	20	35
Heartbreak — GX 101...	20	35
Heartstone — GX-100..	20	35
Hot Racer — LK-115	40	70
Jelly Fish — GK-100 (Clear Tech)	30	50
Jelly Fish — GK-100 (Clear Tech) Green Coil	45	75
Kailua Diver — GB-712.......................................	100	175
Old Bond — GG-102..	90	150
O'Sole Mio — LK-108..	20	30
Liquid Sky — LG-104	40	70
Luna Di Capri — LK-109.....................................	60	100
Midas Touch — LK-112.......................................	20	30
Moneypenny — LB-118..	20	30
Nab Light — LW-118...	20	30
Needles — GB-408..	60	100
Neo Rider — GG-103	90	150
Notebook — LR-108...	20	30
Pink Lolly — LL-104...	20	30
Red Wave — LW-121	20	30
Sign Of Samas — GX-105....................................	45	80
Sloan Ranger — GX-104......................................	30	50
South Moulton — LL-103.....................................	20	30
Speed Week — GK-112..	50	80
St. Catherine Point — GB-121.............................	165	280
Take Off — GK-114...	45	75
Ticker Tape II — GB-713	45	80
Tiger Moth — GX-701	85	140
Tintarella — GK-108...	45	75
Touch Down — GB-409..	45	75
White Knight — GW-110......................................	45	75
White Window — GB-711	60	100

DEEP BLUE, M#SDK-100, Ca.1990 (SCUBA)

SAND STORM, M#SCB-104, Ca.1990 (Chronog.)

HAPPY FISH, M#SDK-101, Ca.1991 (SCUBA)

SIGNAL FLAG, M#SCN-101, Ca.1990 (Chronog.)

MEDUSA, M#SDK-102, Ca.1991 (SCUBA)

SKATE BIKE, M#SCB-105 (Chronog.)

BLACK FRIDAY, M#SCB-100, Ca.1990 (Chronog.)

SKIPPER, M#SCN-100, Ca.1990 (Chronog.)

1989

NAME & GRADE — Description	N-Mint	New + Box
Bar Oriental — GR-104	$210	$350
Boca Verde — GX-402	75	125
Bondi Diver — GK-115	20	35
Beaujolais — LR-109	40	70
Blue Jet — GS-701	45	75
Blue Jet — GS-701 (NO DATE)	150	250
Blue Leaves — GN-104	60	100
Bright Lights — GX-706	20	35
Casbah Rock —LN-105	60	100
Chic-on — Gx-111	45	75
Coldsteel — GY-104	30	50
Color Window — GB-715	30	55
Croque Monsieur — Gx-112	45	75
Croque Moiselle — Ln-107	20	30
Day Off — GY-400	50	80
Eclipses — GB-128	60	100
Figueiras — GB-125	50	80
Geoglo — GW-403	20	35
Glowing Arrow — GX-109	50	80
GOLDEN BOND — GP-101	45	75
Greengo — LW-124	20	30
Greenie — GX-110	45	75
Greenroom — GN-103	45	75
Grey Line — GB-411	30	50
Hang Twelve — GJ-102	50	80
Harajuku — GB-124	120	200
High Flyer — GX-704	25	40
Icebreaker — GX-113	20	30
Kailua Diver — GB-712	50	80
Lemon Iceberg — GK-116	20	35
Lobro — LB-123	20	30
Lucretia — GB-126	45	75
MBA — GX-403	30	45
Medici's — GB-127	75	125
Metalsphere — GY-102	30	50
Metropolis — Gx-405	50	80
Moonquake — Gx-404	45	75
Noblesse Oblige — LX-100	20	30
Petrodollar — GG402	45	75
Petrodollar — GG402 (NO DATE)	200	350
Rosehip — GP-100	50	80
Rush For Heaven — GN-105	90	150
Sandy Mountains — GG-105	75	125
Shibuya — GG-104	90	150
Silver Thread — LB-121	40	70
St. Germain — GB-123	60	100
Steeltech — GY-100	30	50
Stormy Weather — GV-100	75	125
Sun Lady — LB-125	20	30
Tango Azul — GX-401	90	150
Taxi Stop — GB-410	50	80
White Window — GB-711	45	75
Wipeout — GB-714	60	100

WHITE HORSES, M#SCW-100,Ca.1990 (Chronog.)

VELVET UNDERGROUND, M#GZ-999,Ca.1990

THE GLOBE, M#GB-137, Ca.1991

MIMMO PALADINO, M#GX-113, Ca.1990 (ART)

BREAKDANCE, M#GO-001, Ca.1990 (Special)

RORRIM 5, M#GZ-107, Ca.1990 (ART)

MOZART, M#GZ-114, Ca.1990 (Special)

ROSSO ON BLACKOUT, M#GZ-120, Ca.1991 (ART)

SPECIAL EDITIONS

NAME & GRADE — Description	Mint+Box	New + Box
Bergstrussli — GZ-105, 1987, TP.9,999	$900	$1,500
Bonaparte — GX-106, 1988	225	500
Breakdance — GO-001, 1985, TP.9,999	900	1,500
Baby Breakdance —LO-001, TP.9,999	500	900
Chronometers' — SETS	3,000	5,000
Chronometers' — GP-104, BMX, 1990	600	1,000
Chronometers' — GK-124, Jelly Fish, TP.2,000	600	1,000
Chronometers' — GB-719, Knight of Night, 1990	600	1,000
Chronometers' — GK-125, Turbine,1990	600	1,000
Fachhandel Logo — any style , 1983	300	500
Golden Jelly — GZ-115, 1990	300	500
Hollywood Dream — GZ-116, 1990, TP.9,999	800	1,500
Sir Limelight — 1989, any style	500	1,000
Lady Limelight —any style	300	800
Limelight II —any style	500	1,000
Lady Limelight II — any style	300	800
Mozart — TP.7,500	400	700
Olympia — GZ-400 & 402	300	600
Olympia — LZ-100	150	300
Original Jelly Fish — TP.200	3,000	5,000
Pierre Alechinsky — GZ-401, 1988	600	1,000
Pol Bury — GZ-110, 1988	350	600
Pompadour — GX-107	250	500
PUFFS' — any style, 1988, TP.120 ea.	4,800	8,000
Valerio Adami — GZ-111, 1988	350	500
Velvet Underground — GZ-999, Prototype	5,000	9,000
Velvet Underground — BLACK TP.500	2,000	4,000
Velvet Underground — WHITE TP.500	2,500	4,500

ART

NAME & GRADE — Description	N-Mint	New + Box
Folon 1 &2 &3 — SETS	$1,500	2,500
Folon — GZ-109, NO.1	480	800
Folon — GZ-106, NO.2	480	800
Folon — GZ-108, NO.3	480	800
Kiki Picasso — 1985, TP.140	12,000	20,000
Keith Harting — SETS	4,200	7,000
Keith Harting — GZ-104, Blanc Sur Noir, 1986	800	1,500
Keith Harting — GZ-103, Mille Pattes, 1986	800	1,500
Keith Harting — GZ-100, Modele Avec Personnage	800	1,500
Keith Harting — GZ-102, Serpent, 1986	800	1,500
Fondation Maeght — SETS, TP.5,000 ea.	1,200	2,400
Mimmo Paladino —GX-113, TP.120	20,000	30,000
Rorrim — GZ-107, 1987, TP.5,000	1,200	2,000
700 YEARS CONFOEDERATIO HELVETICA (1991) (SWISS ART)TP. 700, set, series 1 signed	3,500	6,000
BLACKOUT — GZ-119	50	80
FLACK — GZ-117	50	80
TEST — GZ-118	50	80
WHEEL ANIMAL — GZ-120	50	80

FLACK, M#GZ-117, Ca.1991 (ART)

NEO WAVE, M#SCJ-100, Ca.1991 (Chronog.)

TEST, M#GZ-118, Ca.1991 (ART)

SILVER STAR, M#SCN-102, Ca.1991 (Chronog.)

WHEEL ANIMAL, M#GZ-120, Ca.1991 (ART)

SPUTNIK, M#PWR-106, Ca.1990 (POP SWATCH)

FLASH ARROW, M#SCL-100, Ca.1991 (Chronog.)

BRAEKDANCE, M#LO-001, Ca.1985

POP SWATCH

NAME & GRADE — Description	N-Mint	New + Box
Aqua Pink — BK-120	$360	600
Diva — BB-106, TP.9,999	350	600
Encantador — TP.9,999	100	175
Haute Couture — any style	100	175
Roses Are Forever — BC-101	120	200
Sputnik—PWR-106	100	175

CHRONOGRAPH

NAME & GRADE — Description	N-Mint	New + Box
Black Friday — SCB-100, 1990	$90	$150
Sand Storm — SCB-104, 1990	300	500
Signal Flag — SCN-101, 1990	300	500
Skate Bike — SCB-105, 1990	300	500
Skipper —SCN-100, 1990	240	400
White Horses — SCW-100, 1990	900	1,500
Chronograph — SETS, 1990	2,000	3,600
Flash Arrow — SCL-100, 1991	75	125
Gold Finger — SCM-100, 1991	90	150
Silver Star — SCN-102, 1991	90	150
Navy Berry — SCR-100, 1991	75	125
Neo Wave — SCJ-100, 1991	75	125
Chronograph — SETS, 1991	480	800

SCUBA

NAME & GRADE — Description	N-Mint	New + Box
Barrier Reef — SDB-100, 1990	$35	60
Bora Bora — SDN-400, 1990	60	95
Deep Blue — SDK-100, 1990	45	75
Merou — SDK-101, 1990	60	95
Blue Moon—SDN-100, 1991	35	60
Happy Fish—SDN-101, 1991	90	150
Hyppocampus—SDK-103, 1991	35	60
Medusa—SDK-102, 1991	35	60

WATCH TERMINOLOGY

ADJUSTED-Adjusted to compensate for temperature, positions,and isochronism.

ALARM WATCH-A watch that will give an audible sound at a pre-set time.

ANNEALING-Heating and cooling a metal slowly to relieve internal stress.

ANTI-MAGNETIC-Not affected by magnetic field.

Arbor

ARBOR-The mechanical axle of a moving part; on the balance it is called the staff, on the lever it is called the arbor.

ASSAY-Analyzing a metal for its gold or silver content.

AUTOMATON-Animated mechanical objects and figures; actuated by the going, striking or repeating train.

AUXILIARY COMPENSATION-For middle temperature errors found on marine chronometers.

Balance Cock

BALANCE COCK-The bridge that holds the upper jewels and the balance and secured at one end only.

Balance Spring

BALANCE SPRING-Also called the hairspring; the spring governing the balance.

Balance Staff

BALANCE STAFF-The shaft of the balance wheel.

Balance Wheel

BALANCE WHEEL-A device shaped like a wheel that does for a watch what a pendulum does for a clock.

Banking Pins

BANKING PINS-The two pins which limit the angular motion of the pallet.

Bar Movement

BAR MOVEMENT-A type of movement employing about six bridges to hold the train also known as a Lepine Calibre.

Barrel

BARREL-Drum-shaped container that houses the mainspring.

BEAT-Refers to the tick or sound of a watch ; about 1/5 of a second. The sound is produced by the escape wheel striking the pallets.

Beetle Hand

BEETLE HAND-Hour hand resembling a stag beetle; usually associated with the poker-type minute hand.

BELL METAL-Four parts copper and one part tin used for metal laps to get a high polish on steel.

BEZEL-The rim that covers the dial (face) and retains the crystal.

BI-METALLIC BALANCE-A balance composed of brass and steel designed to compensate for temperature changes in the hairspring.

BLIND MAN'S WATCH- A Braille watch; also known as a tact watch.

BLUING or BLUEING-By heating steel to about 540 degrees, the color will change to blue.

BOW-The ring that is looped at the pendant to which a chain or fob is attached

BOX CHRONOMETER-A marine or other type chronometer in gimbals so the movement remains level at sea.

BOX JOINTED CASE-A heavy hinged decorative case with a simulated joint at the top under the pendant.

BREGUET KEY-A ratcheting watch key permitting winding in only one direction.

Overcoil Hairspring

BREGUET SPRING-A type of hairspring that improves timekeeping also called overcoil hairspring.

BRIDGE-A metal bar which bear the pivot of wheels and is supported at both ends .(see cock.)

BULL'S EYE CRYSTAL-Used on old type watches; the center of the crystal was polished which achieved a bull's eye effect.

CALENDAR WATCH-A watch that shows the date, month and day.

CAP JEWEL-Also called the endstone, the flat jewel on which the staff rests.

CENTER WHEEL-The second wheel; the arbor for the minute hand; this wheel makes one revolution per hour.

CHAIN (Fusee)-Looks like a miniature bicycle chain connecting the barrel and fusee.

CHAMPLEVE-An area hollowed out and filled with enamel and then baked on.

CHRONOGRAPH-A movement that can be started and stopped to measure short time intervals and return to zero. A stopwatch does not keep the time of day.

CHRONOMETER ESCAPEMENT-A detent escapement used in marine chronometers.

CLICK-A pawl that ratchets and permits the winding wheel to move in one direction; a clicking sound can be heard as the watch is wound.

CLOCK WATCH-A watch that strikes the hour but not on demand.

CLOISONNE-Enamel set between strips of metal and baked onto the dial

CLUB TOOTH-Some escape wheels have a special design which increases the impulse plane; located at the tip of the tooth of the escape wheel.

COARSE TRAIN-16,000 beats per hour.

COCK -The metal bar which carries the bearing for the balance's upper pivot and is supported at one end.

COMPENSATION BALANCE-A balance wheel designed to correct for temperature.

COMPLICATED WATCH-A watch with complicated works;other than just telling time, it may have a perpetual calendar, moon phases, up and down dial, repeater,musical chimes or alarm.

CONTRATE WHEEL-A wheel with its teeth at a right angle to plane of the wheel.

CONVERTIBLE-Movement made by Elgin; a means of converting from a hunting case to a open-face watch or vice-versa.

CRAZE(crazing)-A minute crack in the glaze of enamel watch dials.

Crown

CROWN-A winding button.

Crown Wheel

CROWN WHEEL-The escape wheel of a verge escapement; looks like a crown.

Curb Pin

CURB PINS-The two pins that change the rate of a watch; the two pins,in ef-fect,change the length of the hairspring

CYLINDER ESCAPEMENT-A type of escapement used on some watches.

DAMASKEENING-The art of producing a design, pattern, or wavy appearance on a metal.

DEMI-HUNTER-A hunting case with the center designed to allow the position of the hands to be seen without opening the case.

DETENT ESCAPEMENT-A detached escapement . The balance is impulsed in one direction; used on watches to provide greater accuracy.

DIAL-The face of a watch. Some are made of enamel.

DISCHARGE PALLET JEWEL-The left jewel.

Double Roller

DOUBLE ROLLER-A watch with one im-pulse roller table and a safety roller, thus two rollers.

DRAW-The angular position of the pallet jewels in the pallet frame which causes those jewels to be drawn deeper into the escape wheel under pressure of the escape wheel's tooth on the locking surface.

DROP-The space between a tooth of the escape wheel and the pallet from which it has just escaped.

DUMB REPEATER-One that strikes the hour on the case or block rather than a bell or gong.

DUPLEX ESCAPEMENT-An escape wheel with two sets of teeth, one for locking and one for impulse.

EBAUCHE(ay-boesh)-A movement not completely finished or in the rough; not detailed; a movement made up of two plates ,train, barrel and did not include a dial, case, or escapement.

ECCENTRIC-Non-concentric; usually a cam.

ELECTRONIC WATCH-Newer type watch using quartz and electronics to produce a high degree of accuracy.

ELINVAR-A hairspring composed of a special alloy of nickel, steel, chromium, manganese and tungsten that does not vary at different temperatures.

Endshake

ENDSHAKE-The up and down play of an arbor between the plates and bridge or between the jewels.

END STONE-The jewel or cap at the end of the staff.

EPHEMERIS TIME-The time calculated for the Earth to orbit around the sun.

ESCAPE WHEEL-The last wheel in a going train; works with the fork or lever and escapes one pulse at a time.

Fork

ESCAPEMENT-The device in a watch by which the motion of the train is checked and the energy of the mainspring communicated to the balance. The escapement includes the escape wheel, lever, and balance complete with hairspring.

FARMER'S WATCH(OIGNON)-A large pocket watch with a verge escapement and a farm scene on the dial.

FIVE-MINUTE REPEATER-A watch that denotes the time every five minutes, and on the hour and half hour, by operating a push piece.

FLINQUE-Enameling over hand engraving.

FLY BACK-The hand returns back to zero on a timer.

FOB-A decorative short strap or chain.

FORK-The part of the pallet lever that engages with the roller jewel.

FREE SPRUNG-A balance spring free from the influence of a regulator.

FULL PLATE -A plate (or disc) that covers the works and supports the wheels pivots. There is a top plate, a bottom plate, half, and 3/4 plate. The top plate has the balance resting on it.

FUSEE-A spirally groved, turncated cone used in some watches to equalize the power of the mainspring.

GENEVA STOP WORK-A system used to stop the works preventing the barrel from being overwound.

GILT (or GILD)-To coat or plating with gold leaf or a gold color.

GOING BARREL-The barrel houses the mainspring; as the spring uncoils, the barrel turns, and the teeth on the outside of the barrel turn the train of gears as opposed to toothless fusee barrel.

Foliot

FOLIOT-A straight-armed balance with weights on each end used for regulation; found on the earliest clocks and watches.

GOLD-FILLED-Sandwich-type metal; a layer of gold, a layer of base metal in the middle, another layer of gold-then the layers of metals are soldered to each other to form a sandwich.

GOLD JEWEL SETTINGS-In highgrade watches the jewels were mounted in gold settings.

GREAT WHEEL-The main wheel of a fusee type watch.

HACK-WATCH-A watch with a balance that can be stopped to allow synchronization with another timepiece.

HAIRSPRING-The spring which vibrates the balance.

HALLMARK-The silver or gold or platinum markings of many countries.

HEART CAM-PIECE-A heart-shaped cam which causes the hand on a chronograph to fly back to zero.

HELICAL HAIRSPRING-A cylindrical spring used in chronometers.

HOROLOGY (haw-rahl-uh-jee)-The study of timekeeping.

HUNTER CASE-A pocket watch case with a covered face that must be opened to see the watch dial.

IMPULSE-The force transmitted by the escape wheel to the pallet by gliding over the angular or impulse face of the pallet jewel.

IMPULSE PIN(Ruby pin)(roller pin)-A pin on the balance which keeps the balance going .

INCABLOC-A patented shock absorbing device which permits the endstone of the balance to give when the watch is subjected to an impact or jolt.

INDEX-Another term for the racquet-shaped regulator which lengthens or shortens the effective length of the hairspring.

ISOCHRONISM-"Isos" means equal; chronos means time-occurring at equal intervals of time. The balance and hairspring adjusted will allow the watch to run at the same rate regardless whether the watch is fully wound or almost run down.

JEWEL-A bearing made of a ruby or other type jewel; the four types of jewels include; cap jewel, hole jewel, roller jewel or ruby pin, pallet jewel or stone.

KARRUSEL-An invention of Bonniksen in 1894 which allows the entire escapement to revolve within the watch once in 52 1/2 minutes (in most karrusels), this unit is supported at one end only as opposed to the tourbillon which is supported at both ends and which most often revolves once a minute.

KEY SET-Older watch that had to be set with a key.

LEAVES-The teeth of the pinion gears.

LEVER ESCAPEMENT-Invented by Thomas Mudge in 1760.

Lever

LEVER SETTING-The lever used to set railroad watches.

LOCKING-Arresting the advance of the escape wheel during the balance's free excursion.

MAIN SPRING-A flat spring coiled or wound to supply power to the watch. The non-magnetic mainspring was introduced in 1947

MAIN WHEEL-The first driving wheel, part of the barrel.

MALTESE CROSS-The part of the stop works preventing the barrel from being overwound.

Marine Chronometer

MARINE CHRONOMETER- An accurate timepiece; may have a detent escapement and set in a box with gimbals which keep it in a right position.

MEAN TIME- Also equal hours; average mean solar time; the time shown by watches.

Meantime Screw

MEANTIME SCREWS-Balance screws used for timing, usually longer than other balance screws; when turned away from or toward the balance pin, they cause the balance vibrations to become faster or slower.

MICROMETRIC REGULATOR-A regulator used on railroad grade watches to adjust for gain or loss in a very precise way.

MICROSECOND-A millionth of a second.

MINUTE REPEATER -A watch that strikes or sounds the hours, and minutes on demand.

MOVEMENT-The works of a mechanical watch without the case or dial. (quartz watches have modules)

MUSICAL WATCH-A watch that plays a tune on demand or on the hour.

MULTI-GOLD-Different colors of gold-red, green, white, blue, pink, yellow and purple.

NANOSECOND-One billionth of a second.

N.A.W.C.C.-National Association of Watch and Clock Collectors.address is P.O. Box 33, Columbia, Pa. 17512.

NUREMBURG EGG-Nickname for a German watch that was oval-shaped.

OIL SINK-A small well around a pivot which retains oil.

OVERBANKED-A lever escapement error; the roller jewel passes to the wrong side of the lever notch, causing one side of the pallet to rest against the banking pin and the roller jewel to rest against the other side, thus locking the escapement and stopping the motion of the balance.

PAIR-CASE WATCH-An extra case around a watch-two cases,hence, a pair of cases. The outer case kept out the dust. The inner case could not be dustproof because it provided the access to the winding and setting keyholes in the watch case.

PALLET-The part of the lever that works with the escape wheel-jeweled pallet jewels, entry and exit pallets.

Parachute

PARACHUTE-An early shockproofing system designed to fit as a spring on the endstone of balance.

Pendant

PENDANT-The neck of the watch; attached to it is the bow (swing ring) and the crown.

PILLARS-The rods that hold the plates apart. In older watches they were fancy.

Pinion

PINION-The larger gear is called a wheel. The small solid gear is a pinion. The pinion is made of steel in some watches.

PLATE-A watch has a front and a back plate or top and bottom plate. The works are in between.

POISE-A term meaning in balance to equalize the weight around the balance.

PONTILLAGE(bull's eye crystal)-The grinding of the center of a crystal to form a concave or so called bull's eye crystal.

POSITION-As adjusted to five positions; a watch may differ in its timekeeping accuracy as it lays in different positions . Due to the lack of poise, changes in the center of gravity, a watch can be adjusted to six positions: dial up, dial down, stem up, stem down, stem left, and stem right.

QUICK TRAIN-A watch with five beats or more per second or 18,000 per hour.

RACK LEVER ESCAPEMENT-Developed by Abbe de Hutefeuille in 1722 and by Peter Litherland in 1791; does not use a roller table, but a pinion.

Receiving Pallet

RECEIVING PALLET-Also called left or entrance jewel, the first of two pallet jewels with which a tooth of the escape wheel comes into engagement.

REPEATER WATCH-A complicated watch that repeats the time on demand with a sounding device.

REPOUSSE-A watch with hammered, raised decoration on the case.

ROLLED GOLD- Thin layer of gold soldered to a base metal.

Table Roller

Safety Roller

Crescent
Roller Jewel
Horns
Fork Slot
Guard Pin

ROLLER JEWEL-The jewel seated in the roller table, which receives the impulse from the pallet fork.

ROLLER TABLE-The part of the balance in which the roller jewel is seated.

SAFETY PINION -A pinion in the center wheel designed to unscrew if the mainspring breaks; this protects the train from being stripped by the great force of the mainspring.

SAFETY ROLLER-The smaller of the two rollers in a double roller escapement.

SIDEREAL TIME-The time of rotation of the Earth as measured from the stars.

SIDE-WINDER-A mismatched case and movement.; a term used for a hunting movement that has been placed in an open face case and winds at 3 o'clock position.Open face winds at 12 o'clock.

SILVEROID-A type of case composed of alloys to simulate the appearance of silver.

SINGLE ROLLER-The safety roller and the roller jewel are one single table.

SPRING RING-A circular tube housing a coiled type spring.

SIZE-System used to determine the size of the movement to the case.

SKELETON WATCH-A watch made so the viewer can see the works. Plates are pierced and very decorative.

STACKFREED-Curved spring and cam to equalize the uneven pull of the mainspring on 16th century German movements.

STAFF-Name for the axle of the balance.

SUN DIAL-A device using a gnomon or style that cast a shadow over a graduated dial as the sun progresses, giving solar time.

SKULL WATCH-A antique pendant watch that that is hinged at jaw to reveal a watch.

SWIVEL-A hinged spring catch with a loop of metal that may be opened to insert a watch bow.

SLOW TRAIN-A watch with four beats per second or 14,000 per hour.

TOP PLATE-The metal plate that usually contains the name and serial #.

SNAILING-Ornamentation of the surface of metals by means of a circle design; also called damaskeening.

TORSION-A twisting force.

SOLAR YEAR-365 days, 5 hours, 48 minutes, 49.7 seconds.

SPOTTING-Decoration used on a watch movement and barrel of movements.

TOURBILLON-A watch with the escapement mounted on a platform pivoted at both ends which revolves most often once a minute. This is designed to eliminate position errors.

TRAIN-A series of gears that form the works of a watch. The train is used for other functions such as chiming. The time train carries the power to the escapement.

TRIPLE CASE WATCH-18th and 19th century verge escapement, fusee watches made for the Turkish market. A fourth case sometimes added in Turkey.

UP AND DOWN DIAL OR INDICATOR-A dial that shows how much of the mainspring is spent and how far up or down the mainspring is.

VERGE ESCAPEMENT-Early type of escapement with wheel that is shaped like a crown.

VIRGULE ESCAPEMENT-Early escapement introduced in the mid 1700s .

WATCH PAPER-A disc of paper with the name of the watchmaker or repairman printed on it; used as a form of advertising and found in pair-cased watches.

WIND INDICATOR-A dial that shows how much of the mainspring is spent. (see up and down dial)

WOLF TEETH-A winding wheel's teeth so named because of their shape.

COOKSEY SHUGART RICHARD E. GILBERT

ABOUT THE AUTHORS

The Complete Price Guide To WATCHES welcomes Mr. Richard E. Gilbert as co-author in the 12th edition and is excited to tap the wealth of information and pricing knowledge he has acquired. Mr. Gilbert holds both Bachelor's and Master's degrees in Science. Richard Gilbert is the owner of Ashland a multi-million dollar international mail order business, he has an impeccable reputation for honesty and integrity, and has been sought after for years by other dealers as a guide to establishing prices.

Both authors have been active watch buyers since the early 1960's. The authors have been Horologists and members of the National Association of Watch and Clock Collectors since the early 1970's. Both have searched for fine timepieces all over the world and are the foremost experts in the field of antique pocket and wrist watches. Both have enjoyed broadening their knowledge in horology while traveling in Europe.

The co-authors travel extensively to auctions throughout the United States and Europe, to regional and national conventions, meets and shows, and keep an up-to-date pulse of the watch market. They continually expand their horological reference library and their extensive selection of watch photographs. Because of the unique knowledge of the market these two co-authors possess, this volume should be considered one of the most authoritative watch references on the market today. Each edition contains updated and revised information and prices, and has become the accepted standard reference work of the watch market. "We see this book as an extension of the information we have been gathering for years and take great pride in sharing it with other collectors who have a deep and abiding interest in watches," the authors stated.

Mr. Shugart resides in Cleveland, Tennessee, and Mr. Gilbert lives in Sarasota, Florida.

WHY ME?

Here are some reasons why you might want to call me when you are thinking of selling:

1. To get the pieces I need, I constantly pay the highest prices.

2. You'll like the way I do business. Transactions are pleasant, fast, fair, and confidential.

3. My business was established in 1970. I have a reputation for knowledge, service, and integrity. NAWCC #9849.

4. I'll travel anywhere to inspect your collection.

5. **I buy complicated, early, unusual, or beautiful POCKET WATCHES and small clocks as well as singing bird boxes, gold musical items, movements & parts.** *I also buy select WRISTWATCHES - complicated, rare, unusual or those by important makers.* **I am particularly interested in watches by Breguet, Cartier, Patek, and Lange, as well as wonderful watches by any maker and from any period.**

6. I buy individual items as well as complete collections. Selected items taken on consignment.

7. Since I am a watchmaker, I'm not afraid to buy broken or incomplete pieces.

8. I pay substantial finders' fees.

9. If you're a dealer and you need help to evaluate or purchase a fine piece or an entire collection, call me.

10. The phone call is free. **(800) 776-6575**

Stephen Bogoff
Antiquarian Horologist
P.O. Box 408   Mill Valley, CA 94942   (415) 383-8100   Fax (415) 383-8112

Located 15 minutes north of San Francisco

Switch to Swatch

Timetrax 600 Electronic Timing Machine

The model 600 is our very best machine for fine watches and some smaller clocks, offering features and performance not found in timers costing many times more. New for '92 is a battery compartment and related electronics for portable operation. You can now operate the unit on either wall current or batteries! And best of all we've held the price to the same low $ 595.

State of the art microprocessor design employs software specifically designed for regulating all types of mechanical wrist and pocket watches. The model 600 also features a highly stable TCXO (Temperature Compensated Crystal Oscillator) timebase for extremely reliable readings. The TCXO timebase, accurate to within 2 parts per million, assures you the precision required for fine timepieces.

Our newly designed Model 100 Sensor and Bulova No. 200 Case Holder are included. The system works equally well with or without removing the back of the watch under test. The model 600 calculates and displays timing information in two different formats.

The unit will display the train directly for any train between 7200 and 36000. Once the correct train is known the unit calculates and displays the number of seconds per day gained or lost by the timepiece based on it's present rate.

While other timers calculate seconds per day for a few very standard trains the 600 is preprogrammed with 41 standard watch trains that were chosen from the master balance list and covers virtually all American and European factory watches. If you do run across a train that's not listed it can still be regulated using the direct train readout feature. Watchmakers with their own fixtures will find the direct train readout to be an invaluable aid for trimming hairsprings. Connect your fixture to the 600 and read out directly in beats per hour!

The model 600 is supplied with a case holder, special sensor for wrist and pocket watches, a clip on sensor for pocket watches and small clocks, an earphone, instruction manual w/tables of known trains, and a 1 year hassle-free parts and labor warranty.

Timetrax Model 600 Electronic Timing Machine **$595.00**

TIMETRAX 600 Watch Timer: Specifications

General
A quality instrument designed, engineered & made in the USA.

Operating Modes
Train: direct reading 7200 to 36,000 beats per hour
Sec/Day: direct reading -500 to +500 w/out-of-range indication
Preset Train: 41 standard watch trains, listed separately
Preset Average: 2 to 130 in steps of 2

Timebase
Type: TCXO (Temperature Compensated Crystal Oscillator)
Stability vs temp: +/- 1 ppm 0 to 50 degrees Centigrade
Stability vs age: +/- 1 ppm per year
Freq. adjustability +/- 5 ppm internal trim, factory adjustable

Preprogrammed Wrist & Pocket Watch Trains

7200	15000	18850	20940
9000	15300	18900	20944
10800	15360	19333	21000
11880	15600	19440	21300
12000	16200	19444	21450
12600	16320	19600	21600
13320	16800	19800	25200
13500	17280	19825	28800
14000	17750	20160	30000
14160	18000	20222	36000
14400			

SEND 3 STAMPS FOR OUR NEW 1992 CATALOG OF BOOKS

Horological Literature: Books on Clocks & Watches, Price Guides, Technical & Repairing, Jewelry & Related Subjects. Also featured is our complete line of Electronic Timers.

ADAMS BROWN CO.
Box 357
Cranbury, NJ 08512
609-655-8269

BOOKS on Clocks & Watches - Electronics for Horology

Professional Horology

As with other art forms, international and regional conventions and auctions help determine prices and appreciation for fine watches and clocks almost on a weekly basis.

Professional Horology is a recognized specialist in the evaluation, purchase & sale of fine pocket and wrist watches, clocks, and other ingenious mechanisms from the 15th century to the present.

Clients both here and abroad will attest to the confidential, courteous and patient handling of appraisals as well as purchase and sale negotiations entered into on their behalf.

Victor Kullberg minute repeater, #4000: Presented by King George V of England to Shah Reza I Pahlevi, in 1925, to commemorate the founding of the sovereign nation of Iran: 6 Carats in fine diamonds, ruby eyes, enamel sun, platinum sword.

LeRoy à Paris #3138 (CA1800): Extremely rare example of a first class execution of the Pinwheel Escapement for use in a pocket watch.

If your travels take you to the Boston area, schedule a visit to my premises for an examination of my current inventory. If you are looking for a particular timepiece or wish to discuss the liquidation or sale of a collection, or individual item, please do not hesitate to contact me (interesting trades or upgrades will always be considered). I will gladly travel to facilitate a mutually rewarding transaction.

Joseph Conway, Horologer
Fine Watches & Clocks, Ingenious Mechanisms & Instrumentation

132 River Street, Newton, Massachusetts 02165
(617) 244-0066 (Shop)/(617) 244-5225 (Office)
FAX # (617) 244-5290
Mass & Out-of-State: 1-800-542-7771

JOIN THE NAWCC

The National Association of Watch & Clock Collectors, Inc.
invites you to become an active member of the
world's largest horological association.

BENEFITS OF MEMBERSHIP

Subscription to the BULLETIN
Subscription to the MART
Participation in National Conventions
Participation in Regional Conventions
Participation in local Chapter activities
Advance notice of National Seminars
FREE Research services of the NAWCC Library & Museum
FREE Admission to the Watch & Clock Museum
Use of the NAWCC Lending Library

**Establish friendships with others who share a fascination
for watches and clocks. Time is wasting! JOIN TODAY!!**

Annual NAWCC membership dues is only **$25.00 (US)**
or **$32.00 (Non-US)**. Payment must be in US funds
drawn on a US bank or International money order.

- -

MEMBERSHIP APPLICATION

To enjoy the benefits of membership, please complete this form
and send it, with your check or money order to:
NAWCC, 514 Poplar St, Columbia PA 17512-2130
(717) 684-8261

Name _____

Street _____

City _____ State_____ ZIP_____

Phone ( ) _____ Amt Enclosed $25 [ ] $32 [ ]

Were you previously an NAWCC member? Yes [ ] No [ ]

What was your previous Member Number? _____

If recommended by an NAWCC member, give name and number:
_____

INTERNATIONAL WRISTWATCH
features market and fashion trends, worldwide auction reports, new watch lines, as well as in-depth articles on the great Swiss watch manufacturers.

Subscribe using this coupon and receive 1 *free* issue with a one-year subscription or a *free* binder with every two-year subscription.

Send to: WRISTWATCH - Subscriptions Dept.
c/o PMG Inc - Suite 100 PG - 2001, West Main St - Stamford, CT 06902 - USA

Name _____

Address _____

_____

_____ _____ Zip Code _____

Country _____ Tel No: _____

I enclose a cheque for a subscription covering:
    one year (7 issues for the price of 6): $35 (USA); $48 (REST OF THE WORLD)
    two years **PLUS free binder** (12 issues): $68 (USA); $90 **(REST OF THE WORLD)**
    made payable to WRISTWATCH.

Or pay by: Credit A/C No   AMEX ❏   VISA ❏   MASTER ❏

Expiry date _____ / _____ / _____   Signature _____
If payment is made by credit card, this form may be sent by fax to USA (203) 348-3555.